The Laws of Restitution

The Laws of Restitution

ROBERT STEVENS

Great Clarendon Street, Oxford, OX2 6DP,
United Kingdom

Oxford University Press is a department of the University of Oxford.
It furthers the University's objective of excellence in research, scholarship,
and education by publishing worldwide. Oxford is a registered trade mark of
Oxford University Press in the UK and in certain other countries

© Robert Stevens 2023

The moral rights of the author have been asserted

First Edition published in 2023

All rights reserved. No part of this publication may be reproduced, stored in
a retrieval system, or transmitted, in any form or by any means, without the
prior permission in writing of Oxford University Press, or as expressly permitted
by law, by licence or under terms agreed with the appropriate reprographics
rights organization. Enquiries concerning reproduction outside the scope of the
above should be sent to the Rights Department, Oxford University Press, at the
address above

You must not circulate this work in any other form
and you must impose this same condition on any acquirer

Public sector information reproduced under Open Government Licence v3.0
(http://www.nationalarchives.gov.uk/doc/open-government-licence/open-government-licence.htm)

Published in the United States of America by Oxford University Press
198 Madison Avenue, New York, NY 10016, United States of America

British Library Cataloguing in Publication Data

Data available

Library of Congress Control Number: 2022947801

ISBN 978–0–19–288502–9

DOI: 10.1093/oso/9780192885029.001.0001

Printed and bound by
CPI Group (UK) Ltd, Croydon, CR0 4YY

Links to third party websites are provided by Oxford in good faith and
for information only. Oxford disclaims any responsibility for the materials
contained in any third party website referenced in this work.

Foreword

The creation of the legal category of unjust enrichment, with a conceptual structure based on the four elements of (1) enrichment of the defendant, (2) at the expense of the claimant, (3) an unjust factor, and (4) the absence of a defence, is arguably the most remarkable development in English law in recent times. It was effectively the work of a single legal scholar, Professor Peter Birks, who succeeded in having his ideas accepted by the Law Lords of the day, and whose pupils (and their pupils in turn) have subsequently reinforced his influence through their dominance of scholarship in this area of the law.

A number of factors contributed to this situation. The earlier categorisation of a range of issues in the law of obligations under the catch-all heading of 'quasi-contract' was evidently unsatisfactory and in need of reconsideration. More recent analysis of the law of restitution focused attention on a form of relief and on a description of the variety of situations in which it was available. To a legal scholar disposed towards elegance and simplicity, the search for a unifying legal principle connecting those situations (and others which were thought to display an underlying similarity, such as equitable subrogation or rights of contribution) must have had a strong intellectual attraction.

The field was also one in which the judiciary were particularly liable to defer to scholarly analysis. The subject, insofar as a disparate range of problems could be described as a subject, was scarcely touched on in the legal teaching which the judges had undergone; nor were problems in 'quasi-contract' frequently encountered in practice. There were some aspects of the subject which were familiar, such as claims for the recovery of money paid under a mistake of fact, but the situations giving rise to claims to restitutionary relief had not previously been understood as being connected by a unifying principle. The Law Lords were likely to include people who were attracted by the idea of such a principle. Lord Atkin in *Donoghue v Stevenson* and Lord Wilberforce in *Anns v Merton London Borough Council* had illustrated the susceptibility of senior judges to the attractions of grand unifying theories. In the event, the theory of unjust enrichment went beyond the matters formerly categorised as quasi-contract, and extended to such matters as proprietary claims, remedies in contract, remedies in tort, and a variety of claims in equity.

The 1990s, when the theory of unjust enrichment gained acceptance at the highest level, were also a particularly propitious time for Birks' ideas to be accepted. An influential member of the House of Lords for much of that period, and Senior Law Lord for part of it, was Lord Goff of Chieveley, a former law don who was committed to the idea of partnership between academic lawyers and the judiciary, and had a deep interest in the law of restitution, on which he had himself co-written the leading textbook. He delivered significant speeches in several of the cases which proved to be critical in establishing Birks' theory of unjust enrichment as a legal doctrine. After his retirement, the torch passed to Lord Steyn, another innovative judge with a close relationship with the academic community.

Birks was an exceptional scholar and teacher, but it has to be remembered that his thinking was still in the course of development at the time of his death in 2004, at the early age of 62. He had himself departed in his most recent work, published in the year of his death, from the earlier approach which had by then received the imprimatur of the House of Lords, leading some of the Law Lords to wonder whether they had too readily accepted his previous ideas. Subsequent case law in the Supreme Court and the Judicial Committee of the Privy Council, from the 2013 case of *Benedetti v Sawiris* onwards, has struck a more sceptical note. Some of the decisions of the House of Lords based on Birks' theory have been departed from, and others have been viewed with evident reserve.

One can perhaps apply to legal scholars the remarks which Lord Rodger of Earlsferry once made about appellate courts:

> Part of the function of appeal courts is to try to assist judges and practitioners by boiling down a mass of case law and distilling some shorter statement of the applicable law. The temptation to try to identify some compact underlying rule which can then be applied to solve all future cases is obvious … But the unhappy experience with the rule so elegantly formulated by Lord Wilberforce in *Anns v Merton London Borough Council* [1978] AC 728, 751–752, suggests that appellate judges should follow the philosopher's advice to 'Seek simplicity, and distrust it'.[1]

The present work is written in the spirit of that advice. Professor Stevens challenges the idea that there is a general principle of 'unjust enrichment' which unifies the different areas of the law where restitutionary claims may be made. Rather than there being a single legal category of unjust enrichment, animated by a single unifying theory based on the four elements described above, he argues that different principles underlie restitutionary claims in the different areas of the law where such claims may be made, and seeks to identify those principles.

The subject is divided into six parts, in which Professor Stevens discusses respectively (I) unjustified performance, such as a payment made under a mistake, or a service rendered under a contract that has been set aside; (II) conditional performance, where performance is rendered under an agreement which is subject to a condition, and the condition is not fulfilled; (III) intervention in another's affairs, such as where one person discharges another person's obligation; (IV) property and trusts, where he considers the use of unjust enrichment analyses in those contexts; (V) wrongdoing, where he considers restitutionary responses to torts and other wrongs; and (VI) countervailing reasons, where defences to restitutionary claims are considered.

The book is the product of much thought and careful scholarship. As always with Professor Stevens, it is written in a highly readable style. I have found it to be unusually interesting, not only in its challenge to academic orthodoxy, but also in its exploration of the role of restitution in diverse areas of the law, such as contract, property, equity, and torts. I expect it to be widely read, and to produce much debate. I commend it to anyone interested in this troublesome but absorbing area of the law.

Lord Reed of Allermuir
August 2022

---

[1] *Customs and Excise Commissioners v Barclays Bank plc* [2006] UKHL 28, [2007] 1 AC 181, [51]. The philosopher was A N Whitehead.

Preface

My first encounter with restitution occurred at the age of ten. In 1980, Rubik's cubes were released upon the market, and became a craze across the world, including in my local primary school. My father, an obsessive about such things, deduced an algorithm for solving the puzzle, which he then taught to me. I then set up trade in my school, offering to solve the cubes of others at a rate of two pence each. I advertised my service with posters. I soon had a thriving enterprise, inevitably with many repeat customers.

Unfortunately, the school's headmaster, taking the same Victorian view as that of the Infants Relief Act 1874 (since repealed by the Minors Contracts Act 1987), considered that the agreements with my peers were all void. He required me to repay all of my earnings.

I began teaching the law of restitution on the Bachelor of Civil Law programme at the University of Oxford in 1994, and have taught the subject more or less continuously ever since. Initially, my approach was to pass on what I had learned when studying the course, with a few minor tweaks of my own devising. However, over time I have become an apostate,[1] convinced that what has become the academic orthodoxy in relation to the subject, at least in my own jurisdiction, is seriously deficient. That orthodoxy has, *faute de mieux*, had considerable influence on the judicial development of the law. Although we need not go as far as John Maynard Keynes in thinking that 'madmen in authority, who hear voices in the air, are distilling their frenzy from some academic scribbler of a few years back', it is time for a long form treatment of the law from a new perspective.

This work is not a textbook, although I hope that for many topics it could be used as one. Rather, it is a sustained argument as to how part of the law fits together, and relates to other areas. It is for all those who wish to understand the law(s) of restitution. It is not aimed solely at academics and students. In a review of my previous book, the Scottish judge Lord Brodie stated that for those practitioners 'who prefer to sharpen their presentations with fresh material and the spice of controversy, this is a book which should be on the shelf and kept within easy reach'.[2] I have aimed at the same on this occasion.

I have made extensive use of examples from all common law systems, trying to select the best and most interesting illustrations. Inevitably, there is a bias towards English cases and they predominate in the footnotes. This is because, given English law's long history, there are so many of them, and they are also the ones I know best. In two chapters (Improvements, Illegality) the law of England is out of line both with that elsewhere and the position in principle. I have introduced comparisons to civilian jurisdictions (which differ almost as much between each other as they do with the common law) where I have found it useful to do so.

I hope that even those who do not accept the larger claims about the nature of the subject will find specific insights that are helpful.

---

[1] See also L Smith, 'Restitution: A New Start?' in P Devonshire and R Havelock (eds), *The Impact of Equity and Restitution in Commerce* (2019), 91.

[2] P H Brodie (2009) 13 Ed Law Rev 534.

Acknowledgements

I owe a debt of thanks for help to such an embarrassingly large number of people that the book is, in a sense, crowdsourced.

First, those who taught me the subject. Peter Birks, Andrew Burrows, and Ewan McKendrick.

Second, all those to whom I have taught the subject, and who in return have taught me, over the intervening years, both at the University of Oxford and University College London.

Third, those with whom I have taught. Peter Birks (again), Andrew Burrows (again), Robert Chambers, Mindy Chen-Wishart, Gerhard Dannemann, James Edelman, Charles Mitchell, James Penner, Helen Scott, Lionel Smith, William Swadling, and Frederick Wilmot-Smith.

Fourth, all those whose doctorates I have supervised, in whole or in part, in this and related areas. Elise Bant, Tatiana Cutts, Rory Gregson, Jeroen Kortmann, Krishna Kizhakkevalappil, Timothy Liau, Ali Pirataei, and Chee Ho Tham. All of them will see their influence in this text.

Fifth, I received helpful comments on one or more draft chapters and earlier nascent work from Tariq Baloch, Allan Beever, Jordan English, Alex Georgiou, Rory Gregson (again), Birke Hacker, Matthew Hoyle, George Leggatt, Timothy Liau (again), Rachel Leow, Nick McBride, Jason Neyers, Helen Scott (again), Lionel Smith (again), Steve Smith, Sandy Steel, William Swadling (again), Alexander Waghorn, Sam Williams, and Frederick Wilmot-Smith (again).

Special thanks are owing to Daniel Friedmann and Andrew Kull, who have worked in and thought about this area longer than almost anyone else. Each of them read the entire manuscript in draft as I produced it and gave many pieces of helpful advice.

Sixth, over several years I have developed with Ben McFarlane, under the influence of others, an attempt to re-explain Maitland's conception of Equity and 'equitable property' for a modern audience, which is reflected in this book.

Seventh, thanks to Anirudh Belle for his research assistance.

Eighth, I am very grateful to Lord Reed for writing the foreword. It should be apparent to anyone who reads the book why he was the only person I would have asked to do so (Baron Bowen having inconsiderately died more than a century before I began work).

Finally, thanks to B, E, F, and Z for enriching my life. Justifiably or not.

Robert Stevens
Oxford
1 August 2022

Summary Contents

Detailed Contents	xiii
Table of Cases	xxi
Table of Legislation	xlv
List of Abbreviations	xlix

I. SUMMARY

1. Summary	3
2. Foundations	16

II. UNJUSTIFIED PERFORMANCE

3. Performance	29
4. Reversal	57
5. Theory	71
6. Practice	83

III. CONDITIONAL PERFORMANCE

7. Conditions	109
8. Contract	128

IV. INTERVENTION IN ANOTHER'S AFFAIRS

9. Discharge	153
10. Necessity	173

V. PROPERTY AND TRUSTS

11. Things	191
12. Equity: General	214
13. Equity: Restitution	229
14. Improvements	264

VI. WRONGDOING

15. Wrongs   291
16. Profits   304
17. Damages   332

VII. COUNTERVAILING REASONS

18. Defences   353
19. Illegality   391

VIII. APOLOGIA

20. Conclusion   415

Index   421

Detailed Contents

Table of Cases	xxi
Table of Legislation	xlv
List of Abbreviations	xlix

I. SUMMARY

1. Summary	3
A. Muscle Memory	3
B. Purposes	3
C. The Negative Thesis	4
1. History	4
2. 'Unjust Enrichment'	5
D. The Positive Thesis	9
1. The Dilemma	9
2. Unjustified Performance	9
3. Conditional Performance	10
4. Intervention in Another's Affairs	10
5. Property and Trusts	12
6. Wrongdoing	14
7. Countervailing Reasons	15
2. Foundations	16
A. Law and Justice	16
B. Corrective Justice	19
C. Reasons and Recourse	21
D. Legal Categories	22
E. Quasi-Contract	24

II. UNJUSTIFIED PERFORMANCE

3. Performance	29
A. Introduction	29
B. Red Herrings	30
1. No Loss	30
2. No 'Unjust Factor'	31
3. Grudging Gifts	32
4. No Right Transfer	32
5. Incidental Benefits	34
6. No 'Transfers of Value'	35
C. Performance Defined	36
1. Summary	36
2. Action	38

	3.	Towards	42
	4.	Acceptance	46
D.	Outside of Performance		50
	1.	Other Reasons	50
	2.	'Interceptive Subtraction'	51
	3.	Errors	53
E.	'At the Expense of'?		55

4. Reversal — 57
   A. Enrichment? — 57
   B. Payments — 58
      1. Timing — 58
      2. Counterfactuals — 59
      3. Trustees and Agents — 60
      4. Increases in Value and Interest — 62
   C. Services — 65
      1. The Service and Its Consequences — 65
      2. Enrichment Higher than Market Value of Service — 66
      3. Enrichment Lower than Market Value of Service — 67
   D. The Meaning of Words — 70

5. Theory — 71
   A. *Kelly v Solari* — 71
   B. The Role of Mistake and Similar 'Unjust Factors' — 72
      1. Summary — 72
      2. Negativing — 73
      3. Nullifying — 74
      4. Voluntary Performance — 76
   C. What Is a Good Reason? — 78
   D. The Theory — 79
      1. The Operative Facts — 79
      2. Payments and Services — 80

6. Practice — 83
   A. Introduction — 83
   B. Absence of Good Reason or Vitiation of Consent? — 83
      1. Rescission — 83
      2. Mistakes as to Recoverability — 84
      3. Obligations Performed — 84
      4. Gifts, Wills, and Trusts — 89
      5. Retrospective Changes — 92
      6. Corporate Mistakes — 96
      7. 'Spent' Mistakes — 96
      8. The '*Woolwich* Principle' — 98
      9. The Invention of 'Unjust Factors' — 100
      10. Mispredictions — 101
      11. Different Causal Rules — 102
   C. Comparisons — 103
   D. Birks' Last Work — 104

III. CONDITIONAL PERFORMANCE

7. Conditions	109
A. A New Justification	109
B. Qualified Consent?	110
C. Outside of Contract	111
D. 'Total Failure of Consideration'	115
E. The Meaning of Condition	116
F. Waiver	120
G. The Fiction of Fulfilment	122
H. The Right or Its Performance?	123
I. Relevance of Termination	124
1. Terminology	124
2. Insufficient	125
3. Unnecessary	126
4. Relevance	127
8. Contract	128
A. Introduction	128
B. Breach of Contract	128
1. Claims for Restitution of Services by Party in Breach	128
2. Claims for Restitution of Payments Against Party in Breach	130
3. Claims for Restitution of Services Against Party in Breach	132
4. Claims for Restitution of Payments by Party in Breach	136
C. Frustration	137
1. Money Obligations	137
2. Non-money Obligations	142
3. Other Jurisdictions	146
D. Money, Services, and Penalties	147

IV. INTERVENTION IN ANOTHER'S AFFAIRS

9. Discharge	153
A. The Significance of Discharge of Another's Obligation	153
B. Recoupment	154
C. Contribution	155
D. Methods of Discharge	157
1. Performance	157
2. Joint and Several Obligations	158
3. Conditional Obligations	159
4. Automatic Discharge?	160
E. Volunteers	161
F. Unjust Enrichment?	164
1. Enrichment Insufficient	164
2. Enrichment Unnecessary	167
3. Loss	168
4. The 'Unjust Factor'	169

10. Necessity — 173
- A. Good Samaritans and the Justification for Private Law — 173
- B. Quantification — 176
- C. The Law — 177
  1. Exceptions? — 177
  2. Discharge of Another's Obligation — 178
  3. Reciprocal Duties — 178
  4. Contribution Between Common Interests — 181
  5. Maritime Salvage — 184
  6. Necessaries supplied to Those Incapable of Contracting — 187
- D. Conclusion — 187

V. PROPERTY AND TRUSTS

11. Things — 191
- A. Introduction — 191
- B. Rights — 191
- C. Transfers — 192
  1. Contract and Conveyance — 192
  2. Delivery and Conveyance — 197
- D. Identification — 198
  1. Introduction — 198
  2. Mixtures — 198
  3. Accession — 201
  4. Specification — 203
  5. Fruits — 205
- E. Substitution — 205
- F. Good Faith Purchase for Value — 209
- G. Unjust Enrichment? — 210
  1. Relevance — 210
  2. Ignorance — 211
  3. Defences — 211
  4. Comparisons — 213

12. Equity: General — 214
- A. Introduction — 214
- B. Meta-Law — 215
- C. 'Equitable Property Rights' — 216
  1. Rights to Rights — 216
  2. Common Misconceptions — 219
  3. Significance — 220
  4. The Necessary and Sufficient Duty to be a Trustee — 222
- D. Trusts Arising from Contractual and Other Obligations — 224

13. Equity: Restitution — 229
- A. Trusts and Obligations to Make Restitution — 229
- B. Presumptions of Advancement and of Resulting Trust — 235
- C. Knowing Receipt of Trust Property — 236
- D. Purchase without Notice — 241

E. 'Tracing'	243
1. Substitution	243
2. 'Mixing'	248
3. Wrongdoing	250
F. Subrogation	252
G. Policy?	256
H. Unjust Enrichment?	259
I. Doing without Equity?	262
14. Improvements	**264**
A. Introduction	264
B. Goods	264
1. *Greenwood v Bennett*	264
2. A Freestanding 'Enrichment' Claim?	264
3. A Qualification to a Damages Award	265
4. A Qualification to an Order for Specific Delivery	266
5. A Qualification to Accession?	266
6. A 'Tracing' Claim?	267
7. A Qualification to Priority of Title	267
C. Land	269
1. Introduction	269
2. Evidential Estoppel	269
3. Equitable Estoppel	270
4. Illegitimate Extension	276
5. Australia	285
6. The Future	287

VI. WRONGDOING

15. Wrongs	**291**
A. Introduction	291
B. *Edwards v Lees Administrator*	291
C. Definitions and Distinctions	292
1. Wrongdoing	292
2. Consequential Loss and Wrongdoing	292
3. Consequential Gain and Wrongdoing	294
4. General and Special Damages	295
D. Justifications	297
1. The Obligation to Pay Damages	297
2. Disgorging Gains	299
E. The Wrong or the Right?	302
16. Profits	**304**
A. Introduction	304
B. Information	304
1. Intellectual Property Rights	304
2. Confidential Information	309
3. Private Information	311

	C. Fiduciaries	313
	1. Justification	313
	2. Quantification	317
	3. Constructive Trust?	318
	4. Dishonest Assistance	318
	D. Breach of Contract	320
	1. General Principle	320
	2. *Attorney General v Blake*	323
	E. Torts	326
	1. General Principle	326
	2. Waiver of Tort	328
17.	Damages	332
	A. Introduction	332
	B. Breach of Contract	332
	1. *Wrotham Park Ltd v Parkside Homes Ltd*	332
	2. General Damages: The Contractual Right to Performance	333
	3. Negotiating Damages	338
	C. Torts	344
	1. General Damages	344
	2. User Damages	346
	3. Gain-based?	348

VII. COUNTERVAILING REASONS

18.	Defences	353
	A. Introduction	353
	B. Definitions	353
	C. Specific Defences	354
	1. Change of Position	354
	2. Consent	369
	3. Limitation	371
	4. Passing on	374
	5. Bona Fide Purchase	376
	6. Counter-restitution	378
	7. Bona Fide Payee?	385
	8. Ministerial Receipt	385
19.	Illegality	391
	A. Justification	391
	B. Defence, Denial, or Other?	392
	C. Bribes	393
	D. Reliance	395
	E. Statutory Illegality	396
	F. *Patel v Mirza*	401
	1. The Statute	401
	2. The Minority	402
	3. The Majority	403

		4. The *Ratio*	404
		5. The Future	405
	G.	Summary	408
	H.	Illegality as a Ground of Claim	408
		1. Restitution Founded upon the Statute	408
		2. Withdrawal	409

VIII. APOLOGIA

20. Conclusion	415
A. Comparisons	415
B. 'Unjust Factors' or 'Absence of Basis'?	416
C. Like Contract, Torts, or Neither?	417
D. The Future	418

Index   421

Table of Cases

Abbott Fund Trusts, Re [1900] 2 Ch 326 226
Acme Process Equipment Company v United States 347 F 2d 509 (Ct Cl 1965) reversed on
   other grounds 385 US 138 (1966) 132
Actionstrength v International Glass Engineering SpA [2003] UKHL 17, [2003]
   2 AC 541 .... 112, 286
Admiralty Commissioners v National Provincial and Union Bank (1922) 127 LT 452 389–90
Adras Building Material v Harlow & Jones CA 20/82 (1988) translated in (1995) 3 RLR 235 321
AG v Guardian Newspaper Ltd (No 2) [1990] 1 AC 109 (HL) 299
Agip (Africa) Ltd v Jackson [1990] Ch 265 (Millett J) aff'd [1991]
   Ch 547 (CA) 236–37, 244–45, 387
Agnew v Ferguson (1903) 5 F 879 (1903) 11 SLT 79 84
Aiken v Short (1856) 1 H & N 120, 156 ER 1180 .... 36, 43, 44–45, 73–74, 239, 365
Air Canada v British Columbia [1989] 1 SCR 116 159 DLR (4th) 161 .... 51, 376
Aitchison v Lohre (1879) 4 App Cas 755 186–87
Akers v Samba Financial Group [2017] UKSC 6, [2017] AC 424 .... 219, 223
Akron Securities Ltd v Illife (1997) 41 NSWLR 353 (CA) 370 382
Alan & Co Ltd v El Nasr Export and Import Co [1972] 2 QB 189 (CA) 271
Alati v Kruger [1957] 94 CLR 216 (HCA) 195, 229, 382
Alderson v Temple (1768) 4 Burr 2235, 96 ER 55 408–9
Alesco Corporation Ltd v Te Maari [2015] NSWSC 469 261
Alexander v Vane (1836) 1 M & W 511, 150 ER 537 .... 164, 171
Allcard v Skinner (1887) 36 ChD 145 (CA) 358
Allen v Flood [1898] AC 1 (HL) 284
Alpha Trading Ltd v Dunshaw-Patten [1981] QB 290 122–23
Amalgamated Investment & Property Co Ltd v Texas Commerce International
   Bank Ltd [1982] QB 84 .... 269, 275
Ambrose v Kerrison (1788) 1 H Bl 90, 126 ER 55 154
Ames Settlement, Re [1946] Ch 217 .... 113, 226
Anchor Line (Henderson Brothers Ltd), Re [1937] Ch 483 222
Ancient Order of Foresters in Victoria Friendly Society Ltd v Lifeplan Australia Friendly
   Society Ltd [2018] HCA 43 318–19
Andrew v St Olave's Board of Works [1898] 1 QB 775 10–11
Anglo-Scottish Beet Sugar Corp v Spalding UDC [1937] 2 KB 607 96
Angus v Scully 58 NE 674 (Mass 1900) 143
Anna Wee [2013] SGCA 36, [2013] 3 SLR 801 6
Anns v Merton London Borough Council [1978] AC 728 .... v, 92
Anon Moore 20, 72 All ER 411 204
Apparent from the later decision in The Gloria 286 F 188 (1923) 322–23
Appleby v Myers (1866–1867) LR 2 CP 651 201
Archard v Ring (1874) 2 Asp MLC 422 181–82
Archbolds (Freightage) Ltd v S Spanglett Ltd [1961] QB 374 (CA) 397
Argos, The (1873) LR 5 PC 134 179
Aries Tanker Corporation v Total Transport Ltd [1977] 1 WLR 185 (HL) 381
Armitage v Nurse [1998] Ch 241 223
Armory v Delamirie (1722) 1 Str 505, 93 ER 664 .... 200–1, 213
Armour v Thyssen Edelstahlwerke AG [1991] 2 AC 339 (HL) 204–5
Armstrong v Jackson [1917] 2 KB 822 382–83
Aro Manufacturing v Convertible Top Replacement Co 377 US 476 (1964) 304

TABLE OF CASES

Arrazat case, Cass Req 11 July 1889 43
Arris v Stuckley (1667) Mod 260, 86 ER 1160 52
Asher v Wallis (1707) 11 Mod 146, 88 ER 956 51–52
Athenian Harmony, The [1998] 2 Lloyd's Rep 410 333–34
Atkinson v Denby (1862) 7 H&N 934, 158 ER 749 398
Atlantic Coast Line Railroad Co. v Florida (1935) 295 US 301 60
Atlantic Lottery Corp v Babstock [2020] SCC 19 329
Atlasview Ltd v Brightview Ltd [2004] EWHC 1056 (Ch), [2004] 2 BCLC 191 216
Attorney General of Belize v Belize Telecom Ltd [2009] UKPC 10, [2009]
　1 WLR 1988] 110
Attorney General of Hong Kong v Humphrey's Estate (Queens Gardens)
　Ltd [1987] AC 114 114–15
Attorney General v Blake [2001] 1 AC 268 (HL) 293, 310, 323, 324–25,
332, 333, 419
Attorney General v Observer Ltd. [1990] 1 AC 109 (HL) 311–12
Attorney-General (Hong Kong) v Reid [1994] 1 AC 324 (PC) 227
Australia and New Zealand Banking Group Ltd v Westpac Banking Corp (1988)
　164 CLR 662 389–90
Australian Financial Services and Leasing Pty Ltd v Hill Industries [2014]
　HCA 14, (2014) 253 CLR 560 . . . . 44, 365, 366, 419
Avon CC v Howlett [1983] 1 WLR 605 (CA) 270, 368
Awwad v Geraghty & Co [2001] QB 570 (CA) 393, 399
Ayerst v C&K Construction Ltd [1976] AC 176 219

B Liggett (Liverpool) Ltd v Barclays Bank Ltd [1928] 1 KB 48 160
Bainton v John Hallam Ltd (1920) 60 SCR 325, 54 DLR 537 (SCC) 335
Baird Textile Holdings Ltd v Marks and Spencer plc [2001] EWCA Civ 274, [20002]
　1 All ER (Comm) 737 . . . . 275, 286–87
Baker v Baker & Baker [1993] 2 HLR 408 (CA) 282–83
Baker v TE Hopkins & Son Ltd [1959] 1 WLR 966 (CA) 164, 369
Bakewell Management Ltd v Brandwood [2004] UKHL 14, [2004] 2 AC 519 397
Baldry v Marshall [1925] 1 KB 260 120
Baltic Shipping v Dillon (1989) 21 NSWLR 614 (Carruthers J) 119–20
Baltic Shipping v Dillon (1991) 22 NSWLR 1 (NSWCA) 119–20
Baltic Shipping v Dillon (1993) 176 CLR 3 (HCA) 119–20, 419
Bank of America v Arnell [1999] Lloyd's Rep Bank 399 . . . . 8, 232
Bank of Boston Connecticut v European Grain and Shipping Ltd, The Dominique
　[1980] AC 1056 (HL) 115–16
Bank of Credit and Commerce International (Overseas) Ltd v Akindele [2001]
　Ch 437 (CA) 238, 240
Bank of Cyprus v Menelaou [2015] UKSC 66, [2016] AC 176 . . . . 53–54, 68
Bank Tejarat v Hong Kong and Shanghai Banking Corp (CI) Ltd [1995] 1 Lloyd's Rep 239 39
Banque Belge pour L'Etranger v Hambrouk [1921] 1 KB 321 (CA) 207–8
Banque Financière de la Cité v Parc (Battersea) Ltd [1999] 1 AC 221 (HL) . . . 252, 255, 256, 261, 419
Barclays Bank Ltd v Quistclose Investments Ltd [1970] AC 567 (HL) 218, 225, 227–28
Barclays Bank Ltd v WJ Simms, Son & Cooke (Southern) Ltd [1980]
　QB 677 . . . . 10–11, 45, 96, 160, 239–40, 385
Barclays Bank plc v Boulter [1999] 1 WLR 1919 (HL) 194, 377
Barlow Clowes v Vaughan [1992] 4 All ER 22 (CA) 249–50
Barnes v Eastenders Group [2014] UKSC 26, [2015] AC 1 . . . . 111, 117–18, 147
Baroness Wenlock v River Dee Co (No 2) (1887) 19 QBD 155 (CA) 254
Barr v Crawford 1983 SLT 481 (OHCS) 394
Barron v Cain 4 SE 2d 618 (1939) 122
Barros Mattos Junior v MacDaniels [2005] EWHC 1323 (Ch), [2005] I L Pr 45 392–93
Barros Mattos Junior v MacDaniels Ltd [2004] EWHC 1118 (Ch), [2005] 1 WLR 247 392–93
Barton v Armstrong [1976] AC 104 (PC) 102

Barton v Gwyn-Jones [2019] EWCA Civ 1999, [2020] 2 All ER (Comm) 652 128–29
Basham, Re [1986] 1 WLR 1498 (ChD) 278
Bate v Hooper (1855) 5 De GM & G 338, 43 ER 901 237–38
Bathurs CC v PWC Properties Pty Ltd (1988) 195 CLR 566 257
Batis Maritime Corporation v Petroleos del Mediterraneo SA (The 'Batis') [1990]
   1 Lloyd's Rep 345 114
Bawden v Bawden (CA, Unreported 7 November 1997) 273
Baylis v Bishop of London [1913] 1 Ch 127 (CA) 355
BBMB Finance (Hong Kong) Ltd v Eda Holdings Ltd [1990] 1 WLR 409 (PC) 345
Beale v Harvey [2003] EWCA Civ 1883, [2004] 2 P&CR 18 .... 273, 278
Beasley v Darcy (1800) 2 Sch & Lef 403 380–81
Beck v Northern Natural Gas Company 170 F 3d 1018 (10 Cir 1999) 266, 328
Beevor v Marler (1898) 14 TLR 289 369
Behrend & Co. Ltd v Produce Brokers Co. Ltd. [1920] 3 KB 530 .... 130, 383
Bell v Lever Bros [1932] AC 161 (HL) 72
Bell v Lever Brothers Ltd [1931] 1 KB 557 (CA) 169, 353
Belmont Finance Corpn v Williams Furniture Ltd (No 2) [1980] 1 All ER 393 241
Belmont Park Investments Pty Ltd v BNY Corporate Trustee Services [2011] UKSC 38,
   [2012] 1 AC 383 195
Belshaw v Bush (1851) 11 CB 191, 138 ER 444 .... 160, 239–40
Bence Graphics v Fasson [1998] QB 87 (CA) 335
Benedetti v Sawiris [2010] EWCA Civ 1427 37–38
Benedetti v Sawiris [2013] UKSC 50, [2014] AC 938 .... v–vi, 19, 47, 66, 67, 68,
                                                                           69–70, 113–14, 182
Bentsen v Taylor [1893] 2 QB 274 (CA) 120–21
Berg v Sadler and Moore [1937] 2 KB 158 .... 395, 396–97
Berghoff Trading Ltd v Swinbrook Developments Ltd [2009] EWCA Civ 413, [2009]
   2 Lloyd's Rep 233 171–72
Berkeley Applegate, Re [1989] Ch 32 184
Berridge v Benjies Business Centre [1997] 1 WLR 53 (PC) 269–70
Berry v Barbour 279 P 2d 335 (Okla 1954) 174
Berry, Re (1906) 147 F 208 (2nd Cir 1906) 231
Bettini v Gye (1876) 1 QBD 183 118
BHT (UK) Ltd [2004] EWHC 201 (Ch), [2004] BCC 301 30
Bibby Factors Northwest Ltd v HFD Ltd [2015] EWCA Civ 1908, [2016] 1 Lloyd's Rep 517 381
Bibby v Sterling (1998) 76 P&CR D36 (CA) 272
Bigos v Bousted [1951] 1 All ER 92 398
Bilbie v Lumley (1802) 2 East 469, 102 ER 448 .... 85–86, 88, 93–94, 104–5
Bilta (UK) Ltd v Nazir (No 2) [2015] UKSC 23, [2016] AC 1 401
Binions v Evans [1972] Ch 359 (CA) 280
Binstead v Buck (1777) 2 W Bl 1117, 96 ER 660 180
Birch v Blagrave (1755) Amb 264, 27 ER 176 232–33
Birmingham District Land Co v L&NW Railway (1888) 40 ChD 268 (CA) 272
Black v S Freedman & Co (1910) 12 CLR 105, 110 245
Blackburn v Smith (1848) 2 Ex 783, 154 ER 707 381
Blacklocks v JB Developments (Godalming) Ltd. [1982] Ch 183 230
Blackwell, The 77 US (10 Wall) 1, 14 L Ed 870 (1869) 186
Blakeley v Muller [1903] 2 KB 760n 138
Blue Haven Enterprises v Tully [2006] UKPC 17 .... 48, 274–75
BMP Global Distributions Inc v Bank of Nova Scotia [2009] 1 SCR 504, 304 DLR
   (4th) 292 73
Boardman v Phipps [1964] 1 WLR 993 316
Boardman v Phipps [1967] 2 AC 46 (HL) 314, 315–16, 317, 318
Bofinger v Kingsway Group Ltd [2009] HCA 44; (2009) 239 CLR 269 (HCA) 256
Boissevain v Weil [1950] AC 327 (HL) 396–97, 398, 399, 400, 407
Bolton v Mahadeva [1972] 1 WLR 1009 (CA) 128–29

Bonner v Tottenham & Edmonton Permanent Investment Building Society
 [1899] 1 QB 161 (CA) 166, 167
Boomer v Muir 24 P 2d 570 (1933) 135
Boone v Eyre, (1777) 1 H BL 273n, 126 ER 160n 116
Borden (UK) Ltd v Scottish Timber Products Ltd, [1981] Ch 25 (CA) 204–5
Boscawen v Bajwa [1996] 1 WLR 328 (CA) 254
Boston Deep Sea Fishing and Ice Co. v Ansell (1888) 39 Ch D 339 128–29
Boston Ice Co v Potter 123 Mass 28 (1877) 114
Boughner v Greyhawk Equity Partners Ltd Partnership (Millenium) (2012) 111
 OR (3d) 700; [2012] ONSC 3185; approved [2013] ONC 2, [2013] 5 CBR (6th) 113 250
Boulton v Jones (1857) 2 H & N 564, 27 LJ Ex 117, 157 ER 232, sub nom Boulton v Jones
 3 Jur NS 1156, 6 W 107, 30 LTOS 188 .... 48, 114
Bournemouth and Boscombe Athletic Football Club and Co Ltd v Manchester
 United Football Club Ltd Unreported 21 May 1980 122–23
Box v Barclays Bank Plc [1998] Lloyd's Rep Bank 185 8
Boyd & Forrest v The Glasgow Railway Company 1915 SC (HL) 382
Boyse v Rossborough (1857) 6 HLC 3, 10 ER 1192 90
Boyter v Dodsworth (1796) 6 Term Rep 681, 101 ER 770 52
Boyter v Thomson [1995] 2 AC 628 (HL) 41
BP Exploration Co. (Libya) Ltd. v Hunt (No. 2) [1979] 1 WLR 783 (Robert Goff J) 135, 141–42,
 144, 145, 146, 360
BP Exploration Co (Libya) Ltd v Hunt (No 2) [1983] 2 AC 352 (HL) 145
Bracewell v Appleby [1975] Ch 408 .... 327–28, 332, 343
Bradbury v Taylor [2012] EWCA Civ 1208 .... 280, 282
Bradford v Pickles [1895] AC 587 (HL) 284
Bradshaw v Beard (1862) 12 CBNS 344, 142 ER 1175 154
Brasserie du Pechur (C-46/93) 87–88
Brazil v Durant International Corp [2015] UKPC 35, [2016] AC 297 247
Brewer Street Investments Ltd v Barclay Woollen Co Ltd [1954] QB 428 .... 69–70, 132, 287
Brisbane v Dacres (1813) 5 Taunt 143, 128 ER 641 .... 79, 85–86, 104–5
Bristol and West Building Society v Mothew [1998] Ch 1 (CA) 229, 232
British American Continental Bank v British Bank for Continental Trade [1926]
 1 KB 328 (CA) 389–90
British Motor Transport Association v Gilbert [1951] 2 All ER 641 333–34
British South Africa Co v Companhia de Mozambique [1893] AC 602 (HL) 222
British Steel Corporation v Cleveland Bridge and Engineering Co Ltd. [1984] 1 All ER 504 114
British Steel plc v Customs and Excise Commrs [1997] 2 All ER 366 (CA) 99
Brook's Wharf and Bull Wharf Ltd v Goodman Bros [1937] 1 KB 534 (CA) 171–72
Brown and Davies v Galbraith [1972] 1 WLR 997 (CA) 42, 268
Brown v M'Kinally (1795) 1 Esp 279, 170 ER 356 118–19
Buckley v Gross (1863) 3 B&S 566, 577 122 ER 213 199–200
Buhr v Barclays Bank plc [2001] EWCA Civ 1223 244
Buller v Harrison (1777) 2 Cowp 565, 98 ER 1243 .... 388, 389–90
Bunge SA v Nidera BV [2015] UKSC 43, [2015] 3 All ER 1082 336
Bunnings Group Ltd v CHEP Australia Ltd. [2011] NSWCA 342 347–48
Burdis v Livsey [2002] EWCA Civ 510, [2003] QB 36 .... 296–97, 346
Burgess v Rawnsley [1975] Ch 429 (CA) 111, 114
Burgess v Wheate (1759) 1 Eden 177 242
Burrow's Case (1880) 14 ChD 432 (CA) 242
Burrows and Burrows v Sharp (1991) 23 HLR 82 (CA) 282–83
Bush v Canfield 2 Conn 485 (1818) 130, 133
Butcher v Churchill (1808) 14 Ves Jun 567, 33 ER 638, 641 168
Butler v Egg and Egg Pulp Marketing Board (1966) 114 CLR 185 266
Butterworth v Kingsway Motors Ltd [1954] 1 WLR 1286 383
BV Nederlandse Industrie can Eiproducktion v Rembrandt Enterprises Inc [2020]
 QB 551, [2019] EWCA Civ 596, [2020] QB 551 102

BV v Force India Formula One Team Ltd [2010] EWHC 2373 (QB) 111
Byers v Samba [2022] EWCA Civ 43 .... 236–37, 238, 241

Cahill v Hall 37 NE 573 (1894) 268
Calland v Lloyd (1840) 6 M & W 26, 151 ER 307 192
Campbell Mostyn (Provisions) Ltd v Barnett Trading Co [1954] 1 Lloyd's Rep 65 (CA) 333–34
Campbell v Griffin [2001] EWCA Civ 990, (2001) 82 P&CR DG23 .... 282, 283
Campbell v Mirror Group Newspapers [2004] UKHL 22, [2004] AC 457 .... 215, 311, 312
Canadian Automatic Data Processing Services Ltd v CEEI Safety & Security Inc
    (2004) 246 DLR (4th) 400 (Ont CA) 165
Canadian Pacific Railway v The King [1931] AC 414 (PC) 271–72
Cantiare San Rocco v Clyde Shipbuilding and Engineering Co [1924] AC 226 (HL) 139
Car & Universal Finance Co Ltd v Caldwell [1965] 1 QB 525 (CA) 8, 193–94
Carlill v Carbolic Smoke Ball Co. [1893] 1 QB 256 116–17
Caron v Jahani (No 2) [2020] NSWCA 117, (2020) 382 LR 158 250
Carr-Saunders v Dick McNeil Associates [1986] 1 WLR 922 347
Case of Leather YB 5 Henry VII fol 15 204
Case of Swans (1592) 7 Co Rep 15, 77 ER 435 205
Casey's Patents, Re [1892] 1 Ch 104 (CA) 158
Casson v Roberts [1862] 31 Beav 613, 54 ER 1277 123
Castellain v Preston [1883] 11 QBD 380 (CA) 252
Castle Phillips Finance v Piddington (1995) 70 P & CR 592 (CA) 253
Cave v Cave (1880) 15 Ch D 639 251
Cavendish Square Holdings BV v Makdessi [2015] UKSC 67, [2016] AC 1172 148
Caverley v Green (1984) 155 CLR 242 (HCA) 273
CBS Songs Ltd v Amstrad Consumer Electronics plc [1988] AC 1013 (HL) 41, 158
Celanese International Corp v BP Chemicals Ltd [1999] RPC 203 308
Century (UK) Ltd SA v Clibbery [2004] EWHC 1870 278
Challinor v Juliet Bellis & Co [2015] EWCA Civ 59 61
Chalmers v Pardoe [1963] 1 WLR 677 (PC) 276–77
Chambers v Miller (1862) 13 CB (NS) 125, 143 ER 50 .... 33, 44
Chambers v Miller (1862) 3 F&F 202, 176 ER 91 197
Chandler v Webster [1904] 1 KB 493 (CA) 136, 138, 139–40, 143
Charity Commission for England and Wales v Framjee [2014] EWHC 2507
    (Ch), [2015] 1 WLR 16 249–50
Charlotte, The [1908] P 206 (CA) 346
Chartbrook Ltd v Persimmon Homes Ltd [2009] UKHL 38, [2009] 1 AC 1101 53
Charter plc v City Index Ltd [2007] EWCA Civ 1382, [2008] Ch 313 238
Chase Manhattan Bank NA v Israel-British Bank (London) Ltd [1981] Ch 105 ...... 8, 231, 232–33
Chase v Corcoran 106 Mass 286 (1871) 186–87
Chase v Porter (1877) 69 NY 133 245
Cheese v Thomas [1994] 1 WLR 129 (CA) 358
Chellew v Royal Commission on the Sugar Supply [1921] 2 KB 627 182
Chesterman v Lamb (1834) 2 A & E 129, 111 ER 50 180
Chesworth v Farrar [1966] 2 WLR 1073 331
Chettiar v Chettiar [1962] AC 294 (PC) 395–96
Chetwynd v Allen [1899] 1 Ch 353 254
Chichester Diocesan Fund v Simpson [1944] AC 341 (HL) 39–40
Chief Constable of Greater Manchester Police v Wigan Athletic AFC [2008] EWCA
    Civ 1449, [2009] 1 WLR 1590 .... 37–38, 49
Childers v Childers (1857) 1 De G&J 482, 44 ER 810 232–33
Chillingworth v Esche [1924] 1 Ch 97 113
China Pacific SA v Food Corporation of India, The Winson [1982] AC 939 (HL) 81, 179
Chinery v Viall (1860) 5 H&N 288, 157 ER 266, 321
Church v Lee 5 Johns 348 204
CIA Barca de Panama S.A. v George Wimpey & Co Ltd [1980] 1 Lloyd's Rep 598 (CA) 122–23

xxvi   TABLE OF CASES

Citadel General Assurance Co v Lloyd's Bank Canada [1997] 3 SCR 805 238
Citibank NA v MBIA Assurance SA [2007] EWCA Civ 11 223
Clark v Macourt [2013] HCA 56, (2013) 304 ALR 220 335
Clarke v Dickson (1858) El Bl & El 148; 120 ER 463 .... 8, 381
Clarke v Shee and Johnson (1774) 1 Cowp 197, 98 ER 1041 .... 192, 210, 392–93
Clarke v Swaby [2007] UKPC 1, [2007] 2 P&CR 2 281
Claxton v Kay 101 Ark 350, 142 SW 517 (1912) 53
Clayton's Case Devynes v Noble (Clayton's Case) (1816) 1 Mer 572, 35 ER 781 249–50
Cleadon Trust Ltd, Re [1939] Ch 286 .... 10–11, 160
Cleaver v Mutual Reserve Fund Lie Association [1892] 1 QB 147 300
Clough Mill Ltd v Martin [1985] 1 WLR 111 (CA) 198–99, 203, 204
Cobb v Becke (1845) 6 QB 930, 115 ER 530 38
Cobbe v Yeoman's Row [2008] UKHL 55, [2008] 1 WLR 1752 .... 113, 114–15, 275–76, 279,
    281–82, 284, 286
Cochrane v Moore (1895) 25 QBD 57 (CA) 193
Cohen v Roche [1927] 1 KB 169 191–92
Cohen v Sellar [1926] 1 KB 536 113
Colbeam Palmer Ltd v Stock Affiliates Pty Ltd (1968) 122 CLR 25 (HCA) 307
Cole v Green (1671/2) 1 Lev 309, 83 ER 422 344
Cole, Re [1964] Ch 175 197
Colley v Overseas Exporters [1921] 3 KB 302 122–23
Collier v Collier [2002] EWCA Civ 1095, [2002] BPIR 1057 .... 395–96, 410
Collings v Lee [2001] 2 All ER 332 (CA) 245
Collins v Elstone [1893] P 1 90
Colonial Bank v Exchange Bank of Yarmouth (1885) 9 App Cas 84 (PC) 45
Combe v Combe [1951] 2 KB 215 (CA) 275
Commercial Banking Co of Sydney Ltd v Mann [1961] AC 1 (PC); [1961] AC 1 .... 207, 208
Commerzbank AG v Gareth Price-Jones [2003] EWCA Civ 1663 .... 364, 366
Commerzbank AG v IMB Morgan Plc [2004] EWHC 2771 (Ch), [2005] 1 Lloyd's Rep 298 8
Commissioner of Stamp Duties (Queensland) v Livingston [1965] AC 694 (PC) 40, 226–27
Commissioner of State Revenue v Royal Insurance Australia Ltd [1994] HCA 61,
    (1994) 182 CLR 151 .... 92–93, 376
Commonwealth of Australia v Verwayen (1990) 170 CLR 394 (HCA) 269, 270–71, 275
Concord Coal Co v Ferrin 71 NH 22, 51 A 283 (1901) 114
Continental Caoutchouc & Gutta Percha Co v Kleinwort Sons & Co (1904)
    90 LTR 474 (PC) 389–90
Cook's Mortgage, Re [1896] 1 Ch 923 184
Co-Operative Insurance Society Ltd v Argyll Stores (Holdings) Ltd. [1998] AC 1 (HL) 341–42
Cope v Rowland (1836) 2 M&W 149, 150 ER 707 397
Cotnam v Wisdom 104 SW 164 (Ark 1907) 181
Cotronic (UK) Ltd v Dezonie (t/a Wendaland Builders Ltd) [1991] BCLC 721 (CA) 400
County of Carleton v Ottawa (1965) 52 DLR (2d) 220 (Crt) 162, 171
Couthurst v Sweet (1865–1866) LR 1 CP 649 388
Couturier v Hastie [1856] 5 HLC 673, 10 ER 1065 75
Cox v Prentice (1815) 3 M & S 344, 105 ER 641 .... 62, 389–90
Crabb v Arun [1976] Ch 179 (CA) 277, 280
Craig v Lamoureux [1920] AC 349 90
Crantrave Ltd v Lloyd's Bank Plc [2000] EWCA Civ 127, [2000] QB 917 .... 10–11, 160, 239–40
Craven-Ellis v Canons Ltd [1936] 2 KB 403 48
Creak v James Moore & Sons Pty Ltd (1912) 15 CLR 426 245
Credit Agricole Corp & Investment Bank v Papadimitrou [2015] UKPC 13, [2015] 1 WLR 4265 242
Credit Lyonnais v George Stevenson and Co Ltd (1901) 9 SLT 93 OH, 95 355
Cressman v Coys of Kensington (Sales) Ltd [2004] EWCA Civ 47, [2004] 1 WLR 2775 34
Crippen, Re [1911] P 108 300
Crisan Estate, In re 107 NW 2d 907 (Mich 1961) 181
Criterion Properties plc v Stratford UK Properties LLC [2004] UKHL 28, [2004]
    1 WLR 1846 .... 239, 240–41

TABLE OF CASES   xxvii

Crown Holdings (London) Ltd (In Liquidation), Re [2015] EWHC 1876 (Ch) 8
CTN Cash and Carry v Gallaher [1994] 4 All ER 714 (CA) 77, 99
Cundy v Lindsay (1878) 3 App Cas 459 (HL) 196
Curtis v Groat 6 Johns 169 204
Customs and Excise Commissioners v Barclays Bank plc [2006] UKHL 28, [2007] 1 AC 181 vi
Cutter v Powell (1795) 6 Term Rep 320, 101 ER 573 .... 119, 143, 145–46, 147

D&D Wine International (In Liquidation), Re [2016] UKSC 47, [2016] 1 WLR 3179 ..... 8, 234, 245
Daly v Sydney Stock Exchange (1986) 160 CLR 371 229
Damon Compania Naviera SA v Hapag-Lloyd International SA, The Blankenstein, The
    Bartenstein, The Birkenstein [1985] 1 WLR 435 (CA) 336
Dargamo Holdings Ltd v Avonwick Holdings Ltd [2021] EWCA Civ 1149, [2022] 1 All ER
    (Comm) 1244 110
David Securities Pty Ltd v Commonwealth Bank of Australia [1992] HCA 48, (1992)
    175 CLR 353 .... 72, 77, 355
Davidson v Gwynne (1810) 12 East 381, 104 ER 149 116
Davies v Davies [2016] EWCA Civ 463 .... 279, 282–83
Davis v Bryan (1827) 6 B& C 651, 108 ER 591 123
DD Growth Premium v RMF Strategies [2017] UKPC 36, [2018] Bus LR 1595 .... 85, 237
De Bernardy v Harding (1853) 8 Ex 822, 155 ER 1586 132
Deakins v Hookings [1994] 1 EGLR 190 347
Deering v Earl of Winchelsea (1787) 2 Bos & Pul 270 (ex), 274 126 ER 1276 .... 155, 182
Degelman v Guaranty Trust Co. of Canada and Constantineau [1954] SCR 725,
    [1954] 3 DLR 785 .... 14, 112, 113, 355
Delta Petroleum (Caribbean) Ltd v British Virgin Islands Electricity Corporation
    (British Virgin Islands) [2020] UKPC 23 100
Derby v Scottish Equitable plc [2001] EWCA Civ 369, [2001] 3 All ER 818 368
Deutsche Morgan Grenfell plc v Inland Revenue Commissioners [2006] UKHL 49,
    [2007] 1 AC 558 .... 7–8, 86–87, 88, 89, 373, 419
Devenish Nutrition Ltd v Sanofi-Avenitis SA [2008] EWCA Civ 1086, [2009] Ch 390 326
Dextra Bank & Trust Co Ltd v Bank of Jamaica [2002] 1 All ER (Comm) 193 (PC) 101, 102,
    366–67, 419
Diamond Cutting Works Federation Ltd v Triefus & Co Ltd [1956] 1 Lloyd's Rep 216 333–34
Dies v British International Mining [1939] 1 KB 724, 108 LJKB 398 160 LT 563 136
Dillwyn v Llere Basham [1986] 1 WLR 1498 278
Dillwyn v Llewelyn (1862) 4 De G, F & J 517, 45 ER 1284 .... 270–71, 278
Dimond v Lovell [2002] 1 AC 384 (HL) 133, 346, 400–1, 406
Dimskal Shipping Co SA v International Transport Workers Federation
    (The Evia Luck (No 2)) [1992] 2 AC 152 102
Diplock, Re [1947] Ch 716 (Wynn-Parry J) 39–40
Diplock, Re [1948] Ch 465 (CA) 39–40, 233–34, 248, 267
Diplock, Re [1951] AC 251 (HL) 39–40, 61–62, 233–34, 236, 248, 260
DKLR Holding Co (No 2) Pty Ltd v Commissioner of Stamp Duties (1982)
    149 CLR 431 (HCA) 220
DO Ferguson & Associates v Sohl (1992) 62 Build, LR 95 (CA) 130
Dodsworth v Dodsworth (1973) 228 EG 1115 (CA) 273
Dollar Land (Cumbernauld) Ltd v CIN Properties Ltd 1996 SC 331, 1997 SLT 260 7–8
Don v Trojan Construction Co. 178 Cal App 2d 135 (1960) 294–95
Dorchester Corporation v Ensor (1869) LR 4 Ex 335, 339 327
Donoghue v Stevenson v
Douglas v Hello (No 3) [2005] EWCA Civ 595, [2006] QB 125 312
Dubai Aluminium Co Ltd v Salaam [2002] UKHL 48, [2003] 2 AC 366 156
Dudley v Dudley (1705) Pec Ch 241, 244, 24 ER 118, 119 215
Duke de Cadaval v Collins (1836) 4 Ad & El 858, 111 ER 1006 198
Duke of Beaufort v Patrick, The (1853) Beav 60, 51 ER 954 274
Duke of Norfolk v Worthy (1808) 1 Camp 337, 170 ER 977 387–88
Duncan Fox & Co v North & South Wales Bank (1880) 6 App Cas 1 (HL) 153, 171–72

xxviii　TABLE OF CASES

Durham v BAI (Run-Off) Ltd [2012] UKSC 14, [2012] 1 WLR 867 88–89
Dyer v Dyer (1788) 2 Cox Eq 92, 93, 30 ER 42, 43 230

Earl of Oxford's Case, The (1615) Rep Ch 1, 21 ER 485 272
East Fifty Fourth Street Inc v United States 157 F 2d 68 (USCA, 1946) 376
Eastgate, Re [1905] 1 KB 465 193–94
Eaves v Hickson (1861) 30 Beav 136, 54 ER 840 172
Ebsen Finance Ltd v Wong Hou-Lianq Neil [2022] SGHC (I) 25 .... 7, 371–72
Ecila Henderson v Dorset Healthcare University NHS Foundation Trust [2020]
　UKSC 43, [2020] WLR (D) 592 .... 393, 397, 401, 407
Edelstein v Edelstein (1863) 1 De GJ &S 185, 46 ER 72 307
Edgington v Fitzmaurice (1885) 29 Ch D 459 (CA) 102
Edinburgh and District Tramways Ltd v Courtenay 1909 SC 99 (IHCS) 29, 30, 31
Edwards v Lee's Administrator, 96 SW2d 1028 (Ky Ct App 1936) 8–9, 327, 328
Edwards, Re [2007] EWHC 1119 90
El Ajou v Dollar Land Holdings (No 1) [1993] BCC 698 rev'd on other grounds
　[1994] BCC 143 (CA) 96, 229, 237–38
Electricity Supply Nominees Ltd v Thorn EMI Retail Ltd (1991) 63 P&CR 143
　(CA) 160, 239–40
Elitestone Ltd v Morris [1997] 1 WLR 687 201
Ellis v Goulton [1893] 1 QB 350 387
ENE 1 Kos Ltd v Petroleo Brasileiro SA (The Kos) (No 2) [2012] UKSC 17, [2012]
　2 AC 164 .... 177, 180
Energizer Supermarket Ltd v Holiday Snacks Ltd [2022] UKPC 16 .... 397, 406–7
Equitas Insurance Ltd v Municipal Mutual Insurance Ltd [2019] EWCA Civ 718,
　[2020] QB 418 89
Equuscorp Pty Ltd v Haxton [2012] HCA 7, (2012) 246 CLR 498 400–1
ER Ives Investment Ltd v High [1967] 2 QB 379 272
Eric Bieber & Co Ltd v Rio Tinto Co Ltd [1918] AC 260 (HL) 392, 399
Erlanger v New Sombrero Phosphate Co (1878) 3 App Cas 1218 (HL) 381, 382
Essery v Cowlard (1884) 26 ChD 191 113
Esso Petroleum Co Ltd v Niad [2001] EWHC 458 (Ch), [2001] All ER (D 324 (Ch) 325–26
Esso Petroleum Co Ltd v Southport Corp [1956] AC 218 (HL) 183
Estok v Heguy 40 DLR (2d) 88 266–67
Evans v Bartlam [1937] AC 473 (HL) 269–70
Eves v Eves [1975] 1 WLR 1338 (CA) 278
Exall v Partridge (1799) 8 TR 308, 101 ER 1405 .... 50–51, 154, 167, 169
Exchange Telegraph Co Ltd v Giulanotti 1959 SC 19, 1959 SLT 293 (OHCS) 296 34–35
Experience Hendrix LLC v PPX Enterprises Inc [2003] EWCA Civ 323, [2003] 1 All ER
　(Comm) 830 (CA) 325–26

Faccenda Chicken Ltd Fowler [1987] Ch 117 (CA) 309
Factortame Ltd v Secretary of State for Transport (No.2) [1991] 1 AC 603 (HL) 87–88
Fairchild v Glenhaven Funeral Services Ltd [2002] UKHL 22, [2003] 1 AC 32 88–89
Falcke v Scottish Imperial Insurance Co (1886) 34 Ch D 234 (CA) 31, 32, 160, 175, 183
Farah Constructions Pty Ltd v Say-Dee Pty Ltd [2007] HCA 22, 230 CLR 89 260–61
Farepack Food and Gifts Ltd, In re [2006] EWHC 3272 (Ch), [2008] BCC 22 .... 8, 234
Farmer v Arundel (1772) 2 Black W 824, 96 ER 485 73–74
Farmers' Mart Ltd v Milne 1913 SC (HL) 84, 87, (1914) 2 SLT 153, 154 395
Farquharson Bros & Co v King & Co [1902] AC 325 (HL) 209
Federal Commerce Navigation Ltd v Molena Alpha Inc ('The Nanfri') [1978]
　QB 927 (CA) 380–81
Federal Sugar Refining Co v United States Sugar Equalization Board inc.
　268 F 5775 (1920) 322–23
Ffrench's Estate, Re (1887) 21 LR Ir 283 (CA) 251
FHR European Ventures LLP v Cedar Capital Partners LLC [2014] UKSC 45, [2015]
　AC 250 .... 227, 302, 318, 408

Fibrosa Spolka Akcyjna v Fairbairn Lawson Combe Barbour Ltd [1943]
　　AC 32 (HL) 109, 115, 126, 138, 139
Fisher v Brooker [2009] UKHL 41, [2009] 1 WLR 1764 274
Fitzalan-Howard v Hibbert [2009] EWHC 2855 (QB); [2010] PNLR 11 8
Fitzgerald v FJ Leonhardt Pty Ltd [1997] HCA 17, (1997) 189 CLR 215 400–1
Fivaz v Nicholls (1846) 2 CB 501, 512, 135 ER 1042, 1046 395
Five Steel Barges, Re (1890) 15 PD 142 185–86
Fletcher v Alexander (1867–1868) LR 3 CP 375 182
Flower v Sadler (1882) 10 QBD 572 85
Forbes v Jackson (1882) 19 ChD 615 253
Foreman State Trust & Savings Bank v Tauber 180 NE 827 (1932) 122
Forman & Co. Pty Ltd v The Liddesdale [1900] AC 190 (PC) 128–29
Forsyth-Grant v Allen [2008] EWCA Civ 505 328
Foskett v McKeown [2001] 1 AC 102 (HL) 8, 244–46, 247, 248–49
Foster v Stewart (1814) 3 M & S 191, 105 ER 582 . . . . 322, 329–30
Fowler v Hollins (1872) LR 7 QB 616 211–12
Fox v Mackreth (1789–1791) 2 Bro CC 400, 29 ER 224 315
Fragonard case (Cass le ci, 25 May 1992, Bull Civ I, No 165) 268
Frank Music Corp v Metro-Goldwyn-Mayer Inc 772 F 2d 505 (9th Cir 1985) 308
Freeman v Cooke (1848) 2 Ex 654, 154 ER 652 269–70
Friend v Brooker [2009] HCA 21, 239 CLR 129 164–65
FSHC Group Holdings Ltd v Glas Trust Corporation Ltd [2019] EWCA Civ 1361 53
Fulton Shipping Inc of Panama v Globalia Business Travel SAU ('The New Flamenco')
　　[2015] EWCA Civ 1299, [2016] 1 WLR 2450 335

Gafford v Graham [1999] 3 EGLR 75 (CA) 80 343
Gamerco SA v ICM/Fair Warning (Agency) Ltd [1995] 1 WLR 1226 141–42
Garland v Consumer Gas Co [2004] 1 SCR 629, [2004] 237 DLR (4th) 385 (SCC) 7–8, 30, 73
Gartell & Son (A Firm) v Yeovill Town Football & Athletic Club Ltd [2016]
　　EWCA Civ 62 . . . . 110, 119
Gebhardt v Saunders [1892] 2 QB 452 . . . . 10–11, 159, 162
Gee v Gee [2018] EWHC 1393 279
Geldof Metaalconstructie NV v Simon Carves Ltd [2010] EWCA Civ 667, [2010] 1 CLC 895 381
General & Finance Facilities v Cooks Cars (Romford) Ltd [1963] 1 WLR 644 (CA) 191–92
Gibb v Maidstone & Tunbridge NHS Trust [2010] EWCA Civ 678, [2010] IRLR 786 . . . . 38, 133
Giedo Van der Garde BV v Force India Formula One Team Ltd [2010] EWHC 2373
　　(QB) 336, 343
Gilchrist Watt and Sanderson Pty Ltd v York Product Pty Ltd [1970] 1 WLR 1262 180
Giles v Edwards (1797) 7 TR 181, 101 ER 920 (KB) 109
Gillett v Holt [2001] Ch 210 . . . . 279, 280, 281–82, 283–84
Gillingham Bus Disaster Fund, Re [1958] Ch 300 226
Giumelli v Giumelli (1999) 196 CLR 101 (HCA) 257, 281
Glencore International AG v Metro Trading International Inc [2001] 1 All ER (Comm) 103 203
Glencore v MTI [2001] 1 Lloyds Rep 284 14
Globalia Business Travel SAU v Fultons Shipping Inc of Panama [2017] UKSC 43,
　　[2017] 1 WLR 2581 335
Glubb, Bamfield v Rogers, Re [1900] 1 Ch 354 91
Gnitrow Ltd v Cape plc [2000] 3 All ER 763 168
Gnych v Polish Club Ltd [2015] HCA 23, (2015) 255 CLR 414 . . . . 397, 400–1
Godin et al v London Assurance Co (1758) 1 Burr. 489, 97 ER 419 159–60
Goldburg (No 2), Re [1912] 1 KB 606 192
Goldcorp Exchange Ltd, Re [1995] 1 AC 74 (PC) 233, 248, 257–58, 270
Golden Strait Corpn v Nippon Yusen Kubishka Kaisha, the Golden Victory [2007]
　　UKHL 17, [2007] 2 AC 353 . . . . 334, 335–36
Goldstein v Rosenberg 73 NE 2d 171 (1947) 122
Golightly v Reynolds (1772) Lofft 87, 98 ER 547 192
Google v Lloyd [2021] UKSC 50, [2021] 3 WLR 1268 . . . . 293, 312, 332, 338–39

TABLE OF CASES

Goring, The [1988] 1 AC 831 186–87
Goss v Chilcott [1996] AC 788 (PC) 33–34, 360
Gowers v Lloyds and National Provincial Foreign Bank Ltd [1938] 1 All ER 766 (CA) 389–90
Grainger v Hill (1838) 4 Bing NC 212, 132 ER 769 198
Gray v Johnston 1928 SC 659, 1928 SLT 499 (IHCS). 112
Gray v Thames Trains Ltd [2009] UKHL 33, [2009] AC 1339 407
Greasley v Cooke [1980] 1 WLR 1306 (CA) 269
Great Northern Railway Co v Swaffield (1873–1874) LR 9 Ex 132 .... 7, 178
Green v Portsmouth Stadium Ltd [1953] 2 QB 190 (CA) 409
Green v Weatherill [1929] 2 Ch 213 237
Greenway v Hurd 91794) TR 553, 100 ER 1171 388
Greenwood v Bennett [1973] QB 195 .... 13, 14, 48, 264–65, 264, 265, 266–68
Grey v Hill (1826) Ry & M 420, 171 ER 1070 112
Grey v New Augarita Porcupine Mines Ltd [1952] 3 DLR 1 (PC) 317–18
Grieve v Morrison 1993 SLT 852 (OHCS) 110
Griffith v Brymer (1903) 19 TLR 434 75
Griffiths v Williams (1978) 248 EG 947 (CA) 277
Grimaldi v Chameleon Mining (No 2) (2012) 200 FCR 296, [2012] FCAFC 6 ..... 245, 257
Grobbelaar v News Group Newspapers Ltd [2002] UKHL 40, [2002] 1 WLR 3024 345
Grundt v Great Boulder Pty Gold Mines Ltd (1937) 59 CLR 641 (HCA) 275
Guest v Guest [2020] EWCA Civ 387 283
Guildford BC v Hein [2005] EWCA Civ 979, [2005] LGR 797 180
Guinness Mahon & Co Ltd v Kensington & Chelsea London Borough Council
    [1999] QB 215 123–24
Gulati v MGN Ltd [2015] EWCA Civ 1291, [2017] QB 149 344

Habberfield v Habberfield [2019] EWCA Civ 890, [2019] 2 P&CRDG 13 .... 269, 279, 283–84
Halifax Building Society v Thomas [1996] Ch 217 (CA) 299, 318, 322–23, 326–27, 343
Hall & Baker, Re (1878) 9 Ch D 538 118
Hall v Hebert [1993] 2 SCR 159 .... 392, 403
Hallett's Estate, Re (1880) 13 ChD 696 (CA) 250–51
Halley v Law Society [2003] EWCA Civ 97 245
Halpern v Halpern [2007] EWCA Civ 291, [2008] QB 195 382
Hambly v Trott (1776) 1 Cowp 371, 98 ER 1136 331
Harper v Royal Bank of Canada (1994) 18 OR (3d) 317, 114 DLR 749 (Div Ct) 231
Harris v Hickman [1904] 1 KB 13 162
Harrison, In re; ex p Jay (1880) 14 ChD 19 (CA) 195
Harse v Pearl Life Assurance Co [1904] 1 KB 558 (CA) 400
Hart v EP Dutton & Co Inc 93 NYS 2d 871 (1949) 312
Hartley v Hymans [1920] 3 KB 475 271
Haugesund Kommune v Depfa ACS Bank [2010] EWCA Civ 579, [2012] QB 549 ..... 25, 356–57, 360
Hawkins v McGee 84 NH 114, 146 A 641 (NH 1929) 57, 292–93
Hayim v Citibank N.A. [1987] AC 730 (PC) 217
Hazell v Hammersmith and Fulham London Borough Council [1992] 2 AC 1 (HL) 93, 94, 232–33
Heath v Crealock (1874) 10 Ch App 22 242
Heaton v AX Equity and Law Life Assurance Soc plc [2002] UKHL 15, [2002] 2 AC 329 170
Hedley Byrne & Co Ltd v Heller & Partners Ltd. [1964] AC 465 (HL) 285
Hemmings (t/a Simply Pleasures Ltd) v Westminster CC [2013] EWCA Civ 591 60
Henriksens Rederi A/S v THZ Rolimpex the Brede [1974] 1 QB 233 (CA) 379
Henry v Henry [2010] UKPC 3, [2010] 1 All ER 988 278
Heperu Pty Ltd v Belle [2009] NSWCA 252 214
Herbert v Doyle [2010] EWCA Civ 1095, [2011] 1 EGLR 119 .... 280, 281
Hermann v Charlesworth [1905] 2 QB 123 398
Herne Bay Steamboat Co v Hutton [1903] 2 KB 683 75
Higgs v Holiday (1598) Cro Eliz 746, 78 ER 978 206
High Commissioner for Pakistan in the United Kingdom v Prince Mukkram Jah, The [2016]
    EWHC 1465 (Ch) 390

TABLE OF CASES   xxxi

Hill v Reglon Pty Ltd. [2007] NSWCA 295 200
Hill v Van Erp (1997) 188 CLR 159 53
Hindson v Weatherill (1854) 5 De GM & G 301, 43 ER 886 90
Hingston v Vent (1876) 1 QBD 367 179
Hinton v Sparkes (1868) LR 3 CP 161 136
Hirachand Punamchand v Temple [1911] 2 KB 330 (CA) 160
Hobson v Gorringe [1897] 1 Ch 182 201
Hoechst AG v Inland Revenue Commissioners and A-G (C-410/98) [2001] ECR I-1727 86
Hoffman v Red Owl Stores 133 NW 2d 267 (1965) 285
Holland Hannen & Cubitts (Northern) Ltd v Welsh Health Technical Services Organisation
    (1981) 18 Build L 80 (CA) 128–29
Holland v Hodgson (1872) LR 7 CP 328 201
Holland v Russell (1863) Bes & S 14, 122 ER 365 (KB) 389–90
Hollins v Fowler (1871–1872) LR 7 QB 616, aff'd (1874–1875) LR 7 HL 757 361
Holman v Johnson (1775) 1 Cowp 341, 98 ER 1120 .... 22, 196, 391–92, 397, 398, 403
Holt v Ely (1853) 1 Ellis & Black 795, 118 ER 634 41
Holt v Markham [1923] 1 KB 504 (CA) 367–68
Homburg Houtimport BV v Agrosin Private Ltd (The Starsin) [2003] UKHL 12, [2004] 1 AC 75 386
Hopgood v Brown [1955] 1 WLR 213 (CA) 269–70
Horrocks, Re [1939] P 198 90
Hotham v The East India Company (1787) 1 Term Rep638, 99 ER 1295 122
Hounga v Allen [2014] UKSC 47, [2014] 1 WLR 2889 401
Howard v Pickford Tool Co Ltd [1951] 1 KB 417 (CA) 136
Howard v Wood (1688) 2 Show KB 21, 89 ER 767 52
Howe v Smith (1884) 27 Ch D 89 (CA) 136
Huckle v Money (1762) 2 Wils 205, 95 ER 768 345
Hughes v Asset Managers plc [1995] 3 All ER 669 (CA) 397
Hughes v La Baia Ltd [2011] UKPC 9 371
Hughes v Liverpool Victoria friendly Society [1916] 2 KB 482 (CA) 400
Hughes v Metropolitan Railway Co (1877) 2 App Cas 439 (HL) 270–71, 272
Huning v Ferrers Dann v Spurrier (1802) 7 Ves Jr 231, 32 ER 94 272
Hunt v Silk (1804) 5 East 449, 102 ER 1142 .... 121, 369–70
Hunter v Mann [1974] QB 767 309
Hussain v Lancaster City Council [1999] 2 WLR 1142 (CA) 41
Hussey v Palmer [1972] 1 WLR 1286 (CA) 273, 282–83
Huyton SA v Peter Cremer GmbH [1999] 1 Lloyd's Rep 620 102

IBL v Coussens [1991] 2 All ER 133 (CA) 346
Ibmac Ltd v Marshall (Homes) Ltd, CA (1968) 208 EG 851 128–29
Imperator Realty Co Inc v Tull 127 NE 263, 267 (NYCA, 1920) 272
Independent Trustee Services Ltd v GP Noble [2012] EWCA Civ 195, [2013] Ch 91 ...... 217, 232
Indian Oil Corp v Greenstone Shipp SA (Panama) [1988] QB 345 199–201
Indiana Mutual Insurance Co v Reinsurance Results Inc, 513 F 3d 625 (7th Cir 2008) 48
Ingram v Little [1961] 1 QB 31 (CA) 197–98
Ings v Industrial Acceptance Corp (1962) 32 DLR 2d 611 264
Interfoto Picture Library Ltd v Stiletto Visual Programmes Ltd [1989] QB 433 (CA) 103–4
International Banking Corporation v Ferguson, Shaw & Sons, The 1910 SC 182 (IHCS) 203
International Energy Group v Zurich Insurance [2015] UKSC 33, [2016] AC 509 ...... 88–89, 419
International News Service v Associated Press 248 US 215 (1918) 260, 305
Inverugie Investments Ltd v Hackett [1996] 1 WLR 713 (PC) 349
Investment Trust Companies (in liquidation) v Revenue and Customs
    Commissioners [2017] UKSC 29, [2018] AC 275 .... 30, 31, 34–35, 36–37, 38,
                                                                54, 374, 378, 405, 419–20
Inwards v Baker [1965] 2 QB 29 (CA) 272, 273, 275
Irvine v Talksport [2003] EWCA Civ 423, [2003] 2 All ER 881 345
Isenberg v East India House Estate Ltd (1863) 3 DeG J & S 263, 273, 637, 46 ER 641 342
ITS v Noble [2012] EWCA Civ 95, [2013] Ch 91 244

xxxii TABLE OF CASES

Jackson v Anderson (1811) 4 Taunt 24, 128 ER 235 200
Jacob & Youngs Inc v Kent 23 NY 239, 244, 129 NE 889, 891 (1921) 118, 337
Jacob v Allen (1703) 1 Salk 27, 91 ER 26 51–52
Jacobs v Davis [1917] 2 KB 532 113
Jaggard v Sawyer [1995] 1 WLR 269 (CA) 293, 341, 343, 347
Jamal v Moola Dawood & Sons & Co [1916] 1 AC 175 (PC) 333–34
Jameel v Wall Street Journal Europe Sprl [2006] UKHL 44, [2007] 1 AC 359 344
James Moore & Sons Ltd v University of Ottawa (1975) 5 OR (2d) 162, 49 DLR (3d) 666 126
James Roscoe (Bolton) Ltd v Winder [1915] 1 Ch 62 249
James v Thomas [2007] EWCA Civ 1212 283–84
Jameson v Central Electricity Generating Board [2000] 1 AC 455 170
Jegon v Vivian (No 2) (1870–1871) LR 6 Ch App 742 348
Jenkins v Tucker (1788) 1 Hy Bl 90, 126 ER 55 .... 154, 164, 171, 370
Jennings and Chapman Ltd v Woodman Matthews & Co [1952] 2 TLR 409 69–70
Jennings v Rice [2002] EWCA Civ 159, [2003] 1 P & CR 8 .... 113, 269, 282, 283, 284, 288
Jeremy D Stone Consultations Ltd v National Westminster Bank plc [2013]
    EWHC 208 (Ch) 390
Jerome v Kelly [2004] UKHL 25, [2004] 1 WLR 1409 224
Johnson v Agnew [1980] AC 367 (HL) 341
Johnson v Gore Wood & Co [2000] UKHL 65, [2002] 2 AC 1 292
Johnson v Royal Mail Steam Packet Co (1867–1868) LR 3 CP 38 154
Jones v Barkley (1781) 2 Doug 684, 692; 99 ER 434 118
Jones v Churcher [2009] EWHC 722 (QB), [2009] 2 Lloyd's Rep 94 389–90
Jones v De Marchant (1916) 28 DLR 561 .... 201, 202, 204
Jones v Powles (1834) 3 Myl & K 581, 40 ER 222 242
Jones, Re [1893] 2 Ch 461 184
Jorden v Money (1854) 5 HL Cas 15, 10 ER 868 (PC) 270
Joyce v Epsom and Ewell BC [2012] EWCA Civ 1398, [2013] 1 P&CRDG 1 .... 277, 280
Joyner v Weeks [1891] 2 QB 31 (CA) 336
JS Bloor Ltd v Pavillion Developments Ltd [2008] EWHC 724 (TCC), [2008]
    2 EGLR 85 .... 48, 274–75
JT Developments v Quinn (1991) 62 P&CR 33 (CA) 280

Kammins Ballrooms Co Ltd v Zenith Investments (Torquay) Ltd [1971] AC 850 (HL) 272
Kangaroo, The [1918] P 327 186
Kasumu v Baba-Egbe [1956] AC 539 (PC) 398
Kearley v Thomson (1890) 24 QBD 742 410
Kearns v Andree 107 Conn 181, 139 A 695, 59 ALR 599 (1928) 69, 287
Keech v Sandford (1726) Sel Cas Ch 61, 25 ER 223 314
Keefe v Law Society of New South Wales (1998) 44 NSWLR 451 249–50
Kelly v Fraser [2012] UKPC 25, [2013] 1 AC 450 270
Kelly v Solari (1841) 9 M&W 54, 152 ER 24 .... 71–72, 72, 73, 76, 79, 171, 236, 237, 259, 369
Kendall v Hamilton (1879) 4 App Cas 504 (HL) 158
Kerr v Baranow [2011] 1 SCR 269 257
Kerr v Baranow [2011] 328 DLR (4th) 577 (SCC) 30
Kerrison v Glyn Mills Currie & Co (1911) 81 LJKB 465 .... 101–2, 389–90
Keystone Healthcare Ltd v Parr [2019] EWCA Civ 1246, [2019] 4 WLR 99 317–18
Khan v Permayer [2001] BPIR 95 (CA) 42
Kiam v MGN Ltd [2003] QB 281 (CA) 344
Kinane v Mackie-Conteh [2005] EWCA Civ 45, [2005] WTLR 345 280
King v Alston (1848) 12 QB 971, 116 ER 1134 52
King v Hoare (1844) 13 M & W 494, 153 ER 206 158
Kingston v Preston (1773) 2 Doug KB 689, (1772) 99 ER 437 118
Kingstreet Investments Ltd v New Brunswick (Department of Finance) [2007]
    SCC 1; [2007] 1 SCR 3 .... 19, 99, 376
Kiriri Cotton Ltd v Dewani [1960] 2 WLR 127 (PC) 409
Kleinert v Abosso Gold Mining Co (1913) 58 SJ (PC) 45 122–23

Kleinwort Benson Ltd v Birmingham City Council [1997] QB 380 (CA) 31,375
Kleinwort Benson Ltd v Sandwell Borough [1994] 4 All ER 890 .... 371–72, 378–79
Kleinwort Benson Ltd v South Tyneside Metropolitan BC [1994] 4 All ER 972 .... 375, 378–79
Kleinwort Benson v Lincoln City Council [1992] 2 AC 349 .... 7–8, 76, 86–87, 93–94, 97,
103, 104, 372
Kleinwort Benson v Vaughan [1996] CLC 620 (CA) 154
Kleinwort Sons & Co v Dunlop Rubber Co. (1907) 97 LT 263, 264 389–90
Kolfer Plant Ltd v Tilbury Plant Ltd (1977) 121 SJ 390 180
Krell v Henry [1903] 2 KB 740 .... 75, 139

L Schuler AG v Wickman Machine Tool Sales Ltd [1974] AC 235 (HL) 116–17
LAC Minerals Ltd v International Corona Resources Ltd [1989] 2 SCR 574, (1989)
   61 DLR (4th) 14 .... 257, 266, 300
Lady Hood of Avalon v Mackinnon [1909] 1 Ch 476 91–92
Lake v Bayliss [1974] 1 WLR 1073 321
Lamb v Bunce (1815) 4 M&S 275, 105 ER 836 155
Lamine v Dorrell (1701) 2 Ld Ray 1216, 92 ER 303 .... 206, 328–29
Lamplugh Iron Ore Co Ltd, Re [1927] 1 Ch 308 253
Lampton's Executors v Preston's Executor's 24 Ky 455 (1829) 203
Landmark Land Co v FDIC 256 F 3d 135 (Fed Cir, 2001) 132
Larner v London County Council [1949] 2 KB 683 .... 74, 357–58
Latec Investments Ltd v Hotel Terrigal Pty Ltd (1965) 113 CLR 265 .... 223, 231
Lavoie v Fournier (1924), 37 Que KB 63 (Que KB) 43
Law Society of Upper Canada v Toronto Dominion Bank (1989) 169 DLR (4th) 353,
   (1998) 42 OR (3d) 257 (Ont CA) 250
Layton v Martin [1986[2 FLR 227 278
Leeds Industrial Co-Operative Society Ltd v Slack [1924] AC 851 (HL) 340–41
Leigh v Dickeson (1885) 15 QBD 60 .... 49, 184
Leighton Contractors Pty Ltd v O'Carrigan [2016] QSC 223 261
Les Laboratoires Servier v Apotex Inc [2014] UKSC 55, [2015] AC 430 .... 397, 401
Lester v Woodgate [2010] EWCA Civ 199 274
Lever v Goodwin (1887) 36 Ch D 1 (CA) 304
Lewis v Australian Capital Territory [2020] HCA 26 345
Lewis v Averay (No 1) [1972] 1 QB 198 (CA) 197–98
Lightly v Clouston (1808) 1 Taunt 112, 127 ER 774 .... 322, 329–30
Liggett v Kensington [1993] 1 NZLR 257 (NZCA) 257–58
Lim Teng Huan v Ang Swee Chuan [1991] 1 WLR 113 (PC) 274
Lipkin Gorman v Karpnale [1991] 2 AC 548 (HL) 35, 50–51, 207, 208, 210, 211–12, 236, 237,
259, 355, 357–58, 361–63, 419
Lissack v Manhattan Loft Corporation Ltd [2013] EWHC 128 (Ch) 111
Lister & Co v Stubbs [1890] 45 ChD 1 (CA) 227
Lister v Hodgson (1867) LR 4 Eq 30 53
Little v Courage Ltd. (1995) 70 P & CR 469 (CA), 474 122–23
Livingstone v The Rawyards Coal Co. (1880) 5 App Cas 25 (HL) 57, 266, 298
Llliey v Elwin (1848) 11 QB 742, 116 ER 652 128–29
Lloyd v Dugdale [2001] EWCA Civ 1754, [2002] 2 P&CR 13 280
Lloyd's Bank plc v. Crosse & Crosse [2001] EWCA Civ 366, [2001] Lloyd's Rep PN 452 ... 353
Load v Green (1846) 15 M & W 216; 153 ER 828 .... 8, 193–94, 211–12
Lobb v Vasey Housing Auxiliary [1963] VR 38 142
Lodder v Slowey [1904] AC 442 (PC) 132
Logicrose Ltd v Southend United Football Club Ltd [1988] 1 WLR 1256 382
London Allied Holdings v Lee [2007] EWHC 2061 (Ch) 8
London Joint Stock Bank v Macmillan [1918] AC 777 (HL) 269–70
Lord Cawdor v Lewis (1835) 1 Y & C Ex 427; 160 ER 174 380–81
Lord Churchill, Re (1888) 39 ChD 174 253
Lord Napier and Ettrick v Hunter [1993] AC 713 (HL) 252
Low v Bouverie [1891] 3 Ch 82 (CA), 101 269–70

TABLE OF CASES

Lowick Rose LLP (in liquidation) (Appellant) v Swynson Limited and another (Respondents) [2017] UKSC 32, [2018] AC 313 .... 7–8, 54, 72, 111, 162–63, 256,
Lowther v Carlton (1741) 2 Atk 242, 26 ER 549 242
Lumbers v W Cook Builders Pty Ltd (in liq) [2008] HCA 27, (2008) 232 CLR 635 .... 42, 43
Lumley v Gye (1853) 2 E & B 216, 118 ER 749 .... 218, 329–30
Lunn Poly Ltd v Liverpool & Lancashire Properties Ltd [2006] EWCA Civ 430 .... 338, 343
Lupton v White (1808) 15 Vers J 432, 33 ER 817 200–1
Luxor (Eastbourne) Ltd v Cooper [1941] AC 108 (HL) 122
Lyell v Kennedy (1889) 14 App Cas 437 (HL) 51–52
Lysaght v Edwards (1876) 2 Ch D 499, 506 224

M'Mechan v Warburton [1896] 1 IR 435 53
M'Myn, Re (1886) 33 ChD 575, 578 253
M'Queen v Farquhar (1805) 11 Ves Jr 467, 32 ER 1168 242
Macclesfield Corporation v Great Central Railway [1911] 2 KB 528 (CA) 162, 164
MacDonald Dickens & Macklin v Costello [2011] EWCA Civ 930, [2012] QB 244 .... 36, 37, 42
Mackay v Dick (1881) 6 App Cas 251 122–23
Madden v Quirk [1989] 1 WLR 702 156
Mahoney v McManus (1981) 180 CLR 370 10–11
Mann v Paterson Constructions Pty Ltd (2019) 373 ALR 1 133–34
Marathon Asset Management LLP v Seddon [2017] EWHC 300 (Comm) 339
Marcus Stowell & Beye v Jefferson Investment Corp 797 F 2d 227 (1986) 322–23
Marine Trade SA v Pioneer Freight Futures Co Ltd BVI [2009] EWHC 2656 (Comm); [2010] 1 Lloyd's Rep 631 .... 76, 77
Marles v Philip Trant [1954] 1 QB 29 (CA) 397
Marr v Tumulty, 256 NY 15, 175 NE 356 (CA 1931) 382
Marriot v Hampton (1797) 7 TR 269, ER 443 369
Martin v Pont [1993] 3 NZLR 25 360
Martin v Porter (1839) 5 M&W 351, 151 ER 149 266
Maskell v Horner [1915] 3 KB 106 .... 77, 102
Mason v Le Blaireau (1804) 6 US 238, 266 (2 Cranch 240, 266) 186–87
Mason v New South Wales (1959) 102 CLR 108 (HCA) 376
Master Education Services Pty Ltd v Ketchell [2008] HCA 38, (2008) 236 CLR 101 400–1
Matheson v Smiley [1932] 2 SLR 787 (Mn CA) 181
Max Wayne Cowper-Smith v Gloria Lyn Morgan [2017] 2 SCR 754 .... 275, 281
May & Butcher v R [1934] 2 KB 17n 113–14
Mayson v Clouet [1924] AC 980 136
MCC Proceeds v Lehman Brothers [1998] 4 All ER 675 (CA) 216
McDonald v Dennys Lascelles Ltd (1933) 48 CLR 457 .... 125, 136
McFarlane v Tayside Health Board [2000] 2 AC 59 (HL) 364
McGuane v Welch [2008 EWCA Civ 785, [2008] 2 P&CR 24 282–83
McKeown v Cavalier Yachts Pty Ltd. (1988) 13 NSWLR 303 .... 202, 266–67
McLean v Discount & Finance Ltd (1939) 64 CLR 312 10–11
Menelaou v Bank of Cyprus [2015] UKSC 66, [2016] AC 176 .... 111, 261, 419
Menetone v Athawes (1764) 3 Burr 1592, 97 ER 998 137
Meridian Global Funds Management v Securities Commission [1995] UKPC 5, [1995] 2 AC 500 96
Merrywheather v Nixan (1799) 8 TR 186, 101 ER 1337 156
Mertins v Jolliffe (1756) Amb 311, 27 ER 211 242
Metallgesellschaft Ltd v Inland Revenue Commissioners IRC and A-G (C-397/98) 86
Metcalfe v Britannia Ironworks Co (1877) 2 QBD 423 (CA) 128–29
Metropolitan Asylum District v Hill (1881) 6 App Cas 193 181
Metropolitan Police District Receiver v Croydon Corpn [1957] 2 QB 154 (CA) 165, 165–66
Michael Wilson & Partners Ltd v Nicholls (2011) 244 CLR 427 318–19
Midland Bank Trust Co Ltd v Green [1981] AC 513 (HL) 241–42, 377
Miles v Wakefield Metropolitan DC [1987] 1 AC 539 (HL) 131
Miller v Miller [2011] HCA 9, (2011) CLR 1 .... 397, 400–1

Miller v Race (1758) 1 Burr 452, 97 ER 398 .... 192, 209, 361, 377
Ministry of Defence v Ashman [1993] 32 EGLR 102 (CA) 348–49
Ministry of Defence v Thompson [1993] 2 EGLR 107 (CA) 348–49
Minsky's Follies of Florida v Sennes 206 F 2d 1 (1953) 69
Modelboard Ltd v Outer Box Ltd [1992] BCC 945 204
Moguls Steamship Co v McGregor Gow & Co [1892] AC 25 (HL) 284
Mohamed v Alaga [2001] 1 WLR 1815 (CA) 400
Montagu v Janverin (1811) 3 Taunt 442, 128 ER 175 79
Montagu's Settlement Trusts, Re [1987] Ch 264 .... 237–38, 239, 259
Moore v Erie Ry Co 7 Lansing 39 (NY 1872) 199–200, 280, 281–82
Moore v Fulham Vesty [1895] 1 QB 399 (CA) 369
Moore v Moore [2018] EWCA Civ 2669 .... 279, 280, 281–82
Moore v Scenic Tours Pty Ltd [2020] HCA 17, (2020) 94 ALJR 481, [64] 333
Moore v Sweet (2018) SCC 52 .... 55, 419
Morant, In re [1924] 1 Ch 79 .... 61, 389–90
Morgan Guaranty Trust Co of New York v Lothian Regional Council 1995 SC 151 (IHCS) 30, 76
Morgan v Ashcroft [1938] 1 KB 49 74
Morice v Bishop of Durham (1804) 9 Ves Jun 399, 32 ER 656 217–18
Morrell v Morrell (1882) 7 PD 68 90
Morris, Re [1971] P 62 90
Morris-Garner v One Step (Support) Ltd [2018] UKSC 20, [2019] AC 649 .... 293, 323, 325–26,
   332, 338, 339,340, 341, 342, 343, 347, 348–49, 419–20
Morrison Steamship Co Ltd v Greystoke Castle (Cargo Owners) (The Cheldale)
   [1947] AC 265 (HL) 183
Moses v McFarlane (1760) 2 Burr 1005, 97 ER 676 .... 73–74, 207, 371
Moss v Hancock [1899] 2 QB 111 .... 209, 377
Mouat v Betts Motors Ltd [1950] AC 71 (PC) 333–34
Moule v Garrett (1871–1872) LR 7 Ex 101 166
Mountney v Treharne [2002] EWCA Civ 1174 [2003] Ch 135 227
Mouse's Case, The Gravesend Ferry (1609) 12 Co Rep 63, 77 ER 1341 183
Moynes v Coopper [1956] 1 QB 439 197–98
MSM Consulting v Tanzania [2009] EWHC 21 (QB) 114–15
Munro v Butt (1858) 8 E & B 738, 120 ER 275 128–29
Munroe v Willmott [1949] 1 KB 295 14
Murad v Al-Saraj [2005] EWCA 959 317–18
Murphy Estate [1998] NSJ No 371, 170 NSR (2d) 1 53
Murphy v Brentwood [1991] 1 AC 398 (HL) 92
Muschinski v Dodds (1985) 160 CLR 583l 257
My Kinda Town v Sol [1982] FSR 147 304

N & J Vassopulos v Ney Shipping Ltd [1977] 2 Lloyd's Rep 478 41
Nash v Inman [1908] 2 KB 1 187
National Crime Agency v Robb [2014] EWHC (Ch) 4384 [2015] Ch 520 .... 229, 233, 249–50
National Westminster Bank plc v Spectrum Plus Ltd [2005] UKHL 41, [2005] 2 AC 680 223
National Westminster Bank v Somer International (UK) Ltd [2001] EWCA Civ 970,
   [2002] 1 All ER 198 368–69
Nelson v Nelson [1995] HCA 25, (1995) 184 CLR 538 .... 392, 400–1
Nesbitt v Redican [1924] SCR 135 86
Neste Oy v Lloyd's Bank Plc [1983] 2 Lloyd's Rep 658 234
Neville v Wilson [1997] Ch 144 (CA) 224
New Orleans v Firemen's Charitable Association 43 La Ann 447, 9 So 486 (1891) 126, 336–37
New York Life Assurance Co v Chittenden 134 Iowa 613, 112 NW 96 (1907) 77
Newall v Tomlinson (1871) LR 6 CP 405 389
Newbigging v Adam (1886) 34 Ch D 582 (CA) 69–70, 81–82
Newman v Bourne & Hollingworth (1915) 31 TLR 209 180
Newton v Newton 1925 SC 715, 1925 SLT 476 275
Newton v Porter 69 NY 133 (1877) 206

Nicholson v Chapman (1793) 2 H Bl 254, 126 ER 536 .... 185, 186–87
Nimmo v Westpac Banking Corp [1993] 3 NZLR 218 217
Niru Battery Manufacturing Co v Milestone Trading Ltd (No 2) [2004] EWCA Civ 487,
    [2004] 2 All ER (Comm) 289 171–72,172
Niru Battery Manufacturing Co v Milestone Trading Ltd [2002] EWHC 1425, [2003] 2 All ER
    (Comm) 706, [2003] EWCA Civ 1446, [2004] 1 All ER (Comm) 193 356
Norbury, Nazio & Co Ltd v Griffiths [1918] 2 KB 369 (CA) 158
North v Walthamstow UDC (1898) LJ QB 972 10–11
Norton v Haggett 85A 2d 571 (Vt 1952) 161–62
Norwich Union Fire Insurance Society Ltd v Wm H Price Ltd [1932] AC 455 (PC) 73–74
Nott and Cardiff Corpn, Re [1918] 2 KB 146 (CA) 165
Novoship (UK) Ltd v Mikhaylyuk [2014] EWCA Civ 908, [2015] QB 499 318,319
Nurdin & Peacock plc v DB Ramsden & Co Ltd [1999] 1 WLR 1249 84
NV De Bataafsche Petroleum Maatschappij v War Damages Commission [1956] 1 MLJ 155 203

O'Neil v Armstrong [1895] 2 QB 418 122
O'Neil v Gale [2013] EWC Civ 1554, [2014] Lloyd's Rep FC 202 392–93
O'Sullivan v Management Agency and Music Ltd [1985] QB 428 (CA), [1996] 3 All ER 61 382
Oatway, Re [1903] 2 Ch 356 251
Obbard, assignees of Blofeld (a bankrupt) v Betham (1830) M & M 483, 485, 173 ER 1232 119
Ocean Tramp Tankers Cop v V/O Sovfracht, The Eugenia [1964] 2 QB 226 (CA) 143
Official Custodian for Charities v Mackey (No 2) [1985] 1 WLR 1308 51–52
Ogilvie v Allen (1899) 15 TLR 294 91–92
Ogilvie v Littleboy (1897) 13 TKR 399 91–92
Okedina v Chikale [2019] EWCA Civ 1393, [2019] ICR 1635 397
Ontario Securities Commission and Greymac Credit Corporation (1986) 55 OR (2d) 673;
    (1986) 30 DLR (4th) 1 250
Ontario Securities Commission, Re (1985) 30 DLR (4th) 1 aff'd (1998) 52 DLR (4th) 767 249–50
Oom v Bruce (1810) 12 East 225, 104 ER 87 .... 392, 399
Orakpo v Manson Investments Ltd [1978] AC 95 (HL) 252, 400–1, 406
Orgee v Orgee [1997] EG 152 CS (CA) 283–84
Otis Vehicle Rentals Ltd v Ciceley Commercials Ltd [2002] All ER (D) 203 125–26
Ottey v Grundy [2003] EWCA Civ 1176 283
Oughton v Seppings (1830) 1 B & Ad 241, 109 ER 776 329–30
Owen v Cronk [1895] 1 QB 365 (CA) 389–90
Owen v Tate [1976] QB 402 (CA) 163–64
Owners of the Steamship Mediana v Owners, Masters and Crew of the Lightship Comet
    (The Mediana) [1900] AC 113 (HL) 346
Oxford v Moss (1979) 68 Cr App 183 260

P& O Nedlloyd BV v Utainko Ltd [2003] EWCA Civ 83, [26] 180
Pan Ocean Shipping Co Ltd v Credtrust (The Trident Beauty) [1994] 1 WLR 161 (HL) 45
Pao On v Lau Yiu Long [1980] AC 614 (PC) 158
Papamichael v National Westminster Bank Plc (No.2) [2003] EWHC 164 (Comm),
    [2003] 1 Lloyd's Rep 341 8
Papayammo v Grampian SS CO Ltd (1896) Com Cas 448 181–82
Parfitt v Lawless (1872) LR 2 P & D 462 90
Parkash v Irani Finance Ltd [1970] Ch 101 256
Parker v British Airways Board [1982] 1 QB 1004 (CA), 1017 180
Parker-Tweedale v Dunbar Bank Plc (No.1) [1991] Ch 12 (CA) 217
Parker-Tweedle v Dunbar plc (No 2) [1991] Ch 12 (CA) 216
ParkingEye Ltd v Somerfield Stores Ltd [2012] EWCA Civ 1338, [2013] QB 840 404
Parkinson v College of Ambulance [1925] 2 KB 1 (CA) 394, 394–95, 399, 403, 406, 407, 409
Pars Ram Brothers (Pte) Ltd v Australia & New Zealand Banking Group [2018] 4 SLR 1404,
    [2018] SGHV 60 250
Pascoe v Turner [1979] 1 WLR 431 .... 14, 278,278
Patel v Mirza [2016] UKSC 42, [2017] AC 467 ...... 104, 392, 393, 394–96, 400, 401–8, 409, 411, 419

TABLE OF CASES xxxvii

Patton v Bond (1889) 60 LT 583 253
Patureau-Miran v Boudier, Cass Req 15 June 1892 43
Paul v Speirway Ltd [1976] Ch 220, [1976] 2 All ER 587 256
Pavey & Matthew Pty Ltd v Paul (1987) 162 CLR 221 (HCA) 112, 134
Pavlou, Re [1993] 1 WLR 1046 184
Peachdart, Re [1984] Ch 131 204
Pearce v Brooks (1866) LR 1 Ex 213 395
Peel v Canada (1993) 98 DLR 4th (SCC) 34–35
Pell Frischmann Engineering Ltd v Bow Valley Bros Valley Iran Ltd [2009]
    UKPC 45, [2011] 1 WLR 2370 .... 320, 339–40, 343
Penarth Dock Engineering Co v Pounds [1963] 1 Lloyds Rep 3 (CA) 347
Pendlebury v Walker (1841) 4 Y &C Ex 424, 160 ER 1072 155
Penn v Lord Baltimore (1750) 1 Ven Sen 444, 27 ER 1132 222
Peter Pan Manufacturing Corporation v Corsets Silhouette Ltd [1964] 1 WLR 96 309–10
Pettkus v Becker [1980] 2 SCR 834 117 DLR (3d) 257 .... 6, 30
Philip Collins Ltd v Davis [2000] 3 All ER 808, 831 379
Phillips v Brooks Ltd [1919] 2 KB 243 197–98
Phillips v Homfray (1871) LR 6 Ch App 770 (CA) 330, 348
Phillips v Homfray (1886) 11 App Cas 466 (CA) 304, 328, 330
Phillips v Phillips (1861) 4 De GF & J 208, 45 ER 1164 223
Phoenix Life Insurance Co. Re Burges and Stock's Case (1862) 2 J&H 441, 70 ER 1131 .... 25, 98
Photo Productions Ltd v Securicor Transport Ltd [1980] AC 827 (HL) 124, 135
Pickard v Sears (1837) 6 A&E 469, 112 ER 179 269–70
Piggee v Mercy 186 P 2d 817 (Okla 947) 181
Pilcher v Rawlins (1871–1872) 7 Ch App 259 (CA) 242–43
Pilot Insurance v Cudd 36 SE 2d 860 (1945) (S Ct of S Carolina) 77
Pipkos v Trayans [2018] HCA 39 270–71
Pirie & Co v Middle Dock Co (1881) 44 LT 426 182
Pirie v Pirie (1873) 11 M 941 122–23
Pitt v Holt [2013] UKSC 26, [2013] 2 AC 108 90–92
Planché v Colburn. (1831) 8 Bing 14, 131 ER 305 .... 132, 144, 287
Plimmer v The Mayor, Councillors and Citizens of the City of Wellington (1884)
    9 App Cas 699 (PC) 273
Plimmer v Wellington Corp (1884) 9 App Cas 699 (PC), 710 274
Ploof v Putnam 81 Vt 471, 71 A 188 (Vt 1908) 182–83
Pollard v Bank of England (1871) LR 6 QB 623 .... 44, 389–90
Polly Peck v Nadir (No 2) [1992] 4 All ER 769 (CA) 257
Pordage v Cole (1669) 1 Wms Saund 219, 85 ER 449 118
Portman Building Society v Hamlyn Taylor Neck [1998] 4 All ER 202 (CA) 386, 389–90
Powell v Benney [2007] EWCA Civ 1283, [2008] 1 P &CR DG12 .... 278, 281, 283
Powell v Rees (1837) 7 Ad & El 426, 112 ER 530 329–30
President Insurance Co Ltd v Resha St Hill [2012] UKPC 33, [2021] 2 All ER 1105 95
Prest v Petrodel [2013] UKSC 34, [2013] 2 AC 415 236
Prince Albert v Strange (1849) 1 M&G 25, (1849) 41 ER 1171 309
Prince Jefri Bolkiah v PMG [1999] 2 AC 222 (HL) 309
Proctor v Bennis (1887) LR 36 Ch D 740 (CA) 272
Prudential Assurance Co Ltd v Her Majesty's Revenue and Customs [2018]
    UKSC 39, [2019] AC 929 .... 64,64, 419–20
Queensland Mines Ltd v Hudson (1978) 18 ALR 1 316

R (Best) v Chief of Land Register [2015] EWCA Civ 17, [2016] QB 23 397
R (Hemmings t/a Simply Pleasures Ltd) v Westminster CC [2013] EWCA Civ 591 99
R (Lumba) v Secretary of State for the Home Department [2011] UKSC 12, [2012] 1 AC 245 345
R v Ashwell (1885) 16 QBD 190 197–98
R v Bunkall (1864) Le & Ca 374, 169 ER 1436 206
R v Hinks [2001] 2 AC 241 197
R v Ilich (1987) 162 CLR 110, HCA 33

R v Middleton (1872–1875) LR 2 CCR 38 197–98
R v Prince (1865-7) LR 1 CCR 150, (1868) 11 Cox CC 193 197–98
R v Secretary of State for Transport ex parte Factortame Ltd (No. 4) (C-48/93)
    [1996] QB 404 87–88
R v Secretary of State for Transport ex parte Factortame (No. 5) [2000] 1 AC 524 (HL) 87–88
Radford v de Froberville [1977] 1 WLR 1262 337
Rahimtoola v Nizam of Hyderabad [1958] AC 379 (HL) 389–90
Ramsden v Dyson (1866) 1 LR HL 129 274
Ratcliffe v Evans [1892] 2 QB 524 (CA) 296
Raynor v Preston (1881) 18 Ch D 1 224
RE Jones Ltd v Waring and Gillow Ltd [1926] AC 670 (HL) 45
Reading v Attorney General [1951] AC 507 (HL) 316–17
Redgrave v Hurd (1881) 20 ChD 1 (CA) 354
Redwood Music Ltd v Chappel Ltd [1982] RPC 109 .... 304, 308
Reeves v Drew [2022] EWHC 159 (Ch) 90
Regal (Hastings) Ltd v Gulliver [1967] 2 AC 134 (HL) 314–16
Regalian Properties Ltd v London Docklands Development Corpn [1995] 1 WLR 212 114–15
Registered Securities Commission, Re [1991] 1 NZLR 545 249–50
Regus Ltd v Epcot Solutions Ltd [2008] EWCA Civ 361 336
Relfo Ltd v Varsani [2014] EWCA Civ 360, [2015] 1 BCLC 14 39
Reversion Fund and Insurance Co v Maison Coway Ltd [1913] 1 KB 364 (CA) 162
Rheem Australia Pty Ltd v McInnes [2020] NSWSC 1313 261
Rhodes, Re (1890) 44 Ch D 94 (CA) 164
Rhymney Iron Co v Gelligaer DC [1917] 1 KB 589 10–11
Richdale, ex p (1882) 19 Ch D 409 (CA) 209, 362, 377
Riggs v Palmer 115 NY 506 (1889) 300
Robins v Bridge (1837) 3 M & W 114, 150 ER 1079 41
Robinson v Harman (1848) 1 Ex Rep 850, 154 ER 363 .... 57, 130, 298
Rodocanachi Sons & Co v Milburn Bros (1886) 18 QBD 67 (CA) 337
Rogers v Parish (Scarborough) Ltd [1987] QB 933 (CA) 120
Rogers v Price (1829) 3 Y & J 128, 148 ER 1080 154
Romney Marsh v Trinity House (1870) LR 5 Ex 204 183
Ronex Properties Ltd v John Laing Construction Ltd [1983] QB 398 (CA) 354, 371
Rosenfeldt v Olsen (1984) 25 DLR (4th) 272 (BCCA) 300
Rover International Sales v Cannon Film Sales [1989] 1 WLR 912 125–26
Rowland v Divall [1923] 2 KB 500 (CA) 383
Rowley v Ginnever [1897] 2 Ch 503, 507 266
Roxborough v Rothmans Pall Mall Australia Ltd [2001] HCA 61, (2001) 208
    CLR 516 .... 117, 126, 360, 375
Royal Bank of Scotland v Etridge (No 2) [2001] UKHL 44, [2002] 2 AC 773 (HL) 377
Royal Bank of Scotland v Tottenham [1894] 2 QB 715 (CA) 209, 362, 377
Royal Bank of Scotland v Watt 1991 SC 48 (IHCS) 58–59
Royle v Traff d Borough Council [1984] IRLR 184 336
Ruabon Steamship Company Ltd v London Assurance, The [1900] AC 6 .... 31–32, 81
Rugg v Minett (1810) 11 East 210, ER 985 138
Rural Municipality of Storthoaks v Mobil Oil Canada Ltd (1975) 55 DLR (3d) 1 355
Ruxley Electronics and Construction Ltd v Forsyth [1996] AC 344 (HL) 337

Sabemo Pty Ltd v North Sydney Municipal Council [1977] 2 NSWLR 880 69
Sabo Food Services Inc v Dickinson 280 So 2d 529 (FASC, 1974) 376
Sachs v Miklos [1948] 2 KB 23 (CA) 179
Sadler v Evans (1766) 4 Burr 1984, 98 ER 34 .... 388, 389
Saleh v Romanous [2010] NSWCA 274 286–87
Salsbury v Bagott (1677) 2 Sw 603, 36 ER 745 242
Samsoondar v Capital Insurance Co Ltd [2020] UKPC 33, [2021] 2 All ER 1105 .... 7–8, 95, 419
Sandemans & Sons v Tyzack & Branfoot Steamship Co Ltd [1913] AC 680 199–200
Sanix Ace, The [1987] 1 Lloyd's Rep 465 346

TABLE OF CASES xxxix

Saronic Shipping Co Ltd v Huron Liberian Co [1979] 1 Lloyd's Rep 341 357–58
Savary v King (1856) 5 HLC 627; 10 ER 1046 382
Say-Dee Pty Ltd v Farah Construction Pty Ltd. [2005] NSWCA 800 260
Sayre v Hughes (1867–1868) LR 5 EQ 376 230
Schalit v Joseph Nadler [1933] 2 KB 79 216
School Facility Management Ltd v Christ the King [2020] PTSR 1913, [2020]
　EWHC 1118 (Comm) 384–85
School Facility Management Ltd and others v Governing Body of Christ the King College
　and another (Nos 1 & 2) [2021] EWCA Civ 1053, [2021] 1 WLR 6129 .... 380, 383–85
Scott v Brown [1892] 2 QB 724 (CA) 392, 394, 395
Scott v Pattison [1923] 2 KB 723 112
Scott v Sampson (1882) 8 QBD 491 345
Scott v Southern Pacific Mortgages Ltd [2014] UKSC 52, [2015] AC 385 280
Scottish Equitable plc v Derby [2001] EWCA Civ 369, [2001] 3 All ER 818 364
Scottish Metropolitan Assurance Co Ltd v P Samuel and Co Ltd [1923] 1 KB 348 389–90
Scottish Newcastle plc v Lancashire Mortgage Corporation Ltd [2007] EWCA Civ 684 ... 274
Seager v Copydex (No 2) [1969] 1 WLR 809 310
Seager v Copydex Ltd [1967] 1 WLR 923 (CA) 310
Seath v Moore (1886) 11 App Cas 350 (HL), 380–381 201
Sebel Products Ltd v Customs and Excise Commissioners [1949] Ch 409 98
Secretary of State for Defence v Johnstone 1997 SLT (Sh Ct) 37, 1996 HLR 99 348–49
Sellers v London Counties Newspapers [1951] 1 KB 784 125
Selwyn Benjamin v Stephen Jairam and Ors HCS 1104/ 2000 95
Semelhago v Paramadevan [1996] 2 SCR 415; 136 DLR (4th) 1 (SCC) 342–43
Sempra Metals Ltd v Inland Revenue Commissioners [2007] UKHL 34, [2008]
　1 AC 561 .... 62–63, 64
Severn Trent Water Authority Ltd v Barnes [2004] EWCA Civ 570, [2004]
　2 EGLR 95 .... 327–28, 343,
Shalson v Russo [2003] EWHC 1637 (Ch), [2005] Ch 281 .... 8, 229, 244–45, 249
Shamia v Joorey [1958] 1 QB 448 53
Shand v Grant (1863) 15 CB (NS) 324, 143 ER 809 (CP) 389–90
Sharma v Simposh [2011] EWCA Civ 1383, [2013] Ch 23, [2012] 2 All ER (Comm) 288 ..... 97, 123
Sharp Brothers & Knight v Chant [1917] 1 KB 771 78
Shaw v Groom [1970] 2 QB 504 (CA) 396–97
Shaw v Shaw [1965] 1 WLR 537 (CA) 400
Shaw, Re [1957] 1 WLR 729 230
Sheldon v Metro Goldwyn Pictures Corp 309 US 390 (1940) 308
Shelfer v City of London Electric Lighting Co. [1895] 1 Ch 287 341
Shell UK Ltd v Total UK Ltd [2010] EWCA Civ 180, [2011] QB 86 216
Shelley v Paddock [1980] QB 348 (CA) 398
Shell-Mex Ltd v Elton Cop Dyeing Co. Ltd (1928) 34 Com Cas 39 125–26
Shilliday v Smith 1998 SC 725, 1998 SLT 976 (IHCS) 34–35, 288
Shogun Finance v Hudson [2003] UKHL 62, [2004] 1 AC 919 196
Sigsworth, Re [1935] Ch 89 300
Silsbury v McCoon 3 NY 379 (1850) 204–5
Simpson v Bloss (1816) 7 Taunt 246, 129 ER 99 395
Simpson v Eggington (1855) 10 Ex 845, 156 ER 683 .... 160, 239–40
Sinclair v Brougham [1914] AC 398 (HL) 24, 25, 50, 98, 206
Singer Manufacturing Co v Wilson (1876) 2 Ch D 434 (CA) 305
Singh v Ali [1960] AC 167 (PC) 196, 391–92
Singh v Sandhu (Unreported Decision of the CA, 4 May 1995) 280
Skandinaviska Enskilda Banken AB (Publ) v Conway [2019] UKPC 36, [2020] AC 1111 60–61
Skibinski v Community Living British Columbia [2012] BCJ No 828, 346 DLR (4th) 688 47
Slater v Hoyle Smith Ltd [1920] 2 KB 11 (CA) 335
Slazenger & Sons v Spalding Bros [1910] 1 Ch 257 307
Sledmore v Dalby (1996) 72 P&CR 196 (CA) 281
Smith v Bromley (1760) 2 Doug 696n, 697, 99 ER 441 .... 398, 408–9

xl   TABLE OF CASES

Smith v Hughes (1870–1871) LR 6 QB 597 377
Smith v William Charlick Ltd (1924) 34 CLR 38 77
Snell v Farrell [1990] 2 SCR 311 355
Snepp v United States 444 US 507 (1980) 325
Société Franco Tunisienne d'Armement v Sidermar S.P.A, The Massalia [1961] 2 QB 278 143
Société Générale, London Branch v Geys [2012] UKSC 63, [2013] 1 AC 523 115–16
Solloway v McLaughlin [1938] AC 247 (PC) 345
Sooraj v Samaroo [2004] UKPC 50 224
Sorochan v Sorochan [1986] 2 SCR 38 257
Soulos v Korkontzilas [1997] 2 SCR 217 257
South Australia Asset Management Corporation v York Montague Ltd [1997] AC 191 (HL) 298–99
South Australian Cold Stores Ltd v Electricity Trust of South Australia (1957) 98 CLR 65 77
South Tyneside BC v Svenska International plc [1995] 1 All ER 545 .... 366–67, 375
Southwark London LBC v Tanner [2001] 1 AC 1 (HL) 41
Southwell v Blackburn [2014] EWCA Civ 1347, [2014] HLR 47 282
Space Investments Ltd v Canadian Imperial Bank of Commerce Trust Co (Bahamas)
    Ltd [1986] 1 WLR 1072 (PC) 223, 248
Spalding v Gamage (1915) 32 RPC 273, HL 307
Spaul v Spaul [2014] EWCA Civ 679 .... 111, 114
Spence v Crawford [1939] SC (HL) 52, [1939] 3 All ER 271 (HL) 65, 381
Spence v Union Marine Insurance Co (1867–1868) LR 3 CP 427 199–200
Spenser v S Franses Ltd [2011] EWHC 1269 (QB) 268
SR Projects Ltd v Ramperad [2022] UKPC 24 397
St John Shipping Corp v Joseph Rank Ltd [1957] 1 QB 267 396–97
Stack v Dowden [2007] UKHL 17 [2007] 2 AC 432 236
Stapleford Colliery Co, Barrow's Case, Re (1880) 14 ChD 432, 445 242
Steam Saw Mills Company v Baring Brothers [1922] 1 Ch 244 (CA) 85
Stephen v Camden & Philadelphia Soap Co 68 A 69 (NJ, 1907) 132
Stevenson v Mortimer (1778) 2 Cowper 805, 98 ER 1372 44
Stevenson v Snow (1761) 3 Burr 1237, 97 ER 808 98
Stimpson v Smith [1999] Ch 340 .... 10–11, 171
Stirling v Forrester (1821) 3 Bli 575, 4 ER 712 10–11
Stocks v Wilson [1913] 2 KB 235 196–97
Stocznia Gdanska S.A. v Latvian Shipping Co [1988] 1 WLR 574 125
Stoffel v Grondona [2020] UKSC 42, [2020] 3 WLR 1156 406–7
Stoke on Trent City Council v Wass [1988] 1 WLR 1406 (CA) 327, 343
Story v Windsor (1743) 2 Atk 630, 26 ER 776 .... 209, 242, 362, 377
Stovin v Wise [1996] AC 923 (HL) 173–74
Strand Electric Co v Brisford Entertainments Ltd [1952] 2 QB 246 347–48
Strang, Steel & Co v A Scott & Co (1889) 14 App Cas 601 (PC) 181–82
Strŏms Bruks Aktie Bolag v Hutchinson [1905] AC 515, HL 337
Stubbs v Holywell Ry (1867) LR 2 Ex 311 140
Studdy v Sanders (1826) 5 B&C 628, 108 ER 234 122
Stump v Gaby (1852) 2 De GM & G 623, 42 ER 1015 229
Suggitt v Suggitt [2012] EWCA Civ 1140 281
Sumpter v Hedges [1898] 1 QB 673 (CA) 128, 129, 130, 131–32, 139–40, 147, 383
Surrey Breakdown Ltd v Knight [1999] RTR 84 179
Surrey County Council v NHS Lincoln Clinical Commissioning Group [2020]
    EWHC 3550 (QB) 155, 167
Swan v Swan (1819) 8 Price 518, 146 ER 1281 184
Swan, The [1968] 1 Lloyd's Rep 5 385–86
Sweet v Southcote (1786) 2 BroCC 66, 29 ER 38 242
Swift 1st Ltd v Chief Land Registrar [2015] EWCA Civ 330, [2015] Ch 602 .... 209, 220
Swindle v Harrison [1997] 4 All ER 705 (CA) 317–18
Swordheath Properties Ltd v Tabet [1979] 1 WLR 285 347
Swotbooks.com Ltd v Royal Bank of Scotland Plc [2011] EWHC 2025 (QB) 10–11
Symes v Hughes (1869–1870) LR 9 Eq 465 (Ct of Ch) 410

TABLE OF CASES xli

T&R Duncanson v Scottish County Investment Co. Ltd 1915 SC 1106 122–23
Tamares (Vincent Square) Ltd v Fairpoint Properties (Vincent Square) Ltd [2007]
    1 WLR 2167 347
Tappenden v Artus [1964] 2 QB 185 (CA) 268
Target Holdings Ltd v Redferns [1996] AC 421 (HL) 298
Taylor v Bhail [1996] CLC 377 400
Taylor v Blakelock (1886) 32 ChD 560 (CA) 242
Taylor v Bowers (1876) 1 QBD 291 . . . . 395, 410
Taylor v Caldwell (1863) 3 B & S 826, 122 ER 309 75
Taylor v Chester (1869) LR 4 QB 309 395
Taylor v Laird (1856) 25 LJ Ex 329 . . . . 37–38, 81
Taylor v Motability Finance Ltd [2004] EWHC 2619 (Comm) 133–34
Taylor v Plumer (1815) 3 M & S 562, 105 ER 721 . . . . 206, 207, 209
Taylors Fashions Ltd v Liverpool Victoria Trustees Ltd [1982] QB 133 (CA) 269
Tchenguiz v Grant Thornton UK LLP [2015] EWHC 405 (Comm) 169, 353
Teacher v Calder (1889) 1 F (HL) 39 . . . . 320, 322
Templeton Insurance Ltd v Brunswick [2012] EWHC 1522 (Ch) 238
Test Claimants in the FII Group Litigation v Revenue and Customs Commissioners
    [2008] EWHC 2893 (Ch) 358–59
Test Claimants in the FII Group Litigation v Revenue and Customs Commissioners
    [2014] EWHC 4302, [2015] STC 1471 358–59
Test Claimants in the FII Group Litigation v Revenue and Customs Commissioners
    [2021] UKSC 31, [2021] 1 WLR 4354 . . . . 373, 374, 390
Test Claimants in the FII Group Litigation v Revenue and Customs Commrs [2012]
    UKSC 19, [2012] 2 AC 337 . . . . 88, 99, 358–59, 373
Tetley v British Trade Corp (1922) 10 Lloyd's List LR 678 179
Thoday v Thoday [1964] P 181 (CA) 269
Thogood v Robinson (1845) 6 QB 769, 115 ER 290 204
Thomas v Brown (1876) 1 QBD 714 . . . . 73–74, 114, 123
Thomas v Times Book Co Ltd [1966] 1 WLR 911 197
Thompson & Norris Manufacturing Co v Hawes (1895) 73 LT 369 10–11
Thompson v ASDA-MFI Group plc [1988] Ch 241 122–23
Thorndike v Hunt (1859) 3 De G & J 563 44 ER 1386 242
Thorner v Major [2009] UKHL 18, [2009] 1 WLR 776 . . . . 276, 278–79, 280, 282
Tilley v Bowman [1910] 1 KB 745 193–94
Tinsley v Milligan [1992] Ch 310 (CA) 392
Tinsley v Milligan [1994] 1 AC 340 (HL) 235, 391, 395,396–97, 403, 405, 407
Tito v Waddell (No 2) [1977] Ch 106 . . . . 293, 343
Tojo Maru, The [1972] AC 242 186–87
Tomlinson v Bentall (1826) 5 B and C 737, 108 ER 274 . . . . 155, 171
Tool Metal Manufacturing Co Ltd v Tungsten Electric Co Ltd [1955] 1 WLR 761 (HL) 275
Tootal Clothing v Guinea Property Management Ltd (1992) 64 P & CR 452 (CA) 97
Towers v Barrett (1786) 1 TR 133, 99 ER 1014 116
Townsend v Crowdy (1860) 8 CB (NS) 477 76
Transco plc v Glasgow City Council [2005] CSOH 79, 2005 SLT 958 . . . . 155, 167
Transvaal and Delagoa Bay Investment Co Ltd v Atkinson [1944] 1 All ER 579 389–90
Tri Level Claims Consultant Ltd v Koliniotis (2005) 257 DLR (4th) 291, 201 OAC 282
    (Ont CA) 399
Trial Lawyers Association of British Columbia v Royal & Sun Alliance Insurance Co of
    Canada 2021 SCC 47 271
Tribe v Tribe [1996] Ch 107 (CA) 396, 410, 411
Trident General Insurance Co Ltd v McNiece Bros Pty Ltd (1988) 165 CLR 107 217
Trollope v Koerner 420 P 2d 91 (1970) 69
Trustee of the Property of FC Jones & Sons v Jones [1997] Ch 159 (CA) 208, 209, 244
Tsang Yue Joyce v Standard Chartered Bank (Hong Kong) Ltd [2010] HKCFI 98;
    [2010] 5 HKLRD 217
Tucker v Farm and General Investment Trust Ltd [1966] 2 QB 421 (CA) 205

Turf Club Auto Emporium Pty Ltd v Yeo Boong Hua [2018] SGCA 44 338
Twentieth Century Fox Film Corp v Harris [2013] EWHC 159 (Ch), [2014] Ch 41 302
Twinsectra Ltd v Yardley [1999] Lloyd's Rep Bank 438 (CA) rev'd on other grounds [2002]
UKHL 12, [2002] 2 AC 164 . . . . 225–26, 229
Twinsectra v Yardley [2002] 2 AC 164; [1970] AC 567 225–26
Tyrie v Fletcher (1777) 2 Cowp 666, 98 ER 1297 98

Uglow v Uglow [2004] EWCA Civ 987 278
Ulmer v Farnsworth 80 Me 500, 15 A 65 (SC 1888) 29
Ultraframe (UK) Ltd v Fielding [2007] WTLR 835 318–19
Union Bank of Australia Ltd v McClintock & Co [1922] 1 AC 240 (PC) 207, 208
United Australia v Barclays Bank Ltd [1941] AC 1 (HL) 329–30,331
Unity Joint Stock Mutual Banking Association v King (1856) 25 Beav 72, 53 ER 563, ... 273
Universal Thermosensors Ltd v Hibben [1992] 3 All ER 257 308
Uren v John Fairfax & Sons Pty Ltd (1966) 127 CLR 118, 151 344

Vale v Steinmetz [2021] EWCA Civ 1087 233
Vandervell v IRC [1967] 2 AC 291 236
Vandervell's Trusts (No 2), Re [1974] Ch 269 169
Vercoe v Rutland Fund Management Ltd [2010] EWHC 424 (Ch) 310, 311, 320
Vervaeke v Smith [1983] 1 AC 145 (HL) 269
Vestergaard Frandsen A/S v Bestnet Europe Ltd [2016] EWCA Civ 541, [85] 310
Vhaigley Farms Ltd v Crawford, Kaye & Grayshire Ltd [1996] BCC 957 204
Vickery v Richie 202 Mass 247 (Mass 1909), 88 NE 835 69
Victoria Park Racing & Recreation Grounds Co Ltd v Taylor (1937) 58 CLR 479
(HCA) 51, 294, 305
Vigers v Cook [1919] 2 KB 475 (CA) 128–29
Vincent v Lake Erie Transportation Co 109 Minn 456, 124 NW 221 (Minn 1910) 182–83
Vinogradoff, Re [1935] WN 68 235–36
Vita Food Products Inc v Unus Shipping Co Ltd (1939) AC 277 397
Vodafone v Office of Communications Ltd [2020] EWCA Civ 183, [2020] QB 857 59–60
Voyce v Voyce (1991) 62 P&CR 290 (CA) 270–71

Wah Tat Bank Ltd v Chan Chang Kum [1975] AC 507 (PC) 158
Waikato Regional Airport v AG of New Zealand [2003] UKPC 50, [2003] All ER (D) 399 60
Waldy v Gray (1875) LR 20 Eq 238 242
Walsh v Lonsdale (1882) 21 Ch D 9 (CA) 225
Walter J Schmidt & Co, In re 298 F 314 (1923) 250
Walter v James (1870–1871) LR 6 Ex 124 . . . . 157, 160, 239–40
Walton v Walton (Unreported, 14 April 1994, CA) 278, 279
Waltons Stores (Interstate) Ltd v Maher (1988) 164 CLR 387 . . . . 69, 275, 285, 286–87, 288
Ward v National Bank of New Zealand (1883) 8 App Cas 755 10–11
Waters v Weigell (1795) 2 Anst 575, 145 ER 971 159
Watson Laidlaw & Co Ltd v Pott Cassell & Williamson (1914) 28 RPC 157 (HL) 348
Watson v Shankland (1873) 11 M (HL) 51, (2870–2875) LR 2 Sc 304 115–16
Watts (1996) 112 LQR 39 349
Watts v Story (1983) NLJ 631 (CA) 278
Way v Latilla [1937] 2 All ER 759 (HL) 113–14
Wayne County Produce Co v Duffy-Mott Inc 155 NE 669 (1927) 126
Weatherby v Banham (1835) 5 C & P 228, 175 ER 950 42
Welby v Drake (1825) 1 C&P 557, 171 ER 1315 160
West London Commercial Bank v Reliance Building Society (1885) 29 ChD 954 (CA) 242
Westdeutsche Landesbank Girozentrale v Islington London Borough Council
[1994] 4 All ER 890 (CA) 123–24
Westdeutsche Landesbank Girozentrale v Islington London Borough Council
[1996] AC 669 (HL) 8, 25, 64, 65, 123–24, 231, 232, 235–36, 237, 245
Western Trust & Savings Ltd v Rock (Unreported 26 February 1993, CA) 253

Case	Page
Wetherbee v Green 22 Mich 311 (1871)	204
Whalley v Lancashire and Yorkshire Railway Co (1884) LR 13 QBD 131 (CA)	183
Wharf and Bull Wharf Ltd v Goodman Bros [1937] 1 KB 534 (CA)	370
Whincup v Hughes (1871) LR 6 CP 78	119, 139–40
White and Carter (Councils) Ltd v McGregor [1962] AC 413	136–37, 324–25
White Arrow Express Ltd v Lamey's Distribution Ltd [1995] CLC 1251,	336
White v Garden (1851) 10 CB 919	378
Whitecap Leisure Ltd v John H Rundle Ltd [2008] EWCA Civ 429, [2008] 2 Lloyd's Rep 429	120
Whitehorn Bros. v Davison [1911] 1 KB 463 (CA)	378
Whittington v Seale-Hayne (1900) 82 LT 49	69–70, 81–82, 287
Whitwham v Bullock [1939] 2 KB 81	155
Whitwham v Westminster Brymbo Coal [1896] 2 Ch 538 (CA)	348
Wigan Borough Council v Scullindale Global Ltd [2021] EWHC 779	347
Wilkes v Spooner [1911] 2 KB 473 (CA)	217–18
William Bros v Ed T Agius Ltd [1914] AC 510 (HL)	333–34
William Lacey (Hounslow) Ltd v Davis [1957] 1 WLR 932	114
Williams v Bayley (1868) LR 1 HL 200	85
Williams v Central Bank of Nigeria [2014] UKSC 10, [2014] AC 1189	218, 222–23, 224–25, 372
Williams v Williams [2003] EWHC 742 (K Garnett QC)	358
Willmott v Barber (1880) 14 Ch D 96	272, 274, 275
Willoughby v Willoughby (1756) 1 TR 771, 28 ER 437	242
Wilson v First County Trust Ltd [2003] UKHL 40, [2003] 1 AC 81	400–1, 406
Wilson v Thornbury (1875) LR 10 Ch App 239	91
Wilson v Tumman (1843) 6 Man & G 236, 134 ER 879	41
Wilson's Music & General Printing Co v Finsbury BC [1908] 1 KB 563	10–11
Wiluszynski v Tower Hamlets L.B.C. [1989] ICR 493 (CA)	128–29, 131
Winkfield, The [1902] P 42 (CA)	330, 346
Woolwich Equitable Building Society v Inland Revenue Commissioners [1993] AC 70 (HL)	86–87, 98–100
Workers Trust and Merchants Bank Ltd v Dojap Investments Ltd [1993] AC 573 (PC)	136, 148, 149
Wright v Newton [1835] 2 Cr M & R 124, 150 ER 53	117
Wrotham Park Estate Co Ltd v Parkside Homes Ltd [1974] 1 WLR 798	324, 332–33, 338, 339, 341, 343
Wuhan Guoyu Logistics Group Co Ltd v Emporiki Bank of Greece SA [2013] EWCA Civ 1679, [2014] 1 CLC 40	8
WWF v World Wrestling Federation Entertainment Inc [2008] 1 WLR 445 (CA)	343
XL/Datacomp, Inc. v Wilson (In re Omegas Grp., Inc.) 16 F3d 1443, 1453 (6th Cir 1994)	258
Yango Pastoral Co Pty Ltd v First Chicago Australia Ltd [1978] HCA 42, (1978) 139 CLR 410	400–1
Yaxley v Gotts [2000] Ch 162	280
Yeoman Credit Ltd v Apps [1962] 2 QB 508	121
Yonge v Reynell (1852) 9 Hare 809, 68 ER 744	253
Yorkshire Insurance Co Ltd v Nisbet Shipping Co Ltd [1962] 2 QB 330	252
Zephyrus, The (1842) 1 W Rob 329, 166 ER 596	186

Table of Legislation

UNITED KINGDOM

Statutes

Administration of Estates
    Act 1925 39–40
    s 1 220
    s 32 220
Administration of Justice Act 1982
    s 20 90
Bankruptcy Act 1731 398
Bills of Exchange Act 1882
    s 27(1)(a) 362, 377
    s 27(1)(b) 210, 212
    s 38(2) 209, 377
Building Societies Act 1836 24
Carriage of Goods by Road Act 1965 156
Chancery Amendment Act 1858 (Lord
    Cairns' Act) 330, 340–41
    s 2 340
Civil Liability (Contribution) Act 1978 156
    s 1(3) 170
    s 3 158
Computer Misuse Act 1990 22
Consumer Rights Act 2015
    s 51 113–14
Contracts (Rights of Third Parties)
    Act 1999 227–28
Copyright Act 1709 305
Copyright Designs and Patents Act 1988
    s 90(3) 193
    s 96(2) 304
    s 97(1) 306–7
    s 191I(2) 304
    s 191J(1) 306–7
    s 229(2) 304
    s 233(1) 306–7
Criminal Justice Act 1993 401
    s 57 402
    s 63(2) 401, 402, 406
Criminal Justice Act 1977
    s 1 401–2
Customs and Excise Management
    Act 1979
    s 13A (3) 376
Customs Duties Consolidation
    Act 1876 171–72
Dangerous Dogs Act 1991 22

Exchange Control Act 1947
    s 7 400
Factors Act 1889
    s 2(1) 210
Fraud Act 2006 396
Gambling Act 2005
    s 335(1) 97
Gaming Act 1845 362–63
    s 18 .... 97, 210
Hire Purchase Act 1964
    Pt III 210
Income and Corporation Taxes Act 1988
    s 247 .... 86, 88
Infants Relief Act 1874 196–97
Insolvency Act 1986 258
    s 234(3), (4) 193–94
    s 283(3)(b) 218
    s 306 220
    ss 322–324 220
Judicature Acts 195
Land Charges Act 1972 241–42
Land Registration Act 2002 241–42
    ss 26–29 209
    s 116 280
Landlord and Tenant Act 1927
    s 18(1) 336
Landlord and Tenant Act 1962
    s 4 396–97
Larceny Act 1861 396
Law of Property Act 1925
    s 52 .... 193, 277
    s 53(1)(c) 193
    s 136 .... 161, 220–21
    s 188 199–200
Law of Property (Miscellaneous
    Provisions) Act 1989 270–71
    s 2 97
    s 2(5) 280
Law Reform (Frustrated Contracts)
    Act 1943 .... 137, 371–72,
                              383, 419–20
    s 1(1) 137
    s 1(2) 119–20, 138, 140, 141,
                       144–45, 146, 360, 383
    s 1(3) 143, 145, 146
    s 1(3)(b) 144
    s 2(4) 140

xlvi   TABLE OF LEGISLATION

s 2(5) 137
s 2(5)(a) 141
Law Reform (Married Women and
    Tortfeasors) Act 1935
    s 6 156
Law Reform (Miscellaneous Provisions)
    Act 1934 330
Law Registration Act 2002
    s 27 193
Limitation Act 1980 .... 88, 371–72
    s 3 379
    s 5 371–72
    s 9 371–72
    s 10 371–72
    s 21(1) 372
    s 21(3) 372
    s 28 372
    s 29 372
    s 32(1)(a) 372
    s 32(1)(b) 372
    s 32(1)(c) 86–87, 372–73, 379
Limited Liability Partnership Act 2000 208
Marine Insurance Act 1906
    s 6 181
    s 79 252
Mercantile Law Amendment Act
    s 5 163
Merchant Shipping Act 1995 .... 156, 185
Merchant Shipping (Safety and Load Line
    Conventions) Act 1932
    s 44 396–97
Minors Contracts Act 1987 196–97
Misrepresentation Act 1967
    s 1(1)(b) 86
    s 2(1) 69–70
    s 2(5) 69–70
Patent Act 1946 304
Patents Act 1977
    s 61(1)(d) 304
    s 62(1) 306–7
Police Act 1996
    s 25 49
Proceeds of Crime Act 2002 .... 300, 301
Proceeds of Crime Act 2010 117–18
Public Health (Control of Disease) Act 1984
    s 46(5) 154
Road Traffic (NHS Charges) Act 1999 165–66
Sale of Goods Act 1979
    s 3(2) 187
    s 8(2) 113–14
    s 11(2) 120–21
    ss 12–15 120
    s 16 193
    s 17 193
    s 18, r 1 321
    s 24 .... 195, 210, 321, 377–78
    s 25 .... 195, 210, 377–78
    s 30(1) 130, 383

s 50 336
s 51 336
s 51(3) 296
Social Security Administration
    Act 1992 396
    s 111A 396
Social Security (Recovery of Benefits) Act
    1997 165–66
Solicitors Act 1974
    s 31 399
Statute of Frauds 1677 270–71
    s 4 112
Statute of Monopolies 1624 305
Senior Courts Act 1981 (Supreme Court
    Act 1981)
    s 35A 64
    s 35A(1) 62–63
    s 50 340–41
Supply of Goods and Services Act 1982
    s 15(1) 113–14
Theft Act 1968 396–97
Theft Act 1978 396
Torts (Interference with Goods)
    Act 1977 265
    s 3 191–92
    s 5 191–92
    s 6 14
    s 6(1) 265
    s 6(2) 265
    s 10 200
Trade Marks Act 1994
    s 14(2) 304, 307
Trade Marks Registration Act 1875 305
Value Added Tax Act 1994 (VAT)
    s 80(3) 376
Wills Act 1837
    s 9 222
Wireless Telegraphy Act 2006 59–60

Statutory Instruments

Civil Procedure Rules
    Pt 64 217
    PD 64A
        para1(2)(a)(iii) 217
        para1(2)(c) 217
Defence (Finance) Regulations 1939 398
    reg 2 396–97
Solicitors Practice Rules
    r 3 400
    r 7 400

NATIONAL LEGISLATION

Australia

Banking Act 1959 (Cth) 400–1
Law Reform Act 1995 (Qld)
    Pt 3 Div 2 156

Law Reform (Contributory Negligence and
    Apportionment of Liability) Act 2001 (SA)
    Pt 2, s 6 156
Law Reform (Contributory Negligence and
    Tortfeasors' Contribution) Act 1947
    s 7 156
Law Reform (Misc Prov) Act 1946
    s 5 156
Law Reform (Misc Prov) Ordinance 1955
    s 11 156
Law Reform (Tortfeasors Contribution,
    Contributory Negligence and Division
    of Chattels) Act 1952
    s 5 156
Liquor Act 2007 (NSW) 400–1
New South Wales (Frustrated Contracts)
    Act 1978 146
Taxation Acts Amendment Act 1987 (Vict.)
    s 2(4) 92–93
Tortfeasors and Contributory Negligence
    Act 1954
    s 3 156
Trade Practices Act 1974 (Cth) 400–1
Wrongs Act 1958
    s 24 156
Wrongs Act Amendment Act 1959
    s 25 156

Canada

British Columbia (Frustrated Contracts)
    Act 1974 146
Contributory Negligence Act 1930 (now
    Negligence Act 1970)
    s 2(1) 156
Contributory Negligence Act 1951
    s 2 156
Contributory Negligence Act 1955
    s 2(1) 156
Contributory Negligence Act 1960
    s 5 156
Contributory Negligence Act 1965
    s 3 156
Contributory Negligence Act 1970
    s 3 156
Quebec Civil Code
    ss 1260–1261 220

Cayman Islands

Companies Law
    s 145(1) 61

France

Code Civil
    Art 555 265
    Art 1236 160
    Art 1304-3 122

Art 1583 193

Germany

Bürgerliches Gesetzbuch (Civil Code, BGB)
    § 100 302–3
    § 162(1) 122
    § 226 103–4
    § 267 160
    § 346 135
    § 667 415–16
    § 812 .... 105, 213, 415–16
    § 814 369
    § 823(1) 302
    § 951 .... 202–3, 266–67
Designgesetz (Design Act)
    s 47(2) 306
Markengesetz (Trademark Act)
    s 14(6) 306
Patentgeseetz (Patent Act)
    s 139 306
Urheberrechtsgesetz (Copyright Act)
    s 97(2) 306

New Zealand

Law Reform Act 1936 (no. 31 of 1936)
    s 17 156

Uganda

Rent Restriction Ordinance 1949 409

United States

A Burrows, *A Restatement of the English
    Law of Contract* (2016) 4–5
A Burrows, *A Restatement of the English
    Law of Unjust Enrichment* (2012) 4–5,
                                        34–35
    § 1(3) 291
    § 3(6) 85
A Kull, *Restatement of the Law (Third)
    Restitution and Unjust Enrichment*,
    vol I (2010)
    § 5(2) 72
    § 20 181
    § 20(2) 11–12
    § 21(2) 11–12
    § 21 ill 2 186–87
    §§ 22–25 .... 160, 239–40
    § 22(2)(c) 155
    § 34 146
    § 36 129
    § 37 126
    § 38(2)(b) 135
    § 38 cmt. C illus 9 135
    § 39 illustration 6 323
    § 39 Comment e 300
    § 42 comment g 307

§ 42 comment h 308
§ 44(1) 300, 326
§ 44(3) 326
§ 46 90
§ 53(2) 357–58
§ 64 376
American Law Institute, The Restatement
 (Second) of the Law of Contracts (1981)
 cmt. D, ill 2 135
 § 272(2) 146
American Law Institute, Restatement
 (Third) of the Law of Agency (2007)
 §5.03 96
American Law Institute, Restatement
 Third: Restitution and Unjust
 Enrichment (2011)
 § 45 300
First American Restatement 1937 34–35
Lanham (Trademark) Act 1946 307
Uniform Commercial Code
 § 2-603 180
 § 2-604 180
 § 2-711 130

INTERNATIONAL LEGISLATION

EC Treaty
 Art 81 326
European Convention of Human
 Rights (ECHR)
 Art 8 312
International Convention on
 Salvage 1989 185
 Art 13.1(a) 186
 Art 13.1(b)–(j) 186
 Art 16.1 185
Vienna Sales Convention
 Arts 84–88 180

EUROPEAN UNION

Directive 2004/48EC of the European
 Parliament and the Council of 29
 April 2004 on the enforcement of
 intellectual property rights
 Art 13(1) 306, 307
 Art 13(2) 307

List of Abbreviations

ACT	Advance Corporation Tax
CEO	Chief Executive Officer
CIA	Central Intelligence Agency
CPS	Crown Prosecution Service
ECHR	European Convention of Human Rights
EU	European Union
NHS	National Health Service

PART I
SUMMARY

1
Summary

A. Muscle Memory

One way in which my mid-life crisis manifested itself was in trying to learn how to swim properly. Each Sunday I could be found in the pool at the YMCA on Tottenham Court Road attempting to learn front crawl and breaststroke.

Most of the class were much younger than me and made progress more quickly than I did. One difficulty was that I had learned, badly, how to swim as a child and had been carrying on with poor habits ever since. Forty years of doing something the wrong way made it very hard for me to re-learn the correct way to do things. I could tell that something was wrong with my various strokes, but habits are hard to break, particularly where the old way of doing things so nearly works.

Doing it right is hard. It would have been much easier to have given up and struggled on as before, happily flailing around.

B. Purposes

The negative purpose of this work is to ensure that no further books on this topic are written.

That is not because it is, or could be, definitive. Rather it seeks to show that there is no unified area of law called 'restitution' or 'unjust enrichment'. There are instead (depending upon how you count them) seven or eight different kinds of private law claim, none of which has anything important in common one with another, that have been grouped together by commentators. Few of them have anything very much to do with 'enrichment' as that word is used in everyday speech, and what is restituted differs between them.

Like all private law claims, those gathered here concern (in)justice between individuals, but they have no further unity. Many of them are not based upon an agreement or a wrong, but that negative feature has no utility. 'Restitution' or 'unjust enrichment' should cease to be discussed as unified areas of law.

The positive purpose of this work is to identify and describe the various reasons for 'restitution' that any properly constructed system of private law ought to recognise. Being destructive is easy, and this is the harder but more important goal.

Those readers unfamiliar with this area of law, who merely wish to have an account of it, are advised to skip to the summary of the positive thesis. Those who are familiar with other accounts of it may be assisted by the following explanation of how and why it differs from them.

C. The Negative Thesis

1. History

In the United States this subject is relatively underexamined. The current American Restatement on the topic looks similar to that of the first in 1937 and gathers together almost all private law claims that are not contractual or tortious into one large work.

Outside of the United States, an ambitious, capacious, and well-worked theory of 'unjust enrichment' has arisen in the common law world over the last 40 years. That theory in the Anglo-Commonwealth is largely a product of the work of Peter Birks. Birks' thinking influenced others. He did so both directly, through his pioneering, clearly written publications and charismatic teaching, but also indirectly as his students[1] and others adopted his framework, whilst often disagreeing at a lower level of detail.

Birks' approach was to take the formulation that a claim for restitution concerned the defendant's 'unjust enrichment at the expense of the claimant' and subject it to rigorous linguistic analysis, showing what the elements of this phrase meant in ordinary speech and revealing how this was reflected in the law. His scheme is elegant.

Although Birks himself repudiated much of his earlier work in his final book, most of those who have followed him remain committed to a modified version of his original account, set out in 1998.[2] There he excluded from the subject claims based upon wrongdoing, claiming that the remainder had a much tighter unity. One indication of his influence is that all textbooks written before this date included a section on 'restitution for wrongs', after it no new ones did so.

It is common to start the modern history of the subject in the common law with the publication of Scott and Seavey's American Restatement in 1937,[3] followed in England by *Goff & Jones* in 1966.[4] However, today in the Anglo-common law, textbooks are far more strongly influenced by Birks. This includes the latest editions of *Goff & Jones* itself, under new editors, which, in accordance with Birks' views, has changed its title[5] and scope,[6] and has adopted a completely different structure from that of earlier editions. Very little of the original authors' work now remains in the text.

It is unusual in the common law that the account of an area by academics has had such an influence upon the law itself. One reason for this impact has been the apparent want of any satisfactory comprehensive alternative.[7] Another is that the subject is not taught, save in the

---

[1] Birks counted among his Doctoral students many of those who went on to write extensively on the law of unjust enrichment: Justice Edelman, and Professors Robert Chambers, Simone Degeling, Tomas Krebs, Charles Mitchell, and Lionel Smith. Lord Burrows studied under Birks as an undergraduate and graduate at Brasenose, Oxford. Professor Graham Virgo studied Restitution on the Oxford BCL under Birks. I also did so and taught with Peter Birks on the course for the last decade of his life. Many of these students of Birks went on to have Doctoral students of their own, such as Professors Elise Bant and Helen Scott both of whom produced important work in the area under the supervision of (then) Professor Burrows.

[2] P Birks, 'Misnomer' in W Cornish and others (eds), *Restitution Past, Present and Future: Essays in Honour of Gareth Jones* (1998), 1. See also M McInnes, 'Misnomer: A Classic' (2004) 12 RLR 79.

[3] A Wakeman and S Seavey, *Restatement of the Law of Restitution: Quasi Contracts and Constructive Trusts* (1937).

[4] R Goff and G Jones, *Goff and Jones: The Law of Restitution* (1st edn, 1966).

[5] C Mitchell, P Mitchell, and S Watterson (eds), *Goff & Jones: The Law of Unjust Enrichment* (9th edn, 2016).

[6] Eg the law of attornment, proprietary estoppel, and 'restitution for wrongs' are now excluded.

[7] There is a longstanding body of work which is sceptical as to the utility of 'unjust enrichment'. Most prominent is that of Steve Hedley: S Hedley, 'Unjust Enrichment as the Basis of Restitution—An Overworked Concept' (1985) 5 LS 56; S Hedley, *Restitution: Its Division and Ordering* (2001). See also J Dietrich, *Restitution: A New Perspective*

modern era on some graduate programmes. Practitioners, as a result, lack confidence when dealing with it and will reach gratefully for an account that offers them an apparently easy to apply formula that works in all cases.[8]

Trying to encapsulate the work of several different people will, of course, omit many differences large and small, but the core claims of those who have supported the recognition of a category of 'unjust enrichment' in the Anglo-common law may be summarised as follows.

2. 'Unjust Enrichment'

(a) The four-stage test

In order to make out a claim in unjust enrichment the claimant must show three things: that the defendant was enriched, that this was at the expense of the claimant, and that this was unjust. These three elements of the claim are independent of one another. What constitutes an 'enrichment' may be answered completely separately from the particular reason why it is 'unjust', and so on. The 'core of the core'[9] example of a claim in unjust enrichment is the restitution of a mistaken payment of money that is not due.

The fourth stage is the defences that may be invoked by the defendant to resist a claim that is made out once the three unjust enrichment elements are proven. The most significant defence is that of change of position, which applies to all claims in 'unjust enrichment' save where a specific countervailing policy dictates otherwise.

(b) Enrichment

Enrichment is established by showing that the defendant is factually better off in a financial way than he was. This is determined at the moment of the receipt of any benefit, and not at the later moment of judgment by the court. The receipt of money is a central case because money is always enriching.

Some things, such as services, are not always enriching because the defendant may not have chosen them himself (such as when someone cleans the windows of my house when I personally prefer them to be dirty). In such cases, enrichment may be established by showing either that the defendant was incontrovertibly benefitted (by either having a realised benefit or being saved a necessary expense) or that the defendant requested or freely accepted the service.

(1998); I Jackman, *The Varieties of Restitution* (2nd edn, 2017); P Jaffey, *The Nature and Scope of Restitution: Vitiated Transfers, Imputed Contracts and Disgorgements* (2000); P Watts, ' "Unjust Enrichment"—The Potion that Induces Well-Meaning Sloppiness of Thought' (2016) 69 CLP 289; C Webb, *Reason and Restitution: A Theory of Unjust Enrichment* (2016). It is not at all clear that a headcount shows more proponents than opponents.

[8] I participated in Andrew Burrows' two restatement projects: A Burrows, *A Restatement of the English Law of Unjust Enrichment* (2012) and A Burrows, *A Restatement of the English Law of Contract* (2016). It was noticeable how much more deference the judges and practitioners showed the academics in the former than in the latter.

[9] P Birks, *Unjust Enrichment* (2nd edn, 2005), 73.

(c) At the claimant's expense

The area where there is least unanimity amongst commentators is in relation to this element of the claim, an element which was given very little consideration by Birks in his original work.[10]

Most now accept that it is unnecessary to show that the claimant suffered a loss that correlates to the claimant's gain (at least in the sense in which 'loss' is ordinarily used in English).[11] All also (rightly) accept that it is unnecessary to show that any right of the claimant's was infringed.

At one extreme lies Birks himself, who in his last work argued that a mere causal link between the defendant's enrichment and either an action of the claimant or some asset of his sufficed.[12] If, for example, P mistakenly paid X £1,000, and X, delighted by his good fortune, paid D £750 as a result, on a causal approach P has caused D to be £750 better off, and on its face this should suffice for there to be a claim. This broad starting position was then, he thought, cut back by a number of policy considerations where this would lead to 'too much' restitution.[13] If, for example, P, in performing his contract with X, benefitted D, he argued that P should not be allowed to escape from the bargain he had made with X and be permitted to bring a claim over against the third party to the contract. This, so he argued, was to prevent insolvency law from being circumvented, as P had decided to run the risk of X's insolvency by extending credit to him by performing in advance of counter-performance.

Almost as generous to the plaintiff, although slightly less so in the current edition, are the latest editors of *Goff & Jones* who argue that some kind of series of transactional links between claimant and defendant should suffice, subject to the same kinds of policy cut-backs as Birks invoked.[14]

At the other extreme is Professor Virgo, who argues that enrichment ought always in principle be 'direct'.[15] By 'direct' he means not via a third party, as where P pays money to X, causing X to pay money to D. Lord Burrows in his textbook adopts a similar position (subject to exceptions of uncertain scope and justification),[16] although he has subsequently changed his mind, so as to adopt an approach more closely resembling German law.[17]

(d) Unjust

Obviously, most enrichments at the expense of others cannot be reversed. As Birks epigrammatically said,[18] children in the playground quickly learn that if they give their toys away they cannot get them back. The law maintains the same rule in most cases.

---

[10] P Birks, *An Introduction to the Law of Restitution* (rev edn, 1989), 132–139. The bulk of discussion concerns 'interceptive subtraction', see Chapter 3, Performance.

[11] But see M McInnes, '"At the Plaintiff's Expense": Quantifying Restitutionary Relief' (1998) 67 CLJ 472 reflecting the position stated by the Supreme Court of Canada: see *Pettkus v Becker* [1980] 2 SCR 834. See also *Anna Wee* [2013] SGCA 36, [2013] 3 SLR 801 [128] [147]; E Ball, 'At the Claimant's Expense' (2014) 130 LQR 13; Mitchell, Mitchell, and Watterson, *Goff & Jones: The Law of Unjust Enrichment* (n 5), [6-106]–[6-107]; E Ball, *Enrichment at the Claimant' Expense* (2016).

[12] Birks, *Unjust Enrichment* (n 9), 74–75.

[13] ibid, 75–98, 209–210.

[14] See generally, Mitchell, Mitchell, and Watterson, *Goff & Jones: The Law of Unjust Enrichment* (n 5), [6-07]–[6-117].

[15] G Virgo, *The Principles of the Law of Restitution* (2006), 106–116.

[16] A Burrows, *The Law of Restitution* (3rd edn, 2011), 63–85.

[17] A Burrows, 'At the Expense of the Claimant': A Fresh Look' (2018) 28 RLR 167; A Burrows, 'In Defence of Unjust Enrichment' (2019) 78 CLJ 521.

[18] Birks, *An Introduction to the Law of Restitution* (n 10), 9.

In the central case in unjust enrichment theory of the mistaken payment of money, the orthodox account as to why there is a claim in such a case bases it upon the vitiation of the claimant's consent to the defendant's enrichment. Mistake, so it is said, is one of a number of unjust factors concerned with the plaintiff's voluntariness. Some 'unjust factors' vitiate this consent. In addition to cases of mistake, that the claimant was subject to duress or undue influence, or suffering from an incapacity, and this has caused the conferral of a benefit upon the defendant, are said to justify recovery for the same kind of generic reason. We might broadly say that the justification for any claim is the protection of the claimant's autonomy.

A fortiori from this category of case are those where the claimant has given no consent at all to the defendant's enrichment. So, where the claimant is either ignorant of the defendant's enrichment at his expense, or powerless to prevent it, restitution ought to follow. Although the case law in most jurisdictions has yet to recognise any such 'unjust factors'[19] the logic of the theory requires that the courts do so.

On the other side are cases where the plaintiff has consented, but this consent is qualified or conditional. If I pay a builder in advance for work to be done on my house, if that work is subsequently not done, restitution ought to follow because although there was an initially valid consent to the defendant's enrichment, the failure of the condition renders such consent no longer effective.

Birks initially sought (implausibly) to expand this list of defective consent cases to cover situations where the claimant had been legally or morally compelled to confer a benefit upon the defendant.[20] Although 'legal compulsion'[21] in some form still has its supporters,[22] 'moral compulsion'[23] does not, and today most books seek to explain the cases previously covered by these categories as based upon some kind of policy, external to the relation of the parties.[24] Where the defendant sent his horse by railway but failed to collect it, the plaintiff railway company was entitled to reimbursement for its expenditure in stabling it.[25] Formerly this was explained in terms of the plaintiff's 'moral compulsion', whereas the common approach now is to explain it in terms of encouraging useful interventions. Other 'policy' cases (which here means cases inexplicable as based upon the state of mind of the claimant) include *ultra vires* payments by public bodies, encouragement of withdrawal from illegal transactions, and the recovery of benefits conferred under court judgments that are later reversed.

In his final work, Birks rejected this 'unjust factors' approach, arguing that appellate court litigation in England compelled the adoption of a different, more unified structure, where almost all claims could now be explained in the same way, as based upon an absence of basis for the defendant's enrichment.[26] Few academics, and no textbooks in England,[27]

---

[19] But see *Espben Finance Ltd v Wong Hou-Lianq Neil* [2022] SGCA(I) 1, [251].
[20] Birks, *An Introduction to the Law of Restitution* (n 10), 173–203.
[21] ibid, 185–193.
[22] Eg Burrows, *The Law of Restitution* (n 16), ch 17; *Samsoondar v Capital Insurance Co Ltd* [2020] UKPC 33.
[23] Birks, *An Introduction to the Law of Restitution* (n 10), 193–202.
[24] See, eg, chapters addressing 'necessity' as an 'unjust factor' in Mitchell, Mitchell, and Watterson, *Goff & Jones: The Law of Unjust Enrichment* (n 5), ch 18; Burrows, *The Law of Restitution* (n 16), ch 18; and Virgo, *The Principles of the Law of Restitution* (n 15), ch 11.
[25] *Great Northern Railway Co v Swaffield* (1874) LR 9 Ex 132.
[26] Birks, *Unjust Enrichment* (n 9), ch 6.
[27] McInnes is, again, an exception. M McInnes, *The Canadian Law of Unjust Enrichment and Restitution* (2014) follows this structure as a result of the Canadian Supreme Court's decision in *Garland v Consumer Gas Co* [2004] SCC 25, [2004] 1 SCR 629.

have followed him. Although there was initially some flirtation with Birks' approach by the House of Lords,[28] and it is close to the orthodoxy in Scotland,[29] more recent English authority appears to have firmly rejected it.[30]

(e) Proprietary claims
Unlike in civilian legal systems, where unjust enrichment is seen solely as part of the law of obligations, it is claimed that in common law systems unjust enrichment also generates proprietary rights.[31] The revesting of legal title in a seller where the contract of sale is avoided for the fraud of the buyer is said to be an example at common law.[32] More common are claims in equity, such as the trust that has controversially been held to arise in the payor's favour where money is mistakenly paid.[33]

On this view, as the proprietary claim is to the extent of the enrichment in the defendant's hands, the process of 'tracing' is concerned with identifying where that value has gone when it has been mixed with other value to which the claimant has no entitlement,[34] and is to be distinguished from 'following' value as it is transferred from one person to another.[35]

(f) Restitution for wrongs
Separate from restitution for unjust enrichment properly so-called, are obligations to account for gains made from wrongdoing. An example is the famous *Great Onyx Cave* case.[36] The defendant owned land above an entrance to a cave in Kentucky with spectacular onyx formations. He commercialised it, making profits through tourism. The plaintiff was a neighbour who owned land below which part of the cave ran, and successfully claimed the proportion of the profits attributable to trespass on the portion of the cave that belonged to

---

[28] Eg *Deutsche Morgan Grenfell plc v Inland Revenue Commissioners* [2006] UKHL 49, [2007] 1 AC 558, [155]–[158] *per* Lord Walker.
[29] Eg *Dollar Land (Cumbernauld) Ltd v CIN Properties Ltd* 1996 SC 331, 348–349, 1997 SLT 260, 271 *per* Lord Cullen; *Kleinwort Benson v Lincoln City Council* [1992] 2 AC 349, 408 *per* Lord Hope.
[30] Eg *Swynson v Lowick Rose LLP* [2017] UKSC 32, [2018] AC 313, [32] *per* Lord Sumption; *Samsoondar v Capital Insurance Co Ltd* [2020] UKPC 33, [2021] 2 All ER 1105, [21] *per* Lord Burrows.
[31] But see J Edelman, 'Restitution of (Property) Rights' in E Bant and M Bryan (eds), *Principles of Proprietary Remedies* (2013).
[32] *Load v Green* (1846) 15 M & W 216; 153 ER 828; *Clarke v Dickson* (1858) El Bl & El 148; 120 ER 463; *Car & Universal Finance Co Ltd v Caldwell* [1965] 1 QB 525 (CA).
[33] *Chase Manhattan Bank NA v Israel-British Bank (London) Ltd* [1981] Ch 105. Followed: *Commerzbank AG v IMB Morgan Plc* [2004] EWHC 2771 (Ch), [2005] 1 Lloyd's Rep 298, [36] *per* Lawrence Collins J; *Re Farepak Food and Gifts Ltd (in Administration)* [2006] EWHC 3272 (Ch), [39]–[40] *per* Mann J; and *cf. Re Crown Holdings (London) Ltd (In Liquidation)* [2015] EWHC 1876 (Ch) *per* Murray Rosen QC. Doubted: *Westdeutsche Landesbank Girozentrale v Islington LBC* [1996] AC 669, 704–706 and 714–715 *per* Lord Browne-Wilkinson. See also *Box v Barclays Bank Plc* [1998] Lloyd's Rep Bank 185, 200–201 *per* Ferris J; *Bank of America v Arnell* [1999] Lloyd's Rep Bank 399 (Aiken J); *Papamichael v National Westminster Bank Plc (No.2)* [2003] EWHC 164 (Comm), [2003] 1 Lloyd's Rep 341, [222]–[231] *per* Judge Chambers QC; *Shalson v Russo* [2003] EWHC 1637 (Ch), [2005] Ch 281, [108]–[127] *per* Rimer J; *London Allied Holdings v Lee* [2007] EWHC 2061 (Ch), [268]–[272] *per* Etherton J; *Fitzalan-Howard v Hibbert* [2009] EWHC 2855 (QB); [2010] PNLR 11, [49] *per* Tomlinson J; *Wuhan Guoyu Logistics Group Co Ltd v Emporiki Bank of Greece SA* [2013] EWCA Civ 1679, [2014] 1 CLC 40 [18]–[19] *per* Tomlinson LJ; *cf. Re D&D Wine International (In Liquidation)* [2016] UKSC 47, [2016] 1 WLR 3179, [30]–[32].
[34] See L Smith, *The Law of Tracing* (1997). For a critique, see T Cutts, 'Tracing, Value and Transactions' (2016) 79 MLR 381.
[35] *Foskett v McKeown* [2001] 1 AC 102, 127–128 *per* Lord Millett.
[36] *Edwards v Lee's Administrator*, 96 SW2d 1028 (Ky Ct App 1936).

him. This is said to be one of a large number of cases, where restitution has been awarded for breach of contract, equitable wrongs, and other torts.

(g) Rejection

The central negative thesis of this work is that all six propositions above are both wrong as an account of the positive law in common law jurisdictions and unsatisfactory as an account of the reasons that may justify the rules that there ought to be. Although the model summarised above is not accepted by all and has had little influence in some jurisdictions such as those of the United States, it can serve as a useful hypothesis for contrast in order to get to the correct position.

D. The Positive Thesis

1. The Dilemma

The greatest attraction of the account that this work seeks to reject is its elegance and simplicity. Rather like the framework law students are taught for the 'tort of negligence' (duty, breach, causation of damage, remoteness, defences) it provides a convenient way of dividing up an area that is, at first sight, unmanageable and incoherent. It proffers a model for simplifying and rationalising a large area of law.

The dilemma is that the law, and what it ought to be, is neither as simple nor as elegant. The reality is of different kinds of claim—some are the subject of litigation every day, whilst others have only ever arisen in a few cases and so are of limited practical importance. Many are intimately related to other areas of law that a work of this size cannot adequately encompass (eg all of contract, Equity, property, and agency law). Exposition is therefore hard.

That said, an outline, that follows the chapters of this book, is possible.

2. Unjustified Performance

The largest category of case is that of a performance rendered by the claimant to the defendant for no reason. The classic example is that of a mistaken payment. 'Performance' here is intended to cover not just the payment of money, but also the rendering of a service under a contract that has been avoided. An acceptance by the defendant of the payment or service rendered by the claimant is an essential element of the transactional link between them, so that the performance is the doing of both of them, and not one alone. The reason for its reversal is the lack of any good reason justifying it. Both the performance and the possible reasons that could justify it are objective and apply to both parties. The justification for the claim is not found in the mind(s) of one or both parties.

What is restituted, or reversed, is not any consequent enrichment the defendant may have acquired as a result of the payment or service, but the performance itself. The consequent enrichment may either be much higher, or lower, than the value of the performance. The extent to which the defendant is better off is irrelevant, and so the language of 'unjust enrichment' is unhelpful and has led courts and commentators into error.

3. Conditional Performance

The next largest category, but with a quite different justification, is that of a performance rendered under an agreement, where the parties have stipulated that the performance is conditional, and that condition has failed. This is the subject matter of Chapters 6 and 7. The most obvious examples are cases where payment for a service under a contract is made in advance, and that counter-performance is not rendered, commonly because of the defendant's breach. The law's traditional language is to say that there has been a 'total failure of consideration' for the payment made.

The condition is found in the agreement between the parties, again not in the minds of one or both of them. The agreement may be an enforceable contract, but may not be (because of, eg, lack of intent to create legal relations, absence of consideration, one party lacking capacity to contract, want of certainty, want of form, and so on).

Again, what is reversed is the performance rendered, not any consequent benefit received. Because the reasons for the claim are different, the applicable defences are not the same. It is not therefore possible to reason by analogy between these first two categories, assuming that a rule applicable to one applies to the other.

Although such rights to restitution are not contractual, it is a necessary condition that there is an agreement between the parties. The relation between such rights and those properly called contractual therefore requires careful consideration.

4. Intervention in Another's Affairs

(a) Discharge of another's obligation
Where one person discharges an obligation that ought to be entirely or in part borne by another, the party who has so discharged the obligation should (and does) have a claim for the expense incurred in so doing, to the extent that the defendant has been saved the expense of performance (or, if one prefers, a claim to the value of the obligation the defendant has been relieved from performing, to the extent that the claimant has incurred expense in discharging it).

A claim of this form, unlike the examples considered so far, may be said to be concerned in part with the extent to which the defendant has been left better off in the sense that he has been relieved of an obligation. Its justification is to seek to ensure that the burden of discharging a legal obligation falls upon the right party. It follows that since claims of this kind are confined to cases of discharge, it should not alone suffice that the defendant will not as a matter of fact incur the cost of performance. The obligation relieved must be a legal one. Even here however, the use of 'enrichment' is apt to mislead. If one party discharges another's obligation, she should have a claim over for the cost of doing so. It should not avail the defendant to argue that a wealthy relative would have discharged his obligation for him for nothing.

Discharge may occur in three ways. First, the claimant may perform another's obligation on his behalf. This occurs where either the obligor has authorised the performance in advance, or ratifies it subsequently where it has been done for his benefit.[37] Second, the

---

[37] *Crantrave Ltd v Lloyd's Bank Plc* [2000] EWCA Civ 127, 923 *per* Pill J, [2000] QB 917; *Swotbooks.com Ltd v Royal Bank of Scotland Plc* [2011] EWHC 2025 (QB), [49]–[56]. See also *Re Cleadon Trust Ltd* [1939] Ch 286; *Barclays Bank Ltd v WJ Simms, Son & Cooke (Southern) Ltd* [1980] QB 677, 700 *per* Robert Goff J.

obligation may be conditional (eg an obligation to abate a nuisance is conditional on there being a nuisance to abate) and the claimant removes that condition.[38] Third, the claimant and defendant may owe the obligation jointly (sometimes with just each other, but possibly with third parties) so that performance by one of his obligation automatically relieves his co-obligor.[39]

The justification for such claims is not based upon the claimant having been 'legally compelled' to benefit the defendant, and the presence of a legal obligation on the claimant to discharge the obligation of another is not a necessary condition in this category. Further, in cases of this kind, although there may have been a performance from claimant to defendant (so that alternative explanations for any claim may be available) this is unnecessary. This is because the defendant is not being obliged to do anything that he was not already under a legal obligation to do. The law is not here creating an obligation *de novo* that did not exist before, but rather trying to ensure that the burden of an obligation arising for other reasons falls on the proper person. The conditions and subject matter of the claim are, therefore, quite different from the first two categories above.

(b) Necessity

In civilian legal systems, there is a general rule, originating in Roman law, giving those who intervene in another's affairs a claim against the beneficiary of such intervention.

> When a person is absent and someone looks after his affairs, actions arise reciprocally between them. These are known as the actions on uninvited intervention (negotiorum gestio). The direct action lies for the principal, the person whose business is managed; the intervener has the counter-action. It is obvious that they are not really contractual, because they only lie where the intervener has no mandate. The beneficiary of the intervention incurs his obligations without even knowing the facts. This was accepted as good policy, to ensure that the affairs of the absent were not left untended if they suddenly had to set off abroad without having time to make proper arrangements. Plainly no-one would intervene on their behalf without an action to recoup his outlay. Just as a useful intervention by the intervener puts the principal under an obligation, so the intervener too becomes liable to render an account. (Justinian, Institutes, 3.27.1)

Applying this idea, if my neighbour's fences blow down when he is away, and I repair them so as to prevent his cattle from straying, I may have a claim against him.

If we accept the policy in favour of such a claim, it gives rise to two possible sensible responses. The stronger would be to encourage such useful intervention by allowing the claimant to recover a reward, and this is the approach taken in the law of salvage at sea, both in the common law and in other legal systems. The weaker is to remove any disincentive to intervene, by giving a claim for recompense for expenditure incurred, and this is the form of the civilian *negotiorum gestio contraria*. This policy does not favour stripping the benefitted

---

[38] *Gebhardt v Saunders* [1892] 2 QB 452; *Thompson & Norris Manufacturing Co v Hawes* (1895) 73 LT 369; *Andrew v St Olave's Board of Works* [1898] 1 QB 775; *North v Walthamstow UDC* (1898) LJ QB 972; *Wilson's Music & General Printing Co v Finsbury BC* [1908] 1 KB 563; *Rhymney Iron Co v Gelligaer DC* [1917] 1 KB 589.

[39] Eg *Stirling v Forrester* (1821) 3 Bli 575, 590–591; 4 ER 712, 717; *Ward v National Bank of New Zealand* (1883) 8 App Cas 755, 765; *McLean v Discount & Finance Ltd* (1939) 64 CLR 312, 328; *Mahoney v McManus* (1981) 180 CLR 370, 376; *Stimpson v Smith* [1999] Ch 340, 348.

party of any gain made from the intervention, although this might provide a ceiling on recovery, and indeed no legal system I know of does this.[40]

The problem with the justification for such claims is apparent in the above quotation from the Institutes of Justinian. There is no 'plainly' about whether such a policy does in fact encourage useful intervention, or whether it has marginal, no, or even negative impact on people coming to the aid of one another. Further, such a contentious policy-based right to reimbursement is not of the kind that may be legitimately recognised by judicial creation, and despite the attempts to construct it at common law from various fragments, no such claim exists.

5. Property and Trusts

(a) Things

The most prominent rival to the orthodox account this work seeks to overturn is one that seeks to push 'unjust enrichment' into other categories of law. One such move is to try to expand the category of contract so as to encompass more than simply enforceable agreements.[41] Another is to adopt a broad sense of 'property', and to seek to explain recovery in some, but not all, cases, as based upon the claimant's pre-existing entitlement to what, after a transfer, the defendant acquires.[42] The problems with (and truth behind) these approaches are discussed at various points throughout this work. One problem is that they risk obscuring those cases that genuinely are based upon agreement or the claimant's entitlement to what the defendant has received.

The most straightforward cases are where a claimant has a chattel (that may include cash), that he has title to, stolen from him, which the defendant subsequently receives. The claimant has a right to the thing good against all others, including the defendant, and may bring a claim against the defendant for the value of that right. Again, such a claim is not based upon whether the defendant is factually better off (he may not be) nor does the state of mind of the claimant (his ignorance or powerlessness) form part of what he must assert in order to succeed (although if he consented to what has happened, that may provide a good reason why the claim fails).

It is tempting to extrapolate from this straightforward case to more complex commercial ones, involving, for example, transfers from bank accounts, and beneficiaries under trusts who are defrauded. This is particularly so in a world where transfers using cash are quickly disappearing. These extrapolations are mistaken and obscure other quite different justifications for any claim, governed by different rules.

---

[40] *Cf.* A Kull, *Restatement of the Law (Third) Restitution and Unjust Enrichment*, vol I (2010) §§ 20(2) and 21(2).
[41] Eg P Jaffey, *The Nature and Scope of Restitution* (2000).
[42] S J Stoljar, *The Law of Quasi-Contract* (2nd edn, 1989), esp 5–10, 113, 250; Watts, ' "Unjust Enrichment"— The Potion that Induces Well-meaning Sloppiness of Thought' (n 7); C Webb, *Reason and Restitution: A Theory of Unjust Enrichment* (2016) (esp ch 4); Jaffey *The Nature and Scope of Restitution* (n 41); P Jaffey, *Private Law and Property Claims* (2007) (esp chs 3 and 8); P Jaffey, 'Restitution' in D Campbell and R Halson (eds), *Research Handbook on Remedies in Private Law* (2019).

(b) Equity

Equitable rules have a distinctive form which is a product of their history. They are rules concerning other rules, a form of meta-law.[43]

The most significant example is, of course, the trust. The key to understanding the trust (in common law jurisdictions) is that it concerns rights of a particular form: a duty to another not to use identifiable rights for the rightholder's benefit. Other equitable property rights (such as the fixed charge) also possess this form, whilst differing in other respects (eg charges are defeasible upon performance of the secured obligation, trusts are not).

The beneficiary's interest under a trust does not confer upon her a 'property right' in the same sense as that held (at common law) by someone with the registered title to land, or possession of a bicycle: a right to a *thing* good against the rest of the world. Rather the beneficiaries have a right in relation to a *right* of the trustee,[44] and this may be asserted against anyone who subsequently acquires the right that is the subject matter of the beneficiaries' entitlement, who also has knowledge of the original trustee's duty, save a bona fide purchaser for value without notice at time of acquisition.

Where a rightholder is under a duty to convey a particular right to another, he is also no longer free to use it for his own benefit. A trust therefore arises, even though the parties may not have intended to create it. A familiar example is the trust that arises in favour of a purchaser of land prior to conveyance. Similarly, whenever there is an obligation to re-convey back to someone a right they have acquired (as where a fully executed contract for the sale of land is rescinded because of the fraud of the buyer) a trust arises.

In principle, the duties of a trustee are only imposed upon someone who did not voluntarily undertake them if, once they have acquired from another rights that are the subject matter of a trust, they acquire knowledge of the existence of the trust and have not themselves disposed of the assets before acquiring such knowledge. Knowledge establishes the existence of the trust obligation, liability for breach of trust is itself strict for all trustees.

If a trustee is no longer able to hold trust assets for another, for example because he has sold them, obligations to correct this state of affairs may arise. This may take the form of an obligation to reconstitute the trust, or the trustee may be obliged to hold the substituted or 'traceable' assets for the beneficiary.

None of this has anything very much to do with 'enrichment'.

(c) Improvements

If the above claims are correct, it follows that where a plaintiff mistakenly improves another's property (such as repairing another's car believing it to be one's own,[45] or a window cleaner mistakenly working on the windows of a house wrongly believing he has a contract with the owner to do so), without more there should be no claim, even if the work by the improver leaves the defendant better off than he otherwise would be (eg by selling the car for a higher figure after the work is done, or by saving the homeowner the inevitable cost of employing someone else to do the cleaning job).

---

[43] B McFarlane and R Stevens, 'What's Special about Equity?' in D Klimchuk, I Samet, and H Smith (eds), *Philosophical Foundations of the Law of Equity* (2020). *Cf.* H Smith, 'Equity as Meta-Law' (2021) 130 Yale Law Journal 1050.
[44] See B McFarlane and R Stevens, 'The Nature of Equitable Property' (2010) 4 The Journal of Equity 1.
[45] Eg *Greenwood v Bennett* [1973] QB 195 discussed in Chapter 14, Improvements.

Where the work has been done under an agreement that is conditional, and that condition has failed, a claim for its value should be available, regardless of whether the agreement constituted an enforceable contract, as exemplified by the Supreme Court of Canada's decision in *Degelman v Guaranty Trust Co. of Canada and Constantineau*.[46] If work is done on another's property in the expectation of payment, and the defendant freely accepts the work on that basis, its value should be recoverable regardless of whether or not the defendant is left better off as a result of the work done.

There are, however, also a number of other ways in which the unaccepted improvement of another's property may have legal consequences, even where no cause of action arises. First, the quantum of damages payable for tortious interference by the improver may be reduced by the value of the work done.[47] Second, the law may refuse to give its assistance through an order for specific delivery unless payment is made for the work done.[48] Third, it may determine that a party with prior possession of a thing only retains priority over a subsequent possessor who has improved that thing if he accounts for the value of the work done. Fourth, the person with title to the thing may be estopped from asserting his rights against the improver,[49] although the concept of proprietary estoppel has been expanded on an unprincipled basis in English law in order to give rise to a cause of action unmoored from its original justification.

6. Wrongdoing

Although genuinely gain-based responses to wrongdoing exist, they are a much smaller category than is commonly supposed.

A secure example is the duty to account for profits made from a patent infringement or other intellectual property right. In the intellectual property context this may be seen as an attempt to recreate the principle of *fructus* that operates in relation to the ownership of physical things (ie if I own a tree I own its fruits, if I own a sow I own her piglets). This is reflected in the fact that what must be accounted for is profits attributable to the patent, saved expenses are irrelevant, as is the counterfactual question of what profits the defendant would have made if he had not engaged in the wrongdoing.

Most supposed examples of gain-based responses to wrongdoing are nothing of the kind however. Some are not properly understood as based upon wrongdoing, such as a fiduciary's obligation to account for unauthorised profits. Others are not helpfully conceptualised in terms of gains by the defendant. If I take your bicycle without permission and use it to cycle to work, but leave you no worse off as you would not have used it in the meantime, I must pay you a fee, but this is not quantified by, or justified by reference to, any gain (if any) that I have made.

---

[46] [1954] SCR 725, discussed in Chapter 7, Conditions.
[47] *Munroe v Willmott* [1949] 1 KB 295. See the Torts (Interference with Goods) Act 1977, s 6; *Glencore v MTI* [2001] 1 Lloyds Rep 284, 328 *per* Moore-Bick J.
[48] *Greenwood v Bennett* [1973] 1 QB 195.
[49] *Pascoe v Turner* [1979] 1 WLR 431.

7. Countervailing Reasons

(a) Defences

In law, a defence is a fact that is asserted by the defendant that gives rise to a new reason why a claim should fail. It is not merely a denial of an essential element of the claimant's case. The defence of 'change of position' is, on this view, a true defence. It is not merely a denial of the defendant's 'enrichment'. Its central justification is to ensure that an innocent person is left no worse off by a claim to reverse an unjustified performance between the parties. Its rationale then determines its scope, and the kind of claims to which it is a possible answer.

Similarly, there are several other defences (bona fide purchase, passing on, counter-restitution, consent) that apply to some, but not all, of the claims commonly grouped together under the category 'unjust enrichment'. Disentangling which defence applies to which kind of claim, and how, can only be done by disaggregating the reasons for these different claims.

(b) Illegality

Illegality is not, properly speaking, a defence but a principle required by the need for the reasons underlying legal rules to cohere together. Sometimes those reasons require a claim for restitution of a performance rendered to fail, but they may require such a claim to be available where it would otherwise not exist.

2
Foundations

A. Law and Justice

This is neither merely a work of description, gathering together and setting down the positive law in the field in a particular jurisdiction, nor is it just a work of pure theory untethered by what the positive law in any particular time and place may be. Instead, it attempts to straddle what, as a matter of low brute fact, the positive law actually is in different jurisdictions, and the high principles of justice to which they all aspire. This requires justification.

Scientific theories are predictive, and so are falsifiable.[1] The standard model of particle physics predicted the existence of the Higgs boson, an elementary particle, in the 1960s, that was only observed in 2012. Darwin's theory of natural selection, although supported by evidence when he was writing, has been reinforced over time with material from the fossil record and DNA sequencing. Other scientific theories, such as Lamarck's theory of inherited acquired characteristics, have fared less well as they have collided with inconvenient facts. Scientific theories can be refuted by pointing to facts that they mispredict, without requiring another better theory that explains the world as it is.

Oliver Wendell-Holmes viewed law similarly as a science of prediction.[2] Trying to predict how a judge will decide a case is one of the things practitioners must do for their clients. Central to this process of prediction are several factors such as the justice of the case in the abstract, the relevant positive law, the temperament of the judge, and the quality of the opposition legal team. There is nothing wrong with this predictive approach, which sometimes travels under the name of 'legal realism', but it is not truly a theory of law or justice properly so-called at all, but instead a theory of the behaviour of judges. It is not my enterprise.

It is tempting, but wrong, to think as Holmes did, that legal theories properly so-called are the same as scientific ones. If a legal theory says 'the law ought to be X' but it is in fact not-X, doesn't that falsify the theory in the same way as would a prediction in the scientific field?

The positive law in any particular jurisdiction is a matter of social fact. It is a matter of the rules that have been posited by those in authority, often the legislature but including, in a system of binding precedent such as the common law, the judges. On questions of what the positive law is within my jurisdiction, once the judges have spoken (assuming they have had cited to them the relevant binding legal materials) that is the end of the matter (unless and until reversed by those with authority to do so). On the question of what the law of England is, English judges, in giving the reasons necessary for the outcome of the case before them,

---

[1] K Popper, *The Logic of Scientific Discovery* (1934).
[2] O W Holmes Jr, 'The Path of the Law' (1897) 10 Harv L Rev 457, 458 ('The primary rights and duties with which jurisprudence busies itself again are nothing but prophecies') and 461 ('The prophecies of what the courts will do in fact, and nothing more pretentious, are what I mean by the law').

deserve absolute deference (save from a superior court of appeal). They have sole authority once they have declared the answer.

One job of the jurist has been to make sense of these facts. The legislature and the judges set down their rules in a piecemeal fashion. Indeed, the judges, in deciding cases and giving reasons for outcomes, why one side wins, often do not speak in the language of rules at all. What the positive legal rules are needs to be inferred from the results and the reasons judges give for their decisions (which are not always coherent). These diverse facts needed to be, and to a lesser extent still need to be, collated. In the nineteenth century, and into the twentieth, textbooks on a wide variety of subjects appeared to perform this task. In the United States it is common for 'Restatements' produced by several different hands to perform the same job (which is even more vital with 51 different jurisdictions[3] with no ultimate appellate court tying them together outside of the narrow range of disputes covered by the United States Supreme Court). These works can be wrong to the extent that they misstate the relevant positive law facts at the time of their publication, but they cannot be refuted by subsequent changes in the law as they are works of description, not prediction.

Two styles of fact collation have now emerged. One is the attempt to be exhaustive, exemplified in England by *Chitty on Contracts* or *Dicey, Morris and Collins on the Conflict of Laws*. Nobody alive (save perhaps the General Editor) will ever read these works from cover to cover as they would a novel. They are to be dipped into by those who know what they are looking for on the details of a rule on a specific issue. The other is the more bare bones student textbook for purposes of education, often produced in frequent new editions as a means of extracting money from the young. Once someone has mastered the latter, they are in a position to use the former.

This process of reportage can never be complete; new facts emerge every week. It is, however, far less important than it was a century ago. It is not 'theoretical' in any sense. This work of collation was largely done before I was born. Again, it is not my enterprise.

A quite different question is what justice requires. What the positive law ought to be cannot be derived from what it is. (Conversely, but more controversially, what as a matter of posited fact it is cannot be derived from what it ought to be.) No number of inconsistent statutes and cases can refute a proposition of what justice requires since the legislators and judges have no authority on this question. (Although within our jurisdictions, we all have good reasons for following the law once they have pronounced what it is). Nobody, regardless of their title, is entitled to any deference as to what the best rules may be. Just as a claim about the nature of the world is only falsifiable by proof of an inconsistent fact, so a claim as to a proposition of what justice requires may only be superseded by another and better claim. This is the truth behind the aphorism that it takes a theory to beat a theory. We may be able to falsify a theory without providing another, but without more that leaves us with nothing.

What can the facts of the positive law tell us about justice? Does justice and the posited law in the disparate jurisdictions that there are, with their different histories, have any relationship?

One view is that the posited law is of no (or very little) use in thinking about what justice requires. For some, the range of potential reasons of justice in play are many and the values

---

[3] Fifty states and the federal jurisdiction.

sought to be furthered incommensurable, so that the point of the positive law is to settle disputes about justice with a rule that, without which, disputes cannot be resolved in the abstract. An illustration might be the length of a limitation period. How long should it be? Three years? Ten? Six? There is no right answer to this question (although some such as ten minutes or a thousand years, may be wrong). One of the central points of the positive law is to provide us with a rule that settles questions, like this, that have no single right answer. It is to miss one of the central points of law to think that there is, or could be, a single right answer as a matter of justice to all legal disputes. We need posited rules where there is no one right answer. Comparative law, on this view, is the diverting process of noting that the legal facts in one jurisdiction are different from another.

Is most of private law like this, a set of rules for resolving disputes involving incommensurable values, which may be more or less consistent, or certain, or efficient, but cannot, save at the outer range, be more or less just? Is the specific topic of this work, the law of restitution, of this kind, so that the only remaining job of the jurist is to construct a set of rules from the relevant authorities that are as coherent as possible, but that are no more or less just than a different set of rules that may either exist in another jurisdiction, or which could be constructed?

Part of the point of this book is to try to show that this is not so, that there are principles of justice that underlie the 'law of restitution'. These apply in all times and places. There is some wiggle room at the margin, where different legal systems may make different choices with one being no more right than another. One such large choice, it will be argued, is the institution of the trust as it exists within common law systems, which because of its form, means that personal and proprietary claims that do not exist in other systems arise. Such choices need to cohere together so as to make sense, but they are not as ineluctable as the rules of algebra.

If then the positive law does not settle what it ought to be, why have I included so much of it in a 'theoretical' work?

Trying to answer questions of justice in the abstract, without concrete examples, is extremely difficult. It is for this reason that philosophers who are concerned with ethics or politics often rely upon examples (such as the various trolley problems, or science fiction hypotheticals concerning being hooked up to a violinist). What examples enable us to do is to test abstract principles (such as utilitarianism or the Golden Rule or Kantian right). We can then go back and forth between our stated principle and concrete examples. Sometimes our firm intuitions as to how the examples should be answered will cause us to modify, or even abandon, our principles. Sometimes our principles will cause us to conclude that our instincts as to how the examples should be answered is in fact wrong. This to-ing and fro-ing has been said to be the process of finding 'reflective equilibrium'.[4]

In law, we are lucky enough to have many thousands of real-world examples, from different jurisdictions and times, where intelligent people of sound judgement have given a verdict as to the right result, often independently of one another. This enables us to test our principles of justice against actual cases. Sometimes this process will require us to conclude that our principles need refinement. Sometimes we will conclude that a rule is wrong or a case incorrectly decided because contrary to the applicable principle(s) of justice. It is this

---

[4] J Rawls, *A Theory of Justice* (1971), 65.

approach that enables us to choose between two inconsistent decisions of ultimate appellate courts from different jurisdictions and decide that one of them is wrong as a matter of justice, when they cannot be wrong as a matter of the positive law of their own jurisdiction unless decided *per incuriam*. It enables us to say that an ultimate appellate court was right in deciding to overturn its predecessor, and not simply record the fact as we do with a change in the weather. A theory that claims that some, many, most, or all of the posited legal rules in a jurisdiction are incorrect as a matter of justice may be more or less interesting, but it cannot be more or less wrong because of its inconsistency with the positive law as it is found.

The distinction between the fact of the posited law, and of what justice requires can be lost sight of in common law jurisdictions because we are taught through the case law method. A practitioner in arguing a case for a client, or a judge in deciding the result, often, especially at appellate level, employs a combination of arguments drawing upon both the positive law ('I am bound to follow *X v Y*') and of justice ('Any other result would be unfair on the defendant because … '). Although we can go back and forth between the *is* and the *ought*, we cannot assume anything about one from the other.

B. Corrective Justice

It is often said that 'unjust enrichment' is a form of, or justified by, 'corrective justice'.[5] What this means needs careful treatment as this term is used in a number of different senses.

On one view, any rule that requires something that has happened in the past to be corrected, is a norm of corrective justice. It describes the form of a rule. A rule that says damages for wrongdoing must be paid is a rule that seeks to correct something in the past, and so is a corrective justice rule. A rule that said mistaken payments must be returned would therefore also be a rule of corrective justice. However, what the reason(s) for such rules of correction may be are many and various. On this view, 'corrective justice' is the *explanandum* not the *explanans*. We could have good and bad rules of corrective justice. A rule that said gifts to the poor must be returned would be a rule of corrective justice, albeit a very bad one.

This usage of 'corrective justice' has at least two things to be said in its favour.

First, corrective justice is often seen as contrasted with, and having a family relation to, distributive justice. In distributing a particular human good (land, access to education, a child's birthday cake, etc) the reasonable criteria by which we do so may be many and various (need, merit, ability to pay, etc). Some rules for determining distribution may be bad or arbitrary (height, ethnicity, etc). It would be curious to invoke 'distributive justice' as an explanation, when what needs justifying is why a particular distribution may be just.

Second there are, observably, different kinds of reasons that legal systems (rightly) take as justifying norms of correction, just as there are different kinds of reason that may justify different kinds of distribution of goods. If this is all 'corrective justice' means, rules that require that something that happened in the past be corrected, it can be put to one side.

---

[5] Eg A Burrows, *the Law of Restitution* (3rd edn, 2011), 68–69; *Kingstreet Investments Ltd v New Brunswick (Finance)* [2007] 1 SCR 3, [32] per Bastrache J; *Benedetti v Sawaris* [2013] UKSC 50, [2014] AC 938, [97] per Lord Reed; K Barker, 'Unjust Enrichment: Containing the Beast' (1995) 15 OJLS 457; L Smith, 'Restitution: The Heart of Corrective Justice' (2001) 79 Tex L Rev 2115.

Another view is that corrective justice is a concept applicable only to wrongdoing. When a duty is breached, whether a contractual one to deliver goods at a particular time and place, or a tortious one not to negligently run over a pedestrian while driving, or of any other kind, the reason for the original duty does not disappear. Because of this, the original duty becomes a duty to do the next best thing to having conformed with it.[6] In private law, this most commonly takes the form of a duty to pay compensation for consequential loss suffered as a result of a wrong.

Whatever the merits of this argument, it has no application to many forms of private law, including many obligations to make restitution that are not based upon any breach of a pre-existing duty (such as the obligation of the recipient of a mistaken payment to make restitution).

A third view, most closely associated in the modern era with Professor Ernest Weinrib, is that the form of private law's obligations controls the kind of reasons that can and do justify it.[7] Duties of right are necessarily owed to other people in a way that duties of virtue or public duties need not be. This form imposes a constraint upon the kind of reasons that can correctly, as a matter of justice, justify them. They must be reasons that tie this particular rightholder to this particular duty-bearer. Because rights themselves are bilateral, the reasons that can justify them ought also to be bilateral in form, applying to both parties together. The language of 'correction' is misleading on this usage, as all rights (whether of correction or otherwise) have this bilateral form (although we can infer the bilateral nature of a primary right from the bilateral nature of any secondary obligation of correction that is the form it takes after breach).

Two examples, from outside of the scope of this work, illustrate the significance of this third view.

The first, familiar to torts theorists, is the inadequacy of the reasons commonly given at the start of textbooks on the law of torts that seek to justify the imposition of liability. It is often said, imposing liability for injuries caused by careless drivers serves the goal of deterring prospective defendants from antisocial conduct of this kind. Allowing the injured victim of careless driving to sue serves the useful goal of ensuring those who suffer injury through no fault of their own obtain compensation to counterbalance their loss.

One problem with seeking to justify the law of torts generally, or the tort of negligence specifically, through the goals of deterrence and compensation is that these justifications do not relate the particular plaintiff to the particular defendant in any way. If we took these justifications seriously, it may be better to operate a clearing house system instead, where all the negligent drivers paid a fine into a central fund, and all those who had suffered injury had a claim on that fund. Such a system would look superior to the one we have now because we could tailor the fine on the negligent party to obtain the level of deterrence required, and quantify the compensation awarded to the degree of need. Reasons of deterrence and compensation, at least on their own, are not bilateral in the way that right-shaped reasons need to be. These beneficial consequences may count in favour of any particular rule, but they cannot alone suffice. We cannot simply put together the reasons applicable to the defendant (deterrence) and reasons applicable to the plaintiff (deserving of compensation because of their misfortune).

---

[6] See eg J Gardner, 'What is Tort Law For? Part 1: The Place of Corrective Justice' (2011) 30 Law and Phil 1.
[7] E J Weinrib, *The Idea of Private Law* (rev edn, 2012); E J Weinrib, *Corrective Justice* (2012).

Almost all policy arguments in favour of the torts system (such as loss spreading, risk allocation, or enterprise liability) suffer from the same flaw. They fail to account for a system of rights, because they are not right-shaped. If we take them seriously, which requires exceptional intellectual honesty such as that possessed by the late Patrick Atiyah,[8] they lead to proposals for the abolition of the law of torts in whole or in part, as has happened in relation to liability for personal injuries caused by accidents in New Zealand.

A second example is the law of contract formation. One view of contract is that it is promissory morality given legal form.[9] Good people keep their promises; being resolute is a virtue. Promisees have expectations created that deserve protection.

However, promises alone do not, in England, and should not, give rise to legal rights.[10] They are unilateral. Contract law requires a bargain. There must be an offer and an acceptance: a doing by both parties, a bargain for which they are each responsible. The meaning of that bargain is not found in the subjective intentions of one or other of the parties, or even of both of them where they fortuitously coincide, but in the objective meaning of the bargain that they have made together. It is only this idea of the bargain between them that explains the bilateral form of the right(s) created.

'You wronged me' or 'We agreed' at least potentially suffice to justify private law duties because they are reasons that relate the two parties together.

As this third, substantive, usage of the label 'corrective justice' suffers from the flaw that it does not necessarily concern the correction of anything, some have preferred labels such as 'interpersonal justice'[11] or 'commutative justice'[12] to capture the idea.

We do not need to adjudicate between the different usages of the term 'corrective justice', the label does not matter and I shall make no further reference to it. What is important for the purpose of this work is that what has become the orthodox account of 'unjust enrichment' is defective as failing to take seriously the bilateral reasons that can legitimately justify rights between persons.

C. Reasons and Recourse

Because rights are bilateral, the kinds of reasons that can legitimately justify *them* are also bilateral. Similarly, the kind of countervailing reasons that can show, that, exceptionally, one party has no right, and that the other has a privilege, must also be bilateral. This is not however true of all of the reasons applicable in private law. Some reasons may only apply to one party and not the other, or even to neither party specifically. A corporation or a child may lack capacity to contract for purposes of their protection. This reason applies to one side alone. It is however not a reason that explains the existence of a right, but rather why a claim may not be brought against them. It justifies an immunity from suit.

Another example is limitation statutes. These (generally) bar the bringing of an action to enforce a right after a period of time. They too provide an immunity from suit. They do not

---

[8] Eg P Atiyah, *Accidents Compensation and the Law* (3rd edn, 1980), 627.
[9] C Fried, *Contract as Promise: A Theory of Contractual Obligation* (2nd edn, 2015), esp ch 2.
[10] Under the influence of Stair, who thought the law should track moral virtue, bare promises are in principle enforceable in Scotland without the need for acceptance.
[11] Eg A Robertson, 'On the Function of the Law of Negligence' (2013) 33 OJLS 31.
[12] Eg A Beever, *Forgotten Justice: The Forms of Justice in the History of Legal and Political Theory* (2013).

(generally) concern the rights we have against each other, but rather how long we each have to bring a claim. Their justification too is nothing necessarily to do with what is fair between plaintiff and defendant, considerations completely unrelated to them, sometimes called 'policy' reasons may justify them: most importantly enabling all of us to 'close the books' on past actions. The justification for such immunities need not be, and are not, bilateral.

Similarly, the law of illegality takes its justification from the need to ensure that the reasons for legal duties cohere together. If I pay you for a public honour that is not forthcoming, the traditional rule in England was that bribes are not recoverable where the promised benefit is not received because the claimant would have to rely upon the offence of dishonesty that he had committed in order to make out his claim.[13] The entire point of the illegality rule is to refuse to do justice as between the parties themselves.

The many and diverse reasons why a claim should fail, despite the existence of a right that is *prima facie* deserving of enforcement, usually travel under the label 'defences' and I shall follow this usage. Such defences either give rise to a privilege (ie the claimant exceptionally has no right) or an immunity (ie the claimant exceptionally has no power to sue). The reasons justifying immunities from suit need not be bilateral, but that is not true of the reasons justifying the rights between us *inter se*.

D. Legal Categories

We can divide the law in different ways for different purposes, with categories overlapping with each other. Three kinds of category may be distinguished for our purposes.

The first are contextual categories based around particular sets of facts in the world: 'horse law', 'sports law', 'computer law', and so on. Sometimes particular contexts require special regulatory rules (eg the Dangerous Dogs Act 1991, and the Computer Misuse Act 1990). We cannot however use these categories for purposes of legal reasoning. We cannot assume that one rule that applies to dogs (how they are bought and sold for example) is specific to them or tells us anything useful about other rules applicable to dogs.

The second are categories united by their legal form. The distinction between public duties (which are not owed to identifiable individuals) and private duties (which are) is of this kind. Within private law, we distinguish between rights *in rem* (rights in relation to things and exigible against the rest of the world) and rights *in personam* (rights exigible against specific individuals). As we shall see, 'equitable property rights' are distinguished by their form: they are rights in relation to other rights. Easements, security rights, and tenancies in common are also all kinds of rights that are given unity by their form.

The law of restitution (as opposed to the law of unjust enrichment) also claims to be a subject united by the form of rights that are created. It is said to concern obligations to give up (which for some includes giving back) to another gains made. In this it purports to sit alongside other categories united by the form of the subject matter of any claim. Claims to gains made by the defendant may be contrasted with claims to make good losses incurred by the claimant. As we shall see, the material traditionally treated as making up the 'law of restitution' has no such formal commonality.

---

[13] *Holman v Johnson* (1775) 1 Cowp 341, 343, 98 ER 1120, 1121 *per* Lord Mansfield.

The third kind of category is the most important in legal reasoning: those united by the reason why duties arise. What is meant here is not why as a matter of the positive law they are valid (eg if they are found in a court judgment or in a statute) but rather, the reason of justice why the positive law is right to so recognise them. Contractual obligations may have many different kinds of formal content but they are given unity by the reason why they arise: agreements ought to be kept, *pacta sunt sevanda*.

The law of torts may be described as having a formal unity, being concerned with the secondary obligations created by the infringement of primary rights. Secondary obligations that arise as a result of wrongdoing (usually to compensate for losses caused) may also be said to have a unity of reason. The reason why the primary duty exists does not disappear when the wrong occurs, generating an obligation to do the next best thing now possible. To that extent at least, the law of damages for wrongdoing also has a unity of reason. It is the law of the next best now possible, given where we are after the wrong. Some, of course, maintain that tort law (sic) is a ragbag of completely different things having nothing in common,[14] in which case we should stop talking about it.

'Unjust enrichment', unlike 'restitution', purports to provide us with a unified reason of justice why legal duties arise. Again, it is a central theme of this work that no such unity of reason exists.

One of the difficulties in making good this claim is that proponents of 'unjust enrichment' are sometimes guilty of employing a 'motte and bailey' approach to argument.[15] This takes the form of making the larger (the 'motte') claim that there just is a law of unjust enrichment, and that it is permissible to analogise between all kinds of cases that are alike (as the 'four-stage test' presupposes). Then, when pressed, a retreat is made to the more easily defended position (the 'bailey') that there are in fact many different reasons for recovery in play and that there is no unity of reason that connects them. What links these disparate groups together is then a mystery, and why it is ever permissible to analogise from one group of cases to another unexplained. The problem is not that there may be countervailing reasons in some cases why we may disapply the general default rules, but rather that there is no reason for thinking there should be general default rules (and for determining to which cases they should apply) at all.

What can mislead us is that we often find ourselves using the same kind of reasoning in different areas, and this can trick us into thinking that we are in the same place. My father worked as an electronics engineer from the 1950s until the 2000s. Originally, he had worked with vacuum tube technology (valves) but these were eventually replaced by early bipolar transistors. The former were voltage operated, the latter by current. Much later, a new kind of transistor, field effect transistors, were developed which, because voltage operated, had several of the same features as valves. Those who had started their career with the older technology were then at an advantage because the new device operated in a similar way to the obsolete one. But it would have been a mistake to think that they were the same, and to have worked upon the assumption that one device operated in the same way as another, just because they had certain factual characteristics in common.

---

[14] Eg J Goudkamp and J Murphy, 'The Failure of Universal Theories of Tort Law' (2015) 21 Legal theory 47.
[15] N Shackel, 'Motte and Bailey Doctrines'. Practical Ethics blog, University of Oxford (5 September 2014) <http://blog.practicalethics.ox.ac.uk/2014/09/motte-and-bailey-doctrines/> accessed 26 October 2022.

E. Quasi-Contract

Although having gradually gone into desuetude, the old category of quasi-contracts has strong parallels with the modern category of 'unjust enrichment'. Quasi-contract encompassed a miscellany of private obligations: those created by court judgments, statutory obligations unrecognised by the common law, the duty of those such as innkeepers carrying out a common calling to accept requests for service, the obligation of those under a contractual incapacity to pay for necessaries, the duty through 'waiver of tort' of those who acquire the proceeds of the right to the thing of another, and the obligation to refund mistaken payments.[16]

It is instructive to contrast the French category of quasi-contracts which encompasses quite different claims: liability to reimburse an intervener in another's affairs for his expense, recovery of undue payments, and some cases of unconscionable commercial dealings.[17] French law does not recognise the common callings category, just as, as we shall see, the common law does not recognise the reimbursement entitlement of necessitous interveners. It is a different miscellany.

Once we have before us these lists, it is apparent that the label refers to obligations that are *not* contractual. The only relation between contracts and quasi-contracts is that they both create legal obligations. Within the quasi-contract category, nobody (surely?) would suppose that the same justifying reason for the imposition of an obligation operated in, say, judgment debts and the obligation of minors to pay for the food they buy. As such, this dustbin category of 'other obligations' did no harm. We are not misled into thinking we can analogise from the rules applicable in one category into another.

As 'quasi-contract' was and, where still in use, remains a label for a rag-bag group of obligations with nothing in common save that they are not contractual, problems only arise if we take the label seriously. This appears to have happened in the puzzling House of Lords decision of *Sinclair v Brougham*.[18] The Birkbeck Permanent Benefit Building Society was incorporated under the Building Societies Act 1836. At some point the Society started to operate, and styled itself, as a bank, something which it had no power to do under the statute. The modern law today treats contracts entered into with private companies acting outside of the purposes of their incorporation as valid, but the law then was, and still is in relation to public corporations, that because the contracts entered into were *ultra vires* the corporation they were void. An order for the winding up of the Society was made, and the question arose as to the distribution of its assets. Outside creditors with valid contracts were, by consent, paid, and so the competition was between the bank depositors, whose contracts were void, and the shareholders of the Society. The depositors argued that '[i]f a corporation gets into its hands the money of somebody else for no consideration and on no valid contract, it cannot keep the money but must pay it back; it is liable to an action for money had and received just as much as an individual is'.[19]

This was rejected on the basis that as the imputation of a contract to recover back money paid that was not due was based upon a fictitious promise to do so, this fictitious imputation

---

[16] P Winfield, *The Law of Quasi-Contracts* (1952).
[17] E Descheemaeker, 'Quasi-Contrats et Enrichissement Injustifié en Droit Français' (2013) RTDCiv 1; P Letelier, 'Another Civilian View of Unjust Enrichment's Structural Debate' (2021) 79 CLJ 527.
[18] [1914] AC 398.
[19] *ibid*, 401.

was impermissible where no actual promise would have been valid. The claim for money had and received failed.[20]

This reasoning and result was inconsistent with prior Court of Appeal authority,[21] could not be reconciled with other cases of quasi-contractual liability where no enforceable contract could have existed whatever agreement were proven (as in the case of the obligation of minors to pay for necessaries), and treated the fiction of the promise to repay as having a substantive importance that it did not have. The decision was, and is, wrong. Its basis, albeit not necessarily the result, was subsequently disapproved by the House of Lords,[22] and the Court of Appeal has now held that where money is paid under a contract that is invalidated by statute it is recoverable, save where this is inconsistent with the statute's meaning.[23]

If 'unjust enrichment' were just a re-labelling of the same miscellany covered by 'quasi-contract', to make it even clearer that these claims are not contractual, it would be even more inert and unthreatening than the label it sought to replace. From the start, however, the label has been taken seriously, and the ambition of its proponents has been greater. This is shown by the early exclusion of some cases of quasi-contracts (court judgments, statutory obligations, common callings), the more recent exclusion of others (waiver of tort), and the expansion to cover other categories of claim (often but not always in Equity) that were seen as analogous to mistaken payments and so are now included (such as the right to contribution between co-sureties). This has led to the same error, taking the label seriously, that its champions rightly identified as having arisen in *Sinclair v Brougham*.

---

[20] The decision to allow the depositors' claim *in rem* was equally puzzling.
[21] *Phoenix Life Insurance Co. Re Burges and Stock's Case* (1862) 2 J&H 441, 70 ER 1131.
[22] *Westdeutsche Landesbank Girozentrale v Islington LBC* [1996] AC 669 (HL), 710 *per* Lord Goff.
[23] *Haugesund Kommune v Depfa ACS Bank* [2010] EWCA Civ 759.

PART II
UNJUSTIFIED PERFORMANCE

3
Performance

A. Introduction

In order to understand the reasons why claims succeed, it is often best to start with ones that fail.

A Scottish *obiter dictum*:

> One man heats his house, and his neighbour gets a great deal of benefit. It is absurd to suppose that the person who has heated his house can go to his neighbour and say—'Give me so much for my coal bill, because you have been warmed by what I have done, and I did not intend to give you a present of it.'[1]

A classic American case:

> Two neighbours each owned non-adjoining limestone quarries which were each prone to becoming filled with water. The plaintiffs owned a pump which they used for draining their quarry, thereby also emptying the defendant's. They sought to recover compensation for this service. This was denied on the basis that it was impossible to 'imply a promise' between the parties.[2]

Why should there be no claim in these cases,[3] when we know that the mistaken payment of money is recoverable? What essential element is missing? Put simply, the answer of this chapter is that it is the absence of either a payment by the plaintiff to the defendant, or a service rendered by the plaintiff accepted by the defendant. Where there is a claim, it is to reverse the payment made or service rendered, not to any consequent enrichment the defendant may have. This chapter and the next primarily concern an account of the law, and we shall return to the theoretical justification for this condition at the conclusion of Chapter 5.

We start with a number of other possibilities that have been suggested as to why there is no claim in the examples above. Although these will be discarded, they point towards the correct position. The chapter then proceeds to consider more precisely the meaning and importance of 'performance'. In particular, the often-difficult question of determining to whom a payment or service has been rendered is addressed.

---

[1] *Edinburgh and District Tramways Ltd v Courtenay* 1909 SC 99 (IHCS), 105 *per* Lord President Dunedin.
[2] *Ulmer v Farnsworth* 80 Me 500, 15 A 65 (SC 1888).
[3] It has been argued that a claim should succeed in the latter case when modern restitutionary reasoning is followed: J McCamus, 'The Self-Serving Intermeddler and the Law of Restitution' (1978) 16 Osgoode Hall LJ 517, 524–525.

The Laws of Restitution. Robert Stevens, Oxford University Press. © Robert Stevens 2023.
DOI: 10.1093/oso/9780192885029.003.0003

B. Red Herrings

1. No Loss

The Scottish *dictum* comes from *Edinburgh and District Tramways Ltd v Courtenay*.[4] An advertising firm paid a rental to a tramway company in return for the carrying of adverts on tram cars. Under their agreement, it was necessary for the firm to pay for boards on the tram cars so as to display the advertising. Subsequently, the tramway company ordered new trams that came ready fitted with 'decency boards', obviating the need for the advertising firm to incur this expense. The tramway company brought a claim against the advertising firm for the costs the latter were thereby saved. The claim rightly failed. Lord President Dunedin in holding for the defender stated 'there are certain marks or notes of the situation in which recompense is due, and I think that one mark or note is that the person who claims recompense must have lost something'.[5] This requirement of correlative loss was recently relied upon by the UK Supreme Court in *Investment Trust Companies v HMRC*.[6]

This requirement of correlative loss and gain is sometimes thought to distinguish claims for restitution that are independent of wrongdoing, a right violation, and those that are then said to be 'autonomous'.[7] It also has the apparent benefit of historical pedigree, the Digest quoting Pomponius states '*Jure naturae aequum est, neminem cum alterius detrimento et injuria fieri locupletiorem*' ('it is natural justice that no-one should unjustly enrich himself to the detriment of another').[8]

However, loss in the ordinary sense of that word is neither sufficient nor necessary for a claim to succeed. An example where we introduce this element is as follows:

> P and D each own one of only two examples of a rare collectible stamp worth thousands of pounds. P's stamp is destroyed by fire, which causes D's stamp to more than double in value. D sells his stamp. P seeks restitution from D of the enrichment D has made at his expense.[9]

No claim should succeed in such a case. The correlation between D's factual gain and P's factual loss is insufficient. 'It is not the case that where there is gain on one side and loss on the other the maxim [unjustified enrichment] invariably applies for the connection between loss and gain may not be of that direct and intimate sort to which alone the grounds of duty apply.'[10]

---

[4] 1909 SC 99 (IHCS).
[5] *ibid*, 105.
[6] [2017] UKSC 29, [2018] AC 275, [45] per Lord Reed. See also *Re BHT (UK) Ltd* [2004] EWHC 201 (Ch), [2004] BCC 301.
[7] See also *Morgan Guaranty Trust Co of New York v Lothian Regional Council* 1995 SC 151 (IHCS), 155, 'these actions are all means to the same end, which is to redress an unjustified enrichment upon the broad equitable principle *nemo debet locupletari aliea jactura*', per Lord Hope. Canadian law has, at least formally, adopted such a requirement: *Pettkus v Becker* 117 DLR (3d) 257, 274 (SCC); *Garland v Consumer Gas Co* [2004] 237 DLR (4th) 385, 397 (SCC); *Kerr v Baranow* [2011] 328 DLR (4th) 577, 593 (SCC). Whether it in fact does so is a different matter.
[8] D. 50.17.200.
[9] *Cf.* D Friedmann, 'Restitution of Benefits Acquired Through the Appropriation of Property or the Commission of a Wrong' 80 Col L Rev 504, 532 (at fn 144).
[10] Baron David Hume, *Lectures 1786–1822*, vol III (G Campbell and H Paton eds, Stair Society Vol 15 1952), 170.

A more complex example is the important decision of the Court of Appeal in *Falcke v Scottish Imperial Insurance Co*.[11] A life insurance policy had been repeatedly mortgaged. The plaintiff was the owner of the ultimate equity of redemption who paid a premium to stop the policy from lapsing when none of the incumbrancers were prepared to do so. When the policy paid out, the plaintiff sought a lien over the proceeds. This claim was rejected, Bowen LJ famously saying that '[l]iabilities are not to be forced upon people behind their backs any more than you can confer a benefit upon a man against his will.'[12] The presence of correlative loss and gain did not suffice. Although the case might be thought to be restricted to the question of whether a lien was available, as opposed to a personal claim against the payee of the policy for the gain they had made, there is no indication in the reasons in the judgments that this is the case.

Indeed, as we shall see,[13] there was a loss suffered by the claimant in *Investment Trust Companies v HMRC*, and so the invocation of the idea in that case cannot explain the result.

Conversely, where restitution of a service rendered and accepted succeeds, it has never been required to be shown, and cannot be assumed, that the plaintiff has been left factually worse off by its provision. Similarly, there is (probably) no rule barring recovery where an initial loss has been passed on[14] (eg by a pursuer who has mistakenly paid the defendant, but who then raised his prices to make good the disbursement in a situation of inelastic demand). This is an indication that loss is not a necessary condition of recovery.

It may be objected that a different meaning of 'loss' is here being used. Lord Reed in *Investment Trust Companies v HMRC* makes it clear that he does not intend 'loss' to have the meaning it does in the law of damages (ie being worse off than you otherwise would be).[15] We might seek to explain this by expanding the meaning of loss to include lost opportunities that the claimant had in the past. If I clean your windows, I have lost the opportunity to clean someone else's while I was doing so, although I may not be counter-factually worse off today by the work. By contrast, heating my flat, benefitting my neighbour above, is something I would have done in any event. Similarly, in *Edinburgh and District Tramways Ltd v Courtenay* the new trams with their new fittings would have been acquired in any event, so there is no 'subtraction' in the sense of a lost opportunity to behave otherwise.

If I request the use of your horse for a week, upon its return it may be healthier and better exercised than it would have been absent my use of it. Although the horse owner has not, as things turned out, been prejudiced, but indeed has been benefitted, he would not have given the use of the horse without the request. This action or 'doing' is something for which the party making the request is jointly responsible and that would not have happened without him. If this is what is meant by 'loss', better, less misleading terminology is available to us.

2. No 'Unjust Factor'

A popular answer as to why there is no claim is to focus on the fact that there is no recognised 'unjust factor' in the examples given so far, and to use that both as an explanation for

---

[11] (1886) 24 Ch D 234.
[12] *ibid*, 248.
[13] Below p 37.
[14] *Kleinwort Benson Ltd v Birmingham City Council* [1997] QB 380 (CA). See Chapter 18, Defences.
[15] *Investment Trust Companies v HMRC* [2017] UKSC 29, [2018] AC 275, [45] *per* Lord Reed.

the result and as a defence of a model of the law that seeks to explain recovery as based upon some defect in or qualification of the plaintiff's consent.[16] Such 'unjust factors' are said to include mistakes, as in the case of a mistaken payment of money which is recoverable. The consent of the man who has heated his flat to the benefit of his neighbour above is not 'vitiated'. However, we can adjust the examples to show that this cannot be the explanation.

> *P* and *D* each own one of only two examples of a rare collectible stamp worth thousands of pounds. *P mistakenly* destroys his stamp, which causes *D*'s stamp to more than double in value. *D* sells his stamp. *P* seeks restitution from *D* of the enrichment *D* has made at his expense.[17]

The addition of a mistake by *P* should make no difference.

Similarly, in *Falcke* it was arguable that the claimant was making a mistake in paying the premium, induced by the fraud of a third party, but the Court of Appeal did not discuss this, because it was of no significance.

3. Grudging Gifts

Peter Birks in his final work sought to argue that the person who inadvertently heats the flat above is making a grudging gift.[18] A person who turns the heating on can foresee that heat rises, and that this will leave any neighbour above better off, and that is sufficient to constitute a gift. The gift would then provide a juridical basis for the defender's enrichment, so that restitution would be denied.

This obviously will not do. Gifts, like contracts, cannot be made unilaterally.[19] Foresight of benefit of another is not enough. Further, should a fool who does not know that heat rises, who would never have turned the heating on if he had known that his hated noisy neighbour would thereby benefit, have a claim? Should someone who mistakenly destroys his stamp, reasonably believing it to be the only copy, have a claim against the owner of the other example if he could not have foreseen the consequent enrichment? No.

4. No Right Transfer

A different kind of answer is given by those who wish to tie restitution to the transfer of property rights. An early, albeit crude, version of this view was put forward by Stoljar, who maintained that where P paid D $100 in cash by mistake, P retained title to the cash and so could bring a claim on the basis 'that is mine'.[20] That will not work in cases where what is

---

[16] Eg M McInnes, 'The Reason to Reverse: Unjust Factors and Juristic Reasons' (2012) 92 Boston University Law Review 1049, 1064. *The Ruabon Steamship Company Ltd v London Assurance* [1900] AC 6 might also be attempted to be explained in this way

[17] *Cf.* D Friedmann, 'Restitution of Benefits Acquired Through the Appropriation of Property or the Commission of a Wrong' 80 Col L Rev 504, 532 (at fn 144), emphasis mine.

[18] P Birks, *Unjust Enrichment* (2nd edn, 2005), 158–160.

[19] See Chapter 5, Practice.

[20] S J Stoljar, *The Law of Quasi-Contracts* (1964), ch 1; S J Stoljar 'Unjust Enrichment and Unjust Sacrifice' (1987) 50 MLR 603.

provided is work or a service, but it is then suggested that these cases can be pushed away as being akin to contract in some way.

The Stoljar view suffers from the fatal flaw that where cash is paid by mistake the payor does not retain title to it (save perhaps where the mistake is sufficiently fundamental to prevent title passing).[21] A more sophisticated version of the proprietary theory has been developed by other commentators, with the fullest having been propounded by Professor Webb. On this view, the law may, for good reasons in order to protect third parties, say that title to the cash (or any other transferable right) has passed to the recipient, but also say that whatever justified the transferor's original entitlement to the property also now justifies the obligation of the recipient to make restitution. The reason for the original title persists as against the recipient, even if the legal entitlement itself does not.[22]

This is, on its face, a plausible account of the recovery of the mistaken payment of cash, made more so once it is accepted that it is not intended to be exhaustive (ie that there are several other reasons for restitution which explain other cases such as restitution of the provision of services). It does seem to identify a bilateral reason that ties the claimant to the defendant (the pre-existing property right to the cash which is good against everyone other than the title holder including the payee). Many of the older cases speak of the plaintiff recovering 'his' money. It would also explain why there ought to be no claim in the absence of any transfer of a right, as in the case of the rising heat.

Unfortunately, it only provides an explanation where what is transferred is the right to a thing, such as cash. Where, for example, a debt is mistakenly assigned, the plaintiff transferor only had a right exigible against the debtor, not the transferee, and so this cannot provide the necessary explanation.

Further, it is both radically over- and under-inclusive as an explanation and cannot be made to work outside of simple payments made by cash. An example:

C mistakenly thinking that he owes D £100, asks his mother to pay this sum for him on his behalf. His mother does so with her cash.

Although C has neither lost any right nor transferred one to D, he has a claim for restitution from him. That the mother was acting as the son's agent does not mean that C at any point acquires any right to the cash, but rather that her action in paying is attributed to him. The only transfer of any right is by C's mother to D, but she has no claim against him.

Conversely:

C and D mistakenly believe that C owes D £100. D requests that C pays the money owed to D's brother. C does so with his cash.

Here D has received no right from C or anyone else. The brother's act of acceptance of the payment does not entail that D acquires any right to the cash. Again, C has a claim for restitution against D,[23] but no claim against the party to whom he transferred his right to the

---

[21] *Chambers v Miller* (1862) 13 CB (NS) 125, 143 ER 50; *R v Ilich* (1987) 162 CLR 110, HCA. Discussed in Chapter 11, Things.
[22] C Webb, *Reason and Restitution: A Theory of Unjust Enrichment* (2016), 73–77. Cf. P Jaffey, *Private Law and Property Claims* (2007). For an early version of a similar theory see F C von Savigny, *System des heutigen römischen Rechts*, vol V (1841), 526.
[23] *Goss v Chilcott* [1996] AC 788 (PC).

cash (the brother). One value of Professor Webb's proprietary account is that it shows how obligations to make restitution are compatible with the law on the passing of title.

A similar view to professor Webb's is that the existence of interpersonal claims to reverse unjustified payments of cash and other right transfers removes the injustice that would otherwise result from the operation of the principle of abstraction (ie that the validity of a conveyance is not determined by what is fair as between the parties to that conveyance).[24] For example, in England, title to registrable shares is determined by the name appearing on the share register. Where one party has transferred their right to shares to a fraudster, such a transfer occurs once the register is altered, but this is only justifiable *if* the innocent party also has an interpersonal right to re-transfer back to them.[25] The reason the conveyance is effective despite the fraud is in order to protect third parties. An obligation on the defendant to make restitution of the right acquired softens, and makes justifiable, the operation of the abstract transfer of rights.[26] Without any right to restitution the abstracted rules for the transfer of rights would be unjustifiable.

Important as this argument is, it would only justify an obligation to make restitution where the defendant has acquired an identifiable right from the plaintiff. As the examples above and others show, a payor may have a right to restitution without the payee acquiring any right from her. A payment from plaintiff to defendant is not dependent upon the plaintiff losing, or the defendant acquiring, any right. It is, therefore, again radically under-inclusive as an explanation. This argument from the principle of abstraction is, as we shall see, central to justifying the constructive or resulting trusts that arise where there is an obligation to (re-)transfer identifiable rights acquired.[27] Indeed, such trusts more perfectly 'heal the wound' created by the abstract rules for the transfer of rights than does a mere personal obligation to make restitution.

We shall return to the question of the significance of rights and right transfers at the end of Chapter 5.

5. Incidental Benefits

An explanation of some pedigree as to why the claims in the initial examples fail, is that it is necessary to exclude recovery where the enrichment conferred is an 'incidental benefit', and this was invoked by the First American Restatement in 1937.[28] Scottish law seems to have long recognised such a restriction.[29] More recently, the Canadian Supreme Court[30]

---

[24] *Cf.* B McFarlane, 'Unjust Enrichment, Rights and Value' in D Nolan and A Robertson (eds), *Rights and Private Law* (2012), ch 20.
[25] *Cf. Cressman v Coys of Kensington (Sales) Ltd* [2004] EWCA Civ 47, [2004] 1 WLR 2775.
[26] '[I]n the words of the great pandectist Heinrich Dernburg, it is by means of an enrichment action that the law attempts to heal the wounds that it itself inflicts (by virtue of the abstract transfer of ownership)': R Zimmerman, *The Law of Obligations: Roman Foundations of a Civilian Tradition* (1996), 867.
[27] See Chapter 13, Equity: Restitution.
[28] A Scott and W Seavey, *Restatement of the Law of Restitution: Quasi Contracts and Constructive Trusts* (1937), § 106; rejected in A Kull, *Restatement of the Law (Third) Restitution and Unjust Enrichment*, vol I (2010), 466 as 'a conclusion in place of a reason'.
[29] Hume, *Lectures 1786–1822* (n 10), 166; Niall R Whitty, 'Indirect Enrichment in Scots Law' (1994) JR 200, 239; *Exchange Telegraph Co Ltd v Giulanotti* 1959 SC 19, 26, 1959 SLT 293 (OHCS) 296 per Lord Guest; *Shilliday v Smith* 1998 SC 725, 1998 SLT 976 (IHCS), 980 per Lord President Rodger.
[30] *Peel v Canada* (1993) 98 DLR 4th (SCC).

and the UK Supreme Court have relied upon it,[31] as has Andrew Burrows' *Restatement of Restitution*. According to the last, a benefit is incidental where 'the claimant has an objective unconnected with the defendant's enrichment'.[32]

Although, as we shall see, this idea again points towards the solution, it is at best an inelegant way of expressing the relevant principle.

First, it is not the case that the fact that the conferral of the benefit was done in order to further the pursuer's own interests will, without more, rule out a claim. A person who pays a debt that they think they owe may do so for wholly selfish reasons, for example fear of their own bankruptcy, but we do not for that reason rule out a claim when it is discovered that the money was not due.

Second, we may ask what the benefit is incidental to? One answer in some cases is that it is incidental to the performance of a contract, as where a builder repairs my garden wall benefitting my neighbour, or where the supply of manure to a tenant farmer that is then dug into the ground benefits the landlord. It is sometimes said that we do not want to allow the party performing the contract to be able to escape the contractual allocation of risks, avoiding the risk of bankruptcy of their counterparty, and bring a 'leapfrogging' claim over against a remote party who has incidentally benefitted from the performance.[33] But why not? There seems to be circularity of reasoning here (ie if the law *did* allow the claim against the remote party, the pursuer would not be running the risk of bankruptcy of the counterparty to the same extent as they would know of the ability to claim over). Further there seem to be many examples, such as that of the rising heat, where there is no attempt to leapfrog out of any contract, and yet we think the claim should fail.

Third, there are examples of successful claims said to be based upon 'unjust enrichment' where the defendant's enrichment is unrelated to any objective of the plaintiff, but where recovery is allowed, including the leading case in the area.[34] No explanation is proffered as to *why* incidental benefits as defined sometimes do, and sometimes do not, count.

Fourth, and most importantly, the 'incidental benefits' exception is a description not an explanation. We can see that the claim ought to fail but the theory articulates no reason why. Without some reason, it looks *ad hoc*, introduced to explain away examples that do not fit 'unjust enrichment' theory.[35] What we are really looking for is not a countervailing reason as to why claims should fail in cases such as these, but rather the identification of a constituent element of there being a duty upon the defendant.

6. No 'Transfers of Value'

Another suggestion, now also with the weight of the support of the UK Supreme Court, is to say that what is required is a 'transfer of value'[36] between plaintiff and defendant, sometimes

---

[31] *Investment Trust Companies v HMRC* [2017] UKSC 29, [2018] AC 275, [57] *per* Lord Reed.
[32] A Burrows, *A Restatement of the English Law of Unjust Enrichment* (2011), 54–55.
[33] Birks, *Unjust Enrichment* (n 18), 89–98.
[34] *Lipkin Gorman v Karpnale* [1990] 2 AC 548 (HL). Most cases of discharge of another's obligation are similarly problematic.
[35] L Smith, 'Restitution: A New Start?' in P Devonshire and R Havelock (eds), *The Impact of Equity and Restitution in Commerce* (2019), 91.
[36] *Investment Trust Companies v HMRC* [2017] UKSC 29, [2018] AC 275, [57] *per* Lord Reed.

with the additional qualifier that such transfer be direct.[37] Again, this points towards the correct position, but in language that is unhelpful.

In English, if I transfer something to you, you obtain something that I once had. I could transfer to you the possession of the computer on which I am typing by delivering it physically to you, and you accepting it. In law, some rights are transferable. I could sell to you my right to the computer on which I am typing under a contract, the transfer of the right being possible without physical delivery of the thing. In each case I transfer to you something that I had and now you have (possession of the thing/right to the thing). Again, in English, a 'transfer' does not necessitate the loss of the subject matter of the transfer by the transferor. If I transfer information to you, you acquire information that I had, but I do not lose it by so doing.

The meaninglessness of talk of a 'transfer of value' is most obvious in cases of services. If I clean the windows of your house that may (or may not) leave me worse off and you better off but there has been no transfer between us. What you have (clean windows) is not something I had at the start, nor is something I had (the choice whether to do the work?) obtained by you.

Talk of 'transfers' also (as we shall see) misleads us into misidentifying the subject matter of the claim. It may fool us into thinking that what is to be reversed is the 'value received' or 'value surviving' by the defendant (ie the consequential improvement in his factual balance sheet position, what is obtained because of a transfer). As we shall see, this is a mistake.

Further it will lead us into the error of thinking that where there is a transfer, the transferor is necessarily the correct plaintiff. An example:

P1 mistakenly believes that he owes *D* £1,000. *P1* requests *P2* to pay *D* this sum on his behalf. *P2* pays *D* this sum in cash. *P2* would not have done so if he too had not also mistakenly believed that he owed *P1* this sum.

Who has a claim against *D*?

The law is[38] (and ought to be) that *P1* has a claim against *D*. It is *P1* who has paid *D*. P2 has a claim for reimbursement from *P1*, but no claim against *D*.

The only transfer that has occurred is between *P2* and *D*. *P2* has transferred both possession of the physical notes and the right to them to *D*. The language of 'transfer' is therefore prone to mislead.

C. Performance Defined

1. Summary

The label we put upon the necessary connection between plaintiff and defendant, which captures both the cases of a payment made and of a service rendered by the plaintiff, which has also been accepted by the defendant, is less important than the idea. 'Transfer of value' is

---

[37] *ibid*, [50].
[38] *Aiken v Short* (1856) 1 H & N 54, 156 ER 1180; *MacDonald Dickens & Macklin v Costello* [2011] EWCA Civ 930, [2012] QB 244.

the current terminology of the English courts, but as discussed, this is inexact. The bilateral nature of the necessary relation has caused some to prefer the word 'transaction'.[39] However, a contract is a 'transaction' but where a contract is set aside it is the performance rendered under it that must then be reversed. I shall prefer the term 'performance' because it has the pedigree of usage in German law,[40] does not carry with it the connotations of a contract, is familiar to common lawyers as the subject matter of reversal in the context of rescission of a contract, and is closer in natural English usage as a description of the idea we are trying to capture than any other label. Looking back, the most important of the Roman *condictiones* all involved a performance in the form of a payment of money from one party to another (*condictio indebitti, condictio causa data causa non secuta, condictio ob injustum vel turpem causam, condictio sine causa, condictio ob causam finitam*). This requirement is not a quirk of one system, but an inevitable requirement for all.

'Performance' may be summarised as having three constituent elements. This is for purposes of exposition only; they form an indissoluble sequence.

First, what the plaintiff is seeking to reverse must be his *action*. So:

C pays X £1,000 by mistake. X, delighted by this windfall, pays £200 to D, a charity.

Although D has accepted a payment of £200, this payment was not made by C.[41] Although there is a causal link between D's being better off and C's payment, and a series of transactional links between them, this is insufficient. The payment to D was made by X and was not done, save in a causal sense, by C.

Second, the action C rendered must have been *towards D*. So:

C cuts down the hedge on his land near the boundary with the land of D, his neighbour. C does so in order to improve his view. D thinks the work is being done for his benefit, when it is not, and stands by admiring the work.

Although D may have benefitted from the work, and by standing by might be taken to have accepted it, the work was not done towards or for him, and so its value is irrecoverable. (Notice again that it should not matter whether C was mistaken in cutting the hedge.)

Third, C's action for D must have been *accepted* by D.[42]

C provides heat to a block of flats, mistakenly thinking that he has the agreement of all residents that they will reimburse him for the cost. D, one of the residents, ignorant of C's mistake, is thereby saved the cost of heating his flat.

The 'performance' must have been the doing of both parties together, not one alone. Pollock C B's aphorism that 'One cleans another's shoes, what can the other do but put them on?'[43]

---

[39] *Investment Trust Companies v HMRC* [2017] UKSC 29, [2018] AC 275, [48] *per* Lord Reed.
[40] W Wilburg, *Die Lehre von der ungerechtfertigten Bereicherung* (1934). See J P Dawson, 'Indirect Enrichment' in E von Caemmerer, S Mentshikoff, and K Zweigert (eds), *Ius Privatum Gentium: Festschrift fur Max Rheinstein* (1969), 789.
[41] *Investment Trust Companies v HMRC* [2017] UKSC 29, [2018] AC 275, [51] *per* Lord Reed.
[42] The requirement of acceptance makes the label 'performance' inelegant but is used for want of any better.
[43] *Taylor v Laird* (1856) 25 LJ Ex 329, 333.

reflects what the law is and ought to be. There should be no claim available even where, as things turn out, the cleaning (or heating) leaves the defendant better off than he otherwise would be. In the context of the reversal of services, the courts have described this part of the relation as being the need to establish 'free acceptance'.[44] 'Acceptance' here does not mean mere knowledge, but the opportunity to reject, with a shared responsibility for the payment or service provided.

This is not, as we shall see in the next chapter, the test for determining whether a separate enrichment is 'at the expense' of the plaintiff. Rather the performance received (ie the payment or service) is the subject matter of the claim. The performance is what is reversed, not any consequent enrichment the defendant may or may not have.

In the two examples with which we began this chapter (the rising heat, the drained quarries), although the defendant had been enriched by the plaintiff's actions, this merely causal relation should not and does not in law suffice. No legally significant event has occurred between the parties that the law ought to reverse.

We now consider in detail the three elements in turn.

2. Action

(a) Principle

A straightforward recent example of a claim that should have and did fail is the decision of the UK Supreme Court in *Her Majesty's Revenue and Customs v Investment Trust Companies*.[45] The simplified facts were that the claimants were charged VAT (a sales tax) for the provision of services. The service provider then made periodic VAT returns to the Revenue. It then transpired that the services were exempt from tax under European Union (EU) law. The claimants sought a claim over against the Revenue.

The claim was correctly denied. The claimants did not pay the Revenue anything; they had paid the service provider, not the Revenue. They had paid this money on the basis of the contract of service. Under this contract the payment had been conditional on the VAT being payable, so that they should be entitled to restitution from the provider of that sum. The transfer of the *right* to the money was not so conditional, and so no trust could arise. No claim against the Revenue could be brought even if the provider had used the very money they had been paid to pay the supposed tax to the Revenue.[46]

Similarly, inaction alone does not suffice. Someone with a time limited valuable option to buy an asset from another, who by mistake fails to exercise it within the relevant period, has no claim against the person benefitted. The failure by omission to bring a valuable claim before the expiry of a limitation period gives rise to no claim against the person left better off.[47] The rescission of a wholly executory contract involves the reversal of no performance, it is simply the setting aside of otherwise binding legal obligations.

---

[44] Eg *Chief Constable of Greater Manchester Police v Wigan Athletic AFC* [2008] EWCA Civ 1449, [2009] 1 WLR 1590, [47]; *Benedetti v Sawiris* [2010] EWCA Civ 1427, [118]–[119].
[45] [2017] UKSC 29, [2018] AC 275. *Cf. Cobb v Becke* (1845) 6 QB 930, 115 ER 530.
[46] See Chapter 13, Equity 2: Restitution.
[47] But see *Gibb v Maidstone & Tunbridge NHS Trust* [2010] EWCA Civ 678, [2010] IRLR 786 discussed below 133.

There are, however, other successful claims that might indicate a less restrictive approach. What is their justification?

(b) Complex payments

One example, which also shows the inseparability of the elements summarised above, is that of complex payments, exemplified by *Relfo Ltd v Varsani*.[48] At a time when the company of which they were the sole shareholders and directors was subject to a tax claim of £1.4 million, Mr and Mrs Gorecia caused £500,000 to be paid out of the company's bank account, into a Latvian bank account. On the same day, Intertrade Group LLC made a payment of $878,479.35 from its Latvian bank account to the account of Mr Varsani in Singapore. This sum was the dollar equivalent of £500,000 minus 1.3%. Intertrade Group's bank statement showed that the payment out that it made was funded by payments to it earlier on the same day. It was however not possible to show the link between the initial payment out and the money received by Intertrade Group LLC. Mr Varsani had close links to Mr and Mrs Gorecia, and the following week he paid them $100,000. The payment made by them left Relfo Ltd insolvent, and they went into liquidation shortly thereafter.

The coincidence of the figures, and the relationship between the parties, was enough to demonstrate what had happened. The company had paid Mr Varsani £500,000. Because it rendered the payor company insolvent, a Byzantine mechanism for doing so had been chosen in order to disguise what had occurred. That it was not possible to demonstrate every step in the process that had been employed was irrelevant. What those in control of the company were trying to do, and had succeeded in doing, was pay Mr Varsani. It should not be necessary in a case such as this to 'trace',[49] and it should not matter how many foreign bank accounts or intermediaries are employed.

(c) Maladministered estates

Sometimes the person with the power of suit is not the rightholder, and this has caused confusion.

Where a deceased's estate is maladministered, so that assets are distributed by the personal representative to the wrong person, the recipient comes under a duty to make restitution to the estate. This duty is enforceable at the suit of any of those interested in the correct distribution of the estate, whether as creditors of the deceased, testamentary beneficiaries, or those entitled under the intestate rules of succession. A similar regime applies where a company's assets are to be distributed by a liquidator or administrator.

In *Re Diplock*,[50] the testator, Caleb Diplock, left the residuary part of his estate, amounting to more than £250,000, to such 'such charitable institutions or other charitable or benevolent object or objects' as his executors' chose. From 1936 onwards they distributed this sum to more than 130 charitable institutions. In 1939, one of Caleb's next of kin learned of his cousin's death and informed the executors of his intention to challenge the will. He successfully challenged the clause distributing the residuary estate as void for uncertainty, meaning that the executors had made an incorrect distribution.[51] The executors were sued

---

[48] [2014] EWCA Civ 360, [2015] 1 BCLC 14. See also *Bank Tejarat v Hong Kong and Shanghai Banking Corp (CI) Ltd* [1995] 1 Lloyd's Rep 239.
[49] P Birks, 'Tracing Misused (Bank Tejarat v Hong Kong and Shanghai Banking Corp)' (1995) 9 Trusts Law Int'l 91.
[50] [1951] AC 251 (HL).
[51] *Chichester Diocesan Fund v Simpson* [1944] AC 341 (HL).

for the loss caused by their misadministration, a claim that was compromised for £15,000, a sum paid to the estate. The cousin alongside a large number of other relatives of the deceased, then sought to claw back from the charities the distributed funds into the estate for readministration by the judicial trustee under the Administration of Estates Act 1925. The claim failed before Wynn-Parry J,[52] but his decision was overturned by the Court of Appeal on the basis that 'it is prima facie at least a sufficient circumstance that the defendant, as events have proved, has received some share of the estate to which he was not entitled',[53] a decision that was affirmed by the House of Lords.[54]

On its face this claim might be thought, and has been relied upon by commentators,[55] to establish a more liberal approach to restitution than argued for here. The payments were made by the executors, not the next of kin, and yet a 'direct claim'[56] was permitted. What is wrong with this expansive analysis?

The relief sought and the order made (in this case as in others) was not to make restitution to the next of kin to the extent that they individually have been left worse off by each payment (a complex calculation), but rather to make restitution of the payment made to the estate. This was a claim to reverse the payment made from the estate to the charities. Most of those who were to benefit from the repayment were not parties to the litigation.

The claim was one brought by those interested in the proper administration of the estate to enforce a right to repayment of the estate itself, and not as a claim to enforce a right to restitution that they themselves had.[57] An analogy is the standing that minority shareholders have, subject to conditions, to enforce rights of the company in which they have a stake. The rights they enforce are those of the company, not their own.

Seeing the claim as based upon an exception to the ordinary rules as to who has control over the enforcement of the estate's rights explains two further aspects of the case. First, it explains why, unlike in cases where the plaintiff is seeking to enforce his own rights, the next of kin must first have exhausted their remedies against the executors. This is their primary route for redress, not the exceptional usurpation of control over the enforcement of the estate's rights. Second, as we shall see, a proprietary claim against the recipient charities was also successful. This is explicable if the entitlement is vested in the estate, but not if it is an entitlement of the next of kin personally, as prior to disbursement they have no proprietary right to any part of the estate, but merely a right against the executors that the estate is correctly administered.

The correct position was subsequently expressed most clearly by Viscount Radcliffe:[58]

> The basis of such proceedings is that they are taken on behalf of the estate and, if they are successful, they can only result in the lost property being restored to the estate for use in the due course of administration. Thus, while they assert the beneficiary's right of remedy, they

---

[52] [1947] Ch 716.
[53] [1948] Ch 465, 491 *per* Lord Greene MR.
[54] [1951] AC 251 (HL).
[55] Eg C Mitchell, P Mitchell, and S Watterson (eds), *Goff & Jones: The Law of Unjust Enrichment* (9th edn, 2016), [8–132]; Lord Hoffmann, 'The Redundancy of Knowing Assistance' in P Birks (ed), *The Frontiers of Liability*, vol 1 (1989), 477–478; Lord Walker, 'Dishonesty and Unconscionable Conduct in Commercial Life—Some Reflections on Accessory Liability and Knowing Receipt' (2005) 27 Syd L Rev 187, 202;
[56] [1951] AC 251 (HL), 265 *per* Lords Simonds.
[57] L Smith, 'Unjust Enrichment, Property and the Structure of Trusts' (2000) 116 LQR 412, 437–444. See also T Liau, *Standing in Private Law* (forthcoming).
[58] *Commissioner of Stamp Duties (Queensland) v Livingston* [1965] AC 694 (PC), 714.

assert the estate's right of property, not the property right of creditor or legatee; indeed, the usual situation in which such an action has to be launched is that in which the executor himself, the proper guardian of the estate, is in default, and thus his rights have to be put in motion by some other person on behalf of the estate.

(d) Agents

In law, as outside it, it is possible for one person to act through the agency of another. If one person *(P)* authorises in advance another *(A)* to perform an action on *P*'s behalf, if *A* performs that action, the law attributes *A*'s action to *P*. *Qui facit per alium, facit per se.* This does not mean that the action ceases to be *A*'s but rather that it becomes the doing of both of them jointly.[59] If I authorise you to punch someone else on the nose, and you do so on my behalf, both of us will be jointly liable in battery. It is also possible to ratify the acts of others which are done on our behalf, so that they are attributed to us after performance.

In contract law, if an agent is authorised to negotiate an agreement on behalf of his principal, and does so, the principal is bound just as if he had acted personally.[60] Usually in cases of disclosed agency, the agent will not be bound because it will be clear that his actions are not intended to create any agreement with him personally.[61] Where someone purports to contract on behalf of another, but is acting without authority, the person on whose behalf he purported to act may subsequently ratify what has been done, so as to conclude a contract.[62] (The separate doctrine of ostensible authority is best understood as being an aspect of the objective approach to contract formation: we are bound by the objective impression of agreement for which we are responsible, one aspect of which is the ostensible or apparent authority with which we cloak others to act on our behalf.)

Where an agent purports to act on behalf of another but in circumstances where they lack the authority to do so, this results in both the principal and agent being able to recover. In *Holt v Ely*[63] where an agent was deceived into making a payment, he could personally recover it. As it was unauthorised, he had not made it for and on behalf of his principal. The principal could have chosen to ratify what had been done, the agent had purported to act on his behalf, and sought to bring a claim in his own right.

Where an agent acts within authority, his principal can potentially recover the value of the performance rendered. If therefore *P* mistakenly believes that he owes *D* £1,000, and authorises *X* to pay *D* on his behalf, *P* may have a claim for restitution after payment from *D* because *X*'s actions are attributed to him. It does not and should not matter whether *X* has any entitlement to or will seek reimbursement from *P*, nor that any right *D* acquires comes from *X* and not *P*. Similarly, if *Window Cleaners Ltd* renders a service under a contract to *D* through the actions of its real-world employees who clean windows, and the contract is subsequently avoided for misrepresentation made by *D*, *Window Cleaners Ltd* should be

---

[59] *CBS v Armstrad* [1988] AC 1013 (HL), 1058 *per* Lord Templeman; See also *Hussain v Lancaster City Council* [1999] 2 WLR 1142 (CA); *Southwark London LBC v Tanner* [2001] 1 AC 1 (HL), 22 *per* Lord Hoffmann.
[60] *Boyter v Thomson* [1995] 2 AC 628 (HL), 632 *per* Lord Jauncey.
[61] *Robins v Bridge* (1837) 3 M & W 114, 150 ER 1079; *N & J Vassopulos v Ney Shipping Ltd* [1977] 2 Lloyd's Rep 478; *Boyter v Thomson* [1995] 2 AC 629 (HL), 632.
[62] *Wilson v Tumman* (1843) 6 Man & G 236, 134 ER 879.
[63] (1853) 1 Ellis & Black 795, 118 ER 634.

entitled to restitution of the value of the work performed, because the actions of its workers are attributed to it.

A superficially more complex example is illustrated by the decision of the Court of Appeal in *Khan v Permayer*.[64] Mr Khan and his business partner ran an unsuccessful restaurant that they wished to sell to Mr Eaves. Their landlord, Permayer, made it a condition of the assignment of the lease that he was paid the £40,000 he was owed. It was agreed that Mr Eaves would assume responsibility for the debt by deed, pay it, and be reimbursed by the former owners through deductions from their salaries for running the business in the future. It subsequently transpired that the landlord was owed nothing, the debt having been discharged by earlier insolvency proceedings. Although the claim by Khan for restitution succeeded, the Court of Appeal treated the case as more difficult than it was. Mr Eaves had paid on behalf of the sellers with their authority. The payment was Mr Khan's, just as it would have been if his bank had made the payment for him.

However, where the agent acts within his authority, as in these examples, if he has any recourse it is against his principal alone. Neither Mr Eaves nor the employees of *Window Cleaners Ltd* should have any claim against the defendant in their own right even though the payment and the service were their doing as much as that of their principal.[65] This is not because of the operation of any principle of agency law, but because the performance rendered by the plaintiff must be towards or for the defendant.

3. Towards

There are many examples where a principal has rendered a performance towards another through the agency of someone else. Claims have then been brought by the agent against the recipient of the principal's performance. These claims have rightly failed. The agent is performing towards his principal, not the third party. The clearest illustrative cases, as a matter of authority, concern the provision of services.

The decision of the High Court of Australia in *Lumbers v W Cook Builders Pty Ltd (in liq)*[66] exemplifies the issue. A builder, W Cook & Sons Pty Ltd ('Sons') entered into a contract with Mr Lumbers and his son for the construction of a house outside Adelaide. Most of the work (engagement and payment of sub-contractors, supervision of work) was performed by another related but separate company W Cook Builders Pty Ltd ('Builders') under an agreement with Sons. Builders brought a claim for remuneration for their services against the ultimate employers who had received the benefit of a completed house that cost in excess of A$1 million to build.

Although the Lumbers were unaware of the role of Builders, this should make no difference to the analysis. The court rightly emphasised the importance of the contractual structure the parties had adopted. These contracts showed who was rendering performance, and who it was for. Builders performed its services towards and for Sons,

---

[64] [2001] BPIR 95 (CA).
[65] *Contra* Mitchell, Mitchell, and Watterson, *Goff & Jones* (n 55), [6–59].
[66] [2008] HCA 27, (2008) 232 CLR 635. See in England *Brown and Davies v Galbraith* [1972] 1 WLR 997 (CA); *MacDonald Dickens & Macklin v Costello* [2011] EWCA Civ 930 [2012] QB 244. But compare *Weatherby v Banham* (1835) 5 C & P 228, 175 ER 950.

at their request. That work was attributable to Sons as done at its request and could be relied upon by Sons to show that it had performed its contract with the Lumbers. There were two possible claims, one by Builders against Sons, and one by Sons against the Lumbers. Although Builders had done work, and this had left the landowners better off, this work had not been done for them. Builders had not done the work towards and for the Lumbers.

This decision may be contrasted with the famous French case of '*Boudier*',[67] which appears a misstep. The plaintiffs were small family merchants called Boudier who supplied manure worth 324 Francs to a tenant farmer, who subsequently went into bankruptcy. The landlord had terminated the lease over outstanding debts, and accepted the crop, enhanced with the supplied manure that had acceded to the land into which it was dug, in part payment. The plaintiffs brought a claim over against the landlord and succeeded, purportedly on the basis of the Roman *action de in rem verso*. The case has subsequently been interpreted as embodying a general principle of unjust enrichment unfound in the *Code Civil*.

It is common to seek to justify the result in *Lumbers*, and to criticise that in *Boudier*, on the basis of the reallocation of insolvency risk.[68] The manure suppliers had run the risk of their buyer's insolvency by extending credit on an unsecured basis. Again, circular reasoning of this kind is never satisfactory. If the law does permit a claim against the party ultimately benefitted to whom no performance has been rendered, as it does in France, then that is a factor suppliers will take into account in deciding to extend credit, so that they no longer run the risk of insolvency. It also provides no explanation in cases where there is no contract under which performance is rendered. The better explanation is that the necessary connection between plaintiff and defendant, regardless of the intermediary's potential insolvency, is missing.

In relation to the payment of money, the classic decision is that of *Aiken v Short*.[69] However, the result of the case is capable of being justified in several different ways, so that it is not clear authority for any single one.

The plaintiff bank had purchased property from X, that it believed was subject to a charge securing a debt that X owed to D. The bank paid the debt, having been authorised by X to do so, in order to release its property from the charge. It was subsequently discovered that X had no title to the property that the bank had purchased, so that the bank had paid under a mistake. The claim against the recipient of the payment failed.

Pollock C B stated (emphasis added):

The Bank had paid the money in one sense without any consideration, but the defendant had a perfect right to receive the money from Carter, and *the bankers paid for him*.[70]

---

[67] Cass Req 15 June 1892, *Patureau-Miran v Boudier*. A similar claim had earlier been rejected *Arrazat* case, Cass Req 11 July 1889. *Cf.* the Quebec decision *Lavoie v Fournier* (1924), 37 Que KB 63. Query whether the suppliers had retained ownership of the manure until payment, losing their right of ownership through accession. *Cf.* Chapter 11, Things.
[68] Eg Birks, *Unjust Enrichment* (n 18), 89–94.
[69] (1856) 1 H&N 210, 165 ER 1180.
[70] (1856) 1 H&N 210, 214, 165 ER 1180, 1181.

44 PERFORMANCE

Platt B, stated (emphasis added):

> The money which the defendant *got from her debtor* was actually due to her, and there can be obligation to refund it.[71]

Bramwell B, by contrast, stated:

> In order to entitle a person to recover back money paid under a mistake of fact, the mistake must be as to a fact which, if true, would make the person paying liable to pay the money; not where, if true, it would merely make it desirable that he should pay the money. Here, if the fact was true, the bankers were at liberty to pay or not, as they pleased.[72]

Pollock C B and Platt B are most clearly stating the correct rule. The payment made to the defendant was made by her debtor, through the agency of his bank. The bank had rendered its performance towards *X*, the debtor. The bank's performance was not for the defendant, regardless of the physical movement of cash from the bank to the defendant. The only recourse the bank ought to have had was against the party towards and for whom it had rendered its performance.

Another explanation for the result in *Aiken v Short* is that the payment discharged an obligation owed to the defendant by *X*.[73] Although this may be important on some fact patterns, here the result ought to be exactly the same if we remove the contractual debt from the story. For example:

> *X*, wishing to make a gift to his brother *D*, instructs his bank, *C plc*, to pay *D* £1,000. *C plc*, overlooking the fact that *X* is overdrawn, makes the payment, and now seeks recovery from *D* on the basis that if it had known the truth it would never have paid.

The bank has rendered performance to its customer, through the mechanism of transferring money on its customer's behalf to the defendant. Its only recourse should be against its customer.[74]

In *Stevenson v Mortimer*[75] a Custom House official demanded fees in excess of his entitlement from the Master of a ship, which the Master paid. The ship owner then sought to recover the payment, the Master having done so with the authority of his principal. Lord Mansfield giving judgment held that the owner was entitled to be reimbursed, although he had not personally paid. Although Lord Mansfield stated that the agent could himself have recovered, he did so on the basis that he did so 'from the authority of the principal', that is, on behalf of the principal and not himself.

Aiken v Short also illustrates that the person to whom performance is rendered is assessed objectively (as are all elements of the claim). We are not concerned with the subjective

---

[71] (1856) 1 H&N 210, 215, 165 ER 1180, 1182.
[72] (1856) 1 H&N 210, 215, 165 ER 1180, 1182.
[73] See also the materially identical *Australian Financial Services and Leasing Pty Ltd v Hill Industries* [2014] HCA 14, (2014) 253 CLR 560 discussed critically in Chapter 18, Defences.
[74] *Chambers v Miller* (1862) 13 CB (NS) 125, 143 ER 50 *per* Erle CJ; *Pollard v Bank of England* (1871) LR 6 QB 623; A Burrows, *The Law of Restitution* (3rd edn, 2011), 213–214; Birks, *Unjust Enrichment* (n 18), 90–91.
[75] (1778) 2 Cowper 805, 98 ER 1372.

motives of the plaintiff. That the bank had its own good commercial reasons for wanting the debt discharged is not relevant in determining for whom the performance is rendered. In the context of contractual relationships this issue is most readily answered by asking to whom, construing the objective meaning of the contract, are the obligations which are being performed owing.

An illustration of the objective nature of the enquiry is *Barclays Bank Ltd v WJ Simms & Son and Cooke (Southern) Ltd*.[76] A housing association drew a cheque for £24,000 on its account with the plaintiff bank in favour of a builder. The next day a receiver was appointed over the builder's assets, and the association phoned the bank and gave instructions to stop the cheque, with confirmation given in writing. The same day the receiver presented the cheque and the bank official overlooked the instruction and paid.

Because the bank lacked the actual authority of its customer, the debt owed was not discharged.[77] The bank successfully sought restitution of the payment from the builders. Although the bank staff thought that in making the payment they were doing so on behalf of the bank's customer, in reality they were not as the authority had been withdrawn. Without the agency relationship, we return to the default position: the bank was paying the builder, this was done for no reason, and restitution should follow.

A more difficult case is the decision of the House of Lords in *Pan Ocean Shipping Co Ltd v Credtrust (The Trident Beauty)*,[78] which turns upon the nature of equitable assignment. The claimants hired the Trident Beauty under a time charter at a rate of $6,400 per day. Freight was payable in advance for 15-day periods. When the payment for the third 15-day period was made, the vessel was in fact unavailable for hire because she was awaiting repairs. The claimant sought restitution, which was refused.

One reason for the result, which is irrelevant for present purposes, was that the charter contract itself provided for the recovery of hire paid in advance that was not earned, and this was an agreed complete regime governing repayment.

More interestingly, the owners had assigned all receivables due under the charter as security for a loan from Creditcorp. Creditcorp had notified the charterers of this arrangement and had been paid directly by them. The charterers sought restitution from Creditcorp, the insolvency of the vessel's owners meaning that they were not worth suing. Could they do so?

The conclusion was that no claim was permissible. If the owners had merely asked that all monies due to it had been paid to a third party then clearly the only party against whom a claim should lie would still be the owners. The performance would be rendered to them, even if the mechanism by which that was done was through a payment to a third party.

If the nature of the assignment had been that the person to whom the charterers owed all monies due under the contract had changed (and this is deceptively implied by the law employing the language of 'assignment') so that the contractual obligations were, after assignment, owed to Creditcorp and not the owners, then the result is wrong. The performance

---

[76] [1980] 1 QB 677. See also *RE Jones Ltd v Waring and Gillow Ltd* [1926] AC 670 (HL) where the party the claimants thought they were paying was not the defendant who they were actually paying; *Colonial Bank v Exchange Bank of Yarmouth* (1885) 9 App Cas 84 (PC), remittance by the bank to an unauthorised payee. See generally S Meier, 'Mistaken Payments in Three-Party Situations: A German View of English Law' (1999) 58 CLJ 567.

[77] See Chapter 9, Discharge. *Contra* R Goode, 'The Bank's Right to Recover Money Paid on a Stopped Cheque' (1981) 97 LQR 254. Apparent authority, a doctrine concerned with agreement formation, is irrelevant here.

[78] [1994] 1 WLR 161 (HL).

rendered would have been to Creditcorp. That the obligations were initially owed to the owners would be irrelevant if this had changed before performance had been made.

As we shall see, however,[79] an assignment of property that the assignor does not yet have, as in this case, cannot operate as a transfer. What the assignee acquires is a right in relation to the right of the assignor to be paid as it falls due. Equitable assignment does not operate as a novation, with one contracting party substituting for another. Rather the charterer's obligation remained owing to the owners, with Creditcorp acquiring a right in relation to that right to be paid. Performance was, therefore, still made to the original contracting party, even though they did not ultimately receive the economic benefit of it. The claim against Creditcorp correctly failed.

4. Acceptance

(a) Principle

In principle, in order to justify the defendant being under an obligation to the plaintiff, the performance that is to be reversed must be the doing of both of them. If I heat my flat in order to warm yours above, in the mistaken belief that you have agreed to pay me for the expense you will be saved as a result, no claim should follow even if this does reduce your heating bills. It is not the case, and should not be, that the justification for recovery can be wholly 'plaintiff sided'.[80] Such an approach would be immoral. We would be using the defendant as a mere means to an end, requiring him to correct something that was not his doing.

Conversely, the justification for the imposition of the obligation cannot be wholly 'defendant sided' as, without something that relates the defendant's conduct to the plaintiff, there is no reason for the plaintiff acquiring a right against him.

In relation to the importance of acceptance, there is a division amongst those who seek to explain the law in terms of 'unjust enrichment'. The current editors of *Goff & Jones*, following the view taken by the original authors, adopt a 'free acceptance' principle as follows:[81]

> [A defendant] will be held to have benefited from the services rendered if he, as a reasonable man, should have known that the claimant who rendered the services expected to be paid for them, and yet did not take a reasonable opportunity open to him to reject the proffered services. Moreover, in such a case, he cannot deny that he has been unjustly enriched.

Peter Birks originally took the same view, seeing 'free acceptance' as both a method for establishing 'enrichment', and independently of showing that the enrichment was unjust. He illustrated this view with the following example:

> Suppose that I see a window-cleaner beginning to clean the windows of my house. I know that he will expect to be paid. So I hang back unseen till he has finished the job; then

---

[79] Chapter 12, Equity: General.
[80] See also Chapter 2, Foundations.
[81] See Mitchell, Mitchell, and Watterson, *Goff & Jones* (n 55), [17-103]; see also R Goff and G Jones, *Goff & Jones: The Law of Restitution* (7th edn, 2006), [1-1019]; R Goff and G Jones, *Goff and Jones: The Law of Restitution* (1st edn, 1966), 30–31.

I emerge and maintain that I will not pay for work that I never ordered. It is too late. I have freely accepted the service. I had the opportunity to send him away. I chose instead to let him go on. I must pay the reasonable value of his work.[82]

As others have argued, the example illustrates the problem with a wholly defendant-sided explanation for the creation of a private law obligation. A person who stands by and listens with pleasure to a busker, but does not pay; or who, when driving, stopped at traffic lights, does not object when someone cleans his windshield but then drives off without payment, is behaving in a shabby way.[83] However, want of moral probity by another is insufficient for the justifiable creation of legal rights. If the law does not require us to come to the assistance of babies drowning in puddles when we could easily pick them up, *a fortiori* it should not require us to speak up to stop entrepreneurs who are polishing our shoes in the hope that we will pay them.[84]

Similarly, it is mysterious how the fact of acceptance of or request for a service (or indeed of a payment) suffices to show that the defendant is 'enriched', at least if that word has the meaning that it does in everyday speech. If I request that you paint my coal white, after the work is done, I am left worse, not better, off. I now have a heap of useless coal, when before I had valuable fuel. It may be that, in some circumstances, your doing the work saves me the expense that I would otherwise have incurred in employing someone else to do the work, but this will not always be so[85] and as a counterfactual matter is unrelated to whether I accepted or requested the work or not. The doing by you of unrequested work I know nothing about may also save me an expense I would otherwise have incurred. Conversely, I may never have paid anyone else anything to do the work I have requested of you. What the defendant would have paid for the requested work if the plaintiff had not done it is not something which the plaintiff is required to plead or prove.

'Unjust enrichment' theorists seek to overcome the objection that the defendant's acceptance or request cannot, alone, establish that the defendant is objectively better off by *starting* with the assumption that all services (painting coal white, singing tuneless songs, destroying handsome buildings) and goods (recalcitrant camels, polluted land) enrich the recipient to the extent of the market value of acquiring them.[86] This is then subject to the defendant being able to 'subjectively devalue',[87] by which is meant respecting the defendant's freedom to choose that a particular service or other benefit is not enriching to him. This ability to 'subjectively devalue' is then lost by the party who has freely accepted.[88]

However, this starting assumption is unwarranted. A service *may* result in a defendant being factually better off by increasing the value of assets (eg my car is repaired by you and it is now worth more than it was) or by saving expenses (eg you clean my windows, so that I do not pay someone else to do the work that day). The mere fact that the service has been accepted, requested, or bargained for is not however sufficient to demonstrate the fact of

---

[82] P Birks, *An Introduction to the Law of Restitution* (rev edn, 1989), 265–266.
[83] A Burrows, 'Free Acceptance and the Law of Restitution' (1988) 104 LQR 576, 578.
[84] G Mead, 'Free Acceptance: Some Further Considerations' (1989) 105 LQR 460.
[85] Eg *Skibinski v Community Living British Columbia* [2012] BCJ No 828, 346 DLR (4th) 688.
[86] Eg Burrows, *The Law of Restitution* (n 74), 46–47.
[87] See *Benedetti v Sawiris* [2013] UKSC 50, [2014] AC 938, [15]–[26] (*per* Lord Clarke, with whom Lord Kerr and Lord Wilson agreed), but see at [110]–[119] (*per* Lord Reed).
[88] Strictly, this would entail that 'subjective devaluation' is a defence, with 'free acceptance' a reply: see Chapter 18, Defences.

enrichment. We cannot go from the legal fact that claims are allowed in many such cases, to the conclusion that this is because there must be an enrichment.[89] (Further, as we shall see in the next chapter, the quantum of recovery is determined by the market value of obtaining the goods or service, not the extent to which the defendant is factually better off as a result, which may be a higher or lower figure.)

This creates a problem as there are very many cases indeed where the courts have looked to whether the defendant has requested or freely accepted the service provided and treated that as a necessary condition of a claim's success.[90] Why? The problem is one for 'unjust enrichment' theory, not the law. Some kind of 'acceptance' is required because this is a constitutive element of the action by the plaintiff and defendant together that it is legitimate to reverse. It is not required in order to show that the defendant is enriched, it cannot do so. Still less can the defendant's shabby conduct *alone* suffice to create a right to reimbursement in the plaintiff.

(b) 'Enrichment' insufficient and unnecessary

One way of showing the significance of 'acceptance' is, again, to rely upon claims that fail where this element is missing.

That the defendant has *not* freely accepted a service does not demonstrate that he was not enriched by it, indeed she may have chosen to pay for it if she had been given the option to do so, but where she has not so accepted no obligation arises. If 'while you are sitting on your porch sipping Margaritas a trio of itinerant musicians serenades you with mandolin, lute and hautboy, you have no obligation, in the absence of a contract, to pay them for their performance, no matter how much you enjoyed it'.[91]

In *Blue Haven Enterprises v Tully*[92] the owner of 95 undeveloped acres in Jamaica ripe for redevelopment as a coffee plantation agreed to sell them to the defendant. There was a dispute over the acreage and price, which led to the seller purporting to terminate the deal, but the buyer eventually obtained an injunction restraining the sale otherwise than in accordance with the contract. Unfortunately, in the interim the seller agreed to sell the land to the defendant, who proceeded to make improvements to it before the conveyance, as he was entitled to do under the terms of the agreement, in the mistaken belief that there was no prior purchaser. Sixty acres were cleared and planted, workers cottages, offices, and a road were constructed. A short time after the work was started, the defendant had given notice to the plaintiff of his superior claim to the land, but the plaintiff had carried on regardless. Eventually the defendant obtained court orders in his favour that enabled him to go into possession of the land, now improved by the presence of a coffee plantation.

After the plaintiff learned of the defendant's prior claim, the work done subsequently should, on any view, give rise to no claim. The plaintiff had consented to the position they then found themselves in, knowing the land was someone else's. The work done prior to notification had saved the defendant an expense he would inevitably have incurred, and this

---

[89] Eg A Lodder, *Enrichment in the Law of Unjust Enrichment and Restitution* (2012), 78–79. See also J Edelman, 'The Meaning of Loss and Enrichment' in R Chambers, C Mitchell, and J Penner (eds), *Philosophical Foundations of the Law of Unjust Enrichment* (2009), 211.
[90] Eg *Craven-Ellis v Canons Ltd* [1936] 2 KB 403, 412 *per* Greer LJ, 415 *per* Greene LJ.
[91] *Indiana Mutual Insurance Co v Reinsurance Results Inc*, 513 F 3d 625, 656 (7th Cir 2008) *per* Posner J.
[92] [2006] UKPC 17. See also *Boulton v Jones* (1857) 2 H&N 564, 157 ER 232 (discussed in Chapter 7, Conditions); *JS Bloor Ltd v Pavillion Developments Ltd* [2008] EWHC 724 (TCC), [2008] 2 EGLR 85. *Cf. Greenwood v Bennett* [1973] QB 95 (CA), discussed in Chapter 14, Improvements.

was done by mistake, which has led to some arguing that 'a better understanding of the enrichment requirement'[93] should have led to recovery. Why then was a claim denied?

The court stated that because the defendant had not 'done something, or had [not] just stood by in circumstances where his action, or inaction, would make it unconscionable for him to refuse to reimburse … the cost of development' the claim failed.[94] Indeed, as soon as the defendant learned of the work, he had done his best to notify the plaintiff of his prior interest. Without some conduct on the defendant's part that made him one of those responsible for the work, he was not obliged to pay for it.[95] Although it is often accepted that 'it is an elementary principle of justice that people should not be liable to pay for things that they did not choose'[96] this has nothing to do with whether the defendant is enriched or not.

Similar is the decision of *Chief Constable of the Greater Manchester Police v Wigan Athletic AFC Ltd*.[97] The defendant football club could only play matches if it had a valid safety certificate, which required such numbers of police as the Chief Constable decided were necessary to ensure orderly behaviour. From 2003 the Chief Constable determined that extra policing than before was needed. The Club disagreed and made it clear that they would not pay for any extra policing. The extra policing was provided for two seasons, but would not have been if the Chief Constable had not believed he was entitled to be reimbursed for it. The Court of Appeal held that there was no statutory entitlement to recovery as the extra officers had not been provided at the request of the defendant.[98] The majority also held that as the defendant had not freely accepted the service he could not be required to pay for it. Maurice Kay LJ dissented on the basis that the club was 'incontrovertibly benefitted', as it had been saved a necessary expense as matches could not have taken place without a valid safety certificate. Without some form of acceptance on the part of the defendant however, this enrichment should not suffice.

Conversely, as we shall see in the next chapter, restitution should and is ordered of the performance rendered by the plaintiff and accepted by the defendant regardless of whether the defendant is better off or not.

In practice almost all claims for the recovery of the benefit of a service that have properly succeeded arise in cases where there is an agreement between the parties, which is not necessarily an enforceable contract, that the performance rendered by the plaintiff and accepted by the defendant is conditional. These cases will be discussed in Chapters 7 and 8.

(c) Payments

But what of payments of money? Is it not possible to pay money to a defendant without his acceptance, as where money is deposited into my bank account whilst I am asleep?

I cannot unconditionally transfer to you the title to cash without consent. If I dump a bundle of used £10 notes on your doorstep, intending them to become yours, the cash remains mine without co-operation on your part. The use of agents for receipt does not alter the need for acceptance by the recipient before a payment can be made. If I owe you £100, presenting this sum to you will not alone discharge the debt without your co-operation

---

[93] J Edelman and E Bant, *Unjust Enrichment* (2nd edn, 2016), 182.
[94] See also *Leigh v Dickeson* (1885) 15 QBD 60.
[95] See also generally on improvement of another's property, Chapter 14, Improvements.
[96] Edelman and Bant, *Unjust Enrichment* (n 93), 63
[97] [2008] EWCA Civ 1449.
[98] Police Act 1996, s 25.

through acceptance. (Once sued the debtor may invoke the defence of tender, a defence that would be otiose if it were possible to pay another through unilateral act.) A payment of money requires co-operation on the recipient's part.[99]

Similarly, I cannot discharge my debt to you by paying an equivalent sum to any high street bank at all for your account. If, however, I pay it to your account with *your* bank this is effective because that bank is authorised to receive on your behalf. The bank's acceptance is attributed to its customer because that is what the bank has been authorised to do on its principal's behalf. The customer has accepted because its agent has accepted. Banks are agents for receipt.

Where money is paid the condition of acceptance can be lost sight of because it is impossible to make a payment without acceptance. By contrast I can clean your windows or sing you a song without any co-operation on your part. It is therefore only in the case of services that 'acceptance' is revealed as a freestanding requirement that the plaintiff must prove.

It may be objected that the requirement of 'acceptance' cannot bear the weight being placed upon it. The defendant who accepts a payment, honestly and reasonably believing it is owed, or who opens a bank account, into which unbeknownst to him $1 million is mistakenly deposited, is not morally culpable in any way. Two answers are important. The first is that it is not the acceptance *alone* that justifies the claim. It forms part of an indivisible sequence: a performance rendered by the plaintiff and accepted by the defendant without good reason. Second, in private law we are not generally concerned with want of virtue. Just as the shabbiness of the defendant's conduct is insufficient to impose a legal obligation upon him, so it is that upstanding citizens of unimpeachable moral conduct may find themselves legally obliged to reverse legal actions for which they are jointly responsible with another.

D. Outside of Performance

1. Other Reasons

Several groups of cases do not appear to fit with the performance condition, but a source of confusion has been the lumping together of a number of different kinds of claim with different justifications. Viscount Haldane LC has been (rightly) criticised for claiming that 'the common law of England really recognizes (unlike Roman law) only actions of two classes, those founded on contract and those founded on tort'.[100] The pernicious and now more common variant on this idea is the claim that a tripartite division is possible, so that all (or almost all) actions outside of contract and torts are founded upon a single principle governed by the same rules.[101]

Two large categories of case that do not require any performance between the plaintiff and defendant are those based upon the receipt of a thing to which the plaintiff has superior title,[102] and the discharge by the plaintiff of a legal obligation properly borne by the defendant.[103] Each is given its own chapter in this work, as are other quite separate kinds of

---

[99] On the use of deeds see Chapter 11, Things.
[100] *Sinclair v Brougham* [1914] AC 398 (HL), 415.
[101] Eg W A Seavey and A W Scott, 'Restitution' (1938) 54 LQR 29, 31; A S Burrows, 'Contract, Tort and Restitution—A Satisfactory Division or Not?' (1983) 99 LQR 217. 'Not' is the correct answer.
[102] Exemplified by *Lipkin Gorman v Karpnale Ltd* [1991] 2 AC 548 (HL).
[103] Exemplified by *Exall v Partridge* (1799) 8 TR 308, 101 ER 1405.

claim.[104] Neither category requires there to have been any performance from the plaintiff to defendant, and different rules apply because the reasons for the claim are different.

2. 'Interceptive Subtraction'

(a) The problem

Similar are a group of cases, some now only of historical interest, that have been relied upon by commentators for a principle of 'interceptive subtraction'.[105] Birks sought to argue that whenever wealth 'would certainly have arrived in the plaintiff if it had not been intercepted by the defendant *en route*, from the third party, it is true to say that he plaintiff has lost by the defendant's gain'.[106] This principle has been adopted by some other commentators.[107] Clearly there has been no performance between plaintiff and defendant in such cases, nor any 'transfer of value' or 'transactional link' between them. Some commentators have therefore sought to rely upon them as supporting a wider principle that the factual correlation between the defendant's gain and the plaintiff's loss should suffice.[108] Where it is sufficiently factually certain that the plaintiff would have received an enrichment, and instead the defendant has, it has been argued that a general principle of 'interceptive subtraction' should be recognised.

Taken at its face, such a principle would lead to some surprising results. In the classic High Court of Australia decision of *Victoria Park Racing & Recreation Grounds Co Ltd v Taylor*,[109] the plaintiffs owned a racetrack in south Sydney, charging admission to people who bet on the races inside. Taylor, who owned adjacent land, allowed a radio company to construct a platform from which the races could be viewed, in order to broadcast information about the races, which enabled off track betting. Attendance at the ground fell, causing the plaintiffs a loss. Although the claim that failed was for an injunction, could the racetrack owners have brought a claim for the gain being made at their expense, the profits that they would inevitably have made having been intercepted by the defendant neighbour? The answer is, surely, no. How then can the examples Birks sought to rely upon for this 'interceptive subtraction' principle be explained?[110]

(b) Rental payments to agents

One group of cases concern claims by landowners for rents received from tenants by parties not entitled to them. In *Lyell v Kennedy*[111] a landlord died intestate. The manager of the property who had collected the rents during the deceased's lifetime continued to do so, not informing the tenants of the landlord's death but informing others that he was acting on behalf of the heirs, whoever they may be. The heirs eventually brought an action to recover

---

[104] Eg general average (Chapter 10, Necessity) or knowing receipt of trust property (Chapter 13, Equity: Restitution).
[105] Birks, *An Introduction to the Law of Restitution* (n 82), 133–134.
[106] ibid. See also *Air Canada v British Columbia* [1989] SCJ No 44, 59 DLR (4th) 161, 193–194 *per* La Forest J.
[107] Eg G Virgo, *Principles of the Law of Restitution* (3rd edn, 2015), 108–111.
[108] Eg Mitchell, Mitchell, and Watterson, *Goff & Jones* (n 55), [6-100] but *cf.* [6-609].
[109] (1937) 58 CLR 479.
[110] The examples in equity of secret trusts and secret commissions are considered in Chapter 12, Equity: General. *Cf.* Mitchell, Mitchell, and Watterson, *Goff & Jones* (n 55), [6-98].
[111] (1889) 14 App Cas 437 (HL). *Cf. Official Custodian for Charities v Mackey (No 2)* [1985] 1 WLR 1308 (Nourse J). See also *Jacob v Allen* (1703) 1 Salk 27, 91 ER 26.

the rents, the defendant manager arguing that as more than 12 years had passed since the death, he was entitled to the land and rents through lapse of time and adverse possession. This was rejected on the basis that the heirs 'could and did adopt and ratify his agency, they were in, and never out of, possession'[112] and that where 'the true owner can and does ratify an agency undertaken on his behalf, though without his antecedent authority, the case is the same as if he had himself received the rents'.[113] The entitlement to recovery here is the same as it would be against someone who had been acting as an authorised agent for receipt of the payments from the start.[114] The agent must account because he is acting for another in receiving the payment.

(c) Usurpation of office

More difficult are the now archaic cases concerning holders of public offices, such as the rector of a parish, who were entitled to the payment of a tithe, or local tax, for their support and the carrying out of their work. Where another purported to hold that office, usually by mistake, and received payments as a result, the true holder of that office had a claim against him for the payments received.[115] This cannot be explained on the basis of agency, as above, because the usurper was neither acting nor purporting to act on behalf of another. This can also not be explained as a claim for interference with any right to the office (ie as based upon wrongdoing) as recovery was confined to the payments received, not to the loss suffered as a result of being excluded. If, for example, the defendant did not recover tithes that he could have charged (perhaps out of sympathy for the poor of the neighbourhood) only an action for the payments actually received was possible.[116] Some commentators have therefore sought to rely upon these cases as supporting a wider principle that the factual correlation between the defendant's gain and the plaintiff's loss should suffice.[117]

The limits of the doctrine do not however support this wider proposition. The only payments recoverable were those that the true office holder was entitled to as such (eg a tithe). Gifts to, and payments for work done by, the defendant were irrecoverable even if the same gifts would as a matter of fact have been made to, or the same salary earned by, the true office holder if he had not been usurped.[118]

The reason for recovery in these unusual cases is linked to the fact that payment to the usurper was capable of discharging the obligation to the office holder. Ordinarily if X owes C £100, but mistakenly pays D, the obligation is not released and C's only claim is against the original debtor (X), with X left with a claim against the mistaken payee (D). Unusually, the acts of a *de facto* holder of an office, including the receipt of payments, was binding on the true holder. These cases may therefore be seen as ensuring that the benefit of the performance of an obligation accrues to the party to whom that obligation is owed,[119] an unusual sister category of claim to those concerned with ensuring that the burden of the performance of an obligation falls upon the party subject to that obligation.[120]

---

[112] (1889) 14 App Cas 437 (HL), 456.
[113] *ibid*, 460–461.
[114] Eg *Asher v Wallis* (1707) 11 Mod 146, 88 ER 956.
[115] *Arris v Stuckley* (1667) Mod 260, 86 ER 1160; *Howard v Wood* (1688) 2 Show KB 21, 89 ER 767.
[116] *King v Alston* (1848) 12 QB 971, 116 ER 1134.
[117] Eg Mitchell, Mitchell, and Watterson, *Goff & Jones* (n 55), [6-99]–[6-100].
[118] *Boyter v Dodsworth* (1796) 6 Term Rep 681, 101 ER 770.
[119] *Cf.* L Smith, 'Three-Party Restitution: A Critique of Birks' Theory of Interceptive Subtraction' (1991) 11 OJLS 481, 494.
[120] Chapter 9, Discharge.

(d) Rectification of gifts

Another candidate for the recognition of a looser connection between plaintiff and defendant is the *obiter* suggestion of Lord Romilly MR in *Lister v Hodgson*[121] that where there has been a deed of gift which the donor has mistakenly drawn up in favour of *D* rather than *C*, this may be rectified in favour of *C* if the donor has died before realising her mistake. It is unclear whether Lord Romilly MR thought that the appropriate plaintiff was the representative of the estate of the donor, the intended beneficiary,[122] or possibly both. Whether rectification is available at all depends upon whether it is permissible to give effect to the subjective intentions of the person executing the document, or whether rectification may only be used to set aside a document and thereby give effect to another objectively valid disposition.[123] Gummow J in *Hill v Van Erp* doubted whether, in the case of a mistakenly executed will, an intended beneficiary would have any claim against the actual beneficiary,[124] and his view seems preferable to that of Lord Romilly MR.

(e) Attornment

A fourth group of cases concern where *X* pays money to *D* instructing him to send it to *C*. Here there is no claim by *C* against *D* unless and until *D* attorns to him (ie until *D* tells *C* that he is holding the money for her). It is difficult to understand how on the theory of 'interceptive subtraction' the attornment adds any certainty to the question of whether the money would indeed have been received by *C*, the attornment changes the legal position not the factual one.[125] Where *D* still has the money that has been paid to him it is possible to say that either legal title to it is passed to *C* through the attornment (as with cash) or that the attornment suffices to show the intention to create a trust.[126] Where the defendant does not have the money however it is difficult to conceptualise what the basis of the obligation to *D* created by the attornment might be; it cannot be contractual because of the absence of consideration.[127]

The reason that no general principle of 'interceptive subtraction' can be extracted from these groups of cases is, again, that the rules are different in each of these disparate categories because the reasons for the claims are different.

3. Errors

It is important to acknowledge that it is not possible to reconcile all decisions from all jurisdictions.

The decision of the UK Supreme Court *Bank of Cyprus v Menelaou*[128] is difficult to justify, at least as it is reasoned. The case concerned the decision of parents to sell their home,

---

[121] (1867) LR 4 Eq 30, 34–35.
[122] *Cf. M'Mechan v Warburton* [1896] 1 IR 435, 439 *per* Chatterton V-C.
[123] The objective approach is adopted in *Chartbrook Ltd v Persimmon Homes Ltd* [2009] UKHL 38, [2009] 1 AC 1101, the subjective approach by *FSHC Group Holdings Ltd v Glas Trust Corporation Ltd* [2019] EWCA Civ 1361. The latter is criticised in R Stevens, 'What is an Agreement' (2020) 136 LQR 599.
[124] See also *re Murphy Estate* [1998] NSJ No 371, 170 NSR (2d) 1.
[125] Smith, 'Three-Party Restitution: A Critique of Birks' Theory of Interceptive Subtraction' (n 119), 505.
[126] *Cf. Claxton v Kay* 101 Ark 350, 142 SW 517 (1912). Reward fund created for the successful arrest and conviction of murderers. Reward paid to the defendant who was not entitled to it, successful claim against recipient by person who had caught the criminal.
[127] But see *Shamia v Joorey* [1958] 1 QB 448 (Barry J) which is wrongly decided.
[128] [2015] UKSC 66, [2016] AC 176.

downsize, and buy a house for their daughter, the defendant, Melissa. The claimant bank had a charge over the parents' home. They agreed to the release of their charge on the basis that they would acquire a charge over the daughter's property. The instructed solicitors sent the bank a charge purportedly over the daughter's property, and the bank agreed to the release of its charge over the parents' property. In the event, the second charge was defective as the daughter, although aware of the purchase of the house for her, had never agreed to the creation of the charge, on which her signature was forged. The claim was allowed by reviving the lien by way of subrogation that the seller to the daughter had had before being paid.

The reasoning of Lord Clarke for the majority appears to adopt a straightforwardly causal analysis:

> She was therefore enriched at the expense of the Bank because the value of the property to Melissa was considerably greater than it would have been but for the avoidance of the charge and the Bank was left without the security which was central to the whole arrangement.[129]

This reasoning assumes that a correlative loss suffered by the claimant suffices as a sufficient connection between the parties. If it were to be taken seriously, it would indicate that a claim should be allowed in the example of the two stamps.

In *Swynson v Lowick Rose LLP*[130] Lord Sumption identified the relevant injustice in a way Lord Clarke had suggested in *Menelaou*:

> The bank's consent to the use of the proceeds of the family home to buy the daughter a house had been conditional on it obtaining a charge. That condition had failed and the daughter had consequently been enriched.[131]

This cannot be correct. Uncommunicated conditions in the heads of claimants to which defendants are not party cannot justify imposing obligations upon them.

The best available analysis of the decision is that the proceeds of the parents' property were not at their free disposition after that property was sold. They were not free, for example, to take the proceeds of sale and place bets on the horses. They were not so free *until* the bank had been repaid what they were owed.[132] In other words, it had been agreed that the proceeds of sale were still subject to the charge in favour of the bank. It is entirely orthodox that where a right is subject to a charge, and that right is used to buy another in the name of a donee, the charge continues to bind the purchased asset. If, unbelievably, the bank had mistakenly agreed to release their charge completely, so that the parents had been free to use the proceeds as they saw fit, a purchase by them of a property in their daughter's name should entail no claim against her.

This reasoning is reflected in the explanation for *Menelaou* of Lord Reed in *Investment Trust Companies v HMRC*.[133]

---

[129] ibid, [24].
[130] [2017] UKSC 32, [2018] AC 313.
[131] ibid, [29].
[132] An equitable interest that is defeasible upon the secured obligation being fulfilled is a charge, not as Lord Carnwath supposed, [133]–[135], a trust.
[133] [2017] UKSC 29, [2018] AC 275, [45] *per* Lord Reed.

[The Bank] had mistakenly authorised the use of the proceeds of sale of the first property (*which it could otherwise have required to be applied to discharge the debt owed to itself*) to purchase the second property, thereby providing the defendant with a benefit at its expense.[134]

However, this explanation is not free from difficulty. First, it gives a different result from that reached: a charge over the title to Melissa's house, not a claim by way of subrogation to the unpaid seller's lien. Second, it is at least arguable that the bank had in fact released the charge altogether, in which case the decision is insupportable.[135] There was no performance between the parties, such as a payment, to reverse.

The Supreme Court of Canada has also embarked upon an expansive approach to the law of 'unjust enrichment' in *Moore v Sweet*[136] with unfortunate results. Mr Moore insured his life for $250,000 with his wife named as beneficiary. When they separated, it was agreed that Ms Moore would pay the premiums and would continue to be the named beneficiary. They subsequently divided the remainder of their property, without mentioning the policy. Upon Mr Moore's death, it was discovered that he had irrevocably changed the designated beneficiary to his new spouse, Ms Sweet. Ms Moore succeeded in bringing a claim in 'unjust enrichment' against Ms Sweet.

Again, there was no performance between Ms Moore and Ms Sweet that could form the basis of a claim. This is, again, a case where the court is invoking unjust enrichment as a shortcut to reach the result that seems correct.

The husband had agreed to transfer the rights under the policy to Ms Moore, for which she provided good consideration by paying the premiums. This should give rise to a trust over the policy. This beneficial interest under a trust should have bound Ms Sweet as she was not a bona fine purchaser of the right to the policy, but merely a donee.

E. 'At the Expense of'?

On the dominant view expressed in modern English textbooks, the discussion in this chapter has concerned the meaning of when an enrichment is 'at the expense of' the plaintiff. Andrew Burrows, for example, has sought to distinguish three categories of case where an enrichment is 'at the expense of' the plaintiff, that has echoes of the ordering of this book. He now distinguishes between 'conferrals' and 'takings', whilst also accepting that cases of discharge of another's obligation are subject to special rules.[137]

This attempt to maintain the unity of 'unjust enrichment' fails for two reasons.

First, these different categories of case are not different ways of proving the same generic thing. The reason why there are these different categories is because the reasons for the claims are different.

---

[134] *ibid*, [65]. Emphasis added.
[135] W Swadling, 'In Defence of Formalism' in A Robertson and J Goudkamp (eds), *Form and Substance in the Law of Obligations* (2019), 95.
[136] (2018) SCC 52.
[137] A Burrows, '"At the Expense of the Claimant": A Fresh Look' (2018) 28 RLR 167 Compare the division of the subject by the original authors of *Goff & Jones* beween cases of conferral by claimant on the defendant, the receipt of benefit from a third party, and the acquistion of a benefit though a wrongful act: *Goff & Jones* (7th edn, 2007), [1-93]–[1-95].

Second, the performance between the plaintiff and the defendant, the payment or service, is not merely a necessary element of a cause of action, which once proven can be discarded, like a ladder that is kicked away. Rather it is also the very thing that must be reversed, not any consequential enrichment that the defendant may acquire as a result. It is to that question, 'what is it that is reversed?', that we now turn.

4
Reversal

A. Enrichment?

In English, to be enriched is to be better off. It is the mirror image of being worse off, to suffer a loss. Accountants are familiar with such gains and losses in drawing up a balance sheet. In relation to consequential loss, the law can, and has, adopted a broader approach than that of the accountant, including such items as misery and distress in quantifying the worsening of the plaintiff's position, and there seems no reason why, on the other side of the ledger, we could not include pleasure and happiness. However broadly or narrowly drawn, to be enriched is to have an improvement, in some sense, in one's overall position.[1]

One ambiguity in the claim that the law concerns enrichment is the baseline against which the improvement is to be measured. When quantifying consequential loss (a noun) for wrongdoing, our comparators are the world as it is, and the (hypothetical) world that would have obtained absent the wrong. It is a counterfactual enquiry. The purpose of an award of damages, for both breach of contract and a tort, is to put the claimant in the position he would have been in if the wrong had not occurred.[2]

This is not the baseline we use when we 'lose' something (a verb) in everyday English. If I have lost my reading glasses we are comparing the (actual) world as it once was in the past (when I had them) with today (when I don't).[3] This is an historical viewpoint. In law, it will not avail a defendant to argue that a wrong has not made the claimant worse off than he was beforehand, if today he is worse off than he otherwise would have been.[4]

Similarly, when we talk of 'enrichment', are we asking whether the defendant is better off than they otherwise would have been absent an event (ie counterfactually), or whether they are better off today than they were at some point in the past (ie historically)? The baselines differ, as we shall see. But whichever is chosen, we are comparing the position *today* with another baseline: a point in the past, or the world as it would otherwise have been.

In fact, when the law in England and elsewhere seeks to reverse a performance rendered it is not, and has never been, concerned with the defendant's 'enrichment' in relation to either possible baseline. Instead, the law reverses the performance rendered, and nothing else. This is true both of payments and of services.

---

[1] R Zimmermann and J du Plessis, 'Basic Features of the German Law of Unjustified Enrichment' (1994) 2 RLR 14, 31.

[2] *Robinson v Harman* (1849) 1 Exch 850, 855 *per* Parke B; *Livingstone v Rawyards Coal* (1879–1880) LR 5 App Cas 25 (HL), 39 *per* Lord Blackburn.

[3] For an example of the conflation of these two senses of loss, see J Edelman, 'The Meaning of Loss and Enrichment' in R Chambers, C Mitchell, and J Penner (eds), *The Philosophical Foundations of the Law of Unjust Enrichment* (2007), 211.

[4] Discussed further in Chapter 15, Wrongs. The classic illustration in the context of breach of contract is *Hawkins v McGee* 84 NH 114, 146 A 641 (NH 1929) (the 'hairy hand' case).

B. Payments

1. Timing

In the Scottish decision, *Royal Bank of Scotland v Watt*,[5] payment was made to the defender by the pursuer bank on a cheque that had been fraudulently altered by a third party. The defender, who was not a party to the fraud, had arranged with the wrongdoer to receive payment on his behalf, and to remit to him all but a small proportion, which he did.

The consequence of the payment was that the defender was left factually better off only to the extent of the small balance. Was this the extent of liability, or was it the quantum of the payment itself? The court concluded in favour of the full balance, discounting the fact that this was greater than the extent to which the defender was in fact enriched. This is correct, as a matter of *prima facie* liability. 'The emphasis is not upon the extent to which the party receiving the payment has been enriched, but upon whether that person has any good and equitable reason to refrain from repaying the money to the person who paid it under a mistake.'[6] Here the performance to be reversed is the payment from the pursuer received by the defender. That the consequential enrichment to the defender was much lower than this figure is neither here nor there.

Those who wish to defend the idea that the subject matter of the claim is a factual enrichment, point to the initial or immediate improvement in the defender's balance sheet position.[7] Birks distinguished between 'value received' and 'value surviving'[8] and argued that in simple payment cases, like *Watt*, the law is concerned with the former.

It is however hard to see what the significance of the defendant once having been enriched at some point in the past is. It is possible to see why one person being left better off as a result of another's misfortune (as in the example of the destruction of one of two rare stamps) counts towards the beneficiary being under some obligation to the loser. The significance of someone having been enriched at some point in the past, when as things have turned out they are not now, is mysterious.

It is no answer to say that the cause of action arises as soon as the enrichment occurs (ie when the money is received). In the law of torts, a cause of action will (usually) arise when the wrong occurs (eg at the moment a pedestrian is hit by a negligent driver). That does not mean that we quantify any consequential loss at that moment, rather we assess that at the time of judgment (eg if the pedestrian makes a speedy recovery and so does not suffer the loss of earnings that might have been initially expected, this is taken into account). Why does the law not do the same where a claim to recover back money paid that is not due, if it is genuinely concerned with enrichment?

A different answer is to invoke the defence of change of position which, if relied upon by the defendant, would probably today apply in *Royal Bank of Scotland v Watt*. After a defendant has received a payment, he and not the payor is in a better position to demonstrate

---

[5] 1991 SC 48 (IHCS).
[6] *ibid*, 57 *per* Lord Murray.
[7] A Kull, *Restatement of the Law (Third) Restitution and Unjust Enrichment*, vol I (2010), 7 (commentary to § 1, ch 1): 'Restitution is concerned with the receipt of benefits that yield a measurable increase in the recipient's wealth.'
[8] P Birks, *An Introduction to the Law of Restitution* (rev edn, 1989), 75–77.

what has happened to his overall wealth as a result. Did he spend the money on a holiday he would not otherwise have gone on? Put it into a bank that went insolvent?

Practical considerations of this kind would justify shifting the evidential burden on to the defendant after payment, as in a trial for murder where he is found in a locked room with a stabbed victim and a knife in his hand. It would not justify the existence of any free-standing defence. 'Change of position' would become a denial of an essential element of the claim, the enrichment, not a defence properly so called raising a new reason why an otherwise good claim should fail.[9]

This reconfiguration of change of position into being a denial of enrichment does not fit with the law as it is, nor with what it ought to be. A recipient of a mistaken payment will not have a defence of change of position if when he paid away the money he knew that he ought to pay it back (ie if he was acting in 'bad faith'). Disqualifications from relying upon the defence such as this demonstrate that this is a true defence and not a denial. On what basis is the bad faith defendant still held liable if he is not, as things subsequently transpire, in fact enriched?

The defence of change of position cannot therefore be explicable in terms of 'disenrichment'.[10] It is a genuine defence, raising a new reason why a claim fails.[11] The nature of that reason is explored in Chapter 18.

2. Counterfactuals

A company law example:

> In 2018, *P Ltd* pays out a dividend to shareholders of £1 million. *Q*, the chief executive officer of *P Ltd*, decided to do so without taking into account whether there were any distributable profits, and without consultation with any other director. If these steps had been taken, the same dividend would have been lawfully declared and paid in any event, as the company's accounts for the year disclosed sufficient profits. In 2020, *P Ltd* goes into insolvent liquidation.

There is no legal basis for the payment to the shareholders; the dividend is invalid as not having complied with the (minimalist) requirements of UK company law. Assuming that the shareholders are independent of *Q*, they have committed no wrong through receipt. The payment has not, as a counterfactual matter, left them better off, as if it had not occurred a lawful dividend would have been paid. Restitution of the payment still ought to follow in any event: no lawful (ie valid) dividend was ever paid.

The context in England in which this issue has arisen is in relation to overpaid taxes and other levies. In *Vodafone v Office of Communications Ltd*,[12] mobile phone network operators were charged a licence fee under the Wireless Telegraphy Act 2006. These were calculated

---

[9] See further Chapter 18, Defences.
[10] But see P Birks, *Unjust Enrichment* (2nd edn, 2004), ch 9 and A Burrows, *The Law of Restitution* (3rd edn, 2011), 526–527.
[11] See also E Bant, *The Change of Position Defence* (2009) and S Kiefel, 'Lessons from a Conversation About Restitution' (2014) 88 ALJ 176.
[12] [2020] EWCA Civ 183, [2020] QB 857.

under regulations made by the defendant in 2015 that were subsequently quashed. These had purported to replace an earlier measure. The claimants sought restitution. The defendant argued that the correct measure of recovery was the difference between the sums paid and those that would have been due *if* it had made valid regulations. The court rejected the defendants' counterfactual argument and held that the claimant was entitled to restitution of the sum that could have been lawfully charged under the pre-existing regime. This required no retrospective legal authorisation on their part as the earlier regulations had never been superseded.

Two things restrict the scope of the decision's *ratio*. First, this case, and others like it, may be seen as restricted to the recovery of tax or tax-like levies, where a principle that there should be no taxation without parliamentary authority applies.

Second, the court's formulation seems to bar recovery to the extent a sum *could have been* validly charged, even though as a matter of fact it never was. Earlier cases had limited recovery in this way, albeit often without argument on the point.[13] In *Hemmings (t/a Simply Pleasures Ltd) v Westminster CC*,[14] the claimants were operators of sex shops in Westminster. The defendant council charged them a licence fee, which was found to be invalid. The claimant conceded that they were only entitled to recover the difference between the sums paid and what could be reasonably, and therefore validly, charged. The Court of Appeal stated that this concession had been correctly made, Beatson LJ stating that this result 'reflected the economic reality of what happened notwithstanding the public law flaw in the circumstances of the original payment'.[15] This might indicate a counterfactual analysis was appropriate. However, the trial judge had also ordered for reasonable and therefore valid fees to be determined *retrospectively* by the council, and the Court of Appeal accepted that this could be done.[16] If retrospective determination of the fee cannot be made, restitution in full of the payment made should be ordered. It should not suffice that the payment could have been validly charged, if it never was.

3. Trustees and Agents

One possible response to the fact that we are unconcerned with the counterfactual question of whether the defendant is better off than he otherwise would be as a result of the payment, is that this is the wrong baseline. Perhaps what we should be comparing is the position after the payment has been made with the position before it? Surely, in this sense, the defendant is enriched, even if, as things turned out, counterfactually he is not?

Skandinaviska Enskilda Banken AB (Publ) v Conway[17] is an illustration of why this is also untrue. The defining feature of a trust is that a trustee is under a duty not to use the rights that are held on trust for his own benefit.[18] In economic terms, for non-charitable trusts the parties who are made better or worse off by the increase or decrease in the value

---

[13] *Waikato Regional Airport v AG of New Zealand* [2003] UKPC 50, [2003] All ER (D) 399.
[14] [2013] EWCA Civ 591.
[15] *ibid*, [110].
[16] *ibid*, [132]. See also *Atlantic Coast Line Railroad Co. v Florida* (1935) 295 US 301 (Cardozo J).
[17] [2019] UKPC 36, [2020] AC 1111.
[18] See J Hackney, *Understanding Equity and Trusts* (1987), 20–22; and Chapter 12, Equity: General.

of a trust estate are those to whom the trustee owes his duties, which is why they are called 'beneficiaries'.

The defendants held redeemable shares in the claimant, an investment company. The collapse of Lehman brothers in 2008 caused them (and many others) to seek to redeem their investment, and they sent a request to the company in order to do so. The payments due to shareholders were calculated according to the company's net asset value, and the defendants managed to obtain payment in full. Subsequently it transpired that the company's asset value had been fraudulently inflated. The claimant went into insolvent liquidation. Under section 145(1) of the Cayman Islands' Companies Law 'every conveyance or transfer of property ... made ... by the company in favour of any creditor at a time when the company is unable to pay its debts ... with a view to giving such a creditor a preference over the other creditors shall be invalid'. The liquidator sought restitution of the payments made on the basis that they had no valid basis. The claim succeeded.

One argument for the defendants was that they held the investment in the claimant as bare trustees for two other beneficiaries. They had never therefore personally benefitted from the payments.

This argument, correctly, failed. The court held that the statute merely invalidated the payment; it did not create a statutory regime for its recovery. Therefore the entitlement to recover was governed by the general law. The *payment* was made to the defendants. They were therefore the party against whom the claim could be asserted. Although the (potentially very numerous) beneficiaries of a trust are the parties made better off by a payment to the trustee, no payment had been made to them and so no claim against them is possible.

The court rightly contrasted the position of a trustee with that of an agent receiving a payment for his principal. Where a solicitor receives a payment for their client into a client account they too will hold the money received on trust. No claim should be possible against the solicitor because the payment is not made *to* them, but rather to their client on whose behalf they receive it.[19] When a disclosed agent is authorised to receive a payment on behalf of another, this action of receipt is attributed to his principal. The payor is seeking to pay the principal not the agent, nor is the agent receiving it as made to him. The only claim the payor should have is therefore against the principal, not the agent.[20] This is so even where the agent is not also a trustee.[21] If the agent goes into bankruptcy, with the result that the principal will never in fact be enriched by the receipt of the money as it will never be paid over to him by his agent, a claim is still available against the principal (subject to a potential defence of change of position).

Although the court itself employed the language of 'enrichment',[22] this confuses more than it assists. The parties factually enriched were the beneficiaries, but the payment was not made to them but to the trustees, and that is the subject matter of the claim.

The court also reasoned that the claim was one for 'money had and received' at common law,[23] and that the common law ignores the equitable interest under a trust.[24] Reasoning of this kind, based solely upon the historical divide within common law jurisdictions, is never

---

[19] See Chapter 18, Defences.
[20] *In re Morant* [1924] 1 Ch 79.
[21] *Challinor v Juliet Bellis & Co* [2015] EWCA Civ 59.
[22] [2019] UKPC 36, [2020] AC 1111, [82]–[93].
[23] ibid, [77]–[79].
[24] ibid, [89].

very satisfactory. Equity does not ignore the beneficial interest, but no different result arises in that jurisdiction (as in a case such as *Re Diplock*[25] where an incorrect distribution is made from an estate to a trustee).

In summary, the difference between the receipt by an agent and a trustee is important in illustrating the basis for the claim. A trustee will not be enriched but is liable unless also an agent. A disclosed agent will not be liable because no performance is made to him but may well be 'enriched', at least until he has paid over to his principal.[26]

4. Increases in Value and Interest

An example:

> C pays D £10,000 by mistake. Because he is now able to do so, D invests an equivalent sum in shares in a Biotech company that proves enormously successful. The lack of the equivalent sum causes C to refrain from making an equivalent investment that would have been equally successful.

Ignoring the question of whether the proceeds of the money are held on trust, the only claim C should and, now, does have in England, is to the £10,000 paid. It should not suffice that the greater factual gain the defendant has made correlates with an equivalent loss suffered by the claimant. That there has been a performance for no reason from C accepted by D cannot justify reversal of anything other than the performance itself.

At one time, this did not represent the law in England because of the decision of the House of Lords in *Sempra Metals Ltd v Inland Revenue Commissioners*[27] to award interest in order to prevent the defendant's unjust enrichment.

If a claim for a tort arises on 1 May 2018 for damages for £1 million for losses suffered, and comes to trial on 1 June 2021, interest must be awarded in order to ensure that the claim is correctly valued. A right to be paid £1 million in 2018 is worth more than a right to be paid the same notional figure in 2021. In order correctly to value the claim at today's prices, the notional figure must be revalued to take account of the time value of money. This is nothing to do with any consequential loss suffered by the claimant. If the defendant can prove beyond peradventure that the claimant would have squandered the money gambling, as the claimant did with all his other wealth, if he had paid him when the claim arose, this will not avail him. Similarly, it is not dependent upon any factual gain made by the defendant as a result of not having paid immediately.

The English legislation governing this revaluation awards interest on a simple, and not a compound, basis.[28] It may be that the rationale for this is that we are seeking to revalue the capital sum, not ascertain how much the claimant would now have if he had invested the money paid. However, this seems an uncommercial way of determining the time value of

---

[25] [1951] AC 251 (HL).
[26] *Cox v Prentice* (1815) 3 M & S 344, 348, 105 ER 641, 642 *per* Lord Ellenborough. See further Chapter 18, Defences.
[27] [2007] UKHL 34, [2008] 1 AC 561.
[28] Senior Courts Act 1981, s 35A(1).

money, and in *Sempra Metals* a majority of the House of Lords succumbed to the temptation of circumventing the restrictive statutory rule.

If a debtor fails to pay his creditor, can the creditor bring a claim against him for the benefit he makes from the non-performance? There is no reason for the debtor's 'enrichment', and the creditor may have made a mistake in not pressing for payment earlier. The debtor may have made a gain from his non-payment, and this may correlate with a loss that is caused to the creditor by his failure to pay. However, without a performance between claimant and defendant that requires reversal, there should be no possibility of a claim.

In *Sempra* where the claim was to interest upon corporation tax prematurely paid, there was no dispute as to the recoverability of the capital sum. The majority awarded the claimant compound interest on the basis that the defendant was unjustly enriched through having had the opportunity to use the unjustifiably paid money during the period of prematurity. Title to the money paid had passed; there was no question of the claimants establishing any proprietary right to anything the defendant retained. No argument for a duty to hold the money paid on trust that could also have potentially justified an award of compound interest was made.

The majority took the view that it was unnecessary to show that the claimant had suffered a loss that correlated with a gain of the defendant in order to establish a claim.[29] They also accepted that if the defendant had made profits from the use of the money mistakenly paid this could not have been recovered.[30] Compound interest based on a freestanding claim in unjust enrichment was however awarded. Why was the use of the money over time 'at the expense of' the claimant at all? How did this case differ from the standard one of a debtor who does not fulfil his obligations and is thereby better off?

Lord Nicholls stated:

The benefits *transferred* by Sempra to the Inland Revenue comprised, in short, (1) the amounts of tax paid to the Inland Revenue and, consequentially, (2) the *opportunity* for the Inland Revenue, or the Government of which the Inland Revenue is a department, to use this money for the period of prematurity.[31]

The problem with this reasoning is that it is inaccurate to describe the *opportunity to use* as having been *transferred* by the claimant to the defendant. What is 'transferred' is the capital sum.

How much subsequent use is 'transferred' on the day of payment?

The relevant performance is the payment of the capital sum. The next day, and every day thereafter, there is no fresh performance capable of supporting a claim. As a result of the payment of the capital sum, the defendant has the opportunity to make use of it. The value of the resultant opportunity to use is dependent upon what happens subsequently. If, delighted by their good fortune, the recipient of a mistaken payment gives an equivalent sum away to charity they will no longer have the opportunity to use it. The opportunity to use is not 'transferred' with the capital sum, but arises subsequently from having the money, just as in the simple non-payment of a debt case.

---

[29] [2007] UKHL 34, [2008] 1 AC 561, [30]–[31] *per* Lord Hope, *per* Lord Nicholls [66], [126]–[129].
[30] ibid, [32], *per* Lord Hope, [117] *per* Lord Nicholls.
[31] ibid, [102] (emphasis added). See also [32] *per* Lord Hope.

If, therefore, on 1 January *C* lends £1,000 to *D*, repayable on 1 April, the failure to repay subsequently should give rise to no claim to the time value of money as there is no relevant performance rendered to reverse on 2 April and each following day. The assumption of earlier House of Lords authority that in order, exceptionally, to claim compound interest it was necessary to establish an ongoing fiduciary duty to hold the money received under a trust for the claimant's benefit, so that there would be a duty each subsequent day after payment to account for the use value of the money received, is correct.[32] The authorities relied upon by Lord Nicholls as supporting the result all involved claims based upon wrongdoing, an illustration of the dangers of reasoning by analogy between different kinds of 'restitutionary' claim.[33]

If the subject matter of the claim were genuinely the enrichment the defendant obtains from the claimant, then the use value of the money should be recoverable (at least where the defendant does in fact put the money to good use, as where he is saved a borrowing cost). That this is incorrect is the lesson of the Supreme Court's decision in *Prudential Assurance Co Ltd v Her Majesty's Revenue and Customs*[34] which overruled *Sempra Metals* on this point.

The case itself concerned an attempt to extend *Sempra* to allow interest upon interest, but the court took the step of overturning the previous decision altogether (even though this was not argued for before them). The court rightly held that the 'use value' of the money was not transferred to the defendant, but was a consequence of receipt of the capital sum.[35] Interest could only be claimed on the basis of the statutory authorisation of it, under section 35A of the Senior Courts Act 1981. The purpose of this section is to revalue the right to the return of the capital sum to reflect the time value of money. It does not give rise to a freestanding claim for a gain made or loss suffered.

Lord Burrows has sought to criticise *Prudential Assurance*, and defend the overturned result in *Sempra Metals*, using two examples, which he claims are ones where a claim to the use value of what has been received by the defendant ought to be allowed.[36] Each illustrates the dangers of over-generalisation that 'unjust enrichment' theory leads to. His first example is as follows:

> C transfers a car to D mistakenly believing that D is entitled to the car under the terms of her employment. C discovers the mistake after one year and informs D that she must return the car which she does.

This example is ambiguous because it is not clear whether what is transferred is possession of the car (the physical thing) for a period of time or C's title to the car (the right).

If it is the former, and D accepted the use of the car on the basis that it did not have to be paid for it, there should be no claim. C has consented to D's use, so that no tort is committed. The mere fact that the claimant's mistake has, as a matter of fact, had the consequence of making the defendant better off (here, by allowing her the use of a car which she may otherwise have had to pay for) should not suffice. There should merely be a claim for return of possession of C's vehicle.

---

[32] *Westdeutsche Landesbank Girozentrale v Islington London Borough Council* [1996] AC 669 (HL).
[33] [2007] UKHL 34, [2008] 1 AC 561, [230] *per* Lord Mance in dissent.
[34] [2018] UKSC 39, [2019] AC 929.
[35] *ibid*, [71]–[74].
[36] A Burrows, 'In Defence of Unjust Enrichment' (2019) 78 CLJ 521, 536–541.

If instead D has acquired C's title to the car, C may have a claim for the re-conveyance back of that title, but again this would only give rise to a claim for the use value of what was, at law, D's car in the interim, *if* D was under an obligation to C not to use the title acquired for his own benefit (ie if there is a trust). As we shall see, adopting the position of Lord Browne-Wilkinson in *Westdeutsche*, no such obligation, and hence no trust, arises unless and until D has knowledge of C's mistake.[37]

A similar answer may be given in the second example given by Lord Burrows:

> C is induced to buy a car from D for £5,000 by D's innocent misrepresentation as to the car's mileage. After six months, C discovers the truth and immediately rescinds the contract by returning the car and D returns the £5,000 to C.

If the misrepresentation had been fraudulent, this would have entitled C to rescind the contract and revest title in the car back in himself *ab initio*, possibly thereby enabling a claim in tort for the wrongful use of the car for the six-month period.[38] Where the misrepresentation is innocent, however, only rescission in equity is available (and is done by a court order, not by the innocent party through self-help). No revesting of title to the car should occur, and there will, at most, be a trust over the title to the car from the moment of rescission. Therefore, there should be no claim for the use value of the vehicle for the period prior to rescission. D was using his own car. He was under no obligation to anyone not to use the vehicle for his own benefit. Rescission of a contract reverses the performance rendered under that contract, not the consequence of that performance. Some allowance might be made if D cannot return the vehicle in the same condition as it was in at the time of contracting, but that is all.

In both examples, the mere fact that C's mistake has made D factually better off should not suffice.

C. Services

1. The Service and Its Consequences

Just as with payments, where a service has been provided for no reason, what is reversed is its performance, the service itself, not its consequence, such as any expense saved (where the defendant would have paid for the work if the claimant had not done it) or any realised gain (as where a repaired bicycle is sold for more than it would have been absent the work).

One possible reason for the mistake in thinking that what is reversed is the defendant's consequent enrichment is that whilst an act of payment can appear to be sensibly undone by ordering the same act to be done in reverse (ie repayment) the same is not true of a service. Windows cannot be sensibly unwashed, medical treatment ungiven, buildings unbuilt. Dirtying windows, breaking legs, and demolishing buildings are not washing, healing, and

---

[37] Chapter 13, Equity: Restitution.
[38] For rights that do not automatically revest (ie not title to goods) there will be a trust over the right transferred, and an entitlement to any benefits traceably attributable to the right received: *Spence v Crawford* 1939 SC (HL) 52, 65, 'the beneficial ownership of the shares was in the pursuer; he had no interest in the dividends or in the profits or losses of the company'. See Chapter 13, Equity: Restitution.

building in reverse. It is therefore tempting to focus on the consequence of the service, the factual gain made by the defendant, and think that that is what is being returned, because it can be.

Where a service has been rendered and accepted for what, it is now apparent, is no good reason, a court cannot, absent magic or a time machine, order it not to have been done. We find the same problem in the law of torts where negligently caused death or injury cannot be meaningfully undone. Instead, the law requires the defendant to do the next best thing, which can now be ordered to be done.[39] In our context, that is payment of a monetary equivalent to the service. In placing a figure on the (objective) value of a service our best resort is to look to the market for it at the time rendered. This will often be either a lower or higher figure than the extent to which the defendant has been made better off by the service.

2. Enrichment Higher than Market Value of Service

Both the result reached and the division of approach in getting there in the UK Supreme Court decision of *Benedetti v Sawiris*[40] illustrate the subject matter of the claim. (Although that case concerned work done under an agreed condition that failed, it may here be used as illustrative as on these facts the same result would follow in relation to, say, a contract that was rescinded.) Mr Benedetti worked in the telecommunications business. He performed brokerage services for a group of companies owned or controlled by Mr Sawiris for the successful acquisition of an Italian telecommunications company called Wind. Mr Benedetti performed these services under an agreement, under which a subsequent agreement would settle the quantum of remuneration. Because no such subsequent agreement was ever entered into, the agreed condition for which the work had been done failed. Restitution ought therefore to be awarded. But of what? The members of the court were unanimous in concluding that Mr Benedetti had already been paid for the service a sum greater than its value, and so the court's consideration of how to value this was *obiter dicta*. However, the division within the court on the best approach to valuation is important.

If the law genuinely were concerned with the defendant's enrichment, how might the quantification be carried out? An enquiry ought to be made to ascertain the extent to which each of the defendants respectively had been left better off by what had occurred. Had the deal proven successful or not, so that each had a realised gain (a shareholding worth more than they paid for it)? Alternatively, what expense that they would otherwise have incurred had each company been saved? What proportion of a fee for the brokerage services would each have paid if Mr Benedetti had not rendered it?

Of course, no court in fact reasons like this. What is awarded is the market value of the service, regardless of the degree to which the service has proven beneficial to each of the defendants. In this case, because the deal had gone through, the service had almost certainly proven spectacularly successful for Mr Sawiris and his companies. After the deal was complete, Mr Sawiris had offered to pay Mr Benedetti €75 million for what the latter had done, before negotiations eventually broke down. The trial judge found that a reasonable market value of the service was €36 million, calculated as 0.3% of the transaction's value. Each of

---

[39] J Gardner, 'What is Tort Law For? Part 1: The Place of Corrective Justice' (2011) 30 Law and Philosophy 1.
[40] [2013] UKSC 50, [2014] AC 938.

the defendants was held jointly liable for the market value of the service, although it could not be the case that each would in fact have been enriched to the same degree. A single performance may be rendered to, and accepted by, a number of defendants, each of whom will be jointly liable. Any consequent enrichment, by contrast, would only be obtained by those parties, if any, made better off.

One common way of defending the idea that the law is concerned with 'enrichment' is to argue that this is assessed by reference to what the defendant would have had to pay *ex ante* in order to receive the service. The artificiality of this reasoning is apparent if we try to apply it to payments (which as we have seen may also either not be enriching to the recipient, or far more enriching, than the capital value of the sum paid). Is the correct valuation of the obligation to make restitution the sum that the recipient would have had to pay someone else, in order for an equivalent payment to have been made to them? The action for 'money had and received' becomes an action for 'what would have had to be paid to receive the same sum of money'.

Further, the court does not enquire into whether the defendant would in fact ever have paid someone for the service, if the claimant had not provided it, and if they would, how much that sum would have been. In *Benedetti v Sawiris* itself the brokerage service would never, in fact, have ever been paid for at the rate set by the court, as it would (on the uniform practice) have been performed on the basis of a payment of a reward if the transaction was successfully completed (unsuccessful transactions giving rise to no payment). It was this 'reward' basis, the only sum that would have been paid if agreement had in fact ever been reached between the parties, that Mr Benedetti was trying to claim. It was also not the case that each of the defendants would ever have had to bear the cost of any such payment in full. Each would instead have borne a proportion.

It might be objected that the court does not enquire as to what the defendant would in fact have paid because this is impossible or impractical,[41] but in fact it is neither.[42] Rather, it is irrelevant.

The correct position is that what is being reversed is the service itself, which has been accepted by the defendant, and that we are unconcerned with the extent to which the defendant has in fact been enriched by it. The court, in placing a value on the payment or service that is reversed, necessarily uses the market figure. In the case of services this may have no relation, as in *Benedetti*, to any figure that would, in any conceivable world, ever in fact have been paid for it by the individual defendants.

3. Enrichment Lower than Market Value of Service

The converse situation is where we reverse a performance that is not factually enriching, as where the claimant has painted the defendant's coal white at the other's request. The defendant must pay the market value of the performance, even if, as in this case, it has left him as a matter of fact worse off. A non-contractual claim for a *quantum meruit* is not dependent upon showing a *quantum lucratus*. Again, it is no answer to say that this is what the

---

[41] Birks, *Unjust Enrichment* (n 10), 54.
[42] Edelman, 'The Meaning of Loss and Enrichment' (n 3), 211, 236.

defendant would have had to pay in order to acquire the service if, as a matter of fact, that is not what would otherwise have occurred.

The position of most commentators is that a service is *prima facie* enriching at its market value, unless this particular defendant can argue that he himself would not have chosen it.[43] Birks coined the term 'subjective devaluation' for this idea. However, as we have seen, there is no basis for the premise, that all services received are *ipso facto* enriching.[44] Why should we assume that someone whose coal has been painted white is, without more, enriched by the market cost of employing someone to do such a thing?

The assumption of enrichment subject to the defendant invoking 'subjective devaluation' was adopted by Lord Clarke in *Benedetti v Sawiris*, although he described this terminology as 'misleading'.[45] But what of the case where the defendant accepted the service, evidently placed some value on its performance, but where it was not worth the full market value to him? It might be very expensive to have a huge mound of coal painted white, and the defendant, although placing some small value upon the result, might not value it to the extent of the cost of achieving it. Lord Clarke, following the dominant approach in the textbooks, accepted that evidence of this personal valuation could be used to reduce the award.

Lord Reed, by contrast, saw the award as being one for the monetary value of the service.[46] He considered this basis of assessment as being required to do justice to both parties, regardless of the extent to which the defendant was left better off on his side than he otherwise would have been. In determining the market value of the service to the claimant, his or her characteristics are relevant in assessing the market they are in. So, a film star may not have to pay the same price for a designer dress as the person in the street because wearing the dress may enhance the fashion house's brand image. But what we are seeking to ascertain, because what we are trying to reverse, is the value of the service, not the extent to which this particular defendant is benefitted by it.

The difference between the two judges in *Benedetti* reflects the subsequent difference in approach of the same judges, that of Lord Clarke in *Menelaou* and of Lord Reed in *ITC*, discussed in the previous chapter. Lord Clarke, following the dominant academic approach, is looking at the consequential enrichment of the defendant on his side, and treating that as the significant fact. Lord Reed by contrast is looking, in his preferred language, at the 'transfer of value' between them: the payment or service itself.

An example of the difference the two approaches leads to was given subsequently by Lord Burrows in criticising Lord Reed:

C cleans D's windows mistakenly thinking that D is a client. D allows C to do so knowing that C will want payment (ie D freely accepts). The sum a reasonable person in D's position would pay for the windows would be £10 (ie that is the market rate). There is objective evidence that D is only ever willing to pay £2 for his windows to be cleaned.[47]

---

[43] Eg G Virgo, *Principles of the Law of Restitution* (3rd edn, 2015), 64, 96; Burrows, *The Law of Restitution* (n 10), 61 (see also at 44–45); C Mitchell, P Mitchell, and S Watterson (eds), *Goff & Jones: The Law of Unjust Enrichment* (9th edn, 2016), [4-12]–[4-18], [4-19]–[4-23].
[44] Birks, *An Introduction to the Law of Restitution* (n 8), 109–110.
[45] [2013] UKSC 50, [2014] AC 938, [26].
[46] [2013] UKSC 50, [2014] AC 938, [100].
[47] A Burrows, Inner Temple Lecture on Unjust Enrichment, 17 February 2014. Available at https://www.innertemple.org.uk/education/education-resources/readers-lecture-series/previous-lecture-series-and-speakers/

If D's actions are sufficient for him to be liable, he must pay for the value of the work done, here £10. Burrows' suggestion that D should be able to rely upon his own idiosyncratic valuation, here £2, is wrong.

A litigated illustration is the Massachusetts decision of *Vickery v Richie*.[48] A fraudulent architect, acting as agent for neither party, deceived a landowner and a builder into thinking that they were contracting with each other on different terms. The landowner was deceived into believing the price for the work was for $23,000, the contractor $33,500. After the work had been completed, the land had increased in value by $22,000. The court concluded that no contract had been entered into by the parties. The court awarded the builder the market value of the work, as determined by an expert, concluding that 'the right does not depend upon the ultimate benefit received by the owner'.[49]

Today, because the defendant was wholly innocent and not responsible for the mistake the defendant made, we might reduce the award to ensure that they are left no worse off. This is not however related to the quantification of the claim, which is to the work done, which has an objective value. The dishonest defendant gets no reduction.

Further, although it is uncommon for people to accept services that will not, at least in some sense, benefit them, there are examples of services rendered under bargains which, because incomplete, as things turn out, are not beneficial to the defendant, and which he would not have chosen either initially or now. An example is the important decision of the Court of Appeal in *Brewer Street Investments Ltd v Barclay Woollen Co Ltd*.[50] The plaintiffs were landlords who entered into negotiations with the defendants to lease premises to them. Agreement was reached but expressed to be 'subject to contract'. The plaintiffs undertook to make certain alterations to the premises, with the cost to be borne by the defendants. Subsequent negotiations to conclude the leasehold contract broke down. Considerable work had gone into altering the premises by this point. As the defendants had never gone into possession, they were never in any sense enriched by what the plaintiffs did.

Somervell LJ adopted a contractual approach, stating that 'the defendant undertook responsibility for this work',[51] but this is difficult to reconcile with the usual meaning of 'subject to contract' which is that it is agreed between the parties that there is no enforceable agreement unless and until the formal agreement is executed, and that any contractual action for reasonable remuneration should only be available when the agreed condition precedent for the sum being earned was fulfilled, which it never was as the work was never completed.[52] Denning LJ saw the claim as one for 'restitution', but not one quantified by reference to any gain the defendants made, but rather by the cost of the work.[53]

Again, *Brewer Street*, like *Benedetti*, concerned the failure of an agreed condition of the work, here the condition being the conclusion of a contract between the parties,[54] and it

---

[48] 202 Mass 247 (Mass 1909), 88 NE 835.
[49] 202 Mass 247 (Mass 1909), 253, 88 NE 25 *per* Knowlton CJ.
[50] [1954] QB 428. See also the High Court of Australia's decision in *Waltons Stores (Interstate) Ltd v Maher* (1988) 164 CLR 387 on functionally identical facts, discussed in Chapter 14, Improvements. *Kearns v Andree* 107 Conn 181, 139 A 695, 59 ALR 599 (1928); *Minsky's Follies of Florida v Sennes* 206 F 2d 1 (1953); *Trollope v Koerner* 420 P 2d 91 (1970); *Sabemo Pty Ltd v North Sydney Municipal Council* [1977] 2 NSWLR 880.
[51] [1954] QB 428, 433.
[52] *ibid*, 435 *per* Denning LJ.
[53] *ibid*.
[54] *Cf. Jennings and Chapman Ltd v Woodman Matthews & Co* [1952] 2 TLR 409 where, on similar facts, the work was done on the basis that it would only have to be paid for if the head landlord gave consent to the granting of the lease. The refusal of the landlord meant that the condition never failed.

might be argued that different considerations apply to this different species of claim. But here the valuation of the claim should be the same if what had occurred was the avoidance of the partially executed contract for misrepresentation. An illustration is the classic decision of *Whittington v Seale-Hayne*.[55] The plaintiff, who bred prize poultry, agreed to enter into a lease on the basis of an innocent misrepresentation by the defendant's agent that the premises were in a 'good sanitary condition'. As part of the agreement, the plaintiff covenanted to carry out such works as were required by the local authority to be done. Unfortunately, the water supply was poisoned so that the tenant's manager became ill and most of the birds died. The defendant agreed to rescission, and to pay £20 for the rent and works carried out under the lease. The plaintiff claimed for the full loss they had suffered as a result of entering into the deal, including the loss of stock, removal and medical expenses, and the profits they would have made. These additional losses were denied. Farwell J did so on the basis that to award these additional sums would be to turn a claim for an indemnity into one for damages. An innocent misrepresentation was not, and where the defendant can show he had reasonable grounds for believing the statement to be true, still is not,[56] wrongful, so as to support a claim for damages. Where a contract is rescinded, what is sought to be reversed is the performance rendered under the contract. Only the expenditure that the claimants had been obliged to incur was properly recoverable. The claim is not, therefore, one for compensation for loss absent wrongdoing, based upon some principle of 'unjust sacrifice' or 'estoppel' (sic) as is sometimes claimed,[57] as foreseeable losses that the claimant has incurred are irrecoverable.[58] Rather we are quantifying the value of the performance obliged to be rendered under the agreement,[59] which may be higher or lower than either the gain made by the defendant or the loss suffered by the claimant.

D. The Meaning of Words

'Unjust enrichment' theory might be defended from the criticisms of this chapter by arguing that 'enrichment' in law does not have the meaning that it does in ordinary speech. Instead, it might be said, 'enrichment' is a 'term of art'[60] or has an 'objective' meaning, unrelated to the extent to which the individual defendant is in fact better off.[61] However, the central benefit claimed for 'unjust enrichment' and the move away from older labels such as 'quasi-contract' and *quantum meruit* was that it is a term that reflects the underlying justification for the claim. If it does not, we should abandon it. If we must have a label that covers both payments and services, 'performance' would be better.

---

[55] (1900) 82 LT 49. See also *Newbigging v Adam* (1886) 34 Ch D 582
[56] Misrepresentation Act 1967, s 2(1).
[57] S J Stoljar, 'Unjust Sacrifice' (1987) 50 MLR 603; G A Muir, 'Unjust Sacrifice and the Officious Intervener' in P D Finn (ed), *Essays in Restitution* (1990), 297.
[58] See Chapter 14, Improvements.
[59] *Newbigging v Adam* (1886) 34 Ch D 582 (CA), 589 *per* Cotton LJ, 596 *per* Fry LJ, 592–593 *per* Bowen LJ.
[60] Mitchell, Mitchell, and Watterson, *Goff & Jones* (n 43), [4-403].
[61] Edelman, 'The Meaning of Loss and Enrichment' (n 3), 211, 223–241.

5
Theory

A. *Kelly v Solari*

When Mr Solari died, his widow claimed under his life insurance policy as his executrix. She was paid, but the insurer later discovered that they had not been obliged to do so as the policy had lapsed because of the failure to pay a premium. The policy document had been marked 'lapsed' but not been checked. The plaintiff brought an action to recover the amount paid. At trial the action failed, but Lord Abinger CB gave leave to the plaintiff to move for the amount claimed, which he did. This was the procedure for allowing the claim to be heard before the full court. The Court of Exchequer then ordered a retrial in order to answer the question of whether the directors had known that the policy had lapsed. If they had, no recovery would be allowed.

As part of the full court, Parke B said:[1]

> [If the money] is paid under the impression of the truth of a fact which is untrue, it may, generally speaking, be recovered back, however careless the party paying may have been, in omitting to use due diligence to inquire into the fact. *In such a case the receiver was not entitled to it, nor intended to have it.*

What is the operative reason for recovery? Is it that there was no entitlement to the payment, or that the plaintiff was making a mistake? Or some combination of the two? Has Parke B stated two grounds for recovery, or only one? If the basis for recovery is lack of entitlement, why did the court order a retrial to determine the state of the directors' knowledge at time of payment?

The answer from the judgment is that it is the lack of entitlement that is the justification for the award. As Lord Abinger CB stated, in a judgment concurred with by Parke, Gurney, and Rolfe BB. 'the *defendant* ought to have had the opportunity of taking the opinion of the jury on the question whether in reality the directors had a knowledge of the facts … the knowledge of the facts which *disentitle* the party from recovering must mean a knowledge at the time of payment'.[2] The court, correctly, stated that the state of the mind of the plaintiff in making the payment, whether he paid it knowing that it was not due, was a matter for the *defence* to raise. This state of mind of the plaintiff in paying was, rightly, not considered an essential element of what needed to be established for the claim to succeed. Rather, if the directors had known the money was not due but had still paid, they were *disentitled* from recovery. The basis of recovery therefore, that the claimant had established and that needed to be answered by the defendant, was the lack of entitlement to the payment.

---

[1] (1841) 9 M& W 54, 58, 152 ER 23, 26 (emphasis added).
[2] (1841) 9 M& W 54, 58, 152 ER 23, 26 (emphasis added).

The Laws of Restitution. Robert Stevens, Oxford University Press. © Robert Stevens 2023.
DOI: 10.1093/oso/9780192885029.003.0005

The result in *Kelly v Solari* was right and it was reached for the right reasons.

B. The Role of Mistake and Similar 'Unjust Factors'

1. Summary

Today most commentators, departing from the approach of *Kelly v Solari*, see the state of mind of the claimant as an essential element of the cause of action (ie part of what needs to be proven so as to *entitle* recovery). This is based upon the theory that 'restitution for mistake rests on the fact that the plaintiff's judgment was vitiated in the matter of the transfer of wealth to the defendant'.[3] This claim that the defendant's obligation is based upon the plaintiff's 'vitiation of consent' now has judicial support.[4]

If the law is, as is claimed, correctly concerned with whether there is an absence of entitlement to the performance received, why do the leading cases in the common law world often ask whether the plaintiff was mistaken?[5] What is the explanation if it is not the 'vitiation' of the consent of the plaintiff to the defendant's enrichment?

The plaintiff's mistake plays three quite distinct roles within the law, which may be summarised as follows.

First, that a payment (or other performance) was rendered on the mistaken assumption that there was an obligation to do so is often the best way of proving a negative: that there was no good reason for it. No legal system starts with the assumption that all payments are presumptively recoverable: the lack of entitlement must be proven. Proving that the payment was made for a bad reason establishes, at least on the balance of probabilities, that it was not made for one of the diverse good reasons that exist for establishing entitlement. A mistake as to the existence of an obligation to pay *negatives* any justification for it. The mistake as to whether a payment was owed is not itself the justification for recovery, but the best way of proving that restitution is so justified. It is an heuristic for establishing the lack of entitlement.

Second, although the claimant's subjective state of mind cannot form part of the justification for the imposition of an obligation upon the defendant, it may suffice to invalidate what would otherwise be a good reason for a performance rendered. Our mistakes in making them may sometimes *nullify* contracts, gifts, wills, trust deeds, and other rights of other people that we are responsible for creating.

This distinction between negativing and nullifying mistakes is familiar in contract law from Lord Atkin's speech in *Bell v Lever Brothers*.[6] Indeed, it may be speculated that it was the familiarity with the latter vitiating role of mistake in the law of contract that initially led to the mistaken belief that it always played the same role in the law of *quasi*-contract.

---

[3] P Birks, *An Introduction to the Law of Restitution* (rev edn, 1989), 147. See also A Burrows, *The Law of Restitution* (3rd edn, 2011) ch 9; C Mitchell, P Mitchell, and S Watterson (eds), *Goff & Jones: The Law of Unjust Enrichment* (9th edn, 2016), [9-06]–[9-09].
[4] *Lowick Rose LLP v Swynson LLP* [2017] UKSC 32, [2018] AC 313, [22] *per* Lord Sumption.
[5] Eg *David Securities Pty Ltd v Commonwealth Bank of Australia* (1992) CLR 353 (HCA). See also A Kull, *Restatement of the Law (Third) Restitution and Unjust Enrichment*, vol I (2010) § 5(2).
[6] *Bell v Lever Bros* [1932] AC 161 (HL), 217 *per* Lord Atkin.

Third, a party who pays a sum that they know they do not owe is undeserving of the law's assistance in obtaining its recovery. They have consented to the position they now find themselves in. The claimant's state of mind, their consent, is not what justifies another being under an obligation, it cannot do so. Rather, it provides a defence. Consent is here playing the same role as a defence as it does in the law of torts (*volenti non fit iniuria*) and contract (waiver). This was the issue in *Kelly v Solari*. If the defendant was making a mistake in paying (or was subject to duress or undue influence) then they did not truly consent, and there would be no defence. The state of mind of the claimant is relevant to *disentitle* recovery.

These three roles will now be looked at in detail.

2. Negativing

If a plaintiff makes a payment to which the recipient is not entitled, how does he establish the lack of entitlement? Iacobucci J in the Supreme Court of Canada's decision *Garland v Consumer Gas* stated that the correct approach was as follows:[7]

> First, the plaintiff must show that no juristic reason from an established category exists to deny recovery. By closing the list of categories that the plaintiff must canvass in order to show an absence of juristic reason, [Professor Lionel] Smith's objection[8] to the Canadian formulation of the test that it required proof of a negative is answered. The established categories that can constitute juristic reasons include a contract, a disposition of law a donative intent and other valid common law, equitable or statutory obligations.

This cannot be correct as a matter of practice. The plaintiff who seeks recovery of a payment made could not be expected to show that there was no contract, no gift, no moral obligation, no court judgment, no statute, and no other good reason for why a payment was made. This is especially so as, on Iacobucci J's suggested approach, the list of such justifying reasons is not in fact closed ('include').

If instead the plaintiff shows that she paid because she mistakenly thought she was obliged to do so, then she has shown, at least *prima facie*, that she paid for a bad reason. This on its face suffices to show that she did not pay for any of the multitude of good reasons that there might be. That this is correct is demonstrated by the subsequent decision of the Supreme Court of Canada in *BMP Global Distributions Inc v Bank of Nova Scotia*.[9] This concerned a bank's right to recover payments made under a forged cheque. The focus was upon whether the payment had been made by mistake and, once it was shown that it had been, no further analysis of the want of any other validating reason was needed. The court did not require the plaintiff to go through the list of potentially operative 'juristic reasons' and rebut them all.

The label adopted for the central example of the kind of mistakes that prove the negative in this way is 'liability mistakes'.[10] This unfortunately treats 'liability' and 'obligation' as

---

[7] (2004) 237 DLR (4th) 385, [44].
[8] In L Smith 'The Mystery of "Juristic Reason"' (2000) 12 SCLR (2d) 211, 212–213.
[9] [2009] 1 SCR 504, 304 DLR (4th) 292.
[10] *Aiken v Short* (1856) 1 H & N 210, 215; 156 ER 1180, 1182 per Bramwell B. See also *Norwich Union Fire Insurance Society Ltd v Wm H Price Ltd* [1932] AC 455 (PC), 462, 'The "Fact" which Baron Parke is referring to is one "which would entitle the other to the money" if true' per Lord Wright.

synonyms, which they are not. If an obligation that is unenforceable (ie there is no liability to be sued) is performed, there should, without more, be no right to restitution. The unenforceable obligation provides a good reason for the rendering of performance.[11] As Lord Mansfield said in *Moses v McFarlane*:[12]

> The kind of equitable action to recover back money, which ought not in justice to be kept, is very beneficial, and therefore much encouraged. It lies only for money which *ex aequo et bono,* the defendant ought to refund: it does not lie for money paid to the plaintiff, which is payable in point of honor and honesty, although it could not have been recovered from him by any course of law: as in payment of a debt barred by the Statute of Limitations, or contracted during his infancy, or to the extent of principal and interest upon an usurious contract, or for money fairly lost at play: because in all those cases, the defendant may retain it with a safe conscience, though by positive law he was barred from recovering it.

By contrast, if a payment is made under an agreement between the parties, and the claimant has paid more than was due, this shows that the payment was unjustified.[13] A mistake as to an obligation to pay *negatives* the existence of any entitlement.[14]

For purposes of negativing the existence of a good reason for a performance, not all mistakes suffice. If I mistakenly make a payment to you of money that I owe, it cannot be recovered. There was a good reason for it. If a father makes a gift to his son on his birthday, which he would not have done if he had known that his son had been drinking the night before, he cannot in law recover it.[15] Proving that you made a gift of money by mistake on its face shows that there was a good reason for it, the gift, not that there was not.

If a gun is held to your head, and demand made that you hand over the contents of your wallet to another (who may or may not be the person holding the gun) proof of these facts would also show that any payment was made for a bad reason, and therefore *prima facie* not for one of the diverse good reasons that might have justified it. Most litigated cases of duress or undue influence involve setting aside (ie nullifying) contracts and gifts, but some also operate in this way.

3. Nullifying

An example:

> *P* agrees to provide *D* with financial services in return for a share in a business. *P* discovers that *D* had misrepresented material facts to him before entering into the deal. *P* now seeks to rescind and recover the value of the service provided.

---

[11] Eg *Thomas v Brown* (1876) 1 QBD 714.
[12] (1760) 2 Burr 1005, 1012, 97 ER 676. See also *Farmer v Arundel* (1772) 2 Black W 824, 825–826, 96 ER 485 *per* De Grey CJ.
[13] See eg *Larner v London County Council* [1949] 2 KB 683 where the agreement was binding in honour only.
[14] *Cf.* S Meier, 'No Basis: A Comparative View' in A Burrows and A Rodger (eds), *Mapping the Law: Essays in Memory of Peter Birks* (2006) 343, 351.
[15] *Morgan v Ashcroft* [1938] 1 KB 49, 66 *per* Sir Wilfred Greene MR. But see Burrows, *The Law of Restitution* (n 3), 214–217.

The conditions for the creation of an enforceable contract (offer and acceptance, certainty, consideration, an intention to create legal relations) have been fulfilled. These conditions are bilateral and objective. The subjective error in P's head, for which D is responsible, entitles P to rescind, or avoid the contract. After rescission, the basis for performance that once exists has been retrospectively invalidated, or nullified. Restitution of the performance rendered under the contract then follows. Where, as in this case, we seek to nullify an otherwise valid contract (or gift, will, or trust) the category of mistakes that suffice is not, and has never been, confined to 'liability mistakes', indeed the mistakes will very rarely be of that kind.

A more restricted class of mistakes will nullify a contract where neither party is responsible for a shared mistake.

Another example:

P agrees to hire a Music Hall from D for a hire of £10,000 per month for three months, payment in advance. Unbeknownst to the parties, the music hall had burned to the ground an hour before they entered into their agreement.

Agreements, like the acts of communication that are used to make them, have limits. In some cases, agreements run out and are not (objectively) interpreted as covering the situation the parties now find themselves in. This is most commonly the case where the contract is not possible to perform. Usually in cases of the unforeseen non-existence of the subject matter of an agreement it does not bind.[16] If in the example the fire had occurred two hours later the obligation to provide the Hall would be described as frustrated,[17] but the reasons why the obligations of the parties are released is in principle the same regardless of the moment the fire occurs.[18] The agreement cannot be interpreted as covering the state of affairs that now exists, and so cannot provide a justification for any performance rendered under it. Again, any old mistake will not do, and in order to give a label to the idea that the agreement does not cover the facts as they are now known to be we label the requisite shared mistake a 'fundamental' one.

More difficult are cases where the contract is possible to perform, but its entire purpose has been frustrated or fallen away. This has happened in litigated cases extremely rarely, the most famous English examples being the 'coronation' cases. Where rooms had been hired to overlook the coronation of King Edward VII, when the King fell ill postponing the celebrations, the agreements could still have been performed but no longer had any of the purpose which had formed the common basis upon which they had been entered into. Again, it did not matter whether the agreement was made before[19] or after[20] the unforeseen illness of the King; the agreement did not cover this situation. Where some purpose survives, the contract remains valid,[21] and so any performance made under it cannot without more be recovered.

---

[16] Eg *Couturier v Hastie* [1856] 5 HLC 673, 10 ER 1065.
[17] *Taylor v Caldwell* (1863) 3 B & S 826, 122 ER 309.
[18] See generally Chapter 8, Contract.
[19] *Griffith v Brymer* (1903) 19 TLR 434.
[20] *Krell v Henry* [1903] 2 KB 740.
[21] *Herne Bay Steamboat Co v Hutton* [1903] 2 KB 683.

Mistakes are not, of course, the only way of demonstrating that, despite appearances, there is no responsibility for the putatively valid contractual obligation because of the condition of the state of mind of the person creating it. Duress, undue influence, and incapacity are all methods of invalidating rights that would otherwise be created, nullifying responsibility.

Wills, trust deeds, and gifts can also all be nullified on the basis of the mistakes made by those creating them, or because their creator was subject to duress or undue influence. At least in relation to mistakes however, the rules differ between the different categories.

In relation to the rights of others that are not voluntarily created, such as those created by a court order or a tax statute, no mistake can nullify them, and duress and undue influence are of no relevance. Only a fresh court order (usually an appeal) or new statute, respectively, can overturn them.

4. Voluntary Performance

The third role for 'mistake' is that it shows that the claimant did not consent to the state of affairs he now seeks to correct.[22] It rebuts a potential defence. In pleading terms, it is a reply. An example:

> *D* claims that *P* owes him £1,000 and demands it from him. *P* is certain that he does not owe this sum but pays anyway.

Even if it can be shown that the money is not owing, so that there is no objective reason for the payment having been made, there is no injustice to *P* in refusing to reverse the payment. Just as with *volenti non fit iniuria* in the law of torts, *P*'s subjective consent means that the law has no justification for coming to his aid. The subjective state of mind of the plaintiff may bar the right to restitution, not operate as a ground for its creation.[23] Voluntary payments cannot therefore be recovered.[24] This is a defence, and the focus is solely on the claimant's state of mind. This explains why, in *Kelly v Solari* once it had been shown that the payment was not owed, it was for the defendant to raise that the plaintiff had known this but had paid in any event, so that the plaintiff was disentitled. A possible test would be the position if we continue our example:

> *D* upon discovering that the money was not due, reimburses *P*.

Although *P* could not have compelled *D* to reimburse him, once he has done so *D* should have no claim to recover the payment back again.

---

[22] *Cf. Morgan Guaranty Trust Co of New York v Lothian Regional Council* 1995 SC 151, 165 *per* Lord Hope; *Kleinwort Benson v Lincoln City Council* [1999] 2 AC 349, 408 *per* Lord Hope.
[23] *Kelly v Solari* (1841) 9 M& W 54, 59, 152 ER 23, 26 *per* Parke B. 'If, indeed, the money is intentionally paid, without reference to the truth or falsehood of the fact, the plaintiff meaning to waive all inquiry into it, and that the person receiving shall have the money at all events, whether the fact be true or false, the latter is certainly entitled to retain it.' *Cf. Townsend v Crowdy* (1860) 8 CB (NS) 477, 494 *per* William J.
[24] *Marine Trade SA v Pioneer Freight Futures Co Ltd BVI* [2009] EWHC 2656 (Comm); [2010] 1 Lloyd's Rep 631, [76]–[77] *per* Flaux J.

Duress and undue influence may similarly show that the claimant did not truly consent, and so can recover a performance rendered. As we shall see, some mistakes, most often mistakes of law, are no longer operative at the time of court judgment because the claimant is now in exactly the position he expected to be in, and so the initial mistake should not suffice for the purpose of showing lack of consent.[25]

An illustration of the principle that a plaintiff cannot recover back a payment that he knows the defendant is not entitled to is *CTN Cash and Carry v Gallaher*.[26] A buyer paid a sum of money to his supplier. This sum was not owed. The buyer paid because of threats by the seller to discontinue further supplies which the buyer had no contractual entitlement to. The suppliers made the threats in the honest belief that the sum was owed. A threat to discontinue the conferral of a benefit, as opposed to a threat to cause harm, cannot constitute duress. Recovery was properly denied: the claimants had paid the money knowing full well that it was not due.[27] *If* the buyers had stipulated that they paid reserving their rights to recover the payment at a later date, then recovery should have been allowed because this would have shown that they did not consent to the position that they now found themselves in. But they did not.

A difficult question arises where the payor knows that they may not owe the money but pays anyway, subsequently discovering that they did not.[28] Is their consent sufficient, or not, if they would not have made the payment if they had known the truth? The decision of the Supreme Court of Iowa in *New York Life Assurance Co v Chittenden*[29] is an illustration. Jarvis had a life insurance policy. He disappeared and was not heard of for over seven years. An administrator of his estate was appointed who filed a claim. The insurance company initially refused to pay unless they were given a bond of indemnity for return of the money if Jarvis proved to be alive. This was refused, and the company gave way and paid up. In fact Jarvis was alive. Recovery of the payment was rightly refused. If you pay knowing full well that the existence of a reason for performance is uncertain, and fail to make it clear that the payment is conditional upon there being such a good reason when you have the opportunity to do so, you have consented to the position you now find yourself in and are undeserving of the law's assistance.

Although most litigated cases of duress or undue influence involve the nullification of a contract or gift, some do not. In *Maskell v Horner*,[30] the plaintiff was a trader outside Spitalfields market who had for a dozen years paid tolls demanded by the owner of the market. The plaintiff objected on the grounds that he was not in the market, whereupon the defendant threatened to seize his goods. He paid up and continued to do so but always under protest. Subsequent litigation established that there was no right to the tolls. Rowlatt J refused recovery on the basis that the plaintiff had acquiesced.[31] This was overturned on appeal, Lord Reading CJ stating:[32]

---

[25] See Chapter 6, Practice.
[26] [1994] 4 All ER 714 (CA).
[27] *Smith v William Charlick Ltd* (1924) 34 CLR 38, 51–52 *per* Isaacs J, 51 *per* Knox CJ.
[28] *Marine Trade A v Pioneer Freight Futures Co Ltd BVI* [2009] EWHC 2656, [2010] 1 Lloyd's Rep 631; *South Australian Cold Stores Ltd v Electricity Trust of South Australia* (1957) 98 CLR 65; *David Securities Pty Ltd v Commonwealth Bank of Australia* [1992] HCA 48, 175 CLR 353, 373–374.
[29] 134 Iowa 613, 112 NW 96 (1907); *cf. Pilot Insurance v Cudd* 36 SE 2d 860 (1945) (S Ct of S Carolina).
[30] [1915] 3 KB 106.
[31] [1915] 3 KB 106, 111.
[32] ibid, 118.

> If a person with knowledge of the facts pays money, which he is not in law bound to pay, and in circumstances implying that he is paying it voluntarily to close the transaction, he cannot recover it …[but it can be recovered if] the payment is made for the purpose of averting a threatened evil and is made not with the intention of giving up a right but under immediate necessity and with the intention of preserving the right to dispute the legality of the demand.

C. What Is a Good Reason?

The diversity of good reasons that there may be for making a payment or other performance are so many and various that it is hard to improve upon Iacobucci J's non-exhaustive list. The easiest examples of a good reason for a performance are those that are legally obligatory and enforceable. Payments made under contracts, wills, court judgments, tax statutes, following declaration of a dividend by a company, and so on are not recoverable, regardless of whether mistakenly made, unless and until what justified the payment (the contract, will, court judgment, etc) are set aside.

As we have also seen, legal obligations do not cease to be such simply because they are unenforceable. The most important distinguishing feature of legal obligations that are unenforceable when compared with those that are a nullity (ie that do not exist) is that once performance is rendered it cannot be recovered. The performance of an obligation after the expiry of a limitation period that rendered it unenforceable, or performance of a contract that is unenforceable for want of a formality requirement, cannot without more be reversed.[33]

More difficult as a matter of the common law because underdeveloped (although not problematic in principle) is the performance of natural or moral obligations. We need to draw again the distinction between matters of virtue and matters of right. The question of how I ought, as a virtuous person, to behave is a different question from the rights you have against me. Virtuous passers-by will pick up a baby that is drowning in an inch of water, but the baby has no right to be picked up.

An example:

> C agrees to pay D half of his winnings should he win the lottery. Having done so, and believing that such agreements are enforceable, C pays D.

Had D a right to be paid? If we take the view that consideration goes to enforceability of the agreement and not its validity (as we should) then the answer is yes. Here, D has a right to be paid, albeit an unenforceable one, and no restitution should be allowed. Similarly, executed gifts are irrecoverable, although there was no obligation to make them, unless and until they are set aside.[34]

By contrast, a man who makes a large payment to his daughter on her wedding day may act as *virtue* requires of him, but the daughter has no right to the payment without more.

---

[33] See eg *Sharp Brothers & Knight v Chant* [1917] 1 KB 771 (unenforceable but valid rental payments).
[34] Discussed in Chapter 6, Practice.

If his payment is a gift which can be set aside, because for example he was subject to duress or he was making a sufficiently serious mistake, the mere fact that he had behaved as a virtuous person *should* have done independently of the gift cannot alone provide a supporting reason for the payment.

'Good reasons' then are not moral reasons that apply to one party alone. Nor are they found in the mind of either party. Rather they are objective reasons of entitlement to the performance made, that apply to both parties. They are, in that sense, juridical or legal. They are however wider than the category of obligations that would be enforced if no performance has yet been made (eg they include gifts).

Once we accept that good justifying reasons need not be legally enforceable obligations, the decision in *Brisbane v Dacres*,[35] today usually dismissed as wrong, becomes justifiable.

Masters of ships during the Napoleonic wars could, as now, be ordered by their superiors to do anything lawful. When they were ordered to carry a large amount of public money, a gratuity was paid to them of 0.5% the value. By convention, one third of that sum was then paid over by the Master of the vessel to the Admiral under whom he served. In *Montagu v Janverin*[36] an admiral had brought an action to claim his third when it had not been paid, and Lord Mansfield had refused to enforce the custom. The question that arose in *Brisbane v Dacres* was whether a payment that had been made to an Admiral under the customary convention could then be recovered?

The decision that it could not is justifiable. It is one thing to hold that a convention cannot be enforced, quite another to decide that it provides no justification for payments made under it. Those who make a conventional contribution at the end of a church service should not be able to get their money back on the basis that one of the reasons they had been so generous was that they were making an error of law. If you pay the staff of a restaurant a tip at the end of a meal this is irrecoverable, even if your motivation was that you thought there was a legal obligation to do so.

Finally, a difficult example:

P, a baby, is about to drown but is saved by D who is injured in the process.

Civilian jurisdictions would allow D a claim for compensation on such facts, but, as we shall see, the common law does not.[37] What if P as an adult, believing he is obliged to do so, pays D a sum by way of compensation, should it be recoverable? The answer, in all jurisdictions, should be no.

D. The Theory

1. The Operative Facts

In explaining the law, it is much easier to show than to tell, but we are now in a position to understand the principled basis of recovery in cases like *Kelly v Solari*.

---

[35] (1813) 5 Taunt 143, 128 ER 641.
[36] (1811) 3 Taunt 442, 128 ER 175.
[37] Chapter 10, Necessity.

The current approach in textbooks is to ask three questions in determining whether there is a cause of action in 'unjust enrichment'. Was the defendant enriched? Was the enrichment at the claimant's expense? Is the enrichment unjust? The third question is most commonly answered by looking to the state of mind of the claimant in enriching the defendant. Paradigmatically the enrichment will be unjust if the claimant was making a mistake.

The problem in principle with this approach is that it takes the operative facts to be ones concerned with the defendant (his enrichment) and the claimant (his loss, his mistake) independently of one another. The formula then adds together these factors applying them independently to each party in order to justify the obligation the defendant owes to the claimant. This cannot work as the operative facts are of the wrong form. Rights and obligations in private law are bilateral. We need to identify reasons that are also bilateral, that relate the two parties together. A mistake the claimant makes that enriches another cannot justify imposing an obligation on the enriched party. What has your mistake got to do with me?[38]

This abstract problem may then be illustrated by an example that we have already encountered.

> *P* and *D* each own one of only two examples of a rare collectible stamp worth thousands of pounds. *P* mistakenly destroys his stamp, which causes *D*'s stamp to more than double in value. *D* sells his stamp. *P* seeks restitution from *D* of the enrichment *D* has made at his expense.[39]

No recovery should be allowed. The point of the example is that we have held in place the facts that are often claimed to operate (the mistake, enrichment, and correlative loss) whilst removing those that actually do so (a performance by the plaintiff to the defendant to which the latter was not entitled). We can then see that the former do not suffice.

2. Payments and Services

Many commentators have suggested that there are two separate principles governing the reversal of transfers of property and the reversal of services rendered.[40] As we have seen however, a payment, although it may involve the transfer of a right, often does not. Seeking to explain the recovery of mistaken payments by reference to a right of the plaintiff that has been acquired by the defendant does not map on to either the law or our intuitions as to how it ought to be.

A payment is however legal event. Absent the legal system, or a body of rules as in the game of Monopoly, we could not pay one another anything. Cash would merely be pieces of paper moving from one hand to another. Although, it is possible to pay someone else without either yourself losing any property right, or the payee obtaining one, a payment is a legal event, a juridical act. Those who have sought to explain recovery in mistaken payment cases as based upon a property transfer are correct in seeking to identify a legal, and

---

[38] F Wilmot-Smith, 'Should the Payee Pay?' (2017) 37 OJLS 844.
[39] *Cf.* D Friedmann, 'Restitution of Benefits Acquired Through the Appropriation of Property or the Commission of a Wrong' 80 Col L Rev 504, 532 (at fn 144).
[40] Eg P Watts, 'A Property Principle and a Services Principle' [1995] RLR 49.

not merely a factual, event that requires reversal. If a legal event has occurred that is without justification, the law has good reason for reversing what it has done.

However, that a legal event has occurred that ought not to have done so, is not, on its own, sufficient to impose an obligation upon a defendant to correct it.[41] Why, without more, should individuals be obliged to get the law out of the mess it has created? The juridical act must be that of both the plaintiff and the defendant. It is to meet this condition that the courts, and this work, have insisted upon the importance of a request or acceptance on the part of the defendant where restitution is sought from him, such acceptance always being implicit in the payment of money. From the other side of the relation, the payor has standing to require the reversal of the payment because it was his doing.

Although juridical acts are not confined to payments, and include such things as the transfer of shares in a company, the granting of an easement, or the settlement of a legal dispute, they do not, without more, include services. Cleaning windows, repairing bicycles, and building houses can all be done absent the legal system. As we have seen however, doing these things without more, even by mistake in a way that leaves the defendant better off, does not suffice. If they have been done by mistake, benefitting another party, what business is it of the law to reverse them? 'One cleans another's shoes, what can the other do but put them on?'[42]

Almost all of the example we have discussed so far concerning the reversal of a service rendered were ones where the performance was rendered under an agreement, albeit not an enforceable contract, under which the condition for such performance had failed. As we shall see in Chapter 7, Conditions, in such cases we have another independently sufficient justification for restitution. Similarly, as we shall also see in Chapter 14, Improvements, there are examples of mistaken improvement of the tangible property of another where the improver has an entitlement to reimbursement but this is best explained in terms of competing entitlements to the thing worked or built upon. Not all claims to recover the value of services are however explicable in these alternative ways.

The classic *Whittington v Seale-Hayne*,[43] that was discussed in the previous chapter, is an example of a case that cannot be so compartmentalised. The contract between the parties had been avoided, and so no extant agreement could form part of the justification for the claim. The value of the work done under the now avoided contract was recoverable. Here, however, the value of the work recoverable was that which *the law* had, prior to avoidance, required the plaintiff to render.[44] Again, we have identified a legal event between the two parties, the performance of a once valid legal obligation owed by one party to the other, that ought to be reversed. The suggested important distinction therefore is between juridical

---

[41] *Cf.* B McFarlane, 'Unjust Enrichment, Rights and Value' in Donal Nolan and Andrew Robertson (eds), *Rights and Private Law* (2012).
[42] *Taylor v Laird* (1856) 25 LJ Ex 329, 332 *per* Pollock CB; *Ruabon SS Co Ltd v London Assurance* [1900] AC 6, 12 *per* Lord Halsbury, '[I]f a man built a wall so as to shield his neighbour's house from undue wet or danger from violent tempests, he ought to be entitled to contribution because his neighbour has got an advantage from what he did .... I can find no authority for any principle which includes this case.' *China Pacific SA v Food Corporation of India* [1982] AC 939, 961 *per* Lord Diplock, 'a mere stranger cannot compel an owner of goods to pay for a benefit bestowed upon him against his will'. See also D 50. 17. 69 (*Invito beneficium non dutur* 'no one is obliged to accept a benefit against his consent').
[43] (1900) 82 LT 49.
[44] See also *Newbigging v Adam* (1886) 34 Ch D 582 (CA), 589 *per* Cotton LJ, 596 *per* Fry LJ, 592–593 *per* Bowen LJ.

and non-juridical acts, between legal events and those independent of the legal system. It is not between payments and services as such.

If a payment is rendered by mistake, the payment *itself* is not vitiated. If it were there would be no need to bring a claim in the case of a mistaken payment: nothing would legally have occurred. If, however, a supporting justification in law for a juridical act is removed (eg an executed contract is avoided *ab initio*) or never existed (eg the payment of a sum of money that is not due) and the defendant is jointly responsible for that act, the law ought to reverse what has (legally) happened at the suit of the person who has performed the action. There is no (objectively) good legal justification for the performance rendered between these parties. What is reversed is not a factual state of affairs (eg the defendant being better off than he otherwise would be) but a legal event (eg a payment, the performance of an obligation). The ground for recovery is not found (subjectively) in the plaintiff's mind. The recovery of payments of sums of money that are not due is the core example of this case. The reason for recovery embraces both parties together. We have our bilateral reason.

6
Practice

A. Introduction

It might be objected that the claim so far, whilst of some interest, is as irrelevant as that of the Frenchman whose response upon seeing an early flight of the Wright brothers' aircraft was to object 'That is all very well in practice, but does it work in theory?' Does it make any difference in practice whether it is the mistake or the lack of entitlement that justifies recovery? Is it not the case that, whatever the theoretical niceties, the common law courts today are looking to the state of mind of the claimant as justifying the obligation of the defendant?

The answer is that it does make a difference in practice, and that the role of mistake (and duress, undue influence and so on) in the common law has never been explicable in any way other than that given in the previous chapter. Eleven illustrations follow.

B. Absence of Good Reason or Vitiation of Consent?

1. Rescission

The law of rescission has never been compatible with the proposition that 'vitiation of the claimant's consent' to the defendant's enrichment justifies the claim.[1] An example:

> C agrees to buy a ship from D. During the negotiations, D has misrepresented the size of the propellers of the vessel. This forms part of C's decision-making process to go ahead with the deal. Six months later, C pays the price, at which point he has forgotten about the statement concerning the propellers, and it forms no part of his reason for paying. Having now discovered the misrepresentation, he seeks rescission and repayment.

In a legal system that permits rescission in such circumstances, restitution should follow. It should not matter that the mistake played no part in the decision to perform, so long as it is sufficient to nullify the reason that would have justified that performance.

This pattern is always found within the law of rescission, which is a one-stage process. If a contract is set aside for misrepresentation, duress, undue influence, or for any other reason, restitution of the performance rendered always follows. We do not ask a plaintiff to plead and prove that the misrepresentation, duress, or undue influence that was operative at the time the bargain was entered into, was *also* present at the later time the performance that it is sought to reverse was made. The latter is irrelevant, because it is not the basis of the claim.

---

[1] D Friedmann, 'Valid, Voidable and Non-Existing Obligations: An Alternative Perspective on the Law of Restitution' in A Burrows (ed), *Essays on the Law of Restitution* (1991), 247.

Rescission of a contract itself is not a cause of action. Rescission may operate as a defence (as where a claim is brought to enforce an executory contract and the defendant seeks to set aside the contract based upon misrepresentation, duress, or undue influence). Rescission may also operate as a necessary and sufficient condition of the obligation to make restitution of the value of the performance rendered under a contract (as where a claim is brought to recover payments made under a contract set aside on the basis of misrepresentation, duress, or undue influence).

2. Mistakes as to Recoverability

A nice illustration of the problem with the 'vitiation of consent' approach is *Nurdin & Peacock plc v DB Ramsden & Co Ltd*.[2] The defendant landlord thought that it was entitled to increase the rent due under a lease and did so. It was making a mistake, because no such increase was possible without a rent review. The plaintiffs were presented with invoices for the increased amount, which they paid not realising the need for the review. The plaintiffs were then advised of the need for the review, and that they were not obliged to pay the higher rent. However, they continued to pay five more instalments because they were concerned that the landlord might forfeit the lease but were advised that they would be able to recover any overpayments. The defendants argued that overpayments made because of a mistake as to an entitlement to get it back could not be recovered. They argued that allowing the claim to succeed would involve an inherent contradiction: if there were recovery then there was no mistake, and if there was no mistake there was no right to recovery. Neuberger J whilst accepting that this raised 'an unusual logical problem',[3] held that it should not stand in the way of recovery.

We might recharacterise the kind of mistake the claimant made in order to avoid the problem. If they were advised 'you have a contractual right to recover the money' if that was wrong, no contradiction would arise in allowing a recovery on another basis. But it should make no difference if the advice had been simply 'you will have a right to recover the money', thereby creating the apparent contradiction.

The paradox arises because of thinking that it is the mistake that grounds recovery. The correct analysis is that because the money was not due, it should be recoverable. The claimants had not consented to the state of affairs of the defendants not paying them back, because they thought they would have a right to recovery. That that belief turned out to be true does not contradict the reason for the claim. No logical paradox therefore arose.

3. Obligations Performed

An example:

> *P* owes a number of creditors money, including *D* to whom he owes £10,000. *P* intends to pay all of his creditors except *D*, but by an oversight pays *D* as well as all the others.

---

[2] [1999] 1 WLR 1249. *Cf. Agnew v Ferguson* (1903) 5 F 879 (1903) 11 SLT 79.
[3] [1999] 1 WLR 1249, 1274.

P should not be able to recover the payment made, despite having done so by mistake. There was a good reason justifying the payment: the discharge of the debt that was owed.[4] Similarly, if a debtor pays his creditor because of the threat of criminal proceedings he cannot recover his payment,[5] although if the same threats are used to extort payment from a relative of the debtor who is not liable, restitution follows.[6]

Until relatively recently, academic textbooks on the law of restitution wholly ignored the role of justifying reasons, such as gifts, although current works generally recognise that the presence of an *obligation* to render performance may bar recovery.[7] However, they provide no adequate explanation as to why this should be so. *Goff & Jones* states that 'the defendant can escape liability if another legal rule entitles him to keep the benefit, and this rule overrides the rule generated by the law of unjust enrichment which holds that the defendant should make restitution'.[8] Although they do not classify their proposed rule in this way, such an 'override' would be a defence,[9] which it would be for the defendant to plead and prove. It is unclear how the right to restitution, if it is created by the defendant's vitiation of consent, can in principle be overridden by the obligation to pay. How and why does one obligation override the other? Why should the restitutionary obligation, said to be generated by the mistake, not be the one with priority? Burrows claims that sometimes the restitutionary obligation will be overridden, and sometimes it will not, but provides us with no (convincing) account as to why or when this will be so.[10] Appeals to coherence[11] take us no further as they do not explain why the apparent contradiction should be resolved one way and not the other.

Justifying reasons are not confined to legally enforceable obligations to perform. If I mistakenly pay out on a bet, make a will under which you inherit, declare a trust or make a gift to you, restitution should not follow, without more, despite the absence of any legal obligation on me to have done so. We cannot therefore explain the role of justifying reasons by reference to any principle of subsidiarity of unjust enrichment to other obligations, preventing circularity of action, set off, and so on.

Those who subscribe to a proprietary theory of recovery also struggle to explain this (obvious) limitation upon the recovery of a payment made.[12] If the payment in the above example was made in cash, that theory seems to indicate that the mistake should create a right to recover the value of the right transferred. It cannot be argued that the transfer of *that* right was justifiable, because the obligation was to pay $10,000, not *that specific* $10,000 in cash. Why then is there no recovery?

This lack of focus on justifying reasons caused some of the older cases to be unfairly criticised,[13] as not fitting with vitiation of consent theory. The most notable feature of the

---

[4] *Steam Saw Mills Company v Baring Brothers* [1922] 1 Ch 244 (CA); *DD Growth Premium v RMF Strategies* [2017] UKPC 36, [2018] Bus LR 1595, [62] *per* Lord Sumption.
[5] *Flower v Sadler* (1882) 10 QBD 572.
[6] *Williams v Bayley* (1868) LR 1 HL 200.
[7] Eg A Burrows, *A Restatement of the English Law of Unjust Enrichment* (2012), 32–35.
[8] C Mitchell, P Mitchell, and S Watterson (eds), *Goff & Jones: The Law of Unjust Enrichment* (9th edn, 2016), [2-201].
[9] See Chapter 18, Defences.
[10] Burrows, *A Restatement of the English Law of Unjust Enrichment* (n 7), 32–35 (i.e. commentary to § 3(6)); see also A Burrows, *The Law of Restitution* (3rd edn, 2011), 88–91.
[11] Eg J Edelman and E Bant, *Unjust Enrichment* (2nd edn, 2016), 134.
[12] See generally C Webb, *Reason and Restitution: A Theory of Unjust Enrichment* (2016), 96–102.
[13] See also C Tham, 'Unjust Enrichment and Unlawful Dividends: A Step to Far?' [2005] CLJ 177 arguing that a final declaration of a dividend by a company creates a debt, and so its payment cannot be recovered.

much-maligned *Bilbie v Lumley*,[14] the case usually treated as introducing the so-called mistake of law bar, is that, like the similarly unjustly criticised *Brisbane v Dacres*,[15] it is rightly decided.

The plaintiff insurers had paid out a £100 claim under a contract for the insurance of a ship. The insured had not disclosed to them the sailing time of the ship. As insurance contracts are ones of utmost good faith, if an insured fails to disclose a relevant risk the contract may be set aside. The plaintiff alleged that they had made a mistake as to their liability to pay. The defendant's non-disclosure would have been enough to constitute a defence if any action had been brought against them. The claim for repayment failed.

This error of law was not enough on its own to show that there was no good reason for the payment. If the plaintiffs had sought to *set aside* the contract for non-disclosure, which would have required them also to return the premiums received, then restitution of the insurance pay-out should have been awarded. No recovery back of insurance pay-outs made under a still extant and valid contract should, however, be awarded. There is a large difference between a mistake as to whether you are obliged to pay, and mistakenly failing to take steps to avoid an obligation to pay.

At the time *Bilbie v Lumley* was decided, it was unclear whether a fully executed contract could be avoided for non-disclosure,[16] but, absent rescission, no recovery should be allowed based solely upon the fact that the plaintiff had made an error of law in paying. The money was owing under the contract, and unless it was set aside, it should be irrecoverable.

More complex, but essentially the same case, is the decision of the House of Lords in *Deutsche Morgan Grenfell v Inland Revenue Commissioners*,[17] which is wrongly decided.

Section 247 of the Income and Corporation Taxes Act 1988 provided that, where a subsidiary company paid dividends to its parent company, a 'group income election' could be made. If an election was made and accepted, the dividend could be paid without the subsidiary having to pay Advance Corporation Tax (ACT). If the election was made, the ACT remained payable but was set off against the later liability to pay mainstream Corporation Tax. The right to make an election was confined under the legislation to situations where the subsidiary and parent companies were 'both bodies corporate resident in the United Kingdom'. The Court of Justice of the European Union held that it was unlawful for UK law to deny the right to make an election where the parent company was resident in a member state other than the UK.[18] Such discrimination contravened freedom of establishment.

The claimant had a German parent company and was part of a group of companies which would have made a group income election if the legislation had allowed them to do so. The effect was that the taxation was paid at an earlier point than it would otherwise have been paid. The claim was for the interest representing this early payment.

The claimant argued that its claim for restitution could be based upon the mistake of law made in paying the tax.[19] If it were correct that their claim could properly be so characterised, this had apparent advantages so far as the applicable limitation period was concerned.

---

[14] (1802) 2 East 469, 102 ER 448.
[15] (1813) 5 Taunt 143, 128 ER 641.
[16] A bar to rescission removed in the context of misrepresentation in England by the Misrepresentation Act 1967, s 1(1)(b), though arguably still operative elsewhere: *Nesbitt v Redican* [1924] SCR 135.
[17] [2006] UKHL 49, [2007] 1 AC 558.
[18] Case C-397/98 *Metallgesellschaft Ltd v Inland Revenue Commissioners IRC and A-G* and Case C-410/98 *Hoechst AG v Inland Revenue Commissioners and A-G* [2001] ECR I-1727.
[19] *Kleinwort Benson v Lincoln City Council* [1999] 2 AC 349 (HL).

The period of limitation is, usually, six years. Time would normally begin to run from the moment at which payment is made. If, however, the claim is for 'relief from the consequences of a mistake' time only starts to run from the moment when the mistake could, with reasonable diligence, have been discovered.[20] The claimant argued that the mistake was discoverable only from the moment of the decision of the Court of Justice, thereby allowing payments which had been made more than six years before the commencement of proceedings to be recovered. The defendant argued that a claim based upon mistake could not be brought, although importantly it was conceded[21] that a claim for restitution was possible. The defendant argued that the only ground of restitution available was that based upon the principle that taxes paid following an *ultra vires* demand were recoverable, recognised by the House of Lords in *Woolwich Equitable Building Society v Inland Revenue Commissioners*[22] (discussed later in this chapter). It was argued that the availability of recovery on this basis excluded recovery on the basis of mistake. If this was correct, payments made more than six years before the commencement of proceedings were irrecoverable.

The argument that the only possible claim for restitution was one based upon *Woolwich*, although it was accepted by the Court of Appeal, was solely based upon a literalist construction of certain statements of Lord Goff in *Kleinwort Benson v Lincoln City Council*.[23] When put in context, these statements clearly could not bear the weight placed upon them, and the House of Lords rejected the defendant's argument.

Unfortunately, the concession by the Revenue that a claim for restitution was available, was incorrectly made. Park J at first instance had concluded that the effect of the decision of the Court of Justice, that it was unlawful to deny the claimant the ability to make a group income election, did not prevent the obligation to pay arising. The election was like a lever which, when pulled, could prevent the obligation from arising. The wrongful denial of the opportunity to elect did not mean that the effect of the Court of Justice's decision was that the claimant should be treated as having pulled that lever. Park J concluded that even though the obligation to pay arose, this did not prevent recovery on the basis of the mistake made by the claimant in not opting to defer. This analysis was explicitly accepted by Lord Hope.[24]

If the legislation under which the tax was collected was, to the extent that it contravened European Union (EU) law, a nullity under UK domestic law, the UK would have done nothing wrongful under EU law, and no claim based upon any 'euro-tort' would be available. A claim for restitution of payments made under the invalid provisions would then be possible. By contrast, if the statute was valid under UK domestic law, its enactment was therefore wrongful under EU law. In such circumstances, a claim for damages for a 'euro-tort' based upon the UK's wrongful behaviour was potentially available.[25] However, no claim for restitution should then be available as any payments would have been made under a valid statute. The two ways of putting the claim are mutually inconsistent one with another: either the Act was wrongful (under EU law) or it was a nullity (under UK domestic law), it could not be both. The correct position is that the enactment was wrongful. The EU

---

[20] Limitation Act 1980, s 32(1)(c).
[21] *Deutsche Morgan Grenfell v Inland Revenue Commissioners* [2007] 1 AC 558, [7], [107] and [135].
[22] [1993] AC 70 (HL).
[23] [1999] 2 AC 349 (HL).
[24] *Deutsche Morgan Grenfell v Inland Revenue Commissioners* [2007] AC 558 (HL), [62].
[25] Case C-46/93 *Brasserie du Pechur* and Case C-48/93 *R v Secretary of State for Transport ex parte Factortame Ltd (No. 4)* [1996] QB 404; *Factortame Ltd v Secretary of State for Transport (No.2)* [1991] 1 AC 603 (HL).

is not a federal state. Under UK domestic law, UK statutes are (were) not invalidated by EU law but could be wrongful.[26]

By contrast, the result reached by the court was that there was a current obligation to pay the tax under domestic law, but that the mistake made in not avoiding the obligation was sufficient to justify recovery. This is the opposite to the conclusion in *Bilbie v Lumley* and is incorrect. What if a UK company with a UK parent company had failed to read section 247 correctly and thought that it could not elect to defer? After paying, could it obtain restitution after realising its mistake? No. Although the money would not have been paid absent the mistake, it was due and, therefore, not recoverable.

Lord Hoffmann described Park J's interpretation of the tax statute as 'rather sophisticated'.[27] He continued that the 'mistake was about whether DMG were liable [to pay the tax]' and that 'the election provisions were purely machinery, which DMG would undoubtedly have used, by which it could enforce its right to exemption from liability'.[28] This is no doubt correct, but does not meet the objection to recovery. It is one thing for a claimant to pay mistakenly thinking that they are liable to do so when that is not the case. It is quite another to mistakenly fail to take steps to prevent a liability from arising. Just as in *Bilbie v Lumley*, both may be loosely described as 'liability mistakes', but in the latter situation there is an obligation to pay, which should bar a claim for restitution to get the payment back. Payments made under a mistake as to liability suffice to justify recovery not because the claimant's consent was vitiated, but because they show that there was no good reason for the payment made: which was not the case in *Deutsche Morgan Grenfell*.

Lord Walker and Lord Brown did not address the issue of whether the tax was still due, unsurprisingly given that counsel had not argued the point. Lord Scott dissented. He accepted Park J's interpretation of the tax legislation and found that whilst the tax had been wrongfully demanded, it was still due and payable. As a result, he correctly concluded that the claim for restitution ought to have failed as a matter of domestic law.

Deutsche Morgan Grenfell was subsequently overruled on a different ground by the Supreme Court.[29] The House of Lords had misread the Limitation Act. Time started to run as soon as the claimant discovered or could with reasonable diligence discover that they had a worthwhile claim. This had probably occurred long before the decision of the Court of Justice. Given Brexit, the same kind of issue can no longer arise. *Deutsche Morgan Grenfell v IRC* is best quietly forgotten.

Another decision in error for the same reason still has the power to do damage. In *International Energy Group v Zurich Insurance*[30] insurers had insured an employer against liability for mesothelioma for six years of an employee's work, out of a total period of 27 years of employment. During the remaining years the employer had 'self insured' (ie had no liability insurance). Because of the exceptional rules on proof of injury that had been created by the *Fairchild v Glenhaven Funeral Services Ltd*[31] exception, the employer was liable in full for any period of exposure to asbestos that created a risk of injuring an employee. This, on its face, entailed that the insurer was under a matching liability under the terms of

---

[26] *R v Secretary of State for Transport ex parte Factortame (No. 5)* [2000] 1 AC 524 (HL).
[27] *Deutsche Morgan Grenfell v Inland Revenue Commissioners* [2007] AC 558 (HL), [32].
[28] ibid.
[29] *Test Claimants in the FII Group Litigation v Revenue and Customs Commrs* [2012] UKSC 19, [2012] 2 AC 337.
[30] [2015] UKSC 33, [2016] AC 509.
[31] [2002] UKHL 22, [2003] 1 AC 32.

the insurance policy for the employer's full liability to the employee, regardless of length of cover, as the insured would be liable in full for any of the relevant periods of insurance.[32]

The insurer sought to recover back from the insured a proportion of the amount it had to pay, by way of a 'contribution'. The insured argued, naturally enough, that to allow such a 'contribution' would contradict their right to payment under the contract. The majority, adopting the analysis of Burrows,[33] allowed this 'contribution' on the basis that there was no hard and fast rule barring recovery back of payments owing under a contract, no policy was thereby violated, and that it was required to do equity between the parties.

The minority reached the same result by construing the contract as not entitling the insured to be paid anything more than a proportionate share of the time insured.

If, as the majority concluded, the insured had a contractual right to be paid the money owed, and no agreed condition for its payment had failed, no claim for restitution should follow. The authorities relied upon for the proposition that money unconditionally payable could be deducted from were *Deutsche Morgan Grenfell* and those of payments made on a conditional basis, where that condition had failed.[34] The reason that there is no 'absolute bright-line principle'[35] barring recovery in the latter kind of case is that the justification for restitution is, as we shall see, entirely different. The former is wrong. Allowing further 'exceptions' based upon vague notions of equity does the law no credit. The best that can be said is that the result was an understandable attempt to escape the logic of the earlier decision in *Fairchild*.

Subsequently the same issue came up in relation to contracts of re-insurance of the same risk. The Court of Appeal refused to follow the Supreme Court's lead and rightly denied restitution.[36] As Leggatt LJ stated, 'allowing an equitable principle or restitutionary claim to override a valid and binding contract should in my view be regarded as an absolutely last resort, if not a counsel of despair'.[37] Although this may be thought to have been a robust approach to the principles of *stare decisis*, in principle it is correct.

4. Gifts, Wills, and Trusts

Gifts obviously differ from contracts because they do not create obligations. Gifts are also different at common law from contracts because they are valid without the need to prove consideration (ie something given in exchange) or many of the other conditions of an enforceable contract (eg intention to create legal relations). At common law, a contract may operate as the vehicle for the conveyance of title to goods sold ('property passes when intended to pass') whereas for a gift either delivery or the use of a deed is necessary. However, contracts and gifts both require an offer and an acceptance. I cannot make a gift to you unilaterally. Camels that I dump in your front garden that are intended as gifts are not yours. You must accept my proffered ungulate in order for there to be a gift. Deeds of gift are valid without any acceptance, but unless and until the donee does something to enforce his

---

[32] *Durham v BAI (Run-Off) Ltd* [2012] UKSC 14, [2012] 1 WLR 867.
[33] Burrows, *The Law of Restitution* (n 10), 88–91.
[34] *International Energy Group v Zurich Insurance* [2015] UKSC 33, [2016] AC 509, [69].
[35] ibid, [68].
[36] *Equitas Insurance Ltd v Municipal Mutual Insurance Ltd* [2019] EWCA Civ 718, [2020] QB 418.
[37] ibid, [145].

rights (eg demands delivery of the camel, title to which the deed conveyed to him), alone the deed has no legal consequence (ie the donor still has a title to the camel good against everyone else).

Wills and trusts, by contrast, do not require any acceptance by the intended beneficiary in order to be valid. If *S* settles the title to Blackacre on *T* to be held on trust for *B*, *B* does not need to accept for there to be a valid trust.[38] He does not even need to know he is a beneficiary. If I leave you title to a camel in my will, you may prevent the conveyance to you by refusing it, but your entitlement to it under the will is valid without any acceptance.

Actions that have legal effects such as these are given the useful label 'juristic acts' in civil law systems. None of them can be set aside because of *any* mistake that the person carrying them out made, in either the common law or civilian systems. For example, for wills a restrictive approach is taken to the kinds of mistake that count. In England a will may only be rectified under section 20 of the Administration of Justice Act 1982 in cases of clerical error or failures to understand the testator's instructions. Mistakes the testator himself makes (eg how deserving his eldest son actually is) are never sufficient.[39] This difference of approach is also seen in relation to undue influence. Although a gift or a contract may be vulnerable to be set aside on the basis of undue influence, in England[40] the circumstances in which a will may be so set aside are much narrower.[41]

This poses a problem for 'vitiation of consent' theory as, on its face, a mistake (or any other 'unjust factor') that leaves another better off ought to suffice. There is no obligation to confer the enrichment, and so whatever the justification for countervailing obligations overriding the restitutionary obligation may be, it cannot apply here.

What kind of mistakes should suffice to set aside a gift? Uninformed by unjust enrichment theory, most of us would accept that if I make a Christmas present to my son, I should not ordinarily be able to recover it on the basis that I would not have done so if I had known of some bad conduct on his part.

In many civilian systems, gifts as a species of agreement, are subject to the same rules for invalidation. Common lawyers do not tend to think in this way, but the same should be true in our systems. The law of contract is a subset of the wider law of agreement, of which gifts also forms a part. Gifts are not unilateral: the donee must *accept* what the donor *offers*. The same kind of rules for invalidation ought presumptively to apply to gifts and contracts, subject to good reasons for any difference.

Drawing by analogy upon the contractual rules, if the donor's mistake is induced by the donee, that should suffice to allow recovery. Where the donor's mistake is not so induced, there is no parallel with the contract cases where performance is impossible (eg because of the subject matter's non-existence). Gifts are executed agreements, after performance they cannot be 'impossible'. However, where the entire purpose of an agreement (whether a contract or a gift) does not exist (as in the Coronation cases in contract[42]) we may say that the

---

[38] See Y Liew and C Mitchell, 'The Creation of Express Trusts' (2017) 11 J of Eq 133.
[39] JR Martin, M Oldham, A Learmonth, and C Ford (eds), *Theobold on Wills* (17th edn, 2010), 3-3016; *Morrell v Morrell* (1882) 7 PD 68, 70–71; *Collins v Elstone* [1893] P 1; *Re Horrocks* [1939] P 198; *Morris, Re* [1971] P 62, 79.
[40] *Cf.* A Kull, *Restatement of the Law (Third) Restitution and Unjust Enrichment*, vol I (2010), § 46.
[41] *Hindson v Weatherill* (1854) 5 De GM & G 301, 43 ER 886; *Parfitt v Lawless* (1872) LR 2 P & D 462; *Boyse v Rossborough* (1857) 6 HLC 3, 10 ER 1192; *Craig v Lamoureux* [1920] AC 349. Discussed P Ridge, 'Equitable Undue Influence and Wills' (2014) 120 LQR 617. But see *Re Edwards* [2007] EWHC 1119 (Lewison J); *Reeves v Drew* [2022] EWHC 159 (Ch) (Green J).
[42] Discussed in Chapter 8, Contract.

agreement does not cover the state of affairs as they are now known to be, and so should be set aside. What the purpose of a gift was is a matter of construction and depends upon the context, just as it does with a contract. Whether a gift can be set aside is dependent upon the purpose of the particular gift in issue, just as whether the hiring of a room may be set aside because of the illness of a King depends upon what the purpose of hiring that particular room was. It is for this reason that Lord Walker in *Pitt v Holt*[43] declined to give a view on brief hypothetical examples of mistakes in making gifts, as the purposes of gifts vary, and the construction of the purpose, like that of a contract, is context dependent. If a gift is made by a donor under the belief that the donee is impecunious, when it would not have been made if the donor had realised that the recipient was rich, what was the purpose of the gift? Was it solely to relieve poverty, or partially given out of friendship?

Because gifts are bilaterally made, a mistake made by the donor alone, which is not shared with or at least known to the donee, ought not in principle to suffice. However, a legal system with a doctrine of consideration may rationally choose to be more relaxed about the invalidation of gifts than of contracts because nothing is given in exchange for them. Instead of the *entire* purpose having to be frustrated, we may choose that the main or central purpose suffices. This was not however the traditional approach. In *Wilson v Thornbury*[44] the donor made a gift to the defendant of £300 upon the latter's marriage. Both parties shared the assumption that the marriage caused the defendant to lose an annuity and the life interest in a house. In fact, she only lost the annuity, as she owned the house. An action to recover the gift was denied. The decision is analogous to those in contract where part of the purpose of the bargain survives, so leaving it on foot.

Further refinements might be possible. If a gift is made by way of deed, the law might say that where this formal step has been taken it should be more reluctant to set aside a gift for mistake, than it is for informal gifts. The formality, demonstrating seriousness and that thought had been taken, might be thought a barrier to recovery. The rule for setting aside the terms of a will is, as we have seen, extremely narrow, but we might justify any difference on the basis that the testator is dead and no longer around to tell us what he meant. Perhaps the rule in relation to wills should be adopted in relation to *inter vivos* gifts by way of deed where the donor has now died?

The above is necessarily speculative, or, more positively, argued through on the basis of principle, because of the paucity of litigated cases. We do however have much more authority in relation to trusts entered into by mistake, and in *Pitt v Holt*,[45] the leading decision in England, Lord Walker assumed that the same principles apply to gifts. As seen, trusts, by contrast with gifts, may be created without any participation by the beneficiary at all. As they are unilaterally created, unilateral mistakes that are not shared by the beneficiaries have always sufficed to have them set aside.[46] It has never been the case however that any mistake that the settlor makes suffices to set aside a trust.[47] *Pitt v Holt* set down a 'serious' mistake test.[48] Lord Walker stated that this seriousness test 'will normally be satisfied only

---

[43] *Pitt v Holt* [2013] UKSC 26, [2013] 2 AC 108, [126].
[44] (1875) LR 10 Ch App 239, but see *Re Glubb, Bamfield v Rogers* [1900] 1 Ch 354, 361 where the view that an innocent misrepresentation could not justify rescission of a gift was disapproved.
[45] [2013] UKSC 26, [2013] 2 AC 108.
[46] Eg *Lady Hood of Avalon v Mackinnon* [1909] 1 Ch 476.
[47] *Ogilvie v Allen* (1899) 15 TLR 294.
[48] See also *Ogilvie v Littleboy* (1897) 13 TKR 399, 400 *per* Lindley LJ.

where there is a mistake either as to the legal character of the transaction, or as to some matter of fact or law which is basic to the transaction'.[49] Again, this will entail a construction of the particular trust instrument to ascertain its purpose in any given case.

On this basis, *Pitt v Holt* itself was exceptional, and generous. The Pitts had set up a discretionary trust for themselves and their children following the significant award of compensation for disabling injuries Mr Pitt had suffered. Unfortunately, because of bad advice the settlement had not been set up in such a way as to avoid inheritance tax. The nominal defendant was a trustee of the settlement (the trustees will have shared the error made) but the true opponent was the Revenue who resisted the avoidance of the settlement. Rescission was awarded, although the mistake made was not as to the legal character of what was done, but rather as to its tax consequences, which must have been perceived as basic. The result is probably justifiable because the entire purpose of the settlement was tax efficiency.[50]

For our purposes, we do not have to improve upon the statement of the law given in *Pitt v Holt*. It suffices to observe that not all gifts made by mistake are recoverable, because there remains a good reason why they are performed unless and until they are set aside. The relevant relief is rescission because a gift (or trust) must be set aside; there is no obligation to make restitution because of the mistaken enrichment of another without more ado.

5. Retrospective Changes

Events that have happened cannot now be changed, absent a time machine. Although the posited law is a matter of fact, its *application* today to events that occurred in the past may differ from the law as it was at the time those events occurred. What the law was, as a matter of fact, cannot change, just like any other fact in the past. But the law may posit today that the rule to be applied to events that occurred yesterday is X, although yesterday when the events occurred the posited law was not-X.

If we think that it is important that people should be able to determine what the law is at the time at which they act, these changes of applicable rules with retrospective application may be deprecated. Indeed, 'retrospective change' by the legislature is relatively rare. In a system of binding precedent, where court decisions create rules which apply to the past, judges must change the law with 'retrospective effect'. This is most obvious when a case is overruled. So, when the House of Lords in *Murphy v Brentwood*[51] overruled their previous decision in *Anns v Merton*[52] they (correctly) changed the positive law not just for the future, but also as the law applies today in relation to events that occurred before their decision. That does not and cannot alter the fact that before *Murphy v Brentwood*, *Anns v Merton* was the law. There were good arguments as to why, as a matter of principle, the law was wrong to posit the rule created by *Anns*. But it did. Law applicable with retrospective effect involves no time machine.

An example of a legislative change with retrospective effect, and the problem this gives rise to for those who think that an error in the head of the payor is the basis of the payee's

---

[49] [2013] UKSC 26, [2013] 2 AC 108, [122].
[50] *Cf.* B Häcker, 'Mistaken Gifts after Pitt v Holt' (2014) 67 CLP 333.
[51] [1991] 1 AC 398 (HL).
[52] [1978] AC 728 (HL).

obligation to him, is the decision of the High Court of Australia in *Commissioner of State Revenue v Royal Insurance Australia Ltd*.[53] The Taxation Acts Amendment Act 1987 (Vict.) sought to amend an oversight in the scope of a tax exemption by extending it, and did so with retrospective effect, deeming the change to have come into force two years earlier than the date of enactment.[54] The plaintiffs sought to recover the tax that was overpaid as a result of this change. Mason CJ stated 'the retrospective operation of [the] Act enables one to say that ... the payments of duty were made under a mistake as to the legal liability to pay them'. This is difficult to understand. The retrospective change had the result that the law as it applies today, to the facts as they occurred in the past, meant that there was no good reason according to the law today for what had happened. There was, however, no error in the mind of the payor at the time they paid. As a matter of fact, the positive law at that time was that they owed the tax. What had once been a good reason had been retrospectively removed, but that cannot create an error in the head of the payor at the time of payment.

The other members of the court did not adopt Mason CJ's analysis. Brennan (with whom Toohey and McHugh JJ agreed) and Dawson JJ denied the existence of any mistake,[55] preferring to see recovery as necessity in order to give effect to the retrospective repeal.

Far more common than legislative changes to the law with retrospective effect are those made by the judges. Whenever a decision involves the overruling of a case, and therefore part of the positive law, a prior rule has been abolished and a new one introduced.

However, it will often be the case that, before a decision, no clear rule existed: that is, there was no binding rule on the point in issue, and no prior case to overturn. The judge who decides the case on the point is then creating a rule where none previously existed. The law has still changed, as applied to past and future events, but through addition. A rule now exists where previously there was none; without subtraction, no prior rule has been abolished. When created, all judge made law therefore has the quality of applying rules to past events, rules that did not exist at the time those events occurred. *How* judges make law, and the reasons judges may legitimately rely upon for changing it, differs from the procedure and legitimate reasons of a legislature, but judges do make law with retrospective application.

The creation of a new rule, with no overturning of a prior one, was probably the effect of the decision in *Hazell v Hammersmith and Fulham London Borough Council*.[56] The House of Lords held, overturning the Court of Appeal below but not any prior authority, that interest rate swap contracts entered into by local authorities were *ultra vires* and void. The law was changed in the sense that before the litigation there was no rule, and now there is.[57]

Interest rates swaps are like gaming contracts, one party paying a fixed rate of interest on a capital sum, the other one that varies with interest rate movements. Local authorities had been attempting to evade caps on their ability to borrow imposed by central government by entering into such bargains, with the counterparty bank usually advancing the payment of its side of the deal upfront. In subsequent litigation after the contracts were found to be void, in *Kleinwort Benson v Lincoln City Council*,[58] the issue arose as to whether the banks could recover the payments that they had made. The plaintiffs sought to argue that they had

---

[53] [1994] HCA 61, (1994) 182 CLR 151.
[54] Taxation Acts Amendment Act (Vict.), s 2(4).
[55] [1994] HCA 61, (1994) 182 CLR 151, [16].
[56] [1992] 2 AC 1 (HL).
[57] *Cf. Kleinwort Benson v Lincoln City Council* [1999] 2 AC 349, 411 *per* Lord Hope.
[58] [1999] 2 AC 349 (HL).

been mistaken in order (again) to take advantage of the more generous limitation period that applies where the litigant seeks 'relief from the consequence of a mistake'. (The Supreme Court has subsequently affirmed that the House of Lord had been correct to apply this provision to mistakes of law.) Whether a claim could succeed depended upon whether a claim based upon a mistake of law was permissible. The trial judge had held that he was bound (by, amongst other cases, *Bilbie v Lumley* above) that it was not, and permission was granted to appeal to the House of Lords on this issue. A majority (Lords Goff, Hoffmann, and Hope; Lords Browne-Wilkinson and Lloyd dissenting) allowed the appeal.

The issue of whether, on the facts, the plaintiffs were mistaken was not therefore resolved, but it is possible to argue that they were. The contracts had (eventually) been entered into on the basis of advice from senior counsel that they were valid. It could be said that the banks had paid on the belief that there was a rule to that effect, when in fact until *Hazell* was decided there was no rule at all on the validity of such contracts.

What if, in deciding *Hazell*, the House of Lord had overturned clear ultimate appellate court authority existing before they were entered into that the contracts had been valid? In such circumstances it would no longer be possible to state that any mistake had been made. The rule at the time of payment would have been that performance was due under a valid contract. How a court may legitimately decide to overturn prior authority may be different from the reasons a legislature may invoke in doing so, but there is still a change from one rule to another however it is effected. Should recovery therefore be denied?

It would be unacceptable if it were, even though a payor who pays upon the basis of clear ultimate appellate court authority that they must do so is not making any mistake as to what the law is. The only exception is where that decision is given without relevant binding authority having been cited to the court (ie it is *per incuriam* and so not the law). Otherwise, a court decision is the positive law. There is no shadow law, un-posited existing somewhere in the ether. To think otherwise is to misunderstand the authority of courts to state what the law is. It is astonishing if judges, of all people, make such an error as to the power they wield.

This is not, as is sometimes said, a problem of discoverability of the mistake.[59] Rather, there is no mistake at all.

If a binding rule requiring payment is subsequently overturned (whether by the legislature or a subsequent court) the payor who pays prior to the change is *more* deserving than a party who pays on the uncertain authority of advice from counsel backed up by no judicial or legislative authority. The latter 'mistaken' party might be characterised as having made a voluntary payment, knowing that there was no clear rule one way or the other. The party who pays upon the basis of clear authority, that is subsequently overturned, has not even arguably consented to the state of affairs they now find themselves in. They were also not mistaken.

We might, following Lord Hoffmann, be prepared to speak of a 'deemed' mistake where a rule relied upon is overturned with retrospective effect,[60] but this is a fiction, showing that an actual mistake is not the reason for recovery. The more authoritative the legal source positing the duty to pay, the more deserving the payor is if this is overturned with retrospective effect, but also the more implausible the 'mistake' analysis becomes.

---

[59] *ibid*, 411 *per* Lord Hope.
[60] *ibid*, 400.

A decision illustrating the unacceptable results of seeing the mistake of the claimant as being the operative fact that justifies recovery is that of the Privy Council in *Samsoondar v Capital Insurance Co Ltd*.[61]

The claimant was the third-party loss insurer of the defendant's vehicle. The policy between them was 'owner driver only'. In 2005, the defendant's lorry was in an accident damaging a third party's vehicle, whilst being driven by an employee of the defendant. The defendant sent a claim form under the insurance policy, and the claimants informed the defendant that they were settling the matter with the third party, but that he would have to pay the excess, which he did. In a judgment of 9 June 2006, *Selwyn Benjamin v Stephen*[62] Kokaram J had held that 'owner driver only' policies covered cases of those driving with the permission of the driver, such as this one. By a letter of 10 April 2007, the claimants disputed their liability under the policy on the basis that the defendant had not been personally driving, but then on 21 June 2007 informed the defendant that they had paid $43k in settlement of the claim. In 2012 the Privy Council in *President Insurance Co Ltd v Resha St Hill*[63] overturned the earlier interpretation of policies of this kind, so that cover did not extend to drivers authorised by the owner.

Amongst a number of other claims, the claimants sought restitution of the money paid. The Privy Council overturned the Trinidad and Tobago Court of Appeal and wrongly denied this claim, with the advice of the court given by Lord Burrows.

A complicating distraction is that the payment under the contract was received by the third party whose vehicle was damaged. As we have seen however, the relevant performance the claimant made was to the defendant counterparty under the contract of insurance between them. The claimants were, at the request of the defendant, performing their contractual obligations to them. Just as where a bank makes a payment authorised by its customer to a third party, where it does so by mistake the correct defendant (if any) is its customer, not the third party. The same was true in this case. There were two transactions. The insurer was performing its contractual obligations to its counterparty. The defendant was paying the third party, through its insurer, the money it owed because of the tort. The letter of 10 April initially disputing liability did not end either the request to perform, or the authority to do so. There was therefore a performance, a payment, from the claimant to the defendant. On its face, it was for no good reason. Why then was recovery denied?

The court ruled out the claim on the basis that the claimants had not pleaded and proved that they were making a mistake. Why had they not done so? For the obvious reason that they were not. They had alleged, as Narine JA had stated in the Court of Appeal, that they paid because of their 'inability ... on the state of the law as it then stood, to avoid payment of the third party's claim'. They had paid because the positive law in 2007 in Trinidad and Tobago *was* that they were obliged to do so.

This was a small claim, $43,500. Those responsible for the pleadings just pleaded the facts as they were. Unversed in 'unjust enrichment' theory, they had no idea that they were expected to invoke a fictional 'mistake'. They just told the truth: they paid because that is what the positive law in 2007 was, and now the applicable law has changed so that the defendant

---

[61] [2020] UKPC 33, [2021] 2 All ER 1105.
[62] *Selwyn Benjamin v Stephen Jairam and Ors* HCS 1104/2000.
[63] [2012] UKPC 33, [2021] 2 All ER 1105.

is not entitled to the payment made. Here 'vitiation of consent' theory is giving rise to injustice, and the claim should have succeeded.

6. Corporate Mistakes

Corporations do not have any physical existence in space. They are legal constructs. The actions of real-world persons may be attributed to a corporation, so that it can sign a contract, commit a tort, or occupy land through them, but alone it can do nothing. Similarly, the states of mind of real-world persons may, for the purpose of legal rules, be attributed to a corporation, but alone it cannot know or intend anything.

One approach for attributing knowledge of an individual to a corporation is to ask who is its 'directing mind and will',[64] most obviously a company's Chief Executive Officer. In cases such as *Barclays Bank v Simms*[65] however, the mistake in paying was made by a lowly employee who overlooked a stop instruction. How could their mistake be attributed to Barclays Bank plc? What if the Chief Executive Officer had known that the money was not due, only the low-level employee making any error, would that mean that Barclays made no mistake?[66]

We might adopt a different attribution test, and ask whether the knowledge was material to the agent's performance of his duties to his principal.[67] This might then allow us to attribute the error of the low-level employee to the payor corporation. This approach then creates a larger difficulty. What if the clerk had paid knowing that the money was not due? Should his state of mind still be attributed to the corporation, so that no recovery is then possible? What if the payment had occurred because computer software had become corrupted, so that no real-world person made any identifiable mistake?

If a payment is made to which the payee is not entitled recovery should follow, without the necessity of identifying and attributing any mistake of an employee to the corporate entity. The mistake of the clerk in *Barclays Bank v Simms* showed that there was no good reason for the payment, not that Barclays Bank plc had a mistaken intention. If a low-level employee pays knowing that the money is not due, this alone should also not bar recovery.

7. 'Spent' Mistakes

An example:

> A father declares a trust for his daughter of £100,000 for the sole reason that he believes that she has just got married. In fact, the daughter is unmarried. Shortly after the trust is set up however the daughter meets the partner of her dreams, and after a whirlwind romance, marries. The father now seeks to set aside the trust.

---

[64] *El Ajou v Dollar Land Holding plc* [1994] BCC 143 (CA).
[65] [1980] QB 677 (Robert Goff J).
[66] *Cf. Anglo-Scottish Beet Sugar Corp v Spalding UDC* [1937] 2 KB 607 (Atkinson J).
[67] *Cf.* American Law Institute, *Restatement (Third) of the Law of Agency* (2007) §5.03; *Meridian Global Funds Management v Securities Commission* [1995] UKPC 5, [1995] 2 AC 500; R Leow, *Corporate Attribution in Private Law* (2022), ch 6.

The father should not be able to do so. Although the mistake may have been sufficiently serious to set aside the trust at the time of creation, the father now finds himself in exactly the same position he would have been in if he had made no mistake in the first place. He consented to the current state of affairs, and no rescission should be awarded as he is undeserving of the law's assistance.[68]

The same kind of problem arose in *Sharma v Simposh*.[69] The claimants paid £55,000 under an oral agreement for an option to purchase a block of flats. The defendants agreed in return to complete redevelopment, refrain from selling to anyone else, and to give the claimants the option to purchase for £11 million. The market then fell, and the claimants decided not to go through with the deal and sought to recover their payment. Under section 2 of the Law of Property (Miscellaneous Provisions) Act 1989 such contracts are void unless signed and in writing. The Court of Appeal found that the claimants had 'got what they paid for' and so could not recover.[70] Would it have made any difference if the claimants had alleged that they had known nothing of section 2 of the Law Reform (Miscellaneous Provisions) Act, had thought the agreement was enforceable, and would never have paid upfront if they had realised they acquired no legal rights to performance from the counterparty?

This should make no difference at all. The claimants now find themselves in exactly the position they bargained for. They have consented. That at some point in the past they could not have enforced the counter-performance they have now received is irrelevant. They are now in the same position as if they could have done so, and the mistake should not suffice.[71] Similarly, at one time gaming contracts were void under legislation. Fully executed gaming contracts could not be reversed. 'Stakes' were expressly stated to be irrecoverable,[72] and if a bookmaker paid out winnings he had consented to the position he found himself in.

If this is correct, does it call into question *Kleinwort Benson v Lincoln City Council*? In that case, the swaps contracts had been fully executed. They had been closed out, with no further payments due. Each party had on its face received exactly what they bargained for. It appeared as if the parties now found themselves in exactly the same position as they would have been in if the contracts had been valid. Should this have barred recovery?

That it should not (and did not) is based upon the different reason for invalidity. The bargains were void because the councils lacked the capacity to enter into contracts of this kind. They were in the same position as very small children who sell their toys. This incapacity meant that they, unlike the buyers in *Sharma*, could not validly consent. They were not therefore barred from recovery.

What of the position of the banks where (unusually) they had lost under the 'bet' as to the movement of interest rates once the contract had been fully performed? Where, as in *Kleinwort Benson* itself, they sought restitution, they did not lack capacity, and so had they not consented to the position they now found themselves in?

Although it superficially appeared that they were, in reality they were not. The banks had entered into these deals in order to make money. Usually, their judgement as to the future movement of interest rates under swap agreements proves superior to that of their counterparties, and so they win. In these cases, they never had the opportunity to win. Any

---

[68] *Cf.* invalid payments by corporations, Chapter 4, Reversal.
[69] [2011] EWCA Civ 1383, [2012] 2 All ER (Comm) 288.
[70] *ibid*, [26], [57].
[71] *Tootal Clothing v Guinea Property Management Ltd* (1992) 64 P & CR 452 (CA), 455.
[72] Gaming Act 1845, s 18 (repealed by the Gambling Act 2005, s 335(1)).

payments they received would have to be returned to the local authority. If the local authorities could always recover when it had lost, so too should the banks be able to do so when it did.

Identical in structure is the old decision of the Court of Appeal in *Re Phoenix Life Assurance Co.*[73] An insurance company received premiums under marine insurance contracts. These contracts were *ultra vires* and, as the law then stood, consequently void. It was not alleged that any insured event had occurred. Recovery of the premiums was allowed: the insurer had never been 'on risk' (ie it could always have recovered any payments that it made because it could not validly consent to them). For many years, it was doubtful whether this decision represented the law in England as being difficult to reconcile with *Sinclair v Brougham*.[74] With the disapproval of that case, we can now once again say that *Re Phoenix Life* is good law.[75]

8. The '*Woolwich* Principle'

In the common law, when a legal doctrine is not understood, we adopt three different techniques in giving it a label. The first is to use Latin (eg *res ipsa loquitur, res inter alios acta*). The second is to use antique French (eg 'torts', 'estoppel'). The third is to use the name of the case that is said to have originated it (eg 'the rule in *Rylands v Fletcher*'). The '*Woolwich* Principle' is an example of the third.[76]

The Inland Revenue demanded that the Woolwich Building Society pay them £57 million in tax. The Society denied that they were liable to pay the tax but paid 'without prejudice to any right to recover the payments'. In subsequent proceedings for judicial review, it was established that the Regulations under which the tax was payable were *ultra vires*, and void. The Revenue accepted that they were obliged to repay the capital sum but denied that there was any obligation upon them to do so from the outset.[77] The Society argued that there was a right to restitution as soon as payment was made, so that they were entitled to statutory interest upon the capital sum from that moment. By a majority, the House of Lords upheld the Society's claim.

The basis for restitution could not be 'mistake' as the Society had strongly denied that they were obliged to pay from the outset. No illegitimate pressure had been applied to them, court proceedings being a legitimate way of settling any dispute. Seen as a case of a contractually agreed right to repayment, if the payor's contention that the tax was not due was upheld, time would only start to run for purposes of interest from the moment of successful judicial review proceedings, and not from the earlier point of payment. The court held that 'money paid by a citizen to a public authority in the form of taxes or other levies paid pursuant to an ultra vires demand by the authority is prima facie recoverable'.[78]

---

[73] *Phoenix Life Insurance Co. Re Burges and Stock's Case* (1862) 2 J&H 441, 70 ER 1131.
[74] [1914] AC 398, (HL).
[75] For earlier examples see *Stevenson v Snow* (1761) 3 Burr 1237, 97 ER 808 and *Tyrie v Fletcher* (1777) 2 Cowp 666, 98 ER 1297.
[76] *Woolwich Equitable BS v IRC* [1993] 1 AC 70 (HL).
[77] Cf. *Sebel Products Ltd v Customs and Excise Commissioners* [1949] Ch 409 (Vaisey J).
[78] *Woolwich Equitable BS v IRC* [1993] 1 AC 70, 177 per Lord Goff.

One way of viewing cases such as these is that they are part of 'public law' and so cannot be used for purposes of understanding 'private law'. This gains some support from the approach of the Supreme Court of Canada in *Kingstreet Investments Ltd v New Brunswick (Department of Finance)*[79] where a similar claim was said to be *sui generis* and based upon the constitutional principle that taxes should not be levied without proper authority.

No doubt the claims are part of 'public law' in the sense that the defendant is part of the state. They are also part of 'public law' in the sense that whether a tax statute is constitutionally valid or whether a taxing regulation made under a statute is within the *vires* of the relevant public body, is a public law issue. How could it be otherwise? However, once the public law issue of validity has been answered, there is nothing particularly 'public' involved in the question of whether money paid that is not due (or, more generally, a performance rendered for no good reason) should be reversed.

At the time it was decided, it was plausible to explain the *Woolwich* Principle in terms of a policy of ensuring that public bodies behaved lawfully, characterised by the slogan that there should be 'no taxation without the authority of Parliament'. Since it was decided however, the possible restrictions on the '*Woolwich* Principle' have been washed away, because unjustifiable, making this interpretation unrealistic. So, if a valid tax regulation is misconstrued, rather than being *ultra vires*, payments that are not due are recoverable.[80] The rule also now goes beyond taxes so as to include, for example, sex shop licence fees[81] but it would seem difficult to explain why one kind of payment is within, and another without. Further the '*Woolwich* Principle' probably applies to utility companies, universities, and other bodies with a public flavour, but there seems no principled basis for drawing a line between the public and private defendants.

Most importantly, the possible requirement of a demand has been rejected by the Supreme Court in *Test Claimants in the FII Litigation v HMRC (No 1)*.[82] That court retained a requirement that the state must, in some sense, have stated that the payment was owing,[83] so that an overpayment in cases of self-assessment would not be covered,[84] but it is difficult to see what the principled basis for any such restriction might be.[85] Once the need to show any prior action on the part of the public body making them responsible for the payment made falls away, seeing the claim as based upon the need to regulate the state goes with it.

Explaining recovery as based upon 'public policy' not only requires the drawing of lines that cannot be rationally drawn, doing a legal system no credit, but also gives counter-intuitive results. If, for example, the Woolwich Building Society had paid knowing that the tax was not due without also stating that it did so 'without prejudice', no recovery should follow, although the 'public policy' would still seem to apply. They would have consented. Conversely, if a payment is made following a demand by a private defendant, which it is subsequently shown was not owed, as it was in *CTN Cash and Carry Ltd v Gallaher Ltd*,[86] restitution should follow *if* the payor pays 'without prejudice to any right to recover'.

---

[79] [2007] SCC 1, [2007] 1 SCR 3.
[80] *British Steel plc v Customs and Excise Commrs* [1997] 2 All ER 366 (CA).
[81] *R (Hemmings t/a Simply Pleasures Ltd) v Westminster CC* [2013] EWCA Civ 591.
[82] [2012] UKSC 19, [2012] 2 AC 337.
[83] ibid, [174] *per* Lord Sumption.
[84] ibid, [186] *per* Lord Sumption.
[85] Mitchell, Mitchell, and Watterson, *Goff & Jones: The Law of Unjust Enrichment* (n 8), [22-20]; *Kingstreet Investments Ltd v New Brunswick (Department of Finance)* [2007] SCC 1; [2007] 1 SCR 3, [53].
[86] [1994] 4 All ER 714 (CA).

It would be better to accept that if a payment is made to the defendant to which he is not entitled it is recoverable, without attempting to pointlessly demarcate the boundaries of the '*Woolwich* Principle'.

9. The Invention of 'Unjust Factors'

The '*Woolwich* Principle' is an example of the need to invent specific grounds for recovery to explain away instances of restitution based upon the general principle that payments that are not due are recoverable.

Another example is the recovery of payments made under court orders that are subsequently reversed. The reversal means that there is no longer any good reason for the payment made, and there is no need to search for a public policy explanation for restitution, and until recently nobody had thought to try. As Lord Leggatt has stated 'there is no need to look for any reason to justify restitution beyond the fact that the appellate court has decided that, on a true view of the law and the facts, the order appealed from should not have been made'.[87]

Other examples are the chapters in textbooks dedicated to 'ignorance'[88] and 'powerlessness'.[89] The reason the courts have not recognised such 'unjust factors' is that a payment or other performance must be volitional. A claimant cannot render a performance in a state of ignorance or powerlessness.

Another example:

> The Chief Executive Officer (CEO) of *P plc* purports to negotiate on behalf of the company for the purchase of widgets from *D*. The agreed price is £100 million, several times greater than the market value of the goods. The contract is performed. After the removal of the CEO, *P plc* seeks to recover the payment made under the contract.

Whether the payments can be recovered is determined by whether the contract is valid. This in turn is determined by whether the CEO had the actual or ostensible authority to enter into it on *P plc*'s behalf. In cases of extreme undervalue such as this, the counterparty either knows or ought to know of the CEO's want of actual authority, so that no valid contract has been created. Absent a contract, there is no good reason for any payment made, and restitution follows.

We cannot explain recovery in such cases as based upon 'mistake'. The person whose knowledge is usually attributed to a company, traditionally said to be its 'controlling mind', is the CEO, who is making no mistake.

Some explain cases such as these as based upon 'want of authority',[90] but this is not a state of mind that 'vitiates' consent to an enrichment, but rather a reason why a *contract* or other transaction is invalid, so as to provide no good reason for any performance rendered under

---

[87] *Delta Petroleum (Caribbean) Ltd v British Virgin Islands Electricity Corporation (British Virgin Islands)* [2020] UKPC 23, [50].
[88] Eg Burrows, *The Law of Restitution* (n 10), ch 16.
[89] Eg Edelman and Bant, *Unjust Enrichment* (n 11), ch 12, III.
[90] R Chambers and J Penner, 'Ignorance' in J Edelman and S Degeling (eds), *Unjust Enrichment in Commercial Law* (2008), 174. See also R Goff and G Jones, *Goff and Jones: The Law of Restitution* (7th edn, 2007), ch 22.

it. The payment itself must be authorised in order for the problem of having to obtain restitution of it to arise. If the payment *itself* has been purportedly made without the actual or ostensible authority of those in charge of the company, it has never been made by the company. If those without actual or apparent authority to do so instruct the company's bank to make a payment on the company's behalf, if the bank makes the payment it cannot debit its customer's account.

10. Mispredictions

The theory that recovery of a mistaken payment is based upon 'vitiation of consent' requires the drawing of a line between mistakes and mispredictions, that is, between errors about the present and the future. This is based upon the idea that someone who acts on a prediction about the future runs the risk that they may be wrong and are therefore undeserving of being relieved of a risk knowingly taken.[91]

This distinction was adopted judicially in the decision of the Privy Council in *Dextra Bank & Trust Co Ltd v Bank of Jamaica*,[92] which is wrongly decided. The claimants paid the defendants just short of US$3 million. They did so because they had been induced to believe by a fraudster that they were entering into a loan with the recipient. The fraudster also deceived the recipient into believing that they were entering into a contract for the sale of Jamaican dollars of equivalent value. The court rejected the claim for repayment on the basis that the claimants were merely making a misprediction as to whether a loan would result, which was a result of a misprediction as to whether the fraudster would obey its instructions.

The instability of the distinction is apparent from these facts. Why could it not be said that the mistake was as to the honesty of the intermediary? The premise for drawing the distinction, that the future is so inherently uncertain that decisions based upon it are ones where we always assume the risk of being wrong, is false. All other things being equal, the future will tend to be more uncertain than the present, but this is not a universal truth. I am producing this work on the basis that the sun will rise tomorrow, an event I have no doubt will occur. Conversely the quantum of oil still unextracted under the North Sea is very uncertain, although it is a present fact.

In *Dextra Bank* there was not, as things turned out, any good reason for the payment made and restitution should have followed. The payment executed on the belief that a loan would be subsequently entered into, when it was not, should have sufficed to show that it was made for no good reason.

Earlier authority had not drawn the distinction relied upon. In the House of Lords decision in *Kerrison v Glyn Mills Currie & Co*[93] the plaintiff was the manager in England of a Mexican mine. They were obliged to reimburse New York bankers who honoured cheques drawn by the manager of the mine in Mexico. They were to do this by paying the correspondent bank in London. In anticipation of such obligation, the plaintiff paid to the defendants £500. He did so in the mistaken belief that he would, in the future, be obliged

---

[91] P Birks, *An Introduction to the Law of Restitution* (rev edn, 1989), 147.
[92] [2002] 1 All ER (Comm) 193 (PC).
[93] (1911) 81 LJKB 465. See also Goff and Jones, *Goff and Jones: The Law of Restitution* (n 90), [4-4011].

to reimburse future drawings. In fact, the New York bankers had committed an act of bankruptcy, and so no such reimbursement obligation would ever accrue. Restitution was awarded.

It might be argued that the plaintiffs were making a mistake of present fact (whether the bankers had committed an act of bankruptcy). On its own, however, that did not show that there was no good reason for the payment. If I owe money to a bankrupt, and pay him, it cannot be recovered, even if I would not have done so if I had known of his act of bankruptcy (because eg I would have wished to exercise a right of set off). In *Kerrison v Glynn Mills Currie & Co* what showed the lack of entitlement to the money was that it was paid in anticipation of an obligation that it was mistakenly believed would accrue in the future. This is identical in form to the mistaken belief that there would be a loan in *Dextra Bank*.

11. Different Causal Rules

The claim that restitution is based upon the lack of, or defect in, the consent of the plaintiff to the defendant's enrichment, is based upon the idea that the 'unjust factor', such as a mistake, *caused* the enrichment.[94] This is to misunderstand the different causal rules that there are and ought to be.

Where mistake is serving the purpose of *negativing* the existence of a good reason for a payment, it is necessary to show that the mistake as to whether an obligation was owed *caused* the payment, because this shows that this bad reason was the explanation for what happened. If the mistake did not cause the payment, it may well have been a good reason that did. Exactly the same is true where we rely upon other bad reasons for a payment made. So, in *Maskell v Horner*[95] showing that the payments were made *because* of the illegitimate threats demonstrated that they were not made for a good reason, and it was the difference of opinion as to what caused the payment that had divided Rowlatt J and the Court of Appeal.

When we *nullify* an otherwise valid contract (or a gift) because of a mistake or the application of duress in entering into it, we do not always require it to be shown that they caused the contract to be entered into, still less that they caused the performance rendered under those contracts. The rule in relation to induced mistakes is (in Equity) a generous one. A misstatement is material, and so sufficient for rescission, if it is 'actively present to the mind'[96] of the party to whom it was made, at least where the statement is fraudulent.[97] If it is, rescission is possible even though the contract would have been entered into absent the misrepresentation. Similarly, a contract may be rescinded for duress without needing to show that the contract would not have been entered into but for the illegitimate pressure,[98] at least in cases of duress to the person.[99]

In the context of mistakes that prevent a contract (or a gift) from being formed, causation plays no part in the analysis. For example:

---

[94] Eg see Burrows, *The Law of Restitution* (n 10), 207–217.
[95] [1915] 3 KB 106.
[96] *Edgington v Fitzmaurice* (1885) 29 Ch D 459 (CA), 483 *per* Bowen LJ.
[97] *BV Nederlandse Industrie can Eiproducktion v Rembrandt Enterprises Inc* [2020] QB 551, [2019] EWCA Civ 596, [2020] QB 551.
[98] *Barton v Armstrong* [1976] AC 104 (PC).
[99] *Dimskal Shipping Co SA v International Transport Workers Federation (The Evia Luck (No 2))* [1992] 2 AC 152, 165 *per* Lord Goff; *Huyton SA v Peter Cremer GmbH* [1999] 1 Lloyd's Rep 620, 636 *per* Mance J.

X, a rogue, writes to *P* misrepresenting that he is *Y*, a reputable businessman operating out of new premises. *P* agrees to deliver 1,000 widgets to *X*'s premises on credit terms, believing that he is contracting with *Y*. After delivery, *X* sells on the goods to *D* and disappears.

If the identity of the counterparty forms part of *P*'s offer to contract, as here, there is no contract between *P* and *X*. *P*'s offer was made to *Y*, and so could only be accepted by *Y*. No title to the goods has therefore passed, and *P* may recover them from *D*. (Sometimes we do not offer to contract with specific individuals, usually and most obviously when shop owners agree to sell goods to customers face to face.) The analysis does not change if *P* would have entered into the same contract with *X* in any event. This cannot alter the fact that no such contract was ever entered into. The counterfactual position is irrelevant.

A similar analysis applies in cases of incapacity and undue influence. Where the want of capacity renders an agreement a nullity, and not merely unenforceable, it should not matter whether the want of capacity caused any performance rendered. In *Kleinwort Benson v Lincoln City Council* it should not matter whether the council would have entered into the same contract, and paid the same amounts as they did, if they had had the capacity to do so (as, on the facts, no doubt, they would have done).

Similarly:

C settles a large amount of property on *D*, a religious order of which he has recently become a member. *C* is in thrall to the charismatic religious leader of *D*. Payments have been made under the settlement that *C* now wishes to recover.

Again, if the settlement can be set aside because of undue influence, payments made under it should be capable of being recovered. It should not (and does not) need to be proven whether the same settlement would not, as a counterfactual matter, have been made independently of any undue influence. The relationship of undue influence creates a bilateral incapacity to enter into certain kinds of transaction. If the contract or gift can be nullified, no causal question then arises.

C. Comparisons

The account of the common law rules offered so far has a strong family relation to the same body of rules found in civilian jurisdictions. The usual story that is told is quite different: that the common law adopts a different approach of looking for specific 'unjust factors' whilst the civilian approach is to adopt a broader 'absence of basis' or 'lack of juristic reason' approach.[100]

The usual comparative account appears plausible because it is reflected in other bodies of rules in private law. In the context of 'good faith' in contracting, for example, it is often said that civilian jurisdictions adopt a general rule, subject to exceptions, whereas the common law has 'characteristically'[101] developed a number of more piecemeal solutions, in relation to penalties, exemption clauses, and unconscionable bargains. Similarly, the Anglo-common

---

[100] Eg T Krebs, *Restitution at the Crossroads: A Comparative Study* (2001), 1.
[101] *Interfoto Picture Library Ltd v Stiletto Visual Programmes Ltd* [1989] QB 433 (CA), 439 *per* Bingham LJ.

law world has no general 'abuse of rights' doctrine, unlike many civilian jurisdictions,[102] but does have a group of more specific 'economic torts' that cover much the same field. We can either start with a general principle and carve out exceptions, or instead have many specific rules. Does it matter if we all muddle through to much the same result?

In the area of 'unjust enrichment', however, two incompatible *explanations* for the results we wish to reach are in competition with one another. Is recovery of a sum of money that is mistakenly paid when not due based upon the error in the mind of the plaintiff, or the absence of any good objective reason for having been made? These two explanations give different, incompatible, results. It would be extremely surprising if the same large body of rules had arisen independently of one another in different jurisdictions with completely different underlying justifications. One of these explanations is wrong.

Not only is the 'vitiation of consent' explanation unsatisfactory in principle, it has never accurately represented the common law position. The proper role of mistake, duress, and undue influence has never been to show that the plaintiff's consent to the defendant's enrichment has been vitiated.

D. Birks' Last Work

In his final book, Birks sought to argue that the English law of unjust enrichment had fundamentally changed as a result of a 'cataclysm': the series of cases concerning void interest rate swaps in the 1990s. He argued that (almost)[103] all of the law he had previously described in one way was now better understood in a new one. He did not claim that his earlier account was wrong, or that it had a poor fit with the positive law as it then was. Rather he claimed that the positive law had been changed by the judges.

This was a far-fetched argument. Judges are not legislators. Although it is not unknown for them to engage in the wholesale re-writing of an area of law[104] this is rarely a legitimate exercise of their power. To have done so *sub silentio* would have been very surprising. To have done so whilst expressly disavowing any intention to effect any change would have been utterly extraordinary. In common law jurisdictions outside of England, such as Australia, that had never had the equivalent of the swaps litigation, the idea that their law needed to be radically reconfigured was even less plausible. Further, even in England, the reasoning of the leading cases following the swaps litigation was inconsistent with Birks' new account.[105] The new version looked dramatically different from the old. This made it too easy to dismiss what he had written, and no textbook writers in England or elsewhere in the common law have followed him.

The truth was more prosaic. The earlier account was wrong. The original error in analysis was caused, in part, by the old 'mistake of law' bar. This apparent rule, that payments made because of a mistake of law were irrecoverable, appeared to lead to the result that

---

[102] BGB § 226.
[103] The exception was the area covered in civilian law by the *actio negotiorum gestio contraria* as these are claims for compensation for expenditure—see P Birks, *Unjust Enrichment* (2nd edn, 2005), 22–23—which Birks had previously sought to explain as a claim for restitution based upon 'moral compulsion' (see Birks, *An Introduction to the Law of Restitution* (n 91), 193–203.
[104] Eg *Patel v Mirza* [2016] UKSC 42, [2017] AC 467.
[105] Eg *Kleinwort Benson v Lincoln CC* [1999] 2 AC 349 (HL).

payments not due were not always actionable in England. The reasons for such a bar to recovery (eg 'ignorance of the law is no excuse') were never persuasive, and as we have seen, the leading cases that were said to have introduced the 'bar'[106] were rightly decided, but on other grounds.

Birks had misidentified the different roles that 'mistake' and other 'unjust factors' played in the common law. This error was revealed by the swaps litigation, where it was not possible to explain recovery where the applicable law changed with retrospective effect as based upon an error in the mind of the payor. He then downplayed the role of 'mistake' and other 'vitiating factors' in his final work, giving the impression that a dramatic change of approach was required.

A new error was then introduced. Birks claimed that almost all of the material in the books on restitution could be explained on the basis of a single simple principle: that any enrichment at another's expense for which there was no basis is recoverable. No civilian jurisdiction adopts such a broad approach. Section 812 of the *Bürgerliches Gesetzbuch* (the German Civil Code) on the face of the text adopts a rule coming close to this position, but in fact that is not the law.[107] Other authors rightly saw that there were several other reasons for the defendant's obligation to make restitution, in the jargon different 'unjust factors'. Unfortunately, they have persisted in arguing that many of these reasons are found in the mind of the plaintiff.

The common law should and does allow recovery of 'a payment to which the defendant is not entitled', and this is a *species* of the *genus* of unjustified performance. We now turn to the next largest category of claim.

---

[106] *Bilbie v Lumley* (1802) 2 East 469, 102 ER 448; *Brisbane v Dacres* (1813) 5 Taunt 143, 128 ER 641.
[107] See the important article by N Jansen, 'Farewell to Unjustified Enrichment?' (2016) 20 Ed LR 123 and Chapter 20, Conclusion.

PART III
CONDITIONAL PERFORMANCE

7
Conditions

A. A New Justification

An example:

> In exchange for *D*'s promise to repair the roof of *P*'s house before the winter, *P* agrees to pay *D* £10,000, payment to be made in advance of the work being done. *P* pays, but *D* never does the work.[1]

D must make restitution of the payment made to *P*.[2] One way of explaining this, in accordance with the previous chapters, is that although *D* may have been initially entitled to the payment under the bargain, he no longer is. Although there may once have been a good reason for the payment (the agreement) now the bargain no longer supports it and so restitution follows. In English, if not always in contract law, 'consideration' is synonymous with 'reason' and so rights to restitution created by a 'failure of consideration' for a payment arise because of the failure of the reason for it.

However, an additional justification is created by the agreement between the parties. The parties have agreed that the entitlement to the payment was subject to the condition that the work would be done. Once that condition has failed, reversal of the payment is required because not to do so would be contrary to the agreement between them. Without restitution, a payment agreed to be conditional would become an unconditional one. Usually, but not always, the agreement is an exchange and the condition specified is counter-performance by the other party. The classic statement of this idea in England is that of Lord Wright:[3]

> The payment was originally conditional. The condition of retaining it is eventual performance. Accordingly, when the condition fails, the right to retain the money must simultaneously fail.

Does this additional, new justification for the duty make any difference to the analysis? Two examples side by side:

> *P* mistakenly pays *D* £10,000 that he does not owe. *D*, innocently believing that he is entitled to the payment, spends the money on a holiday for himself and his family that he would not otherwise have been able to afford.
>
> *P* pays *D* a builder £10,000 in advance under a contract. *D* promises to repair the roof of *P*'s house before the winter in exchange. *D*, expecting to do the work the following month,

---

[1] Do not pay builders upfront.
[2] *Giles v Edwards* (1797) 7 TR 181, 101 ER 920 (KB).
[3] *Fibrosa Spolka Akcyjna v Fairbairn Lawson Combe Barbour* Ltd [1943] AC 32, 65.

spends the money on a holiday for himself and his family that he would not otherwise have been able to afford. *D* never does the work.

In both cases the defendant has spent the money received in good faith. In the first example we may choose to allow *D* a defence of change of position to ensure that he is not left worse off. Although the payment was made for no reason, the law may choose to excuse *D* from making restitution. In the second we should not (and do not) allow such a defence. To do so would be to re-write the parties' bargain. Instead of a payment that is conditional upon the work being done, it becomes a payment that is conditional upon the work being done or the builder having gone on a holiday with the money. The extant agreement between the parties should govern their relation, excluding any such excuse. It provides an additional reason for restitution.

B. Qualified Consent?

The dominant academic approach, at least in England, has been to draw a parallel between claims to recover mistaken payments and those based upon a 'total failure of consideration' and to argue that the latter are also based on the state of mind of the claimant. Whereas the former concern 'vitiated' consent, the latter concern 'qualified' consent.[4]

The difference between the two categories is then said to be based upon the distinction between mistakes and mispredictions that we have already seen, and rejected. It is argued that although 'mispredictions' are insufficient to justify recovery as we all run the risk of the future not turning out as we expect, where the plaintiff has made the future condition in his mind apparent to the recipient, he is no longer a risk runner, and so restitution should follow. The condition is, on this view, found, as a matter of psychological fact in the mind of the claimant, but has been made apparent to the defendant.

As we have seen, this distinction between mistakes and mispredictions which is said to be founded upon whether the risk is run is insupportable. If we truly believed that the plaintiff's qualified subjective consent to the defendant's enrichment sufficed, it is unclear why it would need to be communicated, and the risk running justification is open to the usual objection of circularity.

By contrast, the law is, and ought to be, that the condition is found in the agreement between the parties.[5] Whether the party performing believed the performance to be conditional, as a matter of psychological fact, and, if they did, what that condition was believed by them to have been, is irrelevant.

This is most obvious in cases of enforceable contracts. Although it is sometimes somewhat loosely said that when a contract is interpreted the task is to discover the 'intention of the parties', this is misleading. As Lord Hoffmann has said:[6]

---

[4] Eg C Mitchell, P Mitchell, and S Watterson (eds), *Goff & Jones: The Law of Unjust Enrichment* (9th edn, 2016), [12-101]. Now with judicial support eg *Dargamo Holdings Ltd v Avonwick Holdings Ltd* [2021] EWCA Civ 1149, [2022] 1 All ER (Comm) 1244, [79] *per* Carr LJ, *cf.* [133].
[5] Eg *Gartell & Son (A Firm) v Yeovill Town Football & Athletic Club Ltd* [2016] EWCA Civ 62, [29]–[32] *per* Floyd LJ; *Dargamo Holdings Ltd v Avonwick Holdings Ltd* [2021] EWCA Civ 1149, [2022] 1 All ER (Comm) 1244, [133] *per* Carr LJ. *Cf. Grieve v Morrison* 1993 SLT 852 (OHCS), 855 *per* Lord Morison.
[6] *Attorney General of Belize v Belize Telecom Ltd* [2009] UKPC 10, [2009] 1 WLR 1988, [16].

The court ... is concerned only to discover what the [contract] means. However, that meaning is not necessarily or always what the authors or parties to the document would have intended. It is the meaning which the instrument would convey to a reasonable person having all the background knowledge which would reasonably be available to the audience to whom the instrument is addressed .... It is this objective meaning which is conventionally called the intention of the parties.

This is no less true of conditions found in agreements that are not contractual.

Unfortunately, in modern English judicial statements this has now become confused. Although there are statements adopting the view that the condition must be found in an agreement between the parties,[7] including recent ones from the Supreme Court,[8] there are also loose statements that the condition must be 'mutual'.[9] Thinner too are statements that the condition ought reasonably to have been known by the defendant.[10] In the difficult decision of *Menlaou v Bank of Cyprus*,[11] discussed critically in Chapter 3, Lord Clarke suggested that the reason for restitution was 'failure of consideration' although the defendant had had no dealings with the claimant, and had no knowledge that the bank was expecting a charge.[12]

Once it is accepted the agreement forms part of what justifies the obligation upon the defendant, why and how the defendant must be implicated in the condition under which any performance has been rendered becomes obvious.

C. Outside of Contract

Again, it is a mistake to believe that the law of contracts (ie of *enforceable* agreements) exhausts the law of agreement. A contract at common law requires a number of conditions to be satisfied: consideration, capacity to contract, certainty, intention to create legal relations. Some species of contract (commonly guarantees and contracts for the sale of land) are also required to satisfy formality requirements (although this is less common in most jurisdictions today). It is also a necessary condition of all contracts that there is an agreement: an offer and acceptance on the same terms objectively manifested by both parties. However, agreements that do not fulfil the other conditions for their enforceability are not a nullity. Where a performance rendered, whether a payment or otherwise, is agreed to have been conditional, and that condition has failed, restitution follows, regardless of whether the agreement amounts to an enforceable contract or not. Again, we are looking for a bilateral reason justifying the obligation the defendant is under to the claimant, not one found in the mind of the claimant alone.

---

[7] *Spaul v Spaul* [2014] EWCA Civ 679, [46]–[47] *per* Rimer LJ. *Cf. Burgess v Rawnsley* [1975] Ch 429 (CA), 442 *per* Browne LJ.
[8] *Barnes v Eastenders Group* [2014] UKSC 26, [2015] AC 1, [106], [115]; *Giedo Van Der Garde BV v Force India Formula One Team Ltd* [2010] EWHC 2373 (QB) [286] *per* Stadlen J.
[9] *Lowick Rose LLP (in liquidation) (Appellant) v Swynson Limited and another (Respondents)* [2017] UKSC 32, [2018] AC 313. [20] *per* Lord Sumption.
[10] *Lissack v Manhattan Loft Corporation Ltd* [2013] EWHC 128 (Ch), [88] *per* Roth J.
[11] [2015] UKSC 66, [2016] AC 176.
[12] *ibid*, [21].

This species of claim for restitution is not, therefore, one to enforce a contract, nor is it one seeking damages or any other remedy for its breach. It is however based upon there being an agreement, under which the performance rendered was conditional. That a claim is not contractual does not entail that it is not agreement based. Some commentators have been so keen to establish the independence of the law of restitution from the law of contract that they have thrown the agreement baby out with the contractual bathwater.

As we have seen, where an unenforceable agreement is performed it cannot, without more, be reversed.[13] The distinction between enforceability and nullity is of central importance in the law of restitution. Parties generally bargain for counter-performance from the other party, and once an agreement has been fully executed, the fact that such performance was unenforceable at some point in the past cannot justify recovery, unless the performance was subject to a further agreed condition that has failed.

An example, where the agreement was unenforceable for want of form, but where the claim rightly succeeded, is the decision of the Supreme Court of Canada in *Deglman v Guaranty Trust Co of Canada and Constantineau*.[14] The plaintiff lived with his aunt in Ottawa. She owned two houses and agreed that if he was good to her and did such chores as she requested from time to time, she would leave him one of them in her will. The nephew performed his side, taking her on pleasure drives, doing odd jobs, and running errands. The aunt died intestate. The agreement between them, being one to convey land, was unenforceable under section 4 of the Statute of Frauds 1677. Because the house was not conveyed to him, the claimant was held entitled to the value of the service he had provided over the years. The agreed condition under which the work was done had failed.

This may be contrasted with the (assumed) facts of *Actionstrength v International Glass Engineering SpA*.[15] A sub-contractor, not having been paid by the main contractor, threatened the owner of the site that it would stop work. To prevent this, an agent of the site owner promised that if he could not persuade the main contactor to meet its obligations, they would pay the sub-contractors from money to be withheld from the main contractor. Relying on this promise, another month's work was done, but the main contractors eventually went into insolvency proceedings from which no dividend was likely to be paid. The contract of guarantee was unenforceable because not in writing, as required by section 4 of the Statute of Frauds. The sub-contractors argued, unsuccessfully, that the site owner was estopped from relying upon the statute, so that the guarantee was enforceable. To have given effect to the guarantee by way of an 'estoppel' would have been to frustrate the purpose of the statute. It does not follow, however, that no claim at all should be permitted on such facts. If the condition under which it was agreed between the two parties that the work would be done, that the site owner would pay if the main contractor did not, failed then the value of the work done under that agreement between them (but not otherwise) should be recoverable. (The sub-contractor's work constituted a performance both under their contract with the main contractor, and under the agreement with the site owner). Just as in *Deglman*, allowing such a claim does not amount to enforcing the unenforceable contract of guarantee through a sidewind.

---

[13] Chapter 5, Theory.
[14] [1954] SCR 725, [1954] 3 DLR 785. See also *Grey v Hill* (1826) Ry & M 420, 171 ER 1070; *Scott v Pattison* [1923] 2 KB 723; *Pavey & Matthew Pty Ltd v Paul* (1987) 162 CLR 221 (HCA). But see in Scotland *Gray v Johnston* 1928 SC 659, 1928 SLT 499 (IHCS).
[15] [2003] UKHL 17, [2003] 2 AC 541.

Similar cases arise where the parties' agreement is 'subject to contract'. What these words mean is that although the parties may have reached an agreement, they do not intend it to be enforceable. Usually, they intend the contract to arise only upon the subsequent execution of a formal document. An example of recovery of the value of a service provided under an agreement expressed to be 'subject to contract' is the decision of the House of Lords in *Cobbe v Yeoman's Row*.[16] The defendant was the owner of land ripe for redevelopment, which they agreed in principle ('subject to contract') to sell to the claimant developer. The developer was to pursue the application for planning permission for residential redevelopment at his own expense. Once this permission was obtained, the defendant was to sell the land to the claimant for a fee. After the application was successful, the defendant refused to go ahead and sought to renegotiate the price, which the claimant refused to do. The court awarded the reasonable value of the service provided, to be subsequently assessed.

More difficult are agreements that are unenforceable not through the express stipulation of the parties but because informal and so not on their proper construction intended to create enforceable obligations. There must come a point where not only are such agreements themselves unenforceable as contracts, but where the law will not reverse the performance of obligations under them. If I agree to mow the lawn in exchange for my partner doing the washing up, if she reneges on the deal after I have done the work, my claim for restitution seems so trivial that no court would enforce it. Implicitly the parties are agreeing that all legal enforcement is excluded from the relationship created.

However, some examples of successful claims for restitution under informal agreements have succeeded, although sometimes misleadingly labelled in England, but not generally elsewhere, as being concerned with 'proprietary estoppel'. An example is the decision of *Jennings v Rice*[17] that is considered in Chapter 14, Improvements. As discussed there, the expansionary view of the doctrine of estoppel is unfortunate, and the better approach is often that of the Canadian Supreme Court in *Deglman*: restitution of the valuation of the work done.

Examples of cases where there is no contract because of want of consideration, but where an agreed condition fails, are gifts offered and accepted on the basis of an impending marriage. If the marriage does not go ahead, restitution should follow, regardless of the want of any *quid pro quo* in exchange for any payment.[18] Where however the gift is an engagement ring, the giver cannot recover it if he or she backs out of the marriage.[19] There is no right to recover as the token was given as an earnest of seriousness, it is the equivalent of a contractual deposit.

The UK Supreme Court's decision in *Benedetti v Sawiris*[20] is an example where there was no contract because the agreement was insufficiently complete so as to be enforceable. The failure to set a price is not necessarily fatal to the existence of a contract. If *A* agrees to buy goods from *B*, if no price is determined then a reasonable price must be paid,[21] and the same is true for services.[22] If however the parties agree that the price is to be agreed by them at

---

[16] [2008] UKHL 55, [2008] 1 WLR 1752. For the recovery of a payment on similar facts see *Chillingworth v Esche* [1924] 1 Ch 97.
[17] [2002] EWCA Civ 159, [2003] 1 P & CR 8.
[18] *Essery v Cowlard* (1884) 26 ChD 191; *Jacobs v Davis* [1917] 2 KB 532; *Re Ames Settlement* [1946] Ch 217.
[19] *Cohen v Sellar* [1926] 1 KB 536.
[20] Discussed in Chapter 4.
[21] Sale of Goods Act 1979, s 8(2).
[22] Supply of Goods and Services Act 1982, s 15(1); Consumer Rights Act 2015, s 51. See eg *Way v Latilla* [1937] 2 All ER 759 (HL).

some future point, this is fatal to there being a contract.[23] The agreed obligation was not to pay a reasonable sum, which the court can itself fix, but an unknown sum that the parties never in fact agreed. This was the case in *Benedetti v Sawiris* itself where the parties agreed to agree in the future a reward figure for the successful completion of the deal. A contractual *quantum meruit* was therefore unavailable. No figure could be placed upon what they would have agreed. Only a claim for restitution of the value of the performance rendered, which it had been agreed was conditional upon the agreement of a future reward, was therefore possible.

By contrast, in those cases where the parties have agreed that a reasonable sum is to be paid for work, which is then not paid after the work is done, it does not matter whether the claim for *quantum meruit* is seen as contractual or restitutionary,[24] and the courts have as a result often not bothered to differentiate the two.

In the usual case where the condition is counter-performance under the agreement, until that condition fails no restitution follows. Where the defendant remains ready and willing to perform no claim for restitution is possible unless the plaintiff can, through withholding co-operation, cause the condition to fail.[25]

However, the importance for both kinds of claim of there being *an agreement* between the parties is illustrated by the classic decision of *Boulton v Jones*,[26] where the claim failed.[27] Jones ordered hose pipe from Brocklehurst with whom he had regular dealings. Unknown to Jones, Boulton had taken over Brocklehurst's business earlier that day. Boulton upon receipt of the order supplied the pipe, which Jones (probably) consumed in his business. An invoice was then sent to Jones, who refused to pay. As Jones' offer to buy had been made to Brocklehurst, there was no agreement with Boulton, and so no claim. Jones had only accepted the pipe on the basis that it was being supplied by Brocklehurst. He had not manifested an acceptance of anything from Boulton. Again, the mere fact that Jones is left enriched by the pipe supplied by Boulton, the latter supplying it because he thought the other would have to pay for it, did not and should not suffice.[28]

Similar are cases of expenditure incurred in anticipation of there being an agreement between the parties. Work done in tendering for a contract is therefore irrecoverable, even if it does enrich the defendant as things turn out. In *Regalian Properties Ltd v London Docklands Development Corpn*[29] the claimants submitted a successful tender of £18 million for residential redevelopment of part of the Docklands area of London. The tender was accepted but 'subject to contract'. The claimants incurred considerable expenditure in paying architects and other professionals in preparing designs. Ultimately no contract was entered into because of difficulties in obtaining vacant possession and the decline in the property

---

[23] *May & Butcher v R* [1934] 2 KB 17n.
[24] Cases where either analysis seems plausible include *William Lacey (Hounslow) Ltd v Davis* [1957] 1 WLR 932 and *British Steel Corporation v Cleveland Bridge and Engineering Co Ltd.* [1984] 1 All ER 504. For a contractual example see *Batis Maritime Corporation v Petroleos del Mediterraneo SA (The 'Batis')* [1990] 1 Lloyd's Rep 345 (Hobhouse J).
[25] *Thomas v Brown* (1876) 1 QBD 714, 723 *per* Quain J. See Chapter 8.
[26] (1857) 2 H & N 564, 27 LJ Ex 117, 157 ER 232, sub nom *Boulton v Jones* 3 Jur NS 1156, 6 W 107, 30 LTOS 188.
[27] See also *Boston Ice Co v Potter* 123 Mass 28 (1877); *Concord Coal Co v Ferrin* 71 NH 22, 51 A 283 (1901); *Burgess v Rawnsley* [1975] 1 Ch 429 (CA); *Spaul v Spaul* [2014] EWCA Civ 679.
[28] If the pipe had been consumed in the defendant's use of it, it seems doubtful whether any action for conversion could have alternatively succeeded. Boulton had consented to Jones having the pipe.
[29] [1995] 1 WLR 212.See also *Attorney General of Hong Kong v Humphrey's Estate (Queens Gardens) Ltd* [1987] AC 114; *MSM Consulting v Tanzania* [2009] EWHC 21 (QB).

market. The claimant sought restitution on the basis of the mutual understanding that the parties had at the time the work was being carried out that a contract would eventually be entered into. However, these shared subjective intentions did not suffice. Absent an agreement that the work done was to be paid for, or for some other counter-performance to be rendered in return for it as in *Cobbe v Yeoman's Rowe*, the claim rightly failed.

D. 'Total Failure of Consideration'

One of the irritating features of the common law is that it uses a single word (eg waiver) to cover multiple different concepts. An example is the traditional label for claims for the return of payments made conditionally under an agreement, which is that there has been a 'total failure of consideration'.[30] This has not until very recently been the language employed for the recovery of a performance under an agreement other than the payment of money.[31]

As others have explained,[32] the label is misleading in two ways. First, the word 'consideration' is also applied to the necessary element of contract formation that something is given in exchange for a promise (ie that mere acceptance is insufficient). In a wholly executory contract (eg a contract to buy and sell goods at some later date) each party's promise is good consideration for the other, leading to a valid and enforceable contract. In the context of 'failure of consideration' we are not referring to this question of initial enforceability of the contract, but to whether a condition to which it was agreed a performance was subject has failed.[33] The reason (ie consideration) why my promise to you is enforceable (your promise in exchange) differs from the reason (ie consideration) for the performance under an agreement (usually, but not always, the desired counter-performance from you).

The second longstanding error is to conflate the question of whether the condition has failed with the question of whether counter-performance has been rendered. Conditions are digital matters. Either the condition has failed, or it has not. A condition cannot 'partially' or 'totally' fail. Usually, the condition of one party's performance is counter-performance by the other, but this is not always so. If, for example, a buyer pays a 5% deposit for the purchase of title to an area of land, and then chooses to repudiate the deal, if that repudiation is accepted no restitution is available even though he has received no counter-performance for the payment. The nature of a deposit is that it is an earnest of the buyer's willingness to perform. The deposit is not conditional upon any counter-performance being received. It cannot therefore be recovered despite nothing having been done in exchange.

Similar is the unusual case of advanced freight, which is earned upon signing of a bill of lading, and so must be paid once that occurs, and once paid cannot be recovered, even if the goods are not in fact carried.[34] In *Société Générale, London Branch v Geys*[35] a banker's employment contract entitled him to an extremely large bonus simply from being employed

---

[30] *Fibrosa Spolka Akcyjna v Fairbairn Law son Combe Barbour Ltd.* [1943] AC 32, 77 *per* Lord Porter.
[31] See *Yeoman's Row Management Ltd. v Cobbe* [2008] UKHL 55, [2008] 1 WLR 1752, [43] *per* Lord Scott. See also Mitchell, Mitchell, and Watterson *Goff & Jones: The Law of Unjust Enrichment* (n 4), [12-03]–[12-05].
[32] Eg F Wilmot-Smith, 'Reconsidering "Total" Failure' [2013] CLJ 414.
[33] See P Birks, *An Introduction to the Law of Restitution* (rev edn, 1989), 223.
[34] *Bank of Boston Connecticut v European Grain and Shipping Ltd, The Dominique* [1980] AC 1056 (HL). *Cf. Watson v Shankland* (1873) 11 M (HL) 51, (2870–2875) LR 2 Sc 304.
[35] [2012] UKSC 63, [2013] 1 AC 523.

on a particular date, without having to do any work in exchange for it. However, these are unusual bargains.

The language of 'total failure of consideration' originated in Lord Mansfield's judgment in *Boone v Eyre*,[36] a case concerned with a contractual action for the agreed sum, and not recovery of a payment that has already been made. The plaintiff agreed to sell to the defendant the equity of redemption of a plantation in the West Indies, together with title to the slaves upon it, for £500 and an annuity of £160 for life. The defendant failed to pay the annuity and resisted an action for it to be made on the basis that the plaintiff did not have title to the slaves. Lord Mansfield stated (or is summarised in the brief noting of the case as having said):

> The distinction is very clear, where mutual covenants go to the whole of the consideration on both sides, they are mutual conditions, the one precedent to the other. But where they go only to a part, where a breach may be paid for in damages, there the defendant has a remedy on his covenant, and shall not plead it as a condition precedent. If this plea were to be allowed, any one [slave] not being the property of the plaintiff would bar the action.[37]

The best reading of Lord Mansfield that is available from this passage is that failure to fulfil the promise of good title to the slaves was not a condition precedent to the obligation to pay.[38] The breach of some contractual obligations merely gives rise to a right to damages. Lord Mansfield did not state, and could not have meant, that *any* performance by the seller of his obligations, however slight, entitled him to enforce payment.[39] This is also the best interpretation of the 'total' failure requirement: the non-performance of some obligations do not form a condition precedent to the entitlement to payment.

E. The Meaning of Condition

The word 'condition' is also unfortunately used in quite different senses in contract law. Sometimes it is used synonymously with contractual 'term'.[40] The correct usage (ie most useful and consonant with common usage) is that employed so far of an entitlement being conditional upon one or more factual states being met.[41] It may be a condition precedent[42] ('you are obliged to pay £100 if the work is done by 1 April'), or a condition subsequent[43] ('you are obliged to pay £100 in advance of the work being done, there being no entitlement to the payment if the work is not done by 1 April'). For most purposes, whether the condition is precedent or subsequent does not matter.[44] It is meaningless to speak of a condition,

---

[36] (1777) 1 H BL 273n, 126 ER 160n.
[37] ibid.
[38] See *Davidson v Gwynne* (1810) 12 East 381, 389, 104 ER 149, 152 *per* Lord Ellenborough CJ, 'unless the non-performance alleged in breach of the contract goes to the whole root and consideration of it, the covenant broken is not to be considered a condition precedent'.
[39] See also *Towers v Barrett* (1786) 1 TR 133, 99 ER 1014 (recovery of price of rejected goods after three days' use).
[40] Eg *L Schuler AG v Wickman Machine Tool Sales Ltd* [1974] AC 235 (HL).
[41] A L Corbin, 'Conditions in the Law of Contract' YLJ 739.
[42] Called suspensive conditions in civilian jurisdictions.
[43] Called resolutive conditions in civilian jurisdictions.
[44] 'In one sense, all conditions are precedent; in another, all are subsequent.' O W Holmes, *The Common Law* (1881), 279.

in this sense, being breached. The condition is an event, that either occurs or does not. There need not be any promise by, or obligation upon, either party to bring that condition about. Simple non-promissory conditions are found in gaming contracts. If I place a £100 bet at odds of 4/1 that the horse Dobbin will win the 4.30 race, there is no obligation on either party to bring about Dobbin's victory. Rather, the obligation on the bookmaker to pay the winnings is conditional upon the horse winning the race. Similarly, in unilateral contracts (ie contracts where only one party is ever under any obligation) it is a commonplace that the promisor's obligation may be conditional upon the promisee doing something which the promisee is under no obligation to do (eg Mrs Carlill's entitlement to be paid was conditional upon her using the smokeball as directed and contracting influenza, but she was under no obligation to do anything).[45] One party may have promised to bring about a condition, but that is irrelevant to whether it is a condition or not. If there is a breach it is of a promise, not a condition.

A nice example of restitution for the failure of a condition subsequent, that was not promissory, is *Wright v Newton*.[46] The defendant ran a public house and wanted to sell the business, including goodwill and fixtures, to the plaintiff for £120, £50 of which was to be paid to the defendant the following Monday if the landlord gave permission to the change in tenancy. The landlord initially gave his oral consent to the change, and the deposit was paid. The plaintiff acquired the fixtures and fittings and went into possession, but the landlord subsequently withdrew his consent to the change of tenant. The payment was recovered as 'paid on a consideration that has failed'.

This also illustrates that, even where the agreement between the parties is enforceable, as here, the claim for restitution is not one for breach of contract. The defendant committed no breach as he had not promised that the landlord would consent.[47] Nor was the agreement 'frustrated',[48] the circumstances that occurred were expressly provided for in the contract. Recovery was not refused even though the defendant had provided a partial performance (the fixtures and fittings, a short period of occupation) as the condition satisfying entitlement to the payment (the permission to transfer the lease) could not be met by this alone.

Similar is the more recent decision of the Supreme Court in *Barnes v Eastenders Group*,[49] which is important because it is a claim for the restitution of the value of a service where this conditionality reasoning was applied. The Crown Prosecution Service (CPS) suspected that the Eastenders Group were involved in tax fraud. They obtained an order for the appointment of a receiver of the companies' assets under the Proceeds of Crime Act 2010. The CPS requested that the claimant accountant acted as the receiver, with remuneration to be obtained from the companies' property over which he was appointed. Subsequently the order appointing the receiver was quashed on the basis that there was no arguable case of fraud, so that the appointment was invalid and the receiver had no entitlement to be paid from the assets. They had however incurred considerable expense in performing their role by this point. The claim for payment of the value of the service provided against the CPS succeeded because 'the receiver agreed to accept the burden of the management of the companies on the basis that he would be entitled to take his remuneration and expenses from

---

[45] *Carlill v Carbolic Smoke Ball Co.* [1893] 1 QB 256.
[46] *Wright v Newton* [1835] 2 Cr M & R 124, 150 ER 53.
[47] See also *Roxburgh v Rothmans of Pall Mall Australia Ltd* (2001) 208 CLR 516, discussed later in this chapter.
[48] See Chapter 8, Contract, on this terminology.
[49] [2014] UKSC 26, [2015] AC 1.

the companies' assets, and that state of affairs which was fundamental to the agreement has failed to sustain itself'.[50]

Whether a payment or other performance is conditional, and what that condition may be, is irreducibly a matter of construction of the agreement. Although the counter-performance of some obligations of the counterparty may be a condition of his entitlement to the performance he has received, often some are not.[51] In a world where we give the parties unrestricted power to determine those conditions for themselves,[52] caution must therefore be exercised in generalising. However, the law does have various default rules, absent express stipulation by the parties, for determining these conditions.[53] In international sales, for example, under a CIF sale the buyer must pay against conforming documents, and cannot resist payment, and once made cannot obtain restitution, because of other breaches in relation to the goods committed by the seller.

Two simple examples. First:

> P contracts with D, a builder, for the installation of a bathroom floor for a price of £10,000. D installs two thirds of the tiles but does not finish the job.

Here, P has not received what he bargained for: a bathroom floor. If P has not paid in advance, the builder has no claim for the agreed sum. If P has paid in advance, he should be able to recover his payment. In contract cases, whether a payment made is recoverable is simply the flipside of whether a payment not yet made can be claimed. Neither the claim for restitution nor the action for the agreed sum are actions for breach of contract. As Sir George Jessel MR stated, 'if a man engages to carry a box of cigars from London to Birmingham ... he cannot throw the cigars out of the carriage half-way there, and ask for half the money'.[54] Still less, for all of it. The restitutionary action to recover money already paid and the contractual action to recover money unpaid ought to be treated symmetrically.

Second:

> P contracts with D, a builder, for the installation of a bathroom floor for a price of £10,000. The agreement stipulates that the tiles are to be Azure blue. The builder installs flooring of a slightly different shade.

Here P has received what he bargained for: a bathroom floor. The performance of qualitative obligations or ones of description do not, generally, form a condition precedent to the obligation to pay. If P has not paid, an action for the agreed sum is available, if he has paid he cannot recover back the payment.[55] P's only remedy is one for damages for breach. This

---

[50] ibid, [114] per Lord Toulson.
[51] *Jacob & Youngs v Kent* 230 NY 239, 240–241 per Cardozo J.
[52] *Kingston v Preston* (1773) 2 Doug KB 689, (1772) 99 ER 437 cited in argument in *Jones v Barkley* (1781) 2 Doug 684, 692; 99 ER 434 per Lord Mansfield; *Bettini v Gye* (1876) 1 QBD 183, 187 per Blackburn J.
[53] See the influential rules set down by Serjeant Williams in 1798 in his notes to *Pordage v Cole* [1669] 1 Wms Saund 219, 85 ER 449, 451–454. For an historical overview and criticism see S J Stoljar, 'Dependent and Independent Promises' (1956–1958) 2 Syd L Rev 217. For a more modern take see T Baloch, *Unjust Enrichment and Contract* (2009), 106–111.
[54] *Re Hall & Baker* (1878) 9 Ch D 538, 545.
[55] *Brown v M'Kinally* (1795) 1 Esp 279, 170 ER 356.

is reflected in the old law of actions to enforce bills of exchange given for goods, as Lord Tenterden CJ stated (again discussing an action for the agreed sum):

> If the consideration fails partially, as by the inferiority of the article furnished to that ordered, the buyer must seek his remedy by a cross action.[56]

This, obviously, did not and does not mean that if the buyer had received anything at all under the contract that an action for the price is available.[57]

Sometimes a defect in quality may be so serious that it prevents the condition precedent to the entitlement to payment from being fulfilled (eg the work is so bad that *P* has not received the contracted for bathroom floor)[58] but that would not be the case in this example.

Some cases, as a matter of construction, appear doubtful. One infamous example is the decision of the Court of Exchequer in *Whincup v Hughes*.[59] A father apprenticed his son to a watchmaker for a premium of £25 for six years. After one year the watchmaker died, and the father sought to recover the premium paid. Bovill CJ stated that the 'general rule of law of law is, that when a contract has been in part performed no part of the money paid under such contract can be recovered back'.[60] As we have seen, Lord Mansfield and those following him intended no such rule when originally speaking of a 'total failure of consideration'. If the £25 had not been paid upfront, could the estate of the watchmaker have recovered it? The answer is surely no, the recipient only became unconditionally entitled to the payment upon the completion of the six years of apprenticeship. Recovery where payment has been made in advance should therefore have been permitted. It might be arguable that this should have been subject to the estate also having a claim for the value of the work already provided, the parties' bargain no longer governing their relationship because of the frustrating event.[61] What barred this result was the rule (discussed below) that a *quantum meruit* for work done was also unavailable in a contract discharged through frustration, established in *Cutter v Powell*.[62] The result in *Whincup v Hughes* has now been reversed in England through legislation.

Another failure to construe a contract sensibly occurred in the High Court of Australia's decision in *Baltic Shipping v Dillon*,[63] overturning the approach of the New South Wales Court of Appeal and of the trial judge.[64] Mrs Dillon paid A$2,205 in advance for a 14-day cruise in the South Pacific. On the tenth day the ship sank, and she lost her personal possessions and suffered personal injuries. Mason CJ rightly accepted that if payment had not been made in advance no action for its recovery would have succeeded. However, where payment had already been made a different rule was said to apply so that recovery was impermissible where the plaintiff had received any part of the bargained for benefit (relying upon *Whincup v Hughes*). As we have seen, this division is historically inaccurate, the older cases concerning the failure of the 'whole consideration' having been concerned

---

[56] *Obbard, assignees of Blofeld (a bankrupt) v Betham* (1830) M & M 483, 485, 173 ER 1232.
[57] Wilmot-Smith, 'Reconsidering "Total" Failure' (n 32), 424–426.
[58] See *Gartell & Son (A Firm) v Yeovil Town Football & Athletic Club Ltd* [2016] EWCA Civ 62.
[59] (1871) LR 6 CP 78.
[60] ibid, 81.
[61] See Chapter 8, Contract.
[62] *Cutter v Powell* (1795) 6 Term Rep 320, 101 ER 573.
[63] (1993) 176 CLR 3.
[64] (1991) 22 NSWLR 1 (Gleeson CJ, Kirby P; Mahoney JA dissenting), (1989) 21 NSWLR 614 (Carruthers J).

with the action for the agreed sum. It makes little sense to have different results according to the fortuity of whether payment has been made or not. The better view was that of Kirby P in the Court of Appeal (with whom Glesson CJ agreed): 'What she contracted for was a relaxing holiday experience. It is this that she failed to secure.'[65] This was not a mere defect in the quality of performance. This was not just a poor holiday but no holiday at all, and so a failure of the condition the payment was subject to. Further, no deduction ought to have been made for the days before the ship sank. The cruise was provided on the basis that there would only be an entitlement to the payment upon its completion, which never occurred.[66]

F. Waiver

Contracts for the sale or hire of goods differ from those for the installation of bathroom floors or for holiday cruises because goods, unlike services, can be returned after performance by the seller. Sections 12–15 of the Sale of Goods Act 1979 expressly provides for a number of 'conditions' that, if not satisfied, entitle the buyer to reject the tendered goods. It is an implied 'condition' that goods sold by description shall correspond with that description,[67] that goods sold by sample correspond with the sample,[68] and (in certain cases) that goods be of satisfactory quality and fit for purpose.[69]

If the goods are rejected, there is no entitlement to be paid,[70] and any payment made can be recovered.[71] This is so even if the buyer has obtained benefits from the use of the goods in the interim.[72] However, a buyer or hirer may choose to accept non-conforming goods even though under no obligation to do so. In such circumstances he is said to have lost 'the right to reject',[73] and an action for the price is available (or if he has paid in advance, he cannot recover it).

Further, a condition of the entitlement to payment may be waived, and so can no longer be relied upon. It is important to distinguish between the waiver of a duty and the waiver of a condition, as it is possible to waive one but not the other. If *P* contracts to sell 10,000 tonnes of first grade durum wheat to *D* for £100,000, delivery on 1 April, if *D* subsequently states 'delivery by 4 April is fine' if *P* delivers on 3 April, he commits no breach. *D* has consented, the duty to deliver on 1 April has been waived. Further, even if delivery by 1 April was a condition of the obligation of *D* to pay, his statement is also a waiver of this condition.

---

[65] *ibid*, 26.
[66] *Cf.* the position on frustration, see Law Reform (Frustrated Contracts) Act 1943, s 1(2), discussed in Chapter 8, Contract.
[67] Sale of Goods Act 1979, s 13.
[68] Sale of Goods Act 1979, s 15.
[69] Sale of Goods Act 1979, s 14.
[70] If title to the goods has passed prior to rejection, rejection will revest title and the buyer will cease to be liable for the price: *Whitecap Leisure Ltd v John H Rundle Ltd* [2008] EWCA Civ 429, [2008] 2 Lloyd's Rep 429.
[71] *Baldry v Marshall* [1925] 1 KB 260.
[72] *Rogers v Parish (Scarborough) Ltd* [1987] QB 933 (CA) (restitution of price paid for vehicle driven for 5,500 miles before valid rejection).
[73] The 'right to reject' is a misnomer. The acceptance constitutes a waiver. Non-acceptance means that a condition precedent to the buyer's right to payment remains unfulfilled. The buyer is not exercising any right or power in refusing to accept, he is refusing to waive a condition.

If he has not paid he must do so, and if he has paid in advance he cannot recover.[74] Both the duty to deliver on 1 April *and* its being a condition of entitlement to payment have been waived.[75]

By contrast, in the standard case of a buyer who accepts non-conforming goods, he must pay for them (ie any condition precedent to payment is treated as having been satisfied because of the acceptance of the goods) but may still claim damages for breach (ie the duty to supply conforming goods has not been waived). A buyer who takes too long before attempting to reject may be taken to have waived the condition of payment but not of the seller's duties in relation to the goods.

This sense of waiver is not the same as a contractual variation. There is neither need for consideration nor an offer and acceptance. The manifestation of the promisee's consent to the non-fulfilment of the duty or the condition suffices to waive either. A waiver, unlike a variation, is merely suspensive, it may always be withdrawn by the promisee, unless it is now too late to do so and subject to his being estopped from being so able.[76] It is doubtful whether complete waiver of the counterparty's promised performance is possible (eg 'you don't have to deliver the goods') as this would contradict the rule that consideration (in the formation sense) must be provided for a promise to be binding.

An example of waiver in the context of a claim for restitution is *Yeoman Credit Ltd v Apps*.[77] Under a hire purchase agreement, a hire purchase company bought a second-hand car from a dealer, and hired it to the defendant, with an initial payment of £125 followed by 30 monthly instalments of £15. The car was completely unroadworthy, but the defendant kept the vehicle for six months knowing this and paid the first three instalments. Although the defendant could have rejected the car, and recovered the sums paid, his decision to keep it after discovering the obvious defects and to continue to pay the instalments, debarred him from doing so for the period during which he kept the car.

Waiver also provides the best explanation for the otherwise problematic decision of *Hunt v Silk*.[78] The defendant agreed to let to the plaintiff a house for £10, to be paid at the time of execution in ten days' time. The defendant was to repair the house before that date. The plaintiff paid, took immediate possession, and remained for some time, despite the fact that the defendant had neither executed the lease nor effected the repairs. By paying when they did not have to, and staying on, the plaintiff had 'waived'[79] the conditions of payment, and so was confined to damages. Although through their requests for the work to be done the plaintiffs made it clear that they did not waive the duty of repair, they had by their conduct waived the condition of payment.[80]

---

[74] See *Bentsen v Taylor* [1893] 2 QB 274 (CA).
[75] Sale of Goods Act 1979, s 11(2).
[76] Discussed in Chapter 14, Improvements.
[77] [1962] 2 QB 508.
[78] (1804) 5 East 449, 102 ER 1142. See also C B Morison, *Rescission of Contracts* (1916), 180–181. *Cf.* R Goff and G Jones, *Goff & Jones: The Law of Restitution* (7th edn, 2006), [20-2013] where unfortunately waiver of condition is confused with affirmation of the contract.
[79] (1804) 5 East 449, 102 ER 1142, 1143 5 East 448, 452 *per* Lord Ellenborough, *cf.* (1804) 5 East 449, 102 ER 1142, 1143, 'voluntarily consented' *per* Le Blanc J.
[80] *Contra* A Burrows, *The Law of Restitution* (3rd edn, 2011), 343.

G. The Fiction of Fulfilment

In many legal systems, for example those of the United States[81] and in most civilian jurisdictions,[82] the law recognises a doctrine of 'fictional fulfilment': the deliberate prevention by the promisor of the fulfilment of a condition precedent will result in it being deemed to be fulfilled and the promisor's deliberate bringing about of a condition subsequent will result in it being deemed to be unfulfilled.[83] Such a rule reduces the scope and importance of claims for restitution and damages. The condition is treated as fulfilled, and a claim for counter-performance (usually the agreed sum) becomes available.

A classic US illustration is the decision in *Foreman State Trust & Savings Bank v Tauber*.[84] Max and Frances Tauber entered into a pre-nuptial contract. Max agreed to pay his future wife $20,000 in the event of his pre-deceasing her. They then married, and lived together for four years, until Max shot and killed his wife. Her estate then brought a claim for the agreed sum upon the covenant to pay, which succeeded, the wrongdoer being barred from asserting the non-fulfilment of the condition. Conditions have been taken to be satisfied in cases far short of murder, such as where the vendor of a house refused to complete thereby preventing the condition of the real estate agent's commission being fulfilled under the terms of the agreement.[85]

Does such a rule form part of English law? In the Scottish appeal to the House of Lords, *Mackay v Dick*,[86] an excavating machine was sold on condition that it could excavate at a specified rate on the defendant's property. The buyer refused to provide the opportunity for the excavation rate to be tested. The buyer was held liable for the price, Lord Watson stated,

> The [sellers] were only entitled to receive payment of the price of the machine on the condition that ... on trial it should excavate a certain amount ... They have been thwarted in the attempt to fulfil that condition by the neglect or refusal of the [buyer] to furnish the means of applying the stipulated test; and their failure being due to his fault, I am of opinion that ... they must be taken to have fulfilled the condition.[87]

Although such a principle forms part of Scottish law,[88] it probably does not apply in England. McCardie J in *Colley v Overseas Exporters*[89] refused to recognise any such principle. Under an f.o.b. contract the buyers, in breach of contract, refused to nominate a ship to carry the goods. The sellers were consequently unable to load the goods so that property did not pass to the buyers. McCardie J held that the sellers could not claim the price. He interpreted

---

[81] EA Farnsworth, *Farnsworth on Contracts*, vol 2 (3rd edn, 2003), 454.
[82] Eg French Code Civil, Art 1304-3 ('A suspensive condition is deemed to have been fulfilled if the party who is interested in its failing has obstructed its fulfilment'); BGB § 162(1) ('If the fulfilment of the condition is prevented by the party to whose disadvantage it would be contrary to good faith, the condition is deemed to have been met').
[83] G H Treitel, *Remedies for Breach of Contract* (1991), 204–207; G H Treitel, 'Fault in the Common Law of Contract' in Bos and Brownlie (eds), *Liber Amicorum for Lord Wilberforce* (1987) 185, 206–210.
[84] 180 NE 827 (1932). But see *Barron v Cain* 4 SE 2d 618 (1939).
[85] *Goldstein v Rosenberg* 73 NE 2d 171 (1947).
[86] (1881) 6 App Cas 251.
[87] ibid, 270, cf. 264 per Lord Blackburn. See also *Hotham v The East India Company* (1787) 1 Term Rep 638, 645 99 ER 1295, 1298–1299 per Ashhurst J; *Studdy v Sanders* (1826) 5 B&C 628, 639, 108 ER 234, 238 per Holroyd J; *O'Neil v Armstrong* [1895] 2 QB 418; *Luxor (Eastbourne) Ltd v Cooper* [1941] AC 108 (HL), 149 per Lord Wright.
[88] *Pirie v Pirie* (1873) 11 M 941; *T&R Duncanson v Scottish County Investment Co. Ltd* 1915 SC 1106.
[89] [1921] 3 KB 302. See also *CIA Barca de Panama S.A. v George Wimpey & Co Ltd* [1980] 1 Lloyd's Rep 598 (CA), 609 per Bridge LJ.

Mackay v Dick as a case where the obligation to pay the price had accrued as property had passed to the buyers upon delivery and the price was owed. He construed the obligation to pay in that case as subject to a condition *subsequent* that it was to cease to be payable if the test proved unsatisfactory. As no test did or would take place, the price was earned.[90] There are several other statements that the doctrine of 'fictional fulfilment' does not form part of English law.[91] English courts have generally taken the approach of implying a duty of co-operation and holding the defendant liable in damages for preventing the occurrence of the condition precedent,[92] and allowing a claim for restitution of the value of the work done.

H. The Right or Its Performance?

Generally, as we have seen, the condition of entitlement to the performance received by each party under an agreement is counter-performance by them, and the construction issue is concerned with what counter-performance satisfies the condition. But is part of what is bargained for the right to enforce such performance, so that where a contract is unenforceable there is a failure of condition from the start? That it is not, is shown by the decision in *Thomas v Brown*.[93] The plaintiff paid a deposit of £70 for the purchase of the leasehold of a shop. The contract was arguably unenforceable under the Statute of Frauds because of want of adequate writing, but the court held that regardless of whether the contract was valid, it could not be recovered where the counterparty remained ready and willing to perform.

A fortiori where the agreement has been fully performed no restitution ought to follow. Parties to agreements bargain for performance from one another. Once they have received it, they do not care that at some point in the past they could not have used legal process to obtain what they now have.[94]

The English 'swaps' litigation appears difficult to explain because, as has been seen, some of the interest rate swaps had been fully executed.[95] Why then was restitution allowed?

If an agreement is said to exist as a matter of fact between the parties, then we could say that the banks who sought restitution had not got what they bargained for. If the local authorities could recover back the money they paid on the basis that it was not due, and because they could not consent because of their lack of capacity, they were never 'on risk'. Again, we could argue that it was an agreed condition of the bank's payment that it could win under the bargain. Although it appeared that the banks had received what they bargained for once the contracts had been fully performed, in fact they had not.

However, if we take the nullity of the agreements seriously,[96] it is difficult to accept that any claim to recover could be based upon the payments having been subject to an *agreed*

---

[90] [1921] 3 KB 302, 308.
[91] *Thompson v ASDA-MFI Group plc* [1988] Ch 241, 266 *per* Scott J; *Little v Courage Ltd.* (1995) 70 P & CR 469 (CA), 474 *per* Millett LJ.
[92] *Kleinert v Abosso Gold Mining Co* (1913) 58 SJ (PC) 45; *Alpha Trading Ltd v Dunshaw-Patten* [1981] QB 290; *Bournemouth and Boscombe Athletic Football Club and Co Ltd v Manchester United Football Club Ltd* Unreported 21 May 1980.
[93] (1876) 1 QBD 714, *cf. Casson v Roberts* [1862] 31 Beav 613, 54 ER 1277 (vendor no longer able to convey land having been sold by mortgagees).
[94] *Sharma v Simposh* [2011] EWCA Civ 1383, [2013] Ch 23 discussed above. See also *Davis v Bryan* (1827) 6 B& C 651, 108 ER 591. *Contra*, Mitchell, Mitchell, and Watterson, *Goff & Jones: The Law of Unjust Enrichment* (n 4), [13-31].
[95] See Chapter 5, Practice.
[96] In principle, incapacity should lead to the agreement being unenforceable. See Chapter 18, Defences.

condition that failed. Members of the Court of Appeal in *Guinness Mahon & Co Ltd v Kensington & Chelsea London Borough Council*[97] based recovery upon there being a 'lack of consideration'[98] or a total failure of consideration because the contract was void.[99] This is to use 'consideration' to mean 'reason' and not 'agreed condition'. Although the court was right that recovery ought to have been allowed because there was no good reason for the payment, adopting the same terminology ('failure of consideration') to cover two different ideas is unfortunate.

I. Relevance of Termination

1. Terminology

In common law jurisdictions following the English tradition (but not the United States) yet another sense of 'condition' from that used so far has unfortunately entered common usage in contract law. On this usage a 'condition' is an obligation created by a contract the breach of which gives the innocent party a 'power to terminate'.[100] At one time it was common to use a single word 'rescission' to encompass both the avoidance of a contract for, say, misrepresentation and also its termination for breach.[101] As the latter discharges obligations to perform in the future but does not avoid obligations to perform that have already accrued, does not prevent a claim for breach of contract, and leaves in place terms such as exclusions or limitations upon liability,[102] different labels are appropriate. 'Termination' has therefore become the more common terminology in England instead of 'rescission' for breach, although again we are divided by our common language by the fact this is not so in the United States.

Whether termination for breach is an otiose addition to rules better understood in terms of conditions and their waiver, is beyond the scope of this work.[103] Some have argued however that termination for breach operates in the same way as rescission or avoidance of a contract, so that following its occurrence restitution automatically follows.[104] In fact, termination is neither a sufficient nor a necessary condition of restitution. The important question is always whether the agreed condition of performance has failed.

---

[97] [1999] QB 215.
[98] *ibid*, 233 *per* Waller LJ. See also *Westdeutsche Landesbank Girozentrale v Islington London Borough Council* [1994] 4 All ER 890 (CA), 924 *per* Hobhouse LJ.
[99] [1999] QB 215, 230 *per* Morritt LJ, 234 *per* Robert Walker LJ. See also *Westdeutsche Landesbank Girozentrale v Islington London Borough Council* [1996] AC 669 (HL), 683 *per* Lord Browne-Wilkinson.
[100] Eg E Peel, *Treitel's The Law of Contract* (15th edn, 2020), 981, [18-1043].
[101] A Kull, *Restatement of the Law (Third) Restitution and Unjust Enrichment*, vol I (2010) continues to do so, eg at 13, 37.
[102] Eg *Photo Productions Ltd v Securicor Transport Ltd* [1980] AC 827 (HL).
[103] See J English, 'The Nature of Promissory Conditions' (2021) 137 LQR 630 arguing that it is.
[104] P Birks, *Unjust Enrichment* (2nd edn, 2005), 125. See also D Friedmann, 'Valid, Voidable, Qualified, and Non-existing Obligations: An Alternative Perspective on the Law of Restitution' in A Burrows (ed), *Essays on the Law of Restitution* (1991).

2. Insufficient

If I am sacked for gross incompetence by my employer, if I accept their repudiation of our contract, thereby terminating it, does restitution, by either side, follow? No. Indeed, if I am paid a salary, have done the work for several months, and not been paid, I can maintain an action for the agreed sums that are due, even after the contract has been terminated as a result of my repudiatory breach. Rights to payment that have been unconditionally acquired are not divested by termination of the agreement.[105]

Similarly, in *Stocznia Gdanska S.A. v Latvian Shipping Co*[106] the claimant shipbuilders agreed to design, build, and deliver a ship to the defendants. The price was to be paid in four instalments. The second instalment was to be paid when notice of the keel of the ship being laid was given. The keel was laid and notice given but the defendants refused to pay. The claimant terminated the contract for this repudiatory breach. The House of Lords held that the instalments earned could be claimed as an agreed sum. Unlike a standard contract of sale, the part payment was earned not by the passing of property but by the laying of the keel.

It is sometimes argued that if a party would be entitled to recover back money if it had been paid under a contract, he should not remain obliged to pay such sums which had become due, as it would make no sense to hold him liable in one action for payment which he could then claim back in another.[107] Although this reasoning was invoked by the House of Lords in *Stocznia Gdanska S.A. v Latvian Shipping Co*[108] and applied by the Court of Appeal in *Rover International Sales v Cannon Film Sales*[109] it puts the cart (restitution) before the horse (the contract). In *Rover International Sales v Cannon Film Sales* Thorn EMI granted Proper Films Ltd a licence to exhibit nine films on Italian television for a fee of $1.8 million payable in instalments. The fee was payable in advance of Thorn EMI's delivery of the relevant films. Proper refused to pay the final instalment. This was held to be a repudiatory breach which Thorn EMI accepted. Thorn EMI then sought to recover the final instalment, which had fallen due before termination. The Court of Appeal held that as the instalment, if paid, could have been recovered on the basis of a total failure of consideration, it followed *a fortiori* that there was no liability to pay it.[110]

Although it would be absurd that the prospective payee could sue for the money because it was due before breach, while the payor could then sue for its return because part payments can be recovered back by the payor, this fails to explain which of the two actions should have priority. Indeed, if we took seriously the idea that the ability to claim the agreed sum were determined by whether, if paid, it could be recovered, if we combined this with the supposed 'total failure' requirement for the latter, it would lead to ludicrous results.

The better analysis of *Rover International Sales v Cannon Film Sales* is that on the correct construction of the agreement the last instalment was never earned and the action for the agreed sum should have been refused on this basis.[111] That instalment was subject to the

---

[105] *McDonald v Dennys Lascelles Ltd* (1933) 48 CLR 457, 476–477 *per* Dixon J.
[106] [1988] 1 WLR 574; *cf. Sellers v London Counties Newspapers* [1951] 1 KB 784.
[107] *McDonald v Denys Lascelles Ltd* [1933] 48 CLR 457, 479 *per* Dixon J; *Stocznia Gdanska S.A. v Latvian Shipping Co* [1998] 1 WLR 574, 587 *per* Lord Goff.
[108] [1998] 1 WLR 574.
[109] [1989] 1 WLR 912.
[110] *ibid*, 932 *per* Kerr LJ, 937 *per* Dillon LJ.
[111] See also *Shell-Mex Ltd v Elton Cop Dyeing Co. Ltd* (1928) 34 Com Cas 39; *Otis Vehicle Rentals Ltd v Ciceley Commercials Ltd* [2002] All ER (D) 203.

condition that Thorn EMI's performed. By accepting Proper's repudiatory breach, Thorn EMI showed that they no longer intended to do so.

3. Unnecessary

In most cases where restitution of a performance rendered under an agreement is sought it will have been terminated. However, this is not a necessary condition.[112]

Where the failed condition is a counter-performance that was not rendered in the past, restitution should follow. It should not be necessary to bring to an end other, future obligations to render performance under the same contract in order to do so. An example:

> D contract to supply 20 firemen *per annum* to guard P's office buildings at night, for five years, for an annual fee of £100,000. Three years later, P discovers that D provided no fireman in the first year but did do so in the next two years. P does not wish to terminate the contract.[113]

D should not be entitled to be paid for the first year of security as he did not provide it. If the £100,000 for that year has not been paid it should not be recoverable by D, and if paid upfront, that year's fees should be recoverable by P. The passage of time means that D can no longer fulfil the condition for the first year's payment. Termination is therefore irrelevant in this case.

Similar is the decision of the High Court of Australia in *Roxburgh v Rothmans of Pall Mall Australia Ltd*[114] which concerned the failure of a non-promissory condition. The state of New South Wales imposed a licence fee upon the wholesalers of tobacco products. The wholesalers included the tax as an itemised charge in the price that retailers paid to them. Subsequently the tax was declared invalid as contrary to the exclusive power of the Commonwealth Parliament to impose excise duties. The retailers sought restitution of the portion of the price paid representing the tax. The price had not been expressed as one indivisible sum.[115] Because that portion of the price was conditional upon the tax being due, restitution followed. Itemisation may not always be decisive, but as a matter of construction it is a good indication of what each sum is being paid for. Kirby J dissented on the basis that the contract remained valid, and that the 'consideration' for the payment could not have failed because the wholesalers had not undertaken a contractual obligation to pay the tax over to the Revenue.[116] Neither of these grounds for refusal of restitution is correct. If the wholesalers had not been paid and had been suing the retailers for payment of the price, exactly the same end result ought to be reached.

---

[112] But see *Fibrosa Spolka Akcyjna v Fairbairn Lawson Combe Barbour Ltd* [1943] AC 32, 65 *per* Lord Wright, 'no doubt, when money is paid under a contract it can only be claimed back as for failure of consideration where the contract is terminated as to the future'. See also *The Restatement Third*, § 37 which sees the claims for restitution as part of rescission as a remedy for breach.

[113] Cf. *City of New Orleans v Firemen's Charitable Association* 42 La Ann 447, 9 So 486 (1891).

[114] (2001) 208 CLR 516. Cf. *James Moore & Sons Ltd v University of Ottawa* (1975) 5 OR (2d) 162, 49 DLR (3d) 666.

[115] *Wayne County Produce Co v Duffy-Mott Inc* 155 NE 669 (1927), 'where the item of the tax is absorbed in a total or composite price to be paid at all events … the buyer is without remedy, though the annulment of the tax may increase the profit to the seller' *per* Cardozo CJ.

[116] (2001) 208 CLR 516, [166], [177].

The view that the contract must be terminated or discharged before restitution can be awarded probably arises because of a confusion of different reasons for recovery. Where it is sought to recover a payment on the basis that the defendant was not entitled to it, if the payment was made in performance of a contract, then it will be necessary to rescind (in the sense of avoid) the contract. Where, by contrast, recovery is sought of a payment that it had been agreed was conditional, and that condition has failed, then it is not necessary to rescind (in the sense of terminate) the contract. Indeed, the presence of an extant agreement between the parties is an essential element of this kind of claim.

4. Relevance

If termination is neither a sufficient nor necessary condition of recovery, how is it relevant?

If a contract is terminated, future obligations are discharged and can no longer be performed. In the example above for the provision of fireman to protect the building, if the breach in failing to provide any fireman in year two is sufficiently serious to entitle the employer to terminate, and he does so, further performance in subsequent years cannot be made. If payment has been made for all five years in advance, the defendant could not resist repayment for the work not yet done on the basis that he remained willing and able to provide the service. Termination closes off that possibility. The condition of each year's payment (the provision of 20 firemen) will inevitably fail. Termination is relevant therefore *if* it makes the failure of a condition for a performance rendered (here the counter-performance through the provision of firemen) inevitable. If the employer elects to affirm the contract, the condition precedent to payment will only fail if, subsequently, the fireman are not provided.

8
Contract

A. Introduction

The purpose of this chapter is to consider the interaction between contract and restitution. As we have seen, where the claim is based upon an agreed condition that has failed, the nature of that condition is determined by the construction of the agreement. This question of construction is answered in the same way regardless of whether the issue is whether there is an obligation to make restitution of a performance already rendered or an obligation to render a performance not yet made. This is most obvious in relation to payment obligations but for other obligations, such as to provide a personal service or to convey generic goods, it can be lost sight of because the courts will rarely compel the performance of the contractual obligation, instead awarding damages for non-performance as an adequate remedy. Termination of the contract is neither a necessary nor a sufficient condition of recovery. A condition may be waived, sometimes implicitly by continuing to perform after it has become apparent that it will not be fulfilled.

How these seemingly simple propositions then play out varies according to whether the claim is brought against a party who is in breach of contract or by a party who is; whether it is to the return of money or some other kind of performance; or whether the performance of a contractual obligation is frustrated.

B. Breach of Contract

1. Claims for Restitution of Services by Party in Breach

Again, starting with examples where claims fail sheds light on why those that ought to succeed do so. In *Sumpter v Hedges*[1] a builder agreed to construct houses and stables on the defendant's land for £565. When the work was still incomplete the builder told the defendant that he had run out of money and could not finish. The defendant completed the work using materials the builder had left behind. The builder's claim for the agreed sum or reasonable remuneration for the work done was denied. The Court of Appeal held this was so on the basis that the contract between the parties governed their relationship, and that it was not possible to imply any new contract between them under which a reasonable sum was to be paid for the work done. The defendant had to pay for the builder's materials that he had used, which the builder still had had title to, but that was all.

The claim in relation to the work correctly failed. The work was rendered and accepted for a good reason: that is what had been agreed to between the parties. The work was done

---

[1] [1898] 1 QB 673 (CA).

on the basis that it would be paid for if, and *only* if, it was completed. Such obligations to complete performance before any entitlement to payment are labelled 'entire'. There was therefore no failure of any agreed condition where the work was abandoned by the builder still incomplete. The mere fact that the builder received no counter-performance from the defendant did not mean that the condition under which the work was done failed. Since they were never entitled to any such counter-performance, there was no failure to provide it. Part performance under an agreement, where the entitlement to payment from the counterparty is conditional upon full performance, should not and does not give rise to a claim even where the counterparty is left better off by what has been done.[2]

The reasoning of the court in *Sumpter v Hedges* is sometimes criticised on the basis that they thought that a new contract had to be found in order to justify any claim,[3] and there are of course valid claims that do not depend upon there being any contract between the parties. In the United States, the general position is a rejection of this rule that denies restitution in respect of a partial performance of an entire obligation.[4] Absent a new contract however, no claim is justifiable. The defendants never accepted the partial performance received on the basis that they were to pay for it; from the other side the plaintiffs performed on the basis that in order to earn payment it had to be complete. The fact of benefit and correlative loss is insufficient to justify any duty on the defendant.

This argument of principle suffices to justify the rule, but it also makes good sense in policy terms. As many who have employed builders will know, commonly the only practical method of ensuring completion is to withhold payment until the work is done.

By contrast, if the terms of the bargain had been different, so that the builder had an entitlement to be paid a proportion of the overall price as the work was done, or specified amounts as stages were complete, then the fact that they were in breach in abandoning the work still incomplete would not debar any contractual claim for the sums they were entitled to. An example:

> P agrees to paint the interior of D's house, at a rate of £200 per room. P completes four rooms, but then abandons the work.

If completion of the work is not a condition of payment, *P* has a contractual entitlement to be paid £800, and so may bring an action for the agreed sum for this amount. *P*'s breach of contract does not disentitle him to payment of what is due.

The net result is that the party obliged to provide the service, who in breach of contract fails to do so, either has a contractual claim for payment for work done, or no claim at all. There is no logical space for a non-contractual *quantum meruit*.

---

[2] See also *Llliey v Elwin* (1848) 11 QB 742, 116 ER 652; *Munro v Butt* (1858) 8 E & B 738, 120 ER 275; *Metcalfe v Britannia Ironworks Co* (1877) 2 QBD 423 (CA); *Boston Deep Sea Fishing and Ice Co. v Ansell* (1888) 39 Ch D 339; *Forman & Co. Pty Ltd v The Liddesdale* [1900] AC 190 (PC); *Vigers v Cook* [1919] 2 KB 475 (CA); *Ibmac Ltd v Marshall (Homes) Ltd,* CA (1968) 208 EG 851; *Bolton v Mahadeva* [1972] 1 WLR 1009 (CA); *Holland Hannen & Cubitts (Northern) Ltd v Welsh Health Technical Services Organisation* (1981) 18 Build L 80 (CA); *Wiluszynski v Tower Hamlets L.B.C.* [1989] ICR 493 (CA). But see *Barton v Gwyn-Jones* [2019] EWCA Civ 1999, [2020] 2 All ER (Comm) 652.

[3] Eg [1898] 1 QB 673, 674 per AL Smith LJ; A Burrows, *The Law of Restitution* (3rd edn, 2011), 356–361.

[4] See A Kull, *Restatement of the Law (Third) Restitution and Unjust Enrichment*, vol I (2010), § 36 (Restitution to a Party in Default), 590–592.

2. Claims for Restitution of Payments Against Party in Breach

Restitution of money paid against a party in breach has two potential advantages over a claim for damages. First, the claimant is not put to proof of his loss. Second, where the claimant has made a bad bargain, the claim for restitution will often result in a larger award.

The latter is best illustrated by the classic American decision of *Bush v Canfield*.[5] In 1812, Canfield agreed to deliver to Bush 2,000 barrels of flour in New Orleans by 1 May, for $7 per barrel. Bush paid $5,000 in advance, and sued to recover that amount when Canfield failed to deliver. On 1 May the market price for flour stood at $5.50. A claim for loss suffered as a result of breach of contract seeks to put the plaintiff 'in the same situation with respect to damages, as if the contract had been performed'.[6] This would result in damages of $2,000. This is the value of the flour that ought to have been delivered ($11,000) minus the balance of the price that would have had to be paid ($9,000). A claim for restitution of what has been paid by contrast gives an award of $5,000. (The result reached by the majority of the Connecticut Supreme Court of Errors was that $5,000 was awarded, but as damages. Hosmer J rightly dissented on the basis that the claim should have been put as one for money had and received.)

It is sometimes argued, against an award of the higher sum, that what the buyer has bargained for is performance or damages in the alternative. Allowing the plaintiff to recover more than he could obtain by way of damages, so it is argued, disturbs the parties' allocation of risk under their contract. It is hard to understand however why a party who has paid under a valid contract, and so has a claim for damages for breach, should be placed in a worse position than a party who has paid under an unenforceable agreement where the condition of the payment fails. Should the latter have no claim at all? Parties generally bargain for counter-performance, damages being a remedy for the wrongful breach of the agreement. The buyer in *Bush v Canfield* bargained for a quantity of wheat, not for the opportunity to sue for damages if the wheat is not delivered.

What if the payor has received a part of what has been bargained for? What if a buyer pays £100 in advance for 100 widgets, but the seller delivers only 50? Here the buyer has a right to reject and if he exercises it can claim restitution in full of the price paid. If, however, he accepts the 50 widgets, what is the position? Unlike in *Sumpter v Hedges*, the buyer has chosen to accept the part performance. If they do so, they can be taken to have agreed to pay for what they have received. There is, in this situation, a new contract between the parties. Absent an express price agreed for what has been accepted, it is inferred that the buyer agrees to pay for the goods at the contract rate (and not the market rate).[7] If payment has been made in advance, then the appropriate proportion is recoverable.[8] It has never been the case in the sale context that restitution is barred because the buyer has received some part of what he originally bargained for (ie the language of 'total failure' is again misleading). However, the new contract need not be construed as an agreed variation of the old. It should be open to the buyer to accept the short delivery on the basis that he will pay for it but retain his right to damages for breach for the goods not delivered.

---

[5] 2 Conn 485 (1818). See now Uniform Commercial Code, § 2-711; cf. *DO Ferguson & Associates v Sohl* (1992) 62 Build, LR 95 (CA).
[6] *Robinson v Harmon* (1848) 1 Ex 850; 154 Eng Rep 363 per Parke B.
[7] Sale of Goods Act 1979, s 30(1).
[8] *Behrend & Co. Ltd v Produce Brokers Co. Ltd.* [1920] 3 KB 530.

Similar is the situation where employees only tender a part of the work they are obliged to perform. In *Miles v Wakefield Metropolitan DC*[9] the plaintiff was a superintendent registrar of births, deaths, and marriages, who, in accordance with instructions from his trade union, refused to perform weddings on Saturday mornings. His employer made it clear that in such circumstances his attendance at the office during those hours would not be required and he would be considered not to be in performance of his duties. The employer deducted 3/37ths of his salary, the proportion of time not worked during each week, and the plaintiff brought an action to recover this sum. The claim failed, but Lords Templeman and Brightman expressed the *obiter* opinion that an employee whose work fell short of that necessary to give rise to a contractual entitlement to be paid could claim for a *quantum meruit*.[10] Lord Bridge by contrast stated that no such claim could succeed as it would 'presuppose that the original contract of employment had been superseded by a new agreement'.[11]

The view of Lords Templeman and Brightman is justifiable *if* there are sufficient facts from which it may be inferred that the employer has accepted the lesser work from the employee on the basis that it will be paid for. As in the context of sale, the employer must have had the opportunity to reject what is offered. An employer who continues to give an employee tasks to perform and access to work premises, knowing full well that the employee is refusing to fulfil the terms of his contract so as to be entitled to be paid his wage or salary, may be taken to have entered into a new agreement that the work done is to be paid for at the contract rate, just as with a buyer of goods who accepts short delivery. This does not involve the contract of employment being superseded, but merely an agreement that during the period of the dispute that work accepted is to be paid for.

However, in *Wiluszynski v Tower Hamlets LBC*[12] one of the tasks of the plaintiff employed by a council was to answer inquiries from councillors concerning the council housing estates. The plaintiff's union instructed him to refuse to answer such inquiries. The defendant council made it clear that unless he was prepared to answer such inquiries he would not be paid. The plaintiff carried on performing his other tasks, and then claimed his salary at the end of the dispute. His claim was rejected. The result should have been different if the employer had given the employee instructions on work to do and how to do it (ie if there had been a fresh request to do specific work from which a new agreement might have been inferred).[13]

What if in *Sumpter v Hedges* payment had been made in advance of the work being started? This should make no difference to the net result. The builder is not entitled to the payment if the work is not completed, and restitution of it to the employer should follow without deduction. By contrast if we see the payor's claim as determined by the extent to which the defendant builder is 'enriched', it might be said that the claim should be limited to the extent of any net enrichment as a result of the performance of the contract by both parties. This would result in recovery of only the net balance of what had been paid after the expenses incurred by the builder in doing the work had been deducted.[14] Thinking in terms

---

[9] [1987] 1 AC 539 (HL).
[10] *ibid*, 553, 561.
[11] *ibid*, 552.
[12] [1989] ICR 493 (CA).
[13] *ibid*, 501 *per* Fox LJ, 505 *per* Nicholls LJ.
[14] Suggested by B McFarlane and R Stevens, 'In Defence of *Sumpter v Hedges*' (2002) 118 567, 583–584. *Mea culpa*.

of 'enrichment' is misleading. There should be no question of 'counter-restitution' here and the fortuity of payment in advance should not impact the result.

3. Claims for Restitution of Services Against Party in Breach

(a) What is reversed?

In the ordinary case of a contract for the provision of a service for a fee, where that service has been rendered the usual claim will be one for the agreed sum. Where however either the service cannot be completely performed because the counterparty's co-operation is required and this is withheld, or the counterparty repudiates the contract before performance is complete and this repudiation is accepted, a *quantum meruit* may be awarded for the value of the part performance rendered.[15] The work is rendered on the condition that it will be paid for once complete, but also on the basis that the counterparty will allow such completion.

As we have already seen, what is reversed is the performance rendered under the contract, regardless of any benefit that may have been obtained by the counterparty as a result. The traditional illustration of this rule is *Planché v Colburn*.[16] The plaintiff was employed by the defendant to write a book on costume and ancient armour for *The Juvenile Library* for £100. The plaintiff wrote part of the book and was ready to complete it, but the defendant ceased publication of *The Juvenile Library* and refused to pay. The plaintiff was awarded £50 as the reasonable value of the work already done.

Although today it is common to try to re-explain this result as properly explicable as a claim for damages for breach of contract,[17] this was not the basis upon which the court reached its decision.[18] We see the same result, that what is reversed is the value of the performance rendered and not the consequent enrichment obtained, where no claim for damages is possible because the agreement is unenforceable.[19] What is recoverable is the value of the performance rendered, not of acts preparatory to performance that had not been contracted for.

This rule is also connected to the rule that the part performance of an entire obligation is not, without more, actionable. It would (even more) obviously be wrong to permit the party in breach to recover back the value of work done where this has not consequently enriched the counterparty, and so those disapproving the result in *Sumpter v Hedges* combine this with disapproval of *Planché v Colburn*.[20] Both are correctly decided.

As we have seen, generally inaction that results in a benefit to another is not actionable. If the holder of a power mistakenly fails to exercise it, in a way that benefits the party who is subject to the correlative liability, this is not, without more, actionable. The mistaken failure

---

[15] Eg *De Bernardy v Harding* (1853) 8 Ex 822, 155 ER 1586; *Lodder v Slowey* [1904] AC 442 (PC).
[16] (1831) 8 Bing 14, 131 ER 305. See also in the United States *Stephen v Camden & Philadelphia Soap Co* 68 A 69 (NJ, 1907); *Acme Process Equipment Company v United States* 347 F 2d 509 (Ct Cl 1965) reversed on other grounds 385 US 138 (1966); *Landmark Land Co v FDIC* 256 F 3d 135 (Fed Cir, 2001).
[17] Eg Burrows, *The Law of Restitution* (n 3), 346; J Edelman and E Bant, *Unjust Enrichment* (2nd edn, 2016), 70; A Kull, 'Restitution for Breach of Contract' (1994) 67 Southern California Law review 1465, 1487–1488.
[18] For exhaustive discussion see C Mitchell and P Mitchell, '*Planché v Colburn* (1831)' in C Mitchell and P Mitchell (eds), *Landmark Cases in the Law of Restitution* (2006).
[19] Eg *Brewer Street Investments Ltd v Barclay Woollen Co Ltd* [1954] 1 QB 428 (CA), discussed in Chapter 4, Reversal.
[20] Burrows, *The Law of Restitution* (n 3), 46, 356–358

to bring a valuable action within the relevant limitation period, that would have succeeded if brought, thereby benefitting another, gives rise to no claim to the consequent enrichment. A mistaken failure to exercise an option to buy a portion of land at a level below the market price, thereby benefitting the landowner, is not actionable.

Where however it is *agreed* that the plaintiff will forbear from doing something, and this forbearance is subject to a condition that fails, a claim for the value of the forbearance is possible. This is illustrated by *Gibb v Maidstone & Tunbridge NHS Trust*.[21] An NHS Trust entered into a compromise agreement with its former chief executive to settle the level of compensation in lieu of notice. Subsequently the Trust sought to resist payment under the agreement on the basis that it was irrationally generous and thereby *ultra vires* its powers as a public body to have agreed to. Although the trial judge had found for the Trust on this issue, the Court of Appeal overturned this result. However, in the alternative they considered what the position would be if the contract had been *ultra vires* the Trust. The court would have permitted a claim to the value of the statutory unfair dismissal claim that the former chief executive had foregone as a result of the settlement.

Similar is the use value over time of someone in possession of land or goods. If I give you the possession of my car for a period of time by mistake, and you accept it on the basis that it does not have to be paid for, no claim should arise even if my mistake saves you the expense of hiring another. By contrast, if you obtain possession under an agreement, under which the use is to be paid for, if you refuse to pay, a claim to the use value of the vehicle for the period in possession is available.[22] The undisturbed use was what you bargained for under the agreement.

These examples are illustrations of the dangers of over-generalisation, and assuming that what counts as an 'enrichment' (ie the appropriate subject matter of a successful claim) is the same both inside and outside the context of an agreement.

(b) A price ceiling?

A question that has received different answers from different courts, and divided commentators,[23] is whether the claim for restitution of the value of the work done is either capped by, or quantified by reference to, the contract price for the completed work. If the plaintiff has made a bad bargain, so that the work done had a market worth higher than the agreed price, can the plaintiff escape this ceiling? If we see the claim for the value of the work as identical in form to that for the repayment of money, we might think that consistency requires, as we allow the bad bargain to be escaped in one case (as in *Bush v Canfield*), we should allow it in the other.

The decision of the High Court of Australia in *Mann v Paterson Constructions Pty Ltd*[24] provides a useful vehicle for consideration because of the division between the sophisticated views adopted by different members of the court. The simplified facts were that the

---

[21] [2010] EWCA Civ 678, [2010] IRLR 786.
[22] *Dimond v Lovell* [2002] 1 AC 384 (HL) (although the claim failed because of the policy of protection invalidating the contract).
[23] Compare Burrows, *The Law of Restitution* (n 3), 348–350 with C Mitchell, P Mitchell, and S Watterson (eds), *Goff & Jones: The Law of Unjust Enrichment* (9th edn, 2016), [3-12]. Compare also Birks' initial view in P Birks, *An Introduction to the Law of Restitution* (rev edn, 1989), 288 with his subsequent position in P Birks, 'In Defence of Free Acceptance' in A S Burrows (ed), *Essays on the Law of Restitution* (1991), 136. See also the views of the original authors of Goff and Jones, *The Law of Restitution* (7th edn, 2007), 467–468.
[24] (2019) 373 ALR 1.

Manns entered into a contract with a builder for the construction of two townhouses in Victoria. The building contract was divisible into severable entire stages, with the builder entitled to progress payments upon the completion of parts of the overall work. The Manns had excluded the builder from the site, conduct that amounted to a repudiation of the contract. The question arose as to the builder's entitlement to a *quantum meruit* both for the stages of work that it had an accrued right to payment because complete, and those it did not. All members of the court held that where the builder had an accrued contractual right to be paid for work done, the action for this agreed sum was the exclusive remedy available. A majority[25] held, in accordance with English authority,[26] that a *quantum meruit* for the work done under the incomplete stages was available, and three of that majority concluded that any such award should not necessarily be 'capped' at the sum that would have been payable if the work had been finished.[27] Gageler J alone reached the conclusion that a *quantum meruit* was available but that it should never exceed the contract price.[28]

The position of the dissentients was insupportable. Their central argument was that which we have already seen in relation to the recovery of money, that to allow a claim for a *quantum meruit* that exceeds any possible award for damages for breach would fail to respect the parties' contractual allocation of risk. Again however, parties' bargain for performance from their counterparties, not for a particular remedy by way of a court order following breach, and such court orders have not hitherto been restricted to awards of damages in any event. The parties could not therefore have bargained on that basis. The obligation to pay damages does not arise because that is what the parties agreed to, but rather because paying damages is the next best thing to the promisor doing what he agreed to do. The agreement is a necessary condition of the obligation to pay damages, but that is not the same thing as the damages award being part of what was agreed. In the context of an unenforceable contract, a claim for damages for breach is unavailable, and so the only possible award is one for the value of the work provided. It would be incoherent if a party to an unenforceable contract had available a non-contractual *quantum meruit* when a party to an enforceable contract did not. The conclusion of the dissentients that a *quantum meruit* was unavailable in the context of an enforceable contract cannot be satisfactorily squared with the earlier decision of the High Court in *Pavey & Matthews Pty Ltd v Paul*[29] that it is available where a contract is unenforceable.

Once it is accepted that a claim for a *quantum meruit* should be available, should it be capped by the contract price? What was the condition that was attached to the performance of the work? It was that the work would be paid for once complete. At the point at which the builder has been paid this agreed sum, this condition is necessarily satisfied. Any award greater than the agreed sum for full completion cannot therefore be justified. The price for the work should therefore operate as an *overall* cap on what is recoverable. Gageler J's answer was the correct one,[30] with the incidental advantages of commercial certainty and practical convenience for the plaintiff.

---

[25] Nettle, Gordon, Edelman, and Gageler JJ; Kiefel, Bell, and Keane JJ dissenting
[26] *Taylor v Motability Finance Ltd* [2004] EWHC 2619 (Comm) (Cooke J).
[27] Nettle, Gordan, and Edelman JJ.
[28] (2019) 373 ALR 1, esp [82]–[83], see also [19] and [51].
[29] (1987) 162 CLR 221 (HCA).
[30] *Cf.* Kull, *The Restatement (Third) Restitution and Unjust Enrichment* (n 4), 626.

In the classic US decision of *Boomer v Muir*[31] the plaintiffs recovered $275,000 for incomplete work in building a dam, even though only $20,000 remained payable if the work had been completed. However, it seems probable that this was based upon the idea that the breach (or its acceptance) avoided the contract, so that its terms no longer controlled the parties' relation. Although at one time this was arguably the effect of a fundamental breach of a contractual obligation in England and elsewhere, today this is no longer plausible.[32]

The value of the work should be assessed according to the market cost of obtaining it. The contract rate may provide evidence of this market value, but it should not determine it.[33] This may be contrasted with the case of a buyer who accepts a tendered short delivery of goods, where the contract is used to infer the price the parties are agreeing will be paid for the goods accepted. A non-contractual *quantum meruit* should be fixed by the objective value of the service that is sought to be returned, not the contract rate. The contract rate should not therefore operate as a *rateable* limit on what can be recovered, but as an overall cap.[34]

It is unclear what the circumstances in which Nettle, Gordan, and Edelman JJ in *Mann* would have permitted a claim that exceeded the contract price for full completion might have been. Some commentators, who have sought to explain recovery as based upon the enrichment of the defendant, have argued that where the defendant is incontrovertibly benefitted by the part performance of the claimant in a way that is greater than the contract price, there should be no cap.[35] It would then only be where the claimant had to rely upon the terms of the contract to show that the defendant was 'enriched' that it would so operate as a limit. There would, on this view, be a 'valuation' ceiling and not a universal 'contractual' one. An example may illustrate the point.

> *D* employs *P* to construct a building on *D*'s land for £500,000. *P* does two thirds of the work but is then excluded from the site by *D*. *D* subsequently sells the land with the building for £2 million more than would have been obtained without the building work. The market value of the work done is £1.5 million.

Although *D* is, incontrovertibly, £2 million better off than if the work had not been done, *P*'s claim should still be capped at the contract price. The agreed condition under which the work was done cannot fail if he is paid this sum. This avoids the unacceptable paradox, that the plurality of the High Court of Australia left open as a possibility, of a builder being paid more for partial than for completed work.

---

[31] 24 P 2d 570 (1933). See G Palmer, 'The Contract Price as a Limit on Restitution for Defendant's Breach' (1959) 20 Ohio St LJ 264. The Kull, *Restatement Third, Restitution and Unjust Enrichment* (n 4), § 38(2)(b) adopts a price cap, but characterises the claim as one for damages, which would not be accepted in other common law jurisdictions. *Cf.* American Law Institute, *The Restatement (Second) of the Law of Contracts* (1981), cmt. D, ill 2. Discussed D Friedmann, 'Does the Dead Contract Rule Restitution from Its Grave' (2012) 92 Boston Law Rev 811.
[32] *Photo Productions Ltd v Securicor Transport Ltd* [1980] AC 827 (HL).
[33] *BP v Hunt* [1979] 1 WLR 783, 825 *per* Goff J.
[34] But compare the Kull, *Restatement (Third)* (n 4) § 38 cmt. C illus 9 and the German position BGB § 346.
[35] Eg Burrows, *The Law of Restitution* (n 3), 349–350.

4. Claims for Restitution of Payments by Party in Breach

It is important to distinguish between deposits and part payments. A deposit is an earnest, part performance that it is agreed is to be irrecoverable if the payor backs out from completion.[36] If a deposit has become payable, and the buyer repudiates the deal, if the seller accepts the repudiation the deposit is recoverable as an agreed sum, earned without more.[37] Sometimes a deposit paid is recoverable (or ceases to be payable) where it is penal,[38] but this is not based upon any agreed failed condition.

Unless all payments in advance were to be treated as deposits, it follows that other payments in advance are recoverable where the condition fails.[39] This usually occurs where the payor repudiates the bargain, and this is accepted by the payee, so that no further performance will be rendered which will satisfy the condition of payment. The payee then has a counterclaim for damages for the repudiatory breach.

The facts and result, if not the reasoning, of Stable J in *Dies v British International Mining*[40] illustrate this scenario. The plaintiff agreed to buy 20,000 rifles with ammunition from the defendants. The total agreed price was £270,000, of which the plaintiffs paid £100,000 in advance. The plaintiff never paid the balance and was unwilling to accept delivery. In response the defendants elected to treat the contract as at an end. The contract stipulated for the payment of liquidated damages of £13,500 for non-completion, which the plaintiff accepted he was liable to pay and should be deducted from the amount pre-paid. He sought restitution of the balance. The claim succeeded, however Stable J saw the right to recover as 'derived from the terms of the contract' and not based upon a total failure of consideration.[41] This was in an era when the '*Chandler v Webster* fallacy' (discussed in relation to frustration) was alive and well, so it was perhaps thought that the contract had to be a nullity before restitution followed, and is therefore best ignored.

The decision was, however, in one respect an easy one. The defendants had elected to terminate the deal, so that it became certain that no future performance would be rendered. It is orthodoxy that an 'unaccepted repudiation is a thing writ in water'.[42] What if the seller had refused to accept the buyer's repudiation and insisted that they remained ready and willing to deliver the goods? Could they thereby have prevented the condition under which the payment was made from failing, and refused to make restitution indefinitely?

The better view is that in the majority of cases, including that of a sale contract where the seller can only make delivery if it is accepted by the buyer, 'the innocent party cannot perform the contract without the concurrence of the party repudiating the contract'[43] so that the condition cannot be fulfilled. The buyer can withhold co-operation, thereby preventing the payment from being earned. This is sometimes seen as a restriction upon the remedy of the action for the agreed sum where the money is unpaid.[44] However, it is better seen as concerning the parties' substantive contractual rights, and so equally applicable to a claim

---

[36] *Howe v Smith* (1884) 27 Ch D 89 (CA), 95.
[37] *Hinton v Sparkes* (1868) LR 3 CP 161.
[38] *Workers Trust and Merchants Bank Ltd v Dojap Investments Ltd* [1993] AC 573 (PC) discussed in Section D.
[39] *Mayson v Clouet* [1924] AC 980; *McDonald v Dennys Lascelles Ltd* (1933) 48 CLR 475.
[40] [1939] 1 KB 724, 108 LJKB 398 160 LT 563.
[41] ibid, 744.
[42] *Howard v Pickford Tool Co Ltd* [1951] 1 KB 417 (CA), 421 *per* Asquith LJ.
[43] *White and Carter (Councils) Ltd v McGregor* [1962] AC 413, 422 *per* Lord Reid.
[44] E Peel, *Treitel The Law of Contract* (15th edn, 2020), [21-2009].

for restitution of a payment already made. Again, the same end result should be reached regardless of the fortuity of whether the money has in fact been paid. Termination of the contract is unnecessary, and restitution should follow whenever the condition of a performance rendered fails, even if the reason for such failure is the defendant's withholding of co-operation.

C. Frustration

1. Money Obligations

(a) The common law
The common law position on the unwinding of contracts following their frustration has been frequently criticised,[45] but by the time it was largely[46] replaced in England by the Law Reform (Frustrated Contracts) Act 1943 it had reached a position both justifiable and consistent with the treatment of claims outside of the context of frustration. The approach adopted by the Act is to see the contract as a joint venture between the parties and to instruct the judge to share the gains acquired and losses suffered as a result of its unanticipated discharge between them. Unfortunately, it combines complexity, lack of principle, and uncertainty.

In principle, the event of frustration should make no difference to the approach to determining which obligations remain to be performed, and when a performance rendered can be recovered. The issue remains one of contractual construction. On the correct construction of the contract, following the frustrating event, is the promisee entitled to the payment (or other performance) or not? An example:

> *P* agrees to hire a Music Hall from *D* for at a rate of £1,000 per month. After three months, the Music Hall burns down through neither party's fault.

D has become unconditionally entitled to be paid £3,000. If he has not been paid, he should be able to claim this sum.[47] It is not therefore the case in principle that frustration discharges *contracts*.[48] Instead, it discharges specific obligations under a contract, whilst others may remain unaltered. If *D* has been paid more than £3,000 in advance, he must make restitution of any balance. It is not the case that frustration avoids the bargain, rather its interpretation should continue to govern its unwinding.

The entire doctrine of frustration is best understood in terms of whether the *obligations* of the parties are subject to a condition that has failed. We should properly speak of the frustration of *obligations* rather than of contracts.

---

[45] Eg G Williams, 'Partial Performance of Entire Contracts' (1941) 57 LQR 373; Peel, *Treitel The Law of Contract* (n 44), [19-099]; Burrows, *The Law of Restitution* (n 3), 362.
[46] The Act does not apply to the carriage of goods by sea (except for voyage and demise charters) contracts of insurance, and contracts for the sale of specific goods that are destroyed before risk has passed (s 2(5)).
[47] Eg *Menetone v Athawes* (1764) 3 Burr 1592, 97 ER 998.
[48] *Contra* Law Reform (Frustrated Contracts) Act 1943, s 1(1).

138 CONTRACT

Outside of straightforward contracts for the exchange of a single product or service for a price, the parties' obligations will commonly be 'severable' in ways other than temporal. Another example:

> P agrees to hire seven Music Halls from D at a rate of £1,000 per month each. After three months, one of the Music Halls burns down through neither party's fault.

Although it is often said that English law recognises no doctrine of 'partial frustration', here the correct result would be that D's obligation to provide each Hall for hire is conditional upon its continued existence.[49] As a result of the fire, D should be relieved from the obligation to provide the destroyed building, but ordinarily not the others. Whether the obligation to provide the seven Halls is entire or severable is, as always, a matter of contractual construction. The obligation to pay £1,000 per month for each of the Music Halls is capable of performance but is conditional upon each Hall being provided by the counterparty for use. The obligation to pay for the Hall destroyed therefore also ceases after its destruction.[50] Contracts are not impossible to perform, only specific obligations under them. If payment has been made in advance, only the price for the Hall destroyed that has not been earned should be recoverable. The obligation to provide each Hall is (implicitly) conditional upon its continued existence. The obligation to pay the hire is (expressly) conditional upon having a Hall to use. These obligations are not discharged for the same reason (eg impossibility). The usual construction would be that each parties' other obligations were not conditional upon the existence of the one Hall, and so should continue unaltered.

Problems have been introduced by the courts adopting unrealistic constructions in some cases, of which the most infamous example is the decision of the Court of Appeal in *Chandler v Webster*.[51] Chandler agreed to hire a room on Pall Mall from Webster to overlook the King's coronation parade of 1902 for a fee of £141 15s. Chandler's intention was to erect a stand and sell tickets. The entire balance was payable before the procession, which was to take place on 26 and 27 June. On 19 June Chandler paid £100. The King then fell ill, and the procession was cancelled. Chandler claimed restitution of the £100 he had paid, whilst Webster counterclaimed for the £41 15s balance. The court denied the plaintiff restitution, and also ordered that the unpaid balance be paid. The court accepted that if the contract were 'wiped out altogether'[52] or 'rescinded *ab initio*'[53] that the unpaid balance could not be recovered and the payment already made would have to be returned but as the contract was merely discharged by frustration by the King's illness, money payable before the frustrating event could still be claimed, and payments already made could not be recovered.

As the decision to award Webster the unpaid balance of £41 15s shows, the error of the Court of Appeal was not one concerning the principles applicable to a claim for restitution specifically. Rather, it was one of construction of the contract.

---

[49] *Cf. Rugg v Minett* (1810) 11 East 210, ER 985.
[50] R G McElroy, *Impossibility of Performance* (1941) (G Williams ed), 99–100. There is no omission in the Law Reform (Frustrated Contracts) Act 1943. It is the agreement itself which determines which obligations cease, not the Act, save in the mistake that is s 1(2). *Contra* Peel, *Treitel The Law of Contract* (n 44), [19-115].
[51] [1904] 1 KB 493 (CA); See also *Blakeley v Muller* [1903] 2 KB 760n; *cf. Knowles v Bovill* (1870) 22 LT 70. Disapproved *Fibrosa Spolka Akcyjna v Fairbairn Lawson Combe Barbour Ltd* [1943] AC 32 (HL).
[52] [1904] 1 KB 493 (CA), 499, *per* Collins MR.
[53] *ibid*, 501 *per* Romer LJ.

In the earlier 'Coronation case' of *Krell v Henry*,[54] on similar facts, the defendant had paid a deposit of £25, and the plaintiff was seeking to recover the outstanding balance of £75 hire by 24 June. By contrast with the result in *Chandler v Webster*, this action for the agreed sum failed. What was the difference? The proclamation that the procession was cancelled was made on the morning of 24 June, and as the defendant had the whole day on which to pay, no cause of action finally accrued for payment before the moment of discharge by frustration.

These different results cannot be justified. Although the money in *Chandler v Webster* was *payable* before the moment of discharge, the owner's continued *entitlement* to this payment was subject to the condition subsequent that the coronation procession took place. Absent the procession, no action for the outstanding balance should have been possible, and the money already paid should have been ordered to be returned. The date upon which the money was payable should not be determinative of the conditions to which it is subject.

The case is the same as one for the sale of goods where the price is payable in advance. If it subsequently becomes impossible to pass title to the goods because of their destruction, the buyer cannot maintain an action for the agreed sum as the debt is no longer due, and payments already made must be returned. The obligation to pay is defeasible, subject to a condition subsequent that title to the goods passes.

The most difficult issue in the Coronation cases was never litigated. Where part of the price is described as a deposit, as in *Krell v Henry*, must it still be paid after the frustrating event, or, where already paid, can it be recovered? This turns upon the meaning of a deposit. If we interpret it as guaranteeing that the payor will not back out from the deal, an earnest of his performance, then it ought to be recoverable as it, like the other payment obligations, was conditional upon there being a Coronation. Alternatively, if it is construed as being earned as soon as the contract is entered into, regardless of whether the hiring actually takes place, then it should be irrecoverable.

In 1924 the House of Lords held that the supposed rule in *Chandler v Webster* that the 'loss lies where it falls' did not apply in Scotland,[55] and the problem created by *Chandler* was subsequently corrected by them in England in *Fibrosa Spolka Akcyjna v Fairbairn Lawson Combe Barbour Ltd*.[56] The plaintiffs were a textile company in Poland. In July 1939 they entered into a contract with the defendant British firm for the supply of bespoke industrial machines. The overall price was £4,800, with £1,600 payable with the order, the balance payable against shipping documents. The plaintiffs paid £1,000 of the initial sum on account. On 1 September 1939 Germany invaded Poland, and, on 3 September, Britain declared war. The entitlement to the payment was conditional upon the machines being delivered, which could now no longer occur, and so restitution was awarded. *Chandler v Webster* was overruled.

Errors of contractual construction, as had occurred in *Whincup v Hughes*[57] and *Chandler v Webster* are better dealt with through judicial decision than legislative intervention. The mistakes were not about the rules but their application. The common law position after *Fribrosa* is subject to two criticisms,[58] but neither is justifiable. First, it is said,

---

[54] [1903] 2 KB 740 (CA).
[55] *Cantiare San Rocco v Clyde Shipbuilding and Engineering Co* [1924] AC 226 (HL).
[56] [1943] AC 32.
[57] (1870–1871) LR 6 CP 78.
[58] Eg *Chitty on Contracts* (Hugh Beale, ed) (34th edn, 2021), [26-103].

the supposed rule that any counter-performance at all bars recovery survives, the so-called 'total failure' restriction. Of course, the opposite is true on the facts of *Fibrosa*. The sellers had begun manufacturing for the purpose of performance but this did not bar recovery. Second, and inconsistently, it is claimed to be problematic that the common law did not permit the payee to set off the expenditure which he had already incurred in performing. However, in principle there should be no such setting off. The payor's claim is to the return of the performance rendered, not the overall net enrichment of the payee. The payee has incurred the expenditure on the basis that he would be paid as and when he completed performance. There was no agreement in *Fibrosa* that the payee was entitled to anything for part performance, and in this respect the case is the same as *Sumpter v Hedges*. Such setting off should only be permissible if there is an entitlement to be paid for the expenditure incurred.

Unfortunately, the UK legislature decided that further intervention was required. During a World War.

(b) Legislation

The position for most contracts in England is now governed by the Law Reform (Frustrated Contracts) Act 1943. As drafted, the Act makes the opposite error to that made in *Chandler v Webster*. Section 1(2) of the Act commences (emphasis added):

> *All* sums paid or payable to any party in pursuance of the contract before the time when the parties were so discharged (in this Act referred to as 'the time of discharge') shall, in the case of sums so paid, be recoverable from him as money received by him for the use of the party by whom the sums were paid, and, in the case of sums so payable, cease to be payable;

This makes no differentiation between payments that have become unconditionally earned and those that have not by the time of the discharging event. Instead of unconditional payments before discharge being unaffected by the frustrating event, *all* payments due cease to be payable, and *all* moneys paid are recoverable.

This cannot be correct in principle. It is an example of the error we have already seen of seeing termination as equivalent to avoidance, so that any performance under the contract rendered in the past needs to be reversed. An employee's obligations under her contract of employment may be frustrated by her death but that should not mean that wages already earned cease to be payable, still less that all that has been paid over the years before becomes repayable.[59]

Ridiculous results such as these can be avoided by relying upon a subsequent provision. Section 2(4) provides:

> Where it appears to the court that a part of the contract to which this Act applies can properly be severed from the remainder of the contract, being a part wholly performed before the time of discharge, or so performed except for the payment in respect of that part

---

[59] *Stubbs v Holywell Ry* (1867) LR 2 Ex 311.

of the contract of sums which are or can be ascertained under the contract, the court shall treat that part of the contract as if it were a separate contract and had not been frustrated.

This cumbersome provision creates a judicial discretion ('appears to the court') to apply a fiction ('as if it were a separate contract') in order to deal with the overly broad starting point in section 1(2). As its title makes clear, the Act makes the common mistake of thinking that it is contracts, rather than obligations, that are frustrated, and then has to solve the error by allowing the court to create fictional separate 'contracts'.

Section 1(2)'s error may be further illustrated by considering a simple example of the sale of goods, where property and risk have passed to the buyer, but where the seller has not yet delivered the goods themselves as the contract obliges him to do. If the goods are destroyed without fault, the seller will be relieved from the obligation to deliver through its impossibility. The buyer, who was the party on risk, must still pay as the delivery is not a condition of that obligation. If the Act applies, section 1(2) states that the buyer is relieved of the obligation to pay even though he was the party on risk of destruction, unless the sale is artificially treated as a 'separate contract' from the obligation of delivery. Unfortunately, the common law only continues to apply to contracts for the sale of specific goods.[60]

The badly drafted statutory language is best construed wherever possible so as to conform with the correct question: is the payment subject to an agreed condition that has failed? If so, it ceases to be payable if unpaid, and is recoverable if already paid. But not otherwise.

Section 1(2) continues ('the proviso'):

Provided that, if the party to whom the sums were so paid or payable incurred expenses before the time of discharge in, or for the purpose of, the performance of the contract, the court may, if it considers it just to do so having regard to all the circumstance of the case, allow him to retain, or, as the case may be, recover the whole or any part of the sums so paid or payable, not being an amount in excess of the expenses so incurred.

Robert Goff J described this proviso as 'probably best rationalised as a statutory recognition of the defence of change of position'.[61] This was at a time when Robert Goff and Gareth Jones the authors were arguing for the judicial recognition of such a defence. However, the proviso does not operate in the same way as the change of position defence at common law. First, it is narrower, confining recovery to expenditure 'in or for the purpose of the performance of the contract'. If the recipient innocently spends the money paid on a holiday for himself no deduction is permitted under the proviso. Second, there is no need to show any connection between payments made and the incurring of expenditure, which may precede it. Third, it does not merely apply to payments already made, but also enables payments as yet unmade to be recoverable to the extent of the expenditure. The effect is to rewrite the parties' bargain. The buyer must pay for any work that is done, even though under the terms of the contract, as in *Fibrosa*, the obligation to pay anything is conditional upon a completion that has not and will never occur. Why the costs of the lost expenditure should fall on the payor rather that than the payee, and why this should turn upon whether money is paid or payable, is obscure, and the provision presumably allows the court to split the loss

---
[60] Section 2(5)(a).
[61] [1979] 1 WLR 783, 800 *per* Goff J.

between the parties ('if it considers it just'). Again, we have judicial discretion in place of a rule.[62]

In the one decision to actually consider the application of the proviso, *Gamerco SA v ICM/Fair Warning (Agency) Ltd*,[63] the court refused to make any deduction, reaching the same result as would have obtained at common law. The plaintiffs were concert promoters who had paid the defendants, the corporate form of Guns N' Roses, $412,500, with a balance of $362,500 still payable, when the obligation to provide a stadium, where the concert being promoted was to take place, was frustrated by it being declared unsafe a few days before the scheduled performance. The money paid was recoverable under the Act, and in principle this is the right result as the defendants were only entitled to the payment if the concert took place. By this point, the defendants had incurred expenses of $50,000, while the plaintiffs had incurred around $450,000. Garland J chose to exercise his discretion by making no deduction at all. This is the correct result in principle, and it is to be hoped that future courts exercise their choice in the same way.

Whether the approach of the Act in changing the terms of the bargain is thought justifiable probably turns upon what it is thought the basis of frustration is. One account is that the parties through their contract have entered into a joint venture. This venture has now been set aside by the law for reasons of fairness because of an unforeseen event. It may then be thought necessary to equitably share the loss that will be inevitably suffered between the parties to the enterprise. This loss sharing exercise need not, on this view, be constrained by the contract as the impact of the frustrating event is that it no longer governs the parties' relation.

The approach of the common law at the time of *Fibrosa*, by contrast, was to see the parties' relationship as governed by the agreement between them. Frustration does not abrogate the agreement but merely discharges future performance of certain obligations. Frustration occurs because of the agreement itself. Frustrated obligations to perform are, when the contract is properly construed, those that are conditional upon a state of affairs being in existence (eg the Music Hall that had been hired is not destroyed by fire). The restitution of payments made should be governed by the same principles as those applicable outside of the context of frustration.

2. Non-money Obligations

(a) Common law

As we have already seen, the part performance of an entire obligation under a contract, without more, gives rise to no claim for reimbursement. The person providing the service does so on the agreed basis that they must fulfil the contractual condition before they are entitled to be paid anything, and so there is no injustice to correct where they do not do so. Only if the counterparty prevents the fulfilment of the condition (eg by excluding a builder from a site, or refusing to accept the delivery of goods manufactured to order) is a claim for a *quantum meruit* possible. This rule should apply in the context of frustration, as elsewhere.

---

[62] See *Gamerco SA v ICM/Fair Warning (Agency) Ltd* [1995] 1 WLR 1226, 1237 *per* Garland J.
[63] [1995] 1 WLR 1226. See also *Lobb v Vasey Housing Auxiliary* [1963] VR 38.

In *Cutter v Powell*,[64] Cutter was a sailor on a voyage from Jamaica to Liverpool, who was to be paid upon arrival, but who died before the ship docked. His administratrix failed in her claim for a *quantum meruit* for the work done. Whether what is promised is to pay only upon completion or a proportion as the work as it is done (ie whether the obligation is entire) is again a matter of construction. On the facts, that the sailor's right to payment was conditional upon completion was clear because the agreed fee for the voyage was 30 guineas, four times the market rate payable for the time to be served.

It might be argued that in cases of frustration the logic of the entire obligation rule should not apply. Could it not be said that part of the basis upon which Cutter did the work was that he would have the opportunity to complete it, so that when he unforeseeably died should his estate not have a claim for the value of what he has done? Does the frustrating event mean that 'all bets are off'?[65]

The answer is that the defendant only accepted the work on the basis that they would pay if it were completed. To allow a claim for partial performance is to re-write the parties' bargain. The failure of Cutter's expectations cannot justify imposing an obligation on the counterparty. Cutter's contractual obligation to *continue* to work was subject to the condition that he lived. The shipowner's entitlement to the work *already rendered* was only subject to the condition that it was to be paid for once complete.

The decision of Pearson J in *Société Franco Tunisienne d'Armement v Sidermar S.P.A, The Massalia*[66] illustrates how a claim on another basis might succeed but is not, as is sometimes said, an exception to the general rule.[67] A vessel was chartered to carry iron ore from Masulipatan in India to Genoa via the Suez Canal. The canal was closed by the second Arab-Israeli war and the ship had to undertake the voyage via the Cape instead. Pearson J concluded that the obligation of carriage was frustrated (a result overturned on appeal[68] because at the time of contracting the Suez crisis was already within the contemplation of the parties) but allowed a claim for the value of the carriage to Genoa.

Here there was a bailment of the goods to the shipowners at the time of the frustrating event. The shipowners could not have dumped the iron ore into the ocean and performed another contract. As bailees they were obliged to return the goods to the cargo-owners. They were in the same position as other bailees where the contract has come to an end, upon whom the law imposes a duty to incur expenditure on behalf of another.[69] As a result, they should be entitled to recover the expenditure they have been compelled to provide.

(b) Legislation

The scope of the legislation amending the consequences of frustration is wider than the Law Revision Committee report that preceded it.[70] That Committee had been set up to consider 'the rule in *Chandler v Webster*' but the Act also amended the law in relation to the performance of non-money obligations. Section 1(3) of the Act provides:

---

[64] (1795) 6 TR 320, 101 ER 573.
[65] *Cf. Angus v Scully* 58 NE 674 (Mass 1900).
[66] [1961] 2 QB 278.
[67] Burrows, *The Law of Restitution* (n 3), 363; Birks, *An Introduction to the Law of Restitution* (n 23), 241.
[68] [1964] 2 QB 226.
[69] See Chapter 10, Necessity.
[70] The Law Revision Committee, 'Seventh Interim Report (Rule in *Chandler v Webster*)' Cmnd. 6009.

(3) Where any party to the contract has, by reason of anything done by any other party thereto in, or for the purpose of, the performance of the contract, obtained a valuable benefit (other than a payment of money to which the last foregoing subsection applies) before the time of discharge, there shall be recoverable from him by the said other party such sum (if any), not exceeding the value of the said benefit to the party obtaining it, as the court considers just, having regard to all the circumstances of the case and, in particular,—

(a) the amount of any expenses incurred before the time of discharge by the benefited party in, or for the purpose of, the performance of the contract, including any sums paid or payable by him to any other party in pursuance of the contract and retained or recoverable by that party under the last foregoing subsection, and

(b) the effect, in relation to the said benefit, of the circumstances giving rise to the frustration of the contract.

The first thing to note is that the claim is dependent upon establishing that the defendant has obtained a 'valuable benefit' before the time of discharge. The sub-section draws a distinction between the performance and the resultant valuable benefit. The claim is not simply to the reversal of the value of the service itself, as in *Planché v Colburn*, but is instead dependent upon there being a consequential enrichment that results from that service.[71] Conversely the 'valuable benefit' may be vastly greater than the market value of the service itself, as where a prospector discovers a large and unexpected deposit of a mineral, vastly increasing the value of the defendant's land. The 'valuable benefit' provides a 'cap' on recovery, it is not the valuation of the claim,[72] and the valuable benefit that the defendant receives may be transitory, as the frustrating event may destroy it.

It was suggested by Goff J in *BP v Hunt* that it would have been better if the legislature had treated the services themselves as beneficial,[73] but this would have gone much too far. It is one thing to make the defendant give up a factual gain that he has made from the frustration of a joint venture, if it correlates with an expense incurred by the counterparty. It is quite another to make the defendant pay for a partial service that he has not in fact benefitted from, and that he only agreed to pay anything for if it were completed.

Goff J also suggested that if contract work for a building were frustrated by fire which destroyed the building the award would be nil as there would be no valuable benefit.[74] This is a slip, as the sub-section provides for the valuable benefit to be assessed before the time of discharge (ie before the fire), and further provides (s 1(3)(b)) that the effect of the frustrating event is to be taken into account at the next stage of quantifying the 'just sum'. However, this misreading is an understandable mistake as it is difficult to see what the basis for the defendant having to pay for partial work that has not, as things turned out, left him in any way better off, and which he never agreed to pay for, might be.

Second, as with section 1(2), the court is required to 'have regard' to the expenses incurred by the benefitted party before the time of discharge. Again, it seems doubtful whether

---

[71] *BP Exploration Co. (Libya) Ltd. v. Hunt (No. 2)* [1979] 1 WLR 783, 801–802 *per* Goff J.
[72] ibid, 799.
[73] ibid, 802.
[74] ibid, 801.

this is a statutory version of the defence of change of position, as such expenditure must also be 'in, or for the purpose of performing, the contract'.[75] On the statutory language, the expenditure is something the court is supposed to always take into account in quantifying the just sum, it is not a defence to be pleaded and proved by the defendant.

Third, Goff J suggested that in quantifying the 'just sum', the correct approach, having applied the 'valuable benefit' cap, was to adopt the same approach as that at common law and to measure recovery as the 'reasonable value of the plaintiff's performance'.[76] However, there does not seem to be any basis for this assumption in the statutory language. What if this figure is higher than the contract rate for the work? Goff J suggested, surely correctly, that the defendant should not have to pay more than the price he bargained for.[77]

The facts of *BP Exploration (Libya) Ltd v Hunt (No. 2)*, still the only substantive decision to consider the operation of section 1(3), are complex. This complexity hides the injustice the Act gives rise to. It is important to understand not only the result reached but also that which would have been given by the common law (which, as a matter of justice, is the correct one).

Mr Hunt obtained an oil concession from the Libyan government in 1957 but did not have the resources to exploit it himself. He entered into a contract with BP under which he gave them half the concession, and they undertook to do the exploration, and, if oil was discovered, the extraction. Before it was known whether the concession was a productive field, Hunt was paid in money and oil ('farm-in' contributions). Hunt was then obliged to reimburse BP half of the expenditure incurred by them, and the farm-in contributions, plus 25%, from three-eighths of his share of any oil production once it came on stream.

All went well at first. A large field was discovered and went into operation in 1967. Oil and revenue flowed. However, in 1971, the Libyan government expropriated BP's interest, and subsequently, in 1973, Mr Hunt's. At that point BP had received $63 million of reimbursement oil from Mr Hunt for their expenditure. They had in addition also received huge amounts from their half share of the concession.

It was BP's obligations of performance that were frustrated. They were unable to perform any further extraction, and if Mr Hunt had sued them for breach of contract any such claim would have failed. Mr Hunt's obligations to reimburse were always possible to perform but were conditional upon oil continuing to flow which, after expropriation, it did not.

Applying the Act, Goff J (whose decision with minor changes was upheld by the Court of Appeal and House of Lords) identified the 'valuable benefit' obtained by Mr Hunt, as a counterfactual matter as a result of the work, as being $85 million. This was calculated by the oil he had received from the concession and the compensation paid by the Libyan government for the expropriation. The market value of the payments made and work by BP was $98 million[78] but from this was deducted the $63 million already received from Mr Hunt in 'reimbursement oil'. The result was an award of the balance of $35 million, as this was lower than the valuable benefit cap.

At common law, the correct approach would be to identify as a pre-condition of recovery an agreed condition for BP's performance under the contract that had failed.

---

[75] But see *ibid*, 804 *per* Goff J.
[76] *ibid*, 805.
[77] *ibid*, 806.
[78] The $2 million 'farm-in payments' should have been recoverable under s 1(2) of the Act, rather than s 1(3) but Goff J did not differentiate the two. See [1983] 2 AC 352, 370.

What was this condition? Mr Hunt had already paid BP all that they were contractually entitled to under the deal. He never agreed to accept the work on any other basis. In this respect, the case is the same as *Cutter v Powell*. No recovery should have been permitted.

BP would have been contractually entitled to further reimbursement for the work *if* Mr Hunt had continued to receive the oil. What they were doing (and succeeded in getting under the Act) was obtaining reimbursement for their work even though such subsequent revenues were never received by Mr Hunt. The consequence was that they were reimbursed at a higher rate than the contract provided for from the revenues Mr Hunt had obtained before the expropriation by the Libyan government (ie at a greater than three-eighths rate). It is true that Mr Hunt had greatly benefitted from BP's work, but this was not a windfall, but rather what he was contractually entitled to. BP had also enormously benefitted from the oil revenues they had received from the half of the concession transferred to them by Mr Hunt.

The end result was to re-write the parties' bargain, giving BP more than they had earned. The agreed condition under which the work was done, that BP would be reimbursed for its work if and when Mr Hunt received oil revenues overtime, never in fact failed. The result was a kind of one-sided rescission, with Mr Hunt required to reimburse BP for the market value of the work they had done, whilst BP kept the benefit of the half share of the concession they had obtained from him that had been profitable for four years.

The problem with section 1(3) is the same as that we have already seen in relation to section 1(2). It requires *all* benefits received to be reversed, regardless of whether the agreed condition under which they have been rendered has failed. The oddity of *BP v Hunt* is that the logic of this complete unwinding was only applied to the service provided by BP and not to the value of the half share of the concession provided to them by Mr Hunt.

It may be doubted whether the Act can be made to cohere with general principles of contract law. It is not an improvement upon the law as it stood before its enactment. It introduces a quite different regime for restitution in cases of 'frustrated contracts' (sic) than applies outside of that context. That it has survived so long is probably a result of the rarity of its application, frustration in England being exceptional and commercial parties wisely providing for its effect in their agreement.

3. Other Jurisdictions

England is not, of course, alone in having abandoned the traditional common law rules governing the consequences of frustration. The US Second Contracts Restatement abandons any pretence to a rule and states that the courts may 'grant relief on such terms as justice requires'.[79] With no rule, there is nothing much further to analyse. Other Commonwealth jurisdictions have also enacted frustration specific statutes, which are not an improvement upon the common law position.[80]

---

[79] *Restatement (Second) of Contracts* (n XX) § 272(2). But *cf.* Kull, *Restatement (Third) Restitution* (n 4), § 34.
[80] Eg British Columbia (Frustrated Contracts) Act 1974; New South Wales (Frustrated Contracts) Act 1978.

D. Money, Services, and Penalties

One objection to the above analysis is that it does not treat payments and services in the same way. Where the claim is by the party in breach, an advanced payment is recoverable (*Dies*) but when the part performance of entire obligations is a service, it is not (*Sumpter*). The position of the common law following frustration that has been defended was, and where applicable still is, that payments are recoverable (*Fibrosa*) when the part performance of an entire obligation to provide a service is not (*Cutter*). The legislative intervention by contrast, that has been deprecated, treats money and services in (roughly) the same way in cases of frustration.

The explanation for the apparent different treatment lies in the proper construction of the agreement between the parties. Cases like *Sumpter v Hedges* and *Cutter v Powell* are more closely analogous to deposits, which are irrecoverable where the payor backs out, than they are to advanced payments. As with a deposit, the builder or seaman who fails to meet the condition of payment on its face has no complaint if the value of what he has done is 'forfeit' as a result. That was the bargain he made, and it has proven a losing one because of that failure. If the provider of a service has fulfilled the agreed condition of payment, the appropriate remedy is the action for the agreed sum.

Where the *quid pro quo* for a service is not a payment, or other performance that the court will order to be made, restitution should be possible where the condition of counter-performance has been met but has not been provided in return. In the previous chapter we saw examples of this where the agreement was unenforceable, so that the counter-performance could not be ordered to be made.[81] A further example:

> D, an advertising agency, agrees to run a promotional campaign for P's building business if P renovates D's premises. The obligation to run the campaign accrues in stages as the builder completes part of the work. P completes three of the four stages, but then leaves the job. D now refuses to run any part of the campaign.

If the court will not compel D to provide the service, the condition under which P did the work will consequently fail. Restitution ought therefore to follow. This illustrates that one reason for the different treatment of services and payments results from whether the court will compel the contractual counter-performance to which the claimant is entitled to be made. Where it will do so (as it always will with an obligation to pay money) no claim based upon a failure of the condition will usually arise.

A more significant divergence between money and services cases, that is much harder to justify, is that in the case of a deposit, the law does not permit the parties' complete freedom of contract, but instead requires penal deposits to be returned. By contrast, a service provided will always be 'forfeited' by the party who fails to meet the condition of payment. Legal systems, such as the United States, that do not accept the rule represented by *Sumpter v Hedges*, are re-writing the parties' bargain where the effect is harsh, in a way similar to the English rule against penal deposits.

---

[81] *Barnes v Eastenders Group* [2014] UKSC 26; [2015] AC 1: see **pp 117–118** above.

The leading decision on penal deposits is the decision of the Privy Council on an appeal from Jamaica in *Workers' Trust and Merchant Bank Ltd v Dojap Investments Ltd*.[82] A 25% deposit was paid for premises in Jamaica. The contract provided that the balance was to be paid within 14 days, and that time was of the essence. The buyer failed to pay on time, but subsequently tendered the balance. The seller refused to accept late payment and sought to terminate the contract and retain the deposit. The court held that the deposit must be returned, subject to a deduction for any damages suffered as a result of the buyer's breach.

Lord Browne-Wilkinson saw the rule against penal deposits as part of the general rule against giving effect to agreed penalties for breach. Just as a sum payable upon breach could be caught by the penalties rule, so could a sum forfeit upon breach. In principle the court thought that all deposits should be subject to the rule that if they were not a 'genuine pre-estimate of loss' to the vendor following breach, they should be returned. The question was whether the deposit was reasonable as earnest money. This general principle of vulnerability to invalidation has also been overlaid with a rule that a deposit of up to 10% is never susceptible to the penalties rule.

Today, however, the relationship between the rule against penalty clauses and that against penal deposits is not as close or clear, in England, as it was assumed to be when *Workers' Trust and Merchant Bank Ltd v Dojap Investments Ltd* was decided. The leading decision on the penalty clause doctrine is now *Cavendish Square Holdings BV v Makdessi*.[83] There the Supreme Court formulated the test for whether a clause was a penalty as being whether it created a secondary obligation arising upon breach which imposed a detriment on the contract-breaker out of all proportion to any legitimate interest of the innocent party in the enforcement of the primary obligation.

This (new) formulation of the penalties doctrine is best understood as part of the law of court orders or 'remedies'. Although contracting parties have (almost) unrestricted power to determine for themselves what their substantive primary rights and obligations are, they do not have the power to determine the orders a court will give them. The court is not a party to the contract and cannot be bound by the parties to give a court order contrary to what justice now requires. If, for example, a contract of employment stipulates that if the employee refuses to work, specific performance should be available, a court will refuse to give effect to such a term. Such a term purports to bind a third party, the court, and require it to give an order contrary to the principles of justice that the court applies in determining its orders.

A penalty clause similarly seeks to extract from the court an order for the payment of a sum upon breach that it would not otherwise give: a sum of money greater than the damages justice demands to rectify the wrong. Although the parties have some leeway in determining the secondary obligation that the court will order to be performed, they do not have absolute power to do so. Penalty clauses are not therefore void, but merely unenforceable.[84] A party who pays a penalty cannot recover it.

The above explanation has the benefit of explaining most of the features of the penalties rule in England (eg that it is a rule that applies only upon breach of a contract, concerns attempts to fix the secondary remedial obligations, and whether a clause is a penalty is

---

[82] [1993] AC 573 (PC).
[83] [2015] UKSC 67, [2016] AC 1172.
[84] *ibid*, [8], [9], [87] *per* Lords Sumption and Neuberger, [198] *per* Lord Mance, [238] *per* Lord Hodge.

determined at the time of contracting and not when it is relied upon). If it were, as is sometimes suggested, a doctrine concerned to prevent the parties entering into substantively unfair bargains, it might also be expected that such clauses would be wholly void, and the scope of the doctrine be less restricted.

Unfortunately, this (re)formulation of the law of penalties does not fit well with the law of penal deposits. Such deposits are not an attempt by the parties to fix by agreement the secondary obligations arising upon breach. The event upon which they are 'forfeit' may not be a breach. The buyer who pays a deposit to secure counter-performance need not be under any obligation to proceed to completion, so that no claim for breach ever arises when he backs out. Alternatively, as in the Coronation cases, the bargain may not proceed for some reason other than the parties' choice.

The language of 'forfeiture' is also misleading. It would be more accurate to say that a deposit, unlike a part payment, is conditional upon the seller, but not the buyer, going through with the deal, so that if the buyer does not complete for whatever reason no right to restitution of the payment arises. There is no right to restitution that is being lost if the buyer refuses to go ahead. Deposits are not an attempt by the parties to fix the secondary obligation arising upon breach, and they are not an instruction to the court. The 'penal deposits' rule therefore re-writes the parties' primary obligations, not the secondary obligations arising upon breach. The obligation to pay the penal deposit is not merely unenforceable (as penalty clauses generally are) but void, as penal deposits paid must be returned.

The rule against penal deposits also does not closely resemble its cousin, the doctrine of equitable relief against forfeiture. In England, the court only has jurisdiction to grant equitable relief against forfeiture where what is being forfeited is a proprietary or possessory right, whereas in the penal deposit case no right at all is forfeit. Further, the court will only grant relief where the right to be forfeit is to secure an obligation that the obligor remains willing to perform. It prevents forfeiture for purposes other than securing performance of the primary obligation. A classic example is that of a lease, which it is stipulated is to be determined if a tenant is late in paying any rent. If the tenant remains willing and able to pay, equitable relief against forfeiture may be granted. This was also, of course, true on the facts of *Workers' Trust and Merchant Bank Ltd v Dojap Investments Ltd*: the buyer remained willing to complete. However, it has never been thought to be part of the rule against penal deposits that the buyer remains ready to go through with the deal. It is a rule disbarring the seller having 'too much' security, unlike the equitable one that prevents forfeiture for purposes other than securing performance of the primary obligation.

Regardless of these difficulties of reconciliation and justification, in England, the judicial direction of travel is away from the re-writing of agreements so as to prevent commercially 'unbalanced' results. It may therefore be doubted whether the rule against penal deposits will be extended to services, or indeed at all.

PART IV
INTERVENTION IN ANOTHER'S AFFAIRS

9
Discharge

A. The Significance of Discharge of Another's Obligation

Where one party performs, or otherwise discharges, an obligation that ought to have been borne by another, in whole or in part, the party who has discharged the obligation has a claim over against the correct obligor for the expense incurred in so doing, to the extent that the cost of performing the obligation ought to have been borne by the other.

The purpose of this chapter is to articulate when and why this principle operates, and to explain why the invocation of unjust enrichment adds nothing to the analysis.

First an example where the expense ought to be borne fully by the defendant:

> D is obliged to abate a terrible smell caused by a leak of sewage that emanates from his property. P mistakenly believing that the smell emanates from his land, carries out the necessary work to abate the nuisance.

P should (and does) have a claim against D for the expense incurred in abating the nuisance, providing this does not exceed the market cost of doing the work.

Second an example where the expense ought to be shared between different parties including the plaintiff:

> X is injured whilst driving in an accident involving three other drivers, including P. Each of the three drivers had been negligent, and each is partially responsible for what occurred. X brings a claim against P and succeeds in his action.

P has a claim for a contribution against each of the other two drivers for their share of the responsibility for the injury to X.

In these examples the parties have no relationship at all, still less has there been any performance between them. The defendant has had no participation at all in what the plaintiff has done. What can justify these claims?

The best explanation is that we are seeking to ensure that the burden of a legal obligation is borne by the party subject to that obligation.[1] Where it has been borne, in whole or in part, by another party, this can be corrected by allowing that party redress. The obligation discharged need not, in principle, be one owed as a matter of private law at all: any legal obligation ought to suffice. If, in the example with which we began, the bad smell created a public nuisance, with a consequent duty to the public to abate it, and not a private nuisance with a consequent duty of abatement to a particular landowner or other person impacted, this should make no difference to the analysis.

---

[1] See eg *Duncan Fox & Co v North & South Wales Bank* (1880) 6 App Cas 1 (HL), 11 *per* Lord Selborne LC.

Such claims can be seen as a kind of localised distributive justice. We are trying to ensure that burdens fall where they ought to: the 'ought' being answered by the many and various reasons for the creation of legal obligations. We find no necessity for any performance between plaintiff and defendant, and in particular no need for any acceptance by the defendant of what the plaintiff has done, because we are not imposing any new obligation upon the defendant beyond what he was already obliged to do. The law is not trying to go back to the position as if something had never happened (as it does with, eg, a mistaken payment). Rather, it seeks to go forward to the position that there should have been, where the correct party had done what they ought to do.

B. Recoupment

Here are some illustrations of the principle in action.

In the classic *Exall v Partridge*[2] the defendants were three co-lessees of premises. Two of them assigned their interest to the third co-lessee, Partridge, who was the only party in possession. Partridge was a coach-maker, and the plaintiff left his carriage on the premises. The landlord then distrained the carriage for non-payment of rent, and in order to recover his property the plaintiff paid what was due. The plaintiff then sought to recover the payment from all three co-lessees. The question that arose was whether the case was properly pleaded. Were the co-lessees who were not in possession liable to reimburse the carriage owner for the expenditure, or was the only claim available against Partridge who ultimately amongst the three of them would have had to bear the cost of the rent? The Court of King's Bench held that as all three were liable upon the covenant to pay the rent to the landlord, reimbursement was available against all of them.

A still older example is *Jenkins v Tucker*.[3] The defendant had married the plaintiff's daughter. Sometime after the marriage he left her and their child in England and went to his estate in Jamaica. While he was away, she subsequently died. Her father, the plaintiff, incurred the funeral expenses, and successfully sought reimbursement. Lord Loughborough stated:

> There are many cases of this sort, where a person having paid money which another was under a legal obligation to pay though without his knowledge or request, may maintain an action to recover back the money so paid: such as in the instance of goods being distrained by the commissioners of the land tax.

Subsequently, it was established that strangers could similarly recover the costs of burial, provided that they did not aim to prevent the husband from burying his dead wife.[4] Today, of course, married women are no longer a special category of adult, and so these cases are no longer good law, but it remains the case that private individuals and local authorities that discharge another's duty to bury the dead have a claim for reimbursement.[5]

---

[2] (1799) 8 TR 308, 101 ER 1405. See also *Johnson v Royal Mail Steam Packet Co* (1867–1868) LR 3 CP 38; *Kleinwort Benson v Vaughan* [1996] CLC 620 (CA).
[3] (1788) 1 Hy Bl 90, 126 ER 55.
[4] *Ambrose v Kerrison* (1788) 1 H Bl 90, 126 ER 55. See also *Rogers v Price* (1829) 3 Y & J 128, 148 ER 1080; *Bradshaw v Beard* (1862) 12 CBNS 344, 142 ER 1175.
[5] See now Public Health (Control of Disease) Act 1984, s 46(5).

An example of the discharge of a public duty is *Tomlinson v Bentall*.[6] A pauper was injured in the parish of Heybridge, breaking her leg, but was then improperly taken into the parish of Malden. The plaintiff, the local surgeon in Malden, was called, and cared for her for several weeks. He then sought, successfully, to recover his bill from the parish of Heybridge, where the injury had occurred. It was not possible to discern any request for the work to be done by the defendant parish; indeed, by their discreditable behaviour they had made it clear that they did not want the responsibility. Bayley J stated:

> I do not put the case upon the ground of moral obligation ... but I put it upon the ground the law imposed a legal obligation upon the parish officers of Heybridge to employ a surgeon for the cure of the pauper. I think it highly prejudicial to the rights of the poor that when an accident has happened, the question should be agitated or even pass in the minds of those persons in whose power the sufferer is of necessity placed whether a burden which must fall somewhere must be borne by them, or can by any contrivance be shifted to others.[7]

Modern English authority adopting this principle in relation to the performance of public duties that still exist today is lacking,[8] but there is plentiful American case law.[9]

Confusingly, recoupment is sometimes given the different label of 'subrogation'. One example is where a guarantor is given a claim over against the debtor whose debt he has discharged. This is doubly confusing because the label 'subrogation' is also used in other cases, most commonly insurance, where the obligation is not discharged and the plaintiff is given an entitlement to assert the right of another for his own benefit. Where the guarantor is subrogated to any security that the creditor had against the debtor the language of 'recoupment' may be thought inapposite. Throughout this chapter 'recoupment' will be employed.

C. Contribution

Where the payment of one debt discharges another concurrent debt, the position in principle is relatively straightforward. At common law and in Equity, co-sureties who are equally bound are entitled to an equal contribution from each other if they pay.[10] Where co-sureties are bound for differing amounts, the entitlement to contribution varies proportionately.[11] The same principles should be, and have been, applied to other co-debtors.[12]

---

[6] (1826) 5 B and C 737, 108 ER 274. *Cf. Lamb v Bunce* (1815) 4 M&S 275, 105 ER 836.
[7] (1826) 5 B and C 737, 743–744, 108 ER 274. 276. In 1930 the responsibility of parishes for the poor was abolished, essentially transferred to local and central government.
[8] But see *Transco plc v Glasgow City Council* [2005] CSOH 79, 2005 SLT 958 (OHCS, Lord Hodge). *Surrey County Council v NHS Lincolnshire Clinical Commissioning Group* [2020] EWHC 3350 (QB) should have been decided on this basis, but the reasoning is unfortunately confused.
[9] A Kull, *Restatement of the Law (Third) Restitution and Unjust Enrichment*, vol I (2010), see § 22(2)(c), along with commentary and illustrations.
[10] *Deering v Earl of Winchilsea* (1787) 2 Bos & P 270, 126 ER 1276.
[11] *Pendlebury v Walker* (1841) 4 Y &C Ex 424, 160 ER 1072.
[12] Eg *Whitwham v Bullock* [1939] 2 KB 81.

Where two wrongdoers are concurrently liable to make good the same loss to a victim, the position is more complex. Originally, common law systems rejected any contribution claim, on the basis that a wrongdoer could not rely upon his own wrong in bringing an action.[13] This avoids the difficult issue of apportionment that permitting such claims gives rise to, but at the heavy price of allowing the victim to choose to enforce against a single defendant, leaving the latter with no recourse over against another who may have the greater responsibility for the loss suffered. There is an obvious parallel with the common law's historic reluctance to allow an apportionment defence of contributory negligence to a tort.[14] Apportionment rules work less well outside a courtroom than before a judge. In the middle of the twentieth century, in the Anglo-common law world, statutory reform was undertaken permitting contribution between tortfeasors.[15]

In England, the law of contribution outside of the common law is now found in several different statutes. Claims by those who share the same liability for damage with another are now covered by the Civil Liability (Contribution) Act 1978.[16] 'Damage' here includes not only loss caused by a tort, but also loss caused by a breach of contract, breach of trust, or other equitable wrong. A difficult question has arisen as to whether 'damage' can be given a still wider meaning so as to cover claims other than those for loss suffered as a result of a wrong. At least where the plaintiff is not a wrongdoer, however, a contribution claim at common law should be permitted as the old common law rationale for rejecting such claims would not apply.

Where, as is most common, a contribution is sought from one tortfeasor against another, the apportionment of responsibility for the loss is determined by the degree of contribution to the loss and relative fault.[17] This is a different enquiry from that engaged in in determining whether a wrong has occurred. Query whether this approach should be applied to wrongs other than torts, and it seems clearly inappropriate where the concurrent claims are for damages against one party and restitution against another.[18]

---

[13] *Merrywheather v Nixan* (1799) 8 TR 186, 101 ER 1337.

[14] T Wier, 'All or Nothing' (2003) 78 Tul L Rev 511.

[15] England: Law Reform (Married Women and Tortfeasors) Act 1935, s 6; Australia: Australian Capital Territory: Law Reform (Misc Prov) Ordinance 1955, s 11; New South Wales: Law Reform (Misc Prov) Act 1946, s 5; Queensland: The Law Reform (Tortfeasors Contribution, Contributory Negligence and Division of Chattels) Act 1952, s 5; see now Law Reform Act 1995 (Qld) Pt 3 Div 2; Tasmania: Tortfeasors and Contributory Negligence Act 1954, s 3; South Australia: Wrongs Act Amendment Act 1959, s 25; see now Law Reform (Contributory Negligence and Apportionment of Liability) Act 2001 (SA) Pt 2, s 6; Victoria: Wrongs Act 1958, s 24; Western Australia: Law Reform (Contributory Negligence and Tortfeasors' Contribution) Act 1947, s 7; New Zealand: Law Reform Act 1936 (no. 31 of 1936), s 17. Canada: Ontario: Contributory Negligence Act 1930 (now Negligence Act 1970), s 2(1); Alberta: Contributory Negligence Act 1955, s 2(1); British Columbia: Contributory Negligence Act 1960, s 5; Newfoundland: Contributory Negligence Act 1970, s 3; Prince Edward Island: Contributory Negligence Act 1951, s 2; Saskatchewan: Contributory Negligence Act 1965, s 3. The United States position is somewhat Byzantine, with different Acts and judicial approaches across the States.

[16] Carriers who have met a liability for damage to cargo carried by road which ought to be shared with another are covered by the Carriage of Goods by Road Act 1965. Contribution claims by shipowners for death and personal injury by sea are governed by the Merchant Shipping Act 1995.

[17] *Madden v Quirk* [1989] 1 WLR 702; *Dubai Aluminium Co Ltd v Salaam* [2002] UKHL 48, [2003] 2 AC 366, [51] per Lord Nicholls.

[18] See below p 172.

D. Methods of Discharge

1. Performance

An obligation of another may be discharged in three quite distinct ways that it is important to disaggregate. The starting position, at least in England, is that it is not possible to perform another's obligation. Why not?

Some duties are, on construction, personal to us, in the sense that only the individual subject to that duty can perform them. My contractual duty to teach students for the University of Oxford is of this kind. If one of my colleagues, a far better teacher than I am, at my request delivered the tutorials, seminars, and lectures that I am scheduled to do, that would not be a performance of my obligations to my employer, and I would not be owed my salary at the end of the month. Nobody but me can perform these obligations.

Most legal obligations are, of course, not like this. If I employ a builder to build a house for me, I do not expect that he himself will necessarily do the work. If his employees or subcontractors actually do the labour, I must pay. Where the counterparty is a legal construct, such as a company, the only way of it performing its obligations is through the real-world persons authorised to act on its behalf. The action (whether a payment or other performance) by the agent is attributed to his principal.[19] The same is true where the agent acts without authority, but the action is subsequently ratified.

However, it is in the nature of an obligation to do or not do something, both inside and outside the law, that the action (or inaction) must be that of the obligor. To perform is to do. The actions of an agent may be attributed to a principal where authorised in advance, or ratified subsequently if purported to be done on the principal's behalf. The action that constituted performance by the agent is thereby attributed to the principal. An action performing an impersonal obligation may therefore be carried out either by the obligor personally or through the agency of another. Where for example, without authority, a third party pays the debt of another on the debtor's behalf intending a gift, the debtor may ratify or adopt this payment, thereby discharging the debt.[20] Prior to such ratification, it remains open to the creditor to repay the payor, thereby keeping the debt alive. Absent such agency, a party who is not subject to an obligation cannot perform it. If I am obliged to pay you £100, your receipt of that sum of money from other people will not, without more, constitute performance of the obligation I am under.

Where the performance by another is authorised in advance, it will commonly be possible to discover a contractual right to reimbursement. An obvious example is in relation to contracts of guarantee. If a debtor requests that another guarantees his debt, if the guarantee is given and then paid it may legitimately be inferred that there is a contractual right to reimbursement (given the unfortunate label as we have seen of a right to be subrogated to the original debt, which is here discharged). However, whether the claim for reimbursement is contractual or not in such a case does not usually need to be answered, and so the courts have often not bothered to address the question.

---

[19] This does not mean that the debtor becomes party to any contract there may be between creditor and the third party. *Contra* P Birks and J Beatson, 'Unrequested Payment of Another's Debt' (1976) 92 LQR 188; J Beatson, *The Use and Abuse of Unjust Enrichment* (1991), 183–190.
[20] *Walter v James* (1871) LR 6 Ex 124, 128 *per* Martin B.

Where the performance by the defendant is ratified by the obligor, it will usually not be possible to explain the right to reimbursement as contractual. Although the ratification might be interpreted as also constituting a promise to reimburse, no sufficient consideration for this promise would arise because the plaintiff's action of paying or otherwise performing would be in the past.[21] There is however still a right to reimbursement in order to ensure that the burden of performance falls upon the party subject to the obligation.

2. Joint and Several Obligations

Where an *obligation* is joint the parties are bound as if a single person. Whether an *obligation* is joint is a separate issue from whether the *liability* for its performance is also joint (ie whether parties may be *sued* independently of one another). The *liability* to be sued upon an obligation may be joint (so that there is but one cause of action that must be maintained against them together)[22] or several (so that there are two causes of action against each party to have the obligation fulfilled that may be pursued independently against them individually).[23] When we speak of parties being 'jointly and severally liable', which is on its face contradictory, what is usually meant is that they are jointly obliged, but severally liable.

It is of the nature of obligations that are owed jointly by two or more people, regardless of whether their liability is several, that performance by one discharges them all.[24] If a married couple open a joint bank account that is subsequently overdrawn, payment by one so as to put the account in credit will discharge them both. Similarly, in cases of joint tortfeasors, such as where one or more defendants conspires for the commission of a tort against the claimant that one of them carries out, payment by one will discharge the others.

If a joint obligation is released for one obligor by contractual settlement, this will operate as a discharge for all. This is on the basis that the settlement is an agreed substitute for performance. The death or bankruptcy of one obligor, although it may release him, should not discharge the others, as not amounting to a performance by any of them.

At one time, judgment against a joint obligor discharged the others, even where the plaintiff had not obtained the fruits of his judgment. The original obligation to pay was merged into the new obligation created by the court's order.[25] This rule has been abrogated by legislation.[26]

Several obligations by contrast are ordinarily independent of one another. So, trivially, if A borrows £100 from B, and C borrows £100 from B, repayment by either one will not discharge the other.

---

[21] *Re Casey's Patents* [1892] 1 Ch 104 (CA); *Pao On v Lau Yiu Long* [1980] AC 614 (PC).
[22] Eg the case of joint contractual obligations, subject to contrary agreement: *Kendall v Hamilton* (1879) 4 App Cas 504 (HL); *Norbury, Nazio & Co Ltd v Griffiths* [1918] 2 KB 369 (CA).
[23] Eg the case of joint tortfeasors: *Wah Tat Bank Ltd v Chan Chang Kum* [1975] AC 507, 516 (PC); *CBS Songs Ltd v Amstrad Consumer Electronics plc* [1988] AC 1013 (HL), 1058.
[24] G Williams, *Joint Obligations* (1949), 93.
[25] *King v Hoare* (1844) 13 M & W 494, 153 ER 206.
[26] Civil Liability (Contribution Act) 1978, s 3.

3. Conditional Obligations

Quite different are those cases where an obligation is conditional upon an ongoing state of affairs. Another may by his action remove that condition, thereby discharging the obligor from further performance. Here the obligation has not been performed by anyone but is instead discharged because it was conditional and not absolute. This method of discharge therefore rarely applies to simple obligations to pay money.

We have already seen examples of discharge in this way. A straightforward classic example is *Gebhardt v Saunders*.[27] Sewage water collected in the cellar of the building of which the plaintiff was a tenant. The sanitary authority served a notice on the premises requiring the owner or occupier to abate the nuisance. The plaintiff did the necessary work to abate the nuisance, during which it became apparent that the cause of the nuisance was structural defects in the drains, which were the responsibility of the defendant landlord. The plaintiff successfully claimed the cost incurred in abating the nuisance. Anyone who removes the nuisance, whether they are obliged to do so or not, removes the condition of the obligor's duty to abate it, the nuisance existing, thereby discharging it.

The difference between performing the obligation of another and discharging it by removing a condition of its existence, may be further illustrated by an example where the latter should give rise to no claim.

> D agrees with X to demolish a bridge in disrepair on X's land for a fee of £1,000. P, mistakenly believing that the bridge is on his land, demolishes it before D commences work.

D could not claim the agreed sum from X because he (or his agent) has not done the work that was the condition of payment. The agreement was not a gaming contract as to the continued existence of the bridge. Rather D's obligation has been frustrated, it being a condition of his obligation to demolish the bridge that there is a bridge to demolish. Although P's actions relieve D from the burden of his obligation, this is offset by the fact that D will no longer be paid. P should therefore have no claim against D as this would leave D worse off than if he had done the work himself.

In some cases, the performance of one party's obligation will remove the condition of another's existence. This is so in the case of co-guarantors. If one guarantor pays, the underlying debt it is discharged. It is a condition of the duty under all other guarantees that the underlying debt is owing. Payment by one guarantor therefore releases the others, but not through the performance of the others' obligations. The obligations of each guarantor are not ordinarily joint with the others. Rather the condition of the duty of each of them is released. It should not matter therefore whether the guarantees are joint or several, the order in which they arose, or whether or not one guarantor was aware of the existence of another. All are discharged when the debt they secure is paid.

Similar is the situation where two or more insurers have underwritten the same loss, so payment by one of them results in there being no loss. It does not matter that each is liable severally, payment by one removes the condition of the obligation of all others. If recovery

---

[27] See also *Waters v Weigell* (1795) 2 Anst 575, 145 ER 971.

is made from one alone, he is again entitled to a contribution from others equally liable to pay the whole.[28]

Where multiple wrongdoers have committed separate wrongs against a victim, each individual wrong may be sufficient but unnecessary for some or all of the loss suffered as a result of all the wrongs. A simple example is the multiple car pile-up with which we began. Recovery of some, or all, of the loss from one wrongdoer will discharge the others, because to that extent the loss is no longer suffered as a result of each individual wrong. Each tortfeasor is under a separate obligation, and severally liable, to make good the loss that his wrong has contributed to. However, if one wrongdoer compensates the victim for a head of loss, such as lost earnings, each is to that extent discharged as the loss is no longer suffered. The condition of the obligation of the others to pay damages (that the loss exists) has been removed.

4. Automatic Discharge?

Outside of these three situations (agency, joint obligations, removal of conditions) the common law differs from the approach of civilian jurisdictions in not generally allowing for the discharge of another's debt by a stranger. Roman law did so permit, even if the payor did so against the will of the debtor, but the explanation given for this (that it *is* possible to confer benefits upon people behind their backs)[29] seems unpersuasive. Modern civilian systems follow the same Roman rule.[30] In the United States, the approach to discharge has been more liberal than that adopted in England.[31] The relative restrictiveness of the English law of discharge means that claims for contribution and recoupment are also relatively restricted.

Although it is sometimes argued that English law is ambiguous on the issue,[32] there is clear authority of longstanding establishing the no automatic discharge rule.[33] Authorities cited to the contrary[34] are either examples of ratification[35] or are cases where the contrary had been assumed without argument.[36]

The English common law position is justifiable. Promissory obligations to pay sums of money are not best interpreted as promises that a state of affairs (money from someone being received) will obtain at some future event. Payment obligations are not bets about whether something will happen or not. Rather they are obligations that the promisor will

---

[28] *Godin et al v London Assurance Co* (1758) 1 Burr. 489, 97 ER 419, 421 *per* Lord Mansfield. On the indemnity insurer's right to subrogation, where the assured's claim is *not* discharged, see Chapter 13, Equity: Restitution.

[29] D 46.3.53 (Gai. 5 ad ed prov): *Solvere pro ignorante et invito cuique licet, cum sit iure civili constitutum licere etiam ignorantis invitique meliorem condicionem facere.* ('Anyone can make payment on behalf of a debtor who is ignorant of the fact, even against his consent; for it is established by the Civil Law that the condition of a person can be improved who is not aware of it, and who is also unwilling.') *Cf.* D 50. 17. 69 (Paulus) (*Invito beneficium non datur*, 'no one is obliged to accept a benefit against his consent'); *Falcke v Scottish Imperial Ins Co* (1886) 34 Ch D 234 (CA), 248, *per* Bowen LJ.

[30] BGB § 267. Code Civil, Art 1236.

[31] Kull, *The Restatement (Third)* (n 9), §§ 22–25.

[32] A Burrows, *The Law of Restitution* (3rd edn, 2011), 460–468.

[33] Eg *Belshaw v Bush* (1851) 11 CB 191; *Simpson v Eggingon* (1855) 156 ER 683, 684 10 Ex 845, 847 *per* Parke B; *Walter v James* (1870–1871) LR 6 Ex 124; *Barclays Bank Ltd v WJ Simms, Son and Cooke (Southern) Ltd* [1980] QB 677 (Goff J); *Electricity Supply Nominees Ltd v Thorn EMI Retail Ltd* (1992) 63 P&CR 143 (CA), 148 *per* Fox LJ; *Crantrave Ltd v Lloyd's Bank plc* [2000] QB 917 (CA).

[34] Burrows, *The Law of Restitution* (n 32), 466–467.

[35] Eg *Welby v Drake* (1825) 1 C&P 557, 171 ER 1315; *Hirachand Punamchand v Temple* [1911] 2 KB 330 (CA).

[36] Eg *B Liggett (Liverpool) Ltd v Barclays Bank Ltd* [1928] 1 KB 48; *re Cleadon Trust Ltd* [1939] Ch 286 (CA).

do something: pay. Other obligations to pay, outside of contract, seem sensibly construed in the same way. Obligations to render a performance other than a payment of money are even more naturally construed as requiring that the obligor do the act promised. So long as it is understood that it is possible to discharge conditional obligations by the satisfaction of the condition to which they are subject, or non-personal obligations through the agency of another, the English position is coherent.

As an incidental benefit, the English common law rule prevents claims by those who officiously pay the debts of others, exemplified by *Norton v Haggett*.[37] Mr Norton and Mr Haggett had a series of arguments. A bank held a mortgage securing a debt owed by Mr and Mrs Haggett. Norton went to the bank intending to purchase the debt from them, but so conducted himself that the bank reasonably understood that he wished to pay off the debt without taking any assignment of it. No claim was available to Norton whom the court considered an officious intermeddler, when neither the bank nor Mr Haggett had consented to his substitution as a creditor.

It is sometimes argued that the English common law's position is inconsistent with the free assignability of debts.[38] If a creditor and a third party can, by their agreement, change to whom a debtor owes his obligation, what is the objection to permitting the creditor accepting performance from a third party in discharge of the debtor's obligation, with a claim over? No system permits discharge of a debt without the *creditor* accepting the payment as a discharge, why should this not suffice?

However, the common law did not, and does not, permit the free assignment of debts. Where the debt is contractual, the justification for this is that a party who does not satisfy the conditions for the acquisition of contractual rights against another (providing consideration to the other, being the party to an agreement with them) cannot acquire them. Equitable assignment does not contradict this rule. Rather, as we shall see, equitable assignment involves no transfer of the underlying right to the assignee, but rather the acquisition of a right by the assignee to the right of the assignor against the debtor. To whom the debtor owes his obligation does not change as a result of an equitable assignment.

Statutory assignment of debts, by contrast, does involve the transfer of a right to payment. However, this is subject to three conditions for the protection of the debtor.[39] First, the assignment must be in writing. Second, the assignment must be absolute. Partial assignments so that the debtor has multiple creditors substituted for one are not permitted. Third, the assignor must be given notice. If it were always possible for third parties to discharge a debt, thereby rendering the debtor susceptible to a claim for reimbursement, this would circumvent these statutory restrictions on the assignability of debts.[40]

E. Volunteers

Just as a plaintiff who pays money to another which he knows is not due is undeserving of the law's assistance, someone who has voluntarily performed an obligation knowing that it

---

[37] 85A 2d 571 (Vt 1952).
[38] Eg D Friedmann and N Cohen, 'Payment of Another's Debt' in *International Encyclopaedia of Comparative Law* (1991), vol X, ch 10 § 12; Burrows, *The Law of Restitution* (n 32), 461.
[39] Law of Property Act 1925, s 136.
[40] Beatson, *The Use and Abuse of Unjust Enrichment* (n 19), 200–205.

162 DISCHARGE

is owed by another should not be able to obtain recovery. They have consented to the position they now find themselves in. The original authors of Goff & Jones described this as a bar based upon officiousness.[41] It appears, however, usually to be the same limitation based upon consent that we find across private law. The plaintiff in *Norton v Haggett* was not a volunteer as he had expected to be able to bring the claim he asserted.

An illustration of a party who was a volunteer is *Macclesfield Corporation v Great Central Railway*.[42] The defendant company was under a statutory duty to maintain a bridge over a road. The plaintiff highway authority called upon them to make necessary repairs, but then carried out the work itself despite being under no duty to do so, as they knew. The Court of Appeal rejected the claim, Kennedy LJ stating,

> I do not know the legal principle upon which in those circumstances they can throw the burden on someone else who ought in the first instance to have done the work and who therefore is in a position to say, 'You who seek to recover this payment from me have acted as volunteers'.[43]

In civilian systems that adopt the general *negotiorum gestio contraria* principle, the result here would be different. Only where the performance was intended as a gift to the obligor or was one 'officiously' rendered, would recovery be denied.

A party who mistakenly discharges another's obligation believing it to be their own, or who does so under duress or undue influence, does not validly consent, and so recovery is permitted. Again, the role of mistake (or duress or undue influence) in this context is to remove an objection to recovery. These 'vitiating factors' are not themselves part of the justification for the obligation. An illustration is the decision of the Supreme Court of Canada in *County of Carleton v Ottawa*.[44] The defendant City took over an area controlled by the plaintiff County, and as a result came under a statutory duty to care for Norah Baker, an indigent woman. By a mistake, her name remained on the list of those for whom the County was to be responsible, and they provided support for her that the City ought to have provided for a decade. A claim for reimbursement succeeded on the basis that the City could not escape its responsibility for the care. The County's mistake meant that they were not volunteers.

Similar are those cases, such as *Gebhardt v Saunders*, where the plaintiff is under a legal obligation that they have not voluntarily assumed. The tenants had no choice but to abate the nuisance in order to avoid paying a fine.

What of those cases where the plaintiff has voluntarily assumed the obligation, which once performed discharges the obligation of the defendant? Standard examples include a guarantor of another's debt, or an insurer who has undertaken the same risk as another insurer. If the obligation has been voluntarily assumed, why has the plaintiff not consented to the position they now find themselves in when they are compelled to perform it?

The answer is the position the plaintiff expects to be in. The expectation of the guarantor is that they will have a claim over against the debtor if called upon to meet the guarantee. We are not here referring to any agreement between guarantor or debtor, there may not be

---

[41] R Goff and G Jones, *The Law of Restitution* (7th edn, 2007), [15-009]–[15-0014].
[42] [1911] 2 KB 528 (CA). See also *Harris v Hickman* [1904] 1 KB 13.
[43] [1911] 2 KB 528 (CA), 551. But see *Reversion Fund and Insurance Co v Maison Conway Ltd* [1913] 1 KB 364 (CA).
[44] (1965) 52 DLR (2d) 220 (Crt).

one, but rather to the guarantor's expectations. They have not consented to the position of payment with no claim over against the debtor. That is the nature of a guarantee. This explains Lord Sumption's otherwise enigmatic remark that restitution on the ground of failure of basis 'ordinarily requires that the expectation should be mutual, whereas this is not a requirement for equitable subrogation'.[45] However the ground of recovery is not the uncommunicated expectation in the mind of the plaintiff. Rather, such expectation shows that the guarantor did not consent to the position they now find themselves in.

If the above is accepted, the result reached by the Court of Appeal in *Owen v Tate*[46] seems incorrect.[47] The defendants had taken a loan from Lloyd's Bank, secured by a mortgage over the property of a Miss Lightfoot. In order to secure the release of the mortgage, the plaintiff deposited £350 with the bank, and guaranteed the loan up to that amount. He did not inform the defendants before doing this. The defendants, not wishing to lose the security of Miss Lightfoot's property, objected to this course of action at the time. The guarantee was then called upon, and paid.

Scarman LJ refused the claim over by the plaintiff against the defendants on the basis that he was a volunteer.[48] He had not entered into the guarantee at the request of the defendants and had not done so in circumstances of necessity.

However, this seems inconsistent with the rules in relation to co-guarantors, where one guarantor will not usually have requested that the other enter into the obligation, and where there will not usually have been any necessity to have undertaken it. The expectation of the plaintiff in *Owen v Tate* would have been that, as a guarantor, he would have a claim over against the principal debtor. Further the reasoning of the court is inconsistent with section 5 of the Mercantile Law Amendment Act, which confers upon guarantors a right to subrogation. This legislation was not cited to the court, and so the decision appears *per incuriam*.

On slightly different facts the result would have been correct, and the Act inapplicable, on the basis that the debt was not discharged. If, as argued above, the common law justifiably adopts the position that a stranger cannot discharge a debt unless acting with prior authority, or the debtor subsequently ratifying what was done, then the stranger's entering into a contract with the creditor under which he is obliged to pay, and then doing so, can make no difference.[49] It is sometimes stated that whenever a third party pays under 'legal compulsion' this will discharge a debt,[50] but this is inaccurate and misstates when and why being under a legal obligation to fulfil another's obligation will result in its discharge.

However, the defendants in *Owen v Tate*, although protesting at the time the guarantee was entered into, subsequently requested that the bank look to the sums deposited by the plaintiff for payment. That is how they themselves asked that their obligation be met. The court's assumption that the debt was discharged was correct because of this later request. The defendants were not prejudiced by the bank's earlier decision to release Miss Lightfoot's mortgage as they had no right that the bank looked to her for payment before seeking payment from them. Miss Lightfoot's mortgage was for the bank's benefit, not that of the

---

[45] *Lowick Rose v Swynson* [2017] UKSC 32, [2018] AC 313, [30] *per* Lord Sumption.
[46] [1976] QB 402 (CA).
[47] For a defence based upon facts unmentioned by the Court of Appeal, see N McBride, *The Humanity of Private Law Part I: Explanation* (2018), 213–215.
[48] *ibid*, 411–412.
[49] Birks and Beatson, 'Unrequested Payment of Another's Debt' (n 19), 198–199.
[50] Eg Burrows, *The Law of Restitution* (n 32), 466.

defendants.[51] The result looks wrong in principle, regardless of the legislation that the court did not consider.

Often the same analysis as to the plaintiff's expectations will apply where the plaintiff has been morally rather than legally compelled to perform. No doubt the father in *Jenkins v Tucker* always expected to be able to claim over against the husband. However, even where there is no such expectation, moral compulsion should suffice to vitiate the plaintiff's consent to his current position.

This is familiar to torts lawyers in the context of *volenti non fit iniuria*. In *Baker v TE Hopkins*,[52] two employees were overcome by carbon dioxide fumes in a well they were trying to fix. The plaintiff, a doctor, sought to rescue them, despite being warned of the risk and being aware that the fire brigade was on its way. The plaintiff died in the attempt. The fumes had been caused by the defendant's negligence. The circumstances of necessity vitiated any consent to the risk of injury.

The same applies in the context of discharge of another's obligation. The person who buries an abandoned corpse or who cares for an injured pauper does so in such circumstances of necessity that their consent is vitiated. Again, moral compulsion is not the ground of any claim, any more than it was in *Baker v TE Hopkins*. Persons who make large gifts to Oxfam for famine relief cannot recover them.[53] Rather, moral compulsion removes an objection to recovery on another basis. If, in *Macclesfield Corporation v Great Central Railway*, the highway authority had carried out the work in an emergency because of imminent risk of injury to third parties, recovery ought to have been allowed.

A final nice illustration of someone who was not a volunteer because of a moral obligation is *Alexander v Vane*.[54] The plaintiff and defendant went together to a harness maker. The defendant placed an order, and after it had been given the plaintiff stated that if the defendant did not pay, he would. This guarantee was not enforceable as not in writing as required by the Statute of Frauds. When the defendant did not pay, the plaintiff did so and sought reimbursement. His giving the guarantee in the presence of the defendant meant that he had been implicitly given the authority to pay the debt. Upon payment, although not legally compellable, the plaintiff was not a volunteer, but was bound 'in point of honour'.[55] The claim for reimbursement was upheld.

F. Unjust Enrichment?

1. Enrichment Insufficient

The dominant English academic account seeks to explain this area of law in terms of unjust enrichment.[56] This may be contrasted with the position in civilian systems, where the

---

[51] S J Stoljar, *The Law of Quasi-Contract* (2nd edn, 1989), 172.
[52] [1959] 1 WLR 966 (CA).
[53] See *Re Rhodes* (1890) 44 Ch D 94 (CA), discussed in Chapter 10 Necessity.
[54] (1836) 1 M & W 511, 150 ER 537.
[55] (1836) 1 M & W 511, 513, 150 ER 537 *per* Lord Abinger CB (1836) 1 M & W 511, 513 150 ER 537, 538 *per* Parke B.
[56] Burrows, *The Law of Restitution* (n 32), ch 17; C Mitchell, P Mitchell, and S Watterson (eds), *Goff & Jones: The Law of Unjust Enrichment* (9th edn, 2016), ch 20. But see *Friend v Brooker* [2009] HCA 21, 239 CLR 129, [38]–[50] *per* French CJ, Gummow, Heydon, and Bell JJ on equitable contribution.

doctrine of *negotiorum gestio contraria*, permits for the recovery of expenses incurred in intervening in another's affairs, not the enrichment obtained from such intervention, and generally (but not always) provides the vehicle for reimbursement (but not contribution) where one person pays another's debts.[57] As we shall see, the common law recognises no such general principle.[58] The 'unjust enrichment' explanation is unsatisfactory because enrichment is both insufficient and unnecessary.

It seems plausible that the discharged obligation constitutes an enrichment to the defendant, because it saves an otherwise inevitable expense that the defendant is no longer going to incur because of the plaintiff's actions. Indeed, claims of this kind are more naturally expressed in terms of 'enrichment' than are mistaken payment cases. Once we remove the discharged obligation from the story, however, the result changes, even though the defendant may be saved precisely the same expense. This is most obvious in cases where the plaintiff's actions pre-empt the defendant's obligation from arising, saving him a necessary expense but thereby discharging no obligation.

In *Metropolitan Police District Receiver v Croydon Corpn*,[59] the defendants injured a police constable, incapacitating him from work for seven months. During that time the plaintiff police authority had been compelled to pay him his wages, although he did no work. The constable successfully recovered damages from the defendants, but this did not include a claim for lost earnings as he had not suffered any. The authority sought to recover this expenditure, on the basis that their payment had saved the defendants the expense of having to pay for the lost earnings by way of damages. The Court of Appeal rejected the claim. Although the plaintiff's payments had pre-empted a duty that the defendants would otherwise have been under, thereby leaving them better off than they otherwise would have been, no obligation had been discharged because none had ever arisen. The claim therefore failed.

Although often criticised,[60] *Metropolitan Police District Receiver v Croydon Corpn* is rightly decided. Because the conditions for the defendants being under an obligation to the constable in relation to the lost earnings were unsatisfied (he never lost any earnings), there was no justification for imposing such an obligation upon anyone else. It is essential to the justification for this claim that we are not subjecting the defendant to an obligation different from or greater than the obligation he was already under. Similarly, in the example of the mistaken demolition of the bridge given above, *P* should have no claim against the landowners because the latter's obligation to pay for the work never arose; it was not discharged.

The UK legislature has introduced routes for recovery against tortfeasors by the state in analogous cases to *Metropolitan Police District Receiver v Croydon Corpn*. The Department for Social Security may recover against tortfeasors the value of various social security benefits under the Social Security (Recovery of Benefits) Act 1997. The cost of National Health

---

[57] D Friedmann and N Cohen, 'Payment of Another's Debt' in *International Encyclopaedia of Comparative Law*, vol X (1991), ch 10 §§ 9–10. This doctrine is less satisfactory in explaining claims for contribution.
[58] Chapter 10.
[59] [1957] 2 QB 154 (CA). See also *Re Nott and Cardiff Corpn* [1918] 2 KB 146 (CA); *Canadian Automatic Data Processing Services Ltd v CEEI Safety & Security Inc* (2004) 246 DLR (4th) 400 (Ont CA).
[60] Eg Mitchell, Mitchell, and Watterson, *Goff & Jones* (n 56), [4–39]; Burrows, *The Law of Restitution* (n 32), 453.

Service (NHS) treatment received by tort victims injured in road traffic accidents is recoverable from the tortfeasor under the Road Traffic (NHS Charges) Act 1999.[61] If, as many commentators suggest, *Metropolitan Police District Receiver v Croydon Corpn* should be overturned, all costs that the state currently incurs on behalf of tort victims should in principle be recoverable from tortfeasors who are thereby saved the payment of damages.[62] It may be doubted whether moving the cost of support for victims from one collective fund (the state) to another (the insurance pool paid for by liability insurance premiums) is worth the transaction cost. In principle, it is unjustifiable, although with obvious attractions for any government wishing to shift costs.

Similar is the decision in *Bonner v Tottenham & Edmonton Permanent Investment Building Society*.[63] The plaintiff lessees assigned their lease to Edward Price, who then mortgaged his interest to the defendants. The defendants agreed with Price that if he defaulted on the loan, they would go into possession, and pay the rent that Price owed to the landlord. Price was declared bankrupt, and the defendants went into possession, but failed to pay any of the rent. The landlord forced the plaintiff as original lessee to pay, who then sought to recover this expense from the defendants directly.

In economic terms, the defendants were those who, in the end, benefitted from the plaintiff paying. They were the ones in possession of the property, and what ought to have happened is that they should have performed their obligation to Price, by paying the rent on his behalf, thereby discharging both Price and the plaintiff. Their non-payment was what resulted in the plaintiff paying. However, the plaintiff's proper recourse was against the estate of Price.[64] Although Price's obligation to the landlord had been discharged, his obligation to pay the rent persisted as his estate was obliged to reimburse the plaintiff. Price's estate in turn had an action against the defendants, showing that their obligation to him had not been discharged.

Indeed, if the law were concerned with the *fact* of the defendant being enriched, it should not matter if the plaintiff has discharged the defendant's obligation or not. If, for example, the plaintiff without authority pays the defendant's creditor what is owed, if, as a matter of fact, the creditor would no longer pursue his claim against the defendant as a result, the defendant is better off than he otherwise would be. If the necessary element of recovery really were the defendant's enrichment, the rules on when and why an obligation is discharged would be otiose, replaced by the factual enquiry as to whether enforcement would be pursued when it otherwise would not be.

Some commentators have argued for the recognition of such a principle of 'imperfect discharge'.[65] If, without authority, P pays X in purported discharge of a debt owed by D, even if the debt is not discharged, the result, as a matter of fact, will often be that X will not pursue his claim against D. As a result, D is enriched regardless of the legal position. If the law were concerned with the fact of enrichment, this would be correct. As it is not, it is not.

---

[61] See R Lewis, *Deducting Benefits from Damages for Personal Injury* (1999), chs 12–17.
[62] Law Commission, Report 'Damages for Personal Injury: Medical, Nursing and Other Expenses; Collateral Benefits', Law Com no 262, 1999, [3.22]–[3.23].
[63] [1899] 1 QB 161 (CA).
[64] *Moule v Garrett* (1871–1872) LR 7 Ex 101.
[65] P Birks, *Unjust Enrichment* (2nd edn, 2005), 296–298. *Cf.* C Mitchell and S Watterson, *Subrogation: Law and Practice* (rev edn, 2007), [1–107].

2. Enrichment Unnecessary

Conversely, there are cases where an obligation is discharged, but the defendant is not left better off than they otherwise would be. As we have seen, in *Exall v Partridge* it was only Partridge amongst the three co-lessees who would ultimately have borne the cost of the rent. The issue in the case was whether the claim was only available against the party who, as a matter of fact, would in the end have to bear the expenditure, or against all of the parties who were obliged to pay. The claim was available against all of the co-obligors, although as a matter of fact this was not (and could not be) the extent to which each of the co-lessees who were not in possession was each left better off. Again, as in *Bonner v Tottenham*, the law is not concerned with the economic reality of who is enriched, and to what extent, but rather in allocating the burden of an obligation to the person or persons who ought to bear it.

In the context of allocating legal burdens to financially hard-pressed public bodies, it will often be the case that they are not, in fact, enriched through having an obligation discharged. Illustrative are the facts of *Surrey County Council v NHS Lincoln Clinical Commissioning Group*.[66] The Council sought reimbursement from the NHS Group for the costs of accommodation and care for a young man with autism. The NHS Group made an error of public law in declining to assess whether the young man's condition was sufficiently serious to be eligible for NHS care, under the mistake that even if he were they would not be responsible to provide it. The Council continued to pay for the care, until the NHS Group accepted the error of law it had made, and that it was the party responsible under the relevant legislation. The claim for reimbursement rightly succeeded, but it must be doubted whether, as a matter of fact, the party benefitted through the non-performance of the duty was the defendant. Public bodies do not generally run a surplus. Rather they spend all of their income on performance of their duties. The end beneficiary of their not delivering care to one person will be other persons who would either receive no or lesser care otherwise. But this is irrelevant. We are seeking to allocate the burden of the obligation to the obligor, not strip the person who, at the end of the day, gains from the non-performance of the duty.

A hypothetical example making the same point:

C and D are jointly obliged to pay X £10,000. C pays X. If C had not done so, Y, D's generous relative, would have done so on D's behalf.

Again, it does not matter that, as a matter of fact, the burden of paying the debt would not have fallen upon D if C had not paid it. The law is uninterested in the economic reality of who is left better off. Rather the concern is to ensure that the burden of legal obligations is allocated to those responsible for them. C should therefore have a claim for contribution against D. Similarly, there should be no defence of 'change of position' applicable to claims for recoupment and contribution, unless the obligation discharged itself allows for such a defence.

Similarly, if the debtor would not, counterfactually, have been sued by creditor should this matter? This is the converse of the 'imperfect discharge' argument above. Again, the

---

[66] [2020] EWHC 3550 (QB). See also *Transco plc v Glasgow City Council* [2005] CSOH 79, 2005 SLT 958 (Court of Session Outer House, Lord Hodge) where the defender would never have performed their public duty, and so were never in fact enriched, but the claim succeeded.

same commentators argue that this should make a difference.[67] If the plaintiff has discharged a debt properly owed by the debtor, the debtor is not, in fact, better off if it would not as a matter of fact have been enforced against him, but this is irrelevant. Our concern is not with whether, factually, the defendant is better off, but rather with whether, legally, an obligation which he ought to have borne has been discharged by another.

It might be said that 'enrichment' is here a term of art, which (again) does not refer to the fact of being better off. In which case it is misleading.

3. Loss

When an unjustified performance is sought to be reversed, there is no requirement that the plaintiff establishes a loss, in the sense of a factual detriment, that he has suffered that corresponds with a gain made by the defendant. As we have seen, this is most obvious in the case of a claim to recover back the value of a service rendered.

In the context of a recoupment or contribution action, however, the rule is different. If the plaintiff discharges an obligation for a cost lower than the defendant would have incurred had he discharged it (because, eg, the plaintiff was able to settle the sum owed at a figure lower than that which the defendant would have had to pay, or because a non-money obligation was less onerous for the plaintiff to discharge than it would have been for the defendant), this cost limits the amount recoverable. The Court of Appeal has held that where a debtor had entered into a settlement with a creditor, when the debtor seeks a contribution from a co-obligor, the debtor must disclose the settlement's terms because 'the claimant is not permitted to recover more than it has paid'.[68]

Again, the reason for these different rules is that the claims are not of the same kind. It is misleading to analogise from one to the other. Here we are trying to reallocate the burden of performing an obligation. This is only justifiable to the extent that the plaintiff has in fact borne that burden. This 'cap' should operate on a pro-rata basis. For example:

> *P* and *D* each guarantee the sum that debtor owes to creditor. The debtor is bankrupt, and the sum owing is disputed. *P* succeeds in persuading the creditor to accept £1,000 from him in full and final settlement of what is owed.

Here *D*'s liability to make a contribution to *P* should be calculated by reference to his proportionate responsibility with respect to *P*, meaning that his liability is £500, even if the true value of the debt owed was far greater than £1,000.

The claim is therefore neither 'gain' nor 'loss' based. Rather it is a claim to the expense the plaintiff incurred in performing the obligation, to the extent of the defendant's responsibility for such performance (or, if one prefers, the converse).

---

[67] Mitchell and Watterson, *Subrogation: Law and Practice* (n 65), [4.37]; C Mitchell, *The Law of Contribution and Reimbursement* (2003), [3.16].
[68] *Gnitrow Ltd v Cape plc* [2000] 3 All ER 763, 767 *per* Pill LJ. See too the *dicta* in *Butcher v Churchill* (1808) 14 Ves Jun 567, 575–576, 33 ER 638, 641 *per* Sir William Greene MR.

4. The 'Unjust Factor'

(a) Legal compulsion?

At one time a popular academic approach was to align cases such as *Exall v Partridge* with other cases of compulsion, such as duress, and seek to explain all of them in terms of the plaintiff's 'vitiation of consent' to the defendant's enrichment.[69]

This, of course, will not do. If the law compels me to pay you a sum of money, this is a good reason for your retaining it, not returning it. This does not entail that whether the plaintiff was legally obliged to perform the obligation that ought to have been borne, in whole or in part, by the defendant is irrelevant. As we have seen, this can be a relevant consideration in cases of joint obligations in determining whether an obligation of the defendant has been discharged, and it may also show that the defendant is not a 'volunteer', so that a claim that would otherwise fail succeeds. But it is inexplicable how it could itself be the ground of recovery.

Unfortunately, the academic innovation of 'legal compulsion' as a basis of claim has now gained traction with the courts. In *Samsoondar*, discussed in Chapter 6, Practice, the claimant had at the request of the defendant discharged the defendant's obligation to pay tortious damages. In the circumstances, they were clearly not volunteers. This should have provided a sufficient justification for reimbursement. It is a nice example of a claim justifiable upon multiple different grounds. The claim was however denied on the basis that the claimants had not pleaded the 'unjust factor' that they were 'legally compelled' to pay. However, the orthodox position since the abolition of the forms of action is that litigants plead facts not law[70] and all the relevant facts had been put before the court.

Another approach seeking to explain recovery in terms of the state of mind of the plaintiff is to suggest that the plaintiff is 'powerless' to prevent the defendant's enrichment, and that the lack of entitlement to the benefit the defendant has received from the plaintiff as between them means that there is recovery.[71] Again, although more sophisticated, this will also not do. An example:

> C agrees to buy the title to Blackacre from X. C agrees to pay the purchase price of £1m to D, it being agreed that D should not acquire any rights under the contract. After conveyance, X seeks and obtains specific performance against C compelling her to pay D.

As between them, D had no legal right to the payment from C, and C was powerless because of the court order to resist payment. There was however a good reason why the payment was made to D, her obligation to X, and no recovery should follow. (As we have seen, C's performance was rendered to X under the contract between them, not to D as a third-party beneficiary.)

The same kind of objection applies to Birks' attempt to explain the entirety of the law of restitution in terms of there being 'no explanatory basis' for the defendant's enrichment. In

---

[69] P Birks, *An Introduction to the Law of Restitution* (rev edn, 1989), 197–198; G Virgo, *The Principles of the Law of Restitution* (3rd edn, 2015), 227–229.
[70] *Bell v Lever Brothers Ltd* [1931] 1 KB 557 (CA), 582–583 *per* Scrutton LJ; *Re Vandervell's Trusts (No 2)* [1974] Ch 269, 321 *per* Lord Denning MR; *Tchenguiz v Grant Thornton UK LLP* [2015] EWHC 405 (Comm), [1] *per* Leggatt J.
[71] J Edelman and E Bant, *Unjust Enrichment* (2nd, edn, 2016), 291.

the cases where the plaintiff has been legally compelled, such as the payment by a guarantor, there is obviously a good reason why the enrichment has been conferred. That is what the law required. If instead we mean 'no good reason as between plaintiff and defendant', that is also true in the case of the sale of Blackacre with payment to be made to a non-party, who has no entitlement as against anyone.

(b) A rule against accumulation?

More promising, and closer to the approach adopted in this chapter, is the claim that where the plaintiff and defendant are both legally liable to a creditor, and the creditor is forbidden to accumulate recoveries by enforcing his claims against both, where the creditor recovers against the plaintiff alone, the law gives the plaintiff an appropriate right to contribution or reimbursement against the defendant.[72]

It is true that where a creditor is entitled to accumulate claims, this leaves no room for any further adjustment amongst creditors. If a tortfeasor kills someone who carries life insurance, both the tortfeasor and the life insurer must pay in full. Life insurance, unlike indemnity insurance, does not provide compensation for loss. Rather it is a sum payable upon the happening of an event. Neither the tortfeasor nor the life insurer in paying in full has been asked to bear more than his fair share.

However, a rule against accumulation is not a satisfactory explanation for the law overall.

First, a policy against accumulation of recoveries could be equally satisfied by proportionately reducing each defendant's obligation according to the number of co-obligors that there are. Indeed, in some Australian and American states this (disgraceful) step has been taken in some areas.[73] The obligation of a wrongdoer to do the next best thing to the wrong not having occurred (pay damages) is in principle unaltered by the presence of other wrongdoers concurrently obliged to do the same thing. This shows that a policy against accumulation cannot be the whole story.[74]

Second, and most fundamentally, claims for recoupment or contribution are not, and should not be, dependent upon whether a creditor has or could seek to accumulate recoveries from multiple parties who are liable. It should not (and does not) matter that a creditor recovers in full, minus one penny, from one defendant, and subsequently settles the liability of all others for a penny.[75] The debtor who has had to bear more than his share of the obligation may recover against other obligors regardless of whether there is now no possibility of accumulation by the creditor.

---

[72] Mitchell, *The Law of Contribution* (n 67), [3.28].

[73] K Barker and J Steele, 'Drifting towards Proportionate Liability: Ethics and Pragmatics' (2015) CLJ 49; American Law Institute, *Third Restatement of the Law of Torts, Apportionment of Liability* (2000) §17 Comm. a.

[74] R Wright, 'Allocating Liability Among Multiple Responsible Causes: A Principled Defense of Joint and Several Liability for Actual Harm and Risk Exposure' (1988) 21 UC Davis LRev 1141; W McNichols, 'Judicial Elimination of Joint and Several Liability because of Comparative Negligence—A Puzzling Choice' (1979) 32 OklaLRev. 1; A Burrows, 'Should One Reform Joint and Several Liability' in N J Mullany and A M Linden (eds), *Torts Tomorrow: A Tribute to John Fleming* (1998).

[75] Civil Liability Act 1978, s 1(3), a defendant is liable to pay a contribution 'notwithstanding that he has ceased to be liable in respect of the damage in question since the time when the damage occurred': ie a contribution claim is still available even if the defendant has already settled the claim. See further *Jameson v Central Electricity Generating Board* [2000] 1 AC 455, 471 *per* Lord Hope. Of course, the settlement with one party may prevent the creditor from pursuing his claim against another, see generally *Heaton v AX Equity and Law Life Assurance Soc plc* [2002] UKHL 15, [2002] 2 AC 329.

Third, the anti-accumulation idea is dependent upon both parties being legally liable to fulfil the same obligation. This is radically under-inclusive. It makes the common mistake of conflating obligation with liability. In *Stimpson v Smith*[76] the claimant and defendant were jointly obliged under a guarantee, and the claimant settled with the creditor in order to have it released. The defendant resisted the claim for contribution because there was never any liability to pay under the guarantee (ie the creditor never had any power to sue them) because such liability was conditional upon a demand that never occurred. This did not matter because there was an obligation to pay under the guarantee. In determining the appropriate contributions between claimant and defendant, the court was concerned to determine who should bear the cost of the obligation as between the parties, not with whether the claimant was liable to be sued.

Similarly, it is not a requirement of recoupment that the plaintiff was either liable to be sued to perform *or* legally obliged to do so. We have seen several examples of this: *Jenkins v Tucker, Tomlinson v Bentall, County of Carleton v Ottawa*, and *Alexander v Vane*. In none of these cases is a policy against accumulation explanatory, as no such accumulation by the creditor was possible. Rather, the concern is to ensure that the obligor bears the burden of the obligation that is his. This is both a better explanation and more closely follows the reasoning adopted by the courts in each case. The courts have consistently, and rightly, treated cases of discharge of another's obligation as analogous to one another, and not as analogous to mistaken payment cases such as *Kelly v Solari*.

(c) *Secondary liability?*

The labels of 'primary' and 'secondary' are not always misleading,[77] if by that is meant that one party is primarily *responsible*, whilst another is merely secondary. It makes less sense to speak of primary or secondary *liability* in cases where the party with the power to sue is not barred from claiming against either party. In the decision of the Court of Appeal of *Brook's Wharf and Bull Wharf Ltd v Goodman Bros*[78] a question of construction arose as to which of two obligors ought to bear the cost of performance. The defendants were furriers who had imported squirrel skins from Russia. Some of the consignment was stored in the bonded warehouse of the plaintiffs, from which they were stolen, without any negligence on the part of the plaintiffs. The plaintiffs were compelled to pay the customs duty on the goods stolen under the Customs Duties Consolidation Act 1876. The importers were also liable under the Act, and the plaintiffs sought reimbursement. Here the structure of the legislation was to impose the duty on the warehouseman (whose business was in the jurisdiction) in order to secure the obligation of the importer (whose business may not be). The liability of the plaintiffs was 'secondary' in the sense that the party primarily responsible for the tax was the importer, and so they were entitled to reimbursement because the burden of the obligation ought to have been borne by them. This was a matter of construing the statutory obligations. However, those cases where the plaintiff was not obliged or liable, and so not responsible, at

---

[76] [1999] Ch 340 (CA).
[77] Birks, *An Introduction to the Law of Restitution* (n 69), 186–188. See also *Duncan, Fox & Co v North and South Wales Bank* (1880) 6 App Cas 1 (HL), 11 *per* Lord Selborne LC; *Brook's Wharf and Bull Wharf Ltd v Goodman Bros* [1937] 1 KB 534 (CA), 544 *per* Lord Wright MR; *Niru Battery Manufacturing Co v Milestone Trading Ltd (No.2)* [2004] EWCA Civ 487; [2004] 2 All ER (Comm) 289, [68]; *Berghoff Trading Ltd v Swinbrook Developments Ltd* [2009] EWCA Civ 413, [2009] 2 Lloyd's Rep 233, [24]–[26] *per* Rix LJ.
[78] [1937] 1 KB 534 (CA).

all for the performance of the obligation are *a fortiori* from this kind of case, so long as the defendant's obligation is discharged and they were not volunteers.

The language of 'primary' and 'secondary' is also inapposite in some cases of co-obligors. A simplified version of the complex facts of the Court of Appeal's decision in *Niru Battery Manufacturing Co v Milestone Trading Ltd (No 2)*[79] illustrates the point:

> P negligently misrepresents to X that he is obliged to pay D £1 million. X pays D this sum.
> X successfully claims £1 million from P by way of damages for the loss he thereby suffered.

Here P is primarily responsible for what has occurred, both causally and in terms of blameworthiness. D's only participation has been to receive the payment. Despite this, recoupment should follow.

These facts give rise to two injustices that should be corrected. First, the loss X has suffered as a result of the wrong needs to be reversed. Second, the unjustified payment D has received needs to be returned. If X had successfully claimed against D first, both of these objectives would have been fulfilled, subject to there being any further consequential loss as a result of the payment. As it is, only the first objective has been met. In order therefore to achieve the same position as where both objectives are fulfilled, P should have a claim against D for reimbursement. Although expressed in (multiple) different ways, this was the result in *Niru Battery Manufacturing Co v Milestone Trading Ltd (No 2)*.

(d) Policy?

Finally, although it is common to suggest that claims of this kind are based upon 'policy',[80] this is an idiosyncratic use of the word. Reasons of policy are usually distinguished from reasons of principle on the basis that the former are not concerned with the just position as between plaintiff and defendant. A rule that says that if someone pays for another to carry out a criminal act, the payment can be recovered it the payor withdraws from the endeavour before it is carried out could be justified on this basis. We are seeking to encourage persons generally not to carry out crimes, and so we give them all an incentive to withdraw from them. This is nothing to do with what is fair as between the two parties.

However, the justification for reimbursement and contribution is not justifiable by any policy external to the parties. Rather we are seeking to allocate the burden of a legal obligation justly as between them.

---

[79] [2004] EWCA Civ 487, [2004] 2 All ER (Comm) 289. See also *Eaves v Hickson* (1861) 30 Beav 136, 54 ER 840.
[80] Burrows, *The Law of Restitution* (n 32), 436; Mitchell, Mitchell, and Watterson, *Goff & Jones* (n 56), [1–25].

10
Necessity

A. Good Samaritans and the Justification for Private Law

> A lawyer said unto Jesus, And who is my neighbour?
>
> And Jesus answering said, A certain man went down from Jerusalem to Jericho, and fell among thieves, which stripped him of his raiment, and wounded him, and departed, leaving him half dead.
>
> And by chance there came down a certain priest that way: and when he saw him, he passed by on the other side.
>
> And likewise a Levite, when he was at the place, came and looked on him, and passed by on the other side.
>
> But a certain Samaritan, as he journeyed, came where he was: and when he saw him, he had compassion on him,
>
> And went to him, and bound up his wounds, pouring in oil and wine, and set him on his own beast, and brought him to an inn, and took care of him.
>
> And on the morrow when he departed, he took out two pence, and gave them to the host, and said unto him, Take care of him; and whatsoever thou spendest more, when I come again, I will repay thee.
>
> Which now of these three, thinkest thou, was neighbour unto him that fell among the thieves?
>
> And he said, He that shewed mercy on him. Then said Jesus unto him, Go, and do thou likewise. (Luke 10: 29–37)

The facts of the parable of the good Samaritan give rise to two questions that are fundamental in relation to what can legitimately justify duties in private law.[1] First, should there be a legal duty to assist others, especially when it is (or nearly is) cost free for us to do so? Second, if we do rescue another, or assist someone in need, should this give rise to a legal duty upon the person assisted? This chapter concerns the latter question. It argues that there should be no such general duty, and that the exceptional examples in the common law claimed in support of one, either based upon 'unjust enrichment' or otherwise, do not do so.

The two questions are not logically dependent upon one another. A legal system could coherently impose duties of easy rescue, but no duties upon the person assisted, or vice versa. However, they are interrelated.[2] If the law does impose a duty of assistance, it is then easier to see why the law would impose a reciprocal duty on the party assisted. The English

---

[1] For a discussion of the problems in this chapter, that draws the opposite conclusion, see J Kortmann, *Altruism in Private Law* (2005), 82–186.
[2] *Stovin v Wise* [1996] AC 923 (HL), 943–944 *per* Lord Hoffmann.

common law's general position, discussed below, is not to impose duties of assistance, and to give the intervener no rights against the person assisted.

However, other jurisdictions have adopted different approaches. In particular, civilian systems, following Roman law, have adopted a general principle in favour of recompense for the necessitous intervener. An example:

> While D, a farmer, is away a storm occurs that causes the fences of D's farm to be destroyed, causing D's cattle to be at risk of being lost through straying. D's neighbour, P, is unable to contact him, but repairs the fences for him, thereby preventing the livestock from being lost.

Under the traditional *negotiorum gestio* doctrine, if P had damaged D's property in intervening on the other's behalf, the latter would have a claim for compensation (the *directa* action). P also however has a claim against D for the work done on his behalf (the *contraria* action). In the United States, reimbursement for work done has been permitted on similar facts.[3]

What should the law be? Three broad approaches to the justification of private law duties may be distinguished for our purposes.

First is an instrumental approach, most closely associated in the United States in the modern era with 'law and economics'. However, such a conception is as old as law itself.

> When a person is absent and someone looks after his affairs, actions arise reciprocally between them. These are known as the actions on uninvited intervention (negotiorum gestio). The direct action lies for the principal, the person whose business is managed; the intervener has the counter-action. It is obvious that they are not really contractual, because they only lie where the intervener has no mandate. The beneficiary of the intervention incurs his obligations without even knowing the facts. This was accepted as good policy, to ensure that the affairs of the absent were not left untended if they suddenly had to set off abroad without having time to make proper arrangements. Plainly no-one would intervene on their behalf without an action to recoup his outlay. Just as a useful intervention by the intervener puts the principal under an obligation, so the intervener too becomes liable to render an account'. (Justinian, Institutes, 3.27.1)

This justification in the Institutes of Justinian for a claim for reimbursement is that it removes the disincentive to useful intervention, thereby increasing their frequency. This is not a reason that relates the plaintiff to the defendant. It seeks to make society better. In seeking to increase the good things in the world, the instrumentalist need not necessarily think that those good things are reducible to any single thing, such as the dollar or the util.

Second is the idea that law in general, and private law in particular, should track, and give *determinatio* to, our good moral reasons for action. (Of course, the law may not in fact do so, but the idea is that it ought to.) An important point of law is to give us guidance as to how to act. There are so many reasons in play, and the difficulty of co-ordination with others so great, that one of the central points of law is to set down rules to help us to determine what

---

[3] See *Berry v Barbour* 279 P 2d 335 (Okla 1954).

those good reasons for action are. Law settles the issue for us with rules when, as individuals acting alone, we could not.

We all of us have good moral reasons for picking up babies drowning in an inch of water. If another person rescues us, especially if they do so at great cost to themselves, we also have good reasons to express our gratitude by rewarding those who have assisted us. That being so, and subject to any considerations to the contrary, the law ought, on this conception, to track those good reasons by imposing duties upon us to do so.

For some, who see morality in the same instrumentalist terms as they do law, there will be no difference between the first and second view. For example, for the committed utilitarian, the answer to what our good reasons for action as individuals are will be just as much an instrumental question, answered using the same reasoning, as the question of what society's laws ought to be. All that changes on that approach is the context of the analysis.

A third approach sees law generally, and private law specifically, as concerning our entitlements against one another. On this view, law is not properly about making us, or even helping us, to be good or to comply with our good reasons for action, nor is it about instrumentally achieving good ends beyond enforcing those entitlements. Rather it is primarily a system of rights dictated by what is required for each of us to be able to live lives independent of the choices of others. Without law, we could not do so. Good people rescue drowning babies, but babies have no entitlement that strangers rescue them. The terrible result of drowning a baby and not saving one are, in outcome, the same. In consequential terms there is no difference. That does not, on this view, create an entitlement to be saved. To use state power, in the form of private law and its enforcement, to induce us to conform with our good reasons for action or to instrumentally make the world a better place would, without more, be immoral: an attempt to use the individual as a mere means to an end. On this third view, there is a chasm of difference for the law between drowning a baby in a puddle, and not picking one up out of one, smashing another's bicycle and not fixing it, destroying another's reputation and not speaking well of them, making ill and not curing, locking up and not freeing, and so on. On this view the law may legitimately impose duties upon us not to injure others, but not, without more, duties to confer benefits upon them.

These three different approaches to the province of law then also give starkly different answers as to whether the rescuer ought to have a claim against the rescued.

On the first two views the law has good reasons for imposing a duty on the rescued or assisted without more ado, subject to any countervailing reason why not (eg allowing such claims would lead to abuse).[4]

On the third view, we would be crossing the Rubicon by making any award. In the vivid words of Bowen LJ:

> Liabilities are not to be forced on people behind their back any more than you can confer a benefit upon a man against his will.[5]

Birks responded that Bowen LJ's stricture was unhelpful, as 'all restitutionary liabilities are technically imposed without the consent of the defendant'.[6] However, as we have seen,

---

[4] See Kortmann, *Altruism in Private Law* (n 1), 85–90.
[5] *Falcke v Scottish Imperial Insurance Co* (1886) 34 Ch D 234 (CA), 248.
[6] P Birks, *An Introduction to the Law of Restitution* (rev edn, 1989), 195.

it is untrue that the conferral of a benefit upon another, whether by mistake or otherwise, without any participation at all on the part of the defendant or alternatively any pre-existing obligation that he owes, either does or should suffice for the imposition of an obligation. It is to meet this problem that the courts, and this work, have insisted upon the importance of a request or acceptance on the part of the defendant where restitution of the value of a service is sought from him (and that such acceptance is implicit in cases of money payments).

A less fundamentalist approach than Bowen LJ's would be to insist that imposing private law duties for which the defendant has no responsibility, for instrumentalist policy reasons, is a matter for the legislature, not the courts. Only our most basic entitlements, those necessitated by, or at least compatible with, a system of equal freedom are legitimately created judicially. Further, there are reasons to doubt whether giving the rescuer a claim against the rescued does or will entail more rescue. Are neighbours more willing to mend each other's fences in France (where the *negotiorum gestio contraria* action is recognised) than in England (where it is not)? People often do not guide their conduct using legal rules, especially in emergencies. If some kind of claim is allowed, the level of reward also needs to be set with care. Blood donation rates in the United Kingdom (where donors receive a cup of tea and a biscuit) tend to be higher than in the United States (where donors are often paid). The psychological reason seems to be that payment can mask, and undermine, our benevolent motive.[7] The policy questions of whether it is useful to reward, and how much, are ones the courts lack both the technical competence and political legitimacy to assess.

B. Quantification

If a legal system does adopt the approach that the rescuer should have a claim against the rescued, how should this be quantified? At least four different responses may be identified.[8] First, we could allow the rescuer to recover the loss he has suffered, which may go beyond any expenses incurred ('compensation'). Second, they could be entitled to claim the value of the service rendered ('remuneration'). Third, they could be given a 'reward', which may incorporate elements of the first two measures but include other factors in its calculation, such as how risky the rescue was. Fourth, they may be given a claim to the extent that the claimant is in fact enriched by what has been done.

If we accepted, as Birks at one time suggested, that a rescuer's 'moral compulsion' vitiated his consent to the defendant's enrichment, in the same way as would a mistake or duress, then it is explicable how the claim should be quantified by reference to the gain made by the defendant.[9] However, this has never been the law, nor should it be. Large gifts to charity in situations of terrible need are irrecoverable. Care provided to incapacitated loved ones gives rise to no claim against them.

---

[7] Kortmann, *Altruism in Private Law* (n 1), 92–94.
[8] ibid, 81–83.
[9] P Birks, *An Introduction to the Law of Restitution* (n 6), 193–202. See also G Virgo, *The Principles of the Law of Restitution* (3rd edn, 2015), 291–292.

Most commentators today prefer to justify claims by the rescuer in instrumentalist terms, based upon a policy of encouraging useful intervention,[10] but on such an approach a gain-based order is either too low or too high. If the rescue fails, so that the defendant is not in fact better off through the attempt, no encouragement is given. If it succeeds, the ridiculous result that the defendant has to give up the full value of the benefit obtained seems to arise. Where the defendant's life is saved by the plaintiff's heroism this is obviously inappropriate.

A policy of encouraging rescue justifies two possible responses. One response is to give a positive incentive to intervene. This suggests a reward, payable upon success. After all, we wish to encourage successful interventions, not failures. Gain would be relevant to such a reward, but not the sole factor. Another response is to remove the disincentive to intervene, and to award compensation, regardless of success or failure. If compensation is only awarded in cases of success, the disincentive is not fully removed as the rescuer will never be better off through intervention and runs the risk of being out of pocket. Merely remunerating for the service provided would not remove the disincentive as the rescuer may have suffered a loss through intervening, by injuring himself or his property. In theory a legal system could adopt a very strong policy of promoting intervention both by compensating failures and rewarding success.

As would be expected, no legal system that seeks to encourage rescue adopts a gain-based response. The reward payable in maritime salvage cases can be seen as an example of the first response. The civilian *actio negotiorum gestio contraria* is (generally) best seen as an example of the second. Birks therefore (rightly) in his later work excluded all discussion of the topic of necessitous intervention from 'unjust enrichment' as the response is not enrichment based.[11] Other commentators have however persisted in insisting that the topic belongs within 'unjust enrichment'.

C. The Law

1. Exceptions?

The remainder of this chapter concerns the positive law in the Anglo-common law world. It is today common to argue that in the common law the 'exceptions have swallowed the rule'[12] and that a general claim in favour of the necessitous intervener should now be recognised. Further it is also often said that this should be and is based upon 'unjust enrichment'. Neither proposition is correct. All of the 'exceptions' have specific justifications for their existence and are, as a result, governed by disparate rules. They cannot be generalised. Some are more readily reconciled with Bowen LJ's strictures than others. None is straightforwardly gain-based.

---

[10] Eg A Burrows, *The Law of Restitution* (3rd edn, 2011), 480–482; see also C Mitchell, P Mitchell, and S Watterson (eds), *Goff & Jones: The Law of Unjust Enrichment* (9th edn, 2016), [18-01]–[18-04], [18-07]–[18-08], [18-25], [18-76].
[11] Birks, *Unjust Enrichment* (2nd edn, 2005), 22–23.
[12] Mitchell, Mitchell, and Watterson, *Goff & Jones* (n 10), [18-102], see also *ENE 1 Kos Ltd v Petroleo Brasileiro SA (The Kos) (No 2)* [2012] UKSC 17, [2012] 2 AC 164, [19] *per* Lord Sumption.

178   NECESSITY

2. Discharge of Another's Obligation

One group of cases relied upon for the recognition of an equivalent to the civilian *negotiorum gestio contraria*[13] we have already seen: claims for the costs of burial against the party primarily responsible, claims for the care provided for a pauper that ought to have provided by a parish, and other claims based upon the discharge of another's obligation. Such claims for reimbursement are, generally, seen as part of the *actio negotiorum gestio contraria* in civilian jurisdictions. However, in this group of cases we have an independently sufficient reason for recovery, fitting more closely the reasoning in the cases at common law. We also need to do no violence to Bowen LJ's objection to involuntarily imposed obligations. The defendant is not being asked to bear more than the cost of an obligation that was properly his.

3. Reciprocal Duties

(a) Bailees
Another category with an independent sufficient justification is the group of cases where the claimant is, exceptionally, under an involuntary duty to the defendant to assist them and has incurred expense in doing so. It is fair that where we exceptionally impose upon one party the duty to assist another, that other should bear the cost incurred in performing that duty. In those legal systems that do impose general duties of easy rescue, reciprocal duties of recompense are then also more readily justifiable (although *actio negotiorum gestio contraria* has always been more extensive).

The most common example arises from the law of bailment. In *Great Northern Railway Co v Swaffield*[14] the defendant sent a horse by the plaintiffs' railway but failed to collect it at the destination station. The plaintiffs sent the horse to a livery stable. The defendant refused to pay the (reasonable) charges for the care of the animal. Eventually the plaintiffs paid the livery stable keeper's charges and sent the horse to the defendant who accepted it. The claim to be reimbursed the charges paid succeeded. Pollock B stated:

> [I]t was the duty of the plaintiffs, as carriers, although the transit of the horse was at an end, to take such reasonable care of the horse as a reasonable owner would take of his own goods; and if they had turned him out on the highway, or allowed him to go loose, they would have been in default. Therefore they did what it was their duty to do.[15]

Piggot B, by contrast, stated that the plaintiffs were 'bound, from ordinary feelings of humanity to keep the horse safely and feed him'.[16] The narrower view of Pollock CB is the better one, so that mere bystanders who intervene should have no claim. The duty of the bailee in this situation is imposed, not assumed. They never agreed to have possession of the horse after delivery at the destination station and had no contractual right to reimbursement for the expense they were required to incur.

---

[13] Eg Burrows, *The Law of Restitution* (n 10), 470, 476, 477; Mitchell, Mitchell, and Watterson, *Goff & Jones* (n 10), [18-67].
[14] (1873–1874) LR 9 Ex 132.
[15] *ibid*, 137–138.
[16] *ibid*, 137.

THE LAW   179

The problem bailees find themselves in is that they cannot abandon goods that have been bailed to them, even where such bailment is gratuitous. In *Sachs v Miklos*,[17] the lesson of which is never to do anyone a good turn by storing their property, the defendants had stored free of charge the plaintiff's furniture in their house. They then lost touch with him and needed to use the room. They took reasonable steps to contact him, but when they could not do so, sold the furniture at auction. The value of the furniture then rose, and the plaintiff sued for conversion. It was held that if he had not been contacted, the sale was a conversion of his goods and so the defendants were liable for damages. Results such as this are only justifiable if involuntary bailees who are obliged to incur expense in compliance with their duty to safeguard the goods in their possession, should, and do, have a reciprocal entitlement to be reimbursed the expenditure they consequentially incur.

Cases of this kind have most often arisen in the context of the carriage of goods by sea, where masters of ships on the other side of the world have been unable to contact either the shipowner or the cargo owner and have incurred costs safeguarding the property in cases of emergency.[18] At one time the issue of whether the master, acting without authority, could act as agent for the ship or cargo owner, thereby binding them contractually with others, in circumstances of necessity was confused with the issue of whether the master, as the person in possession of the ship and goods, could recover the expense he incurred in safeguarding them. Both issues were treated as concerning 'agency of necessity'. The old rules on when someone could act as an 'agent of necessity', thereby binding their principal to a contractual duty, arose before the modern law of ostensible authority had become established. They are not our concern.[19]

An illustration that the issues of agency and reimbursement are separate is given by the decision of the House of Lords in *The Winson*.[20] The defendants were the owners of a cargo of wheat that had been shipped to Bombay. The ship foundered on a reef in the South China Sea. Over 15,000 tonnes of the cargo were salvaged (by agreement with both ship and cargo owners) and carried to Manila. There the salvors incurred warehouse charges in storing the goods. The cargo owners argued that until the contract of carriage with the shipowner was terminated, the salvors held the goods for the shipowners alone, and their only claim for reimbursement was against the shipowners. Lord Diplock for the court determined that the cargo owners were liable to reimburse the salvors based upon the law of bailment. As soon as the salvors took possession of the goods they owed a duty as bailees to the cargo owners, and as a result had a reciprocal right to reimbursement for the expense incurred in performing their duty.

> The salvors, under the ordinary principles of the law of bailment ... owed a duty of care to the cargo owner to take such measures to preserve the salved wheat from deterioration by exposure to the elements as a man of ordinary prudence would take for the preservation of his own property. For any breach of such duty the bailee is liable to his bailor in damages for any diminution in value of the goods consequent upon his failure to take such measures;

---

[17] [1948] 2 KB 23 (CA).
[18] *The Argos* (1873) LR 5 PC 134, 165; *Hingston v Vent* (1876) 1 QBD 367; *Tetley v British Trade Corp* (1922) 10 Lloyd's List LR 678.
[19] For a court confusing the two separate issues see *Surrey Breakdown Ltd v Knight* [1999] RTR 84, carefully discussed by Kortmann, *Altruism in Private Law* (n 1), 166–169.
[20] *China Pacific SA v Food Corporation of India, The Winson* [1982] AC 939 (HL).

and if he fulfils that duty he has, in my view, a correlative right to charge the owner of the goods with the expenses reasonably incurred in doing so.[21]

No principle of the law of agency is operative here.

Similarly, in *ENE Kos 1 Ltd v Petroleo Braioleiro SA (No 2)*[22] a vessel had been time chartered, the charterers had failed to pay the hire, and so the ship was withdrawn by the owners as they were entitled to do. The claimant owners were then required to keep the vessel in port while the defendant's goods were unloaded. This expense that the owners as bailees were required to incur was held by a majority to be recoverable by way of a contractual indemnity, but all also agreed that, if it were not, it was recoverable regardless of any contractual entitlement. If the shipowners had not agreed to carry the goods after termination for failure to pay the hire, and if as bailees they were compelled to incur costs on behalf of the defendant, they were entitled to be reimbursed.

We find the same principle in the context of the sale of goods. If, after delivery, a buyer rejects non-conforming goods but still has possession of them, he will be under a (positive) duty to take care of them. If the buyer incurs expenditure in performing this duty (which may in some circumstances such as perishable goods include selling them on behalf of the buyer) this should be recoverable.[23] Often such a claim can be bought alternatively as one for damages for the seller's breach,[24] but the expense should be recoverable regardless of the availability of such a claim.

Bailment cases such as these are not situations of a service rendered to the defendant for no reason. The plaintiffs are legally obliged to the defendant to store or otherwise ensure that care is taken of the goods. The imposition of the exceptional duty explains the right to recovery (and also shows that such duties of assistance are the exception).

The scope of the duty to reimburse is therefore co-extensive with the correlative, exceptionally imposed, positive duty to ensure that care will be taken of the goods. In answering whether a stranger who finds goods and takes them into his possession is entitled to claim reimbursement for the costs he incurs in safeguarding them, the answer turns upon whether a finder comes under the same duty as a voluntary bailee. The traditional rule was that finders of stray animals had no claim for reimbursement against the owner for the expense they incurred in keeping them.[25] Today however there is some limited authority for treating finders as bailees. In *Parker v British Airways Board*,[26] Donaldson LJ stated, in *obiter dicta* that a finder of lost goods has a duty to 'care for [them]' and to 'take such measures in all the circumstances as in all the circumstances are reasonable to acquaint the true owner of the finding and the present whereabouts of the chattel'.[27] If this is correct, the cost of this imposed duty ought to be recoverable.

---

[21] *ibid*, 960.
[22] See also *Guildford BC v Hein* [2005] EWCA Civ 979, [2005] LGR 797.
[23] Uniform Commercial Code §§ 2-603 and 2-604; Vienna Sales Convention, Arts 84–88.
[24] *Kolfer Plant Ltd v Tilbury Plant Ltd* (1977) 121 SJ 390. *Cf. Chesterman v Lamb* (1834) 2 A & E 129, 111 ER 50.
[25] *Binstead v Buck* (1777) 2 W Bl 1117, 96 ER 660 (no lien).
[26] [1982] 1 QB 1004 (CA), 1017. *Cf. Newman v Bourne & Hollingworth* (1915) 31 TLR 209; *Gilchrist Watt and Sanderson Pty Ltd v York Product Pty Ltd* [1970] 1 WLR 1262, 1270 per Lord Pearson; *P& O Nedlloyd BV v Utainko Ltd* [2003] EWCA Civ 83, [26] per Mance LJ.
[27] [1982] 1 QB 1004 (CA), 1017.

(b) Legal duties to provide medical care

Outside of bailment, examples of such reciprocal duties are difficult to identify. A surgeon is, or in the era of the National Health Service was, one of a number of 'common callings', such as innkeepers and farriers, who are under a legal duty to provide their service to all who present themselves. In *Matheson v Smiley*,[28] Smiley shot himself with a shotgun. Two friends discovered him, brought in a doctor, who, determining that it was a case for a surgeon, called in the plaintiff, a surgeon. Smiley was taken to hospital, where all that could be done was attempted, but he died. The plaintiff successfully sought to recover his fee from Smiley's estate. Robson JA quoted Lord Blackburn with approval as saying:

> Those who have the charge of a sick person if he is helpless (whether the disease be infectious or not) are, at Common law, under a legal obligation to do, to the best of their ability, what is necessary for the preservation of the sick person.[29]

As the surgeon was under a legal duty to provide the care, he could not refuse, so he should have a right to reimbursement, regardless of the success of the treatment.

4. Contribution Between Common Interests

(a) General average contribution

The Rhodian law decrees that if in order to lighten a ship merchandise is thrown overboard, that which has been given for all shall be replaced by the contribution of all.[30]

(1) General average loss is a loss caused by or directly consequential on a general average act. It includes a general average expenditure as well as a general average sacrifice.
(2) There is a general average act where any extraordinary sacrifice or expenditure is voluntarily and reasonably made or incurred in time of peril for the purpose of preserving the property imperilled in the common adventure.[31]

The current editors of *Goff & Jones*,[32] unlike the view originally adopted,[33] or the authors of other texts in the field,[34] see the law of general average as another example of the 'necessity' principle.[35] This is unconvincing.

The classic situation of general average is where a ship carrying cargo is in danger of foundering, and the master of the vessel throws the plaintiff's cargo overboard in order to

---

[28] [1932] 2 SLR 787 (Mn CA). Equivalent US authority includes *Cotnam v Wisdom* 104 SW 164 (Ark 1907); *Piggee v Mercy* 186 P 2d 817 (Okla 947), *In re Crisan Estate* 107 NW 2d 907 (Mich 1961). See A Kull, *Restatement of the Law (Third) Restitution and Unjust Enrichment*, vol I (2010), § 20.
[29] *Metropolitan Asylum District v Hill* (1881) 6 App Cas 193, 204.
[30] D 14.2.1.
[31] Marine Insurance Act 1906, s 6.
[32] Mitchell, Mitchell, and Watterson, *Goff & Jones* (n 10) [18-37]. See also C Mitchell, *The Law of Contribution and Reimbursement* (2003) [2.22]–[2.26].
[33] R Goff and G Jones, *The Law of Restitution* (6th edn, 2002), [14-042]–140-55] but see R Goff and G Jones, *The Law of Restitution* (7th edn, 2007), [18-024]–[18-026].
[34] Eg Burrows, *The Law of Restitution* (n 10), 475 fn 34.
[35] See also Virgo, *Principles of the Law of Restitution* (n 9), 303.

save the vessel and the other cargo. The plaintiff has a claim for a contribution towards his loss both from the shipowner and the other cargo owners.[36] The plaintiff in this scenario has personally done nothing to save the venture but has had to bear more than his share of the cost of saving it, to the benefits of the others. The claim is not dependent upon agreement as there may be none between the various parties. No public policy of encouraging useful intervention by the plaintiff, or anyone else, on another's behalf can explain this category. If the master of the ship needs to throw the plaintiff's goods overboard to save the vessel, he usually will need no further encouragement to sacrifice the interests of others for those of his principal. What enables him to make such a decision in cases of emergency without fear of the consequences, is the *privilege* to do so because of necessity the law confers upon him (ie he is not a tortfeasor) not the susceptibility to a claim for general average. The other cargo owners have done nothing at all that needs either encouragement or discouragement. Although there are some cases of general average that resemble the self-sacrifice of the *actio negotiorum gestio contraria*, as where a ship is scuttled by its crew in order to extinguish a fire thereby saving the cargo,[37] these are not the usual case.

A closer analogy is, as initially suggested by the original authors of *Goff & Jones*, other commentators,[38] and case law,[39] the law of contribution between co-obligors, most obviously because it too is a claim for contribution. Like that form of contribution, the law of general average is a form of localised distributive justice. Similarly, the claim is quantified taking into account the loss that the claimant has suffered. 'Average' means loss.[40] 'Particular average' is a loss that falls entirely upon a specific owner (eg where a ship is grounded the loss falls on the shipowner). 'General average' is calculated by reference to the value of the claimant's property sacrificed or other loss suffered to bring the common venture to a place of safety, capped rateably by the value of the property of each of the other members of the joint venture.[41] Unlike the position under the civilian *actio negotiorum gestio contraria*, the sacrifice must have succeeded in benefitting the others. If the defendants' ship or cargo is lost before the end of the voyage there is no claim.[42] Like contribution between co-obligors, it is therefore misleading to think of this claim for contribution as either solely loss or gain based; it is in a sense both and neither. The law makes all the parties to a joint venture bear their share of the cost of saving the rest through the sacrifice of one (or more).

Unlike the law of contribution between those jointly obliged, however, we are not simply imposing upon the defendant his share of the burden of a legal duty they were already under. General average gives rise to a new duty, the burden of which the defendant never accepted and for which, at least in the case of other cargo owners, no conduct of theirs results in their being responsible for arising.

Against the person who has sacrificed the plaintiff's goods, usually the carrier, the claim may be explicable by reference to the right to the goods that the claimant has. In

---

[36] *Strang, Steel & Co v A Scott & Co* (1889) 14 App Cas 601 (PC), 606 *per* Lord Watson.
[37] Eg *Archard v Ring* (1874) 2 Asp MLC 422; *Papayammo v Grampian SS CO Ltd* (1896) Com Cas 448.
[38] S J Stoljar, *The Law of Quasi-Contract* (2nd edn, 1989), 179; D Friedmann, 'Unjust Enrichment, Pursuance of Self-Interest and the Limits of Free Riding' (2003) 36, Loy LA L Rev 831, 853.
[39] *Deering v Earl of Winchelsea* (1787) 2 Bos & Pol 270 (ex), 274 126 ER 1276, 1278 *per* Eyre CB.
[40] 'General average loss' is therefore a tautology.
[41] *Cf.* the joint obligation of those receiving a service under a condition that has failed: *Benedetti v Sawiris* [2013] UKSC 50, [2014] AC 938, as discussed in Chapter 4, Reversal.
[42] *Fletcher v Alexander* (1867–1868) LR 3 CP 375, 382 *per* Bovill CJ; *Pirie & Co v Middle Dock Co* (1881) 44 LT 426, 430, *per* Watkin Williams J; *Chellew v Royal Commission on the Sugar Supply* [1921] 2 KB 627.

circumstances of necessity, it may be exceptionally permissible to sacrifice another's property, but the privilege to do so may be subject to the condition that the sacrificed property needs to be paid for. In the classic Minnesota decision of *Vincent v Lake Erie Transportation Co*[43] the crew of the defendant's ship had just finished unloading, when an unusually severe storm arose. The plaintiffs expressly terminated their permission to allow the ship to be tied to their dock, but the crew continued to lash the vessel to it during the storm. The ship repeatedly banged against the dock, causing $500 of damage. The defendants committed no wrong because of the circumstances of necessity, and if the plaintiffs had untied the ship, they would have committed conversion and been liable for the ship's loss.[44] However, the privilege to use the dock was qualified. No wrong was committed, *provided* the damage was paid for.

Claims based upon this 'qualified privilege' reasoning differ from the result reached in cases of general average. First, the claim in *Vincent* should succeed regardless of whether the sacrifice succeeds (ie there should have been a claim for the damage to the dock even if the ship had sunk). Second, under the law of general average there is no obligation on the carrier to reimburse the full value of the loss caused, unlike in *Vincent v Lake Erie*. Third, an explanation, based upon the right to the thing sacrificed also has no force in relation to claims by one cargo owner against another cargo owner where the defendant was not the party who threw the plaintiff's goods overboard. Fourth, at least when not at sea, where the necessary sacrifice is made to save the lives or property of third parties, there is no claim against anyone.[45]

Unlike in cases of necessitous intervention, the general average claimant is not seeking to be reimbursed for anything he did. There is no danger here of rewarding the officious. If we are to justify this category, and not dismiss it as an historical anomaly of the law of the sea, it is on the basis that the commingling of the parties' property, as part of a common adventure, inevitably required one to be sacrificed for the good of the rest. When these rules arose, trade by sea was very dangerous. Parties know that, in a sea voyage, exceptional measures might have to be taken in an emergency and consented to the idea that in a joint enterprise it is fair if all share the risk. The same is not true of someone who stores their goods in a warehouse on land. The rules originated in a world without modern insurance and were a way of collectivising risk which could not be achieved through contract law alone. It is doubtful whether, as a result, they are capable of being generalised from in the modern era.

(b) Other examples?

In the common law, general average contribution is restricted and applies only to sea voyages.[46] Although historically administered by the common law and not the Admiralty courts, it is traditionally seen as part of, and limited to, the law of the sea.[47] On land, if there is a fire which threatens to destroy the property of a number of people, if the plaintiff's property is destroyed so as to create a firebreak in order to save the rest, there is no authority for allowing the plaintiff a claim against those who benefit from the sacrifice of his property.

---

[43] 109 Minn 456, 124 NW 221 (Minn 1910).
[44] *Ploof v Putnam* 81 Vt 471, 71 A 188 (Vt 1908).
[45] *Mouse's Case, The Gravesend Ferry* (1609) 12 Co Rep 63, 77 ER 1341; *Romney Marsh v Trinity House* (1870) LR 5 Ex 204; *Esso Petroleum Co Ltd v Southport Corp* [1956] AC 218 (HL). Cf. *Whalley v Lancashire and Yorkshire Railway Co* (1884) LR 13 QBD 131 (CA).
[46] *Falcke v Scottish Imperial Ins. Co* (1886) 34 Ch D 234 (CA), 248–249 *per* Bowen LJ.
[47] *Morrison Steamship Co Ltd v Greystoke Castle (Cargo Owners) (The Cheldale)* [1947] AC 265 (HL), 310 *per* Lord Uthwatt.

184   NECESSITY

There are however some other cases where the parties' property is commingled where it is the plaintiff who incurs necessary expenditure benefitting himself, which inevitably benefits another the party with whom his interests are intertwined, where he is permitted to recover a rateable proportion of the expenses incurred.[48]

An old example is that of joint tenancies and tenancies in common, where repair expenditures, that are not obligatory, are incurred by one benefitting them all. A claim for contribution is allowed, but only where there is a suit to partition to sell and divide the property. At that point an allowance has to be given for the increase in value caused by the work.[49] It does not matter who sought the sale.[50]

Cases such as these are, like general average, for a contribution, not for the full benefit obtained by the defendant from the work, nor for what it would have cost the defendant to pay for the service to be provided (the latter would shift the full cost on to the defendant, instead of fairly sharing it).

Another possible modern example is *Re Berkeley Applegate*.[51] A liquidator of a company incurred considerable expenditure investigating, ascertaining, and managing its affairs. There were insufficient free assets to cover the liquidator's costs, but the company held assets on trust for the benefit of investors who had substantially benefitted from the liquidator's work. The trust beneficiaries' interests could not have been realised without the work done by the liquidator of the company in realising and separating the assets. As a condition of the beneficiaries realising their interests, they were required to contribute their share of the expense incurred, to the extent that the free assets of the company were insufficient.

5. Maritime Salvage

The law of maritime salvage is best understood as part of the law of entitlement to things.

In the world we find ourselves in, property rights are extremely useful. In the common law, as elsewhere, our default rule for the allocation of rights to things is first possession. If I pick up a block of marble, or occupy an area of land, I acquire a right to exclude all others from the thing. If another person subsequently picks up the block or occupies the land they too acquire such a right, but an inferior entitlement (title) than the one I had. As I was first, I have a better title than them. We determine priority between two or more entitlements to possession through this temporal rule.

This ranking by order of possession is familiar to parents ('your sister had that first'). However, there may be reasons why this first in time ranking should either be reversed or at least qualified. One of these is where land or goods are improved innocently by the person who is second. Improvements are given separate treatment in this work.[52] Another is where goods are salvaged.

If a ship and its cargo would be lost at sea, but for the salvor's actions, the only reason anything still exists that the person with prior possession can assert any title to is because of the salvor's actions. Without his risking his own property and life, at potentially great cost, the

---

[48] Friedmann, 'Unjust Enrichment, Pursuance of Self-Interest and the Limits of Free Riding' (n 38), 852–867.
[49] *Swan v Swan* (1819) 8 Price 518, 146 ER 1281; *Leigh v Dickeson* (1885) 15 QBD 60 (CA), 67 *per* Cotton LJ, 69 *per* Lindley LJ; *Re Jones* [1893] 2 Ch 461; *Re Pavlou* [1993] 1 WLR 1046.
[50] *Re Cook's Mortgage* [1896] 1 Ch 923.
[51] [1989] Ch 32.
[52] Chapter 14, Improvements.

ship and cargo would be at the bottom of the sea. The only reason these things are still capable of being possessed by anyone as a matter of fact is because of the salvor. This provides a good reason if not for ignoring then for at least qualifying the 'first to possess' rule.

This justification for maritime salvage fits with many of its fundamental features.[53]

First, salvage only applies where property is salvaged, and its value limits the quantum of any award. The saving of life alone gives rise to no reward.[54] If lives are saved (eg those of the crew of a salvaged vessel) a reward may now be claimed, but only from the salved property,[55] not from the individuals rescued.[56] This confinement to property makes no sense if the rule is (solely) based upon encouraging useful intervention, but it follows naturally if the rule is part of the law of entitlement to things.

Second, it explains why it is the rule at sea, but not on the land.[57] At sea, if ships and goods are not salvaged they will generally be irreparably lost through sinking. On land, if a farmer's cattle stray because his fences are not repaired, it will rarely be the case that that means they are gone for good. The cattle may cause damage for which the farmer will be liable, or may be harmed or killed, but rarely completely lost, so as to be incapable of possession at all. There are of course examples of goods on land that would be irretrievably lost unless rescued (eg in cases of fire) but these are not the usual case.

It is true that in the modern era another explanation exists for a special rule of the sea. At sea there is no state, with its police force, fire brigade, and ambulance service to rescue people, so that when at sea we are dependent upon private individuals in a way that is not true on land. However, the salvage rule is of such longstanding that it predates the state taking such an active role in the protection of individuals.

Third, it explains why the salvor obtains a 'lien' over the ship and freight salvaged, and why this will be the only method of enforcement absent a contract. The salvor has a title to the property because of the rescue. The superior title of the party prior in time is only permitted to be asserted if he pays the salvor a reward. The prior possessor's title is qualified. A lien is therefore easier to justify than would be a freestanding claim for a reward. We should not think of salvage as a freestanding obligation to pay a reward secured by a lien. Rather, the claimant with prior title is only entitled to recover his property from the salvor in possession *if* he pays a reward. If the person with prior title wishes to abandon the goods, and be subject to no claim, he should be free to do so. No salvage claim greater than the value of the goods successfully saved is therefore possible.

Fourth, it explains why, historically, the salvor's action for reward was *in rem* (ie to the thing) and not *in personam* (ie against the person with prior title himself). Claims *in personam* have been permitted where there is a contract to provide salvage services,[58] but this is not justifiable absent a contract. Beyond the entitlement to a lien over the thing, or a personal claim for payment where there is a contract, the salvor has no freestanding claim. To describe the salvor's possessory right as being a 'lien' is therefore somewhat misleading as

---

[53] The right to salvage has always been part of maritime law, enforced in England by the Court of Admiralty. It was (slightly) extended by statute by the Merchant Shipping Act 1995 which incorporated the International Convention on Salvage 1989 into UK law. For detailed consideration see J Reeder QC, *Brice on the Maritime Law of Salvage* (5th edn, 2011); F D Rose, *Kennedy and Rose on the Law of Salvage* (10th edn, 2021).
[54] Rose, *Kennedy and Rose on the Law of Salvage* (n 53), [4-111]–[4-165], [17-002]–[17-005].
[55] ibid, [4-155]; see also International Convention on Salvage 1989, Art 16.1.
[56] International Convention on Salvage 1989, Art 16.1.
[57] *Nicholson v Chapman* (1793) 2 H Bl 254, 257–258, 126 ER 536, 538–539 per Erle CJ.
[58] *Re Five Steel Barges* (1890) 15 PD 142 (where two of the salvaged vessels had been sold by the counterparty).

that implies a possessory right securing an independent obligation that could be enforced, when in fact it is a possessory right that is released if payment is made.

Importantly for our purposes, such a justification also means that the law of maritime salvage does not conflict with Bowen LJ's assumption as to when it is permissible to impose freestanding obligations upon defendants, an assumption which this work endorses. The salvor acquires his lien even if the salvage was conducted under protest, provided the salvage was necessary.[59] This is not to deny that the rules are framed so as to encourage rescue; they are. However, such encouragement is only legitimate because of the competing interest in the thing salvaged that the salvor has. Although extending the salvor's lien to salvage on land might have been justifiable, further generalisation is not possible.

There are statements consistent with the idea that maritime salvage is based upon unjust enrichment, and so the rule that the salvage must (at least in part) have succeeded was explained by Dr Lushington as based upon the fact that 'salvage reward is for benefits actually conferred, not for a service attempted to be rendered'.[60] However, although in quantification of the reward the gain made from the salvaging of the property is a relevant consideration,[61] the defendant is not stripped of the full gain they made, so for example a shipowner is not required to give up the full value of a ship that would otherwise have sunk. Rarely will the reward exceed more than half the value of the salvaged property. Nor is the claim one for a *quantum meruit*, calculated by reference to the value of the service provided.[62] Rather the gain is part of the calculation for a reward, to the assessment of which also go the expense incurred by the salvor, the risk run, the skill of the salvors and the speed and efficiency of the work.[63] Professional salvors are commonly awarded more because their expenses are higher (they need to keep boats on standby) and because we wish to encourage a salvage industry.

The requirement that the salvage operation must (at least in part) have been a success could be explained in policy terms (we wish to encourage successful rescues, not unsuccessful ones) but it is better explained as being based upon the fact that the salvor must have saved property, over which he can assert a right to possess, for the justification for the rule to apply.

A lien in favour of the person saving property could have been extended outside of the maritime context, and in the United States this has happened, albeit not so as to give the rescuer a reward[64] but only a lien to secure reasonable remuneration for the work done.[65] In England however the extension of the law of salvage was rejected in *Nicholson v Chapman*.[66] The plaintiff's timber was placed in a dock on the banks of the Thames but got loose and floated down the river to Putney, where it obstructed the towing path. The bailiff of the manor then employed the defendant to take the timber away. The plaintiff then demanded the return of his goods, and the defendant refused unless he was paid a sum as salvage. The

---

[59] *The Kangaroo* [1918] P 327.
[60] *The Zephyrus* (1842) 1 W Rob 329, 330–331, 166 ER 596, 597.
[61] International Convention on Salvage 1989, Art 13.1(a).
[62] *The Blackwell*, 77 US (10 Wall) 1, 14 L Ed 870 (1869).
[63] International Convention on Salvage 1989, Art 13.1(b)–(j).
[64] *Mason v Le Blaireau* (1804) 6 US 238, 266 (2 Cranch 240, 266) *per* Marshall CJ: 'If the property of an individual on land be exposed to the greatest peril, and be saved by the voluntary exertions of any persons whatever, if valuable goods be rescued from a house in flames, at the imminent hazard of life by the salvor, no remuneration in the shape of salvage is allowed. It is perhaps difficult, on any other principle, to account satisfactorily for the very great difference which is made between the retribution allowed for services at sea and on land.'
[65] Kull, *Restatement 3rd* (n 28), § 21 ill 2; eg *Chase v Corcoran* 106 Mass 286 (1871).
[66] (1793) 2 H Bl 254, 126 ER 536.

plaintiff refused, and successfully brought an action of trover. Erle CJ held that the action should succeed because the defendant had no lien over the timber, rejecting the application of the law of maritime salvage to navigable rivers. However, the case is not definitive authority against giving the intervener a claim, first because the defendant was acting under the instructions of the bailiff, and not out of a desire to assist the plaintiff, and second because the defendant had not proven the value of the service he had rendered, the burden of which Erle CJ rightly stated should not fall on the owner in any event.[67] Whatever the position in the eighteenth century, today it was accepted by the House of Lords in *The Goring*[68] that the law of salvage does not apply to non-tidal waters, Lord Brandon stating that 'if any such extension is to be made it must ... be left to the legislature to make it'.[69]

6. Necessaries supplied to Those Incapable of Contracting

That those subject to an incapacity must pay a reasonable price for necessaries supplied is not, contrary to the suggestion sometimes made,[70] best understood as based upon any policy of encouraging useful intervention. The counterparty may be wholly unaware of the incapacity when making the supply. Rather it is a qualification upon the unenforceability of contracts entered into by those lacking general contractual capacity. This is demonstrated by the liability of the party subject to the incapacity to pay for necessaries even in the case of executory contracts. This qualification is itself qualified: the liability is capped at, but not fixed by, a reasonable sum.[71] As Buckley LJ stated:

> The plaintiff when he sues the defendant for necessary goods supplied during infancy is suing him in contract on the footing that the contract was such as the infant, notwithstanding infancy, could make. The defendant although he was an infant had a limited capacity to contract ... an infant may contract for supply at a reasonable price of articles reasonably necessary for his support in his station in life if he has not already a sufficient supply.[72]

D. Conclusion

The claim that any of the above examples is a common law instance of the civilian *actio negotiorum gestio contraria*, that is then capable of being generalised, does not withstand scrutiny. Some claims are quantified by reference to the value of the service provided, some are for reimbursement of the cost in discharging another's obligation, others are for a contribution towards a loss suffered rateably attributable to the gain made by the defendants, and

---

[67] (1793) 2 H Bl 254, 259, 126 ER 536, 539.
[68] [1988] 1 AC 831. See also *Aitchison v Lohre* (1879) 4 App Cas 755, 760 *per* Lord Blackburn; *The Tojo Maru* [1972] AC 242, 268 *per* Lord Reid.
[69] [1988] 1 AC 831, 857.
[70] Burrows, *The Law of Restitution* (n 10), 476.
[71] Sale of Goods Act 1979, s 3(2).
[72] *Nash v Inman* [1908] 2 KB 1, 12. See also Mitchell, Mitchell, and Watterson, *Goff & Jones* (n 10), [24-15]–[24-19].

necessaries are calculated by reference to the price agreed, so long as reasonable. Maritime salvage, though quantified on a reward basis, is not the source of a freestanding obligation but, outside of a contract, rather of a privilege to possess the property salvaged until rewarded. None of these is straightforwardly gain based. Some are dependent upon success, while others are not. These different rules reflect the different underlying reasons why each exists. Each has its own independently sufficient justification.

Sometimes legal systems make different choices, and here we come to one where the civil and common law pull apart. It is not true that we always blunder through to the same result in every case. If it were, what would be the point of having legal rules at all?

This difference between the legal traditions may just be an historically contingent accident, like driving on the left or the right. It may also be a product of the different kinds of society in which the rules emerged. In a family, or other small group with close personal bonds, rules for rescue, with correlative rules of compensation, may be thought more appropriate than in large societies where the role of the state is the more minimalist one of trying to hold the ring. In setting down rules for children, parents should be familiar with the fact that the kinds of orders issued ('apologise to your sister', 'eat your greens') are different from the more limited set of duties a modern state can require of us. Once we exclude women, children, and slaves, the Roman Republic in which the *actio negotiorum gestio contraria* emerged was a small society of men. In such a small cohesive society, more can be demanded of one another, and we might expect the legal rules to more closely track our moral duties to each other.

The general rule adopted in the common law world is at least a defensible one, and the various rules examined here are not exceptions but rather examples of other specific reasons for obligations. Each of these rules, and its limits, is supportable although the differences between the rules on the land and on the sea seem to be partly a product of their history. However, path dependency although it may explain how we got here, does not tell us which rule is to be preferred.

Nationalism in law is usually ludicrous and is at best embarrassing. As we shall see, there are areas, such as in relation to improvements to land and the law of 'proprietary estoppel', where English law is now considerably worse than the equivalent rules in other legal systems. But, in generally denying the imposition of obligations to pay upon those who have no responsibility, in any sense, for what has occurred, English law's position is also the preferable one.

This chapter was a small-scale version of the book: the danger of over-generalising different species of rights and obligation.

PART V
PROPERTY AND TRUSTS

11
Things

A. Introduction

This and the next two chapters form a distinct section. They argue that the invocation of 'unjust enrichment' as an explanation for the creation of property rights or the recovery of things is, at best, otiose. We start in this chapter with claims to recover tangible things or their value.

B. Rights

How in the common law, does a plaintiff recover a thing or its value? The claims discussed so far have generally not depended upon any pre-existing right of the plaintiff,[1] and if we accept the viability of the reasons given, we do not need to resort to any analysis based upon pre-existing rights. Some claims are so dependent, however. For example:

> *X* steals *C*'s motorcycle. *X* gives possession of the motorcycle to *D* intending a gift. *C* seeks recovery of the motorcycle or its value from *D*.

There has been no performance from *C* to *D* to reverse. The basis for *C*'s claim against *D*, either to specific return of the thing or to its value, is *D*'s interference with *C*'s prior right to exclude all others from the motorcycle (a right that may arise for a number of different reasons).

Some legal systems have vindicatory claims of the form 'that is my motorcycle, return it'. Common law systems do not recognise direct vindicatory actions in relation to things but require the plaintiff to put the claim in the form of a wrong. The claim is of the form 'I have an immediate right to possess that motorcycle; you committed a wrong by taking possession of it'. The anterior right to immediate possession of the thing is obviously not a secondary obligation created by any wrong.

In the common law, 'personal' property differs (or today in England, more accurately, differed) from 'real' property because the holder of a title to real property (almost always land) who was dispossessed could obtain a court order that he be put back in possession,[2] whereas the holder of a title to personal property was confined to a money order.[3] This has long since ceased to be true however: the courts of Equity made orders for delivery up of goods where a money award was inadequate,[4] and since 1977 the courts in England have

---

[1] With the exception of general average, see Chapter 10, Necessity.
[2] S Bridge, E Cooke, and M Dixon (eds), *Megarry & Wade: The Law of Real Property* (9th edn, 2019), [1-011]–[1-013].
[3] M Bridge, L Gullifer, K Low, and G McMeel, *The Law of Personal Property* (3rd edn, 2021), [1-009]–[1-016].
[4] *Cohen v Roche* [1927] 1 KB 169; *General & Finance Facilities v Cooks Cars (Romford) Ltd* [1963] 1 WLR 644 (CA). See also J Baker, *An Introduction to English Legal History* (5th edn, 2019), 423–426.

had statutory jurisdiction to order the return of goods on the same grounds.[5] Further, the mere fact that the defendant will not be compelled to return a thing (ie he is not liable to such a court order) does not mean that the plaintiff has no right to its return (ie that the defendant is not obliged to return it). Once damages for conversion have been paid, the plaintiff's title to his goods is extinguished.[6]

The civilian division between movable and immovable things roughly maps the common law's distinction between personal and real but is more conceptually appealing (although the classification of 'intangibles', such as intellectual property rights, as 'movables', when they do not relate to things that exist in physical space that can move, may cause some common law eyebrows to be raised).

If the defendant still has possession of the thing, this is significant if the defendant goes into bankruptcy or other insolvency proceeding. If he does, the prior title is capable of being asserted against the insolvency administrator[7] who takes possession of the defendant's estate. If the insolvency administrator then refuses to return the thing, he will be personally liable for a wrong (ie he commits conversion and is liable in damages).[8] In this way, we give effect to the proprietary right the plaintiff has, whilst only awarding personal money orders.

Where the defendant no longer has the thing, the claimant may rely upon an earlier action of the defendant inconsistent with his title (eg the sale of the defendant's title to the thing, or the destruction of the thing) in order to make out a claim for damages. If the defendant goes into bankruptcy when no longer in possession of the thing, this will give the plaintiff no claim against the administrator personally, and no special priority.

Cash (bank notes, coins, and other negotiable instruments) is tangible property and the right of exclusive possession of it is also capable of being vindicated through the torts relating to things.[9] However, cash operates in a slightly different way from rights to other things. Because cash is a medium of exchange, title to cash will generally be lost where it has been acquired by another in good faith and for value.[10] The traditional language of the 'action for money had and received' is unfortunately ambiguous as in some cases what is being asserted is a wrong (nowadays conversion) in relation to a right to physical cash,[11] whereas in others it is to recover a payment the plaintiff made to the defendant where title to the cash has passed. Both kinds of claim involve money, but their justifications are different.

C. Transfers

1. Contract and Conveyance

In the examples examined so far, although the factual possession of a thing may have been acquired by the defendant, the plaintiff's right to possess has not. Whether the plaintiff can

---

[5] Torts (Interference with Goods) Act 1977, s 3.
[6] Torts (Interference with Goods) Act 1977, s 5.
[7] For persons, in England, a trustee in bankruptcy. The equivalent for corporations are liquidators and administrators. For convenience 'administrators' will be used to cover all.
[8] *Re Goldburg (No 2)* [1912] 1 KB 606.
[9] Eg *Golightly v Reynolds* (1772) Lofft 87, 98 ER 547.
[10] *Miller v Race* (1758) 1 Burr 452, 457–458, 97 ER 398, 401. See also *Clarke v Shee* (1774) 1 Cowp 197, 200, 98 ER 1041, 1043.
[11] *Clarke v Shee* (1774) 1 Cowp 197, 98 ER 1041; *Calland v Lloyd* (1840) 6 M & W 26, 151 ER 307.

recover a thing that he no longer possesses, but once had title to, may depend upon whether he has transferred his title to another.

Most of our rights, that are capable of conveyance at all, cannot be transferred by a contract alone. An obvious example is title to land. In England all conveyances of title to land or any interest in it must be made by deed:[12] a formal piece of paper the execution of which symbolically transferred possession of the land. Today in England, and most other legal systems, title to land is usually registered, with any transfer also requiring alteration of the land register.[13] In relation to title to land, the contract to sell is therefore separate from the conveyance. Registrable securities, such as shares, are also transferred by altering a register, as are some forms of intellectual property rights, such as trademarks. Debts are only truly transferable by way of statutory assignment, and this requires writing and notice to be given to the debtor as to the change of creditor. For all of these rights, the contract to transfer and the method of conveyance are separate and independent of one another (ie they are abstracted). This principle of abstraction protects third parties who may be unaware of the existence or terms of any agreement to transfer. A land register, for example, enables third parties to know who has the right to exclude them from the property and who can convey title to the land.

Some other rights, such as copyright[14] and equitable interests[15] in England, whilst capable of transfer by agreement alone without any further step, require that this agreement is in writing and signed.

A conveyance of the title to goods may be made by delivery, where accompanied (either at the time or subsequently) by an agreement to pass title, or by way of deed.[16] However, both as a comparative matter,[17] and within the common law itself, goods are an exceptional case as title to them may also pass under a contract of sale alone without any formality required. This rule is now found in section 17 of the Sale of Goods Act. Where goods are ascertained,[18] the Act states that 'the property in them is transferred to the buyer at such time as the parties to the contract intend it to be transferred'. The relevant intention is that expressed by the parties' agreement, not what they intend as a matter of psychological fact (the subjective intention of each may differ or change after the moment of contracting).[19] That two parties, as a matter of psychological fact, intend title to goods to pass is immaterial: it will not do so absent a contract.[20] Where the parties have not expressly stated the moment for the passing of title, the Act provides various default rules. For the sale of goods therefore, contract and conveyance are not separate: the contract is the thing that does the conveyance, unless the parties agree otherwise. No actual or symbolic delivery, no formality such as a deed, and no registration is required.

This indissolubility of contract and conveyance in the context of the sale of goods has consequences when the contract is avoided, at least where such rescission takes place at common law. At common law, a contract may be avoided where it has been induced by

---

[12] Law of Property Act 1925, s 52.
[13] Law Registration Act 2002, s 27.
[14] Copyright Designs and Patents Act 1988, s 90(3).
[15] Law of Property Act 1925, s 53(1)(c).
[16] *Cochrane v Moore* (1895) 25 QBD 57 (CA), 60–73 *per* Bowen and Fry LJJ.
[17] But see Code Civil, Art 1583.
[18] Sale of Goods Act 1979, s 16.
[19] *Contra* S Zogg, *Effects of Mistake and Other Defects on the Passage of Title* (2019), 31–36.
[20] *Cochrane v Moore* (1895) 25 QBD 57 (CA).

fraud or duress. In *Load v Green*,[21] a fraudster induced the plaintiffs to sell fabrics to him, for which he had no intention of paying. The fraudster went into bankruptcy, and the plaintiffs brought an action in conversion against his assignees in bankruptcy. Parke B held that the sellers could rescind the contract for fraud, and as a result title to the goods revested in them, which title could then be asserted against the defendant assignees. This rule was applied, and (generously) extended, in *Car & Universal Finance Co Ltd v Caldwell*,[22] where the Court of Appeal held that rescission could occur where all possible steps to regain the goods had been taken, even where the rogue himself could not be found so as to be communicated with. If the buyer of goods goes into bankruptcy or other insolvency proceeding, rescission at law will revest title in the seller, and the administrator of the insolvency will be personally liable in conversion if he fails to return the goods.[23] Although there is no authority, other rights that can be transferred by contract alone, such as the right to copyright, should similarly revest where the agreement transferring them is avoided at law.

It has been argued that *Load v Green* and the decisions following it are wrongly decided, because in addition to any transfer because of the contract, the goods had been delivered to the rogue, and delivery can also operate independently as a method for the transfer of title to goods.[24] However, in the context of the sale of goods, the parties have not agreed and do not intend that the delivery operates to transfer the seller's title but merely to pass possession. Beyond that, the delivery is, as agreed, legally inert, and so rescission of the contract ought to revest the seller's title to the goods.

It has been said that prior to rescission the defrauded party has a 'power *in rem*' to regain their title.[25] If by this is meant some kind of interest in the goods themselves prior to rescission, falling short of legal title, this is misleading. There is a power to avoid the contract, and thereby invalidate the conveyance. This power is only exigible against the counterparty to the contract, although it will then have effects upon third parties. Once it is exercised, the right to the thing revests and is binding upon third parties as if no conveyance had occurred. Prior to rescission, the defrauded party has no interest in the thing itself at all.[26] If, however, the rogue has transferred title to the goods to a third party in good faith who gave value, and such transfer occurs before rescission, the third party will be protected.

It follows, although again authority is lacking, that where the contract is the conveyance, its avoidance by either party should reconvey title to the goods sold.[27] If a fraudulent seller induces a buyer to purchase goods from him, and the buyer subsequently chooses to rescind, title to the goods should revest.[28] Just as a buyer may be better off not rescinding because to do so will deprive them of any contractual claim they would otherwise have, they may also hold off from doing so before court proceedings because of the loss of title to the

---

[21] (1846) 15 M&W 216, 153 ER 828.
[22] [1965] 1 QB 525.
[23] *Re Eastgate* [1905] 1 KB 465; *Tilley v Bowman* [1910] 1 KB 745. In relation to corporate insolvency, if the goods have already been disposed of by the administrator, personal liability depends upon negligence: Insolvency Act 1986, s 234(3), (4).
[24] W Swadling, 'Rescission, Property and the Common Law' (2005) 121 LQR 123. *Cf.* B Häcker, 'Rescission of Contract and Revesting of Title: A Reply to Mr Swadling' [2006] RLR 106.
[25] Häcker, 'Rescission of Contract and Revesting of Title' (n 24), P Birks, *An Introduction to the Law of Restitution* (rev edn, 1989), 170–173.
[26] *Barclay Bank v Boulter* [1999] 1 WLR 1919 (HL), 1925 *per* Lord Hoffmann.
[27] S Worthington, 'The Proprietary Consequences of Rescission' [2002] RLR 28, 36–37; *contra* B Häcker, *Consequences of Impaired Consent Transfers: A Structural Comparison of English and German Law* (2013), 201.
[28] *Contra* S Zogg, *Effects of Mistake and Other Defects on the Passage of Title* (2019), 49.

goods bought. This will be replaced with a potentially speculative claim that the proceeds paid are held on trust, which it is only possible to assert where such proceeds are traceable.[29] It is also arguable that the buyer would have a lien over the goods until repaid, but authority on the point is absent. Title is not therefore revesting because of any defect in the transferor's consent, but because the vehicle of conveyance has been set aside. Given the lack of creditworthiness of the typical fraudster, rescission may sometimes be a bad option.

In Equity, rescission is wider than at law and is available in cases of innocent misrepresentation and undue influence. Such rescission, although it will have consequences in Equity (discussed in the next chapter), should not revest title to the goods themselves, as such title is determined by the common law.[30] The Judicature Acts fused the administration of the separate bodies of law, but did not substantively change them, and contracts that may be rescinded in Equity are not voidable at law.

Even under a contract of sale, it is only the title to the goods sold that is conveyed by the contract itself. Title to any cash given in exchange for the goods will not pass until delivery. It is the nature of an obligation to pay a sum that the particular notes, coins, or other forms of money to be paid is unascertained until payment is made (if in cash, by delivery). Gaming contracts were at one time void, but title to cash stakes or to winnings pass by delivery, not under the antecedent gaming agreement.

Further, it may be queried whether title to goods can pass by agreement alone where the contract is one of barter rather than sale.[31] The (peculiar) rule in relation to sale is ameliorated by the protection of third parties, so that for example, a seller in possession (where title has passed but no delivery has taken place)[32] or a buyer in possession (where title has not passed but delivery has occurred)[33] can pass a superior title to that of the possessor to a purchaser in good faith. Such rules should be applied by analogy to other kinds of contract for the transfer of title to goods, such as a barter.

More important commercially, it is unclear what the position is if the agreement stipulates that title to goods is to revest in the seller if a subsequent condition occurs. Where the revesting is to occur on the buyer's bankruptcy, this will be struck down as contrary to the policy of the bankruptcy statutes: it is an attempt to contract out of the collective insolvency regime.[34] This special bankruptcy rule is predicated upon the general position being that such revesting will ordinarily occur because of the agreement. If this is correct, such revesting should be treated as a re-sale, so that either the statutory protections for third-party purchasers, or a common law equivalent, apply.

Further, where the obligations to perform a contract are discharged because of frustration or because of one party's breach, this should not and does not have any impact upon rights transferred under that contract. As we have seen, it is misleading to speak of a contract being frustrated; rather, certain obligations may be conditional upon their being possible to perform and so are discharged. This should not impact upon the validity of any conveyance already made. Similarly, discharge because of breach merely brings to an end

---

[29] Discussed in Chapter 13, Equity: Restitution.
[30] *Alati v Kruger* (195) 94 CLR 216; *contra* E McKendrick (ed), *Goode and McKendrick on Commercial Law* (6th edn, 2020), [3.101].
[31] See Häcker, *Consequences of Impaired Consent Transfers* (n 27), 193.
[32] Sale of Goods Act, s 24.
[33] Sale of Goods Act, s 25.
[34] *Ex p Jay; In re Harrison* (1880) 14 ChD 19 (CA). See now *Belmont Park Investments Pty Ltd v BNY Corporate Trustee Services* [2011] UKSC 38, [2012] 1 AC 383.

(some) obligations of further performance. Such discharge does not avoid the contract and so any conveyance made under it is unaffected.

Where the parties have failed to reach agreement, but the seller delivers goods mistakenly thinking that they have, title should not pass. The classic decision of *Cundy v Lindsay*[35] is illustrative. A rogue called Blenkarn ordered handkerchiefs on credit from the plaintiffs. He signed his name to make it look like 'Blenkiron & Co' a respectable city firm, and he took premises at 37 Wood Street, Cheapside, in the same street from which they traded. The plaintiffs sent the goods to 'Blenkiron & Co, 37 Wood Street', where the rogue took possession of them. He did not pay for them but sold them on to the defendant. In the Queen's Bench Division, three judges concluded that the plaintiffs had expressed an intention to contract with the person carrying on business at 37 Wood Street, and on this view there would be a contract that was voidable for fraud, so that title to the handkerchiefs would pass to the defendant as the agreement had not been set aside before the re-sale. However, both the Court of Appeal and the House of Lords disagreed. The more natural interpretation was that the sellers had offered to sell handkerchiefs to Blenkiron & Co, and they were the only party who could have accepted the offer. Absent a contract, title to the handkerchiefs could not pass by delivery of them because it was never intended that title should pass through such delivery.[36]

Against this analysis might be cited the decision of the Privy Council on an appeal from Malaysia in *Singh v Ali*.[37] The defendant sold title to a lorry to the plaintiff and delivered the vehicle to him. On the vehicle register, which was not a register of title, the lorry appeared in the defendant's name because the plaintiff could not obtain a haulage licence to operate it. The agreement was therefore an illegal conspiracy to evade the road transport regulations. The parties fell out, the defendant repossessed the lorry, and the plaintiff sued successfully for its value. The court held that the fully executed contract had passed the defendant's title to the plaintiff.[38] The best explanation as to how title passed is that the contract was unenforceable, not void as counsel for the defendant had argued. The illegality rule concerns the coherence of the legal system.[39] The courts will not 'lend their aid'[40] to an unlawful act. This is a rule concerning enforcement, not the existence of a bargain between the parties *inter se*. The contract can still operate as the vehicle for a conveyance, just as can a contract unenforceable for want of a required form or for any other reason.

More difficult to explain is the now obsolete decision of *Stocks v Wilson*.[41] A seller sold the title to furniture and delivered it to an infant. The infant sold the title to the furniture before paying for it, and the seller brought a claim against him. Today title to the goods would pass to the minor because, as we have seen, such contracts with minors are unenforceable not void, but at the time the Infants Relief Act 1874[42] was still in force which provided that such contracts were void. Lush J stated that title to the goods had passed by delivery,[43] and

---

[35] (1878) 3 App Cas 459 (HL). See also *Shogun Finance v Hudson* [2003] UKHL 62, [2004] 1 AC 919; defended R Stevens, 'Objectivity, Mistake and the Parol Evidence Rule' in A Burrows and E Peel (eds), *Contract Terms* (2007), 101.
[36] [1878] LR 3 App Cas 459, 464–465 *per* Lord Cairns.
[37] [1960] AC 167 (PC).
[38] *ibid*, 176 *per* Lord Denning.
[39] See Chapter 19, Illegality.
[40] *Holman v Johnson* (1775) 1 Cowp 341, 343, 98 ER 1120, 1121 *per* Lord Mansfield.
[41] [1913] 2 KB 235.
[42] Repealed by the Minors Contracts Act 1987.
[43] [1913] 2 KB 235, 236.

at least in relation to the bulk of the goods this seems unobjectionable because the plaintiff subsequently agreed to the defendant selling the goods.[44] For the quantity of goods sold without such consent the defendant was liable for the price obtained, which was not shown to be below their value, so that the result reached was correct on any view.

Where title is not transferred by the agreement, but by a separate act of conveyance, such as delivery or deed, rescission of any contract between the parties should not alone revest title. For example, as we have seen, who has title to land is determined by the name of the person upon the land register, and so rescission of the contract of sale will not, alone, revest title. However, the buyer comes under a duty to re-convey back to the seller the title to the land. This creates a trust, as will be discussed in the next two chapters.

2. Delivery and Conveyance

A delivery of goods, accompanied by an intent to pass title from deliveror to deliveree, will also convey title.[45] A delivery is a volitional change of possession.[46] The relevant 'intent' for purposes of transfer of title is, again, not a matter of the deliveror's subjective state of mind. If I hand over my hat to a cloakroom attendant intending, as a matter of psychological fact, that title should pass to them, that alone should not do so.[47] The attendant accepted possession on the basis that there was a bailment, and objectively that is what has occurred. 'Intent' therefore means an objective agreement between the parties. This agreement is not contractual, as no consideration is provided, and no obligations are created by the act of delivery, but it shares several features with the law of contract.

As with a contract, whether a mistake as to identity will prevent there being a valid passing of title, depends on whether the delivery agreement between them is to pass title to a particular individual. If I buy title to an ice lolly from an ice cream van, paying in cash, the agreement is that title to the cash is to pass to the person in front of me: the operator of the vehicle. If I thought her to be Mary Jones, when in fact she is Mabel Jones, this will make no difference, as her identity formed no part of the delivery agreement between us. The intent expressed by us is that title is to pass to the person in front of me. A subjective mistake of the deliveror alone, however fundamental, will not therefore without more prevent title passing.[48]

Sometimes, however, just as in contract law, the identity of the deliveree is an essential part of our agreement. Ordinarily this will not be so when the parties deal with each other face to face,[49] but whether it is or not is always a matter of construction.[50] An example is the difficult decision in *R v Middleton*.[51] The defendant had 11 shillings on deposit with the

---

[44] ibid, 248.
[45] See W Swadling, 'Unjust Delivery' in A Burrows and A Rodger (eds), *Mapping the Law: Essays in Memory of Peter Birks* (2006), 277.
[46] *Re Cole* [1964] Ch 175; *Thomas v Times Book Co Ltd* [1966] 1 WLR 911.
[47] But see *R v Hinks* [2001] 2 AC 241, 266–267 *per* Lord Hobhouse suggesting that title does pass, subject to the donee having the power to revest title through rejection. The better view is that upon the donor's intentions becoming apparent, the donee has the power to accept. See also camel dumping in Chapter 3, Performance.
[48] *Chambers v Miller* (1862) 3 F&F 202, 176 ER 91; *R v Prince* (1865-7) LR 1 CCR 150, (1868) 11 Cox CC 193.
[49] Eg *Phillips v Brooks Ltd* [1919] 2 KB 243; *Lewis v Averay (No 1)* [1972] 1 QB 198 (CA).
[50] *Ingram v Little* [1961] 1 QB 31 (CA).
[51] (1872–1875) LR 2 CCR 38. See also *R v Ashwell* (1885) 16 QBD 190 (no agreement to pass title by delivery of that sovereign). *Cf. R v Prince* [1868] LR 1 CCR 150 (mistake as to validity of bank order did not prevent title passing); *Moynes v Coopper* [1956] 1 QB 439 (mistake as to whether obliged to pay did not prevent title passing).

Post Office Savings Bank. He gave notice that he wished to withdraw 10 shillings. A letter of advice was then sent to the Post Office at Notting Hill to pay him this sum. When he presented himself at the Post Office and presented his depositor's book, the clerk referred by mistake to a different letter of advice relating to a different customer to pay nearly £9. This latter sum the clerk placed upon the counter in cash, and the defendant took up. He was charged with larceny, and the question arose whether title to the cash had passed to him. If it had, he could not steal it. The majority concluded that it had not, albeit for several different reasons.[52] In the circumstances, the delivery agreement was to pay the cash not to the man in front of the clerk, but to the person named in the letter of advice for that sum. Middleton knew this, so that no title to the cash passed to him.

Similarly, just as a contract may, at law, be set aside for fraud or duress, so too ought a delivery agreement so procured, so that title will revest in the deliveror upon it being set aside.[53]

D. Identification

1. Introduction

A person with title to a thing may potentially become unable to assert his right to it in the hands of another because the thing has been mixed with other things of the same kind, it has acceded to another thing, or been made into something else through manufacture. The approach of most writers is to accept that Blackstone was right in the *Commentaries on the Laws of England*[54] and that the common law rules are (roughly) the same as those under (late) Roman law. However, the (late) Roman rules are not as ineluctable as the laws of nature, and do not fit well either with modern science or the common law's approach of vindicating rights in relation to goods through damages for the defendant's wrongful interference with an immediate right to possess them.

2. Mixtures

An example:

> X steals four of P's sheep and mixes them with 96 of D's. The sheep are unmarked and indistinguishable.

In resolving the question of entitlement to the sheep in the mixed flock, two solutions seem plausible. Either P has a continuing title to four sheep in the flock of 100, but has no way of proving which, or P has become a co-owner of the title to the entire flock to the extent of his contribution (here 4%). The choice has consequences. If, for example, Y then stole one of

---

[52] Cockburn CJ, Bovill CJ, Kelly CB, Blackburn, Keating, Mellor, Lush, Grove, Denman, Archibald JJ, and Piggott B; Martin, Bramwell, Cleasby BB, and Brett J in dissent.
[53] *Duke de Cadaval v Collins* (1836) 4 Ad & El 858, 111 ER 1006; *Grainger v Hill* (1838) 4 Bing NC 212, 132 ER 769.
[54] Chapter XXXVI, 6.

the hundred, P would have no claim against him on the first approach (as the stolen sheep is not on the balance of probabilities one to which he has title) but could claim as co-owner on the second. The common law rule is in a state of uncertainty.[55]

Roman law drew a distinction between granular and fluid mixtures. Where no new thing was created, as with a granular mixture of things such as two flocks of sheep (*commixtio*[56]), the individual items that are the subject matter of each party's rights still exist, but an evidential problem has arisen because we cannot prove which sheep came from which party. If we developed a method by which we could identify the ancestry of each individual sheep (through DNA testing?) or, more speculatively, where grain is mixed, a method for identifying where each individual grain came from, that should not alter the *legal* position but merely the *evidential* one. It makes little sense to speak of one sheep ceasing to be co-owned if a marking that helps to distinguish it as belonging to one contributor or another pre-mixture is discovered. Rather, an evidential gap is filled and we have proven whose sheep was always whose. Continuing entitlement is therefore the more natural solution in such a case.

By contrast, in a fluid mixture (*confusio*[57]), as where one person's olive oil is mixed with another's, the Romans thought that each contributing unit 'lost their physical integrity and became a single unit as a result'.[58] The mixed fluid was a new thing, created through the destruction of the contributing parts. We could say that the new mixture was a *res nullius*, but it was more natural to say, as the Romans did, that the new thing is owned in common by the two (or more) owners who contributed towards its creation through the destruction of their things.

However, today we know that the Roman view of the physical consequence of fluid mixtures is wrong. The mixed fluid is not a new thing. At a molecular level, each particle of oil is still there, and if we had the evidence and the practical ability they could be separated just as with sheep or grain. The physical world is, at least at one level lower from our perception, granular. Given our knowledge today of the facts, the *commixtio* solution, of continuing entitlement, but faced with an evidential problem of whose sheep is whose, and the further practical problem of separation as with the oil, seems to follow as the natural rule for all mixtures. Evidential problems of identification and the practical difficulty of separation should not alone create co-ownership.

On the common law approach to entitlement to things, the continuing title approach poses few problems. P has a claim in conversion against D if he refuses to return his four sheep, but the only claim will be one for damages for their value, no court will order the delivery up of what cannot be identified.

However, there are many *obiter* statements that the mixture of things creates a co-ownership of title to them,[59] and this is the approach favoured by textbook writers.[60]

---

[55] *Cf. Clough Mill v Martin* [1985] 1 WLR 111 (CA), 124 *per* Oliver LJ, 'English law has developed no very sophisticated system for determining title in cases where indistinguishable goods are mixed or become combined in a newly manufactured article.'
[56] J Inst 2.1.28.
[57] J Inst 2.1.27.
[58] P Birks, 'Mixtures' in N Palmer and E McKendrick (eds), *Interests in Goods* (2nd edn, 1998) 227, 232. See also R Hickey, 'Dazed and Confused: Accidental Mixtures of Goods and the Theory of Acquisition of Title' (2003) 66 MLR 368, 370.
[59] Eg *Buckley v Gross* (1863) 3 B&S 566, 577 122 ER 213 *per* Blackburn J; *Spence v Union Marine Insurance Co* (1867–1868) LR 3 CP 427, 438 *per* Bovill CJ; *Sandemans & Sons v Tyzack & Branfoot Steamship Co Ltd* [1913] AC 680, 694 *per* Lord Moulton; *Indian Oil Corp v Greenstone Shipping SA (Panama)* [1988] QB 345, 370 *per* Staughton J.
[60] Eg M Bridge, L Gullifer, K Low, and G McMeel, *The Law of Personal Property* (2nd edn, 2018), [16.017].

Professor Lionel Smith has convincingly argued that this would be practically problematic,[61] and the references in the case law to 'co-ownership' are probably inexact. Co-ownership would here mean a tenancy in common. A tenancy in common can only generally be divided by a court order sought by a co-owner with a 50% or greater share,[62] whereas it is thought that in a mixture one contributor may remove his share[63] and another contributor preventing this would commit conversion.[64] At a minimum, if D removes one sheep from the flock of 100, he ought to be able to do so as, on the balance of probabilities, any of one of them is his.

Further where there was a tenancy in common at one time one co-owner could never sue another for conversion but one contributor to a mixture could so sue where, for example, the whole mixture was disposed of, indicating that title continued.[65] Although this rule has been restricted, it has not been abolished.[66]

An example of the problem with the co-ownership solution is the decision of the New South Wales Court of Appeal, *Hill v Reglon Pty Ltd*.[67] The plaintiffs gave possession of scaffolding to a hirer who, in breach of contract, gave it to the defendants. The plaintiffs' scaffolding was then mixed with that of the defendants so that who was entitled to which piece could not be identified. The defendants then went into an insolvency proceeding. The court assumed that the parties became co-owners of the title to each piece of the mixture, but also held that the defendants converted the plaintiffs' scaffolding by granting another a licence to use all the scaffolding in their yard. However, if they genuinely were co-owners, no conversion could have taken place as the defendants would be the co-owners of it all.[68] The result is only justifiable if the plaintiffs continued to be entitled to their scaffolding, and the defendants acquired no title to it though mixing. Indeed, it seems intuitively incorrect that others should be capable of becoming co-owners of my property by mixing it with their own.

It cannot, however, be said that the common law has squarely addressed in a litigated case where it mattered the question of whether the *confusio* or *commixtio* rule is to be adopted.

Finally, one question is whether the rules should vary according to whether the defendant himself wrongfully mixed the goods.[69] For example:

D steals 1,000 gallons of P's oil and mixes it with 500 gallons of his own. Half of the mixture is burnt, so that only 750 gallons remain.

If a wrongdoer prevents the innocent party from proving how much of his property has been taken, the wrongdoer is liable to the greatest extent possible in the circumstances.[70] However, this 'presumption' that operates against wrongdoers is evidential; it does not involve the forfeiture of rights contrary to the evidence. Where the wrongdoer has created the uncertainty, the issue is resolved against him, regardless of the most plausible inference

---

[61] See L Smith, *The Law of Tracing* (1997), ch 5. *Cf.* A Waghorn, 'Sorting Out Mixtures of Property at Common Law' (2021) 84 MLR 61.
[62] Law of Property Act 1925, s 188.
[63] *Indian Oil Corp v Greenstone Shipp SA (Panama)* [1988] QB 345, 370–371 *per* Staughton J.
[64] *Moore v Erie Ry Co* 7 Lansing 39 (NY 1872).
[65] *Jackson v Anderson* (1811) 4 Taunt 24, 128 ER 235.
[66] Torts (Interference with Goods) Act 1977, s 10.
[67] [2007] NSWCA 295.
[68] In England, the Torts (Interference with Goods) Act 1977, s 10 would not cover licensing to use.
[69] See Smith, *The Law of Tracing* (n 61), 77–89.
[70] *Lupton v White* (1808) 15 Vers J 432, 33 ER 817.

to be drawn from the facts.[71] Outside of such a case, the law does not distinguish between innocent and wrongful mixing.[72] In this example, the co-ownership and continuing ownership approaches give the same result. On the first, *P* has a two-thirds share of whatever remains under a tenancy in common. On the second, on the balance of probabilities, each party's oil was destroyed in proportion to their contributing shares. If we continued the story, so that *D* continued to add his own oil to the mixture and consume a portion of it, we also know that the highest quantity of oil that remains in the mixture that is attributable to *P* is the lowest intermediate balance.

3. Accession

An example:

> *P*'s car component is stolen by X, who incorporates it through welding into *D*'s vehicle. The component can only be removed by irreparably damaging the car.

Unlike in the case of mixtures of sheep, we are not faced with an evidential problem. We know exactly where the component is, and what has happened to it. Rather, there is a practical problem resulting from the inability to return it save by damage to the principal thing. Three possible solutions present themselves.

The first is that of accession and is the orthodox textbook account in the common law. The accessory item (the component) has ceased to exist because of the practical impossibility of separation and has acceded to the principal thing (the car). *D* has therefore lost his right to the component. However, the support in the case law for a rule of accession to goods in the common law is extremely thin,[73] and Professor Matthews has argued that no such rule exists.[74] A possible example is the decision of the Court of Appeal of Manitoba in *Jones v De Marchant*[75] in which the plaintiff's husband took 18 of her beaver skins, and with 4 of his own, had them made up into a coat which he gave to his mistress, the defendant. The court held that the plaintiff was entitled to delivery up of the completed coat, holding that her husband's contribution had acceded to the greater whole. However, other explanations for the result and the emphasis in the decision upon the husband's wrongdoing mean it is not unequivocal support for an accession rule. The result could be explained on a narrower basis. The husband's duty to return the 18 beaver skins he had taken upon demand was not extinguished by his wrongfully incorporating them into the coat. Where his only method for complying with that duty was to return the entire coat that is what he, and those who obtain possession from him, must do.[76] A claim in conversion should therefore be available.

---

[71] *Armory v Delamirie* (1722) 1 Sre 505, 93 ER 664.
[72] *Indian Oil Corp v Greenstone Shipp SA (Panama)* [1988] QB 345 (Staughton J).
[73] See the *obiter dicta* in *Appleby v Myers* (1866–1867) LR 2 CP 651, 659–660 *per* Blackburn J; *Seath v Moore* (1886) 11 App Cas 350 (HL), 380–381 *per* Lord Watson. The law of fixtures to land is well established but seems based upon different principles from the Roman rule. A party with title to land cannot generally exclude another from entering to re-possess their goods. Someone with title to goods may lose this privilege if the goods have become fixed to the land. See *Holland v Hodgson* (1872) LR 7 CP 328; *Hobson v Gorringe* [1897] 1 Ch 182; *Elitestone Ltd v Morris* [1997] 1 WLR 687; Smith, *The Law of Tracing* (n 61), 107–109.
[74] P Matthews, 'Proprietary Claims at Common Law for Mixed and Improved Goods' [1981] CLP 159.
[75] (1916) 28 DLR 561.
[76] Matthews, 'Proprietary Claims at Common Law for Mixed and Improved Goods' (n 74), 162.

A second solution to our initial example, consistent with the *commixtio* approach above and the common law's vindication of property rights through the law of wrongs, is to say that as the component physically continues to exist, P still, in principle, has title to it. This avoids the difficult line drawing question of which of two things is the principal and which the accessory. Where the defendant, as in the first example of accession, is innocent, he is under no duty to return the component because he has no responsibility for it being in his possession and cannot be expected to destroy his car in order to return it. No action in conversion is therefore possible against him. Where the defendant is a deliberate wrongdoer (as in *Jones v De Marchant*) if the only way of returning the thing (the 18 beaver skins) is to return the thing into which they have been incorporated (the coat) that is what he is now obliged to do.

This solution seems to fit more accurately with the nature of things (the component has not in fact ceased to exist) and to give more acceptable results in certain cases. For example, if we continued the story of the car component:

> Three months later, D's vehicle is in a car accident causing it to be an insurance write-off and only useful as scrap. When the wreck is dismantled, the component is separated undamaged.

The second solution would allow P a claim in conversion in relation to the component, if and when it became possible to possess it separately again.[77] The accession solution would see P lose his right to the component for reasons that are no longer operative in such a case.

The third possibility is that the law could treat all cases of one thing becoming impossible to separate from another as like fluid mixtures in Roman law and give P and D co-ownership to the indissoluble whole.[78] In such cases, the only practical method for severing the co-ownership would then be the sale of the title to the resultant thing and the division of the proceeds.

If we adopt the first, textbook, account that the common law recognises the principle of accession, further problems arise that require solutions. The difference between the three solutions, and the knock-on problems of the first, are well illustrated by the Australian decision of Young J in *McKeown v Cavalier Yachts Pty Ltd*.[79] The defendant boatyard, not knowing that title to a hull belonged to the plaintiff, constructed a yacht worth AU$25,000 upon it. The original hull was worth only AU$1,800. The court applied the accession rule. As the work had been done gradually, as each piece was installed, it acceded to the hull.

Ignoring for the moment the work done,[80] the operation of the accession rule would destroy the boatyard's title to its materials and allow that to accrue to the benefit of the hull owner. Under German law, the party who loses his rights in this way may require that he is reimbursed by the party who has benefitted by the accession.[81] If title to the material incorporated into the hull is to be destroyed through accession, this seems the best available

---

[77] J Inst 2.1.29: 'Suppose that someone builds on his own land with materials owned by another ... This does not mean that the owner of the material loses his ownership of them; but for the time being he cannot vindicate them or bring an action for their production.... If for some reason the building does come down, then ... the owner of the materials can vindicate them.' See also (Gaius) D 41.1.7.10.
[78] Matthews, 'Proprietary Claims at Common Law for Mixed and Improved Goods' (n 74).
[79] (1988) 13 NSWLR 303.
[80] See Chapter 14, Improvements.
[81] BGB § 951.

solution. However, this may be thought generous as the result may be to force the owner of the principal thing to realise it in order to meet any claim. In *McKeown*, Young J imposed as a precondition of the plaintiff's right to recover the yacht *in specie* the payment of the increase in value attributable to the work and materials.

If the second of the three suggested approaches, rejecting accession, were to be adopted in such a case, we would say that the title to the hull alone continued, and the boatyard could not assert that they had no obligation to return it because any inability to do so was caused by their own trespass in making use of it. A court would refuse to order delivery up of the hull *in specie* because the work was done innocently and damage would be required to be done to the yacht through separation, with the result that damages would be payable by the boatyard for conversion quantified as the value of a good title to the hull (or alternatively damages in trespass for making use of the hull in making the yacht).

4. Specification

An example:

> X steals P's block of marble and gives it to D, who is ignorant of the theft. D, a talented sculptor, crafts it into a statue of sublime beauty.

Who has the better title to the sculpture?

In the early years of the Roman empire the resolution of such cases was a disputed question. The Sabinians held that the owner of the material could not be deprived of his rights, whereas the Proculians took the position that if the manufacturer had made a new thing, he became its owner.[82] The view adopted by the time of Justinian was that if the new thing could not be reconverted into its original form, the manufacturer was the owner[83] but not otherwise.[84] An owner whose gold ingot was melted into a statue did not thereby lose his entitlement, but the owner of gold coins melted down in the same way did. Again, if such an approach is adopted, P should have a personal claim against D to the value of the goods thereby lost.

At common law, the textbook account is, again, that the (late) Roman rule has been adopted, and there are also judicial statements to this effect.[85] However this has been doubted,[86] and Professor Matthews has again denied the existence of any such rule at common law.[87] What problems are there with accepting specification as the common law rule?

First, and most obviously, the line between a 'new thing' and a merely improved old one may be hard to draw, complicated by the question of whether reversal is possible.

---

[82] G Inst 2.79.
[83] Cf. *Lampton's Executors v Preston's Executor's* 24 Ky 455 (1829) (clay bricks as yet unfired).
[84] J Inst 2.1.25.
[85] *Clough Mill Ltd v Martin* [1984] 1 WLR 111 (CA), 119 per Goff LJ. It is the rule in Scotland: *The International Banking Corporation v Ferguson, Shaw & Sons* 1910 SC 182 (IHCS).
[86] *Glencore International AG v Metro Trading International Inc* [2001] 1 All ER (Comm) 103, [178] per Moore-Bick LJ. See also *NV De Bataafsche Petroleum Maatschappij v War Damages Commission* [1956] 1 MLJ 155.
[87] P Matthews, 'Specificatio in the Common Law' (1981) 10 Anglo-American Law Rev 121.

Second, the common law courts have not always adopted the specification rule, indeed the early authorities are clearly against it.[88] What modern authority there is, is against such a rule in cases of wrongful manufacture. For example, in the classic New York Court of Appeals decision *Silsbury v McCoon*,[89] corn was stolen from the plaintiff and used to make whisky. The defendant was a judgment creditor of the thief, who had seized it. The court drew a distinction between innocent and wrongful transformation, reasoning that where it was innocent the manufacturer became the owner, but not where it was wrongful.[90] The successful claim for conversion of the coat (a new thing) made from beaver skins in *Jones v De Marchant* was based upon the same idea. In the example with which we began, the sculptor may be morally blameless, but commits trespass by working upon another's marble. Does the (blameless) wrongdoing mean that the sculptor does not acquire a better title than the owner of the marble?

An alternative solution is to avoid the metaphysical question of whether the changed object is 'new' but instead to make it a condition of recovery of possession from an innocent improver, though not a deliberate wrongdoer, that he is reimbursed for the work done.[91]

The modern context in which the problem has arisen is that of retention of title clauses. It is here we find some support for the specification rule.[92] In *Borden (UK) Ltd v Scottish Timber Products Ltd*,[93] the plaintiffs supplied resin under an 'all moneys' retention of title clause under which no title to goods supplied was to pass to the buyer until all invoices had been paid. Where the goods supplied have been unaltered, such clauses are effective to prevent title passing.[94] The resin, with the supplier's consent, had been used in the manufacture of chipboard. Bridge LJ described the case as one 'akin to' consumption[95] and Templeman LJ stated that when 'the resin was incorporated in the chipboard, the resin ceased to exist'.[96] No retention of title was therefore effective. As statements of physical fact, these *dicta* are, of course, untrue,[97] and the analogy Bridge LJ draws between resin being incorporated into the boards and the burning of fuel[98] is inapposite. The resin did not cease to exist, it was incorporated into something else now in the buyer's possession. However, these statements may be taken as adopting the specification rule.

The result could be explained in an alternative way. The supplier's goods had been combined, with their consent, with the buyer's materials. It was now impractical, if not impossible, for the purchaser to return the resin, and the supplier had no right to the return of the other material to which they never had title. The suppliers could not therefore assert

---

[88] In England see *Case of Leather* YB 5 Henry VII fol 15 (leather into shoes); *Anon* Moore 20, 72 All ER 411 (timber into planks). United States: *Church v Lee* 5 Johns 348 (timber into shingles); *Curtis v Groat* 6 Johns 169 (timber into charcoal). It was assumed, albeit in *obiter dicta* in *Thogood v Robinson* (1845) 6 QB 769, 115 ER 290 that the burning of chalk into lime gave the limeburner title to the lime, but this is a process that is readily reversible. In the United States there is modern authority for the *specificatio* rule in cases of *innocent* manufacture: *Wetherbee v Green* 22 Mich 311 (1871) (timber into barrel hoops). See Matthews, '*Specificatio* in the Common Law' (n 87).
[89] 3 NY 379 (1850).
[90] *Cf.* Smith, *The Law of Tracing* (n 61), 113–114.
[91] See Chapter 14, Improvements.
[92] Some decisions turn upon the correct construction of the clause, and so are unhelpful for our purposes, eg *re Peachdart* [1984] Ch 131; *Vhaigley Farms Ltd v Crawford, Kaye & Grayshire Ltd* [1996] BCC 957.
[93] [1981] Ch 25 (CA); *cf. Modelboard Ltd v Outer Box Ltd* [1992] BCC 945.
[94] *Clough Mill Ltd v Martin* [1985] 1 WLR 111 (CA); *Armour v Thyssen Edelstahlwerke AG* [1991] 2 AC 339 (HL).
[95] [1981] Ch 25, 41.
[96] *ibid*, 44.
[97] P Matthews, 'The Legal and Moral Limits of Common Law Tracing' in P Birks, *Laundering and Tracing* (1995) 23, 46 'reinvents the laws of physics'.
[98] [1981] Ch 25, 41.

any immediate right to possess the resin even if they had 'retained title' in some sense to the molecules of which it was composed. A right to possession is dependent upon there being something possible to possess. The resin could no longer be possessed by the supplier without also interfering with the buyer's right to possess his materials. On this approach, the key question is not whether a new thing has been created but whether the admixture was wrongful (as in *Silsbury v McCoon*) or innocent because authorised (as in *Borden (UK) Ltd v Scottish Timber Products Ltd*). Even where innocent, the position of the buyer would be different on this approach where marble is made into a statue, timber into planks, or olives pressed into olive oil. In such cases the immediate right to possess will not be lost because it is still possible to return the physical thing, without depriving another of something to which he has title.[99] The position of an innocent improver in possession is considered in Chapter 14.

It may therefore be doubted whether the common law either should have or does have the Roman *specificatio* rule, at least where the 'new thing' is either created wrongfully or without admixture.

5. Fruits

That the person who owns a tree owns its fruits or that the owner of a sow owns its piglets required for the Romans a new explanation because the fruit and piglets were perceived as new things, separate from the things from which they came, and these are examples of *fructus*. At a molecular level, however, the fruit and piglets are not new things. These are but parts of the pre-existing thing that have been separated from it. It follows from the nature of our common perception of things that someone with title to a tree has title to its fruits once they become detached, just as they would to a branch that was broken off. This rule is undoubtedly one the common law has[100] and is best seen as separate from the doctrine of accession, which is harder to justify. It is not, today, best seen as a rule concerning the creation of a right to a 'new' thing, but rather as based upon the rightholder's title to the original thing persisting in relation to that part of it from which it is detached.

E. Substitution

In principle, it is not possible, at common law, to become automatically entitled to a right for which your right is substituted without your authority. For example:

D steals C's mobile phone and exchanges possession of it with X for X's title to a knife.

---

[99] *Armour v Thyssen Edelstahlwerke AG* [1991] 2 AC 339 (HL) (steel cut into strips).
[100] At least for everything other than swans. The owner of a cock and the owner of a hen co-own any cygnets: *Case of Swans* (1592) 7 Co Rep 15, 77 ER 435. Where livestock is leased the landlord has no title to the offspring. This is explicable on the basis that it is part of the agreement that the revenue from which the tenant will pay the landlord is from selling what the livestock produce: *Tucker v Farm and General Investment Trust Ltd* [1966] 2 QB 421 (CA).

X intended to convey title to the knife to D and has done so. X does not intend to convey anything to C who never has possession of the knife. C has no title to the knife. It should make no difference if in the example we substitute cash for the phone or the knife.[101] C can recover from a thief the amount for which her thing was sold,[102] but has no right to the cash itself. Unfortunately, in England this straightforward proposition has become confused because cases applying principles from the law of trusts (discussed in the next two chapters) have been thought to have been applying common law rules in relation to things. This story of error is now well known.

The source of the mistake, although not itself problematic, is *Taylor v Plumer*.[103] Plumer employed a stockbroker called Walsh. Plumer gave Walsh a cheque for £22,200 and instructed him to buy Exchequer bills. Instead, Walsh cashed the cheque into notes, and bought US stock and gold bullion with it. He then attempted to flee to the United States, but was caught, and surrendered the stock and bullion to Plumer's attorneys. Walsh was bankrupt, meaning that his estate was assigned to his trustees in bankruptcy. The bankruptcy administrators brought an action alleging that they were entitled to the stock and bullion, and that their retention constituted a tort.

Insofar as title to the physical things was concerned, their original sellers had intended to convey title to Walsh, and that is what had occurred. However, as Lord Ellenborough CJ explained (emphasis added):

> If the property in its original state and form was covered with a *trust* in favour of the principal, no change in the state and form can divest it of such *trust*, or give the factor, or those who represent him in right, any other more valid claim in respect to it, than they respectively had before such change. An abuse of *trust* can confer no rights on the party abusing it, nor on those who claim in privity with him.

The result was that title to the stock and bullion, that had been substituted for Plumer's original cheque, was held on trust, and so unavailable for realisation and distribution to creditors. The claim for recovery by the bankruptcy administrators failed. The entitlement to the rights for which Plumer's initial cheque had been substituted arose under a trust, to which the common law court was not blind.[104] It was analogous to a case of a common law court giving effect to rights arising under an entirely foreign legal system. Why and how equitable rights operate in this way is discussed in the next two chapters. Confusion was subsequently caused because the decision was that of a common law court (inevitably as the action had been brought for a common law wrong). This gave rise to the belief that the right in relation to the substituted stock and bullion must also have arisen at common law, and that Plumer had somehow acquired title to the physical stock certificates and bullion themselves.[105] This is incorrect.

---

[101] *Higgs v Holiday* (1598) Cro Eliz 746, 78 ER 978.
[102] *Lamine v Dorrell* (1701) 2 Ld Ray 1216, 92 ER 303. See Chapter 16, Profits.
[103] (1815) 3 M & S 562, 105 ER 721. See also *Newton v Porter* 69 NY 133 (1877).
[104] S Khursid and P Matthews, 'Tracing Confusion' (1979) 95 LQR 78; L Smith, 'Tracing in *Taylor v Plumer*: Equity in the Court of King's Bench' [1995] LMCLQ 240.
[105] *R v Bunkall* (1864) Le & Ca 374, 375–376, 169 ER 1436, 1437 *per* Willes J; *Sinclair v Brougham* [1914] AC 398 (HL), 418–419 *per* Viscount Haldane LC.

The history of subsequent confusion has been set out elsewhere, but for our purposes we can fast-forward to the leading decision of the House of Lords in *Lipkin Gorman v Karpnale Ltd*.[106] Here 'authoritative blessing' was finally given to 'the law of unjust enrichment'.[107] This has always been somewhat embarrassing as the result in the case itself is so difficult to explain.[108]

Cass, a partner in a firm of solicitors, drew down on a client account, of which he was an authorised signatory, to subsidise his gambling. The firm brought an action for money had and received against the club where Cass had gambled the withdrawals away.

Clearly there was no performance by the firm to the club as, though Cass was a partner, he was gambling for his own purposes. Further, the Privy Council had in earlier decisions been taken to have established that where a partner who is an authorised signatory withdraws cash from their firm's account the partner acquires good title to the cash whether he does so for the firm's purposes or not.[109] Cass therefore had title to the cash spent at the club.

Although the House of Lords accepted that Cass had title to the cash, Lord Goff argued that, as the cash was the traceable substitute for the right to a credit balance that the firm had against the bank, it was possible as a result for the firm to establish a proprietary right at common law to the cash withdrawn by Cass and subsequently received by the club. This cannot be correct and Lord Goff's reliance on *Taylor v Plumer* as authority for any such entitlement to the traceable substitute at law was mistaken.

What is the nature of the proprietary right at common law that Lord Goff thought there was? Birks once sought to argue that it was a 'power *in rem*', analogous to the ability to revest title that the seller of a chattel has if a contract under which title has been transferred can be avoided.[110] As we have seen however, the seller has no rights in relation to the goods prior to rescission, and even if we accept the existence of a 'power *in rem*' it is difficult to understand how such a power would arise in this case, or why it would suffice for the purposes of bringing a claim against the club because, as unexercised, the cash was Cass's and not the firm's.

Further, Lord Goff's reasoning is based upon the account with the bank being in credit. If we change the facts, to make the firm's account overdrawn, with further drawings at the bank's discretion, if further withdrawals are made by Cass, the firm has no right at the start that the cash given to Cass is now the traceable substitute for. It would seem absurd that the result should change according to whether the account was or was not in credit.

It has been argued that the result may be explained as common law relief ('money had and received') for a right in relation to Cass's right to the cash that arose in equity.[111] Although some cases are explicable in this way,[112] here plaintiff's counsel had eschewed reliance upon

---

[106] [1991] 2 AC 548 (HL).
[107] A Burrows, *The Law of Restitution* (3rd edn, 2011), 4.
[108] Another foundational case embarrassing for the same reason is *Moses v Macferlan* (1760) 2 Burr. 1005 97 ER 676.
[109] *Union Bank of Australia Ltd v McClintock & Co* [1922] 1 AC 240 (PC); *Commercial Banking Co of Sydney Ltd v Mann* [1961] AC 1 (PC). The cases concerned bank cheques obtained by a fraudulent agent in exchange for cheques drawn on his principal, the claimants. A claim in conversion was brought against the defendant bank where the agent had cashed the bank cheques. The claim was doomed either because the claimants had no title to the cheques cashed because they had not been obtained with their authority, or if they ratified what had been done so as to acquire title they also ratified the agent's subsequent dealing with them by deposit ([1961] AC 1, 11 *per* Viscount Simonds).
[110] P Birks, 'The English Recognition of Unjust Enrichment' [1991] LMCLQ 472.
[111] L Smith, 'Simplifying the Proceeds of Property' (2009) 125 LQR 318.
[112] *Banque Belge pour L'Etranger v Hambrouk* [1921] 1 KB 321 (CA); see Chapter 13, Equity: Restitution.

any equitable interest, and it was not demonstrated that when the defendants became aware of the plaintiff's entitlement, the cash received or its traceable proceeds still remained so as to be capable of being held on trust.[113]

Despite this, the result in *Lipkin Gorman v Karpnale Ltd* is defensible, at least in holding that there was *prima facie* a claim. The key to explaining this is that the claimant was a partnership. Save where legislation stipulates to the contrary,[114] a partnership has no separate legal personality. If a number of partners buy title to a racehorse together, each individual will own it jointly. Each of them has title to the horse, albeit one jointly held. Similarly, if office furniture is bought for and on behalf of an unincorporated solicitor's firm, the title to the furniture will be owned under a joint tenancy by all of the partners. Sometimes an asset that is intended to be a partnership asset will be transferred into the name of one partner alone, requiring the utilisation of a trust for the benefit of the others, but frequently this will be unnecessary.

Where a bank account is opened in the name of a partnership, all the partners will have a joint right to any credit balance. If the bank pays out cash to the partnership, all will be entitled to the cash under a joint tenancy. When Cass withdrew the cash, he did therefore have good title to it. However, when he gambled with it at the Playboy Club he was not spending cash to which he had sole title. The bank intended to pay him the cash in his capacity as partner. He held it under a joint tenancy with his other partners. The cheques Cass signed were made out to cash, not to Cass personally. The cheques were in fact cashed by the firm's cashier, one Chapman, who then took the notes to Cass. The case was not the same as that considered by the Privy Council, where the bank issued drafts payable by itself to named payees.[115] In *Lipkin Gorman*, the unauthorised payment out of partnership assets should have been, and was, a sufficient basis for a claim by the firm (ie all the other partners) against the club that received them.[116] The firm had title to the cash received by the club.

A decision that illustrates the absurdity of 'common law tracing', the idea that unauthorised substitution of a thing to which *P* has title, for another thing gives *P* title to the substitute, is *Trustee of the Property of FC Jones & Sons v Jones*.[117] A partnership of potato growers committed an act of bankruptcy. The defendant's husband drew cheques for £11,700 on the partnership current account in her favour. She paid the proceeds into her account with a firm of commodity brokers for the purpose of speculating on the potato futures market. This proved extremely successful, and she paid the proceeds of £50,760 into a deposit account with a bank. The partnership was then adjudicated bankrupt. Under the law of personal bankruptcy as it then was, all of the firm's property vested from the moment of the first act of bankruptcy in the insolvency administrator, and dispositions by the bankrupt after that moment were void. The cheques had been drawn by the bankrupt husband after the first such act. The Court of Appeal concluded that it was possible to 'trace' at common law so that the deposit account balance standing to the credit of Mrs Jones was, at law, owed to the firm of potato growers.

---

[113] See Chapter 13, Equity: Restitution.
[114] Eg Limited Liability Partnership Act 2000.
[115] *Union Bank of Australia Ltd v McClintock & Co* [1922] 1 AC 240 (PC); *Commercial Banking Co of Sydney Ltd v Mann* [1961] AC 1 (PC).
[116] See also P Watts, 'Unjust Enrichment and Misdirected Funds' (1991) 107 LQR 521.
[117] [1997] Ch 159 (CA).

But how could this be true? A bank account is a contractual relationship between bank and customer. When in credit, the account holder has a right to payment of the balance upon demand. How could the bank's contractual duty to pay be owing to someone other than the party with whom they contracted? Would their debt not have been discharged if they had paid the 'wrong' party? It is possible to understand how the right to be paid could be held on trust by Mrs Jones for the firm,[118] but not how the bank owed its contractual duty to anyone other than her. This conceptual problem was masked because no claim was brought against the bank, who had paid the money into court.

Millett LJ, who accepted that in *Taylor v Plumer* the court had been applying the rules of Equity, thought that it was now too late to correct the error, and this has academic support.[119] However, this can only be done at the price of the law making no sense. Other jurisdictions should not follow the English lead, and eventually English law will have to correct its error.

F. Good Faith Purchase for Value

The general rule is expressed in the Latin maxim used in common law systems *nemo dat quod non habet* (no one can give what they do not have) or more accurately through the longer civilian equivalent *nemo plus iuris ad alium transferre potest quam ipse habet* (no one can transfer to another more rights than they have). In the example of the stolen mobile phone, although the thief acquired a title to it through his taking of possession, all he could convey to X was that inferior title. C's superior title was not lost and could be asserted against X even though X had been unaware of D's theft in taking possession of the phone and had given value in exchange for the thief's inferior title.[120]

Title to land is never lost through a good faith purchase rule.[121] There are however some cases where the effect of good faith purchase is to extinguish the prior title to goods of the person who is out of possession. The most obvious example is cash acquired as currency. Someone who gives value, in good faith, and without notice of any earlier title held by someone other than the transferee, will extinguish such prior title.[122] This is because cash 'value' includes any consideration which would support a contract.[123] This is important for banks. If cash is deposited, the executory promise to pay (or release) given in exchange, through crediting the account, is value without more.[124] The justification for treating cash differently in this regard is that, as already seen, unlike tables, chairs, and mobile phones, it is used as a medium of exchange. In order to facilitate its negotiability, title may be lost through the operation of good faith purchase.

---

[118] L Smith, 'Simplifying Claims to Traceable Proceeds' 125 LQR 338, 347.
[119] [1997] Ch 159(CA), 169; Burrows, *The Law of Restitution* (n 107), 124.
[120] *Farquharson Bros & Co v King & Co* [1902] AC 325 (HL).
[121] It can sometimes be lost through the effect of registration: Land Registration Act 2002, ss 26–29; *Swift 1st v Chief Land Registrar* [2015] EWCA Civ 330, [2015] 3 WLR 251.
[122] Bank Notes: Bills of Exchange Act 1882, s 38(2); *Miller v Race* (1758) 1 Burr 452, 97 ER 398; Coins: *Moss v Hancock* [1899] 2 QB 111.
[123] Bills of Exchange Act 1882, s 27(1)(a); *ex p Richdale* (1882) 19 Ch D 409, 417 (CA); *Royal Bank of Scotland v Tottenham* [1894] 2 QB 715 (CA).
[124] NB the different meaning of 'value' sufficient to defeat a prior equitable interest: *Story v Windsor* (1743) 2 Atk 630, 26 ER 776; see Chapter 13, Equity: Restitution.

One of the difficulties in explaining *Lipkin Gorman v Karpnale* is why it was that the club had not given value for the bets staked, at least in relation to those that were successful, so as to have a complete defence to any claim in relation to the cash it received.[125] If Cass had spent the cash in a restaurant, any title to the cash the firm had would have been lost. Lord Goff reasoned that where a bet placed was unsuccessful, all that had been given in exchange for the stake was a promise to pay winnings. As such a promise was void under the Gaming Acts as in force at that time,[126] nothing was thereby given in exchange. Where the bet proved successful, no value was also given, Lord Goff reasoned, because any payment by the club was 'in law a gift'.[127] The latter conclusion is a difficult one. It does not follow that because a valid contractual *promise* can suffice for purposes of operation of the defence, that the *performance* of an invalid one should not count. The payment of an antecedent debt can also amount to consideration for the operation of the defence, showing that the existence of a valid contract is not a pre-condition of a 'purchase'.[128] If the gaming contracts had been illegal, and not merely void, the defence may have failed on the alternative basis that the defendant could not rely upon his own illegal conduct in seeking to invoke it, but this was not so.[129]

As we have seen, the rule on transfer of title in the sale of goods in the common law is unusual, and we ameliorate the fact that title can pass without any action such as delivery that is discernible by third parties to the transaction, by giving third parties some protection. The party in possession but without title, whether the seller[130] or the buyer,[131] has the power to sell title to the goods to a third party so as to destroy the title of the counterparty. There are also statutory protections for third parties who buy from mercantile agents in possession[132] and for buyers of motor vehicles from hire purchasers.[133] Unlike the cash rule, however, value must have been given by the buyer in exchange, not merely promised.

G. Unjust Enrichment?

1. Relevance

It is unclear how or why it assists to think of the rules considered in this chapter as concerned with 'unjust enrichment', although some but not others are claimed to be. They are all important in relation to the topic of 'restitution' if by that term we mean the recovery of something, here a tangible thing, or its value. However, their justification has no relation to the other kinds of claim we have seen so far.

---

[125] See further Chapter 18, Defences.
[126] Gaming Act, s 18.
[127] [1991] 2 AC 548 (HL), 577.
[128] Bills of Exchange Act, 27(1)(b).
[129] *Clark v Shee and Johnson* (1774) 1 Cowp 197, 98 ER 1041.
[130] Sale of Goods Act 1979, s 24.
[131] Sale of Goods Act 1979, s 25.
[132] Factors Act 1889, s 2(1).
[133] Hire Purchase Act 1964, part III.

2. Ignorance

In the simple case of cash stolen from the plaintiff, the possession of which has been given to the defendant, two kinds of claim as to the relevance of 'unjust enrichment' have been made. The first, weaker, claim is that there should and does exist an alternative claim in unjust enrichment based upon such facts. The defendant is factually better off through the receipt of the cash, and the plaintiff is correlatively worse off. In order to be compatible with the general claim that the defendant's duty is based upon the state of mind of the plaintiff, an 'unjust factor' of 'ignorance' or lack of consent has been proposed, said to follow *a fortiori* from the category of mistake.[134] The second, more important, claim is that in such case, there should be no necessity to demonstrate that the plaintiff had any title to what was received by the defendant.[135] It is argued that a different connection, whether causal or transactional, should suffice. In England, the difficulty of establishing in *Lipkin Gorman*, the leading case, that the plaintiff had a right to the cash received by the defendant, lent credence to this view.

The first claim has led to a sterile debate as to whether someone who has possession of a thing to which another has better title can be said to be 'enriched'. Again, however, this is to focus on the wrong thing. In the absence of any performance from plaintiff to defendant to reverse, what justifies any claim must be the right to the thing, not the extent to which the defendant may be better off.

The second claim has the potential to lead courts into error. It has not hitherto been thought that, in order to bring a claim in relation to something the defendant has received to which the plaintiff has better title, the plaintiff has to plead and prove his state of mind at some point in the past. Whatever the difficulty with its reasoning, the court in *Lipkin Gorman* clearly thought it important to establish that the plaintiffs had some legal entitlement to the cash with which Mr Cass gambled. If, because of his theft from the plaintiffs, Mr Cass had decided to gamble with his own cash, no claim should lie against the club.

3. Defences

Similarly, the title to goods that revests because of rescission of a contract, exemplified by *Load v Green*, has nothing properly to do with 'unjust enrichment'. The range of countervailing reasons why what would otherwise be a contract may be void or voidable is very large. Nothing is gained by stipulating that each such rule and its consequence must be part of the law of 'unjust enrichment'. Indeed, as it is thought that special defences apply in that area (in particular the defence of change of position) it might then be wrongly assumed that the defence applies without further argument.[136] The traditional approach is that we deal with things to which others have superior title at our peril,[137] so that if we dispose of them we are liable for their value, even if that leaves us worse off. Whether, and when, the

---

[134] Birks, *An Introduction to the Law of Restitution* (n XXX), 140–146; Burrows, *The Law of Restitution* (n 107), ch 16; C Mitchell, P Mitchell, and S Watterson (eds), *Goff & Jones: The Law of Unjust Enrichment* (9th edn, 2016), ch 8.
[135] P Birks, *An Introduction to the Law of Restitution* (n 25), 140–146; Mitchell, Mitchell, and Watterson, *Goff & Jones* (n 134), [8-12]–[8-26].
[136] Discussed in Chapter 18, Defences.
[137] *Fowler v Hollins* (1872) LR 7 QB 616.

recognition of a defence of change of position in *Lipkin Gorman* has qualified that approach is considered in Chapter 18, Defences.

A good illustration of why 'unjust enrichment' adds more confusion than it removes is the operation of the defence of good faith purchase for value. An example:

> X steals £1,000 from the petty cash box of his employer P. X uses the cash to purchase a bicycle worth £300 from D, who is unaware of the theft.

The good faith purchase rule operates regardless of whether the consideration given in exchange is equivalent or adequate. Where, as here, it is not, the purchaser will have been left enriched. This expense results from the plaintiff's deprivation of which he is wholly ignorant. Is there, and should there be, a claim?

Attempts have been made to justify the existence of a good faith purchaser defence in the law of 'unjust enrichment'. The primary argument is that the reason behind the rule for the extinction of prior title would be stultified if a personal claim in unjust enrichment were to be permitted.[138] However, if we took this argument seriously, it would lead to the elimination of all claims for restitution that would be 'inconsistent' with the rules for the passing of title by going beyond them. In the usual case of the mistaken payment of cash, title to the cash passes to the defendant. Does it stultify the reasons behind this rule to then permit a claim for restitution of the payment made?

Further if we combine the stultification idea with the suggestion that there should be no requirement to show that the plaintiff had any title to what was received by the defendant, but that a merely causal or transactional link between the plaintiff and the defendant's enrichment should suffice, counter-intuitive results seem to follow. For example:

> Y steals £1,000 from the petty cash box of his employer P and gives possession of the cash to X intending a gift. X, delighted by his unexpected enrichment, buys title to a motorbike from D for £1,000, making the payment by bank transfer using funds he already had.

Here, D's entitlement to the increase in the sums owed to him by his bank is independent of any good faith purchase for value rule. The purchase was not made with P's cash (or even a traceable substitute for it). Does that mean that no such defence should apply?

An alternative suggestion is that the defence protects the sanctity of the contract, in both examples above the relevant contract is between X and D.[139] However, as we have seen, the defence in relation to cash is not dependent upon there being any contract between X and D.[140] Someone who acquires title to the thing from the good faith purchaser is also protected, although they themselves may not be party to any contract at all. Further, although there are good reasons why the parties to a contract should respect its sanctity, there is no good reason why someone who is not a party to it should.

The better view is that there is no need to invoke these explanations for a good faith purchaser defence because there can be no claim to recover stolen cash from someone acquiring

---

[138] Eg P Birks, *Unjust Enrichment* (2nd edn, 2005), 240–245; Burrows, *The Law of Restitution* (n 107), 576–577; Mitchell, Mitchell, and Watterson, *Goff & Jones* (n 134), [29–01].
[139] K Barker, 'After Change of Position: Good Faith Exchange in the Modern Law of Restitution' in P Birks (ed), *Laundering and Tracing* (1995), 191; Burrows, *The Law of Restitution* (n 107), 577–580.
[140] Bills of Exchange Act 1882, s 27(1)(b).

it from a thief, other than one based upon title to that cash. 'Unjust enrichment' can be dispensed with as an alternative explanation.

4. Comparisons

In civilian jurisdictions, the different kinds of claims sometimes grouped together as part of 'unjust enrichment' are solely part of the law of obligations.[141] 'Unjust enrichment' does not create rights to things. Claims to vindicate pre-existing rights to things are not mediated through the law of wrongs as they are in the common law but are also not seen as part of 'unjust enrichment' law.

Within both common law and civilian traditions, the reasons for the creation of obligations (eg contracts, wrongs, and the many diverse reasons set out in this book) are quite different from the reasons for the creation of rights to things (eg *occupatio*,[142] *confusio, accessio, specificatio, fructus*). As we have seen, outside the law of sale of goods, in the common law as in the civil law, the rules for the valid transfer of rights are also different from, and independent of, the rules for obligations to transfer.

Equity, however, is different, and that is the topic of the next two chapters.

---

[141] Eg BGB § 812.
[142] Eg *Armory v Delamirie* (1795) 1 Str 505, 93 ER 664.

12
Equity: General

A. Introduction

On one view, commonly associated with the endorsement of unjust enrichment as an organising idea, the division between the common law and equitable rules is no more than an accidental one arising from the history of a legal system. Equity is, from this perspective, just a body of rules that has its historical source in the Courts of Chancery in England, the ancestor of the Chancery Division of the High Court in our current legal order, with no more unity than, say, the law created by statutory instruments. They are rules distinguished by their source: here a particular group of judges in the past. A common target for 'fusion',[1] ensuring that the rules from different sources are the same so as to ensure that 'like cases are treated alike', is then the apparently different rules for restitution. An example:

> *T* holds the title to a quantity of valuable antique furniture on trust. One of the beneficiaries is *P*. In breach of trust, *T* gives the title to the furniture to *D*. *D* no longer has it, having given title to the furniture away to charity.

The traditional analysis is that if *D* is to be held liable in an action by *P* for the receipt of the trust property, either knowledge by *D* of the breach of trust before disposal must be shown, or at least some kind of 'unconscionable' behaviour on his part. This differs from the rule in relation to mistaken payments at common law, where the defendant may be held liable regardless of any knowledge or blameworthiness. It has then been argued that there is no explanation for the difference between the equitable and the common law rule other than the vicissitudes of their separate historical development.[2] Either, so it is said, the equitable rules should be brought into line with the common law,[3] or a strict restitutionary liability should be recognised alongside the equitable rule (rendering the latter largely redundant).[4] It never seems to have been argued by commentators that recovery at common law should be restricted, so as to conform with the position in Equity.[5]

Similarly, it has been claimed that a number of trusts traditionally labelled either 'constructive' or 'resulting' are best explained in terms of unjust enrichment, and that the rules

---

[1] A Burrows, 'We Do This at Common Law but That in Equity' (2002) 22 OJLS 1.
[2] Eg P Birks, 'Restitution and Resulting Trusts' in S Goldstein (ed), *Equity in Contemporary Legal Developments* (1992), 'these conflicting views cannot stand in one legal system'. The drawing of a parallel between *quasi-contracts* and the liability of an innocent recipient of trust assets to a beneficiary occurred much earlier: J B Ames, 'Purchase for Value without Notice' (1887) 1 Harv Law Rev 1.
[3] P Birks, 'Misdirected Funds: Restitution from the Recipient' [1989] LMCLQ 296.
[4] P Birks, 'Equity in the Modern Law' (1996) 26 UWALR 1, 72; Lord Nicholls of Birkenhead, 'Knowing Receipt: The Need for a New Landmark' in W Cornish *et al.* (eds), *Restitution: Past, Present and Future* (1998), 231. The latter was endorsed by Lord Walker, 'Dishonesty and Unconscionable Conduct in Commercial Life: Some Reflections on Accessory Liability and Knowing Receipt' (2005) 27 Syd LR 187.
[5] But see *Heperu Pty Ltd v Belle* [2009] NSWCA 252, [145] *per* Allsop P.

for their arising should be changed so as to be brought into line with the general pattern of the operation of this 'principle'.[6]

The central argument of this chapter is that there is an important conceptual difference between common law and equitable rules generally, which explains their different scope and operation.[7] In particular 'equitable property' is fundamentally different from rights to physical things at common law. Once these differences are understood, the reason why the rules at common law and in Equity are not the same becomes clear. These conceptual differences are important both within jurisdictions where the common law and equitable rules are perceived as separate but are administered before a single court (eg England), and in those where the divide between the common law and Equity is now often perceived as a matter of historical importance only (eg those of the United States). It is important to understand why the rules are as they are even if the traditional language of Equity is no longer to be employed. In comparing common law and civilian systems, it also explains why there are often such apparently large differences in result.

The importance of these distinctions for the law of restitution will be discussed in the next chapter. The two chapters should be read together.

B. Meta-Law

The common law forms a freestanding system of rules, just as do French law, South African law, or the rules of Monopoly. Equity does not. Equity is the ivy on the common law wall. It is the plant, not the stone, that requires the other in order to stand. Without the background of the common law, Equity makes no freestanding sense.

Confusion is partially caused by the label, 'equity' (*aequitas*) also having been employed in a quite different sense since at least the time of Aristotle's *Nicomachaen Ethics*. In this latter sense, equity concerns the problem arising from creating definite rules to cover future scenarios, not all of which can be foreseen. 'Equity' then involves a discretionary justice in specific hard cases for the judge to disapply the rules when excessively harsh in a particular instance. The multifarious and technical rules that operate in the law of trusts is enough to show that the disapplication of rules has little or no relation to the body of detailed law in Equity as it now exists in the common law world. In order to differentiate the two senses, I shall capitalise Equity in the common lawyer's sense.

The nature of Equity is a product of its history. It is a body of rules introduced to ameliorate the perceived injustice of the common law rules as they had developed.[8] It did not however amend or overturn those rules, which already formed a coherent legal system and remained valid. Where then was the room for Equity? Equity was, and primarily[9] still is, a system of rules relating to those common law rules. This second order, or supplemental nature takes a number of different forms.

---

[6] Eg P Birks, *Unjust Enrichment* (2nd edn, 2005), 193–194.
[7] *Cf*. L Smith, 'Unjust Enrichment, Property and the Structure of Trusts' (2000) 116 LQR 412.
[8] *Dudley v Dudley* (1705) Pec Ch 241, 244, 24 ER 118, 119.
[9] There are exceptions. The equitable wrong of breach of confidence, has, in England, given birth to a freestanding tort of privacy: *Campbell v MGN Ltd* [2004] UKHL 22, [2004] 2 AC 457, [14] *per* Lord Nicholls. Discussed Chapter 16, Profits.

The closest that Equity comes to conflicting with the common law is that sometimes Equity will restrain the enforcement of rights that the common law recognises. Examples of this include equitable estoppel,[10] equitable relief against forfeiture, rescission for innocent misrepresentation and undue influence, and equitable set off.[11]

There is less apparent conflict where Equity operates so as to supplement the law, by providing court orders unrecognised by the common law in order to satisfy common law rights. The common law courts only made money orders, either to pay damages or debts. Orders for specific performance and injunctions are obvious examples of Equity providing orders that the common law did not. As the question of whether these court orders should be made concerns a wide range of considerations beyond what the rights of the parties *inter se* are, the availability of these orders in Equity is possibly what has led to the mistaken belief that whether to apply equitable rules is, in some sense, discretionary or related to *aequitas*.

For our purposes however, the most important addition is 'equitable property rights'. These too could not meaningfully exist without the common law background.

C. 'Equitable Property Rights'

1. Rights to Rights

In order to answer the normative question of when 'equitable property rights' ought to arise it is first necessary to answer the analytic question of the form that such rights take.

It was, and is, the common law that determined rights to tangible things. Equity did not. There was and is no room for it to do so.

The archetype of an 'equitable property right' is that of a beneficiary under a trust. The key to understanding is that a trustee holds rights on trust, not tangible things. A trust is not a bailment. Two examples side by side illustrate the point.

T holds a title to a quantity of valuable antique furniture on trust. One of the beneficiaries is *P*. *D1* steals the furniture.

P has no claim against *D1* to recover the furniture nor for any wrong he has committed in relation to it. This is not (simply) because common law torts are not available to those with equitable rights. Rather *P* has no claim at all, whether at common law or in Equity, against *D1*.[12] *T*, by contrast, may bring an action against *D1* in conversion. This illustrates that it is *T* not *P* who has a right to the things.

---

[10] Discussed in Chapter 14, Improvements.
[11] See R Stevens, 'Set-off and the Nature of Equity' in P Davies, S Douglas, and J Goudkamp (eds), *Defences in Equity* (2018), 42.
[12] *MCC Proceeds v Lehman Brothers* [1998] 4 All ER 675 (CA). See eg *Schalit v Joseph Nadler* [1933] 2 KB 79; *Parker-Tweedle v Dunbar plc (No 2)* [1991] Ch 12 (CA); *Atlasview Ltd v Brightview Ltd* [2004] EWHC 1056 (Ch), [2004] 2 BCLC 191. But see *Shell UK Ltd v Total UK Ltd* [2010] EWCA Civ 180, [2011] QB 86 where the distinction between legal title and the beneficial interest under a trust was considered 'legalistic', [132]. The result in *Shell* is probably *per incuriam* as the earlier decision of the Court of Appeal in *Parker-Tweedle* was not cited to the court. See also J Edelman, 'Two Fundamental Questions for the Law of Trusts' (2013) 129 LQR 66; W Swadling, 'In Defence of Formalism' in A Robertson and J Goudkamp (eds), *Form and Substance in the Law of Obligations* (2019), 95.

P may compel T to bring an action in conversion, and to hold what is recovered on trust.[13] This ability to compel is not, however, a right to exclude all others from the thing. That is vested in T not P. This is not simply a matter of who has the power of enforcement. If P personally suffers consequential loss as a result of D1's wrong, this is not recoverable from D1 even if both P and T are joined in the same action. D1's wrong was in relation to T not P nor any of the other beneficiaries.[14] (This is most often lost sight of where there is only one beneficiary.)[15] P may have a claim against T for loss suffered if the latter has breached any duty of care he was under in relation to the trust rights (eg he was negligent in allowing the furniture to be stolen). It is tempting, but wrong, to think, therefore, that because all P has is a power to sue T, and no right either in relation to a physical thing, nor one exigible against the rest of the world, that all P has is a mere personal right, equivalent to a contractual right.

By contrast:

T holds a title to a quantity of valuable antique furniture on trust. One of the beneficiaries is P. T, in breach of trust, makes a gift of the title to the furniture to his daughter, D2.

The position of the donee is different from that of the thief. If the original trustee T held the title to the furniture on a bare trust for P then D2 may be compellable to transfer the title to the furniture to P just as would the original trustee; otherwise a beneficiary such as P has a power to compel the donee to reconstitute the trust fund. In either case, at least as soon as D2 becomes aware that the rights were transferred to her in breach of trust, she comes under a duty not to use those rights (or their traceable proceeds) for her own benefit. D2 is commonly stated to hold the title to the furniture on constructive trust.[16] Why is the donee (D2) susceptible to a claim by the beneficiary when the thief (D1) is not? Is this paradoxical?

The answer is that the subject matter of the entitlements of the beneficiaries is the *right* to the furniture, not the furniture itself.[17] The thief does not acquire the trustee's right to the furniture. The thief only acquires a title to the thing from his possession of it, a title that is (obviously) inferior to that of the person from whom he stole it (the trustee). By contrast, the donee has acquired the trustee's right to the furniture, and that is the subject matter of the rights[18] of the beneficiaries. The beneficiaries' rights do not operate merely *in*

---

[13] CPR, Pt 64 and Practice Direction 64A—Estates, Trusts and Charities, para1(2)(a)(iii) and (c); *Tsang Yue Joyce v Standard Chartered Bank (Hong Kong) Ltd* [2010] HKCFI 98; [2010] 5 HKLRD, esp [38].
[14] *Hayim v Citibank N.A.* [1987] AC 730 (PC), 747–748; *Parker-Tweedale v Dunbar Bank Plc (No.1)* [1991] Ch 12 (CA), 19–20; *Nimmo v Westpac Banking Corp* [1993] 3 NZLR 218, 236–237.
[15] Eg *Trident General Insurance Co Ltd v McNiece Bros Pty Ltd* (1988) 165 CLR 107, [11] *per* Deane J.
[16] *Independent Trustee Services Ltd v GP Noble Trustees Ltd* [2012] EWCA Civ 195, [2013] Ch 91, [80] *per* Patten LJ.
[17] F W Maitland, *Equity: A Course of Lectures* (1909), 17. See also L Smith, 'Philosophical Foundations of Proprietary Remedies' in R Chambers, C Mitchell, and J Penner (eds), *Philosophical Foundations of the Law of Unjust Enrichment* (2009); B McFarlane and R Stevens, 'The Nature of Equitable Property' (2010) Journal of Equity 1.
[18] More accurately, the power of any individual beneficiary to enforce the duties of the trustee against him or persons acquiring the trust rights from him. Where there are a number of beneficiaries, no individual one may waive the duties of the trustee, nor need any individual beneficiary necessarily have any financial interest or otherwise in the trust in order to enforce it, save for the remotest of contingent entitlements. We may therefore be reluctant to label an individual beneficiary's entitlement as a 'claim-right'. Rather, it is the beneficiaries as a class who have a claim-right against the trustee, not any one individually (unless the class has only one member). Charitable purpose trusts are trusts because there are persons with the power to enforce the duties of trusteeship in relation to the rights held on trust, not because there are individual beneficiaries with specific entitlements. Further, by contrast with contracts, there is no such thing as an unenforceable trust. It is a necessary feature of the trust that there is someone with standing to enforce the duties of the trustee (*Morice v Bishop of Durham* (1804) 9 Ves Jun 399, 405, 32 ER 656, 658 *per* Sir William Grant MR).

personam with respect to the trustee, but also have third party effects: that is, they may be asserted against any person acquiring the rights that are held on trust who has neither provided value in good faith in their acquisition nor acquired them from another person who did so.[19]

The subject matter of a trust may not only be a right to a thing, but other rights, such as intellectual property rights, shares, and receivables. Equitable rights may also be held on trust, enabling sub-trusts, sub-sub-trusts, and so on.

Commercially, the most significant feature of the beneficiaries' entitlement is that it will provide protection for them upon the bankruptcy of the trustee (or any person acquiring the rights held on trust from the trustee otherwise than in good faith and for value or who acquired them from another who so acquired the rights). If an individual goes into bankruptcy, his trustee in bankruptcy has the bankrupt's estate transferred to him, but that puts him in the same position as a donee. If the individual held rights forming part of his estate on trust, the beneficiaries can continue to assert those rights against the trustee in bankruptcy, so that those rights are not available for realisation and distribution to unsecured creditors of the bankrupt.[20]

Because of these third-party effects, and the commercially most significant one of bankruptcy protection, it has become common usage to refer to 'equitable property rights'. However, two fundamental differences from property rights to things at common law (and in civilian legal systems) should be stressed.

First, as we have seen, the subject matter of a beneficiary's rights are specific rights of the trustee, never a physical thing. This distinction is sometimes elided by referring loosely to 'assets' or 'property' to cover both physical things (eg land, motorbikes, bank notes, share certificates) and rights (eg fee simple estates in land, the right to exclude all others from my motorbike, an accountholder's entitlement to be paid against his bank, the various rights that shareholders have against the company and other shareholders). Strictly, physical things may be possessed but rights cannot.[21] Only the latter may be held on trust. The beneficiaries have rights in relation to rights of the trustee. Rights to rights.

Second the beneficiary's powers to enforce the trust, unlike someone with a title to a thing, are not exigible against the rest of the world, but only against the trustee or persons who acquires the trust rights who have neither provided value in good faith in their acquisition nor acquired them from another person who did so. True, a beneficiary has a right that others do not dishonestly assist a trustee in breaching his duties, but that is not the same right as he has against the trustee himself or persons acquiring trust rights from him.[22] Parties to contracts similarly have a right against all others that they do not procure its breach,[23] but that is not the same right that they have as against their counterparty, and does not transform that contractual right into a 'property right', if the qualifier 'property' is to have any utility. Similarly, a right to be paid a sum of money is not transformed into being a right exigible against the whole world through being held on trust.

---

[19] *Wilkes v Spooner* [1911] 2 KB 473 (CA).
[20] Insolvency Act 1986, s 283(3)(b). The position is the same for insolvent companies: *Barclays Bank Ltd v Quistclose Investments Ltd* [1970] AC 567 (HL).
[21] *Cf. Williams v Central Bank of Nigeria* [2014] UKSC 10, [2014] AC 1189, [31] per Lord Sumption.
[22] B McFarlane, 'Equity, Obligations, and Third Parties' (2008) 2 SJLS 308.
[23] *Lumley v Gye* (1853) 2 E & B 216, 118 ER 749.

In order to avoid confusion, it might have been better if we had used an entirely different label in order to capture the idea of 'equitable property rights', and Professor McFarlane has suggested a possible alternative of 'persistent rights'.[24] This is intended to capture the idea that the beneficiaries' rights can be asserted against, or 'persist' in relation to, someone acquiring the rights that are held on trust.[25] However, it is probably too late in the law's development to hope for any shift in usage. 'Persistence' is also, as we shall see, somewhat misleading as the recipient's duty may have a different content from that of the original trustee, does not properly arise without knowledge on their part, and is a new obligation imposed upon them to which nobody was necessarily previously subject.

In *economic*, as opposed to *legal*, terms the label 'equitable property right' is often accurate to capture the value of the beneficiaries' entitlement. Economically, the individuals who will, at the end of the day, enjoy the benefits of the rights forming the trust estate are (usually)[26] the beneficiaries, not the trustee. It is therefore natural to refer to the parties who, in the end, will obtain the fruits of those rights as the 'beneficial owners'. However, focusing exclusively upon this economic reality, at the expense of the law's conceptual structure, will lead into error.

Although the focus of this chapter will be upon trusts, all 'equitable property rights' take the same basic form (ie they involve rights in relation to other rights). They differ between one another because the content of the duty owed differs (eg a chargee's rights are defeasible upon the obligation secured being performed, whereas a beneficiary's rights under a trust are not so defeasible).

2. Common Misconceptions

Two alternative conceptions of 'equitable property' are current that it is important to reject, because so commonly held.

First is the view that two parallel laws of property with the same subject matter exist. On this view, a trustee can hold land or furniture (the things) on trust, and both he and the beneficiary have a right to the things.[27] Just as the person with legal title has the right to exclude all others from the thing, so too would the person with 'equitable title'.[28] This would create a dual system of property law with the common law saying 'the trustee is the rightholder' and Equity saying 'the beneficiary is the rightholder'. On this view we resolve the dispute between the two systems by allowing Equity to trump the common law. However, the equitable property right is in another sense weaker, as it may be lost where the trustee sells to a good faith purchaser for value of the legal title.

---

[24] B McFarlane, *The Structure of Property Law* (2008), 23–26. See also B McFarlane and R Stevens, 'The Nature of Equitable Property' (2010) Journal of Equity 1, 1. *Mea culpa*.
[25] *Cf. Akers v Samba Financial Group* [2017] UKSC 6, [2017] AC 424, [82] *per* Lord Sumption; S Agnew and B McFarlane, 'The Paradox of the Equitable Proprietary Claim' in B McFarlane and S Agnew (eds), *Modern Studies in Property Law*, vol 10 (2019), ch 17.
[26] But see so-called massively discretionary trusts, discussed L Smith 'Massively Discretionary Trusts' (2017) 70 CLP 17.
[27] A W Scott, 'The Nature of the Rights of the "Cestui Que Trust"' (1917) 17 Columbia Law Rev 269, 275. *Ayerst v C&K Construction Ltd* [1976] AC 176, 177 *per* Lord Diplock.
[28] *Cf.* R Nolan, 'Equitable Property' (2006) 122 LQR 232.

If we adopted this approach, someone with title to a thing has (at least potentially) two rights to it, one at common law and another in Equity, which can be separated or split. Our property rights are, on this view, like a banana, with the Equitable right the flesh stuffed inside the common law skin. Under this account, we have two different sets of rules giving different answers to the same question ('Who has title to the thing?') within one legal system. This view is both incoherent and incorrect[29] and, as we shall see, cannot account for the rules as they are.

Second is the view that a trust involves two separate patrimonies. This is a particularly tempting view for comparatists, as civilian legal systems all recognise the idea of an individual person having two or more patrimonies.[30] For common lawyers, this form of holding is familiar from succession and personal bankruptcy law. In England, upon death (or bankruptcy), the estate (the rights) of the deceased (or bankrupt) will vest in an administrator[31] who will have no personal liability for the deceased's (or bankrupt's) debts. The deceased's (or bankrupt's) estate remains subject to claims by the deceased's (or bankrupt's) creditors,[32] but the administrator's personal patrimony is not so subject. The administrator is not entitled to make use of the separate fund for himself but must realise and distribute it (to creditors in the case of bankruptcy, to the legatees in the case of death). In civilian jurisdictions it is common for a deceased's patrimony to pass directly to his heirs, without the intermediation of an administrator.

This second model is not the form of a trust in common law legal systems because a trust, unlike a separate patrimony, is constituted by rights alone, not liabilities.[33] Trusts cannot be sued, only trustees.

3. Significance

The proof, which is also the significance, of the account of 'equitable property rights' given here, may be demonstrated in a number of ways. Not the least of these is its explanatory power in relation to restitutionary obligations. Some other examples will also be provided in brief outline before proceeding, as the idea is so important and, for some, novel: assignment, security rights, secret trusts, and conflict of laws rules.

At one time, contractual debts and other claims could not be assigned, by which in English we mean transferred, at all. In order to acquire a contractual right against another it is necessary to establish that you had an agreement with that other, and that you had provided consideration in exchange for any promise they had made. A purported assignee of a contractual right could satisfy neither of these requirements and did not therefore acquire any contractual right.

Equitable assignment of a contractual right, despite its name, did not involve the transfer of the contractual right, but rather the creation of a new right in the 'assignee', the subject

---

[29] See eg *Swift 1st Ltd v Chief Land Registrar* [2015] EWCA Civ 330, [2015] Ch 602, [41]; *DKLR Holding Co (No 2) Pty Ltd v Commissioner of Stamp Duties* (1982) 149 CLR 431 (HCA).
[30] See Quebec Civil Code, ss 1260–1261; In Scotland see G Gretton 'Trusts without Equity' (2000) 49 ICLQ 599; L Smith 'Scottish Trusts in the Common Law' (2013) 17 Edinburgh Law Review 283.
[31] Death: Administration of Estates Act 1925, s 1; Bankruptcy: Insolvency Act 1986, s 306.
[32] Death: Administration of Estates Act 1925, s 32; Bankruptcy: Insolvency Act 1986, ss 322–324.
[33] L Smith, 'Trust and Patrimony' (2008) Revue Générale de Droit 379.

matter of which was the assignor's contractual right against the promisor. Statutory assignment, possible since 1874, is quite different. It involves the actual transfer of the right being assigned. As the latter offends privity of contract, it was necessary for this change to be made by legislation, and statutory assignment is now found in England in section 136 of the Law of Property Act 1925.

The different rules between equitable and statutory assignment are then explicable because the latter involves a transfer, whilst the former involves the creation of a new right in relation to another right. Statutory assignment (as a transfer) requires formality to be used (signed writing); equitable assignment does not. Statutory assignment requires notice to be given to the debtor as it involves a change in the party to whom the debtor owes his obligation; equitable assignment does not. Statutory assignment, because a transfer, cannot be used to assign debts not yet in existence; equitable assignment has no such restriction. Statutory assignment does not permit the debt to be partially assigned (if it did the debtor could be prejudiced by having multiple different creditors instead of one); equitable assignment has no such restriction because it involves no change in the identity of the creditor. If an equitable assignee wishes to enforce the underlying debt, the assignor must be a party to the action, because the assignor is still the creditor and there are in fact two actions (assignee v assignor; assignor/creditor v debtor), not one. Statutory assignment requires no joinder, because it is a transfer. Commercially, equitable assignment has many of the desired effects of a transfer (most importantly protection against the assignor's bankruptcy) but this should not blind us to its different form. This was possible because of the nature of 'equitable property rights'.

Security rights are defeasible upon performance of the obligation that is secured, whereas a trustee's duty to a beneficiary cannot be released through the doing of anything other than performing the duties as trustee. Security rights, like assignment, also takes different forms. An example:

P who has a title to a Picasso painting mortgages it to *D* in order to secure a loan of £100,000.

The form a legal mortgage takes is that of a transfer. *P* transfers his title to the Picasso to the creditor. This looks like a risky bargain however, because if *P* repays *D*, he runs the risk that *D* may not reconvey back to him the security, and in particular that *D* may be bankrupt before he does so. However, *D*'s obligation to reconvey gives *P* a right in relation to *D*'s right (an *equity* of redemption) that ensures he is protected against this eventuality.

By contrast:

P who has a title to a Picasso painting charges it to *D* in order to secure a loan of £100,000.

An equitable charge, unlike a mortgage, involves no transfer. *P* retains title to the Picasso, and *D* has acquired a new right in relation to that right securing the debt. Charges are often more convenient than mortgages as the right used by way of security may be inconvenient to transfer (eg giving notice to thousands of debtors when a company's receivables are used for purposes of security) or impossible (eg the security includes future rights which, necessarily, cannot be transferred at the time of the creation of the security).[34] Commercially,

---

[34] On the nature of a floating charge see R Stevens, 'Contractual Aspects of Debt Financing' in D Prentice and A Reisberg (eds), *Corporate Finance Law in the UK and EU* (2011).

legal mortgages of rights to chattels and equitable charges over them appear very similar. Legally, they are quite distinct.

Testamentary dispositions must be made by a will, which in England necessarily requires writing, and the signature of the testator and of two witnesses in the presence of the testator.[35] Where however the testator has communicated to a legatee that he wishes the benefit of the disposition to go to another (classically, an illegitimate child the testator did not wish to acknowledge on the face of his will), if the legatee accepts, then a trust over the right acquired under the will arises on receipt by the legatee. Sometimes the existence of such an arrangement, but not its terms, may be disclosed in the will ('half-secret' trusts) sometimes not ('fully secret' trusts). If an equitable interest under a trust involved the acquisition of an interest in the bequest itself, 'fully secret' and 'half-secret' trusts would contradict the policy of formality in section 9 of the Wills Act 1837. Dispositions would be made other than according to the terms of the Act. However, the beneficiary acquires no right to the bequest. Instead, a trust is arising in relation to the bequeathed right because of the legatee's prior acceptance of the condition under which the bequest was acquired.

Finally, the common law courts have long declined jurisdiction over disputes as to title to foreign land.[36] The same is not however true of a claim that such title is held on trust,[37] because a beneficiary has and asserts no right to the land itself, but instead a right in relation to the trustee's title to the land.

4. The Necessary and Sufficient Duty to be a Trustee

Before proceeding further, it is also necessary to resolve a semantic problem. What is a trust? What are the minimum conditions necessary to be satisfied in order to be describe what has arisen as a trust? Trusts are, as we have seen, obligational, although these obligations can bind those who acquire the right that is the subject matter of that obligation upon their acquiring knowledge. What is the content of this obligation?

Express trusts usually carry with them extensive obligations set out primarily in the instrument that specifies their terms. Such trusts often require rights to be invested and distributions to be made to particular beneficiaries. The equitable rights of beneficiaries that are not expressly declared but that instead arise by operation of law independently are not of this kind. Lord Sumption has described someone who knowingly received rights transferred in breach of trust as not a trustee because no trust has been reposed in them.[38] On this narrow usage we would have to abandon the language of 'constructive trusts' altogether, the appellation of 'trust' would be as misleading as that of 'quasi-contracts',[39] and instead use a different label for the 'equitable property rights' that beneficiaries acquire against recipients of rights transferred in breach of trust. In English, the word 'trust' does imply that something has been entrusted by someone to another (eg a settlor to a trustee) and it is a natural thought that any relationship that does not take this form (as self-declared express

---

[35] Wills Act 1837, s 9.
[36] *British South Africa Co v Companhia de Mozambique* [1893] AC 602 (HL).
[37] *Penn v Lord Baltimore* (1750) 1 Ven Sen 444, 27 ER 1132. See also *re Anchor Line (Henderson Brothers Ltd)* [1937] Ch 483 (land and movables in Scotland subject to an English charge).
[38] *Williams v Central Bank of Nigeria* [2014] UKSC 10, [2014] AC 1189, [31].
[39] W Swadling, 'The Fiction of the Constructive Trust' (2011) 64 CLP 399.

declarations of trust do not) are not really trusts at all. In the United States, confining the usage of 'trust' to the case of a right having been 'entrusted' by one party to another is more prevalent than in the rest of the common law world.[40]

However, beneficiaries have the same protection against the recipient's insolvency where the latter still has the rights received (or their traceable proceeds) as they do against the original trustee, the same remedies for breach against the knowing recipient,[41] and Lord Sumption's narrow usage is neither the general one nor one that he himself subsequently employed.[42] This narrow conception, at least as a matter of linguistic usage, will not therefore be adopted.

At the other extreme, a party may be susceptible, or liable, to come under a duty not to use a right for their own benefit, but no such duty has yet arisen. Such 'mere equities' can have third-party effects but will not take priority over subsequently created (obligational) equitable interests if taken for value without notice of the 'mere equity'.[43] As they have this different feature, a label other than 'trust' is preferable for them.

As a semantic matter, the intermediate usage of 'trust', under which expressly settled trusts are not the only form of trust and 'mere equities' are not trusts, has the dual advantage of having the closest relation to general usage and the most utility in separating analytically distinct concepts.

When trusts are expressly declared, it is often commercially useful to allow the trustees a great deal of freedom in their ability to trade with the trust estate. However, it is not the case that there can be a trust where the trustee is completely free to deal with the rights as they see fit. That the parties give their relationship the label of 'trust' (usually in order to give the beneficiaries protection against the trustee's bankruptcy) is insufficient for there to be a trust (just as calling a security right a 'fixed charge' is not determinative of whether that is what has been created). A trustee must be under a duty not to use the rights that are the subject matter of the trust for his own benefit.[44] This is a necessary condition.

The important proposition for our purposes however is not only a duty not to use identifiable rights for one's own benefit a necessary condition for the existence of a trust, it is also sufficient where such duty is indefeasible. This does not entail that such a duty in relation to a right necessarily needs to be specifically enforceable, liability to enforcement not being the same issue as the existence of a duty, still less that there needs to be any court ordered remedy available in relation to a physical thing such as delivery up.[45] In order to make good this proposition of sufficiency, a number of examples will be given, before turning to restitutionary obligations.

---

[40] Eg J Langbein, 'The Contractarian Basis of the Law of Trusts' (1995) 105 YLJ 625.
[41] C Mitchell and S Watterson, 'Remedies for Knowing Receipt' in C Mitchell (ed), *Constructive and Resulting Trusts* (2010), 115, 138.
[42] *Akers v Samba Financial Group* [2017] UKSC 6, [2017] AC 424, [90].
[43] Ie the 'priority in time gives the better equity' rule does not apply: *Phillips v Phillips* (1861) 4 De GF & J 208, 45 ER 1164; *Latec Investments Ltd v Hotel Terrigal Pty Ltd* (1965) 113 CLR 265. See also the priority of fixed charges over prior in time floating charges.
[44] *Space Investments Ltd v Canadian Imperial Bank of Commerce Trust Co (Bahamas) Ltd* [1986] 1 WLR 1072 (PC), 1073–1074 *per* Lord Templeman; *Armitage v Nurse* [1998] Ch 241, 253 *per* Millett LJ; *Citibank NA v MBIA Assurance SA* [2007] EWCA Civ 11. *Cf.* the distinction between fixed and floating charges where a debtor's freedom to use charged rights in the ordinary course of business is inconsistent with the existence of a fixed charge: *National Westminster Bank plc v Spectrum Plus Ltd* [2005] UKHL 41, [2005] 2 AC 680.
[45] *Contra* W Swadling, 'Unjust Enrichment: Value, Rights and Trusts' (2021) 137 LQR 56, 60, 67, 68.

D. Trusts Arising from Contractual and Other Obligations

An example:

> D contracts to sell his title to Blackacre to D. P pays the price, but conveyance of title to the land has not occurred before D goes into bankruptcy.

In (most) common law systems, D will hold his title to the land on trust for P. The vendor-purchaser constructive trust is probably the oldest, and most firmly established, form of constructive trust.[46] It is accepted by almost[47] everyone. Why, however, does one arise? The common invocation of the maxim 'Equity takes as done what ought to be done' appears to provide us with a fiction, in place of an explanation.[48]

Once paid, P is under a duty to convey the title to Blackacre to D. *A fortiori* at the latest from that moment he is under a duty not to use the title to Blackacre for his own benefit. A trust arises because that is what a trust is.

Even at an earlier stage, where the obligation to convey is still conditional upon D's payment or another event, P ought not to dispose of the right to Blackacre or otherwise render it impossible to perform the obligation to convey that will arise once the condition is satisfied. The obligation of the vendor is of this more limited form, from the moment the agreement is concluded until payment has been made.[49] The vendor should remain entitled to any rents received before conveyance because that is what the agreement provides, but is not free to dispose of the right to the land. The right of the buyer at this stage is akin to a charge over the right to the land, to secure the conditional obligation to convey once payment has been made.

It should not matter if what is sold is a specific right other than title to land. For example, a sale by a beneficiary of his interest under a trust should also give rise to a constructive (sub-)trust.[50]

If we took seriously the (rejected) view that legal and beneficial 'ownership' involved two separate laws of property, with the same subject matter, it is inexplicable how or why a vendor-purchaser constructive trust arises. If the purchaser had acquired a right to Blackacre itself (as opposed to a right in relation to the vendor's right to Blackacre), why would this not contradict the rules requiring the transfer of the right to land to be registered and by way of deed? It is no answer to say: 'that is the common law, this is Equity'. How could Equity, legitimately, contradict the answer as to who owns Blackacre, given today by legislation, through the invocation of a maxim ('Equity takes as done what ought to be done') that invokes a transparent fiction?

By contrast, once we accept that a trust is obligational, with third-party effects upon transferees of the right that is the subject matter of the trustee's obligation, then it becomes

---

[46] *Lysaght v Edwards* (1876) 2 Ch D 499, 506, 'settled for more than two centuries' *per* Jessel MR; *Sooraj v Samaroo* [2004] UKPC 50, [15], 'fundamental' *per* Lord Scott. The mortgagor's 'equity of redemption' is of the same form and also arises because of the contractual duty to (re)convey (subject to rules concerning relief against forfeiture and prohibitions on clogs or fetters on the right to redeem).

[47] But not quite: W Swadling, 'The Vendor-Purchaser Constructive Trust' in S Degeling and J Edelman (eds), *Equity in Commercial Law* (2005), 463. See also *Raynor v Preston* (1881) 18 Ch D 1, 10–11 *per* Brett LJ.

[48] But see Chapter 13, Equity: Restitution.

[49] *Cf. Jerome v Kelly* [2004] UKHL 25, [2004] 1 WLR 1409, [32] *per* Lord Walker.

[50] *Neville v Wilson* [1997] Ch 144 (CA).

apparent why contractual obligations that are of the correct *form* create trusts. The purchaser/beneficiary does not acquire any right to the land (the thing) itself, and so no contradiction arises. The vendor 'is not compelled to convey the property because he is a constructive trustee; it is because he can be compelled to convey that he is a constructive trustee'.[51]

If instead of a sale the contract between *P* and *D* was to grant a lease over Blackacre, an equitable lease will arise before execution,[52] and a contract to grant a mortgage will create an equitable mortgage upon payment. Such equitable rights in relation to the right to the land will have third-party effects in the same way that a beneficiary's interest under a trust does. The difference between a beneficiary's interest under a trust, and other equitable rights such as an equitable lease or mortgage, is found in the content of the obligation owed in relation to the right that is its subject. As a matter of their form, they still concern rights in relation to other rights.

The same contractual analysis explains the trust that arose in *Barclays Bank Ltd v Quistclose Investments Ltd*.[53] Rolls Razor Ltd were in serious financial difficulty. Needing £209,719 to pay dividends that had been declared for shareholders, the money was advanced by Quistclose Ltd. It was agreed that the money so paid was to be used only for the purpose of paying the dividend. The advance was paid into a separate account with Barclays Bank that was opened specifically for this purpose. The bank had notice of the nature of this arrangement. Before the dividend was paid however, Rolls Razor Ltd went into insolvent liquidation. The Bank wished to set off the sums owed to it by Rolls Razor Ltd against the amount standing to the company's credit in its account. The House of Lords held that it could not do so, the right to be paid the sum in the separate account being held on trust by Rolls Razor for Quistclose Ltd.

Absent the contractual obligation not to use the deposited money for any purpose other than the payment of the dividend, there would have been no trust.[54] The facts were insufficient to show that there had been an express declaration of trust. From the outset, however, the contract had provided that the sums paid were not at the payee's free disposition. From the moment of payment, therefore, there was a trust in favour of Quistclose Ltd, who were the party with the (contractual) power to enforce it. Before insolvency intervened, Rolls Razor Ltd had the power to use the money paid for the specified purpose, a power that determined upon it ceasing to be possible to fulfil, companies in insolvency proceedings no longer being able to pay dividends to shareholders.[55] Quistclose Ltd had no power to unilaterally vary the terms of the contract, and so could not have demanded repayment of the money unless and until Rolls Razor's power to use it for the particular purpose came to an end.[56] The trust was coextensive with the parties' contractual rights and obligations and was created by it. In *Quistclose* itself, the payee was also under a duty to exercise the power to pay

---

[51] A W Scott, *The Law of Trusts* (3rd edn, 1967), s 462, 3413. 'Obliged to convey' would be better than 'compelled'.
[52] *Walsh v Lonsdale* (1882) 21 Ch D 9 (CA).
[53] [1970] AC 567 (HL). See generally W Swadling (ed), *The Quistclose Trust: Critical Essays* (2004).
[54] See *Twinsectra v Yardley* [2002] UKHL 12, [2002] 2 AC 164.
[55] See also P Millett, 'The *Quistclose* Trust: Who Can Enforce It?' (1985) 101 LQR 269; *Twinsectra v Yardley* [2002] 2 AC 164, [68]–[103] *per* Lord Millett, [13] *per* Lord Hoffmann. This was not the original understanding of Lord Wilberforce in *Quistclose* itself, who thought that, until the purpose failed, the shareholders were the beneficiaries: [1970] AC 567, 580. This seems to have been based upon a misunderstanding of the party with standing to enforce the duty not to use the account for any purpose other than that specified.
[56] Millett, 'The *Quistclose* Trust: Who Can Enforce It?' (n 55), 291. *Contra* J Glister, '*Twinsectra v Yardley*: Trusts, Powers and Contractual obligations' (2002) 16 Trust Law Int'l 223, 228.

the dividend, but this is unnecessary, so long as they are not free to use the money for any other purpose.

The trust in *Quistclose* was resulting in pattern: the right to the bank account was held on trust back for the payor. It arose for the same reason, however, as the pro-sulting vendor-purchaser constructive trust: the contractual obligations of the promisor required that they do not use particular rights for their own benefit, and that entails a trust. If the agreement between Quistclose Ltd and Rolls Razor Ltd had stated 'the proceeds of this payment are to be held on trust, but the payee has the power to use such proceeds for any purpose they see fit' this would not be a trust, despite the express use of that label. The freedom to use the right for the payee's own benefit is incompatible with the existence of a trust.

Expressly declared trusts also sometimes take the same form as so-called *Quistclose* trusts. If, for example, a subscription fund is set up for a non-charitable purpose, the parties with the power to enforce the duties of the payee not to use the funds received for his own benefit will be, from the start, the subscribers. They will be 'beneficiaries' (even though they may expect to get no personal benefit if the purpose is fulfilled). It is a mistake to think that the settlors of a trust are never also members of the class of beneficiaries. The trustees will have the power, that they will usually be obliged to exercise, to use the trust fund for the designated purpose. If the purpose for which the money was paid can no longer be fulfilled, the power of the trustee to use the money received for that purpose comes to an end.[57] What is left is a bare trust for the subscribers. As in *Quistclose* there is but one trust, not an initial express one and a second one springing up upon its failure. The trust that remains is resulting in pattern, but it is not a new trust.

By contrast:

P contracts to sell a one third share of *Enrichment plc* to *D*, intending to transfer to him the one third stake that he owns. *D* pays the price, but before transfer *P* goes into bankruptcy.

Shares in a company are not like the right to land or antique furniture. Any issue of a share in a company is identical to any other of the same proportion. Indeed, if an owner of shares in a company sells his portion to another this is done through novation (ie the cancelling of the seller's shares and the issuing of shares to the buyer). *P* is not therefore under any duty to transfer the specific share in the company that he owns; he could go out into the market and purchase an equivalent proportion from elsewhere in order to perform his contract with *D*. *P* therefore owes no duty in relation to any specific right he has, even though he may intend to use the shares he has for purposes of performance. No trust therefore arises because it is a sale of something generic. Similarly, where generic goods are sold no trust arises. Where the sale is of specific ascertained goods, because 'property passes when intended to pass', title to them is transferred as soon as there is an unconditional contractual obligation to do so, leaving no scope for a trust over the right to the goods.

Further, as we have seen, upon death or bankruptcy the estate of the deceased or bankrupt will become vested in an administrator. This involves the creation of a patrimony separate from that of the administrator. Creditors of the estate, and the legatees of the deceased, have an entitlement against the administrator that the estate is properly administered, but

---

[57] *Re Abbott Fund Trusts* [1900] 2 Ch 326; *Re Ames Settlement* [1946] 1 Ch 217; *Re Gillingham Bus Disaster Fund* [1958] Ch 300.

no right in relation to any specific right or rights forming part of that estate before distribution. They are not therefore beneficiaries under a trust. The administrator of the estate is similar to a charitable trustee, as they are not free to use the estate's rights for their own benefit (hence 'trustee in bankruptcy') but there are no beneficiaries.[58]

Outside of contract, other obligations to transfer rights create trusts. A good example is the decision of the Court of Appeal in *Mountney v Treharne*.[59] As part of relief under legislation concerning the division of property on divorce, a court ordered a husband to convey his interest in the matrimonial home to his wife. Before the transfer occurred, the husband was declared bankrupt. The administrator of his estate claimed that as the conveyance had not been completed, the husband's interest in the matrimonial home remained part of his estate free for realisation and distribution to creditors. The Court of Appeal held that as the court order created an obligation to convey, this created an equitable interest in the wife in relation to the husband's title binding upon the administrator. This is proof that such constructive trusts are not a misnomer for court orders to transfer.[60]

A controversial example:

P a wholesaler employs *D* as an agent for the purchase of goods. *X* bribes *D* with the title to a jade chess set in order to induce him to purchase goods from him.

What ought *D*'s obligation to *P* be in such circumstances? All accept that *D* ought to compensate *P* for any loss his actions cause his principal. He is also, at *P*'s option, alternatively obliged to give up any profits he makes. But what should his duties be in relation to the title to the bribe?

On one view, *D* should only be obliged to account to *P* for the value of the bribe. This would leave *D* free to deal with the title to the chess set as he sees fit (eg he could sell it and spend the proceeds on a holiday).

This seems incorrect. Why should the disloyal agent, as opposed to his principal, be the one who chooses whether he should enjoy the title to the chess set? Further if he dissipates the bribe, there will be an increased likelihood that he will not be able (through bankruptcy) to account for its value. The better view therefore is that the bribed agent should be under a duty not only to account for the value of the bribe, but also not to use the specific rights received (or their traceable proceeds) for his own benefit. Again, this gives rise to a constructive trust, and after a period of uncertainty[61] this is now English law.[62]

Finally, an exception is usually thought to be made in cases of bare promises in a deed to transfer a right (whether to land or anything else).[63] The general rule that an obligation to transfer creates a trust is here qualified. There is no necessary reason why Equity should recognise the creation of the same obligations as the common law, and here it does not. 'Equity will not assist a volunteer' and a mere donee under a deed acquires no rights under a trust and also cannot obtain specific performance of the common law obligation. We may query

---

[58] *Commissioner of Stamp Duties (Queensland) v Livingston* [1965] AC 694 (PC).
[59] [2002] EWCA Civ 1174 [2003] Ch 135.
[60] *Contra* Swadling, 'Unjust Enrichment: Value, Rights and Trusts' (n 45), 76.
[61] Against the imposition of a trust: *Lister & Co v Stubbs* [1890] 45 ChD 1 (CA). For the imposition of a trust: *Attorney-General (Hong Kong) v Reid* [1994] 1 AC 324 (PC).
[62] *FHR European Ventures Ltd v Cedar Capital Partners LLC* [2014] UKSC 45, [2015] AC 250.
[63] The authorities are however ambiguous: B McFarlane, *The Structure of Property Law* (2008), 230–231.

whether third parties to contracts who today acquire rights under the Contracts (Rights of Third Parties) Act 1999 (as eg the shareholders to be paid the dividend may have done in *Barclays Bank Ltd v Quistclose Ltd*) should be denied an interest under a trust on the same basis.

A rightholder may also expressly declare himself a trustee, thereby validly creating a trust. Does this offend the 'equity will not assist a volunteer' rule, as the beneficiaries have provided nothing in exchange? The power of rightholders to do this unilaterally is justifiable because of the nature of the trust. As we have seen, rights at common law are bilateral. By contrast, the trust is concerned with a restriction upon the freedom to exercise a right that the law has already conferred. We allow such a restriction to be imposed by unilateral act provided that objectively clear words are used ('I hereby declare myself a trustee of the title to Blackacre for the benefit of my daughter'). Unlike all the examples so far, an expressly declared trust is not effective because of an independently existing obligation, but rather because we permit the rightholder to impose such an obligation upon himself provided it is declared expressly.

13
Equity: Restitution

A. Trusts and Obligations to Make Restitution

After the last chapter's long, but unfortunately essential, excursus into the nature of 'equitable property rights', we are now in a position to see when and why restitutionary obligations create trusts.

Where the performance from *P* to *D* consists of the transfer of a right, if that right has been conveyed without justification, *D* ought to reconvey that right. An example:

> *D* innocently misrepresents to *P* the possible development purposes for which a portion of land to which *P* has title can be put. *P* agrees to sell title to the land to *D*, subsequently conveying title to him. Upon discovering the misrepresentation, *P* rescinds the contract of sale.

As we have seen, regardless of whether the misrepresentation is innocent or fraudulent, rescission of the contract will not, alone, reconvey title to the land back to *P*. A conveyance of land requires a deed and (usually) the alteration of the land register. Absent those steps, title to the land remains vested in *D*.

However, following rescission *D* ought to reconvey to *P* the title he has obtained. As we have seen, where the unjustified performance *P* has rendered to *D* consists of a service, it is not possible to perfectly undo what has been done, and so the law requires the return of the value of the service. Where, as here, the performance consists of the conveyance of a right from *P* to *D* the closest that is achievable to the reversal of what has happened is for *D* to reconvey back to *P* what he has received.[1] If *D* is under a duty to reconvey a particular right, then *a fortiori* he is under a duty not to use that right for his own benefit. A trust therefore arises.[2]

Outside of the sale of goods, discussed in Chapter 11, Things, the nature of the right *P* has transferred to *D* should not matter for the analysis. For example:

> *D*, an art dealer, innocently misrepresents to *P* the provenance of a landscape painting. *P* pays £5,000 in cash in exchange for *D*'s title to the picture. The next day, *P* discovers the truth and seeks to rescind. *D* still has the cash.

---

[1] *Cf.* R Chambers, 'Two Kinds of Enrichment' in R Chambers, C Mitchell, and J Penner (eds), *Philosophical Foundations of the Law of Unjust Enrichment* (2009).

[2] *Stump v Gaby* (1852) 2 De GM & G 623, 42 ER 1015; *Alati v Kruger* [1957] 94 CLR 216 (HCA), 224; *Daly v Sydney Stock Exchange* (1986) 160 CLR 371; *El Ajou v Dollar Land Holdings (No 1)* [1993] BCC 698, 713 *per* Millett J (rev'd on other grounds [1994] BCC 143 (CA)); *Bristol and West Building Society v Mothew* [1998] Ch 1, 22–23 *per* Millett LJ; *Twinsectra Ltd v Yardley* [1999] Lloyd's Rep Bank 438 (CA) [96]–[100] *per* Potter LJ (rev'd on other grounds [2002] UKHL 12, [2002] 2 AC 164); *Shalson v Russo* [2003] EWHC 1637 (Ch) [120]–[127] *per* Rimer J; *National Crime Agency v Robb* [2014] EWHC 4384 (Ch), [2015] Ch 520, [41]–[50] *per* Etherton C.

Upon rescission what ought D be obliged to do? Clearly £5,000 ought to be returned, but what of the title to the specific cash with which D was paid? If P receives restitution of £5,000 why should he care about the specific cash with which he originally paid? However, if D dissipates the £5,000 cash there will again be an increased likelihood that he will not be able (through bankruptcy) to account for its value. Until repayment is made therefore, he ought not to be free to use the right to the cash he has obtained for his own benefit.

The trust that arises in such cases is both constructive, in the sense that it is not express because neither party declared an intention that a trust should arise, and resulting, in the sense that the equitable right the transferor acquires results back to him.

An illustration in the context of rectification is *Blacklocks v JB Developments (Godalming) Ltd*.[3] The plaintiff mistakenly transferred title to more land to the defendants' predecessor in title than he had intended. Title to the land was then conveyed to the defendants who were registered as proprietors of the entire portion. The power the plaintiff had to rectify what they had done, combined with their actual occupation, meant that they had an overriding interest binding upon the purchaser, and the court held that the right to the portion mistakenly transferred was held on trust, with the result that the land register was ordered to be rectified.

Similar are attempts to settle express trusts that fail from the outset. In *Re Shaw*,[4] George Bernard Shaw in his will directed that funds be settled on trustees for the purpose of undertaking research into the viability of a 40-letter alphabet. However, because the purpose was not charitable the trust failed. The trustees, as they then knew, had as a result acquired the right transferred to them without justification, and a trust resulted back to Shaw's estate.

In the examples given so far, the right that the defendant has acquired is one that was once vested in the plaintiff. This is not however a necessary condition. It suffices if D has acquired a right without justification, as a result of a performance P has rendered. For example:

> As part of a joint venture agreement between P and D, P agrees to purchase title to land from X, title to be conveyed to D. After conveyance is completed, P rescinds the joint venture agreement because of innocent misrepresentations made by D.

The right to the land D has acquired is not one that was ever vested in P. It was acquired by D through P's performance. The right has been acquired from P without good reason, because the contract that justified it has now been avoided. D ought to be under a duty to P not to use the right so acquired for his own benefit.[5]

In the modern era when the use of cash is obsolescent, almost all money payment cases take a similar form. Payment by 'bank transfer' involves the payor's bank account being debited and the payee's account credited. There is, properly speaking, no transfer of anything between payor and payee. Where both accounts are in credit, the sum owing by the payor's bank to the payor has decreased, and the sum owing by the payee's bank to the payee has increased. Although it is common usage to speak metaphorically of a 'transfer' in such a case, any right the payee has acquired is not something that the payor ever had. The resulting

---

[3] [1982] Ch 183.
[4] [1957] 1 WLR 729.
[5] *Cf. Dyer v Dyer* (1788) 2 Cox Eq 92, 93, 30 ER 42, 43 *per* Lord Eyre CB; *Sayre v Hughes* (1867–1868) LR 5 EQ 376, 380 *per* Stuart VC.

credit of the payee's account is a new right he has acquired, a right to be paid £A not being the same as a right to be paid £A+B, but it has not been transferred to him.

An issue that has proven controversial is the moment from which a trust arises in these examples. The better view is that because a trust arises only at the point at which D is under a duty not to use the right for his own benefit, in most of the examples given so far, that is from the point at which the agreement is rescinded in Equity or rectified by court order.

Prior to rescission, the option or power to rescind is also capable of having third-party effects. If the defendant declares bankruptcy prior to rescission, for example, this should not alone prevent subsequent rescission and the creation of a trust. However, this option or power to rescind is more vulnerable than other vested 'equitable property rights'. The priority between competing 'equitable property rights' is generally determined by their order of creation, but a mere option or power to rescind will not prevail over other subsequently created equitable rights, such as that created by a later trust or fixed charge.[6] The interest of the holder of the power to rescind is, before its exercise, an example of a 'mere equity': a tadpole in relation to the frog that is the trust that is created upon its exercise.[7]

If it is true of rights transferred under a contract that is subsequently avoided that a trust arises, ought it not also to apply in cases where rights are transferred under a contract that is void from the outset? Does the lack of reason for the acquisition of a right from the plaintiff from the outset justify the creation of a trust? That alone it does not was established in the important decision of *Westdeutsche Landesbank v Islington London Borough Council*.[8] The plaintiff bank had paid the council £1.2 million more than the council had paid it under an interest rate swap agreement. Two years after entering into the agreement, such contracts were held to be void, as *ultra vires* the councils entering into them. The issue before the House of Lords concerned interest. Accepting that the payment made was recoverable, could the bank claim compound interest or was it confined to claiming statutory simple interest? Compound interest was only available, so the majority held, against a 'trustee or other person owing fiduciary duties who is accountable for profits made from his position'.[9]

The bank argued that a trust arose because it had 'retained' equitable title to the money paid, although legal title had passed to the local authority. Although there was authority supporting this analysis,[10] it is, as we have seen an example of the banana view of 'equitable property': the idea that someone with a right actually has two parallel rights, one at common law and another in Equity, that can be split. Lord Browne-Wilkinson clarified:

> A person solely entitled to the full beneficial ownership of money or property, both at law and in equity, does not enjoy an equitable interest in that property. The legal title carries with it all rights. Unless and until there is a separation of the legal and equitable estates, there is no separate equitable title. Therefore to talk about the bank 'retaining' its equitable interest is meaningless. The only question is whether the circumstances under which the

---

[6] *Latec Investments Ltd v Hotel Terrigel Pty Ltd* (1965) 113 CLR 265.
[7] P Millett, 'Restitution and Constructive Trusts' (1998) 114 LQR 399, 416.
[8] [1996] AC 669 (HL).
[9] *ibid*, 701.
[10] *Chase Manhattan Bank NA v Israel-British Bank (London) Ltd* [1981] Ch 105. *Cf. Re Berry* (1906) 147 F 208 (2nd Cir 1906); *Harper v Royal Bank of Canada* (1994) 18 OR (3d) 317, 114 DLR 749 (Div Ct).

money was paid were such as, in equity, to impose a trust on the local authority. If so, an equitable interest arose for the first time under that trust.[11]

The conclusion reached was that there could be no trust merely by virtue of payments having been made under a void contract, and therefore compound interest was unavailable. How is this to be explained?

The basis for understanding is, again, that a trust is obligational. A trust is not simply a duty to pay a particular sum of money, as is a contractual debt or (as we have seen) an obligation to return a payment to which the defendant was not entitled. Obligations of that kind can never be breached. An obligation to pay a sum of money always remains possible to perform (unlike an obligation to pay a sum of money on a specific date).

The necessary and sufficient obligation of a trustee, by contrast, is to refrain from using a particular right for one's own benefit. If a trustee uses the rights that are held on trust for his own benefit, he will be liable for breach of trust. This is so for all trustees. As we shall see, it is this obligation that creates the potential duty to account for profits,[12] and so is also the explanation for the availability of compound interest against trustees. Absent such an obligation, the award of compound interest without statutory authorisation is unjustifiable. Should someone who does not know the circumstances that may give rise to a trust (such as, in *Westdeutsche* itself, that the payments were made under contracts that were *ultra vires*) be potentially liable for breach of trust if they dissipate the trust assets? Lord Browne-Wilkinson concluded, correctly, that this was inappropriate:

> Since the equitable jurisdiction to enforce trusts depends upon the conscience of the holder of the legal interest being affected, he cannot be a trustee of the property as long as he is ignorant of the facts alleged to affect his conscience: ie until he is aware that he is intended to hold the property on trust for the benefit of others in the case of an express or implied trust, or, in the case of a constructive trust, of the factors which are alleged to affect his conscience.[13]

In the context of rescission, by contrast, the counterparty has been necessarily informed of the invalidity, and so a trust must have arisen at the latest from that point, if the right or its traceable proceeds are still vested in the defendant.

It should not, therefore, suffice for the imposition of a trust that a right is transferred to the defendant without justification. Authority to the contrary was based upon the misconception that we have two titles to a right, one at law and another in Equity, one of which can be 'retained' whilst the other is transferred.[14] There was no sufficient knowledge on the part of the defendant in *Westdeutsche*, at least before the judgment in *Hazell v Hammersmith*

---

[11] [1996] AC 669 (HL), 706. The reference to 'separation of the legal and equitable estates' is, however, misleading. See Chapter 12, Equity: General.
[12] Chapter 16, Profits.
[13] [1996] AC 669 (HL), 705 (Lord Slynn and Lord Lloyd agreeing). See also 689 *per* Lord Goff. See further *Bristol and West Building Society v Mothew* [1998] Ch 1 (CA), 23–24 *per* Millett LJ; *Bank of America v Arnell* [1999] Lloyd's Rep Bank 399; *Independent Trustee Services Ltd v GP Noble* [2012] EWCA Civ 195, [2013] Ch 91, [84] *per* Lloyd LJ. See also B McFarlane, 'Trusts and Knowledge: Lessons from Australia' in J Gleeson and P Ridge (eds), *Fault Lines in Equity* (2012), 170. But see W Swadling, 'Property and Conscience' (1998) 12 Trust Law Int'l 228; B Häcker, 'Proprietary Restitution after Impaired Consent Transfers: A Generalised Power Model' (2009) 68 CLJ 324.
[14] *Chase Manhattan Bank NA v Israel-British Bank (London) Ltd* [1981] Ch 105.

and *Fulham LBC*[15] that declared the contracts void. Again, it does not, however, follow that prior to such knowledge the payor has no interest at all in relation to the right the defendant has acquired. Rather, the recipient is, again, subject to a liability to be under a duty not to use it for his own benefit, and the payor has the correlative power to create it.[16] For purposes of interest, however, this should not suffice.

What if in cases of rescission the defendant knows from the outset that he is liable to make restitution, but is not yet so obliged? For example:

D fraudulently misrepresents to *P* the possible development purposes for which a portion of land to which *P* has title can be put. *P* agrees to sell the land to *D*, subsequently conveying title to him.

Although the obligation to make restitution of the title to the land can only arise upon rescission of the contract, should *D* be free to use his title to the land for his own benefit in the interim? *D* knows he obtained the title fraudulently and is liable to be under an obligation should *P* rescind. He should not therefore be so free from the outset. We may not wish to describe *D* as a trustee at that point,[17] as he should not be compellable to reconvey before rescission occurs. The position of *D* is analogous to that of a vendor in a vendor-purchaser constructive trust before payment has been made, or of a party who has granted another an option to purchase a particular right that has not yet been exercised, so that the obligation to convey has not yet arisen.[18]

It also follows that there can only be an obligation not to use identifiable rights for the defendant's benefit, and so a trust, if the right (or its traceable proceeds, see Section E) are retained by the defendant at the time at which knowledge of the facts sufficient to create the duty as trustee arises. If they are not so retained at the time of the exercise of any power to impose such a duty, no trust arises. In *Re Goldcorp Exchange Ltd*[19] investors had paid for gold bullion that the defendant company represented that it would store on their behalf. In fact, the company held insufficient stock to carry out its undertakings, and did not intend to do so. Upon the defendant's insolvency, the investors sought to bring claims in a variety of ways in order to obtain priority over the general security right granted to the defendant's bank. One way in which this was argued was that they were entitled to rescind for misrepresentation and assert an 'equitable proprietary right' in relation to the defendant's assets. However, amongst several other decisive objections, the inability of the investors to identify any rights transferred, or their traceable product, in the estate of the defendant was fatal to this argument. The defendant company could not hold on trust rights (or their traceable proceeds) they did not have.

The leading authority of a payment made without justification, where knowledge of this was subsequently acquired by the defendant, when the traceable proceeds of the right acquired could still be identified in their estate, is *Re Diplock's Estate*.[20] As we have seen, the

---

[15] [1992] 2 AC 1 (HL).
[16] *Cf. Birch v Blagrave* (1755) Amb 264, 27 ER 176; *Childers v Childers* (1857) 1 De G&J 482, 44 ER 810.
[17] *National Crime Agency v Robb* [2014] EWHC 4384 (Ch), [2015] Ch 520, [44]; *Vale v Steinmetz* [2021] EWCA Civ 1087, [16].
[18] Chapter 12, Equity: General.
[19] [1995] 1 AC 74 (PC).
[20] [1948] Ch 465 (CA).

case concerned a claim by the correct legatees to enforce an obligation to make restitution to a deceased's estate of payments that had been incorrectly made to the defendant charities. Were the charities simply under a personal obligation to make restitution to the estate, or did a trust also arise over the rights that they had acquired, upon their knowing of the mistake that had been made? This issue was not addressed by the House of Lords[21] (which confined itself to the issue of the standing of individual beneficiaries to bring suit to enforce obligations owed to the estate) but was considered by the Court of Appeal. Where the proceeds of the payment could still be traced (discussed in Section E), such as where the cheque paid on behalf of the estate had been deposited by the charities resulting in a bank account in credit that had not subsequently been withdrawn, the estate could, in equity, assert a 'proprietary right' in relation to such proceeds.[22] Just as with the personal claim, the trustee's obligation of restitution was owed in relation to the estate, not the legatees. The legatees, like the creditors of the estate, were not beneficiaries under a trust and were not seeking to assert any obligations owed to them directly.

Finally, in most situations where a payment has been made under an agreement, subject to a condition, that condition will relate to the payment, not to any rights acquired. No trust should or will therefore arise where the condition fails. This is best illustrated with an example:

> *D Ltd*, a furniture manufacturer and retailer, agrees to sell title to a *P* a green sofa, still to be manufactured, with title to pass upon delivery. A deposit of £100 is payable. *P* pays the deposit by transferring the title to £100 in cash. The following day, *D Ltd* ceases trading and subsequently goes into insolvent liquidation. The notes *P* paid with are the only ones in the cash register of *D Ltd*'s shop.

The deposit that *P* has paid was agreed to be conditional upon *D Ltd* supplying him with the sofas, and so he will have a claim for restitution of this sum. This however will be a personal claim, and he will have to prove in *D Ltd*'s liquidation alongside the other unsecured creditors. What of the right to the cash? Although the physical notes are still separate and identifiable, the transfer of title to the cash was not agreed to be conditional. After the cash was paid, *D Ltd* was free to treat the cash as its own. It was not agreed, either expressly or impliedly, that *D Ltd*'s title to the specific notes received was conditional upon the conveyance of a title to a green sofa. No trust will therefore arise, as it is the payment, not the transfer of title to the cash, that is agreed is subject to a condition.

At one time it was thought that if the recipient of the payment in such cases knows that his imminent insolvency will prevent him from performing, from that moment a trust would arise,[23] but this is incorrect as no agreed condition attached to the right acquired.[24] It should also not matter in this example if *P* was mistaken, whether as to *D*'s solvency or anything else, in paying the money.[25] *D* has unconditionally acquired the right to the cash for a good reason: that is what the contract between the parties stipulated.

---

[21] [1951] AC 251 (HL).
[22] [1948] Ch 465 (CA), 556–557.
[23] *Neste Oy v Lloyd's Bank Plc* [1983] 2 Lloyd's Rep 658 (Bingham J).
[24] *Re D&D Wines International Ltd* [2016] UKSC 47, [2016] 1 WLR 3179.
[25] *Cf. ibid*, [32] *per* Lord Sumption. *In re Farepack Food and Gifts Ltd* [2006] EWHC 3272 (Ch), [2008] BCC 22, [39]–[40] *per* Mann J.

A question that the House of Lords did not need to resolve in *Westdeutsche* was whether a trust would ever arise on the facts upon the recipient knowing that it lacked the capacity to enter into such contracts. Again, if we take seriously the orthodoxy that the contracts were void because of the council's lack of capacity, the acquisition of the right from the bank was unjustified, and from the moment of such knowledge should not be used by the recipient council for its own benefit. However, in principle, as with children, the effect of such incapacity should render an agreement merely unenforceable.[26] If this is so, then no trust should ever arise, the acquisition of the right being justified because of the agreement between them and being subject to no agreed condition that had failed.

B. Presumptions of Advancement and of Resulting Trust

The standard textbook account goes like this.[27] Where title to a thing is transferred from *A* to *B* without explanation, or purchased by *A* in the name of *B*, the title acquired by *B* will, because of a presumption, be held on resulting trust for *A*. By contrast where *A* is *B*'s husband or father, the presumption of advancement operates, so that there is presumed to be a gift of the title.

However, it cannot be that both presumptions exist. Either there is a presumption of advancement (ie a presumption of the facts necessary to constitute a gift) or there is a presumption of a trust (ie a presumption of the facts necessary to constitute a trust). There cannot be both. One of these 'presumptions' is otiose.

That there exists a presumption of resulting trust is supported by the now obsolete decision of the House of Lords in *Tinsley v Milligan*.[28] The plaintiff and defendant both contributed towards the purchase of title to a house, the conveyance of title to which was to the plaintiff alone. They lived together in the property as their family home, but pretended that the defendant was a lodger in order to enable the defendant to defraud the Department of Social Security of benefits to which she was not entitled. After they fell out, and the plaintiff moved out, she brought an action for possession, and the defendant counterclaimed that the title to the house was held on resulting trust in proportion to her contribution to its acquisition. At the time, the traditional approach to illegality in private law still prevailed in England. The defendant did not have to rely upon her illegal conduct as showing that the plaintiff's sole title had been acquired (in part) from her contribution to its acquisition, but instead succeeded upon the basis of a presumption of resulting trust.

What fact is being presumed? Three views have been defended, all of which have some support in the case law, but all of which are either normatively or descriptively problematic.

The first, and narrowest view, is that the fact presumed is a declaration of trust.[29] This gains support from the view of Lord Browne-Wilkinson in *Westdeutsche* that the presumption can be rebutted by evidence that what was intended was inconsistent with there being a declaration of trust.[30] On this view not only would evidence of a gift rebut the presumption, but so too would evidence that any transfer was made by mistake. This view is however

---

[26] See Chapter 18, Defences.
[27] Eg J Glister and J Lee, *Hanbury and Martin, Modern Equity* (21st edn, 2021), 226–240.
[28] [1994] 1 AC 340 (HL). See further Chapter 19, Illegality.
[29] W Swadling, 'Explaining Resulting Trusts' (2008) 124 LQR 72.
[30] [1996] AC 669 (HL), 708.

difficult to reconcile with those cases where a presumed resulting trust arises where the recipient lacked the capacity to declare an express trust.[31]

Second is that what is intended is a trust, albeit not a declaration of one.[32] The difficulty is that, absent a declaration, why should a trust arise at all absent either the proof or presumption of the facts that are ordinarily thought to create one? There is, today, some English authority for the creation of trusts based upon intentions as to 'ownership' other than those expressly declared, but they are usually thought to be confined to cases of quasi-matrimonial disputes.[33]

Third, it has been claimed that the fact presumed is either that there was no intention to benefit the recipient[34] or that there was no reason for the recipient's acquisition of the right.[35] Again however, proof of such a fact should not alone suffice for the creation of a trust, absent knowledge on the part of the recipient.

The first of the three views is probably therefore the most readily defensible, but the presumption is so weak, merely a 'long stop',[36] that it should rarely apply in practice whichever view is now adopted.[37] The conclusion that the fact proved by presumption is a declaration of trust is not determinative of the question of when and why trusts arise absent such declaration. As *Re Diplock* and other examples show, (constructive) trusts (resulting) back to the transferor do not necessarily depend upon the making of a declaration of trust, and the fact that there was no such declaration does not prevent one from arising for other reasons.

C. Knowing Receipt of Trust Property

Returning to the first example with which we began the previous chapter:

> *T* holds a title to a quantity of valuable antique furniture on trust. One of the beneficiaries is *P*. In breach of trust, *T* gives the title to the furniture to *D*. *D* no longer has the furniture, having given his title to it away to charity.

There should be no possibility of a claim by *P* against *D* based upon the line of authority exemplified by *Kelly v Solari*[38] in such a case. There has been no unjustified performance between them that is susceptible to reversal. Similarly, *P* had no right to the furniture itself, and so no claim based upon conversion or equivalent, exemplified by *Lipkin Gorman v Karpnale*,[39] is possible.

It may, however, be possible to show that *D* had come under a duty not to use the title to the furniture he had acquired for his own benefit. If *D* knows, either initially or subsequently,[40] that the gift to him was made in breach of trust by *T* then from the moment of

---

[31] *Re Vinogradoff* [1935] WN 68.
[32] J Mee, 'Presumed Resulting Trusts, Intention and Declaration' [2014] CLJ 86.
[33] *Stack v Dowden* [2007] UKHL 17 [2007] 2 AC 432.
[34] R Chambers, *Resulting Trusts* (1997).
[35] R Chambers, 'Is there a Presumption of Resulting Trust?' in C Mitchell (ed), *Constructive and Resulting Trusts* (2010).
[36] *Vandervell v IRC* [1967] 2 AC 291, 313 *per* Lord Upjohn.
[37] But see *Prest v Petrodel* [2013] UKSC 34, [2013] 2 AC 415.
[38] (1841) 9 M&W 54, 152 ER 24.
[39] [1991] 2 AC 548 (HL).
[40] *Agip (Africa) Ltd v Jackson* [1990] 1 Ch 265, 291 *per* Millett J; *Byers v Samba* [2022] EWCA Civ 43, [19].

such knowledge he ought not to use the title to the furniture he then has for his own benefit. If he acquires such knowledge before giving away the title to the furniture to charity, then his actions in so doing were a breach of trust. In such a case he ought to be liable to account for the value of the trust assets that he has disposed of. P's claim against him would then be of the form 'you are obliged to hold title to antique furniture of the value of £x on trust, either do so or, if you cannot, you must hold £x on trust'.

Where therefore D has acquired knowledge of the circumstances that require him not to use the rights he now has for his own benefit, *either* today he must still hold the rights on trust for the beneficiaries, *or* where he has disposed of the rights after acquiring such knowledge he is in breach of trust.[41] Once the facts necessary to give rise to the trust have been proven therefore, it should not be necessary for the plaintiff to plead and prove one or the other in order to ensure that the recipient is liable for the value of the trust rights, as he would still be liable to account regardless of any such breach by disposal.[42] The usual formulation is that the defendant recipient is 'liable to account as a constructive trustee'. Similarly, unless the defendant is insolvent, there is no need to show that he still has the right that ought to be held on trust or its traceable proceeds. The standard of liability of the trustee is strict, just as it is for express trustees, but knowledge is a necessary condition of being a trustee.[43]

The rule that the defendant must have knowledge of the circumstances that require him not to use rights he now has for his own benefit is the same condition as Lord Browne-Wilkinson relied upon in *Westdeutsche Landesbank v Islington London Borough Council*.[44] The traditional label for such claims is 'knowing receipt' although that is misleading as knowledge acquired after receipt suffices, so long as the rights acquired or their traceable proceeds subsist at that time. 'Receipt' also misleadingly implies that the claim is analogous to the common law 'receipt' based claims we saw in *Kelly v Solari* and *Lipkin Gorman v Karpnale*.

It is also perhaps unfortunate that this form of liability has been yoked with that for 'knowing assistance', which is a form of accessory liability imposed upon third parties to the breach of duty of fiduciaries, independent of the defendant acquiring any right that they are not free to use. Only 'knowing receipt' truly involves liability as a trustee, and because the right acquired by the recipient may be one he still has, involves no necessary assertion of wrongdoing.

In England, the above account was the understanding of the law at the time of *Re Montagu's Settlement Trusts*,[45] which held that knowledge was a pre-condition of the recipient defendant's liability. Megarry VC stated that the 'cold calculus of constructive and imputed notice does not seem to me to be an appropriate instrument for deciding whether

---

[41] S Gardner, 'Moment of Truth for Knowing Receipt?' (2009) 125 LQR 20; C Mitchell and S Watterson, 'Remedies for Knowing Receipt' in C Mitchell (ed), *Constructive and Resulting Trusts* (2010), 115; R Chambers, 'The End of Knowing Receipt' (2016) 2 Can J of Comparative and Contemporary Law 1. But see W Swadling, 'The Nature of Knowing Receipt' in P Davies and J Penner (eds), *Equity, Trusts and Commerce* (2017), 303.
[42] Mitchell and Watterson, 'Remedies for Knowing Receipt' (n 41), 115.
[43] *DD Growth Premium 2X Fund v RMF Market Neutral Strategies* [2017] UKPC 36, [2018] Bus LR 1595, [58], 'a custodial liability comparable to that of an express trustee' per Lords Sumption and Briggs.
[44] [1996] AC 669. *Cf. Green v Weatherill* [1929] 2 Ch 213, 222–223 *per* Maugham J.
[45] [1987] Ch 264. See also *Bate v Hooper* (1855) 5 De GM & G 338, 43 ER 901; *El Ajou v Dollar Land Holdings* [1994] BCC 143 (CA), 154 *per* Hoffmann LJ.

a man's conscience is sufficiently affected for it to be right to bind him by the obligations of a constructive trustee'.[46]

Unfortunately, in England the position has now become obscured because the courts have confused cases concerned with knowing receipt of trust property with simple claims for the return of payments made that were not due. An example:

P pays D £1,000 in cash, mistakenly believing that he owes D this sum. D knows of this mistake from the outset. D spends the cash on drink, that he consumes.

If, as has been argued, from the moment D knows that the payment was without justification, he held the title to the cash on trust for P, and should be liable for breach of trust in using the right so held for his own benefit. However, the quantification of any such claim for breach of trust seems, without more, to be the same as that for restitution of the sum mistakenly paid, and so adds little to the analysis. It should make no difference if P is a company, P Ltd, and that the directors have acted in breach of their fiduciary duties in making the payment. A claim for 'knowing receipt' is otiose here.

The leading English decision on 'knowing receipt' is today usually thought to be that of the Court of Appeal in *Bank of Credit and Commerce International (Overseas) Ltd v Akindele*.[47] The directors of the claimant companies pursued a fraudulent scheme to boost the impression of capital in the eyes of regulators, depositors, and the public. To this end, ICIC (Overseas) Ltd (ICIC) entered into agreements with the defendant Chief Akindele, under which in return for an initial payment of $10 million, he would eventually be repaid $16.8 million three years later, a compounded interest rate of 15%, far higher than any investments available to the defendant elsewhere. BCCI (Overseas) Ltd (BCCI), another company in the same group, paid Chief Akindele what he was owed under the contract, apparently on behalf of ICIC. Upon their subsequent insolvency, the claimant companies both sought to recover the $6.8 million balance on the basis of either the defendant's dishonest assistance in the (undoubted) breach by the directors of their fiduciary duties, or on the basis of knowing receipt of the defendant's assets transferred in breach of fiduciary duty.

The claim for dishonest assistance failed on the basis that dishonesty could not be proven. The claim also failed in relation to knowing receipt on the basis that the counterparty only had knowledge as to the BCCI group's general poor commercial reputation, and did not have any basis for thinking the particular transaction was tainted and that the very generous interest rate return was not such as to render it 'unconscionable' for him to receive the payments. The 'unconscionability' test seems to fall somewhere short of Megarry V-C's test of knowledge, whilst providing little guidance as to what precisely constitutes 'unconscionability'. Because the claim in *BCCI v Akindele* failed, the statements as to whether something less than actual knowledge sufficed are *obiter dicta* but the 'unconscionability' test has been applied subsequently.[48]

Courts are constrained by the way in which the case before them is presented, and there seems to have been a misunderstanding by counsel responsible for pleading the claim as

---

[46] [1987] Ch 264, 285.
[47] [2001] Ch 437 (CA); cf. *Citadel General Assurance Co v Lloyd's Bank Canada* [1997] 3 SCR 805.
[48] *Charter plc v City Index Ltd* [2007] EWCA Civ 1382, [2008] Ch 313; *Templeton Insurance Ltd v Brunswick* [2012] EWHC 1522 (Ch) [79]–[83]; *Byers v Samba* [2022] EWCA Civ 43, [18].

to how it ought to have been set out. Should it have been the counterparty to the contract (ICIC), the party from whom the funds had directly come (BCCI), or both who had a claim?[49] What was the correct basis for any claim they had?

If the contract between the ICIC and Chief Akindele had been invalid, ICIC should have had a claim for restitution of any payments they had made under it.[50] The issue of validity is a question of whether the directors had the actual or ostensible authority to enter into the contract. This is properly a question of agency law. As directors do not have the authority to commit fraud, the issue reduces to the question of whether the counterparty knew or ought to known of the lack of authority. If the counterparty ought to know of the lack of actual authority, the contract is invalid, even if the counterparty is not actually aware of this fact. The validity question is separate from that of whether the directors were in breach of their fiduciary duties.

The claim by ICIC should therefore have been pleaded as one for restitution of $6.8 million that the claimant had paid the defendant under a contract invalid because of the lack of authority of the directors to enter into it, ICIC having paid through its agent BCCI. Such a claim would not be, as in *Re Montagu's Settlement Trust*, by a beneficiary seeking to reconstitute a trust fund. It should be unnecessary to show that the defendant knew of the lack of entitlement, closed his eyes to the truth, was recklessly indifferent, careless as to the true state of affairs, or otherwise behaving 'unconscionably'. *If* his counterparty had paid him $6.8 million the correct question should have been whether Chief Akindele was entitled to the payment made to him or not. Whether the (extraordinarily generous) terms of the loan contract, giving him a return far higher than that available elsewhere, meant that Chief Akindele ought to have known that the directors lacked the apparent authority to enter into such a contract was a question of fact. If the contract between ICIC and Chief Akindele was, as found, valid, there should be no claim for repayment, and *a fortiori* no claim that any proceeds were held on trust so as to potentially give rise to a claim for 'knowing receipt'.[51]

But did ICIC pay Chief Akindele anything? If ICIC had validly authorised BCCI to pay on its behalf, ICIC would indeed have so paid and it would have been the correct plaintiff. ICIC would have paid the defendant, through its agent, and BCCI would be rendering its performance to ICIC. BCCI would then have no claim against Chief Akindele, but only a claim for reimbursement from ICIC, for whom it was paying.[52]

However, the directors of ICIC never had any authority to mandate such a payment on their company's behalf. The whole scheme was a fraud. BCCI also knew that the directors never had authority to authorise the fraudulent payment made on ICIC's behalf, the directors of both companies being the same people. The payment made by BCCI was never therefore validly authorised by ICIC. This remained so despite the subsequent refunding of BCCI by ICIC.

Regardless of the validity of the contract between ICIC and Chief Akindele, therefore, as between BCCI and Chief Akindele, the former had paid the latter $16.8 million without justification, there being no contract between them. If (as the Court of Appeal seem to have

---

[49] *Cf.* M Conaglen and R Nolan, 'Contracts and Knowing Receipt: Principles and Application' (2013) 129 LQR 359.
[50] *Criterion Properties plc v Stratford UK Properties LLC* [2004] UKHL 28, [2004] 1 WLR 1846, [4] *per* Lord Nicholls.
[51] ibid.
[52] See *Aiken v Short* (1856) 1 H & N 210, 156 ER 1180, discussed in Chapter 3, Performance.

assumed) the contract between ICIC and Chief Akindele was valid, could the defendant keep the payment on the basis that the payment by BCCI had discharged an obligation owed to him by ICIC? In the United States, the answer would be yes.[53] This is on the basis that an unauthorised payment can discharge another's obligation, and bona fide creditors are given a specific defence as a result. By contrast, in England, as we have seen, payments by a third party do not thereby discharge obligations when unauthorised.[54] No such defence therefore exists. The obligation of ICIC to pay the defendant $16.8 million would never have been performed, and the debt was undischarged.

Should, therefore, BCCI have been awarded restitution of the payment made by it, which on its face was one to which Chief Akindele had no entitlement with respect to them? In most common law jurisdictions, and in England until recently, the answer may still have been 'no' on the basis of the maxim *ex turpi causa non oritur actio*.[55] As BCCI would have to rely, in making out the claim, upon the fraud of its directors, which would be attributed to it, this should rule out success. As we shall see, in England today the operation of the illegality rule is now unclear.

The result reached in *Bank of Credit and Commerce International (Overseas) Ltd v Akindele*, that there was no claim by either BCCI or ICIC, was therefore, defensible, but it was not a case that should have been analysed in terms of 'knowing receipt'.[56] If there had been a claim by either claimant, it should not have been necessary for such a claim to show that Chief Akindele knew of the fraud but that is because the claim was not properly one for 'knowing receipt of trust property' which in England has been employed beyond its proper bounds.

The correct analysis became clear after the decision of the House of Lords in *Criterion Properties plc v Stratford UK Properties LLC*.[57] The claimant company entered into a partnership agreement with the defendant for the purpose of investing in real property. The agreement created a new company in which both parties held shares. By a separate agreement, the claimant granted the defendant a 'put option', requiring the claimant to buy the defendant's interest in the new company upon the happening of certain events. The events were any change in the control of the claimant or either of the two signatory directors ceasing to be directors of the company. The purpose of the put option was to inflict adverse financial consequences on the claimant company should it be subject to a hostile takeover, but it would also prevent or inhibit the dismissal of the two directors who signed the deal. Such a transaction is commonly termed a 'poison pill'. One of the two directors was dismissed, possibly because of his having agreed to the put option. The claimant sought a declaration by way of summary judgment that the put option was unenforceable. As no performance had in fact been rendered, this was not a claim for restitution at all. In answering the question posed, the courts, up to and including the Court of Appeal, had considered

---

[53] A Kull, *Restatement of the Law (Third) Restitution and Unjust Enrichment*, vol I (2010), see §§ 22–25, along with commentary and illustrations.
[54] *Belshaw v Bush* (1851) 11 CB 191, 138 ER 444; *Simpson v Eggington* (1855) 10 Ex 845, 847, 156 ER 683, 684 *per* Parke B; *Walter v James* (1870–1871) LR 6 Ex 124; *Barclays Bank Ltd v WJ Simms, Son and Cooke (Southern) Ltd* [1980] QB 677 (Goff J); *Electricity Supply Nominees Ltd v Thorn EMI Retail Ltd* (1991) 63 P&CR 143 (CA), 148 *per* Fox LJ; *Crantrave Ltd v Lloyd's Bank plc* [2000] QB 917 (CA).
[55] Discussed in Chapter 19.
[56] *Contra* M Conaglen and R Nolan, 'Contracts and Knowing Receipt: Principles and Application' (2013) 129 LQR, 359, 372–374
[57] [2004] UKHL 28, [2004] 1 WLR 1846.

that the question should be answered in the same way as a claim for knowing receipt of trust property, applying a test of 'unconscionability'. As explained by Lord Nicholls, however, the correct issue was the actual or ostensible authority of the directors to enter into any such contract. If there is no such actual or ostensible authority, any payments made would have been recoverable.[58] If there is no reason for the payment, it is recoverable by the payor from the payee. Knowledge is only a condition for the imposition of a trust.

This does not mean that 'knowing receipt' is never relevant in cases of misdirected payments by company directors. It is most important where a defendant is not a party to whom the claimant has made a payment. An example where it was necessary for the result is *Belmont Finance Corpn v Williams Furniture Ltd (No 2)*.[59] The plaintiff company, Belmont, paid £500,000 to purchase shares in another company. The payment was not in fact at the full value of the shares bought but was made in order to provide the owner of the purchased company with the funds to purchase the shareholding of the plaintiff. Of the £500,000 paid, proceeds of £489,000 was then used to purchase these shares from their owner, City Industrial Finance Ltd. This contravened the statutory prohibition of a company providing financial assistance for the purchase of shares in itself that was then in force. In addition to various claims by the plaintiff against the payee and others, a claim was also brought against the previous owner of the shares, City, for the £489,000 that they had indirectly received. The purported contract for the purchase of shares at an undervalue was invalid, as was the purported contract for the purchase of the Belmont shares from the defendant, City. The payment traceably received by City with knowledge[60] of the unlawful scheme meant that they were accountable as a constructive trustee for its value. As the necessary knowledge was present from the outset, it was unnecessary to plead or prove what had happened to the sums paid: either it remained, in which case it was held on trust, or it had been disposed of, in which case there was liability for breach.

D. Purchase without Notice

Once it is accepted that beneficiaries under a trust have a right in relation to a right vested in the trustee, the curious feature of Equity is that it will allow the beneficiaries' right to be asserted against another who acquires the trustee's right from the trustee. This generosity of protection has limits, however, and where the third party has given value without notice of the claimant's 'equitable property right', his subsequent knowledge of the prior existence of such a right will not enable it to be asserted against him.[61] The special feature of Equity is not therefore the existence of the bona fide purchase for value rule, but rather the rule to which it is an exception.

Although usually described as a defence of bona fide purchase for value, it is clear that the necessary condition is merely lack of notice of the right of the beneficiary.[62] There will be no defence where the defendant ought to have known. Usually, however, the enquiries the purchaser ought to have engaged in, such as where a shop accepts a cash payment, will be none.

---

[58] *ibid*, [3]–[4].
[59] [1980] 1 All ER 393.
[60] *ibid*, 405.
[61] *Byers v Samba* [2022] EWCA Civ 43.
[62] But see *Midland Bank Ltd v Green* [1981] AC 513 (HL), 528 *per* Lord Wilberforce.

In relation to the purchase of title to land the defence at one time had much greater scope for operation, but in that context it has now been almost entirely superseded by statutory protections whereby a purchaser usually takes free of unregistered equitable rights.[63]

In *Credit Agricole Corp & Investment Bank v Papadimitrou* Lord Sumption stated that '[w]hether a person claims to be a bona fide purchaser of assets without notice of a prior interest in them, or disputes a claim to make him a constructive trustee on the footing of knowing receipt, the question of what constitutes notice or knowledge is the same'.[64] This is an unfortunate elision of two distinct concepts. In order to impose the custodial duty of trusteeship upon a recipient, knowledge of the circumstances justifying such duty should be required. It needs to be pleaded and proven by the party asserting such knowledge. As we have seen, the knowledge necessary for the imposition of this duty may arise *after* the moment of receipt. By contrast, bona fide purchase for value of the right held on trust is a defence that it is for the defendant to assert. If proven it prevents the beneficiaries from continuing to asset their rights in relation to the rights received. For this purpose, the question of notice, not knowledge, is assessed at time of acquisition.[65] Further another party acquiring from a purchaser without notice acquires a right that is no longer subject to the beneficiary's right, and so can come under no duty to him, regardless of his state of knowledge at the time of acquisition or subsequently.[66] Lord Sumption's unfortunate amalgamation of the two separate questions would lead to 'knowing receipt' becoming akin to a form of negligence liability for economic loss.

The value given by the purchaser need not be full value, indeed it may be a small fraction of the value of the rights held on trust, leaving the defendant greatly enriched.[67] However, the consideration for the right received must not only be paid but paid in full.[68] The rule here is therefore narrower than in relation to the purchase of title to cash, where a mere promise to pay suffices for the prior title to the cash to be lost. This is important for banks, as it means where stolen cash is deposited all prior titles to it will be extinguished, regardless of whether anything more than a contractual promise is given in exchange. This will also defeat any pre-existing right in equity because the bank's right to the cash is not derived from the person from whom it obtained possession, but is a new right as a result of its good faith purchase.[69] Another illustration that rights are held on trust, not things.

Finally, there is authority for the proposition that the defence only applies where what is acquired by the defendant is a legal right. A purchaser of an equitable right that is held under a sub-trust would therefore have no defence on this view.[70] This seems incorrect,

---

[63] Land Registration Act 2002 for registered land. Land Charges Act 1972 for unregistered land.
[64] [2015] UKPC 13, [2015] 1 WLR 4265, [33].
[65] *Willoughby v Willoughby* (1756) 1 TR 771, 28 ER 437 *per* Lord Hardwicke; *Burgess v Wheate* (1759) 1 Eden 177, 195, *per* Sir T Clarke, 246 *per* Lord Henley; *Jones v Powles* (1834) 3 Myl & K 581, 40 ER 222; *Thorndike v Hunt* (1859) 3 De G & J 563 44 ER 1386; *Pilcher v Rawlins* (1871–1872) 7 Ch App 259 (CA); *Heath v Crealock* (1874) 10 Ch App 22; *Waldy v Gray* (1875) LR 20 Eq 238; *Taylor v Blakelock* (1886) 32 ChD 560 (CA).
[66] *Salsbury v Bagott* (1677) 2 Sw 603, 608, 36 ER 745, 747; *Lowther v Carlton* (1741) 2 Atk 242, 26 ER 549; *Mertins v Jolliffe* (1756) Amb 311, 313, 27 ER 211, 212 *per* Lord Hardwicke; *Sweet v Southcote* (1786) 2 BroCC 66, 29 ER 38; *M'Queen v Farquhar* (1805) 11 Ves Jr 467, 32 ER 1168 *per* Lord Eldon; *Burrow's Case* (1880) 14 ChD 432 (CA). Unless the party so acquiring is the original trustee, whose duty as trustee then revives: *Re Stapleford Colliery Co, Barrow's Case* (1880) 14 ChD 432, 445 *per* Jessel MR; *West London Commercial Bank v Reliance Building Society* (1885) 29 ChD 954 (CA).
[67] Eg *Midland Bank Trust Co Ltd v Green* [1981] AC 513 (HL).
[68] *Story v Windsor* (1743) 2 Atk 630, 26 ER 776.
[69] L Smith, 'Unjust Enrichment, Property and the Structure of Trusts' (2002) 116 LQR 412 (at fn 91).
[70] *Pilcher v Rawlins* (1871–1872) 7 Ch App 259 (CA), 269 *per* James LJ but see A Reilly, 'Does 'Equity's Darling' Need a Legal Title? Reassessing *Pilcher v Rawlins*' (2016) 10 J of Eq 89.

and a confusion with a quite separate rule. Where competing equitable rights are created in relation to the same subject matter (eg successive charges are created by a company) their priority is generally determined by order of creation. Second charges do not take priority simply because the second chargee has given value. However, the second chargee has not acquired the right that is the subject matter of the prior equitable interest, but has rather obtained a second equitable right in relation to it.

E. 'Tracing'

1. Substitution

An example:

> *T* holds a title to a quantity of valuable antique furniture on trust. One of the beneficiaries is *P*. *T*, in breach of trust, exchanges the title to the furniture for a title to a jade chess set.

What ought *T* be obliged to do in such a situation?[71]

T ought to be obliged to reconstitute the trust with a monetary equivalent to the value of the title to the furniture. If the title to the chess set is in fact worthless, it is this that the beneficiaries will seek to require *T* to do. If the right to the chess set is greater in value than that of the furniture then he also ought, in the alternative, to be obliged to account for its greater value, rather than keep it for himself. What, however, of the right to the specific chess set he has obtained in exchange for the right he ought to still be holding on trust? Should he be free to use that for his own benefit?

Again, why should the trustee be the one who chooses whether he should enjoy the title to the chess set? Further if he dissipates the right he has obtained there will be an increased likelihood that he will not be able (through bankruptcy) to reconstitute the trust or account for the value of what he has obtained. The trustee should be under a duty not only to account for the value of the rights obtained in unauthorised exchange, but also not to use the specific rights so obtained for his own benefit.[72]

The trustee's duty here is one of next best compliance. The reasons justifying the original obligation do not disappear when they can no longer be perfectly complied with. The reasons persist and create a new obligation. He ought not to have exchanged the title to the furniture but, given that he has, he ought now to do the nearest thing to complying with his original duty. This duty includes, at the beneficiaries' option, not using the right he has obtained in exchange for his own benefit. The choice as to what he must now do in order to comply as nearly as possible with his original duty (eg simply reconstitute the trust fund with a monetary equivalent to the dispersal, or not use the right he has acquired with trust assets for his own benefit) should be that of the beneficiaries.

---

[71] L Smith, *The Law of Tracing* (1997) remains indispensable. The analysis here accords most closely with J English and J Hafeez-Baig, *The Law of Tracing* (2021). See also M Raczynska, *The Law of Tracing in Commercial Transactions* (2018); A Nair, *Claims to Traceable Proceeds: Law, Equity and the Control of Assets* (2018).
[72] *Cf.* C Mitchell, P Mitchell, and S Watterson (eds), *Goff & Jones: The Law of Unjust Enrichment* (9th edn, 2016), [8–162]; L Smith, 'Equity Is Not a Single Thing' in D Klimchuk, I Samet, and H Smith (eds), *Philosophical Foundations of the Law of Equity* (2020), 166.

In contrast to the position at common law, therefore, the obligational nature of the trust explains why beneficiaries may assert their rights in relation to the substitute for the subject matter of their original rights. Further it does not and should not matter whether the original obligation arises because of the settlement of an express trust or for one of the diverse other reasons we have seen so far for the creation of trusts. The trustee ought not to use the unauthorised substitute right for his own benefit, and so it too is held on trust. This explanation conforms with that given by the courts, who have not invoked reasons other than those which applied to the creation of the original trust in justifying the trust over the substitute.[73]

The same analysis applies to other forms of 'equitable property right.' For example:

D agrees to grant P Bank a first fixed charge over D's title to a quantity of antique furniture in exchange for a loan. Without P Bank's permission, D sells his title to the furniture to X for £20,000 in cash.

D ought now to hold the right to the cash by way of security for P Bank: a fixed charge over the proceeds of sale.[74]

Sometimes, a would-be trustee is never capable of perfectly complying with the reasons for his obligation. For example:

T holds a title to a quantity of valuable antique furniture on trust. One of the beneficiaries is P. T, in breach of trust, gives the title to the furniture to D. D, unaware that T transferred title to him in breach of trust, sells it to X for £20,000 in cash.

If D had been aware from the outset that he had obtained title to furniture that was subject to a trust, then from that moment he came under a duty not to use it for his own benefit.[75] What, however, of the situation where he only acquires such knowledge after disposition? Here, it is too late to comply with such an obligation in relation to the title to the furniture but he is now under a duty of next-best compliance. That entails a duty not to use the substitute (the right to the cash) for his own benefit. A trust therefore arises, even though D was never under any duty in relation to the title to the furniture. This illustrates that the beneficiary's entitlement in relation to the substitute is not dependent upon any wrongdoing, as here the party who exchanged the right to the furniture for that to the cash committed no wrong. The same analysis justifies the result, if not the reasoning, of the decision of the Court of Appeal in *Trustee of the Property of FC Jones & Sons v Jones*[76] considered previously in Chapter 11, Things.

This explanation also justifies why the courts have, somewhat loosely, stated that before it is possible to trace in Equity it is necessary to establish that the party substituting one right for another was subject to a 'fiduciary relationship'.[77] The obligation not to use rights for one's own benefit is a prerequisite of asserting a right in relation to substitute rights.

---

[73] See eg *Foskett v McKeown* [2001] 1 AC 102 (HL), 108 *per* Lord Browne-Wilkinson, 127 *per* Lord Millett.
[74] *Buhr v Barclays Bank plc* [2001] EWCA Civ 1223.
[75] *ITS v Noble* [2012] EWCA Civ 95, [2013] Ch 91, [76] *per* Lloyd LJ.
[76] [1997] Ch 159.
[77] *Agip (Africa) Ltd v Jackson* [1991] Ch 547 (CA), 566 *per* Fox LJ; *Shalson v Russo* [2003] EWHC 1637 (Ch), [2005] Ch 281, [102]–[104] *per* Rimer J. *Cf. Foskett v McKeown* [2001] 1 AC 102 (HL), 128–129 *per* Lord Millett.

Once the reasons for the creation of a trust have been established, those reasons will suffice to generate a trust over substitute rights. Reasons sufficient for the creation of a trust must however be established first.

This poses no difficulties provided that we do not have an overly narrow conception of what a trust is, and when one arises. For example:

D steals £100 in cash from P's possession. D uses the cash to buy a title to a watch from X.

At common law, the title to the watch is D's, as X has conveyed his title to D. How then is there any space for a trust, so as to permit P any entitlement in relation to the exchanged title to the watch?

Although P did not lose his title to the cash through the theft, D did acquire *a* title, that of a thief. Should he be free to use *that* title for his own benefit? No, he ought to surrender it by returning possession of the cash. If that is correct, a thief is a trustee of the title he acquires through possession, and there is Australian[78] and US[79] authority to this effect. When therefore the thief uses his title to acquire title to another thing, he ought to hold that new title for the beneficiary: a trust.[80]

The language of 'tracing' to capture these cases is probably (today) inescapable, but it is a metaphor that can lead to confusion. 'Trace' is a transitive verb. What is its object? When, as a child, we trace the outline of a drawing, the original image persists in our new drawing. What object is persisting?

Two answers are common. One is to suggest that the 'property right' persists.[81] This is unobjectionable if it is understood that 'property right' is being used in a specific sense. As we have seen, at common law (as in civilian systems), it is not understandable how it is possible to become, without more ado, entitled to a thing for which your title to a thing has been exchanged. To think that because 'tracing' is possible in relation to 'equitable property' therefore it must be possible in relation to proprietary rights at common law, the latter being in a sense the greater thing out of which the former are carved, is an example of the failure to understand the profound conceptual difference between the different meanings of 'property rights'. In Equity, what is persisting is the reason(s) for the duty not to use a particular right for the obligor's own benefit. What changes is the subject matter of that duty.

Another answer is to say that what is 'traced' is value, and this is commonly associated with the claim that tracing is an aspect of unjust enrichment.[82] However, the value of the original right (eg the title to furniture) may have no relation at all to that of the substitute (eg the title to £20,000 cash for which it is exchanged).[83] Indeed, it should not matter for the analysis whether either the original right or its substitute is valueless. How or why the

---

[78] *Black v S Freedman & Co* (1910) 12 CLR 105, 110; *Creak v James Moore & Sons Pty Ltd* (1912) 15 CLR 426; *Grimaldi v Chameleon Mining (No 2)* (2012) 200 FCR 296, [255]. In England, judicial statements are less clear: *Westdeutsche Landesbank Girozentrale v Islington London Borough Council* [1996]AC 669, 716 *per* Lord Browne-Wilkinson; *Collings v Lee* [2001] 2 All ER 332 (CA), 337 *per* Nourse LJ; *Halley v Law Society* [2003] EWCA Civ 97, [45]–[56] *per* Carnwath LJ; *Re D&D Wines International Ltd* [2016] UKSC 47, [2016] 1 WLR 3179, [30] *per* Lord Sumption. Compare *Shalson v Russo* [2003] EWHC 1637 (Ch), [2005] Ch 281, [108]–[119] *per* Rimer J.
[79] *Chase v Porter* (1877) 69 NY 133.
[80] *Cf.* R Chambers 'Trust and Theft' in E Bant and M Harding (eds), *Exploring Private Law* (2010),ch 10.
[81] Eg A T Denning, 'The Recovery of Money' (1949) 65 LQR 37, 39.
[82] Eg Smith, *The Law of Tracing* (n 71), 119. See also *Foskett v McKeown* [2001] 1 AC 102 (HL), 128 *per* Lord Millett.
[83] T Cutts, 'Tracing, Value and Transactions' (2016) 79 MLR 381.

value moves from one right to the other is also unclear. The value of a right is not, to co-opt a metaphor of Birks, like a leech attached to one thing, but detachable ready to sink its head into the flesh of a passing right for which its original host is substituted.[84] The subject matter of a trust is not 'value'; if it were there would merely be a personal claim.

The language of 'tracing' which implies that something (property? value?) is subsisting as one right is substituted for another, is one possible source of the hostility towards so-called 'backwards' tracing. An example:

> T, a trustee, buys a title to Blackacre using a loan of £100,000 from *Big Bank plc* secured with a legal mortgage. In breach of trust, T repays the loan from funds that he holds on trust. One of the beneficiaries of the trust is P.

What ought T's duty in relation to the title to Blackacre to be? If T had directly used the trust fund to purchase the title to the land, then there would appear to be no difficulty with saying that T ought to hold the substituted right on trust. Here, however, the right to Blackacre was acquired before the breach of trust (indeed it may have been acquired before T became a trustee at all). Should this make any difference?

The language of 'tracing' misleads us into thinking that something the beneficiaries already had (property? value?) is persisting when it causes the acquisition of something else. Like a leech, it is latching on to the substitute as it passes. Where, as here, the acquisition of Blackacre is acquired *before* the dissipation of the trust estate, this seems impossible to apply.

There is, however, no problem analytically with 'backwards tracing' once we put to one side the misleading metaphor 'tracing' seems to invoke. What we are looking for is a transactional link between T's title to Blackacre and the breach of trust, such that what T now ought to do is not use the title to Blackacre for his own benefit. Here this can be established: trust rights were used to repay the loan that was used to acquire Blackacre.

That what we are looking for are transactional, rather than causal, links between the trustee's acquisition of a right and the breach of trust is nicely illustrated by the leading English decision that concerned 'backwards tracing': *Foskett v McKeown*.[85] Mr Murphy insured his life for an annual premium of £10,000. The first two premiums were paid from his own funds (the source of the third were unclear). The fourth and fifth payments were paid with money Mr Murphy obtained by misappropriating rights that a company, that he jointly controlled, held on trust. Subsequently, Mr Murphy committed suicide, and the insurers paid £1 million to a trustee who had been nominated by the deceased to hold the lump sum for his wife and children. The claimants were beneficiaries under the trust from which the last two insurance premiums had been sourced, who claimed that as (at least) 40% of the premiums had been paid from trust funds, 40% of the insurance payout should be held on trust for them. The beneficiaries of the trust (Mr Murphy's family) argued that all the claimants were entitled to was the sum misappropriated. Importantly, if the last two premiums had not been paid the insured would have been entitled to be paid in any event. As a counterfactual matter, the misappropriated trust funds made no difference to what the insurer was obliged to pay.

---

[84] P Birks, 'Property, Unjust Enrichment and Tracing' (2001) CLP 231, 244.
[85] [2001] 1 AC 102 (HL).

A majority of the House of Lords, with the leading speech given by Lord Millett (with whom Lords Browne-Wilkinson and Hoffmann agreed), concluded that it was unnecessary to show any causal link between the misappropriated trust rights and the insurance proceeds. Instead, it sufficed that as a matter of historical fact the rights under the policy had been acquired in consideration for *all* the premiums that had been paid before that date. It was sufficient to show a transactional link to thereby oblige the proceeds of the policy to be held on trust in proportion to the contributions made by the five premiums paid. The Privy Council subsequently held, that in determining what constituted the necessary transactional link, it looked to 'the co-ordination between the depletion of the trust fund and the acquisition of the asset which is the subject of the tracing claim, looking at the whole transaction, such as to warrant the court attributing the value of the interest acquired to the misuse of the trust fund'.[86]

In *Foskett* the link between the proceeds of the policy and the misappropriated trust fund was transactional, not counterfactual. We can give examples of the converse case.[87]

T, a trustee, in breach of trust, pays his arrears of rent using £1,000 cash the title to which he holds on trust. The landlord is unaware of the breach of trust. One of the beneficiaries of the trust is P. If T had not used trust funds to pay his rent, he had £2,000 standing to his credit with *Big Bank plc* that he would have used.

On a transactional approach, there is no identifiable product of the right to the cash for which it has been substituted. It would not therefore be possible to 'trace' and for P to assert that any right that T holds should now be held on trust. On a counterfactual approach, the right that T would have used (the £2,000 bank balance) is one that he only has because he has misused trust rights.

The rejection in *Foskett v McKeown* of the counterfactual approach, and the adoption of a transactional one, also necessarily required a rejection of unjust enrichment as the explanation for the entitlement to recovery. The law's (longstanding) adoption of a transactional approach is inconsistent with the idea that what justifies recovery is the plaintiff's assets having causally increased the defendant's wealth, either in the abstract or in relation to specific identifiable rights. This incongruity has led those who seek to justify such claims in terms of 'unjust enrichment' to call for the law to be changed so as to accord with a counterfactual approach.[88] A possible reason for thinking that 'backwards tracing' is objectionable is the feeling that some kind of causal link between deprivation and acquisition is required, which cannot be the case where the right that is the object of the claim was acquired before the deprivation, time's arrow only moving one way.

However, the law is (rightly) concerned with what actually happened, not with what would have happened if the trust assets had not been dissipated. There is no duty on T not to use the right to be paid £2,000 by *Big Bank plc* for his own benefit because that right does not

---

[86] *Brazil v Durant International Corp* [2015] UKPC 35, [2016] AC 297, [40] *per* Lord Toulson.

[87] See L Smith, 'Tracing' in A Burrows and A Rodger (eds), *Mapping the Law: Essays in Memory of Peter Birks* (2006) from which this example is taken. *Cf. Foskett v McKeown* [2001] 1 AC 102 (HL), 134 *per* Lord Millett.

[88] D A Oesterle, 'Deficiencies of the Restitutionary Right to Trace Misappropriated Property in Equity and in UCC § 9–306' (1983) 68 Cornell L Rev 172; C Rotherham, 'The Metaphysics of Tracing: Substituted Title and Property Rhetoric' (1996) 34 Osgoode Hall LJ 321; S Evans, 'Rethinking Tracing and the Law of Restitution' (1999) 115 LQR 46; J Edelman, 'Understanding Tracing Rules' (2016) 15 QUT Law Rev 1.

represent what was, and should still be, held on trust. The credit balance was not historically acquired using the trust assets. Of course, *T* ought to reconstitute the trust, but there is no reason why this needs to be done using that specific right.

Again, the metaphor of 'tracing value' is deceptive. It is true that there is identifiable wealth *T* has that he would not otherwise have but for the breach of trust (a portion of the credit balance). *T* could however have used any of his free assets to pay the rent. Why should *T* be under a duty not to use the specific right that, as a counterfactual matter, he would have used, when he could have used any other wealth?

A similar explanation applied in *Re Diplock*.[89] Some of the funds mistakenly transferred to the defendant charities had been used either to erect or improve buildings on their land. The Court of Appeal held that the estate had as a consequence no right in relation to the defendants' title to their land.[90] Although it would have been possible to say, in some sense, that the 'value' of the dissipated estate still survived in the defendants' hands, the value of their land was greatly enhanced, there was no transactional link between the title to the land, and the money mistakenly paid to the charities. The subject matter of any trust would have to be the title to the land, not merely value, and the proceeds of the mistaken payment had not in any sense been used wholly or in part to acquire this right.

More plausible in these cases is to argue that *T* should no longer use *any* of his own estate for his own benefit unless and until he has reconstituted the trust fund. As *T* could have used any of his free assets in order to pay the rent or improve the land, therefore, he should not use any of his estate for his own benefit until the trust fund is reconstituted. At one time this 'swollen assets' approach was arguably the law in England,[91] but it has now been rejected.[92]

2. 'Mixing'

Unlike physical things, rights cannot be mixed together. There is no such thing as a generic heap of rights so that we cannot tell which is which (as with sheep); nor can we combine rights together so as to create a new thing (as with eggs and flour producing a cake). However, two or more rights may be exchanged for another right. For example:

> *T* holds a title to £1,000 in cash on trust. One of the beneficiaries is *P*. In breach of trust, *T* gives title to the cash to *D*. Unaware of the breach of trust *D* exchanges the title to the cash, and title to £5,000 of cash which he holds outright, to buy a title to a motorbike from *X*.

Unlike a case of a mixture of physical things such as sheep, no evidential problem of identification arises.[93] We know all the facts that there are relevant to know. Here *D* holds the right to the motorbike that he has acquired on trust, but its acquisition is only partially attributable to the trust assets. Although the beneficiary can require its sale, *D* is then only obliged to account for the portion of the proceeds attributable to the trust rights. The closest (but

---

[89] [1951] AC 251 (HL).
[90] [1948] Ch 465 (CA), 548.
[91] *Space Investments Ltd v Canadian Imperial Bank of Commerce Trust Co (Bahamas) Ltd* [1986] 1 WLR 1072 (PC).
[92] *Re Goldcorp Exchange Ltd* [1995] 1 AC 74 (PC).
[93] T Cutts, 'Dummy Asset Tracing' (2019) 135 LQR 140, 147–149.

still loose) analogy to physical mixtures is to the Roman law rule of *confusio*: a new right has been created through the 'mixture' (really exchange) of the old.[94]

Similarly:

> T holds a title to £1,000 in cash on trust. One of the beneficiaries is *P*. In breach of trust, *T* gives the title to the cash to *D*. Unaware of the breach of trust, *D* deposits the cash, and title to £5,000 of cash which he holds outright, into a bank account in his name, that is now £6,000 in credit.

D has just one right against his bank, to be paid £6,000, not many different rights to be paid fractions of that sum.[95] Again, no evidential problem has arisen. That right will also be held on trust but *D* is only obliged to account for that portion that is attributable to the trust rights. It was this 'proportionate share' rule that the House of Lords applied in *Foskett v McKeown*.

Where the 'mixed' right that is to be held on trust has been dissipated, the greatest amount that can then be attributed to the original trust assets is the lowest intermediate balance. This rule originated in *James Roscoe (Bolton) Ltd v Winder*.[96] The trustee misappropriated £455 of trust assets, which he deposited in his personal bank account. He then made withdrawals from the account so that all that remained was £25. Subsequent deposits and withdrawals were made so that on his death the account was £358 in credit. It was held that the beneficiary could only assert an interest in the account to the extent of £25. This treats the 'mixed' right as analogous to a fluid, such as water in a bath that is being drained and then topped up.

In principle, in more complex cases, these two rules ('proportionate share' and 'lowest intermediate balance') should also apply where funds from multiple different sources are deposited in a single account, from which withdrawals and deposits are subsequently made. As with water being added to and emptied from a bath over time, it should in principle be possible to calculate how much of the fund/water that remains at the end is attributable to which source. This is sometimes called the 'rolling charge' approach (somewhat misleadingly as it involves no charge or security right). Whilst it is true that this calculation may be slightly complex, and may involve some evidential uncertainty, this approach is hardly rocket science and would require no more than a few lines of computer code.[97] Unfortunately, English judges have sometimes balked at applying the logic of the two rules above and two alternative approaches have found support in the case law.

The first, and rightly much deprecated, alternative has been to apply a 'first in first out' rule, said to be derived from *Clayton's Case*.[98] The Court of Appeal in *Barlow Clowes v Vaughan*[99] held that this rule should apply in relation to bank accounts, save where it was impractical or unjust, but subsequent courts have not hesitated to hold that they are within the exception.[100] *Clayton's Case* itself concerned a quite different issue: where a debtor owes

---

[94] *Foskett v McKeown* [2001] 1 AC 102 (HL), 115 *per* Lord Hoffmann.
[95] *ibid*, 128 *per* Lord Hope.
[96] [1915] 1 Ch 62.
[97] Smith, *The Law of Tracing* (n 71), 286. See also *Shalson v Russo* [2003] EWHC 1637 [2005] Ch 281, [150] *per* Rimer J. Contra Mitchell, Mitchell, and Watterson, *Goff & Jones* (n 72), [7–61].
[98] *Devynes v Noble (Clayton's Case)* (1816) 1 Mer 572, 35 ER 781.
[99] [1992] 4 All ER 22 (CA).
[100] Eg *Charity Commission for England and Wales v Framjee* [2014] EWHC 2507 (Ch), [2015] 1 WLR 16, [49] *per* Henderson J; *National Crime Agency v Robb* [2014] EWHC (Ch) 4384 [2015] Ch 520, [64]–[65] *per* Etherton C.

250   EQUITY: RESTITUTION

multiple debts to a single creditor, some of which may be secured and some not, and pays the creditor a sum of money without allocating the payment to any particular debt, which is the one discharged? The (natural) rule here is that the oldest debt by order of creation is the one paid. This case, and the rule for which it stands, has nothing to do with 'tracing' and claims that rights are held on trust. Other jurisdictions rightly do not apply it in that context,[101] and commentators are in agreement that it should have no application.

The second is to apply a simple *pari passu* approach, ignoring withdrawals over time, and to allocate what remains based upon the amount each claimant has contributed. The unfairness of this approach is most obvious in relation to its treatment of the last contributor, whose claim is discounted even though there may have been no subsequent withdrawals.

Neither of these alternatives is consistent with applying the 'proportionate share' and 'intermediate balance' rules, and consequent uncertainty has arisen as to which rule applies when. In the United States the 'rolling charge' approach has long been applied,[102] and it is now the approach in many Commonwealth jurisdictions.[103] It is to be hoped that less numbers averse courts in England eventually drop the alternative approaches altogether.

3. Wrongdoing

Two examples:

> *T* holds a title to £1,000 in cash on trust. In breach of trust, *T* deposits it with his bank for the credit of his current account, which after the deposit has a balance of £2,000. The following week *T* withdraws £500 in cash from his bank and dissipates it gambling.
>
> *T* holds a title to £1,000 in cash on trust. In breach of trust, *T* deposits it with his bank for the credit of his current account, which after the deposit has a balance of £2,000. The following week *T* withdraws £1,000 in cash from his bank and purchases with it a title to piece of antique furniture, with a market value of £5,000. He then withdraws £500 in cash from the account and dissipates it gambling.

Again, unlike cases of physical mixtures of things, no evidential problem arises in these examples. In setting down rules in such cases for what the subject matter of the trust now is, the law is not relying upon any presumption of fact; there is no further fact that could be proved and no possibility of any presumption being rebutted.

In the first example, what ought *T* be obliged to do? Before the withdrawal so as to gamble, he was obliged to hold the bank account on trust in proportion to the contribution

---

[101] Eg *Re Ontario Securities Commission* (1985) 30 DLR (4th) 1 aff'd (1998) 52 DLR (4th) 767; *Re Registered Securities Commission* [1991] 1 NZLR 545; *Keefe v Law Society of New South Wales* (1998) 44 NSWLR 451.

[102] *In re Walter J Schmidt & Co* 298 F 314 (1923) (Learned Hand J). For earlier authority see A W Scott, 'The Right to Follow Money Wrongfully Mingled with Other Money' (1913) Harv L Rev 134.

[103] Australia: *Caron v Jahani (No 2)* [2020] NSWCA 117, (2020) 382 LR 158; Canada: *Pars Ram; Re Ontario Securities Commission and Greymac Credit Corporation* (1986) 55 OR (2d) 673; (1986) 30 DLR (4th) 1; *Boughner v Greyhawk Equity Partners Ltd Partnership (Millenium)* (2012) 111 OR (3d) 700; [2012] ONSC 3185; approved [2013] ONC 2, [2013] 5 CBR (6th) 113. There had been a brief period of uncertainty caused by *Law Society of Upper Canada v Toronto Dominion Bank* (1989) 169 DLR (4th) 353, (1998) 42 OR (3d) 257 (Ont CA) criticised L Smith 'Tracing in Bank Accounts: The Lowest Intermediate Balance Rule on Trial' (2000) 33 Can BLJ 75. New Zealand: *Register Securities Ltd* [1991] 1 NZLR 545; Singapore: *Pars Ram Brothers (Pte) Ltd v Australia & New Zealand Banking Group* [2018] 4 SLR 1404, [2018] SGHV 60.

of the trust assets. What ought he to do after the withdrawal? Because he is a wrongdoer, the expenditure ought to be attributed to his share, not that of the trust, at the option of the beneficiaries. This is the rule in *Re Hallett's Estate*.[104]

In the second example, what ought *T* be obliged to do? Should it be the defaulting trustee, or the innocent beneficiaries, who gets to choose whether the acquisition of the title to the furniture is attributed to the trust assets? Again, the choice should be that of the beneficiaries, and so the wrongdoer ought to be obliged to hold the title to the antique furniture on trust, because that is the better result for them. The choice should be theirs, not that of the defaulting trustee. We do not, therefore, in either of these examples care what it was that he intended. This is the rule in *Re Oatway*.[105]

Again, the language of 'tracing' is unhelpful. Regardless of whether we are 'tracing' rights, property, or value, how can the object of the exercise be in two places at the same time before the beneficiaries choose which option is better for them (ie in the example in both the right to be paid the sum owed in the account and in title to the furniture)? It may not be possible to ascertain which of the two (or more) options is the best one for the beneficiaries until the end of legal proceedings, and they should not be put to any choice before this is concluded. Birks sought to overcome this problem, which he labelled 'geometric multiplication',[106] by arguing that beneficiaries had a power to create an equitable property right in a traceable substitute, the exercise of which would extinguish it in relation to the original right, but that before they exercised that option no vested rights arose. The better view, however, is that the metaphor of 'tracing' is again misleading us. Until the beneficiaries exercise their choice, the trustee should be obliged to use neither what survives of the original right nor the substitute for his own benefit, so that there should be a fully 'vested' interest as soon as any substitution of one right for another occurs.[107] This does not entail that the beneficiaries should then be able to *claim* both rights in full, they must elect, but that is not because the same 'value' is in two places at once.

The context in which it matters whether the beneficiaries have a 'vested' right or a mere power to create one is in relation to priority disputes, where there is a competition with other equitable rights created in favour of third parties. English authority here supports the view that the beneficiaries have a vested interest,[108] with the authority that is sometimes cited to the contrary actually concerning cases of recipients from trustees unaware of the breach of trust, and so not at the point at which equitable rights were granted in favour of others subject to any trust obligation.[109] In the latter case, fully-fledged equitable interests should take priority over the mere possibility of the creation of one.

---

[104] (1880) 13 ChD 696 (CA).
[105] [1903] 2 Ch 356.
[106] P Birks, An *Introduction to the Law of Restitution* (rev edn, 1989), 394.
[107] Smith, *The Law of Tracing* (n 71), 358–361.
[108] *Cave v Cave* (1880) 15 Ch D 639.
[109] *Re Ffrench's Estate* (1887) 21 LR Ir 283 (CA). See also B McFarlane, *The Structure of Property Law* (2008), 325 (at fn 154).

F. Subrogation

Subrogation entails one party being substituted for another, so that the former acquires either the ability to enforce the latter's rights for his own benefit, or new rights equivalent to those the latter had but which have now been extinguished.[110] 'Subrogation' therefore refers to a form of right, much as 'trust' does so. Like the trust, such rights arise for several different reasons. Three different categories of case need, for our purposes, to be distinguished.

First are those most obviously analogous to the examples discussed so far, where one party acquires rights in relation to another's rights, such as an indemnity insurer's rights to take over the assured's claim against a wrongdoer.[111] An assured's claim against the wrongdoer is not extinguished by the indemnity insurance pay-out. Such rights of subrogation to the (still extant) rights against the wrongdoer arise because of the contract of insurance.[112] The (contractual) right of the insurer to take over the assured's right against the wrongdoer then gives rise to special features in Equity similar to a trust. The contract of insurance contains either an express or implied term that the assured will use its rights against the wrongdoer for the insurer's benefit.[113] The insurer, like the beneficiaries under a trust, has the benefit of an expedited procedure to compel the assured to enforce its rights against the wrongdoer, and any proceeds of the right against the wrongdoer will be held for the insurer.[114] The right of the assured in relation to the claim and its proceeds is limited however to the amount paid out under the insurance, any excess accrues to the assured, and it is because the right to any proceeds is limited in this way that the label 'lien' has been employed.[115] The insurer's right in relation to the proceeds is not however a security right: he has no independent personal right to restitution of the insurance pay-out against the insurer that is being secured. The insurer's lien is a right to the proceeds to the extent of the sum paid under the indemnity insurance.[116] Where a contract of insurance provides for an 'excess', any recoveries from the wrongdoer must first be applied to reimburse the insurer, at one time a controversial matter of contractual construction.[117]

More interesting, and difficult, are those cases where the debt of another is discharged, so that the right is extinguished, and a new right, with identical content, is fictionally 'revived' in favour of the claimant. Our second category is the group of such cases we have already seen, where it is the claimant himself who has discharged an obligation that ought to be borne by the defendant.[118] The most common example is in relation to contracts guaranteeing the debt of another. The payment of the creditor by the guarantor discharges the

---

[110] This section largely follows R Gregson, 'Is Subrogation a Remedy for Unjust Enrichment' (2020) 136 LQR 481. The important work in differentiating the different senses of 'subrogation' was done by Charles Mitchell. See now C Mitchell and S Watterson, *Subrogation: Law and Practice* (rev edn, 2007).
[111] B McFarlane, *The Structure of Property Law* (2008) 28–29.
[112] *Yorkshire Insurance Co Ltd v Nisbet Shipping Co Ltd* [1962] 2 QB 330, 339–340; *Orakpo v Manson Investments Ltd* [1978] AC 95 (HL), 104 *per* Lord Diplock; *Banque Financiere de La Cite v Parc (Battersea) Ltd* [1999] 1 AC 221 (HL), 231–232 *per* Lord Hoffmann.
[113] In some cases, the term is now found in legislation (eg the Marine Insurance Act 1906, s 79: 'Where the insurer pays for a total loss, either of the whole, or in the case of goods of any apportion-able part, of the subject-matter insured, he thereupon becomes entitled to take over the interest of the assured in whatever may remain of the subject-matter so paid for').
[114] *Lord Napier and Ettrick v Hunter* [1993] AC 713 (HL).
[115] *Yorkshire Insurance Co Ltd v Nisbet Shipping Co Ltd* [1962] 2 QB 330.
[116] Smith, *The Law of Tracing* (n 71), 363–364; *cf. Castellain v Preston* [1883] 11 QBD 380 (CA).
[117] *Lord Napier and Ettrick v Hunter* [1993] AC 713 (HL).
[118] See Chapter 9, Discharge.

underlying debt, but the guarantor acquires a new identical right of the same content as the original debt against the debtor.

Such a right to subrogation differs in important respects from a simple right to recoupment. First, if the obligation discharged was secured, the subrogated party acquires the same security. Second, even where it is unsecured, the revived subrogated right has the same features as the right extinguished. If the extinguished right carried with it a right to a particular priority upon the debtor's insolvency (such as, today, claims by employees)[119] or a particular rate of interest,[120] this too is acquired by the subrogated party. In the case of a guarantor or equivalent, this attempt to perfectly replicate the discharged obligation is again justified by the law seeking to ensure that the burden of the obligation falls where it ought. We are seeking to create the world where the party who should have performed the obligation has done so. This justifies both the recreation of all the other features of the discharged debt and the 'revival' of any security right the creditor had.[121] As we have seen, such a right to subrogation is often created by contract (the principal debtor having requested the guarantee), but need not be.

Different again, is the third category of case where the debt is discharged not by a payment *by* the subrogated party himself but instead with money in relation to which he has an entitlement, either at law or in Equity. An example:

> *T* mortgages the title of his house to *X Bank* to secure a loan of £100,000. The terms of the loan are very generous to *X Bank*, entitling them to interest of 10% per annum. *T* also holds the sum of £100,000 standing to his credit with *Y Bank* on trust. In breach of trust, *T* withdraws the sum on deposit with *Y Bank* and uses it to pay off his mortgage.

The beneficiaries of the trust have not, themselves, discharged the debt to *X Bank*, but rights that should have been held on trust for them have been used to do so.[122] Just as where the trustee has substituted trust rights for new rights, his duties as trustee justify the creation of a new duty upon him equivalent to the one that he has discharged. The trustee ought, in addition to his duties to reconstitute the trust fund, to be under the following alternative duties (at the beneficiaries' option). First, an identical debt to the one discharged should be owed by the trustee enforceable by the beneficiaries. Second, such debt should also be secured, so that *T* holds his title to the house by way of security for the revived debt. The shorthand way of expressing this position is that the beneficiaries are 'subrogated' to the discharged debt and its security.

Such a duty is a close relation of the duty of trustees to hold rights that they have acquired in substitute for trust rights. There is not, of course, any right that *T* has that has causally been acquired with the withdrawn trust monies. However, the law takes the further step of 'reviving' the discharged debt and securing this obligation with an equivalent security right over the title to the house. Given the breach of trust, this is the 'next best' equivalent to his

---

[119] *Re M'Myn* (1886) 33 ChD 575, 578 (Chitty J); *Re Lord Churchill* (1888) 39 Ch D 174; *Re Lamplugh Iron Ore Co Ltd* [1927] 1 Ch 308.
[120] *Western Trust & Savings Ltd v Rock* (Unreported 26 February 1993, CA); *Castle Phillips Finance v Piddington* (1995) 70 P & CR 592 (CA), 602 *per* Peter Gibson LJ.
[121] Eg *Yonge v Reynell* (1852) 9 Hare 809, 818–819, 68 ER 744, 748–749 *per* Sir GJ Turner V-C; *Forbes v Jackson* (1882) 19 ChD 615.
[122] *Patton v Bond* (1889) 60 LT 583.

having complied with his original duty that is now available. Such cases are analogous to those of so-called 'backwards tracing' that we have seen.

As we have also already seen with regard to claims to traceable proceeds, the same kind of reasoning can also apply against defendants who are not initially trustees. For example:

> D mortgages the title of his house to *X Bank* to secure a loan of £100,000. The terms of the loan are very generous to *X Bank*, entitling them to interest of 10% per annum. D induces P to lend him £100,000 on the basis that he intends to invest the money in a business venture. D instead uses the borrowed money to pay off his mortgage, as he always intended.

P has the power to rescind the contract of loan for D's misrepresentation. If D still had the right to the money lent, then he ought not to use it for his own benefit, and therefore a trust would arise over such a right from that point. Here however the next best that is achievable (at P's option) is that an identical debt to the one discharged should be owed by D to P, an obligation that should also be secured by an (equitable) mortgage over the title to D's house.[123]

In some cases, the same reasoning can apply even where the defendant has not obtained any right from the plaintiff, and this is illustrated by the decision of the Court of Appeal in *Boscawen v Bajwa*.[124]

> D had charged his title to land to a building society (X). D agreed to sell title to the property, but the agreement with the buyer was not in the correct form and was as a result unenforceable. The buyer had previously arranged a mortgage advance with P, another building society. P paid £140,000 to the buyer's solicitors to be held in the solicitors' client account for purposes of completing the deal. The solicitors held the right to be paid this sum on trust for P. In breach of trust, the solicitors paid the money to X in discharge of the debt owed to them by D before completion of the sale. The sale then fell through. What rights, if any, did P have against D?

What should D's duty be, once he knows that rights subject to a trust have been used to discharge a debt that he owes? He ought to reverse what has occurred, just as much as someone who has acquired a specific right transferred in breach of trust should do so. If the solicitors had instead paid D, who had then used the proceeds to discharge his debt with X, the case would be the same as the previous example. The position we are seeking as nearly as possible to put the parties into is one where the money that had been held on trust for P had not been used to discharge a debt owed by D. Given the discharge of D's obligation to X, how can this position now be most closely replicated? The answer, again, is that the next best position achievable is for an identical debt to the one D owed to X now to be owed to P, on both the same terms and subject to the same security, as Millett LJ rightly concluded.

What links together our second and third categories, therefore, is that in both we are seeking to ensure that the burden of an obligation falls where it ought to. In order to achieve this, we 'revive' a debt identical to the one that has been discharged. The only difference is that, in the second group, the plaintiff himself has discharged the debt, whereas in the third,

---

[123] See eg *Chetwynd v Allen* [1899] 1 Ch 353. *Baroness Wenlock v River Dee Co (No 2)* (1887) 19 QBD 155 (CA) is explicable in the same way.
[124] [1996] 1 WLR 328 (CA).

money in relation to which he has an entitlement, either at law or in equity, has been used by another without authority to discharge the debt.

It should not, however, suffice that the plaintiff has merely *caused* an obligation of the defendant to be discharged. This may be illustrated by the Supreme Court's decision in *Swynson Ltd v Lowick Rose LLP*.[125] Swynson Ltd lent a large sum of money to another company (EMSL) on the basis of an accountants' report negligently prepared by the defendants. The claimant was the controlling owner of Swynson, who lent the debtor company money with which to repay the loan, which they did. The debtor company then went into insolvent liquidation. Swynson brought a claim against the negligent accountants, who argued (successfully) that Swynson had no recoverable loss as the loan had been (luckily for them) repaid. The claimant argued that he should have a claim by way of equitable subrogation to the value of the obligation to pay damages that he had caused to be discharged.

The claimant had not, himself, discharged any obligation of the defendants, nor was the money used to discharge the defendants' obligation money in relation to which he had any entitlement. The claimant had lent money to Swynson, and they then used their money to pay EMSL, which relieved the defendants of their obligation to pay damages. Even if we assume that the money the claimant paid Swynson was subject to a trust in his favour, as paid for the sole purpose of discharging the indebtedness to EMSL, this equitable interest was intended to come to an end upon that purpose being fulfilled, which it had. The Supreme Court, overruling the Court of Appeal, rejected the claim. They did so on the basis that the claimant got precisely what he expected to get: discharge of the loan and a right to repayment from EMSL.[126] The mere fact that he had caused the discharge of the defendants' obligation to pay did not suffice to give him a claim against them.

Unfortunately, the earlier decision of the House of Lords in *Banque Financière de la Cité v Parc (Battersea) Ltd*[127]—probably still today the leading case on subrogation in England—adopted a simple causal approach. Banque Financière de la Cité (BFC) agreed to lend money to Parc (Battersea) Ltd (Parc) in reliance on a 'postponement letter' written by Parc, which provided that claims by companies in the same group as Parc would be subordinate to BFC's loan. BFC was mistaken in making the loan on this basis as this letter was not binding on OOL, a company in the same group as Parc, as given without authority of that company. OOL were owed a large sum by Parc secured by a second charge over Parc's main asset, title to a plot of land. Parc used the money BFC had paid it to pay off a bank with a first charge over title to the land. Parc subsequently went into insolvency.[128]

BFC successfully argued that its mistake in making the loan had left OOL unjustly enriched. If the loan had never been made, OOL would have had only a second charge over the land, but the discharge of the first secured loan had improved their position. To prevent this, the House of Lords allowed BFC to be subrogated, as against OOL, to the first charge over the title to the land that the money it lent had been used to discharge. This was a novel use of subrogation. It involved the creation of a new debt owed by Parc to BFC secured not by the first charge of the debt discharged, good against all other creditors, but instead the creation of one that had never previously existed, good only against OOL.

---

[125] [2017] UKSC 32, [2018] AC 313.
[126] ibid, [32]–[35] *per* Lord Sumption, [87] *per* Lord Mance, and [119] *per* Lord Neuberger.
[127] [1999] 1 AC 221 (HL).
[128] The money was lent using an intermediary, but this complication can be ignored.

No money in relation to which BFC had any entitlement was used to discharge the secured loan to the bank, and no obligation that ought to have been borne by Parc was discharged by BFC.

If the contract of loan had been induced by misrepresentation by Parc, then it could have been set aside. There would then have been a claim based upon an equitable entitlement to the proceeds paid over, which would have been used to discharge a secured loan, to which BFC should then be subrogated. However, the contract under which the money was lent was not set aside and could not be. Further, it was not a condition of the loan to Parc that there was a valid subordination agreement with other lenders, the 'postponement letter' being collateral to the loan. No trust over the proceeds paid could possibly therefore have arisen as the money was paid under a valid loan agreement.

This decision cannot be supported and has been doubted by the High Court of Australia.[129] It should not be enough that a mistake in making an unsecured loan to X that leads to D being left better off entails D being susceptible to a claim.[130] As we have seen, if money that C has an entitlement in relation to is used to discharge X's debt, the law may allow C to be subrogated to the debt. Here however, the money used to pay off the secured loan was Parc's, not the claimant's.[131] The result can, formally, be reconciled with *Swynson Ltd v Lowick Rose LLP* on the basis that in the latter the claimant found himself in the position he expected to be in, whereas in *Banque Financière de la Cité v Parc (Battersea) Ltd* the claimant had been mistaken, but the complex facts disguise the difficulty of justifying the latter decision.

G. Policy?

A quite different analysis to the creation and recognition of property rights from the formalistic approach adopted in this chapter and the previous two, is instead to ask directly why a particular claimant would wish to assert such a right, and then to consider whether they are deserving in policy terms of acquiring one. The approach is to reason backwards from the consequence of a claimant having such a right, and to ask whether, when compared to other claimants, they are more deserving than others are.[132]

One significant reason why a claimant wishes to assert that they have title to a thing, an equitable interest under a trust, charge, or lien, or are subrogated to a security right, and not merely a personal claim to be paid a sum of money, is that this protects them upon the defendant's bankruptcy. Things in the possession of a bankrupt to which another has better title, or rights held on trust or subject to a lien or charge, are not available for realisation and distribution to unsecured creditors. Although there are many other reasons why a claimant may wish to be able to assert a 'proprietary' rather than a merely personal claim, this is probably the most commercially significant one.

---

[129] *Bofinger v Kingsway Group Ltd* [2009] HCA 44; (2009) 239 CLR 269 (HCA).
[130] *Parkash v Irani Finance Ltd* [1970] Ch 101; *Paul v Speirway Ltd* [1976] Ch 220, [1976] 2 All ER 587.
[131] But see *Lowick Rose LLP v Swynson LLP* [2018] AC 313, [23] per Lord Sumption.
[132] Eg E Sherwin, 'Constructive Trusts in Bankruptcy' [1989] U of Ill LRD 297; D Paciocco, 'The Remedial Constructive Trust: A Principled Basis for Priority over Creditors' (1989) 68 CBR 315; H Dagan, 'Restitution in Bankruptcy: Why All Involuntary Creditors Should Be Preferred' (2004) 78 Am Bank LJ 247; E Sherwin 'Unjust Enrichment and Creditors' (2007) 27 Rev Litig 141; E Sherwin, 'Why *Omega Group* Was Right' (2012) 92 BU L Rev 885. The longest sustained treatment is C Rotherham, *Proprietary Remedies in Context* (2002).

Related to direct appeals to the 'policy' question of who is in distributive terms the most deserving, is the claim by some commentators, and of some courts outside of England,[133] particular in the United States,[134] that trusts that are not expressly declared are 'remedial'[135] in the sense that they are created by the order of a court, rather than, as argued in this chapter, ordinarily independent of any court order. Four factors have probably led to this error. First is, again, the linguistic trap of thinking that all true 'trusts' require an 'entrustment'. Second is the ambiguity in the meaning of the adjective 'remedial'. Sometimes all that is meant by 'remedial constructive trust' is a trust that arises to correct or remedy something,[136] and this is wholly unobjectionable. Third is, as we have seen, the fact that the courts of Equity supplemented the law with court orders (specific performance and injunctions) that the common law courts did not possess. It can therefore be thought that what is special or different about Equity is that it is part of the law of court orders, rather than of substantive law. In deciding whether to make an order, courts commonly take into account a range of wider reasons that are not relevant in determining what our rights *inter se* are. My employer has a right that I teach law students, but no court will order specific performance of my obligation to do so. I have a right that my neighbour does not commit a nuisance unreasonably disturbing my right to my land, but that does not entail that I will necessarily obtain an injunction to prevent it. If constructive trusts were 'remedial' in the same sense as these equitable court orders, it is a natural thought that a similarly wider range of 'policy' reasons can be taken into account in deciding whether or not to make any award. In particular, if a court has the choice whether or not to create a trust, it may decide not to do so where this would prejudice other creditors of a defendant upon his bankruptcy.[137] Fourth, and most importantly, some constructive trusts *do* only arise because of a court order (eg orders to rectify a contract for the sale of land or to rescind a contract in Equity). However, it is the obligation to (re)convey arising from the court order that creates the trust, not the order *per se*.

Two factors in combination are said to make the 'unjust enrichment' claimant particularly deserving upon the insolvency of the defendant. First, they are often, but not always, involuntary creditors. Unlike a lender of money, the mistaken payor has not run the risk of its debtor not being able to pay through bankruptcy. This is thought to provide a basis for distinguishing claims for restitution by those who have paid for goods or services in advance whilst receiving nothing in return who are not, as we have seen, beneficiaries under a trust, but who are voluntary creditors of the counterparty. Second, unlike many other involuntary creditors, such as victims of torts, the 'unjust enrichment' claimant has swollen the assets of the defendant available for distribution. Giving them a proprietary 'remedy' thereby prevents the 'unjust enrichment' of unsecured creditors.

It was arguments of this kind that persuaded a majority of the New Zealand Court of Appeal,[138] who were to be overturned by the Privy Council, that the defrauded customers in

---

[133] *Polly Peck v Nadir (No 2)* [1992] 4 All ER 769 (CA).
[134] But see A W Scott, *The Law of Trusts* (3rd edn, 1967), 3416. Canada: *Sorochan v Sorochan* [1986] 2 SCR 38; *Lac Minerals Ltd v International Corona Resources Ltd* [1989] 2 SCR 574; *Soulos v Korkontzilas* [1997] 2 SCR 217; *Kerr v Baranow* [2011] 1 SCR 269. Australia: *Muschinski v Dodds* (1985) 160 CLR 583l *Bathurs CC v PWC Properties Pty Ltd* (1988) 195 CLR 566; *Giumelli v Giumelli* (1999) 196 CLR 101; *Grimaldi v Chameleon Mining NL (No 2)* [2012] FCAFC 6.
[135] *Cf.* Mitchell, Mitchell, and Watterson, *Goff & Jones* (n 72), Part 7.
[136] Eg R Pound, 'The Progress of Law' (1920) 33 Harv Law Rev, 420, 420–421.
[137] See *Grimaldi v Chameleon Mining NL (No 2)* [2012] FCAFC 6, [582].
[138] [1993] 1 NZLR 257 (Cooke P and Gault J; McKay J dissenting).

Re Goldcorp were deserving of a 'proprietary remedy' in relation to the general assets of the defendant company. They had never bargained on the basis that they were to be unsecured creditors, but instead had paid for bullion that they believed was being held for them.

The principal objection to arguments of this kind is that they are of the wrong form. Reasons for 'property rights' must either relate a person to a thing ('I had possession of the diamond ring before you') or to a right ('You agreed to transfer title to Blackacre to me, I paid you the price, and you have not done so'). That a creditor is involuntary, has swollen the bankruptcy estate, or both, are arguments for priority upon bankruptcy. They are not arguments for a proprietary right as they do not relate to any specific thing or right.

Reasons for priority such as these are familiar within bankruptcy law as being part of the justification for giving sums owed to employees, or sometimes the obligation to pay tax, by an insolvent company, priority over other unsecured creditors. Employees, unlike other creditors, are unable to diversify the risk of non-payment, and have through their unpaid for work increased the distributable estate. Employees lack the bargaining power to demand payment in advance from their employers for work not yet done, or to require security for unpaid salary. They are, to that extent, involuntary creditors who must work to live. Priority of particularly deserving classes of creditors upon bankruptcy, or their protection by other means,[139] is, in all jurisdictions, set down in bankruptcy legislation (in England in the Insolvency Act 1986). The courts have no proper role in adding to or subtracting from the class of creditors given such priority status.[140] Even if we did consider this issue to be justiciable, what priority should the 'unjust enrichment' claimant have relative to employees? Above, below, or equal?

Conversely, it is not the proper role of the courts to remove property rights from those in whom they are vested upon another's bankruptcy. Legislation does require some rights to be struck down where inconsistent with the purposes of bankruptcy law (most obviously, striking down preferences or transactions at an undervalue which are either by intention or effect unfair in allowing the opting out from the collective insolvency regime). It is not, however, the proper role of the courts to independently determine the policy question of which rights should be invalidated upon bankruptcy.[141] The beneficiaries of express trusts do not, for example, lose their rights because they have provided no value for them.

In English textbooks, more common than using policy reasoning as a justification for the award of a 'proprietary remedy', is to invoke it as a reason for denying one.[142] A claimant who has voluntarily extended credit to the defendant, knowing that they would be unsecured, is undeserving of the law's protection. Reasoning of this kind is, however, circular as it depends upon the legal position being as it currently is. If we gave those who pay for goods in advance of their delivery either a proprietary right in relation to what they have paid, or priority upon the seller's bankruptcy, they would thereby not be running the risk of such bankruptcy.

---

[139] Victims of torts in England are given a statutory entitlement to subrogation to the insolvent wrongdoer's liability insurance, such insurance often being compulsory.

[140] *Cf. XL/Datacomp, Inc. v Wilson (In re Omegas Grp., Inc.)* 16 F3d 1443, 1453 (6th Cir 1994).

[141] P Millett, 'Bribes and Secret Commissions' [1993] RLR 7, 10; P Birks 'The End of the Remedial Constructive Trust?' (1998) 12 Trust Law Int'l 202, 214–215; P Birks, *Unjust Enrichment* (2nd edn, 2005), 375–401.

[142] Eg A Burrows, *The Law of Restitution* (3rd edn, 2011), 176–179; Mitchell, Mitchell, and Watterson, *Goff & Jones* (n 72), [37-18]–[37-20].

Insolvency law is dependent for its operation upon the general law's allocation of legal entitlements. Attempts to determine the latter by reference to the former (or any other consequence) are a dead end.

H. Unjust Enrichment?

Two inconsistent claims are commonly made in relation to the material of this chapter by proponents of 'unjust enrichment' as an explanatory idea. First is that the rules are best understood as being justified in terms of unjust enrichment. Second is that they need to be changed in order to conform with unjust enrichment. It is in this area that there has been least reading 'up' from the cases in understanding the rules, and the most imposing 'down' on to the law of an 'unjust enrichment' framework. This is unhelpful for three reasons: form, content, and justification.

First, and most importantly, the subject matter of a trust, regardless of whether it is express, constructive, or resulting, is always a right. This right may not be 'enriching' in any way. The right that is held on trust may be a right to land that is subject to onerous environmental clean-up costs and so is valueless, or the right to a child's drawing that may have sentimental worth but no market value. The subject matter of a resulting trust is not 'value surviving'[143] in the hands of the defendant, but an identifiable right vested in him.

Birks sought to elide this difference in form by arguing that the subject matter of the claim in cases exemplified by *Kelly v Solari* was the 'value' received by the defendant, whereas in the 'proprietary' cases it was the 'value' surviving. This is misleading in several different ways. As we have seen, the subject matter for reversal of an undue payment is the payment made in the past, not 'value', the subject matter of a claim to recover a tangible thing is the physical thing itself, whereas in Equity the subject matter of a trust is a right. There is no genus to which these three different concepts belong, and none is necessarily an 'enrichment', at least in the ordinary sense of that word.[144]

Second, as we have seen, the content of the duty of a trustee is not simply to repay a sum of money, as was the case in *Kelly v Solari*. Instead of a simple obligation to make restitution, it is a duty not to use an identifiable right for the trustee's own benefit.

This then leads to the third important difference. The different form and content of obligations of this kind leads to different conditions for their acquisition. Most obviously, there must be a right vested in the defendant that is capable of being held on trust. Further, because a trustee is potentially liable if the rights are used in breach of trust, knowledge of the facts potentially giving rise to the duty is required. The mistaken payment of money may give rise, without more, to a liability to repay, but not to a trust. Conversely there may not yet be any duty to return a right received, but a duty not to use it for the recipient's own benefit in the interim. In the example with which we began, the receipt of a right held on trust is not analogous to the receipt of cash to which the plaintiff had a title. Liability in *Lipkin Gorman v Karpnale* did not depend upon proof of knowledge, whereas in *Re Montagu's Settlement Trusts* it rightly did.

---

[143] *Cf.* Birks, *An Introduction to the Law of Restitution* (n 106), 358–402.
[144] *Cf.* R Chambers, 'Two Kinds of Enrichment' in R Chambers, C Mitchell, and J Penner (eds), *Philosophical Foundations of the Law of Unjust Enrichment* (2009).

It is sometimes said that the position in Equity of requiring 'knowing receipt' is not only inconsistent with the common law's strict liability rule, but is also internally incoherent.[145] As we have seen, the correct legatee under a maladministered will has a claim against the recipient of distributions from an estate that should not have been made, provided any claims against the administrator have been exhausted first. This claim, exemplified by *Re Diplock*, is not however that the recipient make restitution to the legatee, but rather that they make restitution to the estate. The claim, although brought on behalf of the estate, is a straightforward one to make restitution of a payment that should not have been made back to the party making it.[146] It is therefore strict and has no relation to the claim by a beneficiary against a third-party recipient of trust property.

An example of a court being led astray by unjust enrichment reasoning is the decision of the New South Wales Court of Appeal in *Say-Dee Pty Ltd v Farah Construction Pty Ltd*.[147] Two companies formed a joint venture to develop a block of land in Sydney. The director of one oversaw an unsuccessful development application to the local council. He learned in the process that if title to adjacent properties were acquired, a revised application would probably succeed. The counterparty company alleged that a breach of fiduciary duty occurred in not imparting this information to them, and instead the director had arranged for a related company, controlled by the director and members of his family, to purchase the title to the adjoining land. The Court of Appeal held that the director's family (the defendants) were strictly liable for receipt of trust rights or in the alternative strictly liable in 'unjust enrichment'. The High Court of Australia overturned both of these conclusions in intemperate terms.[148]

The first ground for doing so was that the defendants had not received any right capable of being held on trust. The director had exploited information he had acquired, and that had benefitted the defendants, but there is no right to information as such.[149] We have intellectual property rights to some species of information, through the law of patents, trademarks, and copyright, but not to information generally. Even if the information had been confidential, that does not give rise to a right to it exigible against others. We hold rights on trust, not 'value'. The defendants had benefitted from the exploitation of the information, but they had not 'received trust property'.

The High Court also rejected the 'radical change'[150] of recognising a strict liability in unjust enrichment. In this respect they were right to do so. Although the defendants were better off, and the plaintiff worse off, because of the director's actions, alone this is insufficient for the creation of a duty on the party enriched. Again, this is a commercially more complex version of the 'two stamps' case.[151] The plaintiff had good claims against other parties, but not against innocent third parties left factually better off by another's wrongdoing. (However, the court's conclusion that the other family members had no notice of the director' breach[152] is insupportable. The director/father was acting as the agent for the mother

---

[145] Eg Burrows, *The Law of Restitution* (n 142), 424–426.
[146] See Chapter 3, Performance.
[147] [2005] NSWCA 800. See also J Edelman, 'A Principled Approach to Unauthorised Receipt of Trust Property' (2006) 122 LQR 174.
[148] [2007] HCA 22, 230 CLR 89.
[149] *Oxford v Moss* (1979) 68 Cr App 183. 'Property depends upon exclusion by law from interference.' *International News Service v Associated Press per* Holmes J 248 US 215 (1918), 246.
[150] [2007] HCA 22, 230 CLR 89, [148].
[151] Chapter 3, Performance.
[152] [2007] HCA 22, 230 CLR 89, [129].

and children in acquiring the property, and his knowledge should have been attributed to them.[153])

The idea that much of the law of Equity is based upon principles of unjust enrichment that it has in common with the common law has then led to calls for one or the other to be changed. The claim that the rules concerning 'tracing' are based upon 'unjust enrichment' would require them to be redrawn. For example, as we have seen, tracing rules require a transactional not a causal link to be shown. This inconsistency with unjust enrichment theory has led to calls for the rules to be changed. Similarly, if we were tracing 'value' or 'enrichment', where rights that ought to be held on trust are used to pay for improvements to a thing to which the defendant has a title, thereby enhancing its value, the value would traceably survive. This has again led to calls for the law to be changed so that the beneficiaries have a right to the title to the thing improved. Indeed, in Australia there is now some authority for doing so:[154] an example of the feedback loop between the law and the theory of it. Similarly, the failure to understand the conceptual difference between right to things at common law and 'equitable property rights' has led to the mistaken view that as claims to substituted rights are possible in relation to the latter, claims to substituted things are possible in relation to the former.

Similarly, the inconsistency of the law of subrogation with claims to reverse payments that are not due has been invoked in order to relax the restrictions upon the latter. If they were genuinely based upon a common general principle of 'unjust enrichment' then there is clearly no requirement of there being a 'performance' by the plaintiff to the defendant nor any 'direct transfer of value' between them. Those cases where this restriction has been required are then thought to be mistaken or based upon an unarticulated policy concern. Here we see how the absence of a condition in one area of law is then invoked to justify its removal in another, through over-generalising.

The potential for 'unjust enrichment' to expand the law of subrogation was seen in *Banque Financière de la Cité v Parc (Battersea) Ltd*.[155] Applying the four-stage test for liability, the court asked whether the defendant was enriched? (yes, the discharge of the first charge left them as second chargee better off) at the expense of the claimant? (yes, in commercial reality) was it unjust? (yes, the claimant was making a mistake) any defence? (obviously not). Giving the wrong result. Similarly, in *Menelaou v Bank of Cyprus*[156] a majority of the Supreme Court used the same box-ticking approach to create a right to subrogation, giving a result that is hard to justify.[157]

The converse problem also arises. Common law jurisdictions today recognise a defence of change of position to claims for restitution of money mistakenly paid. If resulting and constructive trusts, and many cases of subrogation, are based upon the same general 'unjust enrichment' principle, surely they too should be subject to the same defence? Similarly, it has been argued that the bona fide purchase defence should apply to claims in unjust enrichment, but as we saw in the last chapter, how or why this should be so is unclear, and

---

[153] R Chambers, 'Knowing Receipt: Frozen in Australia' (2007) 2 J Eq 40, 47.
[154] *Alesco Corporation Ltd v Te Maari* [2015] NSWSC 469; *Leighton Contractors Pty Ltd v O'Carrigan* [2016] QSC 223; *Rheem Australia Pty Ltd v McInnes* [2020] NSWSC 1313.
[155] [1999] 1 AC 221 (HL).
[156] [2015] UKSC 66, [2016] AC 176.
[157] See Chapter 3, Performance.

whether it should be the common law rule applicable to cash or the equitable version of the rule uncertain.

I. Doing without Equity?

Much of the reasoning of this chapter and the last has proceeded from the premise that trusts (and other 'equitable property rights') exist and take a certain form. It has then sought to deduce when such rights arise and what their effects are. It has been mainly analytical and descriptive rather than normative. Civilian legal systems although sometimes reaching the same result through different routes (eg separate patrimonies), and sometimes employing the language of 'trusts', rarely, if ever, have rights of the same form as Equity's trust. Should it and its equitable cousins be abolished?

A slightly less dramatic position to total abolition is that of Professor Swadling. He has for many years argued that there are no true trusts other than those that are expressly declared. This would mean that, for example, vendor purchaser trusts,[158] the beneficiaries' rights to substitutes acquired through a breach of trust,[159] *Quistclose* trusts,[160] and trusts arising upon rescission of a contract are all unjustifiable, and that the courts in all of these contexts are either mistaken or mislabelling as a 'trust' another kind of relation. On this view, just as 'quasi-contracts' are now recognised as not contracts, so 'constructive trusts' should no longer be seen as trusts. At a descriptive level, this would do considerable violence to our positive law, and, at least in England, to claim that there are no true trusts except those expressly declared is an example of a 'no true Scotsman' argument.[161]

A common argument for trusts, and other equitable rights such as those created by way of charge or equitable assignment, is their utility. Equitable property rights facilitated charitable trusts, the holding of rights to land in commercially useful ways, the creation of security rights over 'future' property, and the insurer's right to subrogation. In the modern era, it has enabled securitisation of debts, and the holding of securities through tiers of intermediaries. Civilian jurisdictions have sometimes enacted legislation to enable legal structures that, in the common law, Equity had already allowed the creation of.

However, many of the 'equitable property rights' in this and the last chapter were not intentionally created, and cannot be justified by direct appeals to their utility. In this context, the principal justification is that the equitable rules soften, and makes justifiable, the rules for the abstract transfer of rights. Returning to an earlier example.

> *D* contracts to sell his title to Blackacre to *P*. *P* pays the price, but conveyance of title to the land has not occurred before *D* goes into bankruptcy.

As between *P* and *D* themselves, *P* has a better entitlement to Blackacre. The justification for the right not having been transferred to *P* is the protection of other parties. We require

---

[158] W Swadling, 'The Vendor-Purchaser Constructive Trust' in S Degeling and J Edleman (eds), *Equity in Commercial Law* (2005), 463.
[159] W Swadling, 'Ignorance and Unjust Enrichment: The Problem of Title' (2008) 28 OJLS 629.
[160] W Swadling, 'Orthodoxy' in W Swadling (ed), *The Quistclose Trust* (2004), ch 2.
[161] Proposition: 'No Scotsman puts sugar on his porridge', Response: 'But my Uncle Angus in Aberdeen puts sugar on his porridge', Rebuttal: 'No *true* Scotsman puts sugar on his porridge'.

formal steps to be taken to convey (a deed, registration) so that third parties are able to discover who can give them permission to enter, or who can convey or grant a right to or an interest in the land. Absent the trust, others could take the benefit of the principle of abstraction who are not the intended beneficiaries of it (most obviously, D's creditors). Central to the purpose of the constructive trust is that D acquires no title to the land itself, which would fatally undermine the purpose of the principle of abstraction, but instead a right in relation to P's title to the land. This is the truth behind the otherwise opaque maxim that 'Equity takes as done what ought to be done'.

Such equitable interests should not be capable of binding those whom the principle of abstraction exists to protect. This class includes bona fide purchasers of the right that is held on trust. Precisely the same justification applies where the trust is not created by a contract, but instead by obligations to make restitution of rights acquired.

14
Improvements

A. Introduction

This chapter has three functions. First, to consider the legal rules applicable where one person through her work or materials improves a thing, whether land or goods, to which another person has better title. Second, to use the multifarious applicable rules to tie together the threads of the material so far considered. Third, to analyse the proper relationship between claims for restitution and the law of estoppel, and to argue that some but not all of what is currently treated as part of the latter would be better seen as an aspect of the former.

B. Goods

1. *Greenwood v Bennett*

A Jaguar car, worth £400 to £550, to which Bennett had title, was stolen, and then crashed by a thief.[1] The thief then sold the nearly-wrecked vehicle to Harper for £75, which was what it was worth in its damaged condition. Harper then repaired the vehicle, spending £226 on labour and materials. He sold it on to a finance company for £450, who leased it out on hire purchase terms. The title was then investigated, and the police took possession of the vehicle.

The police took out interpleader proceedings, and the final question was, as between Bennett and Harper, who had better title to the vehicle? The trial judge held that Bennett had the better title and ordered the vehicle be delivered to him. The Court of Appeal held that it ought to have been a condition of Bennett's recovery that he paid Harper the value of the work done in improvements (the £226) but as that could no longer be done, ordered that that sum now be paid to Harper. What are the possible explanations for this result?

2. A Freestanding 'Enrichment' Claim?

Some commentators have read Lord Denning MR (unlike the other members of the court Phillimore and Cairns LJJ) as supporting a freestanding claim by the improver against the vehicle owner for the value of the work done, based upon 'unjust enrichment'.[2] The unjust enrichment analysis may be bolstered by the fact that, although unmentioned in the judgments, Bennett had after recovery sold the repaired vehicle for £400, so that he was

---

[1] [1973] QB 195. *Cf. Ings v Industrial Acceptance Corp* (1962) 32 DLR 2d 611.
[2] A Burrows, *The Law of Restitution* (3rd edn, 2011), 238.

definitely benefitted by the work.[3] Although Bennett's enrichment as a result of Harper's work was £325 (the sale price minus its unrepaired value) the award of the lower sum of £226 might be defended on the basis that it was only to this extent that the enrichment was at Harper's expense. The rest of the uplift in value was attributable to the potential for improvement of the car to which Bennett had better title.[4]

However, even Lord Denning was of the view that Harper's possession of the vehicle was an important consideration.

> No matter whether the plaintiffs recover it with the aid of the courts, or without it, the innocent purchaser will recover the value of the improvements he has done to it.[5]

In principle, there should be no freestanding claim to the value of the work done, absent some kind of acceptance by the improver.[6] As argued in Chapters 3, 4, and 5, the mere fact that the claimant has mistakenly enriched the defendant should not suffice, and the other members of the court were clear in not supporting such a claim.

3. A Qualification to a Damages Award

If the claim had been for damages against the improver, the value of those improvements should be taken into account in quantifying any award. When Harper sold the improved car to the finance company and transferred possession to them, he committed the tort of conversion. Without further qualification, this would entitle Bennett either to damages reflecting the market value of the title to the car at that time, or to 'waive' the tort and to claim the proceeds of sale.[7]

These awards are however reduced according to a rule that is, today, found in the Torts (Interference with Goods) Act 1977:

> If in proceedings for wrongful interference against a person (the 'improver') who has improved the goods, it is shown that the improver acted in the mistaken but honest belief that he had a good title to them, an allowance shall be made for the extent to which, at the time as at which the goods fall to be valued in assessing damages, the value of the goods is attributable to the improvement.[8]

Absent this kind of rule, the person with better title to the vehicle could take, with the law's assistance, through a claim for damages, the benefit of the work the improver had done. There is a large difference between the law imposing an obligation to make restitution upon

---

[3] [1973] QB 195, 198 (argument of counsel); P Birks, *An Introduction to the Law of Restitution* (rev edn, 1989), 124.
[4] See eg R Stevens, 'Three Enrichment Issues' in A Burrows and A Rodger (eds), *Mapping the Law* (2006). *Mea culpa*.
[5] [1973] QB 195, 202.
[6] For comparison see the French Code Civil, Art 555. On German law see G Dannmann, *The German Law of Unjustified Enrichment and Restitution* (2009), 113–116.
[7] See Chapter 16, Profits.
[8] Section 6(1). This allowance may also be relied upon by a good faith purchaser of the vehicle from a good faith improver: s 6(2).

someone who bears no responsibility for their enrichment at another's expense, and the law's assisting someone with title to a thing to enrich themselves at the expense of another.

Livingstone v Rawyard's Coal Co[9] was the culmination of a long series of cases concerning the mining of coal that disclosed the same principle at common law.[10] The defendant innocently mined coal from under the plaintiff's land and sold the coal. Coal on the surface is worth more than the same coal under the ground. The act of mining did not confer upon the defendant any better title to the coal. When the mined coal was sold, which constitutes a tort, the plaintiff would, therefore, without more, be entitled to the value of the coal at that point as damages. However, the court held that a just allowance for the outlay in mining the coal had to be given in quantifying the award. Where, by contrast, the defendant has mined the coal knowingly trespassing upon the plaintiff's land, he is required to account for the full value of the coal once sold.[11] The deliberate trespasser is liable for the value of the coal at the surface even where the plaintiff could not have mined the coal himself.[12]

However, this kind of qualification of an award of damages cannot explain *Greenwood v Bennett* where no claim for damages was sought.

4. A Qualification to an Order for Specific Delivery

As seen, it was part of the ratio of the decision in *Greenwood v Bennett* that in an action for specific delivery of the vehicle, the court should make it a condition of such an order that the plaintiff reimburse the defendant for the expenditure incurred.[13] This seems to be based upon the same considerations that, as above, apply to any damages award. However, just as with the qualification of an award of damages, this seems to give an incomplete result if the plaintiff is able to repossess the vehicle without the court's assistance. If, for example, Harper had left the vehicle parked on the street, and Bennett had driven it away because still in possession of a set of keys, should the end result differ?

5. A Qualification to Accession?

Another approach, which requires a distinction to be drawn between the labour and the materials, is to qualify a rule of accession. Where an accessory thing has ceased to separately exist and has acceded to the principal thing, causing the party with title to the accessory thing to lose his right, German law requires the party who has lost his rights in this way to be reimbursed by the party who has benefitted,[14] and there is some limited authority for such a rule in the common law.[15] Without qualification however such a rule may operate harshly,

---

[9] (1880) 5 App Cas 25 (HL). See also *Beck v Northern Natural Gas Co* 170 F 3d 1018 (10th Cir 1999).
[10] For examples outside of that context see *Chinery v Viall* (1860) 5 H&N 288, 157 ER 1192 (discussed in Chapter 16, Profits); *Butler v Egg and Egg Pulp Marketing Board* (1966) 114 CLR 185 (High Ct of Australia).
[11] *Martin v Porter* (1839) 5 M&W 351, 151 ER 149.
[12] ibid.
[13] *Cf. Rowley v Ginnever* [1897] 2 Ch 503, 507 per Kekewich J. See also the lien for improvements to land made in *Lac Minerals Ltd v International Corona Resources Ltd* [1989] 2 SCR 574.
[14] BGB § 951.
[15] See *McKeown v Cavalier Yachts Pty Ltd* [1988] 13 NSWLR 303 (Young J); *cf. Estok v Heguy* 40 DLR (2d) 88 (Brown J.).

potentially requiring the owner of the principal thing to realise it in order to meet such a claim, and it is unclear whether the common law has the accession rule and if it does in what form.[16] If the improvements have been done by a third party using the plaintiff's materials without his consent, then such a rule is important if the accession doctrine is adopted. In *Greenwood v Bennett* itself, such a rule would not allow for reimbursement of the labour in repairing the car, and so again alone appears inadequate.

6. A 'Tracing' Claim?

A further possibility is to argue that the improver can 'trace' the value of the work and materials, into the value of the right to the thing and assert that as a result he is entitled to some kind of right in relation to the thing.

The metaphor of tracing value is, again, misleading us here. The improver has not contributed to the acquisition of the right to the thing, as does someone whose money is taken and used to buy the title to a car. Rather he has contributed to the value of the thing itself. On its own this cannot create any duty upon the rightholder in relation to the title he has. No claim in Equity that the title to the car be held for the improver can therefore be asserted,[17] and as we have seen at common law there is properly no such thing as a 'tracing claim'.[18]

7. A Qualification to Priority of Title

Cairns LJ considered that if the car had reached Bennett's possession without the assistance of legal process (eg if Harper had left the car parked in the street and Bennett had driven it away) then 'it is difficult to see that Howard could have any claim against him for the expenditure that he was put to in making the repairs to it'.[19]

That the result should turn upon whether the party with prior title can repossess the vehicle without the court's assistance seems incorrect. A better approach is to return again to the dispute between the Sabinians and the Proculians.[20] Who has better title, the person with prior possession or the person with subsequent possession who has improved the thing? If the rule favours one over the other, should this be without qualification?

In the common law it is somewhat misleading to say that Bennett 'owned' the Jaguar car. The common law is a system of relativity of title. Bennett had *a* title to the vehicle, but so too did Howard from his later possession of it. Where there are two or more valid titles in relation to the same thing, the law needs a rule to resolve any conflict. The justification for resolving priority disputes between persons with rights to a thing by reference to whose title is first in time is relatively weak. If we are to prioritise the first in order of time, where the thing has been innocently improved by the later party with a competing title, it makes sense to qualify this blunt rule by only allowing it to be asserted if the subsequent party who has improved the thing is reimbursed for his work. The later improver not only has a title

---

[16] See Chapter 11, Things.
[17] *Re Diplock's Estate* [1948] Ch 465 (CA). Chapter 13, Equity: Restitution.
[18] Chapter 11, Things.
[19] [1973] QB 195, 203.
[20] See Chapter 10, Necessity.

to the thing through possession, he has also 'mixed' his labour with it, which might be said to make a difference.[21] On this view, it should not matter whether in *Greenwood v Bennett* the car had been sold, so as to leave Bennett 'incontrovertibly' enriched, and no distinction should be made between the labour and the materials. Indeed, factual enrichment should not be the relevant test, and the court was correct that it was irrelevant that Bennett had sold the car.

The better rule here is analogous to that which we saw in relation to the law of salvage.[22] The right to the thing that the improver should acquire is not merely a possessory lien (ie a mere privilege to possess the thing so as not to commit a wrong by so doing) that would be lost when no longer in possession (as it would be if Bennett had driven away the car parked in the street). Rather it should be a superior title to the thing itself, unless and until paid for the expenditure incurred in improving it. A similar rule was found in Roman law.[23]

The position of the improver in possession of a chattel who mistakenly thinks that he owns it is different from that of one who carries out repairs on the instructions of a thief who the repairer mistakenly believes to be the true owner. For example, a garage which carries out repairs on a vehicle acquires a lien to secure the thief's obligation to pay for the repairs, but as there is no freestanding obligation on the party from whom the car has been stolen to pay for the work, no lien with respect to him.[24] The garage repairer has rendered his performance to the thief, and it is from him alone that he must look for payment.

By contrast, in *Spenser v S Franses Ltd*[25] an expert on antiques carried out research work into the provenance of embroideries at the request of the party with title to them. This work considerably increased their value as it revealed that they were medieval and worth a very large sum of money. The court concluded (perplexingly) that the parties had not entered into a concluded contract but did award the expert a non-contractual *quantum meruit* for the work carried out. In addition, the court found that the expert was entitled to a lien over the goods to secure payment. This arises on the same basis as the lien acquired by an unpaid seller, carrier, or repairer. The prior right to possession is qualified, subject to the condition that the work must be paid for before being capable of being asserted. The unusual feature of the decision was that the work had increased the value of the title to the things, without altering the physical things themselves.

Unlike in *Greenwood v Bennett* however, the expert's title to the goods is a security right, securing an independent obligation to pay for the work done. If, by contrast, Bennett had not wished to pay for the work, he could have chosen to abandon any claim to the car. There should be no freestanding claim against him.

---

[21] J Locke, *Two Treatises of Government* (1689), § 27.
[22] Chapter 10, Necessity.
[23] J Inst 2.1.30.
[24] *Tappenden v Artus* [1964] 2 QB 185 (CA). See also *Cahill v Hall* 37 NE 573 (1894) (Holmes J); *Brown and Davies Ltd v Galbraith* [1972] 1 WLR 997 (CA).
[25] [2011] EWHC 1269 (QB). *Cf*. the French *Fragonard* case (Cass le ci, 25 May 1992, Bull Civ I, No 165), where, in a claim for rescission, an allowance was made for the improved value of a painting by the discovery of its true provenance by the buyer.

C. Land

1. Introduction

By contrast with goods, the law in England in relation to improvements to land is, today, usually mediated through the doctrine of 'proprietary estoppel'. This is unfortunate.[26] As a doctrine, it has never been confined to improvements to land,[27] and, at least in the English jurisdiction, it has broken free of its original justifiable scope. The leading textbook on the law of proprietary estoppel rightly identifies that it has three distinct strands.[28] Two of those strands are justifiable. The third, a cause of action now travelling under that name, is not. It in turn involves the confusion of at least two separate ideas. These different strands need to be disentangled if any progress is to be made. Today it is common for the courts to describe the appropriate response as being a matter of discretion.[29] This is an inevitable result of the running together of these distinct concepts.[30]

To be estopped is to be barred or precluded from asserting something. 'Estop' is an old variation on the word stop. In its legitimate forms, a party may either be estopped from asserting a fact or a right. Estoppel *per rem judicatem*, or *res judicata*, is a generic term of which its two species are cause of action estoppel and issue estoppel, each of which bars the assertion of either facts or rights that have been finally determined in earlier judicial proceedings.[31] Such an estoppel, like other legitimate forms, is not itself a cause of action.

That something has gone wrong with the judicial analysis of a rule is apparent when the label no longer reflects the rule for which it stands, where the development is relatively recent, is not reflected in the law of other jurisdictions, and the source of the mistake is possible to identify and explain. The large number of litigated cases concerning the uncertain doctrine of 'proprietary estoppel' over the last 40 years, which has no parallel in other jurisdictions, does not reflect well on English law.

2. Evidential Estoppel

Where *A* makes a clear and unambiguous statement of fact to *B*, intending *B* to rely upon such statement, and *B* believed the truth of the statement and acted upon it, *A* may be estopped from proving that the fact is false in proceedings between *A* and *B*.[32] This is a rule of evidence.[33] It is neither a cause of action nor a defence, although it may allow a cause of

---

[26] '[A]n amalgam of doubtful utility' *per* Robert Goff J in *Amalgamated Investment & Property Co Ltd v Texas Commerce International Bank Ltd* [1982] QB 84, 103 but contrast *Taylors Fashions Ltd v Liverpool Victoria Trustees Ltd* [1982] QB 133 (CA), 151–152 *per* Oliver J.
[27] Eg *Greasley v Cooke* [1980] 1 WLR 1306 (CA).
[28] B McFarlane, *The Law of Proprietary Estoppel* (2nd edn, 2020), [1.03]–[1.04].
[29] Eg *Jennings v Rice* [2002] EWCA Civ 159, [52] *per* Robert Walker LJ; *Habberfield v Habberfield* [2019] EWCA Civ 890, [2019] 2 P&CRDG 13, [87] *per* Lewison LJ.
[30] Eg *Commonwealth of Australia v Verwayen* (1990) 170 CLR 394, 410–413 *per* Mason CJ, 'there is but one doctrine of estoppel'.
[31] *Thoday v Thoday* [1964] P 181 (CA), 197–198 *per* Diplock LJ; *Vervaeke v Smith* [1983] 1 AC 145 (HL).
[32] *Pickard v Sears* (1837) 6 A&E 469, 112 ER 179; *Freeman v Cooke* (1848) 2 Ex 654, 154 ER 652; *Hopgood v Brown* [1955] 1 WLR 213 (CA)
[33] *Low v Bouverie* [1891] 3 Ch 82 (CA), 101 *per* Lindley LJ, 105 *per* Bowen LJ, 111–112 *per* Kay LJ; *London Joint Stock Bank v Macmillan* [1918] AC 777 (HL), 818 *per* Viscount Haldane; *Evans v Bartlam* [1937] AC 473 (HL), 484 *per* Lord Wright. See also H Malek (ed), *Phipson on Evidence* (20th edn, 2021), ch 5. But see *Berridge v Benjies*

action or defence that would otherwise fail to succeed. There is, as a matter of its history, nothing specifically 'equitable' about this rule (although in the United States it has taken on the label of 'equitable estoppel'). It applies across private law and is not limited to disputes concerning property or land. What is estopped from being asserted is a fact inconsistent with the representation. It is irrelevant that the representor was mistaken as to the facts. This form of estoppel is also sometimes called 'common law' estoppel, but this too is misleading as the rule applies across the jurisdictional divide.

Estoppel in this form, estoppel by representation, is an all or nothing digital matter. The effect is to bar the party who has made the representation from proving its falsity. Its scope is fixed by the representation, rather than by the degree of reliance upon it.[34] It can only operate in relation to statements of existing fact, and not promises in relation to behaviour in the future.[35]

When operating in this way, as a rule of evidence, the only party who can (in principle) be estopped from asserting the fact stated is the representor. For example,[36]

D contracts to sell 80 bushels of wheat to *P*. *D* assures *P* that he has appropriated that quantity of wheat to his account, and *P* pays *D*. In fact, *D* has not allocated any wheat to *P*'s order.

If *D* fails to deliver, *P* should have a claim in conversion against him. *D* should be estopped from asserting that title to that quantity of wheat has not passed to *P*. If he has not, as a matter of fact, allocated that amount of wheat to *P*'s order, so as to be identifiable, he should be estopped from disproving the fact represented. By contrast, if a third party had damaged wheat in *D*'s granary, or *D* has gone into bankruptcy, *P* could not rely upon *D*'s representations as against others (the party damaging the wheat, *D*'s insolvency administrator) to show, contrary to the truth, that an appropriation had occurred, so as to confer title to any specific wheat.[37]

3. Equitable Estoppel

The second, equitable, form of estoppel is best understood as an extension of the law of waiver or acquiescence. In this form, what is estopped from being asserted is a right (which includes a power[38] or an immunity[39]).[40] This form of estoppel takes the classic form of

Business Centre [1997] 1 WLR 53 (PC), 57 *per* Lord Hoffmann; P Feltham and others (eds), *Spencer Bower, Reliance Based Estoppel and Related Doctrines* (5th edn, 2017), [1.51]–[1.62].

[34] *Avon CC v Howlett* [1983] 1 WLR 605 (CA), 620–625 *per* Slade LJ; *Kelly v Fraser* [2012] UKPC 25, [2013] 1 AC 450, [17] *per* Lord Sumption.
[35] *Jorden v Money* (1854) 5 HL Cas 15, 10 ER 868 (PC).
[36] Taken from McFarlane, *The Law of Proprietary Estoppel* (n 28), [8.52]–[8.53].
[37] *Re Goldcorp Exchange Ltd* [1995] 1 AC 74 (PC), 94 *per* Lord Mustill.
[38] Eg *Hughes v Metropolitan Rly* (1877) 2 App Cas 439 (HL).
[39] Eg *Commonwealth of Australia v Verwayen* (1990) 170 CLR 394 (HCA).
[40] The equitable jurisdiction to perfect a failed gift, exemplified by *Dillwyn v Llewelyn* (1862) 4 De G, F & J 517, 45 ER 1284, is not therefore a true example of an estoppel. It is analogous to the doctrine of part performance that rendered binding an oral agreement for the sale of land in origin unenforceable for want of form under the Statute of Frauds 1677. That doctrine has been abolished in England in relation to contracts for the sale of land: Law of Property (Miscellaneous Provisions) Act 1989. See *Pipkos v Trayans* [2018] HCA 39 rejecting the assimilation of the doctrine of part performance into estoppel, but contrast *Voyce v Voyce* (1991) 62 P&CR 290 (CA) seeing the two as one.

equitable rules generally that we have seen.[41] A right (usually arising at common law) is barred or restrained from being asserted. Again, a rule about another rule.

It is possible to acquiesce to actions that would otherwise be wrongful with respect to us, thereby making them non-wrongful. At common law it is possible in this sense to waive all of our rights. If I step into a boxing ring wearing gloves, my opponent commits no battery by hitting me. My guests are not trespassing when I invite them into my home, and I will not be falsely imprisoning them if I lock the door behind them. Rights to our bodily safety, to exclude others from your property, not to be detained, or not to be defamed can all be waived. Waiver needs to be differentiated from alienation or transfer. In none of these examples has there been a transfer of a right. Many rights are inalienable, none are unwaivable. Rather the rightholder's manifestation of consent has conferred a privilege. Exceptionally, the rightholder has no right in relation to that person with respect to whom he has waived his right. This is sometimes put in Latin: *volenti non fit injuria*. *Volenti* is not a defence to a wrong, in the same way that contributory fault is. Rather once the right is waived there can be no breach of a duty, and hence no wrong to commit. In the context of land, the same idea is commonly referred to as the conferral of a non-contractual licence (licence being synonymous with privilege).

Precisely the same principles apply to contractual rights. If a carrier has contracted to deliver goods to me on 1 April, if I state that it is fine if they deliver the next day they will not be in breach of contract if they deliver on the 2 April. Waiver is effective without the necessity of proving a new contract or an estoppel. It is unnecessary to show that the carrier has accepted my offer of a delay, it need not be shown that I have been provided any consideration for it. The effect of the waiver is not to vary the contract, any more than my consent to be punched destroys my right to bodily safety, but rather to prevent there from being a wrong committed by the non-performance.[42] Even if, as a matter of fact, the carrier could never have delivered before 2 April in any event, and does not change their behaviour in any way on the basis of the counterparty's assurance, no breach of contract is committed. Similarly, if you grant me permission to enter your land to which you have title, I am not a trespasser if I do so. It does not matter that I would have entered without permission in any event. No reliance is required.[43]

For waiver to be effective there must be a manifestation of a *current* intention to waive the right. If I initially consent to painful surgery and then communicate my change of mind, or if I agree to stay in the Big Brother House for a series but ask to leave after a couple of days, the surgeon would be committing a battery if they go ahead anyway, and the producers of the programme would be falsely imprisoning if they refused to release me. If in our contractual example the carrier is initially told that delivery the next day is fine, but is then immediately told that actually the goods are needed on 1 April after all, delivery on 2 April will constitute a breach of contract. A waiver is therefore suspensory not extinctive of the right and may be withdrawn.

The withdrawal of such consent may operate unfairly if its effect were to immediately return the parties back to the pre-waiver legal position. If you are invited into someone's

---

[41] Chapter 12, Equity: General.
[42] *Hartley v Hymans* [1920] 3 KB 475.
[43] *Alan & Co Ltd v El Nasr Export and Import Co* [1972] 2 QB 189 (CA), 213 *per* Lord Denning MR; *Trial Lawyers Association of British Columbia v Royal & Sun Alliance Insurance Co of Canada* 2021 SCC 47, [75] *per* Karakatsanis J.

home for dinner, and then your permission to enter is withdrawn in the middle of the soup course, you have a reasonable opportunity to leave before becoming a trespasser.[44]

It is the same idea that underlies the extension of waiver now commonly described as 'equitable estoppel'. In the leading decision of the House of Lords in *Hughes v Metropolitan Railway Co*[45] the defendant had leased premises from the plaintiff. In October 1874 the landlords served notice, as they had power to do under the terms of the lease, requiring the tenant to repair the premises within six months, the lease being forfeit upon failure to comply. The tenants replied that the repairs would be carried out, but that the landlord may wish to purchase the surrender of the lease. From November negotiations took place for the landlord to buy out the tenant, but at the end of the year these broke down. The original notice to repair expired in April 1875, and the plaintiff served a writ of ejectment. The repairs, which had been delayed because of the negotiations, were completed in June. The House of Lords granted the defendant relief from forfeiture, the operative principle being subsequently best described by Bowen LJ:

[I]f persons who have contractual rights against others induce by their conduct those against whom they have such rights that such rights will either not be enforced or will be kept in suspense or abeyance for some particular time, those persons will not be allowed by a Court of Equity to enforce the rights until such time has elapsed, without at all events placing the parties in the same position as they were before.[46]

There is nothing necessarily 'promissory' or 'proprietary' about this form of estoppel, and it may apply to restrain the assertion of many kinds of right.[47] On this usage the difference between 'proprietary' and 'promissory' estoppel is that between the kind of right that is barred from being asserted, rather than the operative principle. Describing such cases as 'promissory' misleadingly implies that there must have been a promise, whereas what is required is acquiescence.[48]

Although not originally given this label, the classic form of this kind of estoppel in relation to rights to land arose where someone with title to land stood by while another, who believed that they had title to the land, built upon it.[49] The case that caused the authors of *Snell's Equity* to recognise, for the first time, the term 'proprietary estoppel',[50] which in turn led to its judicial adoption,[51] was *Inwards v Baker*,[52] which concerned improvements to land that were encouraged.

Old Mr Baker had title to six acres of land. His son lived nearby and wished to purchase another area of land on which to build a bungalow. His father said to him 'Why not put the

---

[44] *Canadian Pacific Railway v The King* [1931] AC 414 (PC).
[45] (1877) 2 App Cas 439 (HL).
[46] *Birmingham District Land Co v L&NW Railway* (1888) 40 ChD 268, 281 (CA). See also *Imperator Realty Co Inc v Tull* 127 NE 263, 267 (NYCA, 1920) *per* Cardozo J.
[47] See *Kammins Ballrooms Co Ltd v Zenith Investments (Torquay) Ltd* [1971] AC 850 (HL), 883–885 *per* Lord Diplock. *Proctor v Bennis* (1887) LR 36 Ch D 740 (CA) (estopped from asserting an [IP] right).
[48] *Cf. Wilmott v Barber* (1880) 15 Ch D 96, 105–106 *per* Fry J.
[49] *The Earl of Oxford's Case* (1615) Rep Ch 1, 21 ER 485; *Huning v Ferrers Dann v Spurrier* (1802) 7 Ves Jr 231, 32 ER 94; *Wilmott v Barber* (1880) 15 ChD 96, 105–106.
[50] R Megarry and P V Baker (eds), *Snell's The Principles of Equity* (26th edn, 1966), 629. See McFarlane, *The Law of Proprietary Estoppel* (n 28), 1
[51] *ER Ives Investment Ltd v High* [1967] 2 QB 379, 399.
[52] [1965] 2 QB 29 (CA). See also *Bibby v Sterling* (1998) 76 P&CR D36 (CA).

bungalow on my land and make it a little bit bigger' which is what the son did. The son then lived there for 30 years. The father died, leaving the title to the land to others in his will, who then sought to evict the son. The Court of Appeal concluded that it would be inequitable to allow the assertion of the right to exclude from possession against the son. The court did not enquire into the value of the work the son had put into erecting the property. Again, estoppel in this form is also a digital matter: the rightholder is estopped from asserting the right relied upon. Its degree does not vary according to the quantum of reliance.

By contrast with estoppel in its evidential form, it is not just the party who has given the assurance who is prevented from asserting the right. In *Inwards v Baker* the right to exclude others from the land was incapable of being asserted against the son by the father's successors in title. Their right to exclusive possession of the land was not however lost, the only person against whom Old Mr Baker or his successors in title were estopped from asserting their right to exclude was the son.

A party in possession of land, such as a squatter, acquires a title to the land good against all others, save those with a better prior title. Where the party in possession, such as the son in *Inwards v Baker*, combines the right acquired from occupation with the privilege created by estoppel as against the only party with the better legal title, he will have a right to the land that is similar to the best legal title to it during the currency of the privilege.[53]

It may, in some cases, be fair to allow the rightholder to reassert his right if certain conditions are met (eg if he can readily prove the value of reliance expenditure and any other detriment and reimburse it, thereby placing the other party back in the position he would have been in if no assurances had been given).[54] In the subsequent decision of *Hussey v Palmer*,[55] the plaintiff was an elderly widow who was invited by her daughter to live with her, in the home that her husband had title to. In order for there to be sufficient space, an extra bedroom was built as an extension, which the mother paid for. The parties then fell out, and the mother left. The Court of Appeal concluded that title to the property was held on resulting trust for the mother in proportion to her payment. However, this is in principle incorrect. The husband's title to the land was not acquired in part through any payment by the mother.[56] It should not be possible to 'trace' into improvements to land and thereby claim that the title to it is thereby held on trust. Her contribution had not been to the acquisition of the right to the land, so as to potentially give rise to a trust or equitable lien, but rather to the land, the physical thing, itself. It had never been agreed with the husband that the widow was to acquire any right to the land. A better solution would be that the defendant should be estopped from excluding the plaintiff from the home for the rest of her life, unless and until she was reimbursed for the extension.[57] In the alternative, but not in addition, the plaintiff should have a personal claim for the restitution of the value of the work done. The extension had been paid for under an agreement between the parties on the condition that she was to live there in return for the rest of her life. This condition failed if she was forced to leave. This would have ensured repayment to the widow, which a trust alone does not.

---

[53] *Cf. Unity Joint Stock Mutual Banking Association v King* (1856) 25 Beav 72, 77 53 ER 563, 565 *per* Sir John Romilly MR; *Plimmer v The Mayor, Councillors and Citizens of the City of Wellington* (1884) 9 App Cas 699 (PC).
[54] *Cf. Beale v Harvey* [2003] EWCA Civ 1883, [2004] 2 P&CR 18.
[55] [1972] 1 WLR 1286 (CA).
[56] *Cf. Caverley v Green* (1984) 155 CLR 242 (HCA).
[57] *Cf. Dodsworth v Dodsworth* (1973) 228 EG 1115 (CA); *Bawden v Bawden* (CA, Unreported 7 November 1997).

274   IMPROVEMENTS

The same principle may apply where one party is mistaken either as to his current rights or whether he would be granted an interest in land, and makes improvements to another's land on this basis, even where there has been no positive encouragement by the person with title to the land.[58] In *Ramsden v Dyson*[59] the defendant had improved the plaintiff's land in the belief that he would be granted a long lease. The plaintiff was unaware of their mistake, and taken alone the mistaken improvement did not bar the assertion of the right to the land. If, however, the plaintiff had known of the mistake an estoppel would have arisen. The classic statement of the conditions of when an equitable estoppel would arise in cases of mistaken improvements is that of Fry J in *Willmott v Barber*:[60]

> It has been said that the acquiescence which will deprive a man of his legal rights must amount to fraud, and in my view that is an abbreviated statement of a very true proposition. A man is not to be deprived of his legal rights unless he has acted in such a way as would make it fraudulent for him to set up those rights. What, then, are the elements or requisites necessary to constitute fraud of that description? In the first place the plaintiff must have made a mistake as to his legal rights. Secondly, the plaintiff must have expended some money or must have done some act (not necessarily upon the defendant's land) on the faith of his mistaken belief. Thirdly, the defendant, the possessor of the legal right, must know of the existence of his own right which is inconsistent with the right claimed by the plaintiff. If he does not know of it he is in the same position as the plaintiff, and the doctrine of acquiescence is founded upon conduct with a knowledge of your legal rights. Fourthly, the defendant, the possessor of the legal right, must know of the plaintiff's mistaken belief of his rights. If he does not, there is nothing which calls upon him to assert his own rights. Lastly, the defendant, the possessor of the legal right, must have encouraged the plaintiff in his expenditure of money or in the other acts which he has done, either directly or by abstaining from asserting his legal right. Where all these elements exist, there is fraud of such a nature as will entitle the Court to restrain the possessor of the legal right from exercising it, but, in my judgment, nothing short of this will do.

It is a notable feature of Fry J's five probanda that they are not expressed as being specific to rights to land, but instead as applying to legal rights generally.[61] Since being set down, the condition that the improver be mistaken as to his *current* rights has been relaxed. If she thought that she would be granted an interest in land, and the rightholder has stood by, an estoppel may also arise.[62] Again, the idea that those who are mistaken as to the future are always risk-runners underserving of protection is rejected.

It might be objected that mere passive abstention by the rightholder from asserting his right, without encouragement of either the mistake or the expenditure, is equivalent to

---

[58] But see McFarlane, *The Law of Proprietary Estoppel* (n 28), [2-04]–[2-50] who would confine the operation of the acquiescence principle to such cases.
[59] (1866) LR 1 HL 129, *cf. The Duke of Beaufort v Patrick* (1853) Beav 60, 51 ER 954, restraining repossession but requiring compensation or the right lost. See also *Lim Teng Huan v Ang Swee Chuan* [1991] 1 WLR 113 (PC).
[60] (1880) 14 Ch D 1065–1066. The other much quoted classic statement is by Lord Cranworth LC in *Ramsden v Dyson* (1866) 1 LR HL 129, 140–141.
[61] See also *Fisher v Brooker* [2009] UKHL 41, [2009] 1 WLR 1764.
[62] *Ramsden v Dyson* (1866) LR 1 HL 129 per Lord Kingsdown; *Plimmer v Wellington Corp* (1884) 9 App Cas 699 (PC), 710 per Sir Arthur Hobhouse; *cf. Lester v Woodgate* [2010] EWCA Civ 199; *Scottish Newcastle plc v Lancashire Mortgage Corporation Ltd* [2007] EWCA Civ 684 criticised McFarlane, *The Law of Proprietary Estoppel* (n 28), [2-18]–[2-25].

imposing liability for inaction. Here, however, the law is not imposing upon the landowner any positive duty of action, rather it is a condition of his being able to continue to assert his right against the mistaken party that he speaks up. By contrast, if the mistaken improver wishes to impose a positive obligation upon the landowner to pay for the work done, some kind of request or free acceptance must be shown.[63] Unlike the position in relation to estoppel by representation, the rightholder must know of his right.

Equitable estoppel properly so-called is therefore a 'shield not a sword'[64] as it is a bar to the assertion of rights. It is not a cause of action, although it may allow a claim that would otherwise fail to succeed.[65] It must relate to some pre-existing right as between the parties. It is generally 'suspensive not extinctive'.[66] Equitable estoppel of this kind may arise because of actual encouragement, as in *Inwards v Baker*, or standing by, as contemplated in *Wilmott v Barber*.

However, the above discussion discloses that in England, the approaches to improvements to goods and to land are not the same.[67] In relation to goods the rule is more generous to the improver in one respect. The party with prior title may only successfully assert it against the mistaken improver of goods, who is in possession with their own later title, upon reimbursing the value of the work done. By contrast, in relation to land, the party with prior title may only be barred from asserting it against the mistaken improver in occupation where he knows of the other's mistake and has stood by without correcting it. Perhaps this difference in treatment could be explained on the basis that title to land is more readily discoverable than title to goods. Alternatively, it may be a feature of the fact that a party with better title to land (realty) may obtain specific recovery as of right, whereas in relation to goods (personalty) the court may confine the party with prior title to damages only. The estoppel rule applicable to land also applies, as Fry J intended, to other rights such as to goods as well, so that a party with prior title who knowingly stands by may in some case be absolutely estopped from asserting his rights, regardless of his willingness to reimburse the expenditure.

In *Cobbe v Yeoman's Row*,[68] the defendants had title to a block of flats. They reached an oral agreement in principle, but no concluded contract, for the sale of the flats to the plaintiff, a property developer. Under the agreement, the plaintiff was to pursue the application

---

[63] See *Blue Haven Enterprises v Tully* [2006] UKPC 17; *JS Bloor Ltd v Pavillion Developments Ltd* [2008] EWHC 724 (TCC); [2008] 2 EGLR 85 discussed in Chapter 3, Performance.

[64] *Combe v Combe* [1951] 2 KB 215 (CA); *Baird Textile Holdings Ltd v Marks and Spencer plc* [2001] EWCA Civ 274, [20002] 1 All ER (Comm) 737. For that earlier understanding in Australia see *Grundt v Great Boulder Pty Gold Mines Ltd* (1937) 59 CLR 641 (HCA) but see now *Waltons Stores (Interstate) Ltd v Maher* (1988) 164 CLR 387. In Canada the same restriction on estoppel as a cause of action as requiring promises in relation to property applies: *Max Wayne Cowper-Smith v Gloria Lyn Morgan* [2017] 2 SCR 754, [17] *per* McLachlin CJ.

[65] Eg *Commonwealth of Australia v Verwayen* (1990) 170 CLR 394. See *Amalgamated Investment & Property Co v Texas Commerce International Bank* [1982] QB 84, 105 *per* Goff J.

[66] *Tool Metal Manufacturing Co Ltd v Tungsten Electric Co Ltd* [1955] 1 WLR 761 (HL).

[67] Compare the more generous approach taken in relation to improvers of another's land in § 10 of the US *Restatement of Restitution* (3rd): 'A person who improves the real or personal property of another, acting by mistake, has a claim in restitution as necessary to prevent unjust enrichment.' It is accepted that this departs from the common law's traditional approach § 10 Comment a. In the early history of the United States, in an era of undiscoverable land titles and the 'difficulties of surveying the wide open spaces' perhaps a more generous approach to the improver was justified: A Kull, 'Mistaken Improvements and Restitution Calculus' in D Johnston and R Zimmerman (eds), *Unjustified Enrichment: Key Issues in Comparative Perspective* (2002), 369, 369–370. See also the very generous treatment of the pursuer in Scotland: *Newton v Newton* 1925 SC 715, 1925 SLT 476 (Inner House Ct of Session).

[68] [2008] UKHL 55, [2008] 1 WLR 1752.

for planning permission. If it was obtained, the defendants were to sell the title to the land to him for £12 million, the properties would then be redeveloped, and the flats sold off. Any proceeds over £24 million were to be divided equally between the parties. The defendants then decided that the price was too low, but did not disclose their change of mind, continuing instead to encourage the developer to pursue the application for consent. Once planning permission was secured, the defendants refused to proceed. Etherton J and the Court of Appeal awarded the claimants 50% of the increase in the value of the promised property brought about by the claimant's obtaining of the planning permission on the basis of 'proprietary estoppel'. Lord Scott, with whom Lords Hoffmann, Brown, and Mance agreed, rejected this basis for such an award.[69] The claimants were not asserting that the defendants were 'estopped' from asserting anything, how then could this be a source of a claim for remuneration?[70] Instead, the court, rightly, awarded a *quantum meruit* for the work done at the defendant's request. Lord Scott's speech reflected an earlier, and more coherent, view of the role of estoppel, which confined it to a preclusive role. However, his speech ignored many cases, over several decades, adopting a much more expansive view of the doctrine.

For a brief moment, therefore, it appeared as if estoppel might be re-confined to its proper role of estopping. In *Thorner v Major*[71] however the House of Lords rejected this interpretation of the decision, and so the wider approach, to which we now turn, remains the law.

4. Illegitimate Extension

(a) *'Estoppel' as a cause of action*

The third form that 'estoppel' has taken in recent decades is as a cause of action. In England this has occurred in relation to promises concerning land and is therefore given the label 'proprietary estoppel'. In Australia, as we shall see, 'estoppel' as a cause of action is probably no longer subject even to this limitation.

On any view, when taking this form 'estoppel' is a misnomer. Instead of one party being barred from asserting something against the counterparty, whether a fact or a right, it is an independent source of the acquisition of rights against others. In England, this has taken two forms. The first, much more common, response is by ordering the conveyance of rights in relation to land despite the ordinary conditions for the acquisition of such rights not having been satisfied. The second is requiring the 'estopped' party to compensate the claimant, generally measured by reference to their reliance expenditure. The latter approach is rare, usually only taken where the promise is insufficiently certain to be given effect to (as where, eg, the party with title to two or more premises promises that they will convey one of them without specifying which).

These two strands would be better explained in two quite different ways, without invoking 'estoppel'. First, where it is agreed that a specific right to land will be conveyed (or other interest executed or granted) to another in exchange for work or other consideration, a trust or other equitable right should arise upon the work or other consideration being provided.

---

[69] Lord Walker gave a concurring speech with which Lord Brown agreed.
[70] [2008] UKHL 55, [2008] 1 WLR 1752, [14].
[71] [2009] UKHL 18, [2009] 1 WLR 776.

Its content should be determined by what was promised. Such a constructive trust (or other 'equitable property' right) should depend upon there being an obligation to convey or grant that right but not upon such an agreement being capable of being specifically enforced.[72] It is the equivalent of the vendor-purchaser constructive trust that we saw and justified in Chapter 12, Equity: General. Second, the value of services provided conditionally at the request of another should be recoverable when that condition fails. Such claims for a *quantum meruit* are not and should not be conditional upon establishing that the service provided has enriched the defendant, nor that the claimant has suffered any detriment. There is nothing specifically equitable, in the jurisdictional sense, about the latter claim.[73]

(b) *Estoppel as a source of 'equitable property rights'*
The beginning of estoppel's growth was the decision of the Court of Appeal in *Crabb v Arun*,[74] which took one small step too far. The plaintiff had title to land with one point of access to the highway. Intending to sell a portion of the land that had the access point, he sought the agreement of the defendant council for another point of access to the road. An agreement in principle that there should be such additional access was reached, but no contract was ever entered into nor any grant of an easement made. The council then erected a gate at the entrance at which the plaintiff was to have the new access to the road. The plaintiff then sold the portion with the other access point. A dispute then arose, and the council closed the new access point, requiring £3,000 for the grant of an easement, which was more than the plaintiff wished to pay. Without any access, the use of the plaintiff's land would be sterilised.

The plaintiff sought a declaration that he was entitled to a right of way and an injunction restraining the defendant from interfering with his enjoyment of it.[75] Such relief was clearly appropriate: the defendant should have been estopped or barred from asserting their right to exclude the plaintiff. The court however went one step further than this and granted the plaintiff an easement over the council's land securing the right of access. How, absent the necessary conditions for the grant of an easement,[76] could such a right *erga omnes* be recognised?[77] If a contract for the grant of an easement had been entered into, and the plaintiffs had paid, then an equitable easement would have arisen on the same principle that we have seen applies in the case of vendor-purchaser constructive trusts. Here, however, there was no such agreement and no consideration provided by the plaintiff (ie he was a volunteer). How could such an equitable easement have arisen absent any obligation to grant one?

Further, instead of seeing equitable estoppel's role as being the barring of the assertion of a right, the court saw it as 'equity displayed at its most flexible'[78] allowing the court to make an order to do 'minimum equity to do justice to the parties'.[79] Subsequently, 'estoppel' (sic) as a cause of action 'developed with remarkable speed'.[80]

---

[72] *Cf. Chalmers v Pardoe* [1963] 1 WLR 677 (PC) where there is no mention of 'estoppel'.
[73] But see B McFarlane and P Sales, 'Promises, Detriment and Liability: Lessons from Proprietary Estoppel' (2015) 131 LQR 610.
[74] [1976] Ch 179 (CA). See also *Griffiths v Williams* (1978) 248 EG 947 (CA); *Joyce v Epsom and Ewell BC* [2012] EWCA Civ 1398, [2013] 1 P&CRDG 1.
[75] [1976] Ch 179 (CA), 180.
[76] Eg Law of Property Act 1925, s 52.
[77] An easement over another's title to land gives a right against all others that it is not unreasonably interfered with and will run with the benefitted title to land.
[78] [1976] Ch 179 (CA), 189.
[79] ibid, 198.
[80] McFarlane, *The Law of Proprietary Estoppel* (n 28), [1.17].

The point when the doctrine became fully unmoored, and 'estoppel' became a claim in itself, came in the subsequent decision of the Court of Appeal in *Pascoe v Turner*.[81] The plaintiff man and defendant woman had been living together, when the man began an affair with another woman. He then reassured the defendant that the house to which he had title and everything in it were hers. She stayed on in the house relying upon this reassurance, spending money on redecorations, improvements, and repairs. However, the house was never conveyed into her name, and the plaintiff subsequently gave her notice to quit, and commenced an action for possession. The Court of Appeal concluded that the 'minimum equity' required to give effect to the promise made was to require him to convey to her the title to the property. This is a constructive trust by any other name. There have subsequently been many cases where the courts have given effect to promises to confer rights in relation to land in a similar way.[82]

The uncertain state of the current law may be ascertained by contrasting the subsequent decision of the Court of Appeal in *Powell v Benney*.[83] Mr Powell, a pastor, and his wife, performed numerous chores for the elderly Mr Hobday, shopping and cooking for him, providing nursing care, and giving him money. In 1993 Mr Hobday informed them that he intended to leave them his properties after his death, an intention he repeated before others and in writing. The relationship continued on the same basis, and the couple paid for repair work to one of the properties to the value of £200. Mr Hobday died intestate. The trial judge refused to order the conveyance of the properties, which were worth £280,000, but instead ordered the payment of £20,000, to be paid from the sale of the properties. The Court of Appeal upheld the order. The court emphasised that there had been no bargain between the parties, which is true and should be significant but does not distinguish the decision in *Pascoe v Turner*.

It may be that a better distinction is that *Pascoe v Turner* should be reinterpreted as explicable as an extension of Equity's jurisdiction to perfect a gift where the formalities had not been complied with, but where there was 'part performance' (the standing-by whilst she carried out improvements) sufficient to operate as a substitute.[84] *Powell v Benney* by contrast concerned the promise of a future transfer.

Today, such a distinction is not maintainable as an explanation of the law because of the decision of the House of Lords in *Thorner v Major*.[85] The plaintiff worked for nearly 30 years without pay on the farm of his father's cousin, Peter. No express promise that he would inherit the farm was ever made, instead the impression that he would do so was created obliquely, such as by handing over an insurance policy notice saying 'that is for my death duties'. Peter died intestate, which left his estate to those more closely related to him and the plaintiff sought relief upon the basis of proprietary estoppel. The Court of Appeal, overturning the trial judge, found that the undertaking by the defendant was insufficiently

---

[81] [1979] 1 WLR 431 (CA). See also *Re Basham* [1986] 1 WLR 1498 (ChD); *Dillwyn v Llere Basham* [1986] 1 WLR 1498 but compare *Layton v Martin* [1986] 2 FLR 227. Compare from a few years earlier *Eves v Eves* [1975] 1 WLR 1338 (CA).

[82] Eg *Walton v Walton* (Unreported, 14 April 1994, CA); *Henry v Henry* [2010] UKPC 3, [2010] 1 All ER 988.

[83] [2007] EWCA Civ 1283, [2008] 1 P &CR DG12. See also *Watts v Story* (1983) NLJ 631 (CA); *Beale v Harvey* [2003] EWCA Civ 1883, [2004] 2 P&CR 18; *Uglow v Uglow* [2004] EWCA Civ 987; *Century (UK) Ltd SA v Clibbery* [2004] EWHC 1870 (Blackburne J).

[84] See also *Dillwyn v Llewelyn* (1862) 4 De G, F & J 517, 45 ER 1284.

[85] [2009] UKHL 18, [2009] 1 WLR 776.

certain to be reasonably relied upon. The House of Lords in turn overturned this conclusion, restoring the trial judge's decision, that an 'estoppel' gave rise to an entitlement in relation to the title to the farm, albeit not the rest of Peter's estate.

Lord Scott, whilst agreeing with the majority, in conformity with his prior speech in *Cobbe v Yeoman's Row*, preferred to base his conclusion upon finding that the undertaking that had been relied upon gave rise to a constructive trust. At least as a matter of language, a constructive trust is accurate in describing the result, when 'estoppel' is not.

The courts in more recent cases have exercised a wide-ranging discretion to create property rights that did not represent any promise made by the landowner. In the difficult to defend decision of *Gillett v Holt*,[86] a number of assurances had been given over several years to the plaintiff that the bulk of the defendant's estate, including the farm on which he lived, would be left to him on the defendant's death, which was eventually reflected in a will making the plaintiff the sole beneficiary. The plaintiff had relied upon these assurances for a 33-year period, by accepting a salary below the market value for the work he did on the farm. The parties' relationship then rapidly deteriorated, the plaintiff was dismissed, and by a new will the estate was to be left elsewhere. Amongst other orders, the Court of Appeal, overturning Carnwath J, ordered the conveyance of the farm to the plaintiff. However, the defendant, although elderly, was not at that point dead. The promise of the farm had been conditional upon that event, but the court in its discretion ordered the conveyance anyway.[87] A conditional equitable right to the title to the land, binding upon whoever the defendant left his title to the farm to may have been justifiable, but not the order of conveyance during the defendant's lifetime.

This 'flexible' approach was also adopted by the Court of Appeal in the similarly difficult *Moore v Moore*.[88] The problem that arose was the promise to leave the claimant his father's farm upon the death of both of his parents, which had been relied upon by the son for many years before the relationship between parents and son broke down. Although not determining a final order, the court again contemplated the correct solution as being the order of the immediate conveyance of title to the property despite the condition of the promise not having been satisfied (both parents being alive, although the father was incapacitated). This was to be coupled with financial arrangements to protect the elderly parents to be determined by the trial judge. If the parties' agreement had amounted to an enforceable contract, it is hard to imagine any court ordering a conveyance before the conditions precedent to the obligation to convey had been met. The court re-wrote the parties' agreement, albeit that it was informal, and re-allocated rights to land on a discretionary basis.

In *Walton v Walton*,[89] Hoffmann LJ had earlier stated that the contrast between equitable estoppel and contract was that the former

[d]oes not look forward into the future and guess what might happen. It looks backward from the moment when the promise falls due to be performed and asks whether, in the

---

[86] [2001] Ch 210. *Cf. Gee v Gee* [2018] EWHC 1393 (Birss J).
[87] *Cf. Davies v Davies* [2016] EWCA Civ 463; *Habberfield v Habberfield* [2019] EWCA Civ 890, [2019] 2 P&CRDG 13.
[88] [2018] EWCA Civ 2669.
[89] (Unreported, 14 April 1994, CA).

circumstances which have actually happened, it would be unconscionable for the promise not to be kept.

Today instead, the courts are looking backwards from the moment of the court judgment, which in *Gillett v Holt* and *Moore v Moore* predated the time when the promise fell due to be performed, and adjusting the parties' rights as they consider fair. In both cases, the plaintiff might as things had turned out have pre-deceased the promisor.

It is sometimes said that certainty is particularly valuable in commercial law. In fact, the opposite is true. Hard-headed commercial parties will attempt to settle disputes at an early stage in order to avoid costs. It is in family disputes, where relationships have collapsed into rancour, where clear rules are needed in order to protect litigants from bitterly fighting. Before the case was referred back to the trial judge to review for a second time to determine the 'minimum equity' to do justice between them, the parties in *Moore v Moore* had incurred legal costs of around £2.5 million, consuming the value of the farm.

The courts have proceeded on the assumption that the 'equity' that arises as a result of the promised conveyance or grant and the reliance upon it, arises before the court's order, and is capable of binding third parties who acquire the right that is subject to the 'equity'.[90] Section 116 of the Land Registration Act 2002 is premised on this assumption. (Although this provision confuses the content of the right created by the 'estoppel' and the reason for its existence. Only if the estoppel gives rise to an 'equitable property right' should it potentially bind third parties.) The 'equity' created by an 'estoppel' therefore arises when the facts occur, and not when the court makes its order. The nature of the 'equity' should then be determined by the content of the obligation the party with the title to the land is subject to grant: for example in *Crabb v Arun* an (equitable) easement,[91] in *Thorner v Major* a beneficial interest under a bare trust because of the duty to convey the freehold estate,[92] where appropriate an equitable charge,[93] or where a lease is promised an equitable lease.[94] That the 'equity' can bind third parties in this way is in obvious tension with the recent trend towards the court determining its scope not by interpreting what had been agreed but in a rather more 'flexible' manner.

Classifying all cases such as these as forms of constructive trust, although inelegant, has the benefit of explaining why the formality requirements for the sale or other disposition of an interest in land do not apply, as there is an express saving for the operation of such trusts.[95] Again, what is created is not a right in relation to the land itself, which would be caught by the policy behind the statutory prohibition, but a(n equitable) right in relation to the title to the land. They should not fall within the formality requirements which concern rights to the land itself.

---

[90] *Singh v Sandhu* (Unreported Decision of the CA, 4 May 1995); *Lloyd v Dugdale* [2001] EWCA Civ 1754, [2002] 2 P&CR 13. *Cf. Binions v Evans* [1972] Ch 359 (CA). See also *Scott v Southern Pacific Mortgages Ltd* [2014] UKSC 52, [2015] AC 385.
[91] See also *Joyce v Epsom and Ewell BC* [2012] EWCA Civ 1398, [2013] 1 P&CRDG 1.
[92] See also *Bradbury v Taylor* [2012] EWCA Civ 1208.
[93] *Kinane v Mackie-Conteh* [2005] EWCA Civ 45, [2005] WTLR 345.
[94] *JT Developments v Quinn* (1991) 62 P&CR 33 (CA).
[95] Law of Property (Miscellaneous Provisions) Act 1989, s 2(5); see *Yaxley v Gotts* [2000] Ch 162; *Kinane v Mackie-Conteh* [2005] EWCA Civ 45, [2005] WTLR 345 and *Herbert v Doyle* [2010] EWCA Civ 1095, [2011] 1 EGLR 119.

'Estoppel' in this form, if accepted, ought to be an all or nothing digital matter: the promisee acquires an equitable entitlement in relation to what was promised at the point at which the reliance upon the promise sufficient to create the 'equity' has occurred. It seems likely that the law is that this response is always available when the conditions of the promise have been met, save where giving effect to the promise is out of all proportion to a minor detriment suffered in reliance upon the promise, as in *Powell v Benney*.[96] It may however be that there are third parties with other competing rights in relation to what has been promised (eg other family members in occupation of land that has been promised to one, who have also made improvements to it) such that it may be inappropriate to allow the beneficiary to demand conveyance to them. In such cases, they may be confined to a money order representing the value of the right to which they are entitled.[97]

The justification for the acquisition of such 'equitable property' rights has never been squarely addressed by the courts, because they have proceeded upon the assumption that it is a version of equitable estoppel properly so-called, which has a lengthy historical pedigree and is a rule which is much easier to explain.

Whether such constructive trusts by another name and other 'equitable property rights' are justifiable depends upon the extent to which it is thought that obligations that are unrecognised as enforceable at common law should be given such recognition in Equity. As we have seen, if a party with title to land is under a contractual obligation to convey title to, or confer an interest in, the land, a constructive trust or other 'equitable property right' will arise. However, this is not a freestanding cause of action, but a restriction upon a right that the law already recognises. The law may choose to be more liberal in relation to the latter than the former. A declaration 'I shall pay you £1,000' does not, without more, give rise to an enforceable right, but a declaration 'I will hold my right to be paid £1,000 by X Bank on trust for you' does create a valid trust where there is such a right. Therefore, although gratuitous promises that have been relied upon will not, themselves, be enforced, it is arguable and coherent that they should be sufficient to create 'equitable property rights' such as a constructive trust. In this category, that the promise is certain and made in relation to an identifiable right is therefore essential. The promise must also be in relation to a right that it is possible to hold on trust.[98] Where the promise relates to a right the promisor does not yet have, the promisee's 'equitable property right' can only arise at the subsequent point of acquisition.[99]

How can the conferral of a trust or other equitable property right in the above cases be squared with the result in *Cobbe v Yeomans Row*, which denied any right on this basis? The easiest way of doing so, although not adopted by the court, is through the interpretation of the agreement the parties had entered into. The flats were to be sold to the claimant upon his obtaining planning permission *and* paying £12 million. Although the planning permission had been obtained, payment had not been made and the defendants would refuse to accept any proffered. The condition the promise to convey was subject to could not therefore be satisfied. There was no unqualified promise to convey. A claim for a *quantum meruit* was therefore the only appropriate relief. This explanation does not fit easily with either *Gillett v*

---

[96] *Suggitt v Suggitt* [2012] EWCA Civ 1140, [44] *per* Arden LJ. See also *Sledmore v Dalby* (1996) 72 P&CR 196 (CA); *Clarke v Swaby* [2007] UKPC 1, [2007] 2 P&CR 2.
[97] See eg *Giumelli v Giumelli* (1999) 196 CLR 101 (HCA).
[98] *Cf. Herbert v Doyle* [2010] EWCA Civ 1095, [70]–[72] *per* Arden LJ.
[99] *Max Wayne Cowper-Smith v Gloria Lyn Morgan* [2017] 2 SCR 754.

Holt or *Moore v Moore*, where the condition of the promise had not been satisfied, but those cases are wrongly decided.

Alternatively, Lord Walker placed emphasis on the fact that the commercial parties knew that the obligation entered into was binding in honour only ('subject to contract'). In the context of domestic disputes, the parties' informal arrangements may also fall short of being enforceable contracts, however they may not realise the significance of this.[100] Such an approach requires a distinction to be drawn between commercial cases (where the role of proprietary estoppel is then much reduced) and domestic ones.

(c) *Estoppel and restitution*

An example of the second strand of 'proprietary estoppel' as cause of action, that should instead have been dealt with as a claim for a *quantum meruit*, is *Jennings v Rice*.[101] Mr Jennings worked as a gardener for Mrs Royle, an elderly widow, from 1970, but from the late 1980s had increasingly cared for her. She was running out of money and could not pay him. From the point at which care had started to be provided, she had reassured him that he would 'be alright' and that 'this will all be yours one day'. Nothing was ever put in writing, and she died without leaving a will. The trial judge awarded £200,000 against her estate, which he calculated as being the market cost of the full-time nursing care Mrs Royle had received, a figure lower than the value of the house and furniture vaguely promised (£435,000), a decision that was upheld by the Court of Appeal.

It was not and should not have been possible to find that Mr Jennings had any entitlement under a constructive trust. Mrs Royle's promise as to what property would be left to him upon her death was too vague so as to give rise to such a trust. Mr Jennings would have had no ground for complaint if the will had meant that he was 'alright', even if he had not been left everything.

Seeing claims of this kind as based upon 'proprietary estoppel' is unfortunate.

First, it misleadingly implies that what must have been promised in exchange for the work is an interest in property.[102]

Second, it obscures the correct quantification of the award, which is properly calculated by reference to the value of the work done, and not according to any loss suffered by the claimant in reliance upon the undertaking by the defendant, nor by reference to any gain made by the defendant.[103] A similar confusion between 'estoppel' and a claim for restitution occurred in *Baker v Baker & Baker*.[104] The plaintiff was an elderly man whose son and daughter-in-law lived with their children in rented accommodation. The parties agreed that if he provided the capital towards the house, he should have a separate room for himself to live in rent free for the rest of his life. He provided £33,950 towards the purchase price of a house, and moved in. Unfortunately, the parties' relationship soon broke down, and he moved out. The trial judge reached the correct result and ordered the repayment of the money, which had been paid under a condition in an informal agreement that had

---

[100] [2008] UKHL 55, [2008] 1 WLR 1752, [66], [91].
[101] [2002] EWCA Civ 159, [2003] 1 P & CR 8. See also *Bradbury v Taylor* [2012] EWCA Civ 1208; *Campbell v Griffin* [2001] EWCA Civ 990, (2001) 82 P&CR DG23.
[102] *Thorner v Major* [2009] UKHL 18, [2009] 1 WLR 776, [61] *per* Lord Walker. But see *Southwell v Blackburn* [2014] EWCA Civ 1347, [2014] HLR 47 (promise that claimant would always have 'a home').
[103] *Cf. Davies v Davies* [2016] EWCA Civ 463, [38].
[104] [1993] 2 HLR 408 (CA). See also *Hussey v Palmer* [1972] 1 WLR 1286 (CA) and *Burrows and Burrows v Sharp* (1991) 23 HLR 82 (CA) which is correct in result.

failed.[105] The defendants successfully appealed on the basis that the plaintiff's loss though detrimental reliance was in fact much lower than the amount paid as he was now living in rent-free council accommodation and so his prejudice was reduced for purposes of proprietary estoppel.[106] This decision is incorrect in principle but was reached because of the way the claim was put by counsel.

Third, the approach in *Jennings v Rice* confusingly implies that, as with estoppel properly so-called, some kind of detrimental reliance is a necessary element of the claim. However, it should not matter whether, counterfactually, Mr Jennings would reluctantly have provided the care for Mrs Royle out of affection and a sense of responsibility, even if there had been no agreement between them, so that he was not in fact prejudiced.[107] It should suffice that he did the work under an agreement between them, that the performance he rendered was conditional, and that condition has failed. The compassionate should not be prejudiced. Detrimental reliance is a necessary element of estoppel in both its evidentiary and its true equitable forms, but it is not a condition of the recovery of the reasonable value of work done or other performance rendered at the request of another.

Fourth, there should be no role for any proportionate 'balancing' of the incommensurables of the claimant's detriment and the defendant's gain as the court in *Jennings v Rice* contemplated.[108] The only task, as in the Supreme Court of Canada's decision on materially identical facts to *Jennings v Rice* in *Deglman*, discussed in Chapter 7, Conditions, should be the valuation of the work done. Where the value of what had been promised in exchange is lower than the value of the work done, the party subject to the claim for reimbursement can resist it by giving what had been promised.

Fifth, the cause of action does not arise as and when any detrimental reliance occurs, as it would with any estoppel properly so-called and as it does when it operates to create a constructive trust or other 'equitable property' right. Mr Jennings' work had commenced several decades in the past and if his claim had accrued when it began it should potentially be time-barred. Rather, his claim arose upon the failure of the condition that the performance was subject to. In *Jennings v Rice*, this only occurred upon Mrs Rice's death.

Sixth, unlike the other forms of 'estoppel' we have seen, the claimant's entitlement is not a digital matter determined by what was said or promised to him, but is rather determined by the value of the work done.

Finally, grouping together the two different kinds of claim, one for an 'equitable proprietary right', most typically trusts, and claims for remuneration for work done at another's request, within one umbrella concept of 'proprietary estoppel' is unhelpful because the degree of confidence of what has been promised should not be the same. For the former, there must be a fair degree of certainty as to the right that the landholder has promised to convey or

---

[105] See also *McGuane v Welch* [2008 EWCA Civ 785, [2008] 2 P&CR 24 claim for restitution of conditional expenditure under an agreement treated as based upon 'estoppel'.
[106] [1993] 2 HLR 408 (CA), 413 *per* Dillon LJ, 419 *per* Roch LJ but *cf.* 416 *per* Beldam LJ.
[107] See also *Powell v Benney* [2007] EWCA Civ 1283, [2008] 1 P &CR DG12. *Cf. Campbell v Griffin* [2001] EWCA Civ 990, (2001) 82 P&CR DG23 overturning the trial judge's finding that there had been no detrimental reliance; *Ottey v Grundy* [2003] EWCA Civ 1176.
[108] [2002] EWCA Civ 159, [2003] 1 P & CR 8, [45]. *Cf.* the 'sliding scale' of weighing the clarity of expectations, the degree of detriment, and the length of time those expectations were held in *Davies v Davies* [2016] EWCA Civ 463, [41] *per* Lewison LJ. The resultant figure seems plucked from the air. See also *Habberfield v Habberfield* [2019] EWCA Civ 890, [2019] 2 P&CRDG 13. In *Ottey v Grundy* [2003] EWCA Civ 1176 the claimant was promised an apartment in Jamaica and a life interest in a houseboat in Chelsea, but was awarded the apartment and £50,000. See also *Guest v Guest* [2020] EWCA Civ 387.

confer. If the promise is 'you'll be alright' or 'I'll leave you one of my three properties when I die' this should be insufficient for the creation of a trust or other equitable right.[109] By contrast, if work is done at another's request on the understanding that it will be rewarded, where such reward is not forthcoming there should be a claim for reimbursement of the value of the work, regardless of how vague the promised return was. Similarly, in cases such as *Gillett v Holt*[110] where the promise to convey or confer the right is conditional, the court should not be ordering the promise to be performed if that condition has not been satisfied. If the plaintiff had been unsatisfied with a contingent equitable interest, he should be able to claim in the alternative the value of the work done over the years, with a deduction for the salary that had in fact been paid. Detrimental reliance may be relevant to whether the promise should be compellable to be performed, but is irrelevant to a claim for a *quantum meruit* for work done at another's request.

One of the reasons for the current condition of English law is that, with the exception of the commercial case of *Cobbe v Yeoman's Row*, claims have been solely put on the basis of 'proprietary estoppel' without reliance in the alternative on long-established reasons for restitution. The judges have then often sought to reach the right result, but at the serious cost of distorting the law of estoppel.

Some commentators, recognising that cases such as *Jennings v Rice* cannot be explained upon ordinary estoppel reasoning, have sought to build upon it to argue for the recognition of a new freestanding cause of action based upon the induced detriment or loss the claimant has suffered, sometime thought to be limited by such detriment having been induced by a promise.[111] Seeing the claim in *Jennings v Rice* as based upon a right to compensation for loss suffered as a result of detrimental reliance is however difficult to justify. A claim to compensation is only supportable *if* Mr Jennings had an entitlement to the inheritance. Absent such an entitlement, this is just a further example of *damnum sine iniuria*: loss without the violation of a right. There seems to be no persuasive reason for thinking that loss that takes the form of detrimental reliance is more deserving of protection than loss that is suffered through any other mechanism. If the intentional infliction of loss is not generally actionable, as it is not in England,[112] why should foreseeably causing someone to suffer loss in reliance upon what we have said or promised be actionable without more? The conditions for the creation of contractual rights (agreement, consideration, certainty, intention to create legal relations, etc) could be relaxed, and a new form of promissory liability, a kind of contract-lite, be recognised. But examples such as *Jennings v Rice* provide a weak case for doing so as we can identify an alternative, and long-established, basis for recovery.

In relation to the first strand of proprietary estoppel as a cause of action, the proposed promise-detriment principle is both over- and under-determinative of the law as it is. First, it does not explain why 'proprietary estoppel' should concern promises in relation to identifiable rights, and so it is then suggested that this restriction should be lifted. Second, it does not explain why an award that is compensatory of detrimental reliance is ever insufficient: why should the promisee acquire any 'equitable property' rights at all?

---

[109] *Cf. Orgee v Orgee* [1997] EG 152 CS (CA); *James v Thomas* [2007] EWCA Civ 1212.
[110] See also *Habberfield v Habberfield* [2019] EWCA Civ 890, [2019] 2 P&CRDG 13.
[111] A Robertson, 'The Reliance Basis of Proprietary Estoppel Remedies' [2008] Conv 295; McFarlane and Sales, 'Promises, Detriment and Liability: Lessons from Proprietary Estoppel' (n 73).
[112] *Moguls Steamship Co v McGregor Gow & Co* [1892] AC 25 (HL); *Bradford v Pickles* [1895] AC 587 (HL); *Allen v Flood* [1898] AC 1 (HL).

By contrast, if it is thought that Mrs Rice's behaviour constituted a wrong,[113] because Mr Jennings had an entitlement to the inheritance, the correct response would be to impose a duty of next best compliance. This would place Mr Jennings in the position he would have been in if no wrong had been committed: that is, he would be placed in the position he would have been in counterfactually if he had inherited, so far as money could do so. Awarding damages by reference to the extent he is worse off by comparison with the position at some point in the past seems unjustifiable. A 'reliance' measure cannot therefore be justified on this basis.

This may be contrasted with duties created by an of assumption of responsibility within the law of negligence, most famously invoked in the decision of the House of Lords in *Hedley Byrne & Co Ltd v Heller & Partners Ltd*.[114] A duty to another that care will be taken can be created by an assumption of responsibility to another, regardless of any contract between the parties. If, for example, *P* gratuitously bails his goods to *D*, the bailee comes under a duty that care is taken of the goods that persons generally are not under. If the goods are subsequently lost or damaged, when if care had been taken they would not have been, *P* is entitled to damages putting him into the position that he would have been in if care had been taken. It is irrelevant that the goods would have been lost or damaged if they had not been bailed to *D*. Damages do not necessarily seek to reflect the position *P* would have been in if he had not relied upon *D*, but rather the position he would have been in if he had not been wronged through care not having been taken. Detrimental reliance is not therefore the gist of the action.

5. Australia

The widening gyre of 'estoppel' achieved yet further extension in the decision of the High Court of Australia in *Waltons Stores (Interstate) Ltd v Maher*.[115] The parties had agreed the terms of a lease. Maher was to demolish an existing building, erect a new one in accord with Waltons' specifications, and then lease it to them. Maher's solicitors prepared the necessary documentation and forwarded it for execution and exchange. This never occurred. It was found by the trial judge that it was a prerequisite of the parties agreeing to be bound that an exchange took place.[116] In addition, under the local equivalent to the Statute of Frauds, to be enforceable a lease of land had to be in signed writing, which had also not occurred. Waltons had second thoughts and instructed their solicitors to go slow. Maher, by contrast, began performance, demolishing the building on his land and laying the foundations for the new one. Waltons knew of this but said nothing. The High Court of Australia, upholding both the Court of Appeal and the decision of Kearney J, held that Waltons were estopped from denying that a binding contract had arisen.

If Waltons had represented that an exchange of documents had occurred, and Maher had relied upon that fact by commencing work, then Waltons would have been estopped from denying that fact, and a valid contract would have existed between the parties. If this

---

[113] See eg M Spence, *Protecting Reliance: The Emergence of Equitable Estoppel* (1999).
[114] [1964] AC 465 (HL).
[115] (1988) 164 CLR 387.*Cf.* the classic *Hoffman v Red Owl Stores* 133 NW 2d 267 (1965).
[116] This seems to have been the conventional understanding in conveyancing practice in New South Wales.

were correct, then the decision is entirely orthodox. The defendant would be estopped from proving that no exchange had occurred as a matter of fact, and so there would be both a concluded agreement that the parties intended to be enforceable and compliance with the statutory formality requirement. Gaudron J, endorsing the view of the trial judge, was alone in adopting this view of what had occurred.

By contrast, the majority (Mason CJ, Wilson and Brennan JJ) took the view that the defendants were estopped from denying the existence of a contract because of the promise of a future binding contract that had been relied upon. As a result, the award of damages in lieu of specific performance of that contract was upheld.

Again, instead of barring the assertion of an existing right, 'estoppel' is here being used as a freestanding source for the creation of a new right. That something has gone wrong with the analysis is again apparent from the label ('estoppel') no longer describing the nature of the rule. This can be obscured by saying that the defendants were 'estopped from denying that there is a contract'. This involves 'estopping' the defendants from asserting that there is *no* right.

On the view of the facts taken by the majority, the successful contractual action in *Waltons Stores v Maher* is difficult to defend. It permits contractual rights to be obtained when the ordinary conditions for their acquisition have not been satisfied. It is sometimes thought that promissory estoppel of this form is operating as a substitute for consideration, an aspect of contract law that has fallen somewhat out of favour. In *Waltons Stores*, however, the promises the parties had given in exchange were perfectly adequate to satisfy the consideration requirement (to grant a lease, to pay for it). Here, the reason there was no enforceable contract was because the parties' agreement was that it was only to become binding upon exchange, and that had not occurred. Further, the statutory requirement that this species of contract must be in writing to be enforceable seems to be being by-passed without adequate justification.[117]

To overcome both of these objections, it may be argued that the cause of action was not contractual at all. Instead, there is a new freestanding kind of claim which requires the satisfaction of different conditions. Unlike a contract (which may be enforced even where wholly executory) the claim could be seen as one for compensation for the loss suffered in detrimentally relying upon the defendant's promise. There would be no more need for such an 'estoppel' claim to satisfy the ordinary conditions of a contract than a claim based upon a tort must necessarily do so. The statutory formality requirement for the enforcement of a contract would then present no obstacle because the claim is not contractual at all. On this view 'estoppel' is again a misnomer,[118] and this label should be abandoned in this context. The form of relief is no longer the digital matter of whether a party is barred from asserting a fact or a right, but is instead determined by the analogue question of the degree of detriment that one party has suffered in relying upon another. There is, at least formally, space for such a new liability rule that does not directly conflict with contractual principles

An objection to this analysis is that it is not what the majority in *Waltons Stores* said, unsurprisingly given that the creation of such a new cause of action unrelated to estopping

---

[117] *Cf. Actionstrength v International Glass Engineering SpA* [2003] 2 AC 541 (HL); *Cobbe v Yeoman's Row Management Ltd* [2008] UKHL 55, [2008] 1 WLR 1752, [29] *per* Lord Scott.

[118] B McFarlane, 'Understanding Equitable Estoppel: From Metaphors to Better Laws' (2013) 66 CLP 267, 273, 'verges on the oxymoronic'.

someone from asserting something would be a dramatic step to take. In England, the Court of Appeal has also rejected taking the step that the High Court of Australia took, outside of promises in relation to land.[119] Indeed, even in Australia there are intermediate appellate court decisions reasserting, albeit in *obiter dicta*, the traditional limits upon the doctrine of promissory estoppel.[120]

The important more difficult question is not what the law is in the different jurisdictions, but whether such a step is justified or not. Should we adopt this independent 'promise-detriment' principle?[121]

If it were the case that there was no other avenue to relief in *Waltons Stores*, then the answer would appear to be a clear yes. However, there was an alternative that was not put to the court, the one adopted by the English Court of Appeal on functionally identical facts several decades before in *Brewer Street Investments Ltd v Barclay Woollen Co Ltd*.[122] The work that Maher did was in performance of an agreement that he had with Waltons. It had been agreed between them that an enforceable contract would subsequently be entered into. This was the agreed condition under which the work was done. When that condition failed, the party at whose request the work had been done should be required to pay for its value. It should not matter that their agreement did not amount to an enforceable contract. This should require no invocation of any principle of estoppel: the defendant is not being estopped from asserting either a fact or a right. Rather they must make restitution of the value of the work. It should be no barrier to recovery that the defendant is not, in fact, enriched by that work. The claim should have been conceived as one for a *quantum meruit*, the reasonable value of the service, regardless of the absence of any consequential gain made by the defendant. Nor should such a claim be quantified by the loss or detriment suffered by the plaintiff. Only the value of the work done should be recoverable. If the promisee suffers a greater detriment by, for example, forgoing other work that would we now know have been extremely lucrative, this should be irrecoverable. Such consequential loss, absent the violation of any right, is *damnum sine iniuria*.

6. The Future

A major source of difficulty has been in seeing claims for restitution of the value of work done as based upon 'unjust enrichment', which seems ruled out *ab initio* where there is no factual enrichment of the defendant, as in *Waltons Stores*. Partly as a result, but also through sticking to what they know, practitioners have resorted to ill-suited rules such as 'estoppel' for a solution, and academics have proposed other principles to fill the gap, variously labelled 'unjust sacrifice' or the 'promise-detriment' principle. No such new concept is however required or justified. Less criticism should be directed at courts who are constrained by the way in which cases are argued before them.

---

[119] *Baird Textile Holdings Ltd v Marks & Spencer plc* [2001] EWCA Civ 274.
[120] *Saleh v Romanous* [2010] NSWCA 274, [74]-[75] *per* Handley AJA, the author of Handley, *Estoppel by Conduct and Election* (2nd edn 2016).
[121] McFarlane, 'Understanding Equitable Estoppel: From Metaphors to Better Laws' (n 118), 267, 286–295.
[122] [1954] QB 428; *Kearns v Andree* 107 Conn 181, 139 A 695, 59 ALR 599. See also *Planché v Colburn* (1831) 8 Bing 14 discussed in Chapter 8, Contract; *Whittington v Seale-Hayne* (1900) 82 LT 49 discussed in Chapter 4, Reversal.

What should the law be? The best option is to re-confine estoppel back within defensible limits. It should be possible to be estopped from asserting facts and rights. These two different forms of estoppel (estoppel by representation or convention and equitable estoppel) should also be disaggregated as engaging different considerations and rules. An equitable rule concerned with restraining the assertion of rights has jumped the rails, and been mistakenly treated as a cause of action. The reasons that may legitimately justify restraining the enforcement of rights are different from, and more liberal than, those that may legitimately justify rights themselves.

If 'estoppel' as a cause of action is to be retained it should no longer be labelled 'estoppel' which misleads us into thinking similar rules should and do apply as operate in the other two forms. Although it may be justifiable that a promise to convey or grant an interest in land (or other right) may create an equitable proprietary right, determined by the content of the promise, this should be subject to limitation. First the promise must be sufficiently certain to be given effect to. Second there must have been a degree of reliance upon the promise sufficient for it no longer to be reasonable for it to be withdrawn. Third, where the promise is conditional it should not create an unconditional vested right until that condition has been satisfied.

Cases such as *Jennings v Rice* and *Waltons Stores v Maher* would be better re-conceived as claims to recover the value of work performed conditionally under an agreement, where the condition has failed. A party who has done work in reliance upon a promise of a right to land may be confined to such a *quantum meruit* where the promise was insufficiently certain, or where the promise is conditional and that condition can no longer be fulfilled (as it may not be because the parties' relationship has broken down).[123]

Such a re-configuration of 'estoppel' when it is currently operating as a cause of action into these two distinct forms discloses what the court's task should be in quantifying any award, which the current practice of requiring an enquiry into the 'minimum equity' to do justice does not. Courts should seek to (re-)construct such rules, rather than opting for the soft option, paid for through litigation and costs, of invoking an open-ended discretion to do what is thought just.

---

[123] *Cf. Shilliday v Smith* 1998 SC 725 (expenditure improving future home in expectation of marriage recoverable).

PART VI
WRONGDOING

15
Wrongs

A. Introduction

The material included in this work is mainly determined by the works of others. It has no common theme. Material claimed to have a unity does not belong together, but is instead made up of several different jigsaw puzzles in one box.

One such puzzle has however been separated out by some authors and treated as distinct.[1] These are claims to gains made by a defendant through his wrongdoing. At least some of these cases are, unlike many of the examples considered so far, genuinely concerned with the enrichment of the defendant. If our concern is with enrichment that is unjust, this topic has more claim for inclusion than many others so far covered. It is also no more different from the other kinds of claim we have seen than they are from each other. Unfortunately, the ideas of 'enrichment' and 'wrongdoing' have also been stretched beyond a useful point, so as to encompass claims better understood in other ways.

This chapter concerns the necessary analytical distinctions between wrongs, losses, and gains, and then goes on to consider the arguments for justifying a gain-based response to wrongdoing. The next two consider in detail the law as it is.

B. *Edwards v Lees Administrator*

In order to orientate the reader, we start with one of the most famous examples.

In 1915 the defendant discovered[2] an entrance to what came to be known as the Great Onyx Cave under land to which he had title. This was the only entrance to the cave, and so was the only means by which it could be exploited. He set up tours, and opened an hotel for tourists. The plaintiff, Lee, was a neighbour with title to land underneath which about one third of the cave, including some of the best attractions, lay. Under the *ad coelum* rule, Lee had title to that third, and the defendant Edwards had committed the tort of trespass. The plaintiff was not, however, left worse off counterfactually than they would have been if the cave had not been used: they could not exploit their portion of the cave themselves because they had no entrance to it. The Kentucky Court of Appeal, having first excluded the profits from the hotel, allowed Lee to recover one third of the net profits of Edwards' business.

When and why are claims for gains from wrongs recoverable? Is this result correct? We are not in this section concerned with claims to recover a thing or its value, which as we saw

---

[1] P Birks, 'Misnomer' in W Cornish and others (eds), *Restitution Past, Present and Future: Essays in Honour of Gareth Jones* (1998); C Mitchell, P Mitchell, and S Watterson (eds), *Goff & Jones: The Law of Unjust Enrichment* (9th edn, 2016), [1-01]–[1-05]; A Burrows, *A Restatement of the English Law of Unjust Enrichment* (2012), § 1(3).

[2] Although the court's conclusion that he had done so was probably wrong. It was probably found by someone else, and Edwards' claim that he had done so was false. See R Brucker and R Watson, *The Longest* Cave (2006), 277.

in Chapter 11 are mediated in the common law through the law of torts. Instead, we are concerned with gains consequent upon wrongdoing.

C. Definitions and Distinctions

1. Wrongdoing

To commit a wrong is to breach a duty. Some wrongs are relational, in the sense that the duty is owed to another person. Not all wrongs have this form, either within the law or outside of it. My duty not to park my car on double yellow lines is a public duty, it is not owed to any identifiable individual. In private law, however, our duties are owed to each other. This differentiates private or interpersonal wrongs from public wrongs.

In the common law, it is not a condition of a wrong that the defendant was in any way blameworthy. Although some torts require the defendant's conduct to have been unreasonable, many such as libel, trespass, or conversion, do not.

A relational duty owed to another to do or not do X is, viewed from the other side of the relation, a (claim-)right that the other has that the duty bearer does or does not do X. When used in this sense, a right is the conclusion of the legal analysis. Sometimes, by contrast, we use the term 'right' not to refer to a conclusion, but instead as a reason for the imposition of a duty. A 'right to privacy' or a 'right to life' refers not to conclusions as to our entitlements in relation to the specific behaviour of another person, but rather to reasons or, sometimes more loosely 'protected interests', that can ground such conclusions.

On this account, torts, breach of contract, and equitable wrongs such as breach of confidence are all forms of civil or private wrongdoing. All involve the infringement of a right (in the first sense) of the plaintiff. Such wrongs generate a new obligation of a different content upon the defendant.

2. Consequential Loss and Wrongdoing

When quantifying consequential loss for wrongdoing, our comparators are the world as it is, and the (hypothetical) world that would have obtained absent the wrong. It is a counterfactual enquiry. Such detriments constituting loss neither should be nor are confined to financial disadvantage and may include such off balance-sheet negatives as pain and suffering.[3]

'Loss' in this sense may include items that a plaintiff never, in fact, had. For example:

D2 agrees to repair P's taxi by 1 May. In breach of contract, the work is not complete until two weeks later, during which time P cannot work.

The earnings P would have made were not something P ever in fact acquired. We would not, therefore, in ordinary English when using the word as a verb speak of his having 'lost' them.

---

[3] See eg *Johnson v Gore Wood & Co* [2000] UKHL 65, [2002] 2 AC 1.

Such counterfactual loss (as a noun) is however often recoverable by way of damages.[4] The same counterfactual approach is taken regardless of whether the claim is for breach of contract or other wrongs. If, for example, the taxi is out of action because D2 had negligently damaged it, the profits that would otherwise have been made may also be recoverable.

It is possible to suffer a wrong without being left, counterfactually, worse off at all. For example:

> P is travelling to the airport to catch an aeroplane, when she is negligently injured by D's careless driving, breaking her finger. The incident causes P to miss her flight. In the course of the flight to P's desired destination, the aeroplane is hit by a freak quadruple bird strike whilst over the ocean, causing it to crash, killing everyone on board. It is as certain as anything can be that P would have died in the crash if she had not been injured by D.[5]

Counterfactually, P is better, not worse, off today than if she had not been injured by D. Being alive generally being a better state of affairs than being dead. That does not however mean that P has not suffered a wrong; she has. D's negligent injury of her was wrongful, a violation of a right, regardless of whether counterfactually it leaves her worse off today. Being worse off today than you otherwise would be is not a condition of having been the victim of a wrong at a moment in the past.

We might, instead of employing a counterfactual sense of 'loss', adopt an historical baseline as our comparator. As we have seen,[6] when, in English, 'loss' is used as a verb, this is our usual perspective, and it is therefore easy to slip between the two different senses. Looking back, do I no longer have something that I once did? In the example, is P worse off today than she was before she was hit? She now has a broken finger, when before she did not, and D is responsible for that. It is difficult to identify any judicial or other legal usage of 'loss' in this sense, and it will not be discussed further.

There are however also several judicial statements employing 'loss' in a third different sense. For example, in relation to breach of contract:

> On breach, the innocent party suffers a loss. He fails to obtain the benefit promised by the other party to the contract.[7]

Similarly:

> If the plaintiff has the right to prevent some act being done without his consent, and the defendant does the act without seeking that consent, the plaintiff has suffered a loss.[8]

'Loss' is here being used as a synonym for the wrong that has been suffered in the past. This is a quite different concept from the factual senses of loss. 'Loss' is not here the state of affairs of being counterfactually worse off today.

---

[4] *Hawkins v McGee* 84 NH 114, 146 A 641 (NH 1929) (the 'hairy hand' case).
[5] The example, slightly amended, is from E Weinrib, 'Right and Advantage in Private Law' (1989) 10 Cardozo Law Rev 1283.
[6] Chapter 4, Reversal.
[7] *Attorney-General v Blake* [2001] 1 AC 268 (HL), 282 *per* Lord Nicholls.
[8] *Tito v Waddell (No 2)* [1977] Ch 106, 335 *per* Sir Robert Megarry V-C quoted with approval in *Jaggard v Sawyer* [1995] 1 WLR 269 (CA), 281–282 *per* Sir Thomas Bingham MR; *Morris-Garner v One Step (Support) Ltd*

No single usage of 'loss' is necessarily correct, but we are using a single word to refer to different ideas.

Counterfactual 'loss', in law determined at the time of judgment, is ambulatory. It may increase, decrease, or even disappear as further consequences occur, as the example of the accident on the way to the airport demonstrates.[9] 'Loss', when referring to the wrong suffered in the past, is an immutable sunk cost.

In Latin, we label wrongdoing without consequential loss, such as the accident on the way to the airport, as *iniuria sine damno*. Lawful competition between participants in the same market usually results, for someone, with the converse: consequential loss without wrongdoing. We saw an example of this situation of *damnun sine iniuria* in *Victoria Park Racing & Recreation Grounds Co Ltd v Taylor*.[10] It is easy to elide the difference between *iniuria* and *damnum*, and common lawyers often do so when using the slippery word 'damage', when using 'injury' and 'harm' interchangeably, or when using 'loss' to cover both. However, the distinction is legally important.

Some wrongs, such as breach of contract, are actionable *per se*, by which is meant an action may be brought without proof of consequential loss. Other wrongs are not so actionable, but are dependent upon the happening of adverse counterfactual consequences. In England, libel and slander are still, to an extent, divided in this way. A defamatory statement that is published in print is actionable without more. If, for example, a newspaper publishes that you are a paedophile on its frontpage, this is actionable without adverse consequences (indeed it should ordinarily give rise to a large award of general damages without more ado). Slander, by contrast, outside of specific exceptions, requires consequential loss to have been suffered, such as the loss of employment. Many other kinds of claim are also dependent upon the suffering of consequential loss, such as deceit or, as its name states, the intentional causing of loss by unlawful means.

3. Consequential Gain and Wrongdoing

An example:

> D, a start-up drug manufacturer, brings to market a new drug. In the manufacturing process he violates the patent of P. D's business is a failure, losing £5 million. If he had not used the manufacturing process, D would not have embarked upon the business at all.

Counterfactually, comparing the position he is in now, with that he would have been in if he had committed no wrong, D is worse off, making no gain.

P's consequential loss might be difficult to quantify, and so we might seek to quantify it by reference to the licence or 'release' fee P would have charged D if he had sought permission in advance. This is, however, to use a quite different counterfactual comparator than that

---

Morris-Garner v One Step (Support) Ltd [2018] UKSC 20, [2019] AC 649, [59] *per* Lord Reed. See also *Google v Lloyd* [2021] UKSC 50, [140] *per* Lord Leggatt.

[9] D Nolan, 'Rights, Damage and Loss' (2017) 37 OJLS 255.
[10] (1937) 58 CLR 479 (HCA); see Chapter 3, Performance.

ordinarily employed: not the world absent the wrongful act but the world there would have been if permission had been sought and granted for the wrongful act. Similarly, it could be argued that *D*'s consequential gain is the expense he has saved in not having had to pay the licence or 'release' fee *P* would have charged *D* if he had sought permission in advance. Neither of these measures is necessarily the same as a *reasonable* licence or release fee. *P* might have charged a higher or lower fee, or refused permission in any circumstances.[11] As we shall see, neither of the consequential loss nor gain accounts of 'negotiating' damages fits the law as it is, which is uninterested in the counterfactual question of the sum that would have been charged if permission had been sought.

Sometimes a gain may be attributable to the wrong regardless of the counterfactual position. For example:

D, a start-up drug manufacturer, brings to market a new drug. In the manufacturing process he violates the patent of *P*. *D*'s business is a modest success, making £5milllion. If *D* had not embarked on this venture, which he would not have done absent the patent violation, he would have manufactured a different drug using a different process, that we now know would have been spectacularly successful, making far more.

Counterfactually, *D* is, again, worse off through having committed the wrong. Despite this, as a matter of history he has acquired a profit of £5 million, that is, at least in part, attributable to the wrong committed by violating *P*'s right to his patent. One of the contributors to the profit that has actually been made is the infringement of *P*'s patent.

4. General and Special Damages

Some commentators have argued that we should speak of gain-based 'damages', and the labels 'restitutionary' or 'disgorgement' damages have been proposed.[12] As a matter of ordinary usage, both as a matter of dictionaries and law, employing the word 'damages' to also cover, for example, an order for an account of profits seems inappropriate. 'Damage', from the Latin *damnum*, ordinarily refers to injury or harm.[13] The expansive approach is also unhelpful because, as we shall see, the justifications for such awards are quite different, and so using one word to cover multiple different concepts, contrary to ordinary usage, confuses more than it assists.

In making out a claim for substantial damages, it is often unnecessary for a plaintiff to plead and prove his itemised consequential loss. Take, for example, a straightforward breach of contract case:

---

[11] *Don v Trojan Construction Co.* 178 Cal App 2d 135 (1960) (reasonable licence fee for non-profitable use of an empty lot that would not have been rented out or used).

[12] J Edelman, *Gain-Based Damages: Contract, Tort, Equity and Intellectual Property* (2002), 65–78. *Cf.* L Smith, 'The Province of the Law of Restitution' (1992) 71 Can Bar Rev 672.

[13] The concept of 'nominal damages', which are awarded for nominal injuries, is unobjectionable on this account. If 'exemplary damages' are awarded so as to make an example of the defendant unrelated to any injury suffered by the plaintiff, they are indefensible. It may be that they are a misnomer for damages justified in another way. See R Stevens, *Torts and Rights* (2007), 85–88.

P agrees to buy from *D* 1,000 tonnes of durum wheat for £500 per tonne, delivery on 1 April. *D* fails to deliver. At that date, the market for durum wheat stands at £600 per tonne.

We do not put *P* to proof of the extent to which he is prejudiced by this breach. He may seek damages based upon the difference in value between what he was promised and what he got.[14] Here, that is calculated by reference to the difference between the market price and the contract price for the wheat at the date of breach, here £100 per tonne. This is a claim for 'general damage'.

By contrast, if *P* wishes to claim a sum greater than this figure, by proving, for example, that the non-delivery caused him to lose a lucrative sub-sale contract at above the market rate, he must plead and prove such 'special' consequential loss.[15] The correct date for assessment of such 'special damage' is the time of judgment.

A similar position applies in the law of torts. For example:

In a driving accident that was the result of *D*'s negligence, the car to which *P* has title is damaged beyond repair.

P should be entitled to the market value of his title to the car at the time of the wrong, without having to prove what he paid for a replacement (if anything). By contrast, if *P* is a taxi driver, and is unable to work for a period of time because he has to buy a replacement vehicle, he must plead and prove such consequential 'special' loss.

Such 'general damages' are only available for wrongs that are actionable *per se*. Deceit, for example, does not give rise to a claim for damages without more; consequential loss must be suffered.

The central claim in Chapter 17, Damages is that, in examples such as the last two, *P* is, and should be, entitled to general damages even if it can be shown that he has, as a counterfactual matter, suffered no loss. Compensatory damages for wrongs actionable *per se* are, in the first instance, awarded for the wrong committed. For those wrongs that do not require proof of consequential loss for actionability, general damages constitute a floor below which the award cannot fall. The distinction between general and special damages has unfortunately caused confusion. Because some awards are not quantified by reference to the plaintiff's consequential loss, it has sometimes been thought that they must therefore be justified by reference to consequential gains made. Rather, such awards are not for 'loss' in the counterfactual sense (*damnum*) but for 'loss' in the sense of having been the victim in the past of a wrong (*iniuria*). They may always be said to be compensatory, but in different senses.

Confusingly, a number of different labels have been used to distinguish between damages for the wrong itself and consequential loss. Claims for general damages have also been described as ones for 'direct loss'[16] or an 'objective loss', which may be contrasted with a 'subjective loss'. Following German law's terminology, we might say the distinction is between 'abstract' and 'concrete' measures of loss.[17] Commentators on contract law have referred to

---

[14] Sale of Goods Act 1979, s 51(3). See Chapter 17, Damages.
[15] See also *Ratcliffe v Evans* [1892] 2 QB 524 (CA), 528 *per* Bowen LJ on the distinction between general and special damages.
[16] *Burdis v Livsey* [2002] EWCA Civ 510, [2003] QB 36.
[17] G H Treitel, *Remedies for Breach of Contract* (1988), 111–124.

general damages as reflecting the 'performance interest'.[18] Commentators on the law of torts have written of 'vindicatory damages'.[19] In previous work, I have used the label 'substitutive damages'[20] to refer to damages for the wrong, but this was perhaps a naive suggestion, as it implied something new and unfamiliar. Lawyers are not in the business of making new discoveries. The language of 'substitution' also implies that the right has (literally) been lost which in most cases (as where the defendant makes wrongful use of a thing to which the defendant has a better title) it has not. In this work, the same distinction between different forms of compensatory award will be given the more familiar labels of 'general' and 'special' damages.

D. Justifications

1. The Obligation to Pay Damages

In our personal lives, it is often best for victims to move on from the slights and injustices others commit. The past is so much spilled milk. In morality and law, however, wrongs in the past also have an afterlife. In law, wrongs create obligations to pay damages.[21] How is this obligation justified?

One natural response is to appeal to instrumental or regulatory reasons. If we make the wrongdoer pay a sum by way of damages this will deter him, and other people, from committing similar wrongs in the future. Arguments of this kind do not, however, explain why the correct measure of any such award is compensatory, when a higher or lower award may better achieve our regulatory goal. Nor, alone, do they explain why any such award should be paid to the victim.

Much more promising is the idea that obligations do not disappear into the void once breached. If I agree to deliver the manuscript of a book with a publisher by 1 April, and that date has now passed, what has happened to my obligation? The reasons for my original obligation (here, most obviously *pacta sunt servanda*) have not disappeared. Those reasons mean that I am now under a duty to do the next best thing to having complied with my original obligation to deliver on 1 April. Ordinarily, this means that I must get as close to delivery on that date as I can and apologise for the delay. This is so even though I never agreed to an obligation of that content.

In law, the form of this duty of next-best compliance is constrained by what the law can sensibly require of us. Apologies cannot meaningfully be ordered because it is of the essence of an apology that it is voluntary. Apologies required by law, given through the gritted teeth of the defendant, merely have their outward form and not the substance. (In the exceptional context of libel, prominent published apologies and recognition of falsity may have a reparative effect on the damaged reputation, and so be justifiably ordered.) What the law can require, and courts can readily order and enforce, are money orders. Those money orders

---

[18] Eg D Friedmann, 'The Performance Interest in Contract Damages' (1995) 111 LQR 628; B Coote, 'The Performance Interest, *Panatown* and the Problem of Loss' (2001) 117 LQR 81.
[19] Eg J Varuhas, 'The Concept of "Vindication" in the Law of Torts: Rights Interests and Damages' (2014) 34 OJLS 253.
[20] Stevens, *Torts and Rights* (n 13), ch 4.
[21] S Steel and R Stevens, 'The Secondary Duty to Pay Damages' (2020) 136 LQR 283.

then take the form of the next best now achievable in money to the wrong not having occurred.[22] This principle was stated by Lord Blackburn in a delict action in an appeal from Scotland to the House of Lords:

> [W]here any injury is to be compensated by damages, in settling the sum of money to be given for reparation of damages you should as nearly as possible get at that sum of money which will put the party who has been injured, or who has suffered, in the same position as he would have been in if he had not sustained the wrong for which he is now getting his compensation.[23]

The same principle was stated by Parke B in an action for breach of contract:

> The rule of the common law is, that where a party sustains a loss by reason of a breach of contract, he is, so far as money can do it, to be placed in the same situation, with respect to damages, as if the contract had been performed.[24]

In more recent times the principle has also been stated as applying to claims by beneficiaries under a trust seeking compensation for breach of trust (which are not the same as claims by beneficiaries that trustees reconstitute trusts).[25]

The remedial next-best principle is therefore the same across the law of civil wrongs. What differs is the content of the primary obligations that are beached. The position the plaintiff counterparty to a contract with a garage mechanic, who in breach has failed to renovate his car, ought to have been in may be different from the position he should have been in if a third party had not negligently damaged it initially.

One of the central reasons why we owe obligations to others is the adverse consequences of non-compliance for those to whom we owe our duties. One of the reasons why I owe you a duty not to destroy your car is because, if I do, you may not be able to drive to work, will incur costs of replacement, and so on. Where such consequential loss is suffered, therefore, it generally makes sense to create a secondary obligation to compensate for it. However, sometimes such consequential loss is outside of the purpose of the duty, and is then considered to be 'too remote'. A justly famous example was given by Lord Hoffmann:

> A mountaineer about to undertake a difficult climb is concerned about the fitness of his knee. He goes to a doctor who negligently makes a superficial examination and pronounces the knee fit. The climber goes on the expedition, which he would not have undertaken if

---

[22] For authors from different perspectives making versions of the above argument, see N MacCormick, *Legal Right and Social Democracy: Essays in Legal and Political Philosophy* (1982), 212; E Weinrib, *The Idea of Private Law* (1995), 135; J Raz, 'Personal Practical Conflicts' in P Baumann and M Betzler (eds), *Practical Conflicts: New Philosophical Essays* (2004), 172; Stevens, *Torts and Rights* (n 13), 59; A Ripstein, 'As if it Never Happened' (2007) 48 William and Mary Law Review 1968. The best long treatment of the idea is J Gardner, '"What Is Tort Law For? Part 1": The Place of Corrective Justice' (2011) 30 Law and Philosophy 1.
[23] *Livingstone v The Rawyards Coal Co.* (1880) 5 App Cas 25, 39 (HL).
[24] *Robinson v Harman* (1848) 1 Ex Rep 850, 154 ER 363.
[25] *Target Holdings Ltd v Redferns* [1996] AC 421 (HL), 432 *per* Lord Browne-Wilkinson citing *Livingstone v Rawyard's Coal.*

the doctor had told him the true state of his knee. He suffers an injury which is an entirely foreseeable consequence of mountaineering but has nothing to do with his knee.[26]

The purpose of the duty the doctor assumed was to guard against harm suffered as a result of the failure of the knee. The consequential harm actually suffered, from the ordinary risks of mountaineering, formed no part of the reason why the duty existed, and is therefore too remote to be recovered.

2. Disgorging Gains

(a) The problem

By contrast to claims for damages reflecting the wrong itself and any consequential harm, a gain-based award for wrongdoing is often more difficult to explain. If instead of working on the book manuscript I have promised to deliver, I spend my time earning large sums of money in legal practice, there is no more than a causal connection between the gain I have made and the wrong the publisher has suffered. My wrongdoing consisted of not doing the work on the book, not the doing of the work I did instead. Why should I be required to give up the gain I have made when such gain is not constitutive of the wrong I have committed and was not one of the reasons why the obligation to deliver the book on time was owed? The duty did not exist because there were good reasons for *me* not to make money in commercial practice. It existed in order for the *publisher* to meet its production schedule and to enable them to make as much money as possible. No doubt one of the reasons for my duty to my publisher is to enable them to make money, but it is not to stop me from making money through an entirely different mode of activity. It usually makes sense to say part of the reason why we owe obligations to one another is the possible consequential harm to the rightholder from non-fulfilment. Ordinarily, subject to the exceptions discussed in the next chapter, it makes little or no sense to say that part of the justification for an obligation to be owed is to prevent the duty-bearer from making a gain. As such, any gain seems outside of the range of reasons justifying the primary obligation, and so ordinarily we could not justify stripping the defendant of it. The consequential gain is too 'remote' from the wrong, as it did not form part of the reasons justifying the underlying obligation. On its own, although we all have an interest in not suffering harm, we never have an interest in preventing others from making gains *per se*. Such gain remains 'too remote' regardless of whether the wrong committed is deliberate or not.

What other justifications can there be to require a wrongdoer to disgorge his gain? A number of reasons have been canvassed, some more plausible than others.

(b) 'No man shall profit from his own wrong'

Although often given as an explanation,[27] this slogan is an assertion of the proposition that needs to be justified.[28] On its own, it also does not say to whom the wrongdoer should give up his gain.[29]

---

[26] *South Australia Asset Management Corporation v York Montague Ltd* [1997] AC 191 (HL), [19].
[27] *AG v Guardian Newspaper Ltd (No 2)* [1990] 1 AC 109 (HL), 262 *per* Lord Keith, 286 *per* Lord Goff.
[28] N McBride, 'Restitution for Wrongs' in C Mitchell and W Swadling (eds), *The Restatement Third: Restitution and Unjust Enrichment Critical and Comparative Essays* (2013), 255, 267–275.
[29] *Halifax Building Society v Thomas* [1996] Ch 217 (CA), 229 *per* Glidewell LJ.

This maxim has more force as a general principle in the context of the criminal law. Under Roman law the property of an executed criminal went to the emperor (regardless of whether he obtained it though a crime). Similarly, in English law the property of a felon went to the King (or sometimes the felon's Lord). The abandonment of these harsh rules then required the adoption of the so-called 'slayer rule': prohibiting a killer from inheriting property upon the death of his victim.[30] This rule aims to ensure equality of punishment for criminals. If we did not take away from those criminals who gain from their crimes what they had thereby obtained, some would suffer a lesser punishment than others.[31] In England, today, the mechanism for recovering the proceeds of crime by the state is governed by legislation.[32]

(c) A proxy for loss

Sometimes, proving consequential loss may be problematic as a matter of evidence. This is especially so in cases of competition or intellectual property infringements, where the defendant's profits actually made may be readily identifiable but the defendant's counterfactual losses difficult to prove.[33] It is therefore tempting to see a gain-based award as a kind of next-next-best award. This is, however, obviously unsatisfactory. In a competitive market, a gain made by one may be evidence of loss by another, but there is no necessary correlation.

(d) Deterrence

A common argument associated with those who see private law in instrumental terms,[34] is that a gain-based award is justified through its regulatory effect on the future behaviour of the wrongdoer and others.[35] This argument takes a strong and a weak form.

The strong version is to argue straightforwardly that gain-based damages are similar to exemplary damages. The sanction of gain stripping will deter people in the future, including the wrongdoer, from committing the wrong. This view is also sometimes coupled with the claim that gain-based awards are justifiable where the defendant's wrongdoing is morally reprehensible.[36] If what we are trying to control are the defendant's deliberations, deliberate wrongdoing may seem a prime candidate for such an award.

Whether, in fact, such awards do have this effect is somewhat speculative. Indeed, if our goal were deterrence, we might expect the award to be tailored more precisely to achieving that goal. It might be responded that a gain-based award is more certain in quantification than one fine-tuned for purposes of deterrence, but this seems an unpersuasive reason for selecting this method of calculation rather than another aimed at the justificatory goal. A fixed sum fine would be even more certain.

---

[30] *Cleaver v Mutual Reserve Fund Lie Association* [1892] 1 QB 147; *Re Crippen* [1911] P 108; *Re Sigsworth* [1935] Ch 89; *Riggs v Palmer* 115 NY 506 (1889); see American Law Institute, *Restatement Third: Restitution and Unjust Enrichment* (2011), § 45. *Cf. Rosenfeldt v Olsen* (1984) 25 DLR (4th) 272 (BCCA).

[31] McBride, 'Restitution for Wrongs' (n 28), 251.

[32] Primarily the Proceeds of Crime Act 2002.

[33] *Cf. LAC Minerals Ltd v International Corona Resources Ltd* (1989) 61 DLR (4th) 14, 50 *per* La Forest J.

[34] Eg Edelman, *Gain-Based Damages: Contract, Tort, Equity and Intellectual Property* (n 12), 16; *cf.* A Kull, *Restatement of the Law (Third) Restitution and Unjust Enrichment*, vol I (2010), § 44(1) but see the qualification of § 39 Comment e.

[35] Edelman, *Gain-Based Damages: Contract, Tort, Equity and Intellectual Property* (n 12), 83–86.

[36] P Birks, *Civil Wrongs: A New World* (Butterworths Lectures 1990–1991) (1992), 97; Edelman, *Gain-Based Damages: Contract, Tort, Equity and Intellectual Property* (n 12), 84–85, J Edelman, J Varuhas, and S Colton (eds), *McGregor on Damages* (21st edn, 2021), [15–1007].

The weaker, and more intuitively appealing, version of the argument is that a gain-based award removes the incentive to commit the wrong, at least where the possible motivation is profit making. Why bother committing the wrong if you will be placed back in the position you were in before?

There are several well-known problems common to both of these arguments.

First, a gain-based award seems peculiarly ill suited to achieving either the strong or the weak objective. For the wrongdoer, the wrong is a one-way bet. Many wrongs are not discovered, and even when they are the rightholders often do not pursue a claim. The worst that can happen for the wrongdoer is that they are no worse off through the attempt. If our goal really were deterrence, other stronger sanctions seem more readily justifiable.

Second, on its own, such an argument does not justify giving the award to the plaintiff. It is another argument of the wrong form. All it would justify is the defendant giving up the gain, not the award going to the rightholder. We could have a gain-stripping policeman, and indeed in England we have such a system in relation to crimes under the Proceeds of Crime Act 2002. Perhaps giving the rightholder the award could be seen as an incentive to bring the action, an inducement to operate as a private policeman, and the rightholders are also often the party best placed to determine whether a claim is worth bringing.

Third, the pattern of law, found in all jurisdictions, is that gains made from some but not all right infringements are recoverable. Without further argumentation, deterrence alone gives us no reason for selecting some wrongs as deserving of a gain-based award and not others, and so commentators taking this view often urge, contrary to the positive law, that it should be available for all wrongs.[37]

Fourth, and most fundamentally, simplistic deterrence arguments such as these are open to the objection that they involve using the defendant as a mere means to an end. The attitude that sanctions for purposes of deterrence alone are justifiable was mocked by Voltaire in *Candide*. Admiral John Byng was court-martialled and executed in 1757 for his part in the failure of the British to prevent Minorca falling to the French. In the novel, Candide witnesses the execution in Portsmouth and is told that in England it is good to kill an admiral from time to time *pour encourager les autres*. It is to be hoped that even the English have left that world behind.

Deterrence may play a role in shaping, or helping to justify the expense of enforcing, rules explicable on other grounds. The enforcement of laws may be costly for the state, and so the incidental benefits of deterrence are not to be discounted in justifying the cost of justice. However, deterrence of future wrongdoing is never, alone, a sufficient justification for a court-ordered remedy.

(e) Institutional protection

A somewhat more sophisticated specific form of the deterrence argument, that seeks to answer the third problem of identifying the particular wrongs that generate a gain-based response, is that certain legal institutions are so deserving of protection that gains made from inadvertent wrongdoing that does not harm an individual plaintiff, requires the stripping of gains.[38] Jackman has argued that where a plaintiff has not suffered any harm, a gain-based

---

[37] Eg Edelman, Varuhas, and Colton, *McGregor on Damages* (n 36), [15-100], 'there is no reason why disgorgement damages should not be concurrently available for common law wrongs just as they are for wrongs historically originated in Chancery'. J McCamus, 'Waiver of Tort: Is There a Limiting Principle?' (2014) CBLJ 333.

[38] I M Jackman, 'Restitution for Wrongs' [1989] CLJ 302.

award may be justifiable in order to protect one of the law's 'facilitative institutions': property, relationships of trust and confidence, and (sometimes) contract. On its own however, we are not given sufficient reasons for selecting one 'facilitative institution' as deserving of protection whilst another is not. Again, why the plaintiff should be the beneficiary of any award if its justification is unrelated to him is unanswered, and why a gain-based response is appropriate, rather than one tailored to deter damage to the 'institution', is unclear.

(f) Fruits

If I own a sow, I own her piglets. If I own an apple tree, I own the apples that fall from it. If this is so, does it follow that if I have title to land, I am entitled to the profits that result from the use of that land?

There are several problems with relying directly in this way upon an analogy with the *fructus* rule in relation to physical things. First, the rule in relation to things seems to be required by the physical nature of such things. If we separate a branch from a tree, the branch is not a new thing but rather a separated part of the old. This does not apply to profits through use. Second, the *fructus* rule where applicable justifies a proprietary right to a thing (the piglets, the apples) good against all others. What we are seeking to justify is a personal obligation to account for gains made by wrongdoing, not why the rightholder 'owns' the profits.[39] The analogy is not therefore a complete one.

However, as we shall see, this idea does point towards a justification for a gain-based award in relation to some rights. One of the central reasons for the existence of certain kinds of rights is not (solely) the prevention of injury or consequential harm, but rather to allocate the benefit of exploitation to the rightholder.[40] This is most obviously so in relation to most forms of intellectual property right. Where the profit from exploitation of the information protected by the right has been made by a party other than the rightholder, the reason for the right justifies the reallocation of this profit to the rightholder. The profit is the piglet of which the right is the sow.

This justification is of limited scope, however, and does not apply to most forms of wrongdoing.

E. The Wrong or the Right?

German law, in common with other systems such as Scots law, possesses a law of delict that is comparatively narrow compared with the common law.[41] Liability is generally confined in three ways. First, injury must have been intentional, negligent, or independently unlawful. The common law's strict duties not to trespass, for example, are generally not found. Second, liability is confined to compensation for resultant damage. Third, there are defences, such as incapacity, that do not generally apply in the common law.

A party in possession who uses another's thing without permission is not therefore in such a system necessarily a wrongdoer. However, they must still pay for the use of the thing.

---

[39] *Cf. Twentieth Century Fox Film Corp v Harris* [2013] EWHC 159 (Ch), [2014] Ch 41. See now *FHR European Ventures LLP v Cedar Capital Partners LLC* [2014] UKSC 45, [2015] AC 250.
[40] *Cf.* P Birks, *An Introduction to the Law of Restitution* (rev edn, 1989), 328–330.
[41] BGB § 823(1).

The right to the thing is conceived as grounding the obligation to pay even though the interference is considered non-wrongful.[42] Outside of cases of possession, the interference with another's right (*Eingriffskondiktion*) is seen as the basis of restitutionary liability, outside of the law of delict.

Some writers have argued that the claims for gains that are in England sometimes categorised as based upon wrongdoing would be better seen, as in German law, as based upon the interference with another's right.[43] For most, but not all, purposes in the common law this is a distinction without a difference; the interference with another's right is, as a matter of definition, a wrong.

Two important comparative lessons are usefully drawn from the German approach however, and similar results are reached when compared with the common law. First, it is not necessarily the case that because a claim for compensation for loss is unavailable as a possible remedy that an account of profits is also ruled out. Although relatively unusual in the common law, as we shall see this does arise in the context of intellectual property rights, and, despite criticism, is justifiable. Second, German law asks whether the gain that was made was attributable to the right interfered with, the so-called *Theorie vom Zuweisungsgehalt*.[44] This does not entail that the interference with all rights gives rise to a gain-based award. This purposive approach, looking to the reasons for the right protected and asking whether a gain is properly attributable to the rightholder, also has explanatory force in the common law. That is the focus of the next chapter.

---

[42] BGB § 100. G Dannemann, *The German Law of Unjustified Enrichment and Restitution: A Comparative Introduction* (2009), 89–90.

[43] J Beatson, 'The Nature of Waiver of Tort' in J Beatson, *The Use and Abuse of Unjust Enrichment* (1991), 206; D Friedmann, 'Restitution of Benefits Obtained through the Appropriation of Property or the Commission of a Wrong' (1980) Col LR 505; D Friedmann, 'Restitution for Wrongs: The Basis of Liability' in W R Cornish and others (eds), *Restitution: Past Present and Future* (1998) 133; D Friedmann, 'The Protection of Entitlements via the Law of Restitution—Expectancies and Privacy?' (2005) 121 LQR 400; T Krebs, 'The Fallacy of Restitution for Wrongs' in A Burrows and A Rodger (eds), *Mapping the Law* (2006), 379.

[44] G Dannemman, *The German Law of Unjustified Enrichment and Restitution: A Comparative Introduction* (n 42), 94; T Krebs, 'The Fallacy of Restitution for Wrongs' in A Burrows and A Rodger (eds), *Mapping the Law: Essays in Memory of Peter Birks* (2006), 379, 389.

16
Profits

A. Introduction

The purpose of this chapter is to describe and, where possible, provide the justification for profit-stripping awards. We start with the most unequivocally secure examples: the infringement of an intellectual property right, breach of confidence, and the fiduciary's duty to account for profits. We then go on to consider when, if ever, the purpose of the underlying duty justifies such an award for breach of contract or torts more generally. Finally, the nature and scope of the doctrine of 'waiver of tort', which permits the recovery of sums that represent the proceeds of a right of the plaintiff, is discussed.

B. Information

1. Intellectual Property Rights

(a) Purpose of the right
Although an account of profits has long been thought available in Equity for the violation of intellectual property rights, today in England, the availability of remedies for their infringement is usually set down in the same legislation that creates and regulates such rights. This is so for trademarks,[1] patents,[2] copyright,[3] design rights,[4] and performers' rights.[5] The formulation in relation to each is that 'all such relief by way of damages, injunctions, accounts or otherwise is available as is available in respect of the infringement of any other property right'. This makes an account of profits depend upon its general availability in relation to other proprietary rights. As an account is available where the defendant has taken and sold a thing to which the plaintiff had better title,[6] it seems to be assumed that an account of profits is generally available for these statutory wrongs,[7] although as we shall see it is not available generally for all wrongs in relation to rights to physical things. Such an award has also been made for the tort of passing off without any such statutory foundation.[8]

---

[1] Trade Marks Act 1994, s 14(2).
[2] Patents Act 1977, s 61(1)(d).
[3] Copyright, Designs and Patents Act 1988, s 96(2).
[4] Copyright, Designs and Patents Act 1988, s 229(2).
[5] Copyright, Designs and Patents Act 1988, s 191I(2).
[6] *Phillips v Homfray* (1886) 11 App Cas 466 (CA).
[7] Eg *Redwood Music Ltd v Chappel Ltd* [1982] RPC 109 (Goff J). In the United States an account of profits is not available for a patent infringement: Patent Act 1946 as interpreted *Aro Manufacturing v Convertible Top Replacement Co* 377 476 (1964).
[8] *Lever v Goodwin* (1887) 36 Ch D 1 (CA); *My Kinda Town v Sol* [1982] FSR 147.

Although an order for an account of profits, an unequivocally gain-based calculation, is unavailable as an award for the commission of most wrongs, it is generally thought to be appropriate in relation to the infringement of intellectual property rights. Why?

Some wrongs are *mala in se*. They are wrongful independently of the law in any particular time or place. Killing and injuring others, defaming them so that they cannot form relationships with members of their community, breaking agreements, burning down a farmer's crops, telling lies, and detaining people against their will are all, without more ado, *prima facie* wrongful.

We have good moral reasons for obeying the law in a generally just system, and so breaking the law is, in a sense, always *malum in se*, but some wrongs exist only because of the positive law. They are in that sense *malum prohibitum*. Absent the positive law stipulating that we ought to pay a tax, there is no obligation to do so.

It is possible to imagine a civilised society that permitted the unlimited copying of books or works of art. Having two versions of the Mona Lisa is, on its face, better than having one. Copying information is quite different from stealing things. Some societies never had any patent, trademark, or copyright laws. Before the modern era of harmonisation, there were wide divergences between the intellectual property rules of different systems. Today, there are serious groups that campaign for the abolition or drastic restriction of the law of copyright,[9] that it is impossible to imagine for rights to tangible things.

Intellectual property rights are primarily justifiable because of the good consequences that follow from legal recognition.[10] The United Kingdom's Industry Trust for Intellectual Property Awareness ran a series of advertisements called 'You make the movies' satirising films such as *Reservoir Dogs*, *The Lord of the Rings*, and *Toy Story* by arguing, rightly, that infringing copyright deprives the producers of important revenues and, as a result, will lead to fewer good films being made. Trademarks enable purchasers of goods to make educated choices in the market and rewards producers of quality products by creating brand loyalty. Patents encourage innovation by securing for researchers a reward for their endeavour. The violation of such intellectual property rights is not usually therefore *malum in se* (which does not diminish their importance). It is no accident that the origins of the general law of patents was in the Statute of Monopolies 1624, of copyright in the Copyright Act 1709, and of our modern system of trademarks in the Trade Marks Registration Act 1875, rather than in judge-made law. Equivalent bodies of law also did not exist in Roman law. Because rights of this kind cannot be justified absent any appeal to instrumental reasoning, their recognition was the proper province of the legislature, not the courts at common law. Some related wrongs were justifiable independently, such as passing off which involves a form of lying, and so were the creation of judicial decisions.[11] It follows that the majority decision of the United States Supreme Court in *International News Service v Associated Press*,[12] that conferred upon a news agency a right exigible against competitors not to reproduce valuable information that it had already published, which fell outside of the classes of intellectual property right mandated through legislation, is indefensible.

---

[9] Eg Pirate Party Australia: <http://www.pirateparty.org.au>.
[10] For a non-instrumental account of copyright, see A Drassinower, *What's Wrong with Copying?* (2015).
[11] On the history of passing off see *Singer Manufacturing Co v Wilson* (1876) 2 Ch D 434 (CA), 453–457 *per* Mellish LJ.
[12] 248 US 215 (1918), Holmes and Brandeis JJ in dissent. *Cf. Victoria Park Racing & Recreation Grounds Co Ltd v Taylor* (1937) 58 CLR 479 (HCA).

However, although rights of this *kind* are primarily justifiable in this way, who specifically acquires such rights, who they are exigible against, their content, and the appropriate remedies are determined by what is just as between persons. The reasons why *I* have a particular right against *you* must be relational (eg I invented that widget and registered it before you; I have been trading under that name before you and have created brand loyalty; I originally authored stories featuring the character Sherlock Holmes, you did not). Such rights must also be compatible with, even if not necessarily required by, our each possessing equal freedom. If it could be shown that executing a few errant copyright infringers led, in the long run, to a happier and more efficient society it would still be unacceptable to do so. The law may rightly choose to forgive blameless infringements, or to require such rights to be registered so as to be discoverable, or to place limits upon such rights by allowing 'fair use'. The content of intellectual property law, and why one person may acquire a specific right against another, is not therefore understandable in blunt instrumentalist terms all the way down. However, one thing 'moral rights' are not is moral rights, just as 'software piracy' does not involve the robbing of ships at sea. Intellectual property law employs the language of moral rights and wrongs (eg 'property') in order to create association and induce compliance.

This reason for the existence of such rights (if accepted) then gives content to the appropriate remedial response for their infringement. Central to the point of intellectual property rights is to secure for the rightholder the profits from their exploitation. We do so in order to encourage the useful activities that justify why each right exists. The carrot of attributing the benefit to the rightholder encourages the creation of novels, well designed shoes, and innovative medical treatments. If, therefore, another profits from violation of the right it follows that that other ought to disgorge the gain to the rightholder. The justification for an account of profits is therefore not the stick of deterrence of wrongdoing, but rather the encouragement of the activity that the right is there to secure. This entails that an account of profits may in some situations be justifiable even where the infringement was entirely blameless, although a claim for loss suffered may not be. The remedy of an account of profits is here the continuation of the reason for the right.

Put another way, profit-making activities, unlike those which cause others loss, are, all other things being equal, things we wish to encourage. Despite this, in some cases it makes sense to allocate that profit to particular rightholders.

Common law systems therefore adopt the same approach as generally do civilian jurisdictions[13] in requiring those who profit through the infringement of intellectual property rights to disgorge such gains to the rightholder.

(b) Fault

In relation to patents, neither damages nor an account of profits are available against a party who did not know and had no reasonable grounds for knowing of the patent's existence.[14] In

---

[13] But see Directive 2004/48EC of the European Parliament and the Council of 29 April 2004 on the enforcement of intellectual property rights, Art 13(1) requiring the courts of Member States to 'take into account' 'unfair profits made' in quantifying damages. On German law see (1895) RGZ 35 63 (*Ariston* case, infringement of copyright), but see today *Urheberrechtsgesetz* (Copyright Act), s 97(2); *Designgesetz* (Design Act), s 47(2); *Patentgeseetz* (Patent Act), s 139; *Markengesetz* (Trademark Act), s 14(6) all of which use the same formulation, following the Directive, that in calculating compensation 'consideration may also be given to the profit which the infringer has obtained by infringing the right'. How and why profits are to be so taken into account and when they are unfair is obscure on the Directive's unfortunate formulation.

[14] Patent Act 1977, s 62(1).

relation to the other rights, however, an innocent infringement will not give rise to a claim for damages, but the defendant is still required to account for any profits made.[15] (It might be said however that nobody innocently copies another's work). Although some commentators disapprove of this latter rule,[16] and it is clearly wrong if our goal were straightforward deterrence, it is justifiable. Requiring the innocent infringer to compensate the rightholder for loss suffered may leave him worse off than he otherwise would have been, an account of profits will not do so. An account of profits does not occupy a 'mid-position'[17] between compensation and punishment. It is not the case that compensation for loss is a necessary feature of liability for wrongs, nor does the availability of an account of profits necessitate the availability of a claim for damages. As it does in other jurisdictions, the law may legitimately choose to allocate profits from exploiting certain information to particular people in order to encourage useful activity, whilst also protecting the innocent from claims for damages.

In relation to both passing off and the infringement of a trademark however a different pattern is found. Here the jurisdiction to award an account of profits is not found in legislation, but in Equity's jurisdiction to make an award, which arose prior to the system of registration disclosing to third parties the existence of such rights. Understandably therefore, absent a system of registration, liability required knowledge of the right's existence on the part of the defendant. Therefore, knowledge is still also required for an account of profits[18] whereas under the legislation this is unnecessary for a claim for damages for infringement of a registered trademark.[19]

However, it may be queried whether these differences between the various forms of intellectual property right is a conscious policy choice by the legislature or an historical accident.

(c) Quantification

The reason for an account of profits is reflected in its quantification. The relevant inquiry is not a counterfactual one, as it is in relation to consequential loss. Rather, we are seeking to ascertain the profits attributable to the right infringed. This is reflected in several different ways.

First, the concern is with profits made, not gains in the abstract. If the infringement results in no profits, but instead reduces the losses that the defendant counterfactually would otherwise have suffered if he had employed non-infringing means, no claim to the expense so saved is possible. We are seeking to encourage the creation of profit-making information, not the doing of useless things more cheaply.

---

[15] Copyright, Designs and Patents Act 1988, s 97(1) (copyright), s 191J(1) (performer's rights), s 233(1) (design right).
[16] A Burrows, *Remedies for Torts, Breach of Contract, and Equitable Wrongs* (4th edn, 2019), 343.
[17] *ibid*. See also Law Commission, *Aggravated, Exemplary and Restitutionary Damages* (Law Com No 247, 1997), Part III.
[18] *Edelstein v Edelstein* (1863) 1 De GJ &S 185, 46 ER 72; *Slazenger & Sons v Spalding Bros* [1910] 1 Ch 257; *Colbeam Palmer Ltd v Stock Affiliates Pty Ltd* (1968) 122 CLR 25 (HCA), 34 *per* Windeyer J. Compare Council Directive (EC) 2004/48 on the Enforcement of Intellectual Property Rights, Art 13.1 ('damages' *shall* reflect 'unfair profits' where the infringer knew or had reasonable grounds to know) and 13.2 (Member States *may* require the recovery of profits where the infringer did not know or have reasonable grounds to know), emphasis added. In the United States, a deliberate but not an innocent trademark infringement may give rise to an award of an account of profits under the Lanham (Trademark) Act 1946: A Kull, *Restatement of the Law (Third) Restitution and Unjust Enrichment*, vol II (2010), § 42 comment g.
[19] *Spalding v Gamage* (1915) 32 RPC 273, HL; Trade Marks Act 1994, s 14(2).

Second, the rule is one of historical attribution, not simply one of counterfactual profits.[20] Although the profit must have been made because of the wrongdoing,[21] that does not mean that all such counterfactual profits are recoverable. For example:

P1 holds the patent for a method of spinning washing that extracts all moisture from clothing. *P2* holds the patent for a method for a machine effectively washing using half as much detergent. *D* holds the patent for a method of silently spinning washing. *D* employs all three innovations in producing his new *Washo* machines for sale in the UK market, violating *P1* and *P2*'s patents. The machines prove remarkably successful, resulting in net profits of £100 million. Without any one of the three innovations incorporated, the machines would have been heavily loss making.

Counterfactually, the net profits of £100 million would not have been made but for the infringement of *P1*'s patent. However, that sum is not solely attributable to *P1*'s patent. That is determined by the degree of contribution *P1*'s patent made to the overall profits compared to the other inputs.[22]

In the classic decision of the United States Supreme Court in *Sheldon v Metro Goldwyn Pictures Corp*[23] the defendants had infringed the copyright to the plaintiff's play 'Dishonored Lady' in producing the Joan Crawford movie 'Letty Lynton'.[24] Negotiations had taken place for the acquisition of the rights for a price of $30,000 but these had fallen through and the studio had proceeded to make the film in flagrant breach of copyright. The total net profits were $587,604. Although this was an example of deliberate plagiarism, the plaintiff was not awarded the entire net profits made. As a counterfactual matter what profits would have been acquired but for the infringement was not determined. An apportionment was made, allowing the defendants to keep the proportion attributable to their original and creative work that had gone into the adaptation. Although no profits at all may have been made without the (mis-)use of the plaintiff's play, the value of the input of Joan Crawford and others from the film studio was greater. The plaintiff was awarded 20% of the profits (still considerably higher than a reasonable licence fee). The same rule has been applied to innocent wrongdoers.[25]

Conversely, the defendant cannot bring into account opportunities that were foregone as a result of the infringement. If the infringement results in profits of £1 million, the award is not reduced if the defendant can show, counterfactually, that he would have done another unrelated non-wrongful activity that would have netted profits of £700,000.[26] The process of attribution is analogous to the 'tracing' exercise in relation to equitable rights, where as we saw the law is looking for a transactional rather than a causal one between a right and its substitute.[27]

---

[20] Kull, *The Restatement (Third)* (n 19), § 42 comment h.
[21] *Universal Thermosensors Ltd v Hibben* [1992] 3 All ER 257 (Sir Donald Nicholls V-C).
[22] Cf. *Redwood Music Ltd v Chappel Ltd* [1982] RPC 109, 132 *per* Goff J.
[23] 309 US 390 (1940). See also D Friedmann, 'Restitution for Wrongs: The Measure of Recovery' (2001) 79 Texas L Rev 1879, 1889–1890.
[24] The film has been unseen since 1936 because of the litigation.
[25] *Frank Music Corp v Metro-Goldwyn-Mayer Inc* 772 F 2d 505 (9th Cir 1985).
[26] *Celanese International Corp v BP Chemicals Ltd* [1999] RPC 203, [39]–[40] *per* Laddie J.
[27] *Foskett v McKeown* [2001] 1 AC 102 (HL).

2. Confidential Information

Outside of the boundaries of intellectual property rights, we do not have general rights exigible against all others in relation to information. If I have valuable information that is commercially useful, I have no claim against you if you subsequently discover the same information independently and exploit it. There are however interpersonal rights, that are not exigible *erga omnes*, that are similar in content. To describe a duty as one of confidence is to describe its content, not the reason for its existence. Such a duty is in the same sequence as duties of care, or fiduciary duties. All are duties of a particular content that arise for a number of different reasons.

Parties may between themselves create by agreement a right that one of them is not entitled to use information, nor disclose it to others, in order to secure for the other party the benefit of its exploitation. The typical commercial context of such agreements is joint ventures. As with fiduciary duties, some relationships also necessarily import such obligations of confidence (eg lawyer and client,[28] employer and employee,[29] clergy and congregation[30]). Outside of such relationships, the acquisition of information in certain ways may also impose a duty not to disclose or exploit it, such as where one party to litigation acquires information through a process of discovery. In principle, the kind of information in relation to which a duty of confidence may be owed is unrestricted.

The duty of confidence in relation to the information creates, between the two parties to the relation, the equivalent of the duty owed by everyone to the holder of an intellectual property right. The duty of confidence is not part of 'property law' therefore: its entire point is that it is a special duty in relation to information unrecognised by (intellectual) property law. However, the confidential relation has third-party effects. Third parties who acquire the information from a party subject to the duty of confidence are also subject to equivalent duties not to exploit or disclose it as soon as they know of the duty of confidence.[31] It is therefore the duty of confidentiality that has third-party effects, not any right in relation to the information itself. Such third-party effects strongly resemble those upon a knowing recipient of trust property, although as we have seen information cannot be held on trust as there is no right to it as such.[32] The close analogy with the trust shows that it is no accident that this area of law arose in Equity. If the information is acquired by a third party independently of the party subject to the duty of confidence, by for example discovering it for themselves, they are free to exploit or disclose it.

Given that a central purpose of the duty of confidentiality is commonly to secure for the rightholder the benefits of the exploitation of the information that is its subject matter, an account of profits is an appropriate remedy in the same way as it is in cases of intellectual property right infringements. In *Peter Pan Manufacturing Corporation v Corsets Silhouette Ltd*[33] the defendants had shown to the plaintiff samples for their new design for styles of brassieres. The defendants had then made use of this confidential information in manufacturing and selling two styles of brassieres based upon the plaintiff's patterns. The

---

[28] *Prince Jefri Bolkiah v PMG* [1999] 2 AC 222 (HL), 235 *per* Lord Millett.
[29] *Faccenda Chicken Ltd Fowler* [1987] Ch 117 (CA).
[30] *Hunter v Mann* [1974] QB 767, 772 *per* Boreham J.
[31] *Prince Albert v Strange* (1849) 1 M&G 25, (1849) 41 ER 1171.
[32] Chapter 13, Equity: Restitution.
[33] [1964] 1 WLR 96.

plaintiff opted to claim for an account of profits, and Pennycuick J held that they were entitled to do so 'as a matter of right'.[34]

However, whether such an account of profits is always available for breach of confidence has, since then, been called into question. In the Court of Appeal's decision in *Seager v Copydex Ltd*[35] the plaintiff was the inventor of a form of carpet grip that he had patented. He met with the defendants to discuss their manufacturing and marketing it. During negotiations he revealed an alternative design that would be easier to manufacture. Negotiations broke down. The defendants then went on to develop and manufacture their own carpet grip, employing the design the plaintiff had orally suggested. The defendants had believed, wrongly, that they were free to do so provided that they did not infringe the plaintiff's patent.

Although barely considered by the court, an account of profits was not ordered, but instead an order that damages were to be assessed. Lord Denning MR stated that the award reflected that the plaintiffs 'would not have got going so quickly except for what they had learned in their discussions with him'.[36] Subsequently such damages were assessed at the market value of the innovation, a capitalised form of a royalty payment.[37] This may be reconciled with *Peter Pan Manufacturing* on the basis that the plaintiff's idea had only made a *contribution* to accelerating the production of the defendant's product, and so requiring an account of *all* profits made was therefore inappropriate. The result reached was probably identical to the appropriate proportion of any profits. Alternatively, it might be said that the defendants were morally blameless, not having realised that they were not permitted to exploit the information they had obtained. However, even if an analogy with the rule applicable in the law of patents were thought appropriate, here the defendants had known of the confidential nature of the information. Their mistake was one of law in thinking that they were legally free to exploit it.

Subsequently, in *Vercoe v Rutland Fund Management Ltd*[38] Sales J expressly held that an account of profits for breach of confidence could be refused. He refused an account of profits where the plaintiffs had marketed a valuable management buy-in opportunity to the defendant venture capital company. The defendant had proceeded to exploit the information obtained for its own benefit without including the plaintiffs. Relying upon what are, as we shall see, today the insecure foundations of Lord Nicholls' speech in *Attorney General v Blake*,[39] he saw the duty of confidentiality as existing on a spectrum, with some cases being closer to fiduciary duties (where an account of profits would be appropriate) and others being closer to a breach of contract (where an award of damages would be appropriate).[40] This view is difficult to accept. As we shall also see, the fiduciary's duty to account for profits is based upon a quite different principle, and the entire point of a contractual duty of confidence may be to allocate the benefit from the exploitation of information to one party. An order for account of profits does not resemble other equitable relief, such as specific performance, in requiring a potentially wide range of considerations to be taken into account so that it may be appropriate to withhold it.

---

[34] ibid, 106.
[35] [1967] 1 WLR 923 (CA).
[36] ibid, 932.
[37] Seager v Copydex (No 2) [1969] 1 WLR 809.
[38] [2010] EWHC 424 (Ch).
[39] ibid, [337]–[339].
[40] [2010] EWHC 424 (Ch), [343]. See also *Vestergaard Frandsen A/S v Bestnet Europe Ltd* [2016] EWCA Civ 541, [85] *per* Floyd LJ.

Sales J expressed the relevant test as being whether 'it is just and equitable that the defendant should retain *no* benefit from his breach of that obligation'.[41] However, this misunderstands how an account of profits ought to be quantified. As we have seen, it is not a matter of stripping the defendant of *all* the profit that, counterfactually, he would have made, but rather of requiring him to account for that portion of the profit that is properly attributable to the plaintiff's right. The denial of an account of profits in this case was therefore based upon a mistake as to the scope of such an award.

Finally, whilst it is readily understandable how an account of profits is appropriate where the information is commercially valuable, so that the purpose of the duty is to allocate the profits from exploitation to one party rather than another, a further step is required in relation to non-commercial information such as state secrets. This was taken by the House of Lords in *Attorney General v Observer Ltd*.[42] The *Sunday Times* was held liable for the profits made from publishing extracts of Peter Wright's book *Spycatcher*, publication having taken place when they knew that the disclosures the book contained constituted a breach of confidence by Wright to the Crown, before the information published had reached the public domain. We may justify this extension on the basis that the purpose of the duty of confidence is to secure the benefit (broadly conceived) of the information to the rightholder, and that although the commercial profits made would never have been obtained by the Crown, they are the poisoned form of the fruits that the duty was intended to secure.

3. Private Information

In *Campbell v Mirror Group Newspapers*[43] the supermodel Naomi Campbell sought damages for the publication by *The Mirror* newspaper of photographs of her leaving a drug rehabilitation clinic. The House of Lords allowed her claim by recognising for the first time a general right not to have information about one's private life published, a step that had already been taken in the United States. In doing so Lord Nicholls held that the claim for breach of confidence had 'shaken off the limiting shackles of the need for an initial confidential relationship'[44] so as to mandate the recognition of such a general right to private information.

This cannot, however, be true. If *P* has commercially valuable information concerning the development potential of a piece of land, then another who independently discovers the same information is under no duty to *P*. By contrast, if *D* acquires that information from someone who owed *P* a duty of confidence in relation to that information, *D* may also be bound by such duty upon acquiring knowledge of *D*'s duty. It is only those who acquire the information from another who is also subject to a duty of confidence who can potentially come under a duty in relation to it.

Lord Nicholls' authority for the proposition that the right to information of this form had broken free of the initial duty of confidence, and been transformed into a right *erga omnes*, alongside our short list of intellectual property rights now found in legislation, was an *obiter*

---

[41] [2010] EWHC 424 (Ch), [339] (emphasis added).
[42] [1990] 1 AC 109 (HL).
[43] [2004] UKHL 22, [2004] AC 457.
[44] ibid, [14] *per* Lord Nicholls.

dictum of Lord Goff in *Attorney General v Observer Ltd*[45] where he suggested that if 'an obviously confidential document is wafted by an electric fan out of a window into a crowded street, or where an obviously confidential document, such as a private diary, is dropped in a public place, and is then picked up by a passer-by' a duty of confidence would be imposed upon the recipient. In both Lord Goff's examples however the duty of confidence would be imposed because of the way the information is acquired. In the first, the recipient knows that the information has come from a confidential relationship between others, even if the party subject to a duty of confidence in that relationship has not deliberately communicated it to him. In the second, the duty is also imposed because of the way the information is acquired, here because of the nature of the document in which it is contained.

The further suggestion in *Campbell v Mirror Group Newspapers* that such a new right to personal information exigible against all others was mandated because of the right to respect for private and family life in Article 8 of the European Convention of Human Rights (ECHR) is also doubtful. The Convention concerns rights against signatory states that they secure particular human goods for those within their jurisdiction. It no more mandates or requires a right to privacy *erga omnes* than does the citizen's right against the state to education under the Convention require the imposition of duties upon all of us to educate one another.

The newly minted right to 'private information' recognised in *Campbell v Mirror Group Newspapers* is better seen as entirely independent of the old law of breach of confidence, which was not a proper vehicle for its recognition and should not be distorted by its creation. The kind of information that may be subject to a duty of confidence is far wider than the narrow category of 'private information' deserving of protection against all others. If this is correct, it also follows that the remedies for infringing one should not necessarily be available for the other. The new wrong has a much closer family relation to defamation, in relation to which what little authority as there is states that a gain-based award is unavailable.[46]

If Naomi Campbell had sought an account of the profits from publication from Mirror Group newspapers, should this have been available? Is an account of profits appropriate for a wrong of this kind? If we were guided by the apparent source in the wrong of breach of confidence and Equity more generally, we might conclude that we should. The Court of Appeal in *Douglas v Hello (No 3)*[47] stated in *obiter dicta* that if profits were made from the infringement of a right to privacy, this should be recoverable to deter future wrongdoers. This *obiter dictum* was in the context of the court's rejection of the view that damages assessed on a 'licence fee' basis was inappropriate. Subsequently, however, the Supreme Court disapproved of this rejection stating that the courts should not be 'prissy' about placing a commercial value upon the right for the purpose of damages.[48]

If we are to justify the new right to private information, it is to allow people a private sphere in which to behave as they choose without fear of intrusion. Ms Campbell's ability to lead her life as she chooses is set back if she is humiliated by the details of her personal life being disclosed. The distress she would suffer through publication of the information would deter her from seeking assistance with her drug dependency. The purpose of the duty was

---

[45] [1990] 1 AC 109 (HL), 281.
[46] *Hart v EP Dutton & Co Inc* 93 NYS 2d 871 (1949).
[47] [2005] EWCA Civ 595, [2006] QB 125, [249].
[48] *Google v Lloyd* [2021] UKSC 50, [142].

not to secure for her the profits or other benefits capable of being extracted from the information, rather its point is to prevent the information from being published. To recognise a freestanding right to 'personal information' was a bold step, to treat it as equivalent to an intellectual property right, securing for its holder the profits made from it, bolder still. The goal of attributing profits in order to encourage the creation of intellectual property does not apply to celebrity status, of which there is an inexhaustible supply. It is tempting to conclude that because a wrong may be very serious or malicious, therefore a gain-based award should be available to redress it. However, where such gains fall outside of the purpose of the duty they should not be recoverable. The appropriate monetary remedy for the misuse of private information is one of damages only.

C. Fiduciaries

1. Justification

Although it has become common today to speak of a duty to account for profits arising because of a breach of fiduciary duty, and such a duty to account does often coincide with the fiduciary being in breach of his duty of loyalty, the duty to account is independent of any wrongdoing.[49] Such a duty to account is a primary one, not a secondary duty arising because of a wrong.

An example:

T holds 40% of the shares in *Duff Ltd*, a widget manufacturer, on trust for a large number of beneficiaries. *T* is a world-renowned expert in the commercial exploitation of widgets. *T* concludes that the management of the company is about to make a catastrophic commercial misjudgement. She has the ability to use her control of the 40% block to secure membership of the company's board for herself, so as to change the company's commercial direction of travel. She judges that she is easily the best person to perform this role. Such membership carries with it remuneration of £500,000 per annum.[50]

What ought *T* to do in such a situation?

T is under an obligation to exercise her control of the block of shares in the interests of the beneficiaries. She cannot recuse herself and give over the task to someone else. To choose someone else to sit on *Duff Ltd*'s board would be a breach of that duty. She is obliged to make the decision that will result in her making a profit. The profit she would thereby obtain cannot therefore have been obtained through the breach of any duty owed. Should she then be free to keep the proceeds?

The correct answer is no. She owes a duty of loyalty to the beneficiaries. An aspect of that duty is that if she does benefit in an unauthorised way in performing her role, she must

---

[49] This section adopts wholesale the work of Professor Lionel Smith. See L Smith, 'Deterrence, Prophylaxis and Punishment in Fiduciary Obligations' (2013) 7 J of Eq 87; L Smith, 'Fiduciary Relationships: Ensuring the Loyal Exercise of Judgement on Behalf of Another' (2014) 130 LQR 608, 625–632; L Smith, 'Prescriptive Fiduciary Duties' (2018) UQLJ 261, 285–286; L Smith, 'Conflict, Profit, Bias, Misuse of Power' in P Miller and M Harding (eds), *Fiduciaries and Trust: Ethics, Politics, Economics and Law* (2020) 149, 165–168.

[50] I am grateful to Professor Lionel Smith for this example.

account for that benefit to them. She would be behaving wrongfully if she did not give up the gain, but the duty to give up the gain cannot itself be sourced in any anterior wrong.

It might be argued that D's wrong would not be in having herself appointed but in failing to disclose her interest or in not seeking permission to profit from the beneficiaries in advance. However, making disclosure should make no difference, and seeking permission may be impossible. Merely disclosing that she was going to make a profit should not enable her to keep it. Further, it may be impractical, if for example a board decision is imminent, to obtain the necessary permission from all of the beneficiaries in time.

Alternatively, it might be argued that her wrong would be in not waiving any remuneration. However, it is in the best interests of the beneficiaries that she earns the remuneration, provided that she accounts to them for it. If she were to waive the remuneration this would then accrue to the benefit of non-beneficiaries.

The example illustrates that the duty of the fiduciary to account for profits is not based upon any wrong committed. Although it may in many situations be possible to identify a wrong by a fiduciary who has made profits, this is neither a necessary nor sufficient ground for the duty to account. It is no sin to make a profit, but that does not mean that the fiduciary gets to keep it.

The fiduciary 'no profit rule' is a rule, it is not a duty not to profit that is breached by a fiduciary who does so. It arises because a fiduciary's duty is to act in another's interests.[51] Being subject to such a duty requires that you subordinate your interests to those of another. It may be that in some cases, such as in the example, the *only* way a fiduciary can loyally serve the beneficiaries' interests is one that involves making an unauthorised profit for herself. But so long as she proceeds to account for that profit, no wrong ever occurs. The logic of this rule has nothing to do with its historical origins in the courts of Equity.

Like a duty of confidence, a fiduciary duty may arise for a number of different reasons. However, the 'no profit' rule follows from the content of the obligation, not the reason for its existence. The leading authorities in England[52] are the decisions of the House of Lords in *Regal (Hastings) Ltd v Gulliver*[53] and *Boardman v Phipps*.[54]

In the former, the plaintiff company, Regal, owned one cinema, and its directors wished it to acquire two more. For this purpose, the company formed a subsidiary, but was then unable to raise the finance for the acquisitions itself. The directors therefore personally subscribed to 3,000 shares in the subsidiary, whilst their company took 2,000. The shares in both companies were later sold at considerable profit. As a matter of fact, the profit that the directors made was not one that could have been obtained for Regal itself. Under new control, Regal brought an action to recover from the directors the profits they had made. The House of Lords unanimously held them accountable. The relevant principle was most accurately stated by Lord Russell:

> The rule of equity which insists on those, who by use of a fiduciary position make a profit, being liable to account for that profit, in no way depends on fraud, or absence of *bona fides* or upon such questions or consideration as whether the profit would or should otherwise

---

[51] *Cf.* P Finn, 'The Fiduciary Principle' in T Yourdan (ed), *Equity Fiduciaries and Trusts* (1989), 1, 32.
[52] Although the rule is much older. Eg *Keech v Sandford* (1726) Sel Cas Ch 61, 25 ER 223.
[53] [1967] 2 AC 134 (HL).
[54] [1967] 2 AC 46 (HL).

have gone to the plaintiff, or whether the profiteer was under a duty to obtain the source of the profit for the plaintiff... The liability arises from the mere fact of a profit having, in the stated circumstances, been made.[55]

This 'no profit' rule is separate from the 'no conflict' rule with which it is sometimes yoked. First, and most obviously, the 'no profit' rule applies regardless of any actual or possible conflict between the interests of the fiduciary and the beneficiary. The fiduciary must account for profits even where it is in the beneficiary's interests that she make such a profit, as in *Regal (Hastings) Ltd v Gulliver* itself. Second their effect is quite different. A situation of conflict arises where a fiduciary is under an obligation to exercise a power for another's benefit, but has a personal interest that interferes with the selfless exercise of this power. Such a conflict may *disable* a fiduciary from perfectly exercising such a power. A sale by a trustee of trust assets to himself is, for example, vulnerable to be set aside, however fair the price and regardless of the trustee's honesty.[56] By contrast, the 'no profit' rule cannot be explained as a 'disability' in exercising a power. No power is necessarily being exercised,[57] and the 'no profit' rule gives rise to a *duty* to account not a vulnerability to having a transaction set aside, as does a disability.

The difficulty with the second decision, that of the House of Lords in *Boardman v Phipps*,[58] is not its result, which is correct, but rather that the speeches of the majority appear so unpersuasive compared to those of the dissentients. Charles Phipps died, leaving a minority stake in a company that owned a textile business to the Phipps family trust. The defendants were a solicitor to the family (Boardman) and one of the beneficiaries under the trust (Tom). They attended the general meeting of the company on behalf of the trustees, and concluded that the company was mismanaged and that a controlling stake should be acquired. Although never appointed as such, the basis for the conclusion that Tom owed a duty of loyalty was that he had taken on for himself the position of agent for the trustees.[59] The same was true of Boardman, but he was also acting as solicitor for the trustees. During negotiations for a buy-out with the company's directors when representing the trustees as minority shareholders, Boardman acquired valuable information as to the true value of the company. After the buy-out fell through, Boardman and Tom then personally acquired a majority stake in the company, proceeding to liquidate its assets and distribute the proceeds to shareholders, ensuring a profit both for themselves, and the trust as minority shareholders. John, another beneficiary under the trust, then brought a claim against Boardman and Tom, with the surviving trustees as co-defendants, for an account of the profits they made from the majority shareholding acquired.

Unlike in *Regal (Hastings)* it seems likely that *Boardman v Phipps* was a case where it was legally, not just factually, impossible for the party to whom the duty of loyalty was owed to have obtained the profits made by Boardman and Tom for itself. The purchase of the majority stake was not one authorised by the trust's investment clause, and a court would not

---

[55] [1967] 2 AC 134 (HL), 144–145. See also 153, the issue was not 'whether they had acted in breach of duty' *per* Lord Macmillan, 159, 'Their liability in this respect does not depend upon breach of duty' *per* Lord Porter.
[56] *Fox v Mackreth* (1789–1791) 2 Bro CC 400, 29 ER 224.
[57] Contra C Mitchell, 'Causation, Remoteness and Fiduciary Gains' (2006) 17 KCLJ 325, 329–330.
[58] [1967] 2 AC 46. For a detailed consideration of the facts see M Bryan, 'Boardman v Phipps (1967)' in C Mitchell and P Mitchell (eds), *Landmark Cases in Equity* (2012), 581.
[59] Bryan, 'Boardman v Phipps (1967)' (n 59), 587–588. Alternatively, Tom had profited, as he knew, from information obtained by Boardman in a fiduciary capacity.

have approved investing in a badly managed company in any event. As a matter of fact, the trust also lacked the ability to raise the necessary funds in any event.

One complexity is the question of the party to whom the defendants owed their duty of loyalty. Boardman and Tom were acting 'for the trust' by which is meant for the trustees, who were the beneficiaries of their duty. The duty to account for profits was owed to the trustees, not to John personally as a beneficiary. The trustees as a class could have consented to their dealings[60] (which may in turn be a breach in some situations of their duties as trustees, but which does not thereby render such consent invalid) but as one of the trustees had lost mental capacity this would have required court proceedings, that never occurred. However, the trustees had probably not been kept fully informed so as to be able to consent in any event.[61]

The dissentients' view was that as there was no actual or potential conflict between the personal interests of the defendants and the interests of the trust, no duty to account for profits should therefore arise.[62] This is, however, an elision of two quite separate rules. The duty of loyalty that Boardman and Tom owed entailed that the benefits from the exploitation of the information they acquired when acting for the trustees should be held for them. Further, once it is accepted that the rule is independent of wrongdoing, so that it was not necessary to identify any breach of fiduciary obligation by Boardman and Tom, the criticisms of the result in *Boardman v Phipps*,[63] fall away. It should not matter that they were in good faith, caused no actual or potential prejudice to the trust, or even conferred a benefit upon the party to whom they owed their duty that could not otherwise have been obtained. Unlike in the case of breach of confidence, the information Boardman and Tom had acquired had not been confided in them by the trust, nor was it acquired from the trust in any other way. Nor was it within one of the defined classes of information constituting intellectual property in the sense of giving rise to rights *erga omnes*. However, the duty of loyalty they owed entailed that the fruits of exploitation of the opportunity they had acquired in acting for the trust also properly belonged to the trust. Their duty of loyalty therefore entailed that they accounted for the profits made.

Finally, most fiduciaries, such as trustees or agents, hold powers that they owe a duty to loyally exercise on another's behalf. As we have seen, the 'no conflict' rule applies where the fiduciary has a personal interest in the exercise of that power that interferes with the judgement as to whether to act, and so renders it vulnerable to be set aside when he chooses to do so. A duty of loyalty is also independent of there being any such power held for another.[64] That it is the duty of loyalty that necessitates the obligation to give up the gain, not the conflict of interest in exercising any power, may be further illustrated by *Reading v Attorney General*.[65] A sergeant enriched himself by accepting bribes to guide smugglers through army check posts in Cairo. He had worn his army uniform so as to ensure that the lorries carrying alcohol in which he rode would not be stopped. The military authorities seized the cash with which he had been bribed, and he was imprisoned following a court-martial.

---

[60] Cf. *Queensland Mines Ltd v Hudson* (1978) 18 ALR 1.
[61] [1964] 1 WLR 1012, 1017 *per* Wilberforce J.
[62] [1967] 2 AC 44 (HL), 88 *per* Viscount Dilhorne, 123, 126 *per* Lord Upjohn, *cf*. 103–104 *per* Lord Cohen.
[63] Eg G Jones, 'Unjust Enrichment and the Fiduciary's Duty of Loyalty' (1968) 84 LQR 472.
[64] But see I Samet, 'Guarding the Fiduciary's Conscience—A Justification of a Stringent Profit-stripping Rule' (2008) 28 OJLS 763.
[65] [1951] AC 507 (HL).

Upon release he brought a claim for the return of the cash, which was denied. All members of the House of Lords accepted that the sergeant was accountable for the money received in Equity, although the sergeant was only a fiduciary in a 'wide and loose sense'.[66] This was because the sergeant had no legal power, and could not have been exercising one, such that the 'no conflict' rule could have been engaged. Rather he was obliged to be loyal, a duty that now required him to account for the bribe received.

2. Quantification

As with other duties to account for profits, the inquiry is not a counterfactual one, but instead one of historical attribution. The rule did not result, and should not have resulted, in *Boardman v Phipps* of the stripping from the defendants of all of the profits that they made. This is so even though, counterfactually, they would have made no profits at all absent the information they had acquired from their positions. The profits they made were partly attributable to the information Boardman had acquired, but also to their own skill and judgement in exploiting it. There is, of course, no mathematical formula for assessing how much of the resulting profit is attributable to the work of the defendants such that they may retain it. Profits attributable to other sources should however not be recoverable. Further, that this is a rule of attribution, and not a form of set off or counter-claim for the value of the work done by the fiduciary, is shown by the result that both Boardman and Tom obtained the benefit of the same 'generous allowance' for the work done, even though it was Boardman and not Tom who had done almost all the work.

A further illustration that the quantum of recovery is not a counterfactual matter, but which also sometimes thereby gives a greater not a lesser award, is *Murad v Al-Saraj*.[67] The defendant proposed to the claimants that they should buy a hotel together, for a total price of £4.1 million, £1 million to be paid by the claimants, £500,000 by him from his own funds, with the balance raised with a bank loan. The deal went through, but the defendant had in fact paid nothing. Instead, the seller had released him from various unenforceable obligations equivalent to that sum including a £369,000 commission for introducing the claimants as buyers. It was found that a fiduciary relationship had arisen, and that the defendant ought to have disclosed the form of his contribution to the purchase. The hotel was eventually sold for a profit of £2 million. However, the trial judge found that had disclosure been made of how the defendant had made his contribution, the deal would still have proceeded, albeit that the share of profits that it would have been agreed that the defendant would receive would then have been lower. A majority of the Court of Appeal held that the defendant was liable to account for all of the unauthorised profits made, subject to an account for the defendant's contribution, not merely the extent to which they were counterfactually better off as a result of their non-disclosure.[68] The majority unfortunately stressed the deterrent effects of such a rule, and stated that it might be relaxed where the defendant was more deserving. The better view is that the duty to account for unauthorised profits follows from the

---

[66] *ibid*, 516 *per* Viscount Jowitt LC and Lord Porter.
[67] [2005] EWCA 959. See also *Grey v New Augarita Porcupine Mines Ltd* [1952] 3 DLR 1 (PC); *Keystone Healthcare Ltd v Parr* [2019] EWCA Civ 1246, [2019] 4 WLR 99.
[68] Arden and Jonathan Parker LJJ; Clarke LJ dissented.

defendant's duty of loyalty today to give up the gain made from the transaction, rather than from the amount of gain counterfactually resulting from a wrong committed in the past.[69] Any incidental deterrence effect of the rule counts in its favour, but is not its justification. Where a claim for consequential loss is brought against a fiduciary for his breach of duty, the approach to quantification is the ordinary counterfactual one, and this is not abandoned for reasons of deterrence.[70]

3. Constructive Trust?

Wilberforce J in *Boardman v Phipps* had held at first instance that the shares acquired by Boardman and Tom were held on constructive trust, subject to a lien for their outlay on the shares, and this decision was affirmed by the House of Lords. Although at one time controversial, following *FHR European Ventures v Cedar Capital Partners*[71] it is no longer in any doubt in English law. From the moment at which they acquired the shares, Boardman and Tom ought not to have used them for their own benefit, and so a trust arose.

4. Dishonest Assistance

On the approach adopted here, that seeks to explain the duty to account for profits as based upon the fiduciary duty of loyalty, a problem then arises in explaining any equivalent obligation of third parties who dishonestly assist in a breach of fiduciary duty. The assistant does not owe the duty of loyalty, and so why should he be obliged to account for the profits he makes? It has now been accepted by the English Court of Appeal[72] and the High Court of Australia,[73] that a dishonest assistant can in principle be liable to account for the profits he makes, but those courts took quite different approaches to the scope of such a rule.

Of course, at one level the problem may be thought trivial. As the claim against the third party is dependent upon their dishonesty, we may be willing to overlook the theoretical niceties. It is not the case elsewhere however that a defendant's dishonest wrongdoing alone suffices to justify an account of profits.[74]

It cannot be said, as has been suggested,[75] that the fiduciary's liability is attributed to the assistant, as the assistant is not jointly liable for any profits the fiduciary may have made.[76] Further it cannot simply be assumed that because 'dishonest assistance' is an equitable and not a common law wrong that the remedial rules are different without more ado. Another, although still unsatisfying, explanation is that we have good reasons for treating the

---

[69] [2005] EWCA 959, [82], [121].
[70] *Swindle v Harrison* [1997] 4 All ER 705 (CA).
[71] [2014] UKSC 45, [2015] AC 250.
[72] *Novoship (UK) Ltd v Mikhaylyuk* [2014] EWCA Civ 908, [2015] QB 499.
[73] *Ancient Order of Foresters in Victoria Friendly Society Ltd v Lifeplan Australia Friendly Society Ltd* [2018] HCA 43.
[74] See eg *Halifax Building Society v Thomas* [1996] Ch 217 (CA).
[75] S Elliot and C Mitchell, 'Remedies for Dishonest Assistance' (2004) 67 MLR 16. *Cf.* P Ridge, 'Justifying the Remedy for Dishonest Assistance' (2008) 124 LQR 445.
[76] *Ultraframe (UK) Ltd v Fielding* [2007] WTLR 835, [1589]–[1601] *per* Lewison J. *Michael Wilson & Partners Ltd v Nicholls* (2011) 244 CLR 427, [106].

dishonest assistant *as if* they were the fiduciary.[77] It could be argued that we do not wish to allow the dishonest participant in a breach of fiduciary duty to obtain a more advantageous position than would arise if they were themselves subject to that duty. Scenarios can be constructed where a party avoids undertaking any duty of loyalty themselves, through the use of intermediaries, and thereby obtains a profit that they could not otherwise retain.

Although accepting that there is potentially a duty to account for profits, the view that the assistant's duty to account for profits should be the same as if he were himself a fiduciary was rejected by the Court of Appeal in *Novoship (UK) Ltd v Mikhaylyuk*.[78] The plaintiff was a shipping company. Its agent in negotiating charters had been in breach of his fiduciary duties, and the defendants had dishonestly assisted in that breach. The charters entered into had proven profitable for the defendants, but this was primarily because they had judged the charter market well, and it had moved in their favour. The charters they had obtained were at the then prevailing market rate. The court correctly stated:

> The essence of the relationship between a fiduciary and beneficiary is that the latter has placed his trust in the former. The core duty of the fiduciary is single minded loyalty to his beneficiary. Thus the breach of duty does not consist in the making of a profit by the fiduciary, but in the keeping of it for himself.[79]

They also, again correctly, endorsed the earlier approach of the same court in *Murad* to the quantification of an award made against fiduciary.

However, as they also rightly noted, this reasoning does not apply to non-fiduciaries. This led them to conclude that as the 'real or effective cause'[80] of the defendants' profits was the movement of the charter market, no recovery was permitted. The difference in these approaches to the fiduciary and the assistant, although criticised,[81] is defensible because only one of them is subject to a duty that clearly justifies an account of profits. It may be queried whether and when third parties should ever be liable for profits made. Outside of those cases where they have acquired information, or the traceable proceeds of rights held on trust from a trustee, the benefit of which should have accrued to the trust, the most readily justifiable case is where the third party is only not personally a fiduciary through the use of intermediaries who are.

In Australia, by contrast, a majority of the High Court showed little reluctance in holding a knowing assistant liable to account for profits,[82] drawing no distinction between the fiduciary and the third party, explaining the liability for profits of both in terms of deterrence of wrongdoing.[83] The more circumspect English approach of looking to the nature of the duty, and not the moral culpability of the defendant, is to be preferred.

---

[77] *Williams v Central Bank of Nigeria* [2014] UKSC 10, [2014] AC 1189, 1198 [9] *per* Lord Sumption; *Ancient Order of Foresters in Victoria Friendly Society Ltd v Lifeplan Australia Friendly Society Ltd* [2018] HCA 43, [77] *per* Gageler J.
[78] [2014] EWCA Civ 908, [2015] QB 499.
[79] *ibid*, [104].
[80] *ibid*, [115].
[81] W Gummow, 'Dishonest Assistance and Account of Profits' (2014) 74 CLJ 405.
[82] *Ancient Order of Foresters in Victoria Friendly Society Ltd v Lifeplan Australia Friendly Society Ltd* [2018] HCA 43, Kiefel CJ, Gageler, Keane, and Edelman JJ, Nettle J dissenting.
[83] *ibid*, [9] *per* Kiefel CJ, Keane and Edelman JJ. *Cf.* [77]–[78] *per* Gageler J.

D. Breach of Contract

1. General Principle

Outside of intellectual property rights, the kinds of duty that are amenable to an award for an account of profits are distinguished by their content. A duty of confidence is a duty not to disclose or exploit information. A fiduciary duty is a duty of loyalty. Each such duty arises for a number of different reasons. By contrast, contractual duties are distinguished by the reason for their existence: *pacta sunt servanda*. Parties may, by agreement, impose upon themselves duties of confidence or fiduciary duties of loyalty. The scope of such duties will then be determined by the parties' agreement.

Confusion arises because duties of the same content may arise either because of or wholly independently of any contract between the parties. An express trust gives rise to a fiduciary duty on the trustee but requires no contract, and a party who receives information from another who is subject to a duty of confidence comes under the same duty upon knowledge of the relevant facts. However, just as a duty of care may arise either independently of a contract or because of one, so too may other duties that are distinguished by their content.

It is therefore a category error to think of contractual duties as necessarily distinct from duties of confidence or loyalty. Sometimes duties of confidence or loyalty *are* contractual duties. Where they are, there is just one duty. Cautious competent lawyers can lose sight of this by pleading a claim in the alternative as one for breach of contract or for breach of confidence, but this is duplication where the duty of confidence is contractual.[84]

Once it is accepted that the breach of some contractual duties does require the obligor to account for profits, and that this is justifiable because of the purpose of the duty assumed, are there others? In the following examples there is no doubt that P is entitled to damages for any consequential loss he may have, but is an account of profits also available?[85]

Usually, it will be impossible to establish any link between the purpose of the duty and the profit by the defendant. In the Scottish appeal to the House of Lords in *Teacher v Calder*[86] the defendant financier broke a contractual duty to invest £15,000 in the business of the pursuer, a timber merchant, and instead invested the same sum in a distillery. The award was limited to the loss suffered through the lack of investment, not extending to the much larger profits the financier had derived from the distillery. As the breach consisted in not investing £15,000 in the timber business, the pursuer would have had no grounds for complaint if the defendant had done so and also invested £15,000 in the distillery. The investment in the distillery was therefore not constitutive of the breach, and it was no part of the purpose of the duty to invest in the timber business to allocate the gain made from the distillery business to the pursuer.

Similar results follow in standard contracts for the sale of goods.

D agrees to sell to *P* 1,000 tonnes of durum wheat for £250 per tonne delivery on 1 April. On 30 March *D* delivers 1,000 tonnes of durum wheat to *X* for a contract price of £500 per

---

[84] Eg *Pell Frischmann Engineering Ltd v Bow Valley Bros Valley Iran Ltd* [2009] UKPC 45, [2011] 1 WLR 2370; *Vercoe v Rutland Fund Management Ltd* [2010] EWHC 424 (Ch).
[85] See also the helpful discussion in D Friedmann, 'Restitution of Benefits Obtained through the Appropriation of Property or the Commission of a Wrong' (1980) Col LR 505, 513–526.
[86] (1889) 1 F (HL) 39.

tonne. On 1 April D fails to deliver any wheat to P the market rate on that day being £300 per tonne.

Although, as a counterfactual matter, it may be that had D not delivered to X he would have used the same consignment to fulfil his obligation to P, he was under no duty in relation to that specific consignment. D could have gone into the market and obtained 1,000 tonnes of durum wheat from elsewhere in order to fulfil his contractual obligation to P.[87] D's breach was constituted by not delivering the wheat to D, not by his delivering other wheat to P, nor indeed by anything else he did. It was not part of the purpose of the duty to D to allocate the profits P made from his sales to anyone else.[88]

This may be contrasted with a contract for the sale of specific goods where title has passed.

D agrees to sell his Picasso miniature hanging in his dining room to P for £500,000. Before delivery, D receives an offer for the painting of £600,000 from X, which D accepts. D delivers the painting to X, who is unaware of the prior agreement.

The default rule in the Sale of Goods Act for the transfer of title to specific goods is that it will pass upon contracting, regardless of whether payment or delivery has been made.[89] D has therefore sold goods to which P has better title, but as a seller in possession has passed good title to X.[90] As we shall see, this entitles P either to claim damages for the tort reflecting the market value of the title to the thing at the time of wrongful sale or to 'waive the tort' and claim payment of the proceeds of sale, here £600,000. If, however, P has not yet paid D the price for the goods, this is deducted from the sum payable.[91] Absent such an entitlement to the goods sold, however, no profit-based award is available.

Where the contract is one for the sale of land, a similar result may be reached because a trust arises. For example:

D agrees to sell title to Blackacre to P for £500,000. After payment, but before conveyance, D receives an offer of £600,000 for title to the land from X. D accepts X's offer and conveys the title to the land to him.

As we have seen, a vendor-purchaser constructive trust arises because of D's obligation to convey to P, such that D should also hold the proceeds of the right that is the subject matter of the trust upon sale.[92]

The general rule of unavailability of a gain-based award also applies to obligations to provide services. For example:

D is employed as a law tutor by P, a College, on a three-year contract. D's extreme beauty is identified by a scout for a modelling agency, and D in breach of contract quits his job

---

[87] On contracts for the sale of specific goods, see Chapter 17, Damages.
[88] *Contra* the decision of the Supreme Court of Israel in *Adras Building Material v Harlow & Jones* CA 20/82 (1988) translated in (1995) 3 RLR 235.
[89] Sale of Goods Act 1979, s 18, r 1.
[90] Sale of Goods Act 1979, s 24.
[91] *Chinery v Viall* (1860) 5 H&N 288, 157 ER 1192.
[92] *Lake v Bayliss* [1974] 1 WLR 1073.

to pursue this opportunity. *D* is phenomenally successful, earning a large fortune in a short time.

No part of the purpose of the duty owed by *D* to *P* was to secure for *P* the fruits of *D*'s potential as a model. Unlike in either *Teacher v Calder* or the example of the sale of generic goods, the work as a model necessarily entails a breach of the contractual duty to teach, *D* being unable to be in two places at once. However, it is still *D*'s failure to teach that is constitutive of the wrong, not his modelling work, and part of the purpose of his duty to *P* was not to allocate such a gain to *D*.

More difficult is the following case.

D1 is employed as an opera singer agreeing to perform in *P*'s opera house for a season. In breach of contract, *D1* accepts an offer from *D2* to sing in his competing opera house in the same season.

Should *P* be entitled to recover from *D1* any amount paid by *D2* in excess of the fee originally agreed between *P* and *D1*? It might be said that this case is different, because part of the purpose of the agreement between *P* and *D1* was to secure for *P* the profits from *D1*'s singing for that season. Instead, *D1* has obtained part of the profit from her singing for herself by performing elsewhere. This case looks more closely analogous to the examples of breach of confidence that we have seen. However, it remains true that *D1*'s breach was constituted by not singing for *P*, not through singing for *D2*. *P* should be able to recover as damages the profits that he would have made, but now cannot. The issue of the recovery of *D1*'s gain only becomes significant where *D1* has made a profit greater than *P* could have done. Although part of the purpose of the duty *D1* was to secure for *P* profits from her singing, this should not catch profits that *P* could not have secured for himself.

D2 will also be liable for procuring *D1*'s breach of contract, and on its face it does seem that an account of profits is a plausible remedy. The point of the contractual duty that *D2* was under an obligation not to procure the breach of was to secure for *P* the gains from *D1*'s performance, the very kind of gain that *D2* has secured for himself.[93] Should this then be recoverable?

This issue arose in the New York District Court decision in *Federal Sugar Refining Co v United States Sugar Equalization Board inc*.[94] The plaintiffs contracted to sell sugar to the Norwegian government for 6.60 cents per pound. The defendant was alleged to have induced the buyer to repudiate the contract, and instead to buy the same quantity of sugar from them for 11 cents per pound. This is of course very unusual. Usually, the party procuring a breach of contract does so by offering a better deal, not a worse one. The defendant was able to force its own worse terms on to the buyer because it had exclusive power to issue a licence for the export of sugar from the United States. The price of sugar at the date the plaintiff would have been obliged to deliver was 8.12 cents per pound,[95] so that their contract had been a losing one for them, giving rise to no claim for damages against the party

---

[93] *Cf.* the cases awarding the value of the labour of a servant seduced away: *Lightly v Clouston* (1808) 1 Taunt 112, ER 774; *Foster v Stewart* (1814) 3 M& S 191, ER 582.
[94] 268 F 5775 (1920). Disapproved *Halifax Building Society v Thomas* [1996] Ch 217 (CA), 230 *per* Glidewell LJ.
[95] Apparent from the later decision in *The Gloria* 286 F 188 (1923).

in breach. Although the District Court concluded that a claim for the profits that the defendant had made in procuring the breach were recoverable, this seems incorrect. The original contract did not secure for the plaintiff any entitlement to be paid 11 cents per pound against anyone, and other courts in the United States have not reached the same conclusion.[96] Again, the purpose of the duty owed to the promisee was not to secure for him profits beyond those he could have made. In cases of uncertainty, the profits that the procurer has made may provide evidence of the profits the promisee would have made if the promisor had not been lured away, but it is only in this indirect way that it should be of relevance.

Finally, an easier example to which we shall return.

D sells his business, including its goodwill to *P*, agreeing not to operate a similar business in the same market for a period of five years. In breach of contract, six months later *D* opens a new identical business that directly competes with *P*'s. *D*'s business proves spectacularly successful.

Here the purpose of the duty was clearly not to allocate to *P* the profits *D* has made. Rather the purpose of a no-compete agreement is to prevent harm to the business *P* has acquired. *P* should therefore be confined to recovering the loss he has suffered as a result.[97]

2. *Attorney General v Blake*

In England, the leading case on account of profits for breach of contract is, still, the poorly reasoned decision of the House of Lords in *Attorney General v Blake*.[98] Today, the correctness of that decision is in doubt, and much of the reasoning of Lord Nicholls for the majority has subsequently been disapproved by the Supreme Court.[99] In principle whether a claim for profits made by the promisee in breach of contract should be recoverable by the promisor should be determined by whether part of the purpose of the contractual duty was to allocate such profits to the promisor. That such claims may, albeit rarely, be available has been hidden by seeing claims for profits based upon duties of loyalty and confidence as belonging to a different area of law, when such duties are sometimes, but not always, contractual. How, if at all, did *Blake* depart from this approach?

George Blake was a 'notorious and self-confessed traitor'.[100] From 1944 to 1961 he was a member of the security services, for the last ten years of which he was an agent for the Soviet Union. He was caught, sentenced to 42 years' imprisonment, but escaped to Moscow. In 1989 he entered into a publishing contract with Jonathan Cape, under which they were to pay him £150,000 for his memoirs. £60,000 had already been paid by the time of publication, and the claim by the Crown was to stop the balance from being paid to Blake, but instead for this amount to be paid to it.

---

[96] *Marcus Stowell & Beye v Jefferson Investment Corp* 797 F 2d 227 (1986).
[97] Cf. *Morris-Garner v One Step (Support) Ltd* [2018] UKSC 20, [2019] AC 649. But see Kull, *Restatement (Third)* (n 19), § 39 illustration 6.
[98] [2001] 1 AC 268 (HL).
[99] *Morris-Garner v One Step (Support) Ltd* [2018] UKSC 20, [2019] AC 649, [66]–[82] *per* Lord Reed.
[100] [2001] 1 AC 268 (HL), 275 *per* Lord Nicholls.

The House of Lords rejected any 'public law' claim by the Crown on the basis that there was no jurisdiction to award a criminal confiscatory order without legislative authority. The Crown conceded that no claim for breach of confidence was available. The information had long since ceased to be secret. The story Blake had to tell had been in the public domain for many years; he had no more secrets to disclose. Even if it could be said that Blake remained under a duty not to exploit the information he had acquired while in service, the profits he could make were not attributable to that information. Jonathan Cape was not prepared to pay him £150,000 because he was saying something unknown. Rather they were prepared to pay him this sum because of who was saying it: the notorious traitor George Blake. A majority of the House of Lords ordered Jonathan Cape to pay the Crown the £90,000 balance in order to anticipate any profits Blake would make through his breach of contract (although an order simply restraining such payment would also have prevented it).

Blake could be dismissed as either *per incuriam* or wrong. It seems doubtful whether members of the security services have contracts of employment at all. Rather they are office holders[101] against whom a claim for breach of contract does not lie. Further the decision of *Wrotham Park Estate Co Ltd v Parkside Homes Ltd*,[102] where a reasonable licence fee had been awarded as a remedy for a breach of covenant, far from being, as claimed by the majority, a 'solitary beacon'[103] justifying a gain-based award, is now recognised as having been compensatory, as we shall discuss in the next chapter. If *Blake* is correct, how is it to be justified?

One difficulty in construing the majority's decision is that Lord Nicholls gave different formulations of when an account of profits should be available for breach of contract. First was the suggestion that an account of profits is appropriate where damages are an inadequate remedy, drawing by analogy upon the rule governing the availability of specific performance.[104] However, in relation to specific relief the reason for such a rule is that damages for consequential counterfactual loss may be inadequate to secure the plaintiff's interest in performance where such an interest goes beyond such loss. A profits-based award will neither secure nor reflect such interest in performance, and so the test seems inapt here. Of course, a damages award will often be inadequate for the different purpose of ensuring that the defendant is stripped of his gains, but when that is justified is the question that needs to be answered.

A second similar formulation, stated to be a 'useful general guide', is to ask whether the plaintiff had a legitimate interest in preventing the defendant's profit-making activity, and hence in depriving him of his profit.[105] This 'legitimate interest' must be thought to be something over and above that created by the agreement itself, if it were not then all contractual obligations to refrain from action would be susceptible to a profits-based award. Lord Nicholls also stated that the award was 'exceptional'[106] in *Blake*, and expressly rejected the

---

[101] A W B Simpson, 'A Decision Per Incuriam' (2009) 125 LQR 433.
[102] [1974] 1 WLR 798, discussed in Chapter 17, Damages.
[103] [2001] 1 AC 268 (HL), 283 *per* Lord Nicholls.
[104] ibid, 281–284.
[105] ibid, 285. The language of 'legitimate interest' has echoes of the approach of Lord Reid in *White & Carter v McGregor* [1962] AC 13 (HL) where, in *obiter dicta* (431) he suggested that a contracting party may only be able to refuse a counterparty's repudiation and continue to perform and claim the agreed sum instead of damages, where he had a legitimate interest in doing so. In that context it has the different meaning of the promisee's legitimate interest in continuing to perform.
[106] [2001] 1 AC 268 (HL), 286.

suggestion by Lord Woolf MR in the Court of Appeal that such an award should be available where the profit was made by 'doing the very thing he contracted not to do'.[107] What may positively constitute a legitimate interest was unfortunately left undefined.

Most promising, but also difficult, was the third formulation that Blake's duty 'if not a fiduciary obligation, was closely akin to a fiduciary obligation'.[108] It is true that the relationship between the parties that was constitutive of the fiduciary duty of loyalty had ended many years in the past. However, the case was structurally similar to that of a company director who, in that role, discovers a profitable business opportunity, and resigns her post. If she then proceeds to personally exploit the opportunity, she will be accountable for the profits she makes, even where she employs no confidential information in doing so. The fiduciary is not permitted to exploit for her own benefit opportunities acquired during the currency of the fiduciary relationship even after the conclusion of that relationship.

Blake's position was analogous. His opportunity to make the profits arose because of his gross treachery in the 1950s. Without the notoriety created by his extreme disloyalty, Jonathan Cape would not have been prepared to pay Blake £150,000. If correct, the result follows from the original duty of loyalty that Blake owed, and the result would be the same even if it is correct that there was no contract between the parties. That the duty to account for profits arose because of the fiduciary relationship between the parties was also the analysis of the US Supreme Court in *Snepp v United States*[109] in requiring a former employer of the Central Intelligence Agency (CIA) to account for the profits made in publishing an unauthorised book concerning the activities of the Agency and the US Government in Vietnam.

That this is the best explanation available may be illustrated by an example.

> *D* a long-retired member of MI6 with a distinguished service record, publishes a book about the security services, in breach of a contractual obligation not to do so. He uses information that is all now in the public domain, and does not disclose his former employment. The book is spectacularly successful.

Although the profits made would not have been made but for the breach of contract, these profits are not attributable to the duty to be loyal. Unlike in the case of a notorious, self-confessed traitor cashing in on his own infamy, the profits are not attributable to an earlier act of treachery, but rather because of the book itself. They should not be recoverable.

Alternatively, if it is not accepted that the duty of loyalty can have such an afterlife many years beyond the ending of the relationship which gave rise to it, it may be best to accept that Lord Hobhouse in dissent was correct, and that *Blake* is wrongly decided. Indeed, the case was not argued in the way suggested above. Lord Hobhouse would have been prepared to award a solatium for the wrong of breach of contract itself, the quantification of which we shall discuss in the next chapter.

In its immediate aftermath, *Blake* was followed once at first instance, in a case where profits had been made through breaching a contractual obligation not to sell at levels higher

---

[107] ibid.
[108] ibid, 287, see also 291–292 *per* Lord Steyn.
[109] 444 US 507 (1980).

than those set by a price control scheme.[110] Today, following the disapproval of much of Lord Nicholls' reasoning by the Supreme Court in *One Step*,[111] there is no prospect for its being built upon further.

E. Torts

1. General Principle

It has been suggested that an account of profits should be available for all torts,[112] but this does not represent the law, nor should it do so. Indeed, outside of intellectual property rights, it is difficult to identify any where it would clearly be appropriate.

A good illustration of why not is the decision of the Court of Appeal in *Devenish Nutrition Ltd v Sanofi-Avenitis SA*.[113] The defendants had entered into worldwide cartels to raise the price of vitamins in breach of the competition provisions of Article 81 of the EC Treaty. This gave rise to a claim for breach of statutory duty before the English courts. The claimants had had to pay higher prices than they should have done as a result of the defendants' conspiracy. A claim for damages for consequential loss was potentially valueless as the claimants had passed on the high prices to their customers, and so they sought, *inter alia*, an account of profits. The court refused such an award.

The purpose of the duty breached in *Devenish* may be contrasted with that in relation to the intellectual property wrongs with which we began. Was the purpose of the duty to secure for the claimants the profits made from operating a cartel? Clearly not. The duty was regulatory. It was there to ensure fair competition between all market participants, not to secure the benefit from running a cartel to any one of them.[114] It should not and does not suffice for a gain-based award that the defendant's wrongdoing was deliberate.[115] The only appropriate remedy was damages for consequential loss.

Similar is the decision of the Court of Appeal in *Halifax Building Society v Thomas*.[116] The defendant fraudulently obtained a loan from the plaintiff secured by a mortgage to finance the purchase of a flat by misrepresenting his identity and creditworthiness. When the defendant defaulted, the plaintiff obtained possession, sold the flat, and recouped in full the mortgage debt. The plaintiff sought a declaration that it was entitled to keep the surplus for its own benefit. The declaration was refused.

Deceit is not actionable *per se*; it requires proof of consequential loss. It is closely related to the 'economic tort' of causing loss by unlawful means. It is far removed from the

---

[110] *Esso Petroleum Co Ltd v Niad* [2001] EWHC 458 (Ch), [2001] All ER (D 324 (Ch), criticised E McKendrick, 'Breach of Contract, Restitution for Wrongs and Punishment' in A Burrows and E Peel (eds), *Commercial Remedies—Current Issues and Problems* (2003), 93, 112. See also the rejection of an account of profits in *Experience Hendrix LLC v PPX Enterprises Inc* [2003] EWCA Civ 323, [2003] 1 All ER (Comm) 830 (CA).
[111] [2018] UKSC 20, [2010] AC 649, [48] *per* Lord Reed.
[112] See, on its face, Kull, *Restatement (Third)* (n 19), § 44(1) but see the important qualification of § 44(3); J Edelman, J Varuhas, and S Colton (eds), *McGregor on Damages* (21st edn, 2021), [15–1029]; P Maddaugh and J McCamus, *The Law of Restitution* (2004, looseleaf edn), ch 24.
[113] [2008] EWCA Civ 1086 [2009] Ch 390.
[114] T Krebs, 'The Fallacy of Restitution for Wrongs' in A Burrows and A Rodger (eds), *Mapping the Law: Essays in Memory of Peter Birks* (2006), 379. 394.
[115] [2008] EWCA Civ 1086 [2009] Ch 390 [390] *per* Arden LJ.
[116] [1996] Ch 217 (CA).

intellectual property wrongs where an account of profits is appropriate, as there is no identifiable right here the purpose of which is to allocate profits to a particular person. It has been argued that *Halifax Building Society v Thomas* is only correct because the gain the defendant made would be taken from him because of criminal process.[117] However, deceit is only actionable if consequential loss is shown, and the plaintiff should always be confined to claiming such loss. For example:[118]

> *P* and *D* are interested in buying the same work of art at auction from *X*. *D* fraudulently misrepresents to *P* that an auction for its sale was cancelled. *P* would only have been prepared to pay £1,500 for the artwork, whereas *D* would not have gone as high as £1,500. Without *P* present at the auction to drive up the price, *D* acquires the work for £1,000.

D has made a gain of at least £500 from his deceit, but as *P* has suffered no loss she should have no claim. The only possible plaintiff is *X* who has been caused loss of £500 through *D*'s use of unlawful means.

A slightly more difficult question of construing the purpose of the duty arose in *Stoke on Trent City Council v Wass*.[119] The defendants had run a market in contravention of the plaintiff council's right to do so. A profits-based award was refused. As the right only protected the plaintiff against being disturbed in operating a market, and did not confer a right that others did not operate a market without more,[120] it could not be said that the purpose of the duty was to secure for the rightholder the profits from operating markets in the area.[121] Its purpose was to allow the rightholder to operate a market undisturbed if they chose to do so, not to allocate to them the profits others made in doing so. Again, it did not suffice that the wrongdoing was deliberate, nor did it matter that the wrong was, in some sense, 'proprietary'. The wrongfulness of the defendant's actions was not, at law, changed by whether it was deliberate or not, and its purpose is not determined by whether it relates to a physical thing such as an area of land.

Should wrongs in relation to corporeal things, such as trespass and private nuisance, outside of unusual cases such as *Stoke on Trent City Council v Wass*[122] generally require the defendant to account for profits?

Unlike intellectual property rights, we do not justify such rights in order to incentivise the creation of their subject matter. The same kind of purposive reasoning that justifies an account of profits in that context seems here to have no traction. Is *Edwards v Lee's Administrators* rightly decided?

In England, it seems clear today that the courts will not award an account of profits for trespass to land, but will instead award damages. Such damages may be for consequential loss but may, as we shall see in the next chapter, also be calculated by reference to the market value of such use or, where there is no market figure, by reference to a reasonable licence fee for such use. For example, in *Severn Trent Water Authority Ltd v Barnes*[123] the defendant

---

[117] Burrows, *Remedies for Torts, Breach of Contract, and Equitable Wrongs* (n 17), 349, J Edelman, *Gain-Based Damages: Contract, Tort, Equity and Intellectual Property* (2002), 146–114.
[118] Taken from D Friedmann, 'Restitution of Benefits Obtained through the Appropriation of Property or the Commission of a Wrong' (1980) Col LR 505, 549.
[119] [1988] 1 WLR 1406.
[120] *Dorchester Corporation v Ensor* (1869) LR 4 Ex 335, 339 *per* Channell B.
[121] [1988] 1 WLR 1406 (CA), 1418 *per* Nicholls LJ.
[122] [1988] 1 WLR 1406 (CA).
[123] [2004] EWCA Civ 570, [2004] 2 EGLR 95. See also *Bracewell v Appleby* [1975] Ch 408.

trespassed on a corner of the claimant's land in laying a water pipe. The Court of Appeal upheld a claim for £610 as a reasonable negotiation fee but refused to uphold the trial judge's award of £1,560 as a small proportion of the defendant's profits through the laying of the pipe. Rather the 'only relevance of the defendant's profits is that they are likely to be a helpful reference point for the court when seeking to fix upon a fair price for a notional licence fee'.[124]

Similarly, the leading decision on private nuisance is the decision of the Court of Appeal in *Forsyth-Grant v Allen*,[125] where an account of profits was rejected as a remedy for the interference with a right to light, albeit that the possibility of such a remedy was not closed off for any possible case.

In deciding whether to strip D of the gain they have made from the wrong, the correct starting point is not 'why not?' but 'why?'. The best justification for any secondary obligation created by the wrong is that it arises because the reasons for the original duty do not disappear upon its breach. They require the defendant to do the 'next best' now available to be done. Where part of the reason for the duty is the possible consequential harm that may be suffered if it is breach, this can then justify a compensatory award. Where preventing the gains the defendant has made do not form part of the reason for the original duty, as almost always they do not, there seems to be no good reason for making a gain-based award. Outside of the cases of intellectual property rights, and duties of confidence and loyalty, the English courts have consistently refused to award an account of profits, despite strong academic support for doing so. This approach is correct.

In *Edwards v Lee's Administrators*, where an account of profits was awarded, the English authority of *Philips v Homfray*[126] was cited as justifying the award. But that case, as we shall see, concerned waiver of tort and a claim to the proceeds of sale of minerals extracted from the plaintiff' land to which the claimant had title, rather than a claim for profits from wrongful use of land. The other authority relied upon by analogy was the availability of account of profits for intellectual property wrongs, where different considerations apply. In the case of innocent trespass, the 10th Circuit of the United States Court of Appeals has refused to award an account of profits where this is greater than a reasonable rental value,[127] and this should be true of all trespasses.

2. Waiver of Tort

When goods to which the plaintiff has title are sold, the traditional analysis is that he is entitled to 'waive the tort' and bring an action for the price obtained. In the classic *Lamine v Dorrell*[128] the defendant had converted Irish debentures to which the plaintiff had a better title. The plaintiff brought an action to recover the price received in *indebitatus assumpsit* for money had and received. The defendant argued that the claim was in the wrong form, that the action should have been brought in tort. This objection failed, and the defendant

---

[124] [2004] EWCA Civ 570, [2004] 2 EGLR 95, [41] *per* Potter LJ.
[125] [2008] EWCA Civ 505.
[126] (1886) 11 App Cas 466 (CA).
[127] *Beck v Northern Natural Gas Company* 170 F 3d 1018 (10 Cir 1999).
[128] (1706) 2 Ld Raym 216, 92 ER 303.

was held liable for the sale price obtained without inquiry as to the market value of the debentures.

Indebitatus assumpsit involved the assertion that the defendant was indebted for a sum of money (*indebitatus*), had promised to pay, and had failed to do so. As such, the form of action in *Lamine v Dorrell* involved a fiction, there being no actual promise to pay. What then was, and is, the actual basis for the obligation to account for the proceeds received?

On any view, the justification for the obligation to account for the sale price is rooted in the right to the thing sold. One natural conclusion therefore is that the obligation to pay arises from a wrong committed in relation to that right. On this view 'waiver of tort' is a misnomer,[129] the claim is based upon the tort committed by selling the thing to which the plaintiff had superior title. This may then be an instance of 'restitution for wrongs', that could operate as a bridgehead for the recognition of further instances of such relief.

A second view however is that the obligation to account is not based upon the wrong committed in the past.[130] Rather, as between plaintiff and defendant, the plaintiff has a better entitlement to the proceeds produced in exchange for his right than does the defendant. This would be so even if the proceeds could be, or have been, obtained non-wrongfully by the defendant. If the defendant in *Lamine v Dorrell* had been the plaintiff's agent and had been authorised to sell the debentures on the plaintiff's behalf, no wrong would have been committed, but the plaintiff would still have had a better entitlement to the proceeds as between them. The defendant cannot be in a better position than he would have been in if the action were authorised. If therefore he has sold the goods he must account for their proceeds, as would an agent. Importantly, it does not follow that an award can be made on the same basis if he has merely made use of a thing to which the plaintiff had better title, as an authorised agent would also not be accountable in such a case. The relevant counterfactual is the position the defendant would have been in if the action had been authorised in advance. On this second view, the language of 'waiver of tort' is not a misnomer: the plaintiff asserts a better entitlement to the proceeds as between the two parties without relying upon any wrong committed by the defendant, and the court was right to reject the defendant's objections as to how the case was pleaded in *Lamine v Dorrell*.

The latter is the better view. First, it explains why the plaintiff is not free to 'waive the tort' whenever the defendant makes a gain through a wrong. It should not, for example, be available for profits made through libel, trespass to the person, or malicious prosecution.[131] Rather it should, and does, only apply where the defendant has obtained, through exchange, the proceeds of a right to a thing to which the defendant had superior title.[132] The outer limit of the rule was *Lightly v Clouston*[133] where Lord Mansfield held that it was possible for an employer of an apprentice who had been seduced away by the defendant to waive the tort and claim the profits thereby made. This was based upon the idea that the employer 'owned'

---

[129] *Atlantic Lottery Corp v Babstock* [2020] SCC 19, [29].
[130] D Friedmann, 'Restitution of Benefits Obtained through the Appropriation of Property or the Commission of a Wrong' (1980) Col LR 505; D Friedmann, 'Restitution for Wrongs: The Basis of Liability' in W R Cornish and others (eds), *Restitution: Past Present and Future* (1998) 133; D Friedmann, 'The Protection of Entitlements via the Law of Restitution—Expectancies and Privacy?' (2005) 121 LQR 400; J Beatson, 'The Nature of Waiver of Tort' in J Beatson, *The Use and Abuse of Unjust Enrichment* (1991), 206.
[131] *United Australia v Barclays Bank Ltd* [1941] AC 1 (HL), 13 *per* Viscount Simon LC.
[132] See also *Oughton v Seppings* (1830) 1 B & Ad 241, 109 ER 776; *Powell v Rees* (1837) 7 Ad & El 426, 112 ER 530.
[133] (1808) 1 Taunt 112, 127 ER 774. Doubted *Foster v Stewart* (1814) 3 M & S 191, 105 ER 582 *per* Lord Ellenborough.

330   PROFITS

the services of his employees in the same way as he had title to goods[134] and is unlikely to be followed today.

Second, it explains why the principle applies to the proceeds of sale, and not gains through the saving of expense. The subject matter of the claim is the specific payment received in exchange for the thing, not the enrichment the defendant has obtained in overall abstract terms.

Third, we see the same idea operate where the defendant has committed no wrong at all. For example:

> P bails his ship, *The Intrepid* to D. In a collision with X's ship, *The Intrepid* is sunk. The responsibility for the collision was entirely X's.

D, as bailee, may recover the full value of the ship from X, even though he may have had a good answer to any claim for damages by P. X cannot invoke P's superior title to the ship in any action by D against him. D must however account to P for the proceeds recovered in respect of the thing bailed to him, despite having committed no wrong with respect to P.[135] Just as P had a better title to the ship than D, he has a better entitlement as between them to the proceeds representing such a right than does D.

Fourth, it explains the operation of the now defunct *actio personalis* rule in the leading decision of *Phillips v Homfray*.[136] Originally, a claim was brought by those with title to a farm against three partners, Forman, Homfray, and Fothergill, operating a neighbouring colliery. It was alleged that considerable minerals had been extracted from beneath the farm by surreptitious extension of the mining operations. The Vice Chancellor ordered three inquiries to be made: first, as to the quantity of minerals removed by the colliers from under the farm; second, the quantity of coal from the colliery that had been conveyed through passages under the farm; and third, the amount that ought to be paid for an easement for carriage of the coal through such passages (a 'wayleave'). This order was affirmed by the Lord Chancellor.[137] The second and third orders were made in order to assess a claim for damages for trespass, such order being available from the Courts of Equity before the Judicature Acts as damages in lieu of an injunction under Lord Cairns' Act.[138]

One partner, Forman, had died and only the first inquiry was ordered against his estate, all three were ordered against the two surviving partners. Ten years later another partner, Fothergill, died, and his executor moved for a stay of the ordered inquiries, which the Court of Appeal ordered to be done in relation to the second and third orders.[139] This was based upon the now obsolete *actio personalis* rule:[140] claims for damages for torts died with the tortfeasor, and so the claims based upon trespasses committed in the past did not survive.

---

[134] *Cf. Lumley v Gye* (1853) 2 El & Bl 216, 118 ER 749.
[135] *The Winkfield* [1902] P 42 (CA).
[136] (1886) 11 App Cas 466.
[137] (1871) 6 Ch App 770 (Lord Hatherley LC). See W Gummow, 'Unjust Enrichment, Restitution and Proprietary Remedies' in P Finn (ed), *Essays on Restitution* (1990), 60–67; W Swadling, 'The Myth of *Phillips v. Homfray*' in W Swadling and G Jones (eds), *The Search for Principle: Essays in Honour of Lord Goff of Chieveley* (1999) 277, 289–292.
[138] See Gummow, 'Unjust Enrichment, Restitution and Proprietary Remedies' (n 138), 60.
[139] (1886) 11 App Cas 466 (Cotton and Bowen LJJ, Baggallay LJ dissenting).
[140] Abolished by the Law Reform (Miscellaneous Provisions) Act 1934.

The first inquiry had been ordered in order to support an action in Equity for an account of proceeds of sale made from the trespass, rather than a claim at law for money had and received. However, for our purposes nothing turns upon this. The important point is that the claim to the proceeds did not die with the death of the defendant, because it was not a claim for trespass. The plaintiff's entitlement to either any minerals the defendants still retained *or* to the proceeds of their sale was independent of any wrong committed in the past. Baggally LJ dissented on the basis that the claim for the wayleave could similarly be treated as independent of the wrong, and this did have the support of Lord Mansfield's judgment in *Hambly v Trott*.[141] The majority, Cotton and Bowen LJJ, rightly rejected it. A claim for wrongful use alone must be based upon the tort as there are no proceeds now representing the right that the defendant now has.

Fifth, although the *actio personalis* rule may be dead and gone, limitation periods currently applicable to claims for damages for past wrongs should not apply to claims to recover the proceeds of sale. Just as the right to recover the original thing should not be lost through lapse of time, nor should the right to recover the proceeds of its sale. In *Chesworth v Farrar*[142] the plaintiff had been the deceased defendant's tenant, running an antique shop from the leased premises. The latter had obtained possession by court order, and the plaintiff alleged that goods left on the premises had been converted and that the defendant was accountable for the proceeds of sale. At the time, claims for torts against a deceased's estate were subject to a limitation period of six months after commencement of its administration, and the question arose whether a claim to the proceeds was caught by this rule, Edmund Davies J holding that it was not. Although some commentators have doubted this result,[143] it is correct.

The defendant does not 'waive the tort' in the sense of forgiving its commission. Rather, he elects not to rely upon it in bringing the claim for the money received. In *United Australia v Barclays Bank*[144] a cheque payable to the plaintiffs was fraudulently endorsed by their secretary in favour of another company. Barclays Bank collected and paid on the fraudulently endorsed cheque. The plaintiffs commenced an action against the payee, either on the basis of money had and received based upon the 'waiver' of the tort or for money lent, but these proceedings were discontinued. Another action was then brought against Barclays for conversion of the cheque. Barclays argued that as the initial action had relied upon 'waiver of tort' this had extinguished the tort so that no such action could then be maintained against them. The House of Lords correctly concluded that the earlier proceeding involved no extinction of the wrong committed by the bank. This result has been relied upon by commentators for the broader proposition that the initial claim against the payee must also have been based upon a tort,[145] but this does not follow.

---

[141] (1776) 1 Cowp 371, 98 ER 1136.
[142] [1966] 2 WLR 1073.
[143] Eg P Birks, *An Introduction to the Law of Restitution* (rev edn, 1989), 348.
[144] [1914] AC 1 (HL).
[145] Eg Birks, *An Introduction to the Law of Restitution* (n 144), 316.

17
Damages

A. Introduction

In addition to claims for an account of profits, and to the proceeds of the right to a thing, discussed in the previous chapter, some commentators have also identified as gain-based those claims for damages that are calculated by reference to a hypothetical release or licence fee for otherwise wrongful conduct. The courts have given such damages a variety of labels. Sometimes they are called 'user damages' because they often but not always arise in relation to the use of a thing, but this is inappropriate in relation to other wrongs such as the breach of a negative covenant. As damages for use may also be determined by the market for such use where there is one, this label is both too narrow and too wide. In England, it was at one time common to refer to such claims as *Wrotham Park* damages, named after the case[1] that was the most prominent example of their being awarded, but again such a label is a giveaway sign of our not knowing what their true basis is. Today, following the Supreme Court's decision in *Morris-Garner v One Step*[2] such damages are (inelegantly) called 'negotiating damages'.[3] This label reflects how they are calculated, albeit that it leaves obscure what their normative basis is.

This chapter considers such damages for breach of contract and torts and argues that the Supreme Court was correct in *One Step* to reject the argument that they are based upon the defendant's gain. Their correct rationale is only clear when such damages are put into the context of the award of general damages. Such damages are not quantified by reference to any counterfactual consequential loss suffered.

B. Breach of Contract

1. *Wrotham Park Ltd v Parkside Homes Ltd*

Although often cited as a leading example of the award of negotiating damages for breach of contract, and as we have seen cited by Lord Nicholls in *Blake* as the 'solitary beacon' justifying a gain-based award in such cases,[4] *Wrotham Park Ltd v Parkside Homes Ltd*[5] itself was not a claim for a remedy for breach of a contract. Nor was it a claim to any gain made.

The Stafford family owned several thousand acres of land outside of Potters Bar. For some time, starting before the First World War, they sold off the land in parcels for development. As portions were sold off, the purchasers were required to agree to a restrictive covenant not

---

[1] *Wrotham ark Estate Co v Parkside Homes Ltd* [1974] 1 WLR 798.
[2] [2018] UKSC 20, [2019] AC 649.
[3] But see *Google v Lloyd* [2021] UKSC 50, [2021] 3 WLR 1268, [139]–[143] ('user damages').
[4] [2001] 1 AC 268 (HL), 283.
[5] [1974] 1 WLR 798. See also *Bracewell v Appleby* [1975] Ch 408.

to develop the land save in accordance with an approved lay-out plan. The purpose was to prevent over-development on any particular portion. The defendant was a developer who was the successor in title to the original purchaser of one such parcel. The plaintiff was the successor in title to the original vendor, the sixth Earl of Strafford. The defendant began the construction of 14 houses and an access road, and the plaintiffs sought a mandatory injunction for the demolition of any building constructed in breach of the restrictive covenant (but did not seek an interim order restraining the building work). The claim therefore was for breach of a covenant that ran with the title to land, between two parties who had no agreement between them.

Brightman J refused the mandatory injunction, and the plaintiffs could not prove any consequential loss as a result of the breach of covenant. Damages were awarded based upon 'such sum of money as might reasonably have been demanded by the plaintiffs from [the defendant] as a quid pro quo for relaxing the covenant'.[6] This was not a sum that the parties would, counterfactually, themselves ever have agreed upon as the plaintiffs 'rightly conscious of their obligations towards existing residents, would clearly not have granted any relaxation'.[7] The correct figure was determined as being 5% of the defendant's anticipated profits (ie not according to any actual gain that the defendant either had or would in fact make as a result of the breach of covenant).

2. General Damages: The Contractual Right to Performance

Once put into the wider context of general damages for breach of contract, the result in *Wrotham Park* is clearly correct, and not best explained in terms of any gain that the defendant could be deemed to have made. In the first instance, the point of damages is to put a figure on 'what the plaintiff ought to have had but did not get'.[8] Such general damages are available not only without proof of loss in the counterfactual sense, but even where loss in this sense can be shown not to have occurred. Where greater counterfactual loss is proved to have been suffered it is recoverable as special damages, subject to the rules of remoteness and mitigation. In English law, the most instructive cases on contractual damages concern the sale of goods and their carriage.

Where a seller in breach of contract fails to deliver, and the buyer has not yet paid, the buyer is entitled to the difference between the market value of the goods and the contract price. This rule cannot be displaced by showing that the buyer suffered no or less consequential loss as a counterfactual matter.

The leading decision establishing this proposition is that of the House of Lords in *William Bros v Ed T Agius Ltd*.[9] However, its facts are complex[10] and the more straightforward

---

[6] [1974] 1 WLR 798, 815.

[7] *ibid*.

[8] *Attorney General v Blake* [2001] 1 AC 268 (HL), 298 *per* Lord Hobhouse, dissenting. See also *Moore v Scenic Tours Pty Ltd* [2020] HCA 17, (2020) 94 ALJR 481, [64] *per* Edelman J.

[9] [1914] AC 510 (HL). See also *Diamond Cutting Works Federation Ltd v Triefus & Co Ltd* [1956] 1 Lloyd's Rep 216 (Barry J); *The Athenian Harmony* [1998] 2 Lloyd's Rep 410 (Colman J). For cases where the buyer rejects, where the market subsequently rises so that consequential loss is avoided, see *Jamal v Moola Dawood & Sons & Co* [1916] 1 AC 175 (PC); *Campbell Mostyn (Provisions) Ltd v Barnett Trading Co* [1954] 1 Lloyd's Rep 65 (CA).

[10] Discussed R Stevens, 'Damages and the Right to Performance: A Golden Victory or Not?' in J Neyers, R Bronaugh, and S Pitel (eds), *Exploring Contract Law* (2009).

decision of the Privy Council in *Mouat v Betts Motors Ltd*[11] is a simpler illustration. In the 1950s, the sale price of American cars in New Zealand, then in short supply, was controlled by legislation. In 1955 the defendant bought the title to a new Chevrolet for £1,207 but agreed not to resell within two years unless he offered it back to the dealers for the purchase price, less a stipulated allowance for depreciation. In breach of the agreement to offer to resell, the defendant sold the title to the car to a third party three months later for £1,700. The agreed depreciation figure was £50. If the Chevrolet had been sold back to the dealer, they in turn could not have re-sold it for a figure higher than the controlled price for a new vehicle, £1,207, and so the defendant argued that the consequential loss was £50. The Privy Council concluded that the plaintiff was entitled as damages to the difference between the market value of the vehicle (£1,700) and the contract price (£1,157).

It is sometimes suggested that this market-based rule is adopted for reasons of commercial certainty.[12] However, the difference in value between what was promised and what was received provides a floor for, not a ceiling upon, what can be awarded. This may be illustrated by the decision of the House of Lords in *Re Hall (R and H) Ltd and Pim (WH)(Jnr) and Co's Arbitration*.[13]

The defendant agreed to sell to the plaintiff a cargo of Australian wheat CIF UK ports at 51s 9d per quarter. The market rose, and the plaintiffs subsequently sub-sold wheat of the same quantity and description at 56s 9d per quarter. The market continued to rise, and the defendant bought a cargo of wheat on board *SS Indianic* at 60s a quarter, and gave notice appropriating the *Indianic* cargo to its contract with the plaintiff, and such notice was then given by the plaintiff to the sub-buyer down the chain. The defendant then sold the *Indianic* cargo to a third party. When the cargo on the *Indianic* arrived the market price had fallen back to 53s 9d a quarter. Having sold the cargo, the defendant was unable to deliver the documents covering the cargo to the plaintiff, who were consequently unable to perform their sub-sale of the same cargo. The Court of Appeal held that Hall's damages were limited to the difference between the contract price (51s 9d) and the market price (53s 9d) at the date of the breach. The plaintiff claimed the difference between the contract price (51s 9d) and the price under their sub-sale (56s 9d).

The House of Lords restored the decision of Rowlatt J that the plaintiff was entitled to recover the difference between the price at which it had bought and the price at which it had resold the cargo together with indemnity for the damages and costs which the plaintiff would have to pay to the buyers who had bought from them. Where what is claimed is consequential loss over and above the market value of the goods this should be recoverable unless too remote. It was well known to both parties that it was common practice to resell cargoes whilst afloat. Apart from common knowledge, the contract itself showed this, and the correspondence as to the actual appropriation of the vessel was additional proof, if proof were needed, of the familiarity of the defendant with the practice of successive re-sales of cargo afloat. The defendant knew as soon as it nominated a cargo that only delivery of that cargo could satisfy the sub-sale, and it was sufficient to give rise to liability for the consequential loss of the profitable sub-sale.

---

[11] [1950] AC 71 (PC). See also *British Motor Transport Association v Gilbert* [1951] 2 All ER 641.
[12] M Bridge, 'Defective Goods and Sub-sales' [1998] JBL 259; *Golden Strait Corpn v Nippon Yusen Kubishka Kaisha, the Golden Victory* [2007] UKHL 17, [2007] 2 AC 353, [9]–[11] *per* Lord Bingham, dissenting.
[13] [1928] 30 Ll L Rep 159 (CA).

Precisely the same entitlement to the difference in value between what was promised and received applies in the case of defective goods.[14] The best recent example is the decision of the High Court of Australia in *Clark v Macourt*.[15] The plaintiffs were doctors who ran fertility clinics. They bought a quantity of frozen donor sperm from the defendants. In breach of warranty, a portion of the frozen sperm supplied was unusable as it failed to comply with identification guidelines. The plaintiffs as a result bought replacement sperm from an American supplier. As was foreseeable, however, the cost of the substituted sperm was passed on to the plaintiffs' patients. Demand for treatment was inelastic, and so the plaintiffs suffered no consequential loss as a result of the defendants' breach.[16] The majority[17] correctly awarded damages reflecting the difference in value between what should have been and what had been provided.

The same result was reached in the context of time charters in the Supreme Court's decision in *The New Flamenco*.[18] The owners accepted the repudiation of a charter by the charterer, but were unable to charter out the vessel elsewhere. As a result, shortly before redelivery the owners sold the vessel for $23.7 million. Although they were free to sell the vessel during the currency of the time charter in any event, it was found that without the charterer's repudiation the owners would not have done so.[19] The market value of ships of this kind then collapsed because of the 2008 global financial crisis, so that on redelivery the vessel would only have been worth $7 million. As a counterfactual matter, therefore, the owners were better off as a result of the breach. However, the court held that the owners were entitled to damages calculated as the difference between the contract rate for hire and the market rate for the duration of the contract.

It is sometimes claimed that the earlier time charter decision of the House of Lords in *The Golden Victory*[20] is inconsistent with this analysis.[21] Again, the owners accepted the charterer's repudiation of a time charter. The contract still had four years left to run at this point, and the owners claimed damages calculated by reference to the difference between the contract rate and market rate for that period. However, 14 months after the repudiation was accepted, the second Gulf War broke out which would have given either party the option to lawfully terminate the contract, an option that the charterers would undoubtedly have exercised. The defendants therefore argued that no loss was suffered by the owners after the outbreak of war, so that no damages should be payable. The plaintiff owners sought to argue that the risk of future war affected the market value of the charter, but as war was far less than certain at the time the repudiation was accepted, substantial damages should be awarded representing the entire value of the contract at that point. A majority[22] found that

---

[14] *Slater v Hoyle Smith Ltd* [1920] 2 KB 11 (CA); *Bainton v John Hallam Ltd* (1920) 60 SCR 325, 54 DLR 537 (SCC). But see *Bence Graphics v Fasson* [1998] QB 87 (CA) criticised G H Treitel, 'Damages for Breach of Warranty of Quality' (1997) 113 LQR 188; C Hawes, 'Damages for Defective Goods' (2005) 121 LQR 389; M G Bridge, 'Defective Goods and Sub-sales' [1999] JBL 259; Stevens, 'Damages and the Right to Performance: A Golden Victory or Not?' (n 10).

[15] [2013] HCA 56, (2013) 304 ALR 220.

[16] Such passing on was entirely foreseeable: *cf.* A Dyson and A Kramer, 'There is No "Date of Breach Rule"' (2014) 130 LQR 259.

[17] *Per* Hayne, Crennan, Bell, and Keane JJ, Gageler J dissenting.

[18] *Globalia Business Travel SAU v Fultons Shipping Inc of Panama* [2017] UKSC 43, [2017] 1 WLR 2581.

[19] *Fulton Shipping Inc of Panama v Globalia Business Travel SAU* ('*The New Flamenco*') [2015] EWCA Civ 1299, [2016] 1 WLR 2450, [11].

[20] *Golden Strait Corpn v Nippon Yusen Kubishka Kaisha, the Golden Victory* [2007] 2 AC 353 (HL).

[21] A Burrows, *Remedies for Torts, Breach of Contract, and Equitable Wrongs* (4th edn, 2019), 47.

[22] *Per* Lords Scott, Carswell, and Brown, Lords Bingham and Walker dissenting.

damages should be reduced to reflect the lower counterfactual loss suffered as a result of the outbreak of war.

The correctness of the decision, indeed what the disagreement between the majority and minority had actually been about, was best explained subsequently by Lord Sumption in *Bunge SA v Nidera BV*.[23] The value of the entitlement to performance should be quantified at the time at which such performance ought to be rendered. As he explained:

> The real difference between the majority and the minority turned on the question what was being valued for the purpose assessing damages. The majority were valuing the chartered service that would actually have been performed if the charterparty had not been wrongfully brought to a premature end. On that footing, the notional substitute contract, whenever it was made and at whatever market rate, would have made no difference because it would have been subject to the same war clause as the original contract ... The minority on the other hand considered that one should value not the chartered service which would actually have been performed, but the charterparty itself, assessed at the time that it was terminated, by reference to the terms of a notional substitute concluded as soon as possible after the termination of the original. That would vary, not according to the actual outcome, but according to the outcomes which were perceived as possible or probable at the time that the notional substitute contract was made. The possibility or probability of war would then be factored into the price agreed in the substitute contract ... Sections 50 and 51 of the Sale of Goods Act, like the corresponding principles of the common law, are concerned with the price of the goods or services which would have been delivered under the contract. They are not concerned with the value of the contract as an article of commerce in itself.[24]

We find the same position, that the promisee is entitled to the difference in value between what he was promised and what he got, in relation to other contracts to provide services. Illustrative is *Giedo van der Garde BV v Force One Team Ltd*.[25] The plaintiff, a motor racing driver, contracted with the defendant, who owned and operated a Formula One motor racing team, that he would be drive a Formula One car for 6,000 kilometres for $3 million. In breach of contract, the plaintiff was only permitted to drive for 2,004 kilometres. Although it was not shown that the plaintiff intended to purchase any test mileage elsewhere, the value of the lost driving distance was calculated at $500 per kilometre. Stadlen J held that the plaintiff was entitled to damages reflecting the failure to provide the service bargained for, calculated as the value of the kilometres unprovided.

This may be contrasted with the famous *New Orleans v Firemen's Charitable Association*[26] where the plaintiff paid for firefighting services but later discovered that the defendant had

---

[23] [2015] UKSC 43, [2015] 3 All ER 1082. See also Stevens, 'Damages and the Right to Performance: A Golden Victory or Not?' (n 10), 195–198.

[24] *Cf. Damon Compania Naviera SA v Hapag-Lloyd International SA, The Blankenstein, The Bartenstein, The Birkenstein* [1985] 1 WLR 435 (CA) (damages reflecting obligation to pay deposit, not lower value of contract as an asset).

[25] [2010] EWHC 2372 (Stadlen J). See also *Joyner v Weeks* [1891] 2 QB 31 (CA); *Royle v Trafford Borough Council* [1984] IRLR 184; *White Arrow Express Ltd v Lamey's Distribution Ltd* [1995] CLC 1251, 1255 *per* Sir Thomas Bingham MR; *Regus Ltd v Epcot Solutions Ltd* [2008] EWCA Civ 361. Damages in relation to tenant in breach of a covenant to repair (*Joyner v Weeks* [1891] 2 QB 31 (CA)) are now confined to the diminution in value of the reversionary interest: Landlord and Tenant Act 1927, s 18(1).

[26] 43 La Ann 447, 9 So 486 (1891).

not used the men, horses, and equipment stipulated under the agreement. No fire occurred, and the court awarded no damages. The better result would have been, as it would have been in the context of a sale of goods, to award the difference in value between the service promised and that provided.

Finally, *Rodocanachi Sons & Co v Milburn Bros*[27] concerned an action for non-delivery under a voyage charter of a cargo of cotton shipped at Alexandria on account of the charterer and bound for the United Kingdom. Owing to the Master's negligence the cargo was lost. The charterer had sold on the cargo on a 'to arrive' basis, relieving the charterer of any obligation should the goods fail to be delivered. The sub-sale was at a price considerably below the market price when the goods should have arrived in the United Kingdom. The contention of the defendant that the plaintiff ought not to be placed in a better financial position than would have obtained if the contract had not been broken was rejected by the Court of Appeal. The value of the goods at the time and place of delivery was recoverable 'independently of any circumstances peculiar to the plaintiff and so independently of any contract made by him for the sale of the goods'.

If then damages are to be awarded for the 'loss' of not receiving what was promised, without more, how is this to be quantified? In the cases discussed so far this was calculated by reference to the market value of the performance promised, with a deduction made for the value of the performance received. This is correct, as we are seeking to compensate for the wrong itself, not any adverse consequences that follow from it. Some commentators, by contrast, have argued instead that the correct measure of recovery should be the cost of correcting or curing the defective performance.[28] Often, of course, no such cure will be possible as no substitute may be available, or the time for performance may have passed. Sometimes the two figures will coincide but often they will not. In principle, it is incorrect to value the promised performance by reference not to its objective market figure, but instead by references to the expense that would have to be subsequently incurred in putting right non-performance. Aside from those case where the courts use the costs of cure as a proxy for the market value (as may be appropriate where there is no ready market in use for purposes of calculation) the costs of cure or correction are a measure of consequential loss. As such, costs of cure should only be recoverable where they either have been or will be incurred, and where such expenditure is reasonable. Unreasonably incurred costs of cure (eg the knocking down and rebuilding of buildings constructed with marginally different bricks from those a builder had contracted to use) are not losses attributable to the wrong (ie their recovery is inconsistent with the 'duty' to mitigate consequential loss).[29]

---

[27] (1886) 18 QBD 67 (CA). See also *Ströms Bruks Aktie Bolag v Hutchinson* [1905] AC 515, HL.
[28] B Coote, 'Contract Damages, *Ruxley* and the Performance Interest' (1997) 56 CLJ 537; B Coote, 'The Performance Interest, *Panatown* and the Problem of Loss' (2001) 117 LQR 81; S Smith, 'Substitutionary Damages' in C Rickett (ed), *Justifying Private Law Remedies* (2008), 93; C Webb, 'Performance and Compensation: An Analysis of Contract Damages and Contractual Obligation' (2006) 26 OJLS 41; D Winterton, *Money Awards in Contract Law* (2015).
[29] *Jacob & Youngs Inc v Kent* 23 NY 239, 244, 129 NE 889, 891 (1921), 'grossly and unfairly out of proportion to the good to be attained' (Cardozo J); *Radford v de Froberville* [1977] 1 WLR 1262 (Oliver J); *Ruxley Electronics and Construction Ltd v Forsyth* [1996] AC 344 (HL).

3. Negotiating Damages

(a) One step

Put into the context of general damages, therefore, the award of 'negotiating' damages in *Wrotham Park* is easily understood. Again, the award is not compensatory in the sense that it makes good counterfactual loss. Rather it is an award reflecting the wrong suffered. Like other such awards, the focus is on the claimant and the wrong done to him, rather than upon the defendant and any gain that he has made. The difference from the other examples considered so far is the lack of any market by which to measure the value of the covenant (ie there is no ready market for building otherwise than in accordance with the planned layout on a specific plot of land in Kent). Absent such a market figure, the court artificially creates one by asking what reasonable parties would agree as a release fee to permit the wrong suffered.[30]

At one time, it was therefore arguable that such damages should always be available wherever a breach of contract occurred, but where there was no market figure to use for purposes of quantification. That this is not the law in England was established by the Supreme Court's decision in *Morris-Garner v One Step (Support) Ltd*.[31]

The defendant sold her share in a care-home business to the claimant for £3.15 million. As part of the sale, the defendant agreed to three-year non-compete, non-solicitation, and confidentiality covenants. In breach of contract, the defendant set up a rival business within a year, and sold it for £12.8 million after the expiry of the covenants. Phillips J awarded substantial damages on a '*Wrotham Park*' basis, a decision upheld by the Court of Appeal. The Supreme Court overturned this decision, holding that damages for counterfactual loss only should be awarded, which should be quantified. Lord Reed gave the leading judgment in which the majority of the court concurred,[32] and it is this that represents the law as it now stands. Lord Reed accepted that there are 'circumstances in which the loss for which compensation is due is the economic value of the right which has been breached considered as an asset'[33] but restricted the circumstances in which negotiating damages are available. He stated:

> [W]hat is important is that the contractual right is of such a kind that its breach can result in an identifiable loss equivalent to the economic value of the right, considered as an asset, even in the absence of any pecuniary losses which are measurable in the ordinary way. That is something which is true of some contractual rights, such as a right to control the use of land, intellectual property or confidential information, but by no means of all. For example, the breach of a noncompete obligation may cause the claimant to suffer pecuniary loss resulting from the wrongful competition, such as a loss of profits and goodwill, which is

---

[30] *Lunn Poly Ltd v Liverpool & Lancashire Properties Ltd* [2006] EWCA Civ 430, [19] per Neuberger LJ, 'really a way of defining market value.'
[31] [2018] UKSC 20, [2019] AC 649. *Cf. Turf Club Auto Emporium Pty Ltd v Yeo Boong Hua* [2018] SGCA 44.
[32] Lady Hale, Lord Wilson, and Lord Carnwath agreeing. Lord Sumption gave a concurring judgment.
[33] [2018] UKSC 20, [2019] AC 649, [91].

measurable by conventional means, but in the absence of such loss, it is difficult to see how there could be any other loss.[34]

Lord Reed is here using 'loss' in two different senses.[35] 'Loss' measured in the 'ordinary way' is here referring to counterfactual consequential loss. 'Loss' measured as the value of a contractual right 'considered as an asset' refers to an award for the wrong of breach of contract itself.

The best way of understanding this passage is that contractual obligations that the promisor does *not* do something (here compete with the promisee) are often quite different from an obligation to convey land or goods, or to perform a service. Land, goods, and services are not merely means to securing something else. They are the very thing that the promisee seeks to secure. By contrast, a promise that another refrains from doing something is not (usually) something that the promisee values in and of itself (almost all others will also not be doing the same thing).[36] Rather it is a means to an end: in *One Step* the prevention of consequential economic loss from the competition. Awarding damages for the wrong itself would, therefore, over-compensate as the purpose of the duty was to prevent the buyer of the care-home from suffering consequential economic loss. It was not the lack of competition itself that the buyer of the business wanted, but to avoid the loss that would be suffered as a result of any such competition. By contrast, in *Wrotham Park* the purpose of the negative covenant was to stop excess housing in one portion of a development impacting upon existing and future homeowners. The rightholder wanted the covenant respected for the benefit of all those who acquired a portion of the overall development, their own possible consequential economic loss being irrelevant to the purpose of that right. This purposive approach is a superior way of demarcating those cases where only consequential economic loss is recoverable than a fruitless enquiry as to when a contractual right is an 'asset' or analogous to 'property'.

(b) Uncertain future loss

Lord Sumption, by contrast with Lord Reed, in a judgment with which the other members of the court did not concur, saw negotiating damages as serving as an 'evidential technique' for estimating what the claimant could reasonably be supposed to have lost. Sometimes this is so, particularly where at the time of judgment such loss is still uncertain because it lies in the future (as it usually, but not exclusively, will be in cases where an injunction is sought to restrain future wrongdoing). On this approach the notional release fee is a surrogate for the consequential loss that would otherwise be suffered.[37] Lord Reed for the majority accepted that a judge might give the reasonable release fee some weight when quantifying consequential loss, but said that it was not itself the measure of loss that was sought to be ascertained.[38]

That negotiating damages are not, or at least not just, a proxy measure for consequential loss in cases of evidential uncertainty is well illustrated by the decision of the Privy Council in *Pell Frischmann Engineering Ltd v Bow Valley Iran Ltd*.[39] The plaintiffs were an

---

[34] *Cf. Google v Lloyd* [2021] UKSC 50, [2021] 3 WLR 1268 *per* Lord Leggatt.
[35] See Chapter 15, Wrongs.
[36] See also *Marathon Asset Management LLP v Seddon* [2017] EWHC 300 (Comm) (Leggatt J).
[37] [2018] UKSC 20, [2019] AC 649, [115] *per* Lord Sumption.
[38] *ibid*, [100] *per* Lord Reed.
[39] [2009] UKPC 45, [2011] 1 WLR 2370.

engineering company who had invested time and money in establishing good relations with the state-owned National Iranian Oil Company for the potential development of an oil field. The plaintiffs entered into a joint venture agreement with the defendants to form a consortium to undertake the project, such agreements including duties of confidence. As time went on, however, delays caused the parties' relationship to deteriorate, and the defendants proceeded to enter into a contract for the development of the field without the plaintiffs' involvement. It was found that in so doing they breached their duty of confidence, and the question arose as to the correct quantification of damages. Subsequently to the wrong however, the field proved disappointing, and the defendants only made between $1 million and $1.8 million in profits.

The important quantification question was whether the subsequent fact of the disappointing returns from the field should be taken into account in assessing the reasonable release fee or not? If the negotiating figure were merely a proxy for calculation of loss, then it would be highly relevant that the actual loss that it is now known would have been suffered was low because the field proved to be of little value. The court however ignored this fact, instead awarding $2.5 million as the figure that reasonable parties would have agreed as a release fee at the earlier time of breach;[40] a higher figure than any possible consequential loss (as it was then known) that would have been suffered.

(c) Damages in lieu of specific relief

The correct relationship of 'negotiating' damages and the availability of an award in lieu of specific relief is determined by the purpose for which the legislation enabling such awards was enacted. In *One Step* Lord Reed posited that one exceptional case where negotiating damages could be awarded was under Lord Cairns' Act as a monetary substitute for the withholding of specific relief.[41] Based upon the purpose of the legislation, and in principle, this is incorrect.

The court's jurisdiction to award damages in addition to or in substitute for an injunction or specific performance was originally found in the Chancery Amendment Act 1858 (Lord Cairns' Act) but is now found in near identical terms in section 50 of the Senior Courts Act 1981. This *procedural* reform served two purposes, only one of which is today of any significance. If, before 1858, a plaintiff wished to stop a wrong, such as a private nuisance, from being committed and also to claim damages either in the alternative or in addition to a claim for an injunction, this would require two sets of proceedings. An injunction could be sought from the court of Chancery, but damages for the tort had to be sought from the common law courts. This problem of the necessity of multiple court actions arising from a single incident was abrogated by section 2 of Lord Cairns' Act which enabled the court of Chancery to award common law damages. Today this purpose is of no significance. The later and more general procedural reform of the Judicature Acts, conferring on all courts the same concurrent jurisdiction, meant that all courts could award specific relief and damages in the same set of proceedings.

What then is today the (procedural) justification for what is now section 50 of the Senior Courts Act? The second purpose of Lord Cairns' Act was that it enabled (and enables)

---

[40] See also *One Step* [[2018] UKSC 20, [2019] AC 649, [159] per Lord Carnwath, *cf.* [56] *per* Lord Reed, 'inclined to agree'.
[41] [2018] UKSC 20, [2019] AC 649, [95](3).

damages to be awarded for wrongs that have not yet been committed. Absent the Act, there is no difficulty in awarding damages for consequential losses that have not yet been suffered if the wrong has already occurred. If a victim is negligently injured by the driver of a car they may recover for future loss of earnings and costs of cure even where, at the time of judgment, these losses have not yet been suffered. However, where an injunction is sought to prevent a threatened nuisance that has not yet been committed (or an order for specific performance is sought of a contractual obligation that has not yet fallen due) then absent legislation no damages could be awarded as there is not yet any wrong.[42] If an injunction or specific performance for an anticipated wrong were to be refused the claimant would have to wait, absent the Act, and recommence litigation on the same facts from the moment the wrong occurred.

It follows therefore that the purpose of the statutory provision was not to enable the award of damages on a different basis from that available at common law. It was and is a procedural addition to the availability of damages to prevent multiplicity of actions. It was not intended to alter the substantive basis upon which they are awarded. The decision of the House of Lords in *Johnson v Agnew*,[43] delivered by Lord Wilberforce, was therefore correct that the Act gave 'no warrant for awarding damages differently from common law damages'.[44] (Similarly, the Court of Appeal were correct a century earlier in concluding that the Act did not mandate withholding an injunction or other specific relief in circumstances when it would previously have been awarded.)[45]

Unfortunately, in *One Step* Lord Reed cast doubt upon Lord Wilberforce's earlier statement of principle, stating that damages under the Act could be awarded 'on a different basis'[46] from those at common law: as a monetary substitute for the court order that was refused.[47] This, it was suggested, is one exceptional category of case where 'negotiating damages' are appropriate.[48] The better view however is that damages are not measured by the value of court orders,[49] but rather by reference to the value of the rights those court orders are supposed to vindicate. One explanation for Lord Reed's view was the need to explain cases such as *Wrotham Park* itself where damages had been ordered under the Act, but the same result should have obtained in that case regardless of whether an injunction had been sought.

Indeed, the availability of specific relief may enable a promisee to extract from a promisor as a 'release' fee a sum greater than his right is worth. This provides a good reason for the refusal of such specific relief, not for the award of a higher sum by way of damages. The blackmail problem created by the availability of specific relief was central to the judgment of Lord Hoffmann for the House of Lords in *Co-Operative Insurance Society Ltd v Argyll Stores (Holdings) Ltd*.[50] The defendants were the anchor tenants of a shopping centre operating a supermarket, which was the largest shop and a commercial benefit to the other smaller shops nearby. A term of the lease was that they would keep the shop open for retail

---

[42] *Leeds Industrial Co-Operative Society Ltd v Slack* [1924] AC 851 (HL).
[43] [1980] AC 367 (HL).
[44] ibid, 400.
[45] *Shelfer v City of London Electric Lighting Co.* [1895] 1 Ch 287.
[46] [2018] UKSC 20, [2019] AC 649, [47].
[47] ibid, [44]. See also K Barker, 'Damages Without Loss: Can Hohfeld Help?' (2014) 34 OJLS 631.
[48] [2018] UKSC 20, [2019] AC 649, [95](4) *per* Lord Reed.
[49] Cf. *Jaggard v Sawyer* [1995] 1 WLR 269 (CA), 282–283 *per* Sir Thomas Bingham MR.
[50] [1998] AC 1 (HL).

trade during ordinary hours of business. While 16 years of the lease remained, the closure of the store (and many others in the same group) was announced, and the plaintiff landlords sought specific performance of the covenant to continue to trade. One reason for the refusal of the order was that to do so

> may cause injustice by allowing the plaintiff to enrich himself at the defendant's expense. The loss which the plaintiff may suffer through having to comply with the order (for example, by running a business at a loss for an indefinite period) may be far greater than the plaintiff would suffer from the contract being broken.[51]

The reason for the possibility of 'unjust enrichment' if such court orders are generally given is that they operate as a sword of Damocles over the defendant: the remedy for the breach of the new duty created by any court order eventually being contempt of court, which is punishable as a crime. That is something a commercial party will seek to avoid at all costs. Where the losses of the promisor from keeping the agreement far exceed those the promisee will suffer from its being breached, if specific relief were readily available the promisee could thereby extract as a 'negotiating' fee far more than his contractual right was worth to him. It would be unacceptable if the law were that specific relief were to be refused on this basis, only for the court to then award damages calculated by a fee representing the value of such an order.

The invocation of Lord Cairns' Act ought, in principle, to be irrelevant to the availability of 'negotiating damages'. However, if the contractual obligation is of the kind that specific relief would in principle be available, this is a clear case where the purpose of the duty is not merely to prevent consequential economic loss (as it was in *One Step* itself) so that damages should not be confined to such losses. Specific performance is not available where damages are an adequate remedy: that is, where the purpose of the contractual duty is no more than the prevention of consequential economic harm. There should therefore be a correlation between the availability of negotiating damages and damages in lieu of specific relief. However, it should not matter for purposes of the award of negotiating damages that such specific relief is no longer available in the particular case (eg because of laches or some other rule applicable to the court order).

The only qualification to the above is that when damages are awarded in lieu of specific performance or an injunction, the correct moment for assessing the value of the right is the time of judgment. This may be contrasted with a claim based upon a pre-trial breach, where such wrong is valued at the time of such earlier breach. This can give rise to a different quantification of award, but not because the applicable principles are different. This may be illustrated by the decision of the Supreme Court of Canada in *Semelhago v Paramadevan*.[52] The plaintiff agreed to buy title to a house from the defendant in the Toronto area for $205,000. The defendant seller reneged on the deal, and conveyed the property to a third party. The value of the property rose between the time of repudiation and trial to $325,000. However, as a result of the seller's repudiation, the plaintiff, who was a domestic buyer in a chain, did

---

[51] Citing R Sharpe, 'Specific Remedies for Contract Breach' in B Reiter and J Swan (eds), *Studies in Contract Law* (1980), 129. See also *Isenberg v East India House Estate Ltd* (1863) 3 DeG J & S 263, 273, 637, 46 ER 641 *per* Lord Westbury LC.
[52] [1996] 2 SCR 415; 136 DLR (4th) 1 (SCC). See L Smith, 'Understanding Specific Performance' in N Cohen and E McKendrick (eds), *Comparative Remedies for Breach of Contract* (2005) 221, 228–230.

not sell the title to the house he already owned, which also rose in value during the same period from $190,000 to $300,000. The defendant argued that in calculating damages the court should take into account the fact that, had the contract been performed, the plaintiff would not have acquired the benefit of the increase in value of his old property because he would have sold it. The court refused to make such a deduction, awarding damages in lieu of specific performance calculated by the difference between the contract price and the market value of the house at the time of judgment.

(d) Gain-based?

Why have so many commentators argued that negotiating damages are gain-based when the courts have repeatedly stated that they are compensatory,[53] albeit not for counterfactual consequential loss suffered? There seems no reason to think that the judicial characterisation is in error, as the award can be either lower than the gain in fact made by the defendant (as in *Wrotham Park*) or higher (as in *Pell Frischmann*).

First is the mistake of thinking that because the award is not measured by reference to any counterfactual loss being suffered, therefore it must be gain-based. Such measures, however, are not the only two alternatives. Second is the motivated reasoning of seeking examples of gain-based awards for wrongdoing from which can be generalised a straightforward overall principle that 'no one shall gain from his own wrong'. Third, and more charitably, there is a sense in which all wrongs are gains to the wrongdoer. The wrongdoer has 'taken' a liberty that he does not have with respect to the rightholder. The 'gain' is, in this sense, a normative rather than a factual one, in the same way that all civil wrongs involve a normative 'loss'.

As we have seen, however, it is very difficult to justify a generalised actual gain-based response to wrongdoing (by contrast with a consequential loss-based response). The most common justification invoked by commentators, deterrence, being wholly unsatisfactory. By contrast, seeing negotiating damages as being awarded for the wrong itself, and as a continuation of the reasons for the duty that has been breached, fits more comfortably both with the more general law of damages as it is, and with the best justification that can be given for it.

The danger from thinking that negotiating damages are 'gain based' is that it may then be concluded that where the defendant actually has made a gain from a wrong (as, eg, the profits made by the defendants in *Stoke on Trent City Council v Wass*,[54] *Halifax Building Society v Thomas*,[55] or *Severn Trent Water Authority Ltd v Barnes*[56]) the defendant should be liable to give it up. This danger manifested itself in the decision of the House of Lords in *Blake*.

---

[53] See also *Giedo Van der Garde BV v Force India Formula One Team Ltd* [2010] EWHC 2373 (QB), [549] per Stadlen J.
 Tito v Waddell (No 2) [1977] Ch 106, 335 per Megarry VC; *Jaggard v Sawyer* [1995] 1 WLR 269 (CA) 281 283 per Sir Thomas Bingham MR, 291 per Millett LJ; *Gafford v Graham* [1999] 3 EGLR 75 (CA) 80 per Nourse LJ; *Lunn Poly Ltd v Liverpool & Lancashire Properties Ltd* [2006] EWCA Civ 430, [29] per Neuberger LJ; *WWF v World Wrestling Federation Entertainment Inc* [2008] 1 WLR 445 (CA) [29], [38] to [39], [47], [56], [58] per Chadwick LJ; *Pell Frischmann Engineering Ltd v Bow Valley Iran Ltd* [2011] 1 WLR 2370 (PC) [48], [50] [60] per Lord Walker; *Morris-Garner v One-Step (Support) Ltd* 2018] UKSC 20, [2019] AC 649, [58]-[60], [79], [91], [95]. [97] per Lord Reed.
[54] [1988] 1 WLR 1406 (CA).
[55] [1996] Ch 217.
[56] [2004] EWCA Civ 570, [2004] 2 EGLR 95. See also *Bracewell v Appleby* [1975] Ch 408.

(e) Blake revisited

Negotiating damages were inappropriate in *Blake*. Neither the actual government nor a hypothetical reasonable one would have agreed a release fee to permit the publication of the work. Nor, plainly, is there a market in the ordinary sense for the buying from governments the treachery of their agents. That does not mean that no substantial award is justifiable in such a case.

Two of Lord Nicholls' formulations of when an account of profits should be available: the possibility of specific performance and the 'legitimate interest' in stopping the activity, focus upon the inadequacy of damages that compensate for consequential loss. Lord Hobhouse, in dissent, thought that, by 1989, Blake's original 1944 undertaking to the Crown was unenforceable, but accepted that if it were still valuable this solatium ought to have been assessed on a 'compulsory purchase' basis. If we are to put a figure upon the Crown's interest in performance that went beyond the consequential loss that they could prove to suffer, what should it be?

The contingent profits that Blake made as a result of his wrong seem ill suited to quantify the award. What if the facts of *Blake* were to recur, but the traitor refused the payment proffered by the publisher on the basis that, if it were accepted, such profits would have to be given up? What damages should be payable in *Blake II*?

One way of assessing the value of Blake's duty, absent an actual or hypothetical market, is to ask what someone would be prepared to pay him to breach it. If we see the award as being made to reflect the legitimate interest in performance that the Crown had in his keeping his undertaking, which could not be reflected in compensation for consequential loss, the same sum should be payable regardless of whether Blake accepted the payment or not. In which case, the better analysis is that if a substantial award is justifiable, regardless of any duty of loyalty, it is independent of his making any gain at all.

C. Torts

1. General Damages

For most torts, as was also the case in *Blake*, nobody would think it appropriate to award 'negotiating' or 'licence fee' damages. It is not the case that reasonable people who are assaulted, detained against their will, or libelled would, if asked in advance, have agreed to a fee to permit such behaviour by the wrongdoer. This does not mean that the plaintiff is always confined to damages for counterfactual consequential loss. Rather, it means that general damages awards for the wrongs themselves are not calculated by reference to hypothetical bargains so as to artificially create a market. Substantial damages awards in the absence of proof of consequential loss have however been made for libel,[57] misuse of private information,[58] waste,[59] and a variety of other wrongs.[60]

---

[57] Eg *Kiam v MGN Ltd* [2003] QB 281 (CA); *Uren v John Fairfax & Sons Pty Ltd* (1966) 127 CLR 118, 151 *per* Windeyer J (HCofA); *Jameel v Wall Street Journal Europe Sprl* [2006] UKHL 44, [2007] 1 AC 359.
[58] *Gulati v MGN Ltd* [2015] EWCA Civ 1291, [2017] QB 149.
[59] *Cole v Green* (1671/2) 1 Lev 309, 83 ER 422.
[60] R Stevens, *Torts and Rights* (2007), 62–63.

However, this also does not entail that substantial general damages are available for all torts, even for those actionable *per se*. A good illustration of why not is the High Court of Australia's decision in *Lewis v Australian Capital Territory*.[61] If an innocent person is detained against their will for six months but incarceration transforms their life for the better, enabling them to recover from their drug addiction, learn new professional skills, and upon release leave a happier and richer person than they otherwise would have been, substantial damages should still be awarded despite the absence of counterfactual loss.[62] Looking at the past, they have been deprived of their liberty and damages should reflect that. By contrast, in *Lewis* a criminal was permitted to serve his sentence on the basis of periodic detention at weekends but failed to meet the terms of his sentence. He was then subject to full-time imprisonment because of the breach of the terms. However, the decision to change the terms of his sentence was invalid as having been made without giving him proper notice. He had therefore been unlawfully detained for 82 days. Here, however, the plaintiff had suffered no loss in either the factual or normative senses. Counterfactually, he was no worse off. Looking to the past, he *ought* to have been imprisoned full-time, which is what would have occurred if proper notice had been given. He had not, therefore, been deprived of a valuable liberty he should have been free to exercise, and so no substantial damages were payable. His position was the same as that of a person with a justifiably very low reputation who is subject to a further libel. Although they are wronged, their loss is nominal because their right is of only nominal value,[63] as the court concluded.

Where wrongs are committed in relation to rights to things or intellectual property rights, rights that are commonly sold and licensed, general damages are appropriately calculated by reference to the market value of the right, or, where there isn't one, by constructing such a market figure through a reasonable release fee.[64] We find precisely the same distinction between general damages for the wrong and special damages for loss consequent upon the wrong as we saw in relation to breach of contract. For example:

On 1 May 2021, *D* takes and gives away possession of collectible gold coins, to which *C* has a better title, to *X*. At the time of conversion, the coins had a market value of £100,000. *C* discovers what has happened several months later. *X* and the coins can no longer be found. At the time of judgment, the value of such coins has declined to £25,000. It is clear that, absent the wrong, *C* would not have disposed of the coins.

The general damages payable by *D* should be, and are, calculated by reference to the market value of the title to the coins at the time of conversion, here £100,000. It should not, and does not, matter that the consequential loss as a counterfactual matter that *C* has suffered is much lower.[65]

This may be contrasted with the case where the consequential loss is higher than the market value figure at the time of the wrong. For example:

---

[61] [2020] HCA 26. *Cf. R (Lumba) v Secretary of State for the Home Department* [2011] UKSC 12, [2012] 1 AC 245.
[62] *Cf. Huckle v Money* (1762) 2 Wils 205, 95 ER 768.
[63] [2020] HCA 26, [6], [19] *per* Kiefel CJ and Keane J, [42] *per* Gageler J, [95] *per* Gordon J; *cf. Scott v Sampson* (1882) 8 QBD 491; *Grobbelaar v News Group Newspapers Ltd* [2002] UKHL 40, [2002] 1 WLR 3024.
[64] Eg *Irvine v Talksport* [2003] EWCA Civ 423, [2003] 2 All ER 881 (passing off).
[65] *Solloway v McLaughlin* [1938] AC 247 (PC); *BBMB Finance (Hong Kong) Ltd v Eda Holdings Ltd* [1990] 1 WLR 409 (PC).

On 1 May 2021, *D* takes and gives away collectible gold coins, to which *C* has a better title, to *X*. At the time of conversion, the coins had a market value of £100,000. *C* discovers what has happened several months later. *X* and the coins can no longer be found. At the time of judgment, the value of such coins has increased to £300,000. It is clear that, absent the wrong, *C* would not have disposed of the coins.

Here, because *C*'s counterfactual loss is higher than the value of the title to the coins at the time of conversion, he should be and is entitled to claim such further consequential loss as special damages.[66]

Similarly, where *D* damages or destroys a thing to which *C* has better title, *C* should be awarded general damages reflecting the difference in value between the right to the thing before and after the wrong, regardless of whether any counterfactual loss is suffered.[67] By contrast if a taxi driver wishes to recover for his lost earnings because of the defendant's negligent damage of his vehicle, he should have to plead and prove such further consequential loss. Again, where special damages are suffered in addition to general damage for the same wrong, this does not lead to double recovery, every penny recovered on one basis reducing the loss suffered on the other.

Sometimes there will be no ready market by which to calculate the difference in value between the thing in an undamaged and damaged state (there will often be no market for damaged things) and so the cost of repairs may be used in some cases as a proxy for this figure. However, that awarding such costs may be inadequate is reflected in the House of Lords decision in *The Mediana*.[68] The claimant harbour authority's lightship was damaged in a shipping accident caused by the negligence of the defendant's ship. The lightship was withdrawn for repairs, the cost of which were awarded in damages. In addition to the cost of repairs the plaintiffs sought damages for loss of use of the ship, even though it was not profit making and they had no need to hire a replacement as they had a spare that covered for the other when not in service. Damages were awarded on the basis of the use value of having the spare lightship for the period of time the damaged ship was out of action.

Costs of repairs will often, as here, be lower than the difference in value, and thereby give too low an award, as they do not reflect the value of being dispossessed of the thing during the period of repairs. In order to get at the correct figure, therefore, the plaintiff should be awarded both the costs of repairs and the use value over time of the thing during the period of repairs, so as to approximate the difference in market value.

2. User Damages

When a defendant trespasses on another's land, the ordinary method of assessment of damages for the wrong will be the market rental value of the property, save in the rare case where

---

[66] *IBL v Coussens* [1991] 2 All ER 133 (CA).
[67] *The Winkfield* [1902] P 42 (CA); *The Charlotte* [1908] P 206 (CA); *The Sanix Ace* [1987] 1 Lloyd's Rep 465. *Burdis v Livsey* [2002] EWCA Civ 520, [2003] QB 36; cf. *Dimond v Lovell* [2002] 1 AC 384 (HL) (a claim for consequential loss that had not been suffered).
[68] *Owners of the Steamship Mediana v Owners, Masters and Crew of the Lightship Comet (The Mediana)* [1900] AC 113 (HL). For the argument that the award was for consequential corporate upset, see A Burrows, 'Damages and Rights' in D Nolan and A Robertson (eds), *Rights and Private Law* (2012) 275, 282–283.

there is no such market in which case a hypothetical reasonable negotiation fee will have to be used.

At one time it was common to argue that damages for such use were gain-based and although there are still hold outs,[69] this is no longer a tenable view following the decision of the Supreme Court in *One Step*.[70] The better view was expressed by Megarry VC in a passage subsequently quoted with approval by Sir Thomas Bingham MR[71] and Lord Reed:[72]

> If the plaintiff has the right to prevent some act being done without his consent, and the defendant does the act without seeking that consent, the plaintiff has suffered a loss in that the defendant has taken without paying for it something for which the plaintiff could have required payment, namely, the right to do the act.

Again, the 'loss' in this passage is not loss in the counterfactual sense of being worse off today than you otherwise would be, but rather the 'loss' of having had, at a point in the past, a right that the other did not do as she did, which has not been respected. Where the wrong consists of the use of a thing, this 'loss' has been described as the loss of 'dominium'.[73] If there is a 'gain' here it is the taking of a freedom that, with respect to the rightholder, the wrongdoer did not have. These formulations are, once again, synonymous with saying the award is for the wrong itself. The loss or gain is normative,[74] rather than for any counterfactual actual consequences.

A nice illustration of the difference between general and special damages in this context is *Swordheath Properties Ltd v Tabet*.[75] The defendants were trespassers who had remained in occupation of premises after the expiry of a residential lease. At trial, the judge denied an order for damages on the basis that the plaintiff landlord had not shown that he would have been able to let the premises to anybody else during the period of trespass. If the only award possible were one for special damages suffered as a consequence of the wrong, this would have been the correct question to ask. However, the Court of Appeal correctly allowed the appeal, awarding damages assessed as the ordinary letting value of the property (ie the market rate).[76]

Similarly, in relation to goods, is the decision of the New South Wales Court of Appeal in *Bunnings Group Ltd v CHEP Australia Ltd*.[77] The defendants had converted pallets to which the plaintiffs had a better title. The plaintiffs operated a pallet hiring business, holding a stock of pallets that were hired out to others for use. At no point during the defendants'

---

[69] C Mitchell and L Rostill, 'Making Sense of Mesne Profits: Remedies' (2021) CLJ 130.
[70] See also A Burrows, *Remedies for Torts, Breach of Contract and Equitable Wrong* (4th edn, 2019), 326–327.
[71] *Jaggard v Sawyer* [1995] 1 WLR 269 (CA), 281–282.
[72] *Morris-Garner v One Step* [2018] UKSC 20, [2019] AC 649, [59].
[73] M McInnes, 'Gain, Loss and the User Principle' [2006] RLR 76, 81, 85. C Michell and L Rostill, 'Making Sense of Mesne Profits: Causes of Action' [2021] CLJ 130 claim that the loss of control is factual not legal, but it is mysterious how, absent a right to it, there is any factual control of the thing used that is 'lost'.
[74] See also N McBride, 'Restitution for Wrongs' in C Mitchell and W Swadling (eds), *The Restatement Third: Restitution and Unjust Enrichment* (2013) 251, 273.
[75] [1979] 1 WLR 285. See also in relation to the wrongful interference with a right to light *Carr-Saunders v Dick McNeil Associates* [1986] 1 WLR 922; *Deakins v Hookings* [1994] 1 EGLR 190; *Tamares (Vincent Square) Ltd v Fairpoint Properties (Vincent Square) Ltd* [2007] 1 WLR 2167. But see *Wigan Borough Council v Scullindale Global Ltd* [2021] EWHC 779, [122]–[128] where the market value of the use of hotel premises was, in the circumstances of a global pandemic, nil.
[76] See also *Penarth Dock Engineering Co v Pounds* [1963] 1 Lloyds Rep 3 (CA).
[77] [2011] NSWCA 342. See also *Strand Electric Co v Brisford Entertainments Ltd* [1952] 2 QB 246.

possession of a number of the plaintiffs' pallets was there insufficient stock to meet demand, meaning that such possession did not, counterfactually, prejudice the plaintiffs. Allsop P for the court ordered damages to be paid on the basis that the 'wrongdoer should pay a price for using the goods of another as a matter of compensation for the denial of the right concerned'.[78]

Some earlier cases concerned damages for crossing land, as opposed to continuous occupation, and they also illustrate the relationship of such damages to claims for consequential loss. In *Whitwham v Westminster Brymbo Coal*[79] the plaintiffs owned land near a colliery that the defendants had used for years for purposes of tipping spoil. It was admitted that the defendants were liable for the diminution in value of the land, but the plaintiffs successfully claimed in addition damages for the use of the land for years. Such damages for wrongful use were independent of the damage to the land itself, so that both were recoverable. Here the award was for two different wrongs in relation to the land: use and damage, so that recovery of one did not reduce the loss of the other.

Finally, the operation of the same principle in the context of patents is shown by the Scottish appeal to the House of Lords in *Watson Laidlaw & Co Ltd v Pott Cassell & Williamson*.[80] The defendants infringed the plaintiff's patent in selling 130 machines for the use of processing sugar in what was then the country of Java. It was assumed that the plaintiff would not have traded in Java, and so was not counterfactually worse off as a result of the wrong. A substantial award as compensation was upheld by the majority.[81] No inquiry was made at any stage as to what any release fee might, as a counterfactual matter, have been and the question of profits was not enquired into as it was not relevant.

3. Gain-based?

We have already seen one danger of understanding awards such as these as gain-based, which is the awarding of sums reflecting actual gains made that exceed any loss in either sense. The opposite problem is that the court may be misled into reducing the award where the gain actually made by the defendant is lower than the market figure. This occurred in the Court of Appeal's decision in *Ministry of Defence v Ashman*,[82] which, following *One Step*, is now of doubtful authority. The Ministry of Defence let housing to serving officers at a rate below the market value. The defendant was the wife of such an officer who had left the family home. The plaintiffs gave her notice as landlords to vacate the premises but she did not. The Ministry claimed mesne profits representing the market value of the use she had made of the property after the expiry of the lease. A majority of the Court of Appeal refused to award the market figure. The defendant argued that she would not have been able to afford the open market figure. Instead, if she had been rendered homeless, she would have been housed by the local authority for a rent below the market rent for the property

---

[78] [2011] NSWCA 342, [175].
[79] [1896] 2 Ch 538 (CA). See also *Jegon v Vivian (No 2)* (1870–1871) LR 6 Ch App 742; *Phillips v Homfray* (1871) LR 6 Ch App 770 (CA).
[80] (1914) 28 RPC 157 (HL).
[81] Lord Kinnear, Lord Atkinson, and Lord Shaw, Earl of Halsbury dissenting.
[82] [1993] 32 EGLR 102 (CA). See also *Ministry of Defence v Thompson* [1993] 2 EGLR 107 (CA). The Scots law is to be preferred: *Secretary of State for Defence v Johnstone* 1997 SLT (Sh Ct) 37, 1996 HLR 99.

she occupied. Adopting an enrichment-based approach, Hoffmann LJ accepted this argument, which he characterised as one of 'subjective devaluation', confining the plaintiffs to the expense the defendant had been saved in not paying for local authority accommodation. Lloyd LJ dissented.

Ashman may be contrasted with the subsequent advice of Lord Lloyd, as he had become, for the Privy Council in *Inverugie Investments Ltd v Hackett*.[83] In a hotel complex of 164 apartments, the defendants legitimately occupied 134 but wrongfully occupied another 30 that were held by the plaintiff under a lease. During the period of trespass, the defendants ran the hotel at a loss, achieving an occupancy rate of 35–40%. Counterfactually, the defendants were worse off through having committed the trespass than if they had not done so. Lord Lloyd concluded that a reasonable rent for the premises wrongfully occupied must be paid even though the plaintiff had not suffered an '*actual* loss'[84] and the defendant had not obtained an 'actual benefit'.[85] No inquiry was made as to what rent would, as a counterfactual matter, have been charged if a lease had been sought. The different approach of the court in *Ashman* was not discussed on the questionable basis that that case concerned 'a restitutionary claim as an independent cause of action'[86] whereas *Inverugie* concerned damages.

Finally, as we have seen, the mistaken view that the use of 'property' is *ipso facto* an enrichment was unfortunately relied upon by Lord Nicholls in the now discredited decision of *Sempra Metals* as a reason for allowing a claim in 'unjust enrichment' for the use value of money over time that a payee had had. The authorities that Lord Nicholls relied upon for this proposition were those concerning damages for the wrongful use of tangible things, and were not analogous.

Some commentators still maintain that Lord Nicholls' view was correct, at least as to what constitutes an 'enrichment' so as to justify a claim, but an example illustrates the dangers of reasoning across from entirely different kinds of claim in this way.

> *P* mistakenly believes that *D* has agreed to hire his lorry. *D* mistakenly believes that *P* has asked him to store his lorry. *P* delivers his lorry to *D* who stores it in his garage for six months.

If no agreement has been reached between the parties because they are reasonably at cross purposes, no claim by either against the other should be possible, save that *P* has an action to recover his vehicle. *P* should have no claim against *D* for the six months of use of the lorry that the latter has obtained because of the former's mistake. *P* has consented to *D*'s possession and *D* has committed no wrong. *D* should not be put to proof that he obtained no benefit in fact from having had possession of the thing, and even if he did benefit no claim should lie. If, by contrast, *D* has had the use of a thing under an agreement with *P*, and the condition under which *D* had such use from *P* has failed, a claim for the market value of such use should be possible regardless of the extent to which *D* is, as a matter of fact, better off. These rules differ because the reasons for the claims differ.

---

[83] [1996] 1 WLR 713 (PC), Watts (1996) 112 LQR 39.
[84] *ibid*, 718 (emphasis in original).
[85] *ibid*, 718.
[86] *ibid*, 715.

PART VII
COUNTERVAILING REASONS

18
Defences

A. Introduction

If there were, or ought to be, a unified area of law explained by reference to 'unjust enrichment', it might be expected that the same defences would and should apply across it, subject to any countervailing reason why not. If, by contrast, as this work maintains, there is no such unity but instead several different kinds of claim justified in a multiplicity of ways, it would be surprising if the same defences applied uniformly to them all. This chapter seeks to establish that the law is and ought to be one of diversity and difference.

B. Definitions

Any fact[1] that the defendant pleads, that can in whole or in part resist the plaintiff's action, that does not constitute a mere denial of an element of the claim, but that instead raises a new reason why the claim should fail, is a defence. Not everything that a defendant may raise in his pleaded defence is, therefore, a defence properly understood. If, for example, the claim is that the defendant negligently injured the plaintiff in a driving accident, if the defendant relies upon new facts unmentioned by the plaintiff in his pleadings, such as the condition of the road, the erratic driving of the plaintiff, and that the defendant was travelling at well within the speed limit, in order to deny that he negligently injured the plaintiff, this is not a defence. Even though new facts are asserted, it is instead a denial of an element of the claim (here negligent conduct causing injury). If, by contrast, in a claim for defamation the defendant asserts that the statement was true, this in England is a defence: the truth or falsity of the statement not being part of the gist of the action. The sequence may also continue with replies, that show why a defence should fail, rejoinders to such replies, and so on.

As discussed in the next chapter, on this definition, illegality is not (or, at least, is not only) a defence. Illegality as a topic has therefore been given separate treatment.

The general rule in private law is *ei incumbit probatio qui dicit*: he who asserts must prove. In practice, the most important effect of characterising an issue as being a defence is that it will determine who has to prove what as a matter of evidence. However, who has the onus of proof is not determinative of whether something is a defence, and there are exceptions to the general position. In relation to limitation of action, it is for the defendant to plead the relevant time-bar but for the plaintiff to show that his claim is still within the relevant period.[2] Limitation is a defence, albeit one that does not follow the general pattern in relation to onus of proof.

---

[1] We plead facts, not law: *Bell v Lever Brothers Ltd* [1931] 1 KB 557 (CA), 582–583 *per* Scrutton LJ; *Re Vandervell's Trusts (No 2)* [1974] Ch 269 (CA), 321 *per* Lord Denning MR; *Tchenguiz v Grant Thornton UK LLP* [2015] EWHC 405 (Comm), [1] *per* Leggatt J.

[2] *Lloyd's Bank plc v. Crosse & Crosse* [2001] EWCA Civ 366, [2001] Lloyd's Rep PN 452.

On this definition, the rescission of a wholly executory contract, on the grounds of duress, undue influence, or misrepresentation, will usually operate as a defence to a contractual action,[3] rather than as a 'claim' in unjust enrichment.

In the criminal law, it is common, and correct, to distinguish between justifications and excuses. This is best understood as being the difference between those defences which, if established, show that, all things considered, no wrong was committed and those which establish that the defendant should be relieved from punishment, despite behaving wrongfully. In private law, the same division is reflected in the language of privilege and immunity. As we have seen, the manifestation of acquiescence or consent confers a privilege, entailing that the other is, exceptionally, under no duty. In the law of torts this is usually expressed as *volenti non fit iniuria*. The expiry of a limitation period, by contrast, confers an immunity from suit. It goes to the enforceability of the duty, the liability, rather than to whether there is a duty.[4] As we have also seen,[5] this distinction between no-duty and no-liability is important within the law of restitution. The performance of an unenforceable obligation is not, without more, recoverable.

The reasons supporting excuses or immunities need not relate the defendant to the claimant. An immunity may be justified because of reasons to do with the defendant alone (eg incapacity), the plaintiff alone (eg comparative fault), or for reasons of policy that are not necessarily related to the two parties at all (eg limitation periods, formality requirements for contracts). By contrast, reasons that operate as justifications or privileges must relate the two parties together, just as the reasons that may legitimately justify rights must do so. Acting reasonably in self-defence may render the defendant's actions justified with respect to his attacker, whereas the same actions mistakenly done when not in fact being attacked can only operate as an excuse. We shall see the same pattern of privileges and immunities in the law of restitution.

Further some defences are claim specific whilst others are general. Just as the defence of truth is specific to the tort of defamation, so the defence of change of position is specific to some claims for restitution, although which ones is, as we shall see, a difficult question. Consent or waiver seems to apply generally across private law, including claims for restitution. It might be expected that limitation periods would operate generally in relation to all actions. However, in England this is not so with a patchwork of applicable rules.

C. Specific Defences

1. Change of Position

(a) Defence or denial?
On one view, a change of position rule is a necessary feature of a law of unjust enrichment.[6] If, for example, a defendant was, initially, enriched by a mistaken payment, but at the time of judgment no longer is, because for example he subsequently had the money paid stolen

---

[3] Eg *Redgrave v Hurd* (1881) 20 ChD 1 (CA).
[4] *Ronex Properties Ltd v John Laing Construction Ltd* [1983] QB 398 (CA), 404 *per* Donaldson LJ.
[5] Chapter 5, Theory.
[6] Eg "The independence and necessity of the law of unjust enrichment derives from the peculiar normativity of extant gain": P Birks, *Unjust Enrichment* (2nd edn, 2005), 207.

from him so that he is not counterfactually better off than if the payment had not been made in the first place, if the basis of the claim is 'enrichment' then there should be no claim in such a case. If the claim is one for 'unjust enrichment' why should those who are not, as things have turned out, enriched be liable?

At one time there was no change of position rule, and those who received mistaken payments could not resist claims for repayment on this basis.[7] In England[8] and Australia[9] courts independently recognised both that a number of claims were best understood in terms of unjust enrichment, and that a defence of change of position applied to them, simultaneously.[10] That the two developments occurred together in single judicial decisions in the two separate jurisdictions was no coincidence. Without a coherent body of law of 'unjust enrichment', it could not be readily determined to which claims the change of position rule applied. Until recognition that the gist of the action was enrichment, why should its negation matter? Without a change of position rule, people who were not actually enriched were being held liable. The two issues appear therefore to be dependent upon one another. At that time, this development was an almost unquestioned academic orthodoxy. It is natural to think, adopting an unjust enrichment approach, that the change of position rule is based upon the defendant's 'disenrichment'.[11] We have, so it seems, answered both why there should be such a defence, and the kinds of claim to which it should apply.

Viewed in this way, however, change of position is not a defence but a denial.[12] A new reason is not being invoked as to why the claim should fail but rather an element of the claim is being disproved. As we have seen, today the dominant academic account is that 'enrichment' is assessed at time of receipt and 'change of position' takes into account what has happened since that time and the date of judgment. However, there is no new countervailing reason being relied upon in order to explain the existence of the change of position rule. It is, as we have seen, difficult to understand, if the normatively significant fact is the defendant's enrichment, why this should be assessed at a moment in the past if this does not reflect the reality today? More readily explicable is a shift in the evidential onus.[13] The defendant is in a better position to show what has happened to the wealth he has obtained after he has received it. We may then require him to prove his 'disenrichment' after this point rather than requiring the claimant to establish the defendant's continued enrichment. Such a shift in the evidential onus would not however constitute a defence.

Even accepting, *arguendo*, contrary to the central claim of this work, that enrichment is the relevant factor linking together the diverse claims considered, problems then arise that cannot be overcome.

---

[7] *Baylis v Bishop of London* [1913] 1 Ch 127 (CA). In Scotland, the defence has long existed: *Credit Lyonnais v George Stevenson and Co Ltd* (1901) 9 SLT 93 OH, 95 *per* Lord Kyllachy.
[8] *Lipkin Gorman v Karpnale Ltd* [1991] 2 AC 548 (HL), 578 *per* Lord Goff, "the underlying principle of recovery is the principle of unjust enrichment".
[9] *David Securities Pty Ltd v Commonwealth Bank of Australia* [1992] HCA 48, (1992) 175 CLR 353, [45] *per* Mason CJ, Deane, Toohey, Gaudron, and McHugh JJ, "unjust enrichment is a definitive legal principle".
[10] In Canada the judicial recognition of the defence in *Rural Municipality of Storthoaks v Mobil Oil Canada Ltd* (1975) 55 DLR (3d) 1 came after the endorsement of the unjust enrichment principle in *Deglman v Guaranty Trust Co of Canada* [1954] SCR 725.
[11] P Birks, *Unjust Enrichment* (2nd edn, 2005), 208–209; A Burrows, *The Law of Restitution* (3rd edn, 2011) 526–527; J Edelman, 'Change of Position: A Defence of Unjust Disenrichment' (2012) 92 Boston U La Rev 1009.
[12] C Webb, *Reason and Restitution* (2016), 220–221.
[13] Although this terminology may be thought inexact. See the careful discussion of Sopinka J in *Snell v Farrell* [1990] 2 SCR 311.

An example:

P pays *D* £1,000 mistakenly believing that he owes *D* that sum. In fact, *P* had repaid *D* what he owed him the previous week. *D*, knowing that *P* must be mistaken, spends the money on a holiday that he would not otherwise have gone on.

It is generally thought that had *D* innocently incurred the extraordinary expenditure on the holiday because of the payment, honestly believing that he was entitled to it, that the defence of change of position should apply. There is, however, no difference in terms of 'disenrichment' according to whether he spent the money knowing of the mistake or not. If *D* gives away the payment or incurs extraordinary expenditure in reliance upon its receipt, what separate principle then explains why he remains liable if he knew[14] that he was not entitled to the payment? It cannot be 'unjust enrichment' because he is not, as things have turned out, enriched.

Alternatively, it might be said that where he has chosen to spend money on a holiday, he cannot deny that he has been enriched by that holiday. He cannot, in the jargon, 'subjectively devalue'. Just as, so it is said, he cannot deny his enrichment where he has requested another to provide him with a service such as a holiday, he cannot do so when he has spent money received on a holiday. If, however, this is correct, why can the party who spends the money innocently believing that he is entitled to the payment rely upon any defence? Why is he permitted to deny that he is enriched through having chosen to go on a holiday?

The better analysis is that change of position is a defence. It can be best justified as ensuring that innocent defendants are not left worse off, rather than as a form of 'disenrichment'. This may be justifiable where the defendant's moral responsibility for what the plaintiff seeks to reverse is low, and the lack of any wrongdoing on their part. It is not tied to 'enrichment' at all.

Seen in this way, when applied to cases such as mistaken payments, it is not a countervailing reason that justifies what would otherwise be unjustified, such as where a blow is given in genuine self-defence. Rather it is an immunity or excuse. The payment or other performance received in the past remains without justification. The defendant is no more entitled to it today than previously. Instead, we forgive the defendant the burden of restitution where she is innocent and this would leave her worse off. One of the situations in which this is significant is where the defendant repays after having changed her position. If the defence operates as an excuse, so as to create an immunity from suit, its effect is to bar the enforcement of any claim, so that repayment would remain justified. If, by contrast, change of position nullified or eliminated the injustice that there would otherwise be, by eliminating any enrichment required to be reversed, such a repayment ought to be recoverable.

(b) Scope of application
(i) Unjustified performance

Once change of position is untied from the concept of enrichment, its scope of application appears problematic to determine. Today, there is judicial support for the proposition that

---

[14] Bad faith in the sense of 'failure to act in a commercially acceptable way' suffices to disqualify the application of the defence: *Niru Battery Manufacturing Co v Milestone Trading Ltd* [2002] EWHC 1425, [2003] 2 All ER (Comm) 706, [135] per Moore-Bick J approved [2003] EWCA Civ 1446, [2004] 1 All ER (Comm) 193.

'change of position is a general defence to all restitution claims (for money or other property) based in unjust enrichment'.[15] If by this is meant that it applies to all of the claims gathered together by commentators as covered by the omnibus 'unjust enrichment' principle, it would go much too far. Cases of mistaken payments are often used, as above in this chapter, as illustrative of when the defence ought to apply. In such cases the defendant's responsibility for the payment that ought to be reversed is low, the principal responsibility resting with the mistaken payor. However, this will often not be the case.

In England, the starting point for discerning the scope of the defence of change of position is the decision of *Lipkin Gorman v Karpnale*[16] that introduced it, in particular the speech of Lord Goff. For good or ill, in that decision Lord Goff refused to be specific as to the contours of the rule preferring not to 'inhibit the development of the defence on a case by case basis'.[17] He did state that the defence should be ruled out 'where the defendant has paid away the money with knowledge of the facts entitling the plaintiff to restitution; and it is commonly accepted that the defence should not be open to a wrongdoer',[18] but went no further. Today, the approach of most English commentators is that the defence should be disqualified in these two categories of case, but not generally elsewhere.[19] However, this seems too broad and would allow many of those who are the party primarily responsible for the payment or other performance that they have received to be relieved from an obligation to make restitution.

An example:

D represents to P that the latter owes him £1,000. As a result, P pays D this sum. Because of the receipt of the payment, D spends an equivalent sum on a holiday for himself that he would not otherwise have taken. In fact, no such sum was owing, although D honestly and reasonably believed that it was.

Although there are judicial statements denying that a defence of change of position should apply where the recipient had induced the payment, albeit innocently, these pre-date the English recognition of the defence in *Lipkin Gorman*.[20] The US Restatement (Third) of Unjust Enrichment and Restitution would, correctly, deny restitution in such a case as D is the party 'primarily responsible' for the payment.[21] In selecting which of two innocent parties should bear the cost of wealth now dissipated, a choice needs to be made. Where the recipient has obtained a payment or other performance through misrepresentation, duress, or the application of actual undue influence for which he, and not a third party, is responsible, any loss should be allocated to him, and the law should not provide him with any defence, even if he has committed no wrong and is morally blameless. Responsibility is here determined not by moral culpability (a misrepresentation for example may be entirely blameless)

---

[15] *Haugesund Kommune v Depfa ACS Bank* [2010] EWCA Civ 579, [2012] QB 549, [122] *per* Aikens LJ.
[16] [1991] 2 AC 548 (HL).
[17] *ibid*, 580.
[18] *ibid*, 580.
[19] Eg C Mitchell, P Mitchell, and S Watterson (eds), *Goff & Jones: The Law of Unjust Enrichment* (9th edn, 2016), [27-40]–[27-53]; Burrows, *The Law of Restitution* (n 11), 537–544.
[20] *Larner v London County Council* [1949] 2 KB 683 (CA), 688–689 *per* Denning LJ.; *Saronic Shipping Co Ltd v Huron Liberian Co* [1979] 1 Lloyd's Rep 341 (Mocatta J).
[21] A Kull, *Restatement of the Law (Third) Restitution and Unjust Enrichment*, vol I (2010), § 53(2).

nor by wrongdoing (even duress need not necessarily constitute the breach of a duty) but rather by whose actions primarily contributed to the loss that has to be distributed.

More difficult is the situation where the plaintiff and defendant are in a relationship of presumed undue influence, exemplified by *Allcard v Skinner*,[22] but where the defendant has in no way exploited the dominance they have over the plaintiff. In this foundational case, the plaintiff joined a religious order, 'The Sisters of the Poor', under the rules of which members undertook a vow of poverty. Having inherited considerable wealth from her father, the plaintiff paid large sums and transferred valuable railway stock to the defendant, the lady superior of the order. The plaintiff left the order, and six years later sought to set aside the gift on the basis of undue influence, and to obtain repayment of the money and re-transfer of the shares. Although no criticism of the defendant's conduct was made, the court concluded that rescission of the gift ought in principle to be available because of the infantilising relationship and the large size of the gift. In the meantime, the sisterhood had acted on the assumption that the gift did not need be returned, and had entered into commitments on this basis. A majority[23] of the court held that setting aside of the gift was barred through the doctrine of laches or acquiescence: the plaintiff had delayed too long in bringing her claim. Absent the delay, should the change of position made by the sisterhood, today, have provided them with a defence? Does the law's policy of protecting the subordinate party extend not only to reversing the transaction, but to leaving the dominant but innocent party worse off? In principle, it should not do so, the defendant not being responsible for the consequential loss. However, in the case of a gift of title to land that was set aside for want of capacity of the donor, there is some limited authority rejecting the application of the defence.[24]

This all or nothing approach to the defence may be contrasted with the approach of the Court of Appeal in *Cheese v Thomas*.[25] The plaintiff, then 85 years old, paid the defendant, his great-nephew, £43,000 for the purchase of a house, which was bought in the latter's sole name for £83,000, the balance financed with a mortgage loan. The arrangement was that the plaintiff was to live in the house for the rest of his life, but that upon his death it would be owned by the defendant. Unfortunately, the defendant did not keep up the mortgage payments, and the plaintiff, feeling his security under threat, sought successfully to rescind the arrangement on the basis of undue influence. The house had now declined in value, so that £25,000 less was recovered than had been paid after the repayment of the mortgage. The court did not enquire into the counterfactual question of the extent to which the defendant would be left worse off if full restitution were required than they would have been if the payment had never been made. Instead, it divided the loss caused by the decline in value of the property between the two parties according to their relative contributions. It may be that, absent evidence as to what the counterfactual position was, as would be usual applying the change of position defence, this loss-splitting approach was the fairest available.

Finally, there is authority at first instance for the proposition that where the claimant relies upon the so-called '*Woolwich* principle' against a public authority, the defence of change of position should not apply because 'such a claim is founded on the unlawful levying of tax

---

[22] (1887) 36 ChD 145 (CA).
[23] Lindley and Bowen LJJ, Cotton LJ dissenting.
[24] *Williams v Williams* [2003] EWHC 742 (K Garnett QC).
[25] [1994] 1 WLR 129 (CA).

and therefore the commission of a legal wrong'.[26] This justification is however incorrect, and seems to come from the ambiguity in the meaning of 'unlawful'. That the levying of a tax is *ultra vires*, beyond power and so invalid, does not render it a breach of a duty, a wrong, although the word 'unlawful' is used to cover both 'invalid' and 'wrongful'. At the time this view was taken, it was unclear whether the '*Woolwich* principle' required there to have been a demand for payment from the defendant authority. Where there is such a demand, regardless of the nature of the defendant, it is understandable how, just as in a case of misrepresentation, it may be concluded that the party primarily responsible for any consequential loss is the defendant, to whom it should then be allocated. Today, however, it is now clear that the public body need not have made any demand for the 'principle' to apply.[27]

Making any exception to the change of position defence turn upon the scope of the '*Woolwich* principle' would make the 'principle' of legal significance, which would be best avoided given its uncertain scope. Either public authorities should be generally barred from invoking the defence, on the basis of a policy of ensuring that they do not receive tax or other income without legal authority, or they should be treated in the same way as any other defendants. The latter is the better default position. For the Revenue, establishing that any receipt, however large, altered the state's behaviour will ordinarily be impossible to establish in any event.

(ii) Conditional performance

By contrast with the case of a performance rendered without justification, exemplified by mistaken payments, and contrary to the view of most commentators,[28] there should be no defence of change of position that applies to claims to recover a performance that has been rendered conditionally under an agreement, where that condition has failed. A variation on an example, that we have already seen:

> *P* pays *D* a builder £10,000 in advance under a contract. *D* promises to repair the roof of *P*'s house before the winter in exchange. *D*, expecting to do the work the following month, spends the money on a holiday for himself and his family that he would not otherwise have been able to afford. *D* dies before doing the work, frustrating his obligation to do so.

Here *D* is not a wrongdoer, nor has he spent the money with the knowledge of the facts entitling *P* to restitution. If, however, we deny restitution in such a case we would be rewriting the parties' agreement. Instead of a payment conditional upon building work, it becomes a payment conditional upon building work or *D* spending the money on a holiday. It should not matter whether the reason the work is not done is *D*'s breach of contract in choosing not to carry out the work, the frustration of the obligation to work through *D*'s death, or *P*'s repudiation of the deal and exclusion of *D* from the site (although the last may entail a counterclaim for damage for breach). It should also not matter what *D* in his mind

---

[26] *Test Claimants in the FII Group Litigation v Revenue and Customs Commissioners* [2008] EWHC 2893 (Ch), [339] (Henderson J). See further *Test Claimants in the FII Group Litigation v Revenue and Customs Commissioners* [2014] EWHC 4302, [2015] STC 1471, [310]–[315] *per* Henderson J.
[27] *Test Claimants in the FII Group Litigation v Revenue and Customs Commissioners* [2012] UKSC 19, [2012] 2 AC 337.
[28] Eg Burrows, *The Law of Restitution* (n 11), 545–547.

thought the terms of the bargain were, nor whether the agreement between the parties was enforceable or not.

In *Goss v Chilcott*[29] money was advanced by the plaintiffs to the defendants under a mortgage secured over the latter's property. However, as the instrument creating the mortgage was subsequently altered by a fraudulent solicitor, the defendants were discharged from repayment under it from the moment of alteration. The plaintiffs therefore resorted to claiming for restitution on the ground that the money had been paid for a consideration that had failed (the repayment of the loan). The defendants argued that they had on-lent the funds they had received to the fraudster, thereby changing their position. The Privy Council rejected this on the basis that they had done so 'in circumstances in which, as they well knew, the money would nevertheless have to be repaid'.[30] This was so even though the defendants had been acting in good faith in paying the fraudster. Even if the defendants had not (subjectively) realised that repayment would have to be made, this should make no difference. The (objective) agreement between the parties should be determinative of whether restitution must be made, not what the defendant knows or does with the payment received.

Similar is the decision of the New Zealand Court of Appeal in *Martin v Pont*.[31] The plaintiffs paid funds to their accountant for the purpose of investing it with a nominated finance company. The accountant's daughter, who was also an employee, misappropriated most of the money. As the condition under which the money had been paid had failed, the accountant was obliged to make restitution, regardless of the fact that he was not in any sense enriched and would be left worse off as a result.[32]

It has been argued, as we have seen, that in the context of frustration, a change of position defence should apply[33] and that the proviso to section 1(2) of the Law Reform (Frustrated Contracts) Act 1943 incorporates such a rule.[34] As discussed in Chapter 8, neither proposition is correct.

(iii) Discharge of another's obligation

When reallocating the burden of performance of an obligation to the party who ought to have borne it, it should be insufficient for the true obligor to escape the burden to show that he has changed his position. There are no litigated decisions on the point, and so hypotheticals must be used to consider the position as a matter of principle. For example:

> D is obliged to abate a terrible smell caused by a leak of sewage that emanates from his property. P, mistakenly believing that the smell emanates from his land, carries out the necessary work to abate the nuisance. D, believing that the nuisance has naturally dissipated, and delighted that he will no longer have to meet the expense, pays for and goes on an expensive holiday he would not otherwise have booked.

Or

---

[29] [1996] AC 788 (PC). *Cf. Haugesund Kommune v Depfa ACS Bank* [2010] EWCA Civ 579, [2012] QB 549, [109]–[129] *per* Aikens LJ.
[30] [1996] AC 788 (PC), 799 *per* Lord Goff.
[31] [1993] 3 NZLR 25.
[32] See also *Roxborough v Rothmans Pall Mall Australia Ltd* [2001] HCA 61, (2001) 208 CLR 516, [71] *per* Gummow J.
[33] Eg J Edelman and E Bant, *Unjust Enrichment* (2nd edn, 2016), 353.
[34] *BP Exploration (Libya) Ltd v Hunt (No 2)* [1979] 1 WLR 783, 800 *per* Robert Goff J.

D and *P* each independently guarantee *X*'s debt to *Y*. *X* goes into bankruptcy, and *P* is required to pay under the guarantee. *D*, mistakenly believing that it is *X* and not *P* who has paid the debt, and delighted that he is no longer potentially liable, pays for an expensive holiday for himself.

It should not matter in these examples whether *D* knows that he is obliged to reimburse *P* or not. No defence should apply. Change of position should no more be a defence than it would have been to evade the original obligations that *D* ought to have performed. There seems to be no good reason for shifting the expense *D* ought to have incurred on to *P*. If, as argued in Chapter 9, such claims for reimbursement and contribution are not based upon the defendant's enrichment, the defendant's 'disenrichment' should also be of no relevance.

(iv) Restitution of the value of rights to things
Where the plaintiff's claim is based upon a right to a thing that has been received by the defendant, the general position ought to be that the defendant's innocent change of position after the time of receipt should afford him no defence. For example:

X steals *P*'s Ferrari and gives it to *D* as a present. *D*, who is unaware of the theft and had been intending to buy a car, is delighted, and because he will no longer have to meet that expense, pays for and goes on an expensive holiday he would not otherwise have booked. Three months later, *D* sells the car for £250,000.

The traditional view is 'that persons deal with the property in chattels or exercise acts of ownership over them at their peril'.[35] The blameless person will be liable for the value of the thing in such a case, even where such a claim will leave them worse off. The interest in our rights to things is given priority over the protection of the morally blameless. If this is accepted, it should not matter whether the defendant still retains the thing or not. It has been suggested that the defence of change of position might be extended to cover cases of conversion, such as this example, where the defendant is an innocent wrongdoer,[36] but this would be a bold development. 'Innocent' here means without personal moral blame, but as between a wrongdoer and his victim the responsibility for the loss that will be suffered by one of them rests with the wrongdoer, just as it does in claims for consequential loss suffered by the rightholder.

If, in the example, we substitute the stolen car for stolen cash, should that make any difference? In principle it is hard to see why it should. Title to cash will generally be lost where it has been acquired by another in good faith and for value,[37] because cash, unlike Ferraris, is a medium of exchange, but it has not hitherto been thought that any other peculiar defence applies.

Looked at from this perspective, therefore, the leading decision of *Lipkin Gorman v Karpnale* becomes difficult to explain if, as argued, the defendant club's liability was based upon the title to the cash with which the rogue Cass was gambling that the plaintiff firm had. Why did the court think a defence of change of position was appropriate when it would

---

[35] *Hollins v Fowler* (1871–1872) LR 7 QB 616, 639 *per* Cleasby B (decision affirmed (1874–1875) LR 7 HL 757).
[36] E Bant, *The Change of Position Defence* (2009), 171–172, 210.
[37] *Miller v Race* (1791) 1 Butt 452, 97 ER 398. See p xxxx.

generally be thought not to apply in other cases based upon the plaintiff's right to a thing that the defendant had received?

Indeed, how the defence, as it is usually conceived, could have applied on the facts in the way it did is also difficult to understand. Cass had withdrawn £222,908 from the firm's bank account that was unaccounted for. Overall, Cass had lost, and the casino won, £174,745. With Cass having personal resources of £20,050, it was accepted that, overall, £154,695 of what the casino received was attributable to the sums withdrawn from the firm's account. It was this sum that the plaintiffs successfully claimed.

Lord Templeman, unlike Lord Goff, did not invoke any defence of change of position, instead looking at the overall consequential enrichment of the defendant from what had occurred as the measure of recovery. The majority (Lord Ackner and Lord Bridge expressly agreeing with Lord Goff on this point) preferred to analyse the result in terms of a defence of change of position. However, how did the application of the defence arrive at the net figure? Taking (simple, hypothetical) figures to illustrate the problem:

Gambler steals £100 in cash from P. Gambler stakes £10 of what has been stolen with casino D, winning £60. He then stakes £90 of what has been stolen, losing.

If we take the net overall position, D is 'enriched' by £40 (£100 minus £60). However, the payout of £60 was only caused by, or related to, the stake of the initial £10. The club did not 'change its position' in any way following the subsequent stake of £90. If P's claim against D is based upon D's title to the cash staked, how and why is D able to bring into account the £60 payout in relation to the later stake of £90? Lord Goff held that it was possible to aggregate the bets, accepting that doing so 'may not be entirely logical; but it is surely just'.[38]

An alternative, but also rough and ready, explanation for the result is that the court was too quick to dismiss the application of the defence of bona fide purchase. As we have seen,[39] the defence of bona fide purchase as it applies to cash differs from how it operates in Equity to prevent an equitable interest from being asserted against the party who acquires a legal right that is its subject matter. In Equity, the consideration provided by the purchaser must not only be paid but paid in full,[40] whereas for cash a contractual promise to provide consideration suffices,[41] even where wholly executory. Whilst Lord Goff was correct, therefore, that the mere promise to pay out on the bets was incapable of operating as a purchase, as the contracts were void under the Gaming Act 1845, it did not also follow that paying out on the bets was not capable of operating as a purchase. For which of the bets had there been any such payout in return, and which other stakes had been gratuitously made with nothing given in return? It was impossible to know, and so perhaps the best solution available was the overall netting out that the court adopted.

Today, with the repeal of the Gaming Act 1845, the gaming contracts would have been valid and enforceable, and so the club would have had a complete defence. The use of cash is also rapidly disappearing. How the result generally, and the defence of change of position specifically, can be justified in *Lipkin Gorman* may not therefore arise for a subsequent court

---

[38] [1991] 2 AC 548 (HL), 583 *per* Lord Goff.
[39] Chapter 11, Things and Chapter 13, Equity: Restitution.
[40] *Story v Windsor* (1743) 2 Atk 630, 26 ER 776.
[41] Bills of Exchange Act 1882, s 27(1)(a); *ex p Richdale* (1882) 19 Ch D 409, 417 (CA); *Royal Bank of Scotland v Tottenham* [1894] 2 QB 715 (CA).

to reconsider. However, it provides a very uncertain basis for the application of a 'change of position' defence where the claim is based upon the plaintiff's right to a thing received by the defendant.

(v) Trusts and other equitable property rights

Still more difficult is whether the defence should now apply where a trust is asserted based upon a duty to make restitution of a right received. For example:

> *T* holds a title to a quantity of valuable antique furniture on trust. One of the beneficiaries is *P*. In breach of trust, *T* gives the title to the furniture to *D*. *D*, had been intending to buy furniture for his home, but unaware of the breach of trust and delighted by his good fortune pays for and goes on an expensive holiday he would not otherwise have booked instead. *P* then informs *D* that the title to the furniture, that he still has, was transferred to him in breach of trust.

Should there be a defence of change of position?

D might argue that his position is no different from that of a mistaken payee. Why then should he be denied a defence? Here however the plaintiff beneficiaries have no responsibility, unlike a mistaken payor, for inducing *D* to go on a holiday. As they have no responsibility for the loss which the defendant seeks to shift on to them, should the defence apply? Further, any claim, whether to knowing receipt of trust property or that the title to the furniture be held on trust, would have been defeated if neither title to the furniture nor traceable proceeds remained in the estate of the defendant at the time at which knowledge of the breach of trust was acquired. Should any such claim in addition be vulnerable to a separate defence of change of position? If the defence were to apply, it would presumably operate in a way akin to a charge. *D* would be under a duty not to use the title to the furniture for his own benefit, but this duty would be defeasible upon *D* reconstituting the trust fund with a monetary equivalent, minus the extent of any relevant change of position.

In the absence of judicial authority establishing any change of position defence to a claim that rights are held on trust, or for knowing receipt of trust property, the positive law presumably remains that no such defence currently applies. Given the beneficiaries' lack of responsibility for the defendant's change of position, and that there seems to be no good reason for classifying the claim as analogous to ones where such a defence applies, this ought to remain the law.

(vi) Wrongdoing

In *Lipkin Gorman*, Lord Goff stated that 'it is commonly accepted that the defence should not be open to a wrongdoer'.[42] This formulation is ambiguous. Does it mean that it is unavailable where the cause of action is based upon a wrong, or where the defendant has committed a wrong (in relation to the plaintiff?) regardless of whether the cause of action asserted itself involves any breach of duty? In discussing the case before him, Lord Goff stated that '[t]he claim for money had and received is not ... founded upon any wrong committed by the club'[43] which indicates the former.

---

[42] [1991] 2 AC 548 (HL), 579.
[43] *ibid*, 578.

To an extent, this restriction is misleading. For those wrongs where an account of profits is available, the appropriate date for attribution of the profits made is that of judgment, not another moment of time, so that whether the profits were higher (or lower) at an earlier point does not alter the quantification. If, for example, the manufacturer of a product infringes another's patent in their production, if the product is initially extremely profitable, but subsequently loss making, it is the portion of the profits today that are attributable to the plaintiff's right that the judge must determine, not the profits, whether higher (or lower), made at some point in the past. Unlike, for example, the case of a mistaken payment, we are here concerned with the defendant's enrichment as a result of what has occurred, which is not best assessed from the perspective of a moment in the past.

By contrast, if the infringing activity made substantial profits, if the defendant then dissipated the profits through an unrelated activity (eg gambling), this should make no difference to the quantum of any award.

(vii) Conclusion

The above review reveals that far from being a general defence applicable to all claims for restitution, change of position is a defence that only securely applies in cases where *P* has made a payment that was not due to *D*, and *D* is not the party primarily responsible for the payment. The core example is that of a spontaneous mistaken payment that was not induced by *D*. The assumption that there is a much wider law of 'unjust enrichment' to which such a defence ought to apply, is incorrect.

(c) Which changes count?

If the rationale for the defence is a concern to ensure that a blameless defendant is not left worse off, what should be sufficient and necessary is to establish counterfactual prejudice, regardless of how improbable or unforeseeable such prejudice was at the time of payment.[44] It should not matter, on this view, that the defendant's change in circumstances occurred because of her own reliance expenditure, or because of the actions of a third party (eg a thief stealing the very cash which had been paid to the defendant, who would not otherwise have stolen anything else). Indeed, in cases where the change occurs without the defendant acting in reliance upon receipt, it may be arguable that she bears less, not more, responsibility for it, and is more unequivocally 'worse off' than where he has spent resources on something of his choosing.

Although the defence does require some causally related change in the defendant's circumstances following the moment of receipt, it may be doubted whether it is always necessary for the defendant to put a figure upon the extent of this change.[45] If, for example, the defendant receives a large payment by mistake and as a result decides to conceive a child based upon her new financial security, putting a figure on the degree to which the defendant is 'worse off' as a result of the child's conception or birth may be both impossible and invidious.[46] Where this is not therefore possible to quantify, it may be concluded that the loss should fall upon the party primarily responsible: the mistaken payor.

---

[44] *Scottish Equitable plc v Derby* [2001] EWCA Civ 369, [2001] 3 All ER 818, [30]–[34] per Walker LJ; *Commerzbank AG v Gareth Price-Jones* [2003] EWCA Civ 1663.
[45] *Cf.* Bant, *The Change of Position Defence* (n 36), 134–138.
[46] *Cf. McFarlane v Tayside Health Board* [2000] 2 AC 59 (HL).

An apparently very generous approach was adopted by the High Court of Australia in *Australian Financial Services & Leasing Pty Ltd v Hill Industries Ltd*.[47] The plaintiffs were a finance company and the defendants were suppliers of commercial equipment. A group of companies controlled by a fraudster (the 'fraudulent group') created a number of false invoices purporting to show the purchase of equipment from the defendants. The plaintiffs agreed to purchase the equipment from the fraudulent group, and to lease it back to them. They paid the defendants the amounts owing on the false invoices in order to buy the equipment from the fraudulent group. Upon receipt, the defendants, ignorant of the fraud, applied the payment in discharge of the fraudulent group's debts to them, and abandoned efforts to pursue enforcement proceedings against them or their directors. The defendants argued that this constituted a change of position providing a defence. The plaintiffs contended that a mere book entry, which could be reversed, could not amount to a change of position, the debts discharged were valueless in any event, and that the prospects of recovery from the fraudulent group or its directors that had been foregone was of negligible value because of their inability to pay them. The possible claims against the fraudulent group and its dishonest directors were no lower in true worth now than they had been in the past.

The High Court held that 'under Australian law, a mathematical assessment of enduring economic benefit does not determine the availability of restitutionary remedies'.[48] The possibility that the defendants would be left worse off meant that allowing the claim would be inequitable, without the defendant needing to demonstrate the degree of actual prejudice.

This decision is explicable because of the way it was argued by counsel for the litigants. It should not have been necessary to invoke such a tenuous 'change of position' in order to conclude that the claim should fail. The facts were materially identical to *Aiken v Short*,[49] discussed in Chapter 3, Performance. The plaintiffs had made the payment in performance of their contract with the fraudulent group to buy the (non-existent) equipment. Although there had been a bank transfer between the plaintiffs and defendants, the performance of the plaintiffs had been rendered to their counterparty. The correct defendant in any claim for restitution was the fraudulent group at whose request and for whom the payment had been made. No claim in addition should therefore have succeeded against the actual (solvent) defendants, who had received the payment as being made on behalf of the fraudulent group, and the claim should also have failed in the era before the recognition of any 'change of position' defence.

Should a 'change of position' that precedes the receipt of any payment suffice? In principle the answer should turn upon who is responsible for any consequential loss, but the current state of English law is unsatisfactory. An example:

D mistakenly believing that he is owed £1,000 by P, gives £500 to charity believing that as the debt is bound to be repaid he can, as a result, afford to do so. Subsequently, P, independently making the same mistake, pays D £1,000. In fact, P does now owe D anything.

---

[47] [2014] HCA 14, (2014) 253 CLR 560.
[48] *ibid*, [84] *per* Hayne, Crennan, Kiefel, Bell, and Keane JJ.
[49] *Aiken v Short* (1856) 1 H & N 54. See also *Lumbers v W Cook Builders Pty Ltd (in liq)* [2008] HCA 27, (2008) 232 CLR 635.

Here *P* has no responsibility for *D*'s gift to charity.[50] The payment he has made cannot have caused the earlier gift.

By contrast:

> *P* informs *D* that he will be paying him £1,000. *D*, believing that the payment is for a sum he is owed, gives £500 to charity believing that as the debt is bound to be repaid he can as a result afford to do so. Subsequently, *P* pays *D* £1,000 believing that he owes him this sum. In fact, no sum was owing.

Here it is *P* not *D* who is primarily responsible for the gift to charity, and to that extent *D* should have a defence. The payment made by *P* did not induce the earlier gift, time's arrow going only one way, so that this result cannot be explained in terms of 'disenrichment'. However, the gift is *P*'s responsibility because it was induced by a statement that he made, however blamelessly. There should be a defence if the innocent *D* is not to be left to suffer a loss that is primarily *P*'s responsibility.

Unfortunately, the leading decision considering the issue is that of the Privy Council in *Dextra Bank v Bank of Jamaica*[51] (which may also usefully be contrasted with *Australian Financial Services & Leasing Pty Ltd v Hill Industries Ltd* above). The plaintiff bank was deceived by a third party into believing that it was entering into an agreement of loan with the defendant bank. Under this mistaken belief it paid to the defendant $3 million. The defendant in turn was also deceived into believing that it was buying this sum in exchange for the equivalent amount of Jamaican dollars from the plaintiff, which it paid to individuals it believed were nominees of the plaintiff. The intermediate fraudster was not acting as the agent for either party. The payments out that the defendant bank made preceded the payment by the plaintiff to them of the $3 million. The claim for restitution was denied.

One basis for the court's decision, that was criticised in Chapter 6, Practice, was that, despite the payment from plaintiff to defendant having been made without justification, it had been done on the basis of a 'misprediction' which was insufficient to ground recovery. It was also further concluded that the defendant's payments out in expectation of receipt of the funds were sufficient to constitute a change of position.[52] This too is difficult to accept. The payments out by the defendant cannot have been caused by the payment received from the plaintiff, the latter coming after the former. Further, the plaintiff was not in any way responsible for the payments that the defendant had made; no representation had come from them but rather from a fraudster who was not their agent. The court seems to have been influenced by its judgment as to which of the parties was more blameworthy[53] but as the plaintiff was not responsible by their actions for the loss suffered by the defendant, this should not have been a relevant consideration. The claim should have succeeded.

A superior approach to that adopted in *Dextra Bank v Bank of Jamaica*, was taken in the earlier decision of *South Tyneside BC v Svenska International plc*,[54] where such 'anticipatory reliance' was excluded but which Lord Goff described as based upon 'exceptional facts'.[55]

---

[50] *Cf. Commerzbank AG v Gareth Price-Jones* [2003] EWCA Civ 1663.
[51] [2002] 1 All ER (Comm) 193 (PC).
[52] ibid, [38] *per* Lord Goff.
[53] ibid, [16], [41] *per* Lord Goff, whilst also rejecting the relevance of relative fault, [40]–[46].
[54] [1995] 1 All ER 545.
[55] [2002] 1 All ER (Comm) 193 (PC), [39] *per* Lord Goff.

There, in one of the many 'swaps' cases, the defendant bank had, in addition to the void swap entered into with the plaintiff council, entered into a matching hedging contract on identical terms with another bank. Every penny it received from the local authority under the void swap was therefore matched by a penny that the bank paid out to its counterparty under the hedging agreement. As a result, the defendant bank argued, it had changed its position. The defence was rightly denied.

The correlation between the payments the defendant received from the plaintiff and those they paid to their counterparty under the hedging agreement did not show causation. If the agreements had been wholly executory at the time the head swap had been discovered to be void, what would have happened? The head swap would have been unperformed, but the hedging contract would have carried on unaltered as it would still be valid. The payments received under the head swap did not cause the payments to be made under the hedging agreement. Although there was a causal relation between the two agreements (ie the hedge would never have been entered into absent the swap) there was no such causal relation between the payments received under the one and paid out under the other. The plaintiff was not, therefore, responsible for the payments made under the hedge, which were rightly not brought into account in the claim for restitution.

(d) Relationship with estoppel

As we have seen, estoppel by representation is a rule of evidence that applies across private law. It is, therefore, neither a defence nor a cause of action. It may result in a cause of action that would otherwise fail, succeeding, or a defence that would otherwise have succeeded, in failing. As a rule of evidence, it is digital: the assertion of the fact contrary to that represented is barred.[56]

In the context of restitution, however, there is authority that estoppel operates in a different way than in the rest of private law. Instead of a digital, all or nothing, rule of evidence, it has operated as an analogue partial defence to the extent of reliance expenditure.

It is arguable that in some cases before the recognition of the change of position defence, the estoppel rule had been stretched beyond its proper bounds, in order to protect innocent recipients, by the finding of representations where none existed. In *Holt v Markham*,[57] the plaintiffs were the agents for the government in making payments for earnings and allowances to Air Force officers after the First World War. Two years after paying the defendant officer, they wrote to say that he had been overpaid. However, their explanation as to why this was so was wrong, and the defendant wrote in reply correcting their error by return. Two months then passed before they replied, again asking for repayment but on a different accurate ground. In the interim, assuming the matter was then concluded, the defendant had sold his war bonds, and invested a considerable sum in a company that subsequently failed. The Court of Appeal inferred a representation that he was entitled to the money through the failure to respond expeditiously to his initial explanation, which the defendant had then relied upon to his detriment. The plaintiffs were therefore estopped from asserting that they had paid under a mistake as to entitlement. At least nowadays, inferring such a representation from a two-month delay in the failure of officials in charge of public disbursements to

---

[56] J Hudson, 'Estoppel by Representation as a Defence to Unjust Enrichment—The Vine Has Not Withered Yet' [2014] RLR 19.
[57] [1923] 1 KB 504 (CA).

respond seems somewhat surprising. Today, it might be better not to be as generous in discerning a representation made, but to deal with the case as one of change of position.

The orthodox understanding of estoppel was subsequently applied by the Court of Appeal in *Avon CC v Howlett*,[58] albeit that the reasons given by the court were qualified. The defendant was overpaid £1,000 in sick pay by his employer, the plaintiff. He made inquiries of the plaintiff, who informed him that the payments were correct. He bought himself a suit and a secondhand car for £460, and did not claim social security benefit of £80. The trial judge limited the claim to the balance of £460, but the Court of Appeal overturned this decision holding that the claim failed in its entirety based upon estoppel, which was, applying the orthodox approach, seen as a digital rule of evidence, the fact barred from being asserted being determined by the representation made.

More recent authority has however departed from the traditional understanding of estoppel by representation as a rule of evidence. The claimants in *Derby v Scottish Equitable plc*[59] informed the defendant both orally and in writing that he was entitled to £202,000 under a pension policy when in fact he was only entitled to £30,000. They then overpaid the claimant £172,000. The defendant, naïve but honest,[60] spent £9,600 on improvements to his lifestyle, £41,700 in paying off a mortgage, and £121,000 on another pension policy. As the last two were readily reversible, only the first was held to constitute a detrimental change of position. The court, relying on statements in *Avon CC v Howlett* that estoppel should not be permitted to allow the representee to 'make a profit'[61] or allowed where the detriment was disproportionate to the size of the payment made,[62] denied its application. The surprising conclusion that a rule of evidence is disapplied in the context of this particular species of claim was thereby reached. Estoppel by representation may, in other contexts, also give rise to a financial benefit to the representee far exceeding the cost of any detrimental reliance, and this has not hitherto been thought a good reason for its disapplication. What constitutes such a disproportion is unclear.

An alternative argument, that Walker LJ found 'ingenious but also convincing', but that he did not find it necessary to adopt, was that the existence of the change of position defence entailed that the representee was unable to establish that there had been *detrimental* reliance. Instead, the defendant had spent £9,600 on improving his lifestyle that he did not have to return. However, the evidential rule, determining what the facts found are, necessarily precedes the inquiry as to what the parties' rights and obligations are in relation to the facts as found. Rules of evidence in private law should not therefore vary according to the substantive law rule to be applied. It may be that it is thought that estoppel by representation is not, contrary to orthodoxy, a rule of evidence, but if this is so, it is obscure what its justification may be.

A similar approach was adopted by the Court of Appeal in *National Westminster Bank v Somer International (UK) Ltd*[63] where Peter Gibson LJ held that the plaintiff should only be estopped to the extent that this was 'unconscionable or inequitable'.[64] This appears to

---

[58] [1983] 1 WLR 605 (CA).
[59] [2001] EWCA Civ 369, [2001] 3 All ER 818.
[60] ibid, [8] *per* Walker LJ.
[61] [1983] 1 WLR 605, 608 *per* Cumming-Bruce LJ.
[62] ibid, 624–625 *per* Slade LJ.
[63] [2001] EWCA Civ 970, [2002] 1 All ER 198.
[64] ibid, [68].

confuse estoppel by representation with the equitable version of estoppel which, unfortunately, travels under the same name.

It seems unjustifiable that this rule of evidence should be disapplied in the specific context of restitution, and the better view is that it should always apply, but that the court should not infer representations where none truly exists.

2. Consent

The role of the plaintiff's consent is the same in the law of restitution as it is in the rest of private law. As we have seen throughout this work, the plaintiff's consent to the situation he is now in operates as a defence to a possible claim based upon another reason. The label the law employs to capture this idea varies. As we saw, the *ratio* of the decision in *Kelly v Solari* was that the defendant should have had the opportunity to establish that the plaintiff had known that the policy had lapsed. Whenever the defendant has received a performance to which he is not entitled, it should be a defence that the plaintiff knew that there was no such entitlement.[65] One possible response to such a defence, as it is elsewhere in the law such as the law of torts,[66] is that the defendant's consent was vitiated, most commonly by mistake, duress, or undue influence. Formally, it is as a reply to a defence of consent that such 'unjust factors' may be relevant to show that the apparent consent was 'vitiated'.

Again, it would be wrong to think that any causative mistake suffices to show that the claimant's consent was vitiated. In *Moore v Fulham Vesty*[67] the defendant issued a summons against the plaintiff demanding payment of a statutory duty to contribute towards street improvements. The defendant paid before any hearing took place, and the summons was withdrawn. The money was not however owing as the plaintiff's house did not abut the relevant street. The claim for restitution was refused. Lord Halsbury stated the law as follows:

> [W]hen a person has had an opportunity of defending an action if he chose, but has thought proper to pay the money claimed by the action, the law will not allow him to try in a second action what he might have set up in the defence to the original action.[68]

That the plaintiff would not have paid if they had known for certain the truth was insufficient.

We saw the same idea in the context of a performance rendered conditionally under an agreement. The plaintiff may waive the condition, so that no claim will then succeed. Such a waiver need not amount to a contractual variation of the contract: no agreement or fresh consideration is required. The plaintiff in *Hunt v Silk*,[69] by choosing to pay when they did not have to, and staying on in the house in its unrepaired state for a period of time, had 'waived'[70] the condition or 'voluntarily consented'[71] to the position they now found

---

[65] *Cf.* BGB § 814, 'what has been performed for the purpose of fulfilling an obligation cannot be claimed back if the person who performed knew that he was not obliged to perform'.
[66] *Cf. Baker v TE Hopkins & Son Ltd* [1959] 1 WLR 966 (CA) (moral compulsion to rescue disqualifies defence of *volenti non fit iniuria*).
[67] [1895] 1 QB 399 (CA). See also *Marriot v Hampton* (1797) 7 TR 269, ER 443; *Beevor v Marler* (1898) 14 TLR 289. See also Chapter 5, Theory.
[68] [1895] 1 QB 399, 402.
[69] (1804) 5 East 449, 102 ER 1142.
[70] *ibid*, 452 *per* Lord Ellenborough CJ.
[71] *ibid*, 453 *per* Le Blanc J.

themselves in. As we also saw, where the plaintiff has a claim both to recover back a conditional performance, and concurrently one for damages for breach of contract, it is possible that her claim will fail for one but not the other, it being possible to waive either the condition or the duty independently of one another.

In the context of the discharge of another's obligation, we again saw that volunteers, that is, those who have consented to the position they now find themselves in by performing an obligation that they know should properly be borne by another, should have no claim. Again, such consent may also be vitiated by duress, undue influence, or mistake. Unlike in the case of unjustified performance, however, that the defendant was legally or morally compelled may also vitiate such consent. The reason for the difference is that where such reasons apply as between the plaintiff and defendant themselves, they provide a justification for the performance rendered. Payments of debts legally owed, and gifts to Oxfam to assist in famine relief are not therefore recoverable. A party legally compelled to pay a customs duty properly borne by another,[72] or a father morally compelled to bury his dead daughter when her husband ought to have done so,[73] may by contrast recover the costs they incur in doing so. As between the plaintiff and the defendant, the legal or moral duty owed to a third party provides no justification.

Contrary to the position taken in most English texts, it cannot be that the claimant's lack of consent is the operative reason for the imposition of an obligation on the defendant. This is most obvious in cases of 'legal' or 'moral' compulsion where the obligation provides a justification for what has been done, not a reason for its reversal. In cases of discharge of another's obligation the plaintiff does not seek to reverse what has happened, but rather to go forward to the state of affairs where the correct party had fulfilled the obligation.

It is in the context of wrongdoing that we are more familiar with consent operating as a defence, and there we give it the Latin tag *volenti non fit iniuria*. It should also apply in those few cases where the plaintiff may claim the defendant's profits as a result of a wrong suffered.

Consent should be irrelevant in those cases where the claim is based upon reasons or policies unconnected with justice as between the parties. If, for example, contrary to the claim of this book, claims based upon the '*Woolwich* principle' are genuinely concerned to ensure government legality in the levying of taxes and equivalent payments, it should make no difference whether a payor, who knows that the recipient public body has no entitlement to a payment, pays 'without prejudice' (as in *Woolwich* itself) or not. The public policy, if it were accepted, should operate regardless of the payor's consent.

Similarly, if there were, contrary to the argument of Chapter 10, Necessity, a common law equivalent to the civilian *actio negotiorum gestio contraria*, the plaintiff's consent in coming to the aid of the defendant should be irrelevant. Any claim to compensation for expenditure incurred and other losses would be based upon a policy of encouraging useful intervention, in relation to which the claimant's consent is irrelevant.

As we have also seen, a trustee's duties are owed to the beneficiaries as a class, not to any single beneficiary (save where the class of beneficiaries has only one member). The consent of one beneficiary of a class cannot therefore suffice to absolve what would otherwise constitute a breach of trust.

---

[72] *Wharf and Bull Wharf Ltd v Goodman Bros* [1937] 1 KB 534 (CA).
[73] *Jenkins v Tucker* (1788) 1 H Bl 90, 126 ER 55.

Finally, in relation to events that occurred in the past, the presence or absence of consent at the relevant time is the important issue, rather than today or at a later point in time. As we have seen, in relation to current rights, I may consent or waive them in relation to a particular duty-bearer, but this consent may be withdrawn, subject to the limitation of equitable estoppel.

3. Limitation

The law of limitation of action in England is in a bad state, and this has bled into the substantive law of restitution.

Limitation statutes generally set down bright line rules that are not tailored to what is fair as between the two litigants to any individual dispute. They are there to enable all of us to close the books on the past. As a result, their effect is, generally, to provide an immunity from suit, and not to invalidate the underlying duty.[74] As we have seen, where an unenforceable duty is performed the general rule is that no restitution of it is possible.[75] Because of their policy purpose, limitation rules were properly introduced by legislation, rather than by the courts at common law.

Generally, claims in Equity are only barred by laches, which covers delay that prejudices the defendant or third parties. This doctrine looks towards the fairness as between the parties, so that mere lapse of time, as opposed to delay in bringing an action, should not bar the bringing of an action.[76] For the doctrine to apply, the plaintiff must either be aware, or ought to be aware, of the claim.

Ideally, we should have a default limitation period that applies to all causes of action that can be asserted, subject to appropriate exceptions. The English Law Commission sensibly proposed a rule that a claim must be brought within three years from when a claimant either knows or ought reasonably to know the facts giving rise to the cause of action, the identity of the defendant, and, where for consequential loss or gain, that such loss or gain was significant.[77] This, it was proposed, should be subject to the further long-stop limitation period of 10 years from the date of the accrual of the cause of action. This default position could then be subject to further refinement in relation to particular kinds of claim as thought appropriate.

Unfortunately, under the current law, the Limitation Act 1980 makes different provision in relation to specific causes of action, with no general default rule. This, inevitably, leads to gaps and confusion as claims that do not comfortably belong within any specific provision are forced into one category or another. This is particularly problematic in relation to the diverse claims for restitution as their correct categorisation is a matter of such controversy. Many claims are covered by section 5 of the Limitation Act, which sets a six-year limitation period from the accrual of the cause of action for actions 'founded on a simple contract'. The history of this section makes it clear that it was intended to cover claims once commonly

---

[74] *Ronex Properties Ltd v John Laing Construction Ltd* [1983] QB 398 (CA), 404 *per* Donaldson LJ.
[75] *Moses v McFarlane* (1760) 2 Burr 1005, 1012, 97 ER 676.
[76] *Hughes v La Baia Ltd* [2011] UKPC 9, [36] *per* Lord Walker, endorsing R P Meagher, W M C Gummow, and J R F Lehane, *Equity: Doctrine and Remedies* (4th edn, 2002), [36.050]. See also W Ashburner, *Principles of Equity* (1902), 721–729; J L Brunyate, *Limitation of Actions in Equity* (1932), 1–23.
[77] Law Commission, *Limitation of Actions* (Law Com No 270, 2001).

described as quasi-contractual.[78] In Singapore, in a striking commitment to theory, this sensible approach has been abandoned on the basis that claims in unjust enrichment are, conceptually, not contractual and therefore not subject to any limitation period at all.[79] This is a particularly extreme example of the dangers of taking too seriously the claim that such a unified and separate area of law exists. Statutory claims, such as under the Law Reform (Frustrated Contracts) Act 1943 are also subject to a specific six-year period,[80] whereas statutory contribution claims are restricted to two years.[81]

Under section 21(3) of the Limitation Act, an action by a beneficiary to recover trust property, or in respect of any breach of trust, is subject to a limitation period of six years. This rule is however disapplied where the trustee is a party to fraud, or where the action is to recover from the trustee the trust property or its proceeds in his possession, or previously received by the trustee and converted to his use.[82] This displacement rule was read narrowly in *Williams v Central Bank of Nigeria*[83] so as to apply to neither a dishonest assistant to a breach of trust, nor a knowing recipient of trust property. The former is easier to defend, dishonest assistants not receiving any right that could be held on trust. Treating knowing recipients as not trustees on the basis that they have not been entrusted with the rights is to adopt a very narrow conception of the meaning of 'trust'.

None of the above raises any fundamental issue of principle for this work, save to observe that there is no general limitation rule applicable to an omnibus 'unjust enrichment' principle. However, a difficulty that would have been best avoided has been introduced because of an expansive reading of provisions allowing for the postponement of the running of the period of limitation.

Limitation may be postponed from running on a number of grounds, including disability,[84] acknowledgment or part payment,[85] fraud,[86] or deliberate concealment of any fact relevant to the cause of action by the defendant.[87] Most importantly, however, section 32(1)(c) provides that time shall not begin to run where the action is for 'relief from the consequences of a mistake' until the plaintiff has discovered the mistake or could with reasonable diligence have done so. It was in order to take the benefit of this provision that the plaintiffs in *Kleinwort Benson v Lincoln City Council*[88] successfully challenged the mistake of law bar.

On the approach argued for in this work, allowing claimants who have mistakenly paid money that is not due to take the benefit of section 32(1)(c) is generous as a matter of statutory interpretation. Where a contract or gift is *nullified* by a common mistake or one induced by the counterparty, and the plaintiff seeks restitution as a result, it may be readily said that the mistake forms a necessary element of the cause of action. Without the mistake, the contract or gift could not be set aside and so no recovery succeed. Where, however, the mistake as to the obligation to pay merely *negatives* the existence of any entitlement to the payment, there may be other alternative ways for the plaintiff to establish this, other than

---

[78] *Kleinwort Benson Ltd v Sandwell BC* [1994] 4 All ER 890, 942–943 *per* Hobhouse J.
[79] *Ebsen Finance Ltd v Wong Hou-Lianq Neil* [2022] SGHC (I) 25.
[80] Limitation Act 1980, s 9.
[81] Limitation Act 1980, s 10.
[82] Limitation Act 1980, s 21(1).
[83] [2014] UKSC 10, [2014] AC 1189.
[84] Limitation Act 1980, s 28.
[85] Limitation Act 1980, s 29
[86] Limitation Act 1980, s 32(1)(a).
[87] Limitation Act 1980, s 32(1)(b).
[88] [1998] UKHL 38, [1999] 2 AC 349.

relying upon the mistake. In particular, in the 'swaps' cases, the contracts were invalid because the local authorities were acting *ultra vires* in entering into them, not because of any mistake. If the ground of recovery was the invalidity of the contracts under which the payments were made, relief need not necessarily have been understood as following 'from the consequences of mistake'.

The Supreme Court subsequently (correctly) interpreted section 32(1)(c) as only applying where the mistake made by the claimant formed a necessary element of the cause of action,[89] but generously continued to allow it to be relied upon by claimants who had alternative ways of proving their lack of entitlement other than their mistake as to their obligation to pay. This then gives rise to difficulties where the defendant's lack of entitlement arose because of a clarification of, or change to, the law through judicial decision. When was the mistake discoverable? Was it when the law was clarified or changed by the court, or at an earlier point when proceedings could have been issued to establish the lack of entitlement to the payment, and hence claim restitution?

Initially, the House of Lords held (or, perhaps more accurately, assumed) that the payor's 'mistake' was only discoverable from the moment at which the judicial decision clarified or changed the law as to whether the defendant was entitled to the payment, such that time only started to run from the moment of that decision.[90] As a matter of statutory language this was however hard to sustain as there must have been a point before that moment where proceedings could reasonably have been brought to establish that there was no such entitlement to the payment, and hence a right to restitution. In *Test Claimant in the FII Group Litigation v Revenue and Customs Commissioners* a majority[91] held that the 'mistake' as to lack of entitlement was discoverable when the claimant could, with reasonable diligence, have known that a worthwhile claim had arisen.

The current state of English law is very unfortunate, caused in part by the insistence upon seeing the mistake as central to the existence of the cause of action. Two examples illustrate the difficulties.

> In 1990, relying upon the decision of the House of Lords *A v B*, which establishes that he owes *D* £1 million, *P* pays *D* this sum. *A v B* is subsequently overturned, wholly unpredictably and to the shock of the legal profession, by the decision of the Supreme Court in *X v Y* in 2022.

The English courts have now held that *P* was mistaken for the purposes of limitation, even if only in a fictional 'deemed' sense, in 1990. It is also assumed that such a mistake is a necessary element of *P*'s claim so as to be within section 32(1)(c). Such a 'mistake' was only discoverable in 2022, if the decision of *A v B* was so secure that it was not thought it could be challenged. There is no 'long-stop' limitation period to prevent the bringing of such long stale claims in these circumstances.

A better solution would have been that any cause of action was based upon *D*'s lack of entitlement to the payment. The cause of action in relation to such lack of entitlement arose in

---

[89] *Test Claimants in the FII Group Litigation v Revenue and Customs Commissioners* [2012] UKSC 19, [2012] 2 AC 337.
[90] *Deutsche Morgan Grenfell Group plc v Inland Revenue Com'rs* [2006] UKHL 49, [2007] 1 AC 558.
[91] *Test Claimants in the FII Group Litigation v Revenue and Customs Commissioners* [2021] UKSC 31, [2021] 1 WLR 4354.

1990: the retrospective nature of judicial decisions meaning that the law today is that *D* was never entitled to the payment. No extended deferment of the running of time based upon mistake should be permitted.

A second example:

In 1990, relying upon the decision of the House of Lords *A v B*, which establishes that he owes *D* £1 million, *P* pays *D* this sum. *A v B* is subsequently overturned by the decision of the Supreme Court in *X v Y* in 2022. This decision does not come as a complete shock, recent academic criticism in specialist journals, and hints from some judges in the preceding years, having given reason to believe that a challenge to *A v B* might be possible.

The effect of *Test Claimant in the FII Group Litigation v Revenue and Customs Commissioners* is that the limitation period starts to run from when, as a matter of law, it was knowable that a worthwhile claim could be brought. This involves the judge deciding the moment in time legal practitioners at some point in the past would have formed the view that it was arguable that *A v B* should be overturned. Rules of limitation, which are supposed to operate as bright lines to enable all of us to close the books on the past, should not turn upon such factual subtleties which it is artificial to expect judges to determine.

A better solution would have been, again, not to have permitted any extension of time based upon such a fictional 'mistake'. Legislative intervention is now required.

4. Passing on

'Passing on' of any loss suffered should not operate as a defence, save that the idea of ensuring that the burden of an obligation falls upon the right party is important in the context of contribution claims.

If it were the case, as the UK Supreme Court has stated, that a claim for restitution is conditional upon the claimant having suffered a 'loss',[92] then if an initial 'loss' is suffered, that subsequently disappears, it might follow that as a result any claim should also fail as a result. In such a case 'passing on'[93] would be a denial: a necessary element of the cause of action would no longer be capable of being made out. However, as discussed in Chapter 3, Performance, the court's reference to 'loss' did not mean factual detriment, in the same sense as in the law of damages, and it is very doubtful whether the court intended any substantive change, so as to make factual prejudice a pre-condition of recovery in straightforward payment cases.

Alternatively, if loss is not a necessary condition of a claim, the law could determine that a claimant who is not, as things have turned out, in any way prejudiced by the event that she seeks to reverse, is undeserving of the court's assistance. Viewed in this way, 'passing on' would be a defence, similar to change of position. Such a rule would give rise to an immunity, the law refusing to assist those who are unharmed.

---

[92] *Investment Trust Companies v HMRC* [2017] UKSC 29, [2018] AC 275, [45] *per* Lord Reed.
[93] Arguably more accurately 'disimpoverishment' if the loss can be eradicated without pushing it on to another party: M Rush, *The Defence of Passing On* (2006), 11–17.

It is very difficult to construct examples where, as a matter of principle, such a defence should apply. Although it has been rejected in a number of cases, none are examples of where it would have been plausibly appropriate to adopt it, even if it were thought an appropriate rule.

In England, the leading decision is thought to be *Kleinwort Benson v Birmingham City Council*[94] where the Court of Appeal rejected any such defence. The facts were, however, the converse case to *South Tyneside BC v Svenska International plc*, where the change of position defence also rightly did not apply. *Kleinwort Benson v Birmingham City Council* was similarly an inappropriate case for the application of any passing on defence even were such a rule thought justified in general. As in *Svenska*, a bank, but here the claimant, had entered into an interest rate swap with a local authority, but also a hedging contract on matching terms with another counterparty bank. The claimant bank sought restitution from the defendant local authority of the net amounts of payments it had made under the invalid swap, and the local authority sought to rely upon the matching receipts the bank had made as establishing a defence of passing on. Evans LJ, in language with echoes of that subsequently used by the UK Supreme Court in *ITC*, held that for an action to succeed, the only 'loss' that was necessary to establish was that the payor had made a payment to the payee that it was necessary to reverse.[95] He also stated that the hedging contracts were 'too remote' to be taken into account.

It may be that the latter argument again refers to the lack of any causal connection between the payments made under the head swap and that under the hedging contract. Just as in *Svenska*, although the two agreements were causally related, payments made under them were not. As a result, it was not possible to say that the initial 'loss' caused by payment had been made good: precisely the same payment under the hedge would have been received even if the main contract had never been performed. As Morritt LJ stated, any analogy with the law of mitigation in relation to damages was misplaced as the hedging agreement was not entered into as a result of having suffered loss, but as a result of having, so the claimant thought, entered into a valid swap agreement. This was an inappropriate case for the application of any 'passing on' defence in the same way that in *Svenska* change of position was rightly denied.

Similarly implausible as a candidate for the operation of the defence was the decision of the High Court of Australia in *Roxborough v Rothmans Pall Mall Australia Ltd*.[96] The claim was for the recovery of a payment by retailer to a wholesaler made conditionally under a sale agreement. The condition was a tax being payable by the recipients, a tax that was invalid under the Australian constitution. The defendants argued that the plaintiffs had passed on the cost of the sum representing the tax to their customers, and so should have no claim in the absence of any loss. This was rejected.

Just as with the defence of change of position, there should be no such passing on defence in cases where the parties' relation is governed by the agreement between them. To have allowed the defendants to keep the payment made to them where the cost of it had

---

[94] [1997] QB 380 (CA). See also *Kleinwort Benson Ltd v South Tyneside Metropolitan BC* [1994] 4 All ER 972 (Hobhouse J).
[95] [1997] QB 280 (CA), 742.
[96] [2001] HCA 61, (2001) 208 CLR 516.

been passed on by the retailers to their consumers would have been to re-write the parties' bargain.

More debatable are cases of overpaid taxes. In the United States, but not in other jurisdictions, a 'passing on' rule has been applied to tax payers in many such cases (although even there the authorities do not speak with one voice).[97] At one time the defence also applied in Canada in relation to the payment of undue tax[98] but more recent Canadian Supreme Court authority has rejected it.[99] Australian authority has never accepted the defence in such cases.[100] In England, unsurprisingly, tax legislation sometimes, but not always, provides that undue tax payments cannot be recovered where the cost has been passed on to a third party.[101] If, as is sometimes claimed, the so-called '*Woolwich* principle' is based upon a public policy of ensuring state legality, the operation of the defence specifically in this context appears peculiarly inapt.

It is in the context of contribution, which is concerned with ensuring that the burden of discharging obligations fall where it should, that a 'passing on' rule is most easily justifiable. For example:

> X owes Y £1,200. X's debt is independently guaranteed by P, D1, and D2. X defaults and goes into bankruptcy. P is compelled to pay the debt in full.

Recovery of a contribution by one co-guarantor against another, passing on the burden, should proportionately reduce the sum recoverable from another co-guarantor. As between P and D1, as co-guarantors, they are each equally responsible for the burden that has fallen solely upon P. P should therefore be able to recover half of the sum he has paid from D1. If, however, he does so, this reduces the extent to which the burden has fallen upon him, correspondingly reducing the contribution P should be able to recover from D2, to a sixth of the sum P paid to X (and creating an entitlement in D1 to a contribution from D2 to a sixth of that sum). Assuming the solvency of all three co-guarantors, the end result should be that each bears one-third of the burden of paying the debt. Precisely the same rules should apply to other examples of contribution, for example as between multiple tortfeasors or in the context of general average. Different rules apply in the context of contribution compared to mistaken payments because the justification for the claim is different.

5. Bona Fide Purchase

It is a mistake to think of bona fide purchase as a single defence, operating in the same way in the context of the different claims for restitution.

---

[97] Compare *East Fifty Fourth Street Inc v United States* 157 F 2d 68 (USCA, 1946) and *Sabo Food Services Inc v Dickinson* 280 So 2d 529 (FASC, 1974). A Kull, *Restatement of the Law (Third) Restitution and Unjust Enrichment*, vol II (2010), § 64; Rush, *The Defence of Passing On* (n 93), 52–61.
[98] *Air Canada v British Columbia* [1989] 1 SCR 1161.
[99] *Kingstreet Investments Ltd v New Brunswick (Department of Finance)* [2007] SCC 1, [2007] 1 SCR 3.
[100] *Mason v New South Wales* (1959) 102 CLR 108 (HCA); *Commissioner State Revenue (Victoria) v Royal Insurance Australia Ltd* (1994) 182 CLR 51 (HCA).
[101] Eg Customs and Excise Management Act 1979, s 13A (3) (excise duty); Value Added Tax Act 1994, s 80(3) (VAT).

First, and most obviously, where the claim is based upon a performance rendered by the claimant to the defendant, or upon the claimant having discharged an obligation properly borne by the defendant, bona fide purchase has no relevance. It is only in the context of claims based upon the defendant having received cash from another to which the claimant asserts a prior title, or to claims based upon 'equitable property' rights that the defence has any application.

In some cases, it may be sought to set aside a contract on the basis of misrepresentations, or duress or undue influence applied by a third party. Generally, absent knowledge on the part of the counterparty it should not be possible to do so. An example:

P agrees to buy oats from D. P mistakenly believes that D has warranted that the oats are old.

If P wishes to rely upon his mistake as to the contract's terms in order deny that he is bound, the orthodox position is that he must show that D knew of his mistake.[102] If P's mistake has been induced by the misrepresentation of a third party, for whom D has no responsibility, the rule should be the same. In the context of contracts of guarantee, however, the rule in England is different, and 'notice' of the misrepresentation or undue influence by the third party has been held sufficient to set the contract aside.[103] This is presumably on the basis that guarantees are suspicious, and so subject to a special rule. (Indeed 'notice' is a misnomer, as it suffices that a creditor bank has not ensured that the guarantor has obtained independent advice from a solicitor, regardless of whether any reasonable bank would have suspected a mistake or undue influence). In any event, these rules for setting aside contracts are not examples of a bona fide purchase defence.[104] The onus for showing that the counterparty knew (or ought to have known) of the mistake ought to be upon the party seeking to set aside the contract.

Second, as we have seen, the rule in relation to cash differs from the bona fide purchase rule in relation to equitable rights. For cash, value given in exchange, in good faith, and without notice of any earlier title held by someone other than the transferee, will extinguish such prior title.[105] 'Value' includes any consideration which would support a contract,[106] such as a promise to give something in exchange in the future.[107] By contrast, where a buyer acquires a legal title that is subject to an equitable interest, the equitable right will only be extinguished if consideration for the right received is not only paid, but paid in full.[108]

Third, there are similar related rules which also differ in their details. The general rule in relation to goods, *nemo dat quod non habet*, is subject to exceptions.[109] Familiar examples are the ability of a seller in possession after title has passed through sale,[110] or a buyer in possession before title has passed through sale[111] to pass good title to a good faith purchaser

---

[102] E Peel, *Treitel the Law of Contract* (15th edn, 2020), 343; *Smith v Hughes* (1870–1871) LR 6 QB 597.
[103] *Royal Bank of Scotland v Etridge (No 2)* [2001] UKHL 44, [2002] 2 AC 773 (HL).
[104] *Barclays Bank plc v Boulter* [1999] 1 WLR 1919 (HL), 1924–1925 *per* Lord Hoffmann.
[105] Bank Notes: Bills of Exchange Act 1882, s 38(2); *Miller v Race* (1758) 1 Burr 452, 97 ER 398; Coins: *Moss v Hancock* [1899] 2 QB 111.
[106] Bills of Exchange Act 1882, s 27(1) (a); *ex p Richdale* (1882) 19 Ch D 409, 417, CA; *Royal Bank of Scotland v Tottenham* [1894] 2 QB 715 (CA).
[107] Eg *Midland Bank Trust Co Ltd v Green* [1981] AC 513 (HL).
[108] *Story v Windsor* (1743) 2 Atk 630, 26 ER 776.
[109] E McKendrick (ed), *Goode and McKendrick on Commercial Law* (6th edn, 2020), 16.25]–[16.93].
[110] Sale of Goods Act 1979, s 24.
[111] Sale of Goods Act 1979, s 25.

without notice of the previous sale. These exceptions only apply where there has been delivery of the goods, or the transfer of a document of title representing them.

Similarly, a person who has been induced by fraud to sell goods cannot rescind the contract of sale after the goods have been bought by a third party who had no notice of the fraud.[112] In such a case, the defrauded seller retains no title to the goods, and loses his right to rescind *unless* the third party had no notice. This is not therefore a defence. The onus of proving that the purchaser had notice of the fraud is therefore on the defrauded party.[113]

If it were the case that, independently of any right that the claimant had in relation to what was received, a claim for restitution were available against a remote enriched party to whom the claimant had rendered no performance, by payment or otherwise, then an apparent anomaly would arise. The rules for the passing of title in relation to cash through good faith purchase or the protection given to 'Equity's darling' could, at least in part, be circumvented by bringing a claim in 'unjust enrichment'. It might then be thought necessary to introduce a parallel defence of 'bona fide purchase' to such claims to prevent such evasion. However, following *Investment Trust Companies v HMRC*,[114] it is now established, at least in England, that no such claims exist, and so there is no need to expand one or other version of the bona fide purchase rule.

6. Counter-restitution

(a) Introduction

Where a performance has been rendered under a contract, or other bargain, a problem arises that does not occur in relation to other claims for restitution. Should and does the plaintiff have to make restitution of the counter-performance he has received in exchange, as a pre-condition of his entitlement to recover the performance he has rendered? The rules should and do differ according to whether the contract is void, voidable, or valid.

(b) Void

Where each party has rendered a performance under a bargain that is, as things have turned out, void, then in principle the performance of each should be reversed, as provided without justification.

This can however give rise to difficult issues where one party's claim for restitution would be subject to a defence, when the other party's would not. An example is the decision of Hobhouse J in *Kleinwort Benson Ltd v Sandwell Borough*.[115] Payments had been made by both parties under an interest rate swap contract, but some of the payments made by the defendant had been made more than six years earlier, and so were potentially time-barred. Hobhouse J held that restitution was available only to the extent the plaintiff 'gives credit for any benefit which he has received' and that 'in so far as the recipient has made cross-payments to the payer, the recipient has ceased to be enriched'.[116] Hobhouse J is here

---

[112] *White v Garden* (1851) 10 CB 919.
[113] *Whitehorn Bros. v Davison* [1911] 1 KB 463 (CA).
[114] [2017] UKSC 29, [2018] AC 275.
[115] [1994] 4 All ER 890.
[116] *ibid*, 929.

endorsing the view that the plaintiff's claim is to the net consequential enrichment that the defendant has acquired (the *Saldotherie* in German law).[117] In *Sandwell*, the writ was issued in April 1991, and so any cause of action that accrued prior to April 1985 was time-barred. However, under the swap as it operated from 1983 onwards, the defendants were not, in net terms, enriched until 1988, the defendants having paid more to the plaintiffs initially.[118] Hobhouse J held that as a result it was only payments made by the plaintiffs after the point of net enrichment that they were relying upon, their claim was not as a result time-barred but was only available to the net balance of receipts.

If, as this work maintains, the subject matter of the claim is the payment made, and not the net consequential enrichment received, what should the position have been? Here there was such a close connection between the demands for repayment of each of the parties that an equitable set-off should have arisen, one demand impeached upon the other.[119] The payments of each party were conditional upon the sums either paid or to be paid by the counterparty. Equitable set off is a substantive, and not a merely procedural defence.[120] It is not sufficient to deny an equitable set off that the cross demand upon which it is based is no longer enforceable by action.[121] For purposes of equitable set off no question of the defendant asserting any claim arises, so as to be caught by the limitation statutes.[122] The defendant should therefore be able to bring into account payments it made outside of the limitation period as a defence to the plaintiff's claim for repayment of sums it made within the limitation period.

This approach then leads to a different result. In *Sandwell*, the only payments the plaintiff should have been able to assert a claim in relation to were those within the six-year limitation period.[123] The recovery of earlier payments made by the plaintiff should have been time-barred. By contrast, the defendant should be able to bring into account, for purposes of equitable set off, all of the payments it has made, including those outside the relevant limitation period. This gives a different, lower, figure than the net balance approach.

A similar, and similarly difficult, issue arises in relation to the interaction of counter-restitution with the defence of change of position. An example:

P, a charity, agrees to exchange its title to a portrait by Rembrandt for D's title to a painting by van Gogh. The artworks are of identical market value. Six months after exchange takes place, the Rembrandt is destroyed by fire. The agreement between them is subsequently determined to be void because of P's incapacity to enter into the deal.

---

[117] His reasoning is more clearly summarised in *Kleinwort Benson v South Tyneside* [1994] 4 All ER 973, 978–979. For a different reading see Burrows, *The Law of Restitution* (n 11), 570–571. On *Saldotheorie* see G Dannemann, *The German Law of Unjustified Enrichment and Restitution: A Comparative Introduction* (2009), 141–146.

[118] [1994] 4 All ER 890, 941.

[119] The *Zweikondiktionlehre* (ie the doctrine of two *condictiones*) in German law, see also T Krebs, *Restitution at the Crossroads* (2001), 101–104.

[120] See generally, R Derham, *The Law of Set Off* (4th edn, 2010), ch 4.

[121] *Henriksens Rederi A/S v THZ Rolimpex the Brede* [1974] 1 QB 233 (CA), 245–246, 249 per Lord Denning MR (but see 254, 264 per Cairns and Roskill LJJ.) Cited with approval by Hobhouse J. See also *Philip Collins Ltd v Davis* [2000] 3 All ER 808, 831 per Jonathan Parker J.

[122] [1994] 4 All ER 890, 943–944. The reference to 'set-off' in Limitation Act 1980, s 3 refers to statutory set off. 'Equitable set-off' is a misnomer as it involves no netting out, see further R Stevens, 'Set-Off and the Nature of Equity' in P Davies, S Douglas, and J Goudkamp (eds), *Defences in Equity* (2018).

[123] Subject to the extension under Limitation Act 1980, s 32(1)(c).

Cases of this kind are much discussed by German commentators. *If* we assume that title to each of the paintings passes,[124] despite the nullity of the bargain, how should counter-restitution relate to the change of position defence? Should the change of position or the counter-restitution defence be applied first? If the former, it may seem that *D*'s liability in relation to the value of the Rembrandt is extinguished, because of the destruction, whereas *P*'s liability in relation to the value of the van Gogh persists. On its face this implies that no set off is available. By contrast, if the counter-restitution rule is given priority, then the value of the two paintings would be set off, and no claim by either party would survive.

The best solution to the problem is the same as that we have already seen in relation to limitation. The operation of the defence of change of position, like that of limitation, is not to extinguish the obligation to make restitution, but rather to provide an immunity from suit. If this is so, it should have no impact upon the need to set off two obligations that impeach one upon another. Here, as each performance was conditional upon the other, they do so. No claim should therefore be permitted for restitution of one party's performance without bringing into account the value of the counter-performance of the other.

A potential difficulty then arises as to the necessary relation between each side's performance for the purpose of such equitable set-off. An example, borrowed from Popplewell LJ,[125] is as follows:

A engages B as a labourer at a daily rate of £200 per day payable weekly in arrears, and the value of the labour is £150 per day. B works for two (five-day) weeks and three days. A pays for the completed two weeks but not for the final three days. The contract is then discovered to have been void from the outset. B has spent the money he received, in such a way as to ordinarily constitute a change of position defence to A's claim for restitution of all the payments made.

If we assume that *A* has a claim for restitution of the payments made (£2,000) and *B* a claim for restitution of the value of the work provided (£1,950), should these be set off one against another? Popplewell LJ suggests that they should not, and that *B*'s claim to the last three days' work (£450) should be seen as independent 'because there is no relevant connection between the earlier week's payments and the labour provided in the last week. The earlier payments were exclusively referable to work in those earlier weeks.'[126]

The best solution to problems such as this one is again to see it as part of the wider law of cross claims that arise between parties. The question then arises as to whether it is fair to allow one claim to proceed independently of the other, applying the general rules governing this issue. In England, this is a matter of equitable set off, which may arise where one claim is contractual and the other tortious,[127] a claim for improvements to land with a cross claim for tortious use of that land,[128] or cross claims based upon a contract.[129] Here the issue is

---

[124] But see Chapter 11, Things.
[125] *School Facility Management Ltd and others v Governing Body of Christ the King College and another (Nos 1 & 2)* [2021] EWCA Civ 1053, [2021] 1 WLR 6129, [80].
[126] *ibid.*
[127] *Beasley v Darcy* (1800) 2 Sch & Lef 403 (Ireland).
[128] *Lord Cawdor v Lewis* (1835) 1 Y & C Ex 427; 160 ER 174 (Exchequer).
[129] *Federal Commerce Navigation Ltd v Molena Alpha Inc ('The Nanfri')* [1978] QB 927 (CA).

one of equitable set off between two restitutionary obligations, but there seems to be no reason in principle why it should operate differently from the rule in other contexts.

On the traditional understanding of the equitable set off doctrine, it does not suffice that the two claims arose from the same transaction.[130] Rather the counterclaim needed to impeach the claim, most obviously where the claim against the defendant (potentially) arose because of the claimant's conduct that gave rise to the counterclaim.[131] The issue is whether the two claims are dependent upon one another, so that it would be unfair to allow one to proceed without the other. It is this traditional understanding that Popplewell LJ is adopting in treating the claim for the last three days as independent of the payments received under the same transaction.

In more recent authority, however, the courts have required that there be a 'close connection' between claim and counterclaim and that it be 'manifestly unjust' not to allow a set off.[132] This is a different test, and that two claims arise from the same transaction seems to have often been treated as sufficient (contrary to the approach of Popplewell LJ).

(c) Voidable

Where a claimant has an entitlement to avoid a contract at common law, for deceit or duress, the traditional rule has been that the impossibility of giving back what has been received has operated as a bar. This is not in principle a defence to a claim for restitution, but a bar that prevents any obligation to make restitution from arising.[133] A simple illustration:

> In negotiations for the sale of the title to a pig, the seller, *D*, fraudulently misrepresents the pig's provenance. *P* buys, partially on the basis of the fact misrepresented. *P* subsequently discovers the truth, but in the interim has eaten the animal. *P* seeks to rescind.

In such circumstances, the common law rule is that because *P* cannot return the pig, rescission is barred.[134] At common law, rescission occurred and occurs, without a court order. It is an act of self-help, usually exercised through informing the counterparty. Its operation is then automatic. That being so, there is no scope for any monetary adjustment, and so the availability of rescission is accordingly fragile.[135] It would be unfair, even on a fraudster, to require *D* to repay and receive nothing back. Rescission's relatively narrow scope at common law is then supplemented by the ability to claim damages for wrongdoing.

Like the defence of change of position, which is applied to claims for restitution, the purpose of the rule is to prevent rescission operating so as to unfairly prejudice the counterparty. Unlike that defence, it is a pre-condition of rescission even where the counterparty is a wrongdoer, even one of high culpability.[136]

---

[130] *Aries Tanker Corporation v Total Transport Ltd* [1977] 1 WLR 185 (HL) (No set off of a voyage charterer's claim for short delivery of oil, against the carrier's claim for freight).
[131] *Beasley v Darcy* (1800) 2 Sch & Lef 403 (Ireland) (Landlord claimed for rent, tenant had a claim for landlord's wrongful cutting of timber, landlord's claim restrained as being unable to pay rent related to the degradation of the property).
[132] *Geldof Metaalconstructie NV v Simon Carves Ltd* [2010] EWCA Civ 667, [2010] 1 CLC 895; *Bibby Factors Northwest Ltd v HFD Ltd* [2015] EWCA Civ 1908, [2016] 1 Lloyd's Rep 517.
[133] The fullest consideration is D O'Sullivan, S Elliott, and R Zackrzewski, *The Law of Rescission* (3rd edn, 2021), ch 18.
[134] *Clarke v Dickson* (1858) EB & E 148, 120 ER 463; *Blackburn v Smith* (1848) 2 Ex 783, 154 ER 707.
[135] *Erlanger v New Sombrero Phosphate Co* (1878) 3 App Cas 1218 (HL).
[136] *Spence v Crawford* [1939] 3 All ER 271 (HL) 288.

In Equity, however, rescission takes place as a result of the court's order. Because the court was, and is, able to set aside the contract on terms, making monetary adjustments for what has happened, rescission was and is more readily available despite changes that have occurred. The House of Lords in *Erlanger v New Sombrero Phosphate Co*,[137] when setting aside, for non-disclosure, a contract for the sale of a phosphate mine that had been mined for a number of years, did so on terms requiring the buyer to return the mine in its now altered state whilst also accounting for the profits made from its operation. A similar flexible approach has been adopted in the context of agreements set aside for undue influence.[138] Where rescission is sought by a court order, therefore, the equitable rule subsumes that at common law.

The rescinding party must account for the performance it has received from the counterparty, but not for other benefits acquired as a result of the contract. If for example the counterparty has bribed an agent of the rescinding party, and the rescinding party recovers that bribe from the agent, this does not have to be brought into account when the contract is set aside.[139] There is Australian authority for ignoring tax relief benefits the rescinding party acquires as a result of a contract whilst it was still in place.[140]

The most difficult issue is whether a monetary substitute always suffices, as it did in *Erlanger*, where it is impossible to return precisely what has been received. In the example of the consumed pig, although it no longer exists, its monetary value at the time of performance could be returned instead. Should rescission in Equity always therefore be available, a monetary adjustment always being possible? The traditional approach is that it is not, and that 'Courts of Equity, when they set aside contracts, direct [a monetary adjustment] as ancillary to the main relief but never in substitution for it'.[141] There are however several cases where a buyer seeks to rescind a purchase of title to goods or other right, but where in the interim he has sold or conveyed away the right acquired, but where the court has permitted rescission upon accounting for the proceeds of sale.[142] These are best understood as cases where both parties had anticipated that what was bought would be re-sold in the way it was. Should the same approach be adopted in cases of anticipated consumption? Further, where what has been transferred is a fungible there seems to be no reason to refuse monetary substitution.

In some cases, however, the valuation of what has been received, which can no longer be returned, may be extremely uncertain and difficult to ascertain. In such circumstances, the risk of prejudice to the counterparty may be high, and it is legitimate for a court then to refuse rescission on this basis.[143]

Conversely, it may be possible to return the very thing received (eg the pig) but the right to it may have declined in value since the time of conveyance. The traditional rule is that such decline in value should not operate as a bar to rescission.[144] This is correct if the

---

[137] (1878) 3 App Cas 1218 (HL), 1278 *per* Lord Blackburn.
[138] *O'Sullivan v Management Agency and Music Ltd* [1985] QB 428 (CA), [1996] 3 All ER 61.
[139] *Logicrose Ltd v Southend United Football Club Ltd* [1988] 1 WLR 1256 (Millett J); *Marr v Tumulty*, 256 NY 15, 175 NE 356 (CA 1931) (Cardozo J).
[140] *Akron Securities Ltd v Illife* (1997) 41 NSWLR 353 (CA) 370.
[141] *Boyd & Forrest v The Glasgow Railway Company* 1915 SC (HL) 20, 30 *per* Lord Atkinson.
[142] *Savary v King* (1856) 5 HLC 627, 667; 10 ER 1046, 1063; *Alati v Kruger* (1955) 94 CLR 216 (HC of A).
[143] *Cf. Halpern v Halpern* [2007] EWCA Civ 291, [2008] QB 195.
[144] *Armstrong v Jackson* [1917] 2 KB 822.

counterparty would not, counterfactually, have disposed of the title to the goods or other right at a higher price in the interim, but operates unfairly where this is not so.

(d) Valid

By contrast, where a contract is valid (even if unenforceable) the agreement should determine the scope of restitution. An example:

> P agrees to build a stable for D for £100,000. P does two-thirds of the work, and leaves the site.[145]

Once it is accepted that P is entitled to no remuneration for the incomplete work, whether under the contract or otherwise, should the result differ if payment had been made by the employer in advance? In principle this should make no difference, the employer should be entitled to repayment without deduction. As we have seen, the formulation for the recovery of payments as based upon a 'total failure of consideration' appears to rule out recovery where any counter-performance at all has been received, but as argued in Chapter 7, Conditions, no such bar should or does exist. A seller of a car to which he does not have the best title must make restitution to the buyer of the price paid, and there is no allowance for the months of use the buyer may have had of the vehicle prior to its recovery by the person with better title.[146]

By contrast, as we have seen, the Law Reform (Frustrated Contracts) Act 1943, departing from the common law rule, in awarding restitution of money paid gives the court the power to set off against the sums paid the expenses the counterparty has incurred in performance.[147] This enables the court to apply the approach more appropriately adopted in relation to the avoidance of contracts. As argued in Chapter 8, Contract, the common law rule is the better one.

Where what has been received is readily returnable, the claimant must do so or pay for it. For example:

> P agrees to buy 500 widgets from D for £100,000. D delivers 200 widgets but then repudiates the deal.

If P does not return the widgets, he must pay for them at the contract rate.[148] If payment has been made in advance, then the appropriate proportion is recoverable.[149] The obligation to give allowance for the widgets kept at the contract rate reflects the (contractual) obligation to pay for them, rather than the operation of a separate principle of restitution.

(e) Schools Facility Management Ltd v Christ the King

The leading English decision on 'counter-restitution' is that of the Court of Appeal in *Schools Facility Management Ltd v Christ the King*.[150] As reasoned, it does not fit easily into

---

[145] *Cf. Sumpter v Hedges* [1898] 1 QB 673 (CA).
[146] *Rowland v Divall* [1923] 2 KB 500 (CA); *Butterworth v Kingsway Motors Ltd* [1954] 1 WLR 1286.
[147] Law Reform (Frustrated Contracts) Act 1943, s 1(2) ('the proviso').
[148] Sale of Goods Act 1979, s 30(1).
[149] *Behrend & Co. Ltd v Produce Brokers Co. Ltd.* [1920] 3 KB 530.
[150] [2021] EWCA Civ 1053.

the threefold scheme set out above. The College agreed to 'hire' a modular building from a building firm. The builders installed the building on the College's land. The College was to pay hire for it annually for 15 years, and then dismantle and return it. The building was opened in 2013, and the College paid for the first four years. It then stopped paying. It was subsequently held that the contracts were *ultra vires* the College (a charity) and so void. In return for the payments, the College had had, and still had at the time of litigation, the use of the building. Indeed, as it had become a fixture, which is not determined by what the parties themselves intended, the claimants had no right to the return of the building itself.[151] How should the case be decided?

If we take seriously the orthodoxy that contracts such as these are void, what would the result be? The College would have a claim for restitution of the payments, to which the builders were not entitled, but what of the building? If the contract is genuinely a complete nullity, it would be as if strangers had trespassed on to the College's land and erected a building upon it. As a fixture, there would be no claim available for its return, and the College would be committing no wrong in continuing to make use of the building. No counter-restitution issue therefore arises.

If, by contrast, the contract is merely unenforceable, as it would today uncontroversially be if the lack of capacity had been that of a minor, the result is different. The payments were made in performance of a contractual obligation that the College was under, and should be irrecoverable. The College had agreed to make these payments in return in return for the use of the building, a condition that had not failed. The College would therefore have no right to restitution of the payments made, but the building, as a fixture, could not be recovered and they could continue to make use of it. However, the building had been constructed and installed on the agreed condition that the College paid an annual fee for 15 years, a condition that had failed. The College ought therefore to have to make restitution of the value of the work and materials rendered, to the extent not already paid for.

Despite using the language of nullity, the court actually proceeded on the basis that the contract was merely unenforceable, using the terms of the agreement to determine what had, and had not, been paid for.[152] Again, in principle, this is correct, the protective incapacity of one party, at least where unknown to the other, should not operate so as to nullify their agreement altogether. The position is quite different in public law where, if a person or body given a *special* power fails to validly exercise it, the *ultra vires* action is a nullity.

The result reached by the Court of Appeal was that the College should have to pay for the use it had made of the building after it stopped paying for it in 2017 until the date of judgment. The payments already made were unrelated to this use, and so could not be set off against or otherwise be brought into account.

This is a result of the way the claim was put by counsel, but it misidentifies the proper subject matter of the builder's claim. The claim should have been seen as one to the work and materials rendered under the agreement. Instead, the focus was on the consequence for the College (ie the subsequent use, their 'enrichment') as a result of the work and materials. The result appears generous to the College, who obtained the building, whilst only paying four instalments and the market value of its use from 2017 until the date of judgment. Foxton J

---

[151] R Gregson, 'Building Unexpectedly Accedes to Land' (2021) 80 CLJ 449.
[152] See the use made of the agreement's terms [2021] EWCA Civ 1053, [86]–[94].

contemplated that a claim for the use value of the building after the time of judgment might have been possible,[153] but the difficult question of its valuation was never investigated.

7. Bona Fide Payee?

In the United States, unlike in England, it is possible as we have seen for a party without authority to discharge an obligation owed by another. If such a rule is accepted (and this work has rejected it) then a defence of bona fide discharge of another's debt is appropriate. For example:

> X owes D £1,000. X instructs its agents P Bank to pay D this sum, but then countermands the instruction. P Bank pays D $1,000 ignoring the countermand.

If the debt is not discharged, because unauthorised, P Bank should have a claim for restitution from D.[154] If, by contrast, the debt is discharged, it would be unfair to require D to repay in circumstances where they have lost their right to payment against X,[155] unless the debt could in some way be revived (the doctrinal basis for which is unclear).

8. Ministerial Receipt

(a) Introduction

Where a payment (or other performance) has been rendered to an agent acting for someone else, most often a bank receiving a payment for its customer, a difficult question arises as to whether the principal, agent, or both is potentially liable for its return. The final claim of this chapter is that 'unjust enrichment' reasoning cannot helpfully answer this question, and that, returning to the theme of Chapter 3, the relevant question is who is the payee (or to whom has another kind of performance been made)?

(b) Defence or denial?

Outside of the context of restitution, whether an agent acting for his principal 'drops out' and cannot be sued, when his principal can, varies according to the nature of the claim. The agent's liability depends upon the applicable rules of the relevant area of substantive law.

Two examples, the first contractual:

> A, acting, as she discloses, on behalf of, P, agrees on P's behalf to buy 1,000 tonnes of durum wheat from X.

Where an agent makes a contract on behalf of a disclosed principal, whether named or unnamed, he is not liable to be sued upon it (nor can they sue the counterparty upon it). Even

---
[153] [2020] PTSR 1913, [2020] EWHC 1118 (Comm), [430]–[440].
[154] *Barclays Bank Ltd v WJ Simms & Son and Cooke (Southern) Ltd* [1980] QB 677 discussed in Chapter 3, Performance.
[155] Kull, *Restatement (Third)*, vol II (n 97), § 67.

if A lacks the actual authority of P, but has apparent authority for which P is responsible, P will be the party to the contract but A will not. A's lack of contractual responsibility is not dependent upon a special 'agency' defence, but is rather determined by who it has been agreed are the parties to the contract. An element of any contractual claim cannot be made out as against the agent who is not a party to the agreement. It is, of course, possible for the agreement to stipulate that the agent is to be concurrently entitled to sue or be sued alongside or to the exclusion of the principal.[156]

Where the fact that A is acting for another is undisclosed to the counterparty, the agreement will, objectively, be between the agent and the counterparty, so that the agent can sue and be sued. The identity of the parties to the agreement is determined by what is (objectively) apparent to each of them, and is settled by the proper construction of the agreement, just as it is for any other contractual term.[157]

By contrast, an example involving the law of torts:

> A, an auctioneer, acting with P's authority, sells a quantity of furniture on P's behalf. X has a better title to the furniture than P.

A commits the tort of conversion by selling a thing to which another has superior title, and cannot avoid liability by asserting that he acted on behalf of another. P will also be liable. A's authorised actions in selling are attributed to P, and if those actions constitute a tort he too commits the same tort jointly with A. *Qui facit per alium facit per se.* Whether the agency is disclosed or undisclosed is irrelevant, and A merely having apparent authority to carry out the sale would not be sufficient for P to be liable.

In claims to reverse a performance, as we saw in Chapter 3, a difficult question often arises as to the correct party to whom performance has been rendered. A payment or other performance may have been rendered to someone who is acting as an agent acting for another. Where the principal is non-justiciable, most obviously because of insolvency, a plaintiff may prefer to seek restitution from the agent, who may respond that they are not the correct defendant.[158] The agent may argue that the performance that the plaintiff seeks to reverse was not made to them. Outside of such performance cases, 'ministerial receipt' is of no relevance.

Where the agency is undisclosed, the position should be that the agent remains liable, unless able to invoke another defence such as change of position. Objectively, the performance has been rendered to the agent, who should not be able to rely upon the fact that they were acting for another, any more than should an agent against whom all the elements of a tortious action can be established.

Where the agency is disclosed however, the position becomes more difficult. Has the performance been rendered to the principal alone, so that the agent is not liable? If so, such agency would operate as a denial of an essential element of the claim, not a defence. Such a rule would not (and could not) be based upon any policy of agency law under which persons acting as agents generally escape liability for their actions.[159] Instead it would operate in the same way as the contractual example above.

---

[156] *The Swan* [1968] 1 Lloyd's Rep 5, 12–15 *per* Brandon J.
[157] *Homburg Houtimport BV v Agrosin Private Ltd (The Starsin)* [2003] UKHL 12, [2004] 1 AC 75.
[158] *Portman Building Society v Hamlyn Taylor Neck* [1998] 4 All ER 202, 207 (Millett J).
[159] *Contra* Mitchell, Mitchell, and Watterson, *Goff & Jones* (n 19), [28-204].

Alternatively, has the performance been rendered both to the agent and the principal, the agent's act of receipt being attributed to her principal? In which case the agent would remain liable unless able to invoke a defence, such as change of position by having paid over what she received to her principal. Such a rule would operate in the same way as the tortious example above.

Outside of identifying the correct defendant to whom a performance has been rendered, agency is irrelevant. Where an obligation that ought to be borne by the defendant has been discharged, it is meaningless to say that they owed the obligation 'as an agent' and so should not be liable. Where the defendant has received a thing to which another has better title, he cannot escape liability by arguing that he received it ministerially. In Equity, if the defendant acquires a right that ought to be held on trust for another, he cannot avoid liability by saying that he has acquired it as the agent of or for someone else if it is vested in him.[160] Often (as with banks) it will be impossible to identify any right that they ought to currently hold on trust, or to identify one that in the past they ought to have so held, so that a claim for knowing receipt will be unavailable against them, but this is not determined through recourse to agency reasoning.

(c) Scope
(i) Conditional performance
The most straightforward situation is that of a conditional performance rendered under an agreement, and so that is the easiest place to begin. Illustrative is *Ellis v Goulton*.[161] The plaintiffs had contracted to buy title to a portion of land, and paid £100 as a deposit to the defendant, a solicitor, the disclosed agent of the sellers. The sale fell through as the sellers had no title to the land. The trial judge held that the defendant solicitor, in order to resist a claim for repayment, had to show that he had paid over the money received to his principal. This was overturned on appeal, Bowen LJ stating that 'the money cannot be recovered from the solicitor, whether he has paid it over to his principal or not'.[162] The solicitor was not party to the agreement under which the payment of the deposit to his principal was conditional. That the agent knew that the deposit was so conditional with respect to his principal was insufficient to show that he had agreed that it was conditional with respect to him. As Bowen LJ stated, 'it is impossible to treat money paid under these circumstances and remaining in the hands of the agent as there under any condition or subject to any trust in relation to the payer'.[163]

Conversely, the receipt by the agent on behalf of the principal, under the agreement between payor and principal, entails that the performance is rendered to the principal regardless of whether there is any payment over by the agent. In *Duke of Norfolk v Worthy*[164] a payment was made to the defendant vendor's agent for purchase of title to land. The deal was not performed as the plaintiffs discovered that the land was located in a different place than agreed, and sought restitution from the counterparty. Lord Ellenborough concluded that the defendant was liable, regardless of whether the agent had accounted for what he

---
[160] *Cf. Agip (Africa) Ltd v Jackson* [1990] Ch 265 (Millett J) aff'd [1991] Ch 547 (CA).
[161] [1893] 1 QB 350.
[162] *ibid*, 353–354.
[163] *ibid*, 353.
[164] (1808) 1 Camp 337, 170 ER 977.

received or not. The action of receipt by an authorised agent also constitutes receipt by the principal. If the agent went into bankruptcy, resulting in no payment over to the principal, the principal should remain liable, despite the absence of any enrichment. The choice to use the agent is the responsibility of the principal.

Just as with a contract, it is possible for the parties to agree that the payment is conditional not only with respect to the principal but with respect to the agent, so that the agent will be jointly obliged if the agreed condition fails.

If the agency is undisclosed, the agent should be the party liable where the condition of any performance rendered fails, as they are the party to the agreement. Objectively, the counterparty entered into an agreement with them, and not the party for whom they were, unbeknownst to the other side, acting. The undisclosed agent should have no defence based upon any payment over to their principal, just as a change of position defence should not apply. To allow any such defence would be to re-write the parties' bargain.

(ii) Unjustified performance

The law in relation to cases of unjustified performance, exemplified by mistaken payments, is more difficult to state.

A good starting point, and correct in result, is the decision of Lord Mansfield in *Sadler v Evans*.[165] The plaintiff paid 1s 6d to the rent collector for Lady Windsor, in the mistaken belief that he owed it to her. Perrot B non-suited the claim against the agent, despite it not being shown that any payment over had been made. The appeal was dismissed, Lord Mansfield giving the judgment for the unanimous court said (emphasis added):

> The money was paid to the known agent of Lady W. He is liable to her for it; whether he has actually paid it over to her, or not: he received it for her … Where 'tis to a *known* agent; in which case, the action ought to be brought against the principal, unless in special cases, (as under notice, or mala fides).[166]

In principle, this is correct. The principal should be liable because the payment was made to them, the receipt of the agent being attributed to the principal.[167] The payment was rendered to Lady Windsor. The agent of a disclosed principal should not be liable, regardless of payment over, as the plaintiff was making no payment to or for them.

By contrast, 12 years later, in *Buller v Harrison*,[168] the defendant, an insurance broker, entered into a contract of insurance on behalf of his principals, who were resident in New York, with the plaintiff insurers. The defendant informed the plaintiffs that an insured event had occurred, and the plaintiff paid them £2,100. The defendant was owed £3,000 by his principals, and credited the sum received against this amount, without paying over. It was discovered that no insured loss had occurred, and the plaintiff successfully sought restitution from the defendant agent. Lord Mansfield said (emphasis again added):

---

[165] (1766) 4 Burr 1984, 98 ER 34.
[166] (1766) 4 Burr 1984, 1986, 98 ER 34, 35. See also *Greenway v Hurd* 91794) TR 553, 555, 100 ER 1171, 1173–1174 *per* Lord Kenyon CJ (although payment over had been made).
[167] *Couthurst v Sweet* (1865–1866) LR 1 CP 649 (duress of goods).
[168] (1777) 2 Cowp 565, 98 ER 1243.

The whole question at the trial was, whether the defendant, who was an agent, had paid the money over. Now, the law is clear, that if an agent pay over money which has been paid to him by mistake, he does no wrong; and the plaintiff must call on the principal... But on the other hand, shall a man, though innocent, gain by a mistake, or be in a better situation than if the mistake had not happened? Certainly not. In this case, there was no new credit, no acceptance of new bills, no fresh goods bought or money advanced.

What then is the case? The defendant has trusted [the principals] and given them credit. He trafficks to the country where they live, and has agents there who know how to get the money back. The plaintiff *is a stranger to them and never heard of their names.* **Is it conscientious then, that the defendant should keep money which he has got** *by their misrepresentation,* **and should say, though there is no alteration in my account with my principal, this is a hit, I have got the money and I will keep it?**

If there had been any new credit given, it would have been proper to have left it to the jury to say, whether any prejudice had happened to the defendant by means of this payment: but here no prejudice at all is proved, and none is to be inferred.[169]

Although *Sadler v Evans* was not cited, the decision may be reconciled with it in three ways. First, and most importantly, where the identity of the broker's principals was unknown to the defendant it may be said to be no longer possible to say that the plaintiff was rendering his performance to them.[170] Second, as between the plaintiff and defendant, the party responsible for the payment was the defendant, who had induced it through his misrepresentation. Third, but less principled, the principals were in New York and not readily justiciable before the English courts, and the presence of English agents for receipt of foreign principals seems to have influenced the subsequent development of the law.

The agent of an undisclosed principal should in principle, remain liable. As between the plaintiff and themselves, the payment was made to them, and not to their principal of whom the payor is unaware. The agent should then be confined to a defence of change of position,[171] most obviously available where they have paid over money received to their principal which they would not otherwise have done.[172]

However, *Buller v Harrison* has subsequently been interpreted, in a long line of cases, as standing for the wider proposition that an agent, even where acting for a disclosed principal, is liable unless there has been payment over without notice of the plaintiff's claim.[173]

---

[169] (1777) 2 Cowp 565, 568, 98 ER 1243, 1244–1245.
[170] See also *Newall v Tomlinson* (1871) LR 6 CP 405; *Portman Building Society v Hamlyn Taylor Neck* [1998] 4 All ER 202, 207 (Millett J).
[171] *Portman Building Society v Hamlyn Taylor Neck* [299] 4 All ER 202, 207 (Millett J).
[172] *Cf. Transvaal and Delagoa Bay Investment Co Ltd v Atkinson* [1944] 1 All ER 579 (Atkinson J).
[173] *Cox v Prentice* (1815) 3 M& S 344, 348, 105 ER 641, 642 *per* Lord Ellenborough (query if the agency was disclosed); *Pollard v The Bank of England* (1871) LR 6 QB 623, 630, *per* Blackburn J; *Continental Caoutchouc & Gutta Percha Co v Kleinwort Sons & Co* (1904) 90 LTR 474 (PC); *Kerrison v Glyn Mills, Currie & Co* (1911) 81 LJKB 465 (HL); *Admiralty Commissioners v National Provincial and Union Bank* (1922) 127 LT 452 (Sargant J); *Scottish Metropolitan Assurance Co Ltd v P Samuel and Co Ltd* [1923] 1 KB 348 (Bailhache J); *British American Continental Bank v British Bank for Continental Trade* [1926] 1 KB 328 (CA); *Rahimtoola v Nizam of Hyderabad* [1958] AC 379 (HL); *Australia and New Zealand Banking Group Ltd v Westpac Banking Corp* (1988) 164 CLR 662 (HCofA); *Jones v Churcher* [2009] EWHC 722 (QB), [2009] 2 Lloyd's Rep 94. See *Holland v Russell* (1863) Bes & S 14, 122 ER 365 (KB); *Shand v Grant* (1863) 15 CB (NS) 324, 143 ER 809 (CP); *Owen v Cronk* [1895] 1 QB 365 (CA); *In re Morant* [1924] 1 Ch 79; *Gowers v Lloyds and National Provincial Foreign Bank Ltd* [1938] 1 All ER 766 (CA); *Traansvaal & Delagou Investment Co Ltd v Atkinson* [1944] 1 All ER 579 (Atkinson J); *Portman Building Society v Hamlyn Taylor Neck* [1998] 4 All ER 202 (CA), where payment over was successfully invoked.

The leading authority adopting this rule in the context of a mistaken payment is that of the House of Lords in *Kleinwort Sons & Co v Dunlop Rubber Co*.[174] A simple crediting of the money received in the books of the agent would not suffice on this view, but instead an actual payment over is necessary for the agent to drop out. Book entries alone can always be simply reversed. This rule is especially important for banks, of course, who are the most important agents for receipt. Before the recognition of the defence of change of position, the rule requiring payment over appears to be based upon the view that the payment was made to the agent, and had not irrevocably reached the principal before payment over.

It can be objected that such a rule places the recipient agent in an invidious position as they may, unlike their principal, not know whether their principal is entitled to the payment made or not.[175] Should they pay on to their principal, or pay back to the payor? The obvious solution is that the agent should interplead in such a situation, leaving any dispute to be resolved between payor and principal. This rule should not, therefore, in the end prejudice the agent recipient (they must pay away to someone).

The most recent authority has, however, departed from this longstanding rule by applying enrichment reasoning. In *Jeremy D Stone Consultations Ltd v National Westminster Bank plc*[176] Sales J held that a defendant bank could not be liable for a mistaken payment that had been credited to its customer's account. Sales J reasoned that, in net terms, the bank was never enriched and so no claim should lie. The bank's assets had increased by the receipt of the payment, but there was a corresponding liability to its customer for the same amount. In balance sheet terms, the bank was therefore not enriched and no claim should lie against them.[177]

Sales J's view could be dismissed as either *per incuriam* (the many cases to the contrary were not cited) or an *obiter dictum* (the defendant bank had paid away the money on its customer's instructions). It certainly goes too far where the agency is undisclosed, as the balance sheet enrichment approach would draw no distinction in such a case. However, it has been cited with approval by the Supreme Court (albeit in an *obiter dictum*).[178]

The better solution would be to return to the views of Lord Mansfield, so that disclosed agents for receipt are not liable, whilst undisclosed ones are.

---

[174] (1907) 97 LT 263, 264 *per* Lord Atkinson.
[175] Mitchell, Mitchell, and Watterson *Goff & Jones* (n 19), [28-204].
[176] [2013] EWHC 208 (Ch). *Cf. The High Commissioner for Pakistan in the United Kingdom v Prince Mukkram Jah* [2016] EWHC 1465 (Ch) (Henderson J), [140]–[150].
[177] [2013] EWHC 208 (Ch), [242]–[243].
[178] *Test Claimants in the FII Group Litigation v Revenue and Customs Commissioners* [2021] UKSC 31, [2021] 1 WLR 4354, [172] *per* Lord Reed and Lord Hodge.

19
Illegality

A. Justification

Illegality, at least as traditionally conceived, operates so as to negative otherwise good reasons why a plaintiff (and possibly a defendant) should win in legal proceedings. The justification for this principle is the coherence of the reasons justifying legal rules. The same reasons why the (criminal) law prohibits murder, theft, bribery, and fraud, also justify the (private) law refusing the assistance of state resources through its powers of enforcement to acts of murder, theft, bribery, and fraud. Hitmen cannot therefore recover their unpaid fees. If we have good reasons for treating conduct as criminal and deserving of serious condemnation, those reasons also suffice for the law to deny assistance to such conduct.

The justification for the illegality rule is not, therefore, unlike almost all other rules in private law, one that seeks to do justice as between the parties to a particular dispute. Indeed, it follows from its justification and formulation that its only effect is to withhold justice as between them, giving rise to a different result from that which fairness as between the parties themselves requires.[1] It is this unusual feature that has led to its unpopularity, and the reluctance of some courts to apply it. Lord Mansfield famously stated in *Holman v Johnson* that the rule is 'founded in general principles of policy, which the defendant has the advantage of, *contrary to the real justice*, as between him and the plaintiff'.[2] It is not a serious objection to the rule that it is capable of preventing the just result as between the two parties:[3] that is its entire point. It may be felt that it is perverse for a legal system to prioritise the law over justice in this way, but here the injustice that would be permitted if the party relying upon her own illegal behaviour were allowed to do so would be suffered by all other non-parties.

The ordinary effect of the illegality on otherwise valid legal obligations should, in principle, be that it renders them unenforceable, and not void. The law's coherence requires that the courts will not 'lend their aid'[4] to an unlawful act. A policy rule concerning the systemic coherence of the law, external to the parties' relation, does not, generally, nullify the reasons applicable as between the parties themselves. As we have seen, title to goods should and does pass under a contract for an illegal purpose,[5] and a fully executed, but at one time unenforceable, contract should not without more be subject to reversal. Society's resources, through the state's enforcement of our rights and obligations, should not however be used to reward or assist acts of murder, theft, bribery, and fraud. It may be that in cases of extremely

---

[1] *Cf.* Law Commission, *The Illegality Defence* (Law Com 320, 2010), [2.15].
[2] *Holman v Johnson* (1775) 1 Cowp 341, 343, 98 ER 1120, 1121 *per* Lord Mansfield (emphasis added).
[3] *Tinsley v Milligan* [1994] 1 AC 340 (HL), 364 *per* Lord Goff.
[4] *Holman v Johnson* (1775) 1 Cowp 341, 343, 98 ER 1120, 1121 *per* Lord Mansfield.
[5] *Singh v Ali* [1960] AC 167 (PC), see Chapter 11, Things.

serious illegality, agreements to commit murder for example, each party's promise creates no good reason for its performance even as between them, and so no obligations at all.[6]

Sometimes the effect of the illegality may be to discharge the obligations of one or both parties to a contract, and so enable restitution of a performance rendered. In *Oom v Bruce*[7] the plaintiffs, as agents for a Russian subject abroad, had paid a premium to insure goods on board a ship to sail from St Petersburg to London. Unknown and unknowable to the parties, at the time of contracting Russia had declared war against Great Britain. The Court of King's Bench held that the plaintiff was entitled to recovery of the premiums. Here the contract was never capable of performance, meaning that the insurer was never on risk, so that the payment had been made 'without consideration',[8] in this case under an agreed condition that had failed. Neither party had, themselves, committed any illegal act.

The illegality rule may also have a number of incidental benefits in some cases. It may deter wrongdoing in some situations (although in others it may actually encourage it). It may provide a further punishment for criminals (although in some it may operate to the advantage of one wrongdoer). It may prevent the legal system from falling into disrepute, as it would if it enforced agreements to murder[9] (but in many cases what the public opinion of enforcing or not enforcing may be is unknowable). It may strip a wrongdoer of his gains (although in some cases it will allow a wrongdoer to keep them). None of these incidental benefits is, alone, sufficient to justify the injustice that the illegality rule requires to be done, and each is contingent for its applicability on the facts of each case. Unfortunately, some commentators, the English Law Commission, and at least a majority of one panel of the Supreme Court in England,[10] see the rule as based upon a basket of these incommensurable policy concerns, which inevitably pull in different directions in any individual case. Other ultimate appellate courts take a different approach.[11]

B. Defence, Denial, or Other?

The illegality rule is not properly speaking a defence, or at least not just a defence. If both parties to an agreement to assassinate a prominent politician want to have the proper construction of its terms resolved by a court, it will not do so. The justification for the rule is not based upon reasons to do with one party or the other. The defendant need not (indeed cannot) plead any fact in his defence for the rule to apply, and the court should of its own motion apply it.[12] However, it often operates as a reason why a claim that would otherwise succeed should fail, and so it is as a consequence often mistakenly classified as a defence.

Because of its justification, illegality may also have other effects.

First, it may operate so as to cause a defence to fail, particularly that of change of position, where expenditure is for an illegal purpose.[13] In the decision of Laddie J in *Barros*

---

[6] F Wilmot-Smith, 'Illegality as a Rationing Rule' in S Green and A Bogg (eds), *Illegality after Patel v Mirza* (2018), 107, 114–115.
[7] (1810) 12 East 225, 104 ER 87. *Cf. Eric Bieber & Co Ltd v Rio Tinto Co Ltd* [1918] AC 260 (HL).
[8] (1810) 12 East 225 104 ER 87 *per* Lord Ellenborough CJ.
[9] *Cf. Tinsley v Milligan* [1992] Ch 310 (CA), 319 *per* Nicholls LJ.
[10] *Patel v Mirza* [2016] UKSC 42, [2017] AC 467.
[11] *Hall v Hebert* [1993[2 SCR 159; *Nelson v Nelson* [1995] HCA 25, (1995) 184 CLR 538.
[12] *Scott v Brown* [1892[2 QB 724 (CA), 728 *per* Lindley LJ.
[13] See also *O'Neil v Gale* [2013] EWC Civ 1554, [2014] Lloyd's Rep FC 202. See also the failure of the defence of bona fide purchase in *Clarke v Shee and Johnson* (1774) 1 Cowp 197, 98 ER 1041.

Mattos Junior v MacDaniels Ltd[14] the defendants had changed their position in good faith by exchanging dollars into Nigerian currency, which were then withdrawn and dissipated by fraudsters. The defendants were held to be disqualified from relying upon the defence because the exchange violated Nigerian foreign exchange laws. However, this is difficult to justify. No offence was committed under English law, and there seems to be no reason for giving such recognition outside of Nigeria to the Nigerian criminal statute, unless that law is the *lex causae*.[15]

Hypothetical cases of expenditure for illegal purposes (expenditure on illegal drugs, etc) may be given where it is more defensible that the defence should be ruled out, but save possibly in very extreme cases (paying for hitmen) it seems unjustifiable that it should do so. The justification for the illegality rule goes to the enforceability of obligations, the use of state resources to assist serious criminality. The invocation of a defence does not ask for the assistance of the legal system in that sense. It may be doubted therefore whether there should be symmetry between the operation of the illegality rule in disqualifying claims and defences.

Second, as we shall see, the reasons why the defendant's conduct is unlawful may also justify an obligation to make restitution of a performance rendered. Arguably, the withdrawal from an illegal transaction before it is performed may also operate as a ground for restitution.[16]

Given its justification, and in principle uniform application across private law, illegality as a disqualifying rule should not merit separate treatment in a book on restitution. However, its application in this field is the one that has caused most difficulties. It has even been proposed that it is an area where completely different rules should apply,[17] and in England, but not elsewhere, its application has been apparently reset by the Supreme Court on a novel basis.[18]

Understanding how claims for restitution in the context of illegality *should* operate involves carefully considering how they relate to any legislation that creates the illegality and the agreement under which the performance that it is sought to reverse is made.

C. Bribes

In theory, the illegality rule could apply to any form of restitutionary action. In practice, the claims that have arisen concern those to recover payments or services[19] rendered conditionally under contracts that are illegal for one or both parties to enter into or perform. A simple illustration of where the rule should apply to a claim for restitution (but arguably no longer does in England) is in attempts to recover a bribe where the illegal purpose is not fulfilled.

---

[14] [2004] EWHC 1118 (Ch), [2005] 1 WLR 247.
[15] *Cf. Barros Mattos Junior v MacDaniels* [2005] EWHC 1323 (Ch), [2005] I L Pr 45.
[16] See Section H.
[17] *Patel v Mirza* [2016] UKSC 42, [2017] AC 467, [197] *per* Lord Mance, [253] *per* Lord Sumption (Lord Clarke agreeing).
[18] *Patel v Mirza* [2016] UKSC 42, [2017] AC 467. A major difficulty is the weight of this authority in other areas, see *Henderson v Dorset Healthcare University* [2020] UKSC 43, [2020] WLR (D) 592.
[19] Eg *Awwad v Geraghty* [2001] QB 570 (CA).

In *Parkinson v College of Ambulance*[20] the secretary of a charity fraudulently misrepresented to the plaintiff that if he made a substantial donation to the charity, in return it would be arranged for him to receive a knighthood. When no such honour was forthcoming, he claimed against the charity in the alternative for damages, for deceit or breach of contract, or restitution of the money paid. All of these claims rightly failed: in claiming restitution the defendant would have to rely upon the agreed dishonest illegal condition, which had failed, in order to recover, which he was precluded from doing.

It is difficult to justify this result in instrumental terms. By refusing recovery it may be that this deters people from paying bribes, but equally it might be that this rule encourages fraudsters into deceiving others into paying them. The briber suffers a further sanction as a result of the rule, but the fraudulent bribee (whose moral turpitude may be thought greater) is rewarded by it. It may be that it would lower the law's esteem to allow recovery, but equally some may think this is generous to the fraudster and so think worse of them. Its effect in *Parkinson v College of Ambulance* was to allow a wrongdoer to profit. None of these incidental issues is properly the justification or concern of the rule, which solely concerns the need for the reasons for our laws to apply coherently.

The English Law Commission, in contrast with the suggested rationale for the law given above, when reviewing the area consistently proceeded on the basis that the courts needed to take into account a range of reasons, that were not limited to the law's coherence.[21] Their proposals at each stage proceeded on the assumption that the true rationale for the illegality doctrine is a range of factors that the courts had not articulated and that needed to be brought out into the open and relied upon more expressly. In their Report they state:

> On the one hand, the courts should attempt to do justice between the parties, enforcing the rights set down by law. On the other hand, the courts must not permit a claimant to profit from a wrong. They should deter illegal conduct and not allow the legal system to be abused by criminals.[22]

In its consultation process, the Commission had identified a somewhat different list of six policy concerns:[23] (1) furthering the purpose of the rule which the claimant's illegal behaviour has infringed; (2) consistency; (3) the need to prevent the claimant profiting from his or her own wrong; (4) deterrence; (5) maintaining the integrity of the legal system; and (possibly) (6) punishment.

How these various factors could be determinative in a case such as *Parkinson* is difficult to understand. Justice as between the parties would result in the illegality being ignored. The defendant was permitted to profit from his fraud, but does that outweigh the goal of deterring the giving of bribes? Asking for the weighing up these incommensurable concerns is like expecting the judge to decide whether three kilogrammes or fifty yards is greater. The factors invoked have no yardstick in common with one another, and no rational

---

[20] [1925] 2 KB 1 (CA). See also *Scott v Brown* [1892] 2 QB 724 (CA). Scotland: *Barr v Crawford* 1983 SLT 481 (OHCS).
[21] Law Commission, *The Effect of Illegality on Contracts and Trusts* (LCCP 154, 1999); *The Illegality Defence* (LCCP 189, 2009), *The Illegality Defence* (Law Com 320).
[22] *The Illegality Defence* (Law Com 320), [1.4].
[23] *The Illegality Defence* (LCCP 189, 2009), [2.5].

balancing of them is possible.[24] The problem is not one of uncertainty[25] but of impossibility. Problems of incommensurability of different values can be overcome with a rule, a central point of law in giving us guidance for action where no right answer is available to us. The Commission rejected this legalistic approach. All that is left is judicial discretion.

D. Reliance

If, as argued, the sole justification for the illegality rule is that the law's reasons for the condemnation of serious criminal conduct also suffice for it to deny assistance to such conduct, the crucial question then becomes whether the plaintiff (or defendant) is invoking such conduct in the proceedings. It should not suffice to deprive someone of their private law rights of action that they have committed a crime, however serious, if it is unrelated to the issue before the court. A rule for determining whether the illegal conduct is sufficiently connected to the claim before the court is inescapably necessary. The necessary condition for determining whether it is so related is whether the illegality is being relied upon.[26] In civilian jurisdictions, the Latin phrase used to capture this idea is *nemo auditur propriam turpitudinem allegans* ('no one shall be heard who invokes his own turpitude'). Two examples from our context, with different results, may stand as illustrative.

In *Berg v Sadler and Moore*[27] the plaintiff was a tobacconist who had been placed on a stop-list as a 'cut-price' retailer by the Tobacco Trade Association. The plaintiff used a member of the association in good standing as his undisclosed agent to buy on his behalf cigarettes from the defendants, who were also members of the association. He did so in cash, with which the intermediary paid, taking a commission for himself. The defendants then grew suspicious and, having been paid a further £73, refused to proceed with another sale. The plaintiff then sought restitution of the money paid. However, in order to make out his claim he had to show how it was that he had paid £73 to the defendant, and that in turn meant establishing that he was engaged in a criminal attempt to obtain goods by false pretences. The claim failed.[28]

The second, is *Tinsley v Milligan*.[29] A couple bought a house together with the help of a mortgage. The balance of the purchase price was provided by them equally, but the title to the house was transferred into the sole name of the defendant. This was done so that the plaintiff could misrepresent to the Department of Social Security that she had no stake in the property and so make a false benefit claim. The parties fell out, and the defendant sought possession of the house. The plaintiff successfully counterclaimed that the title to the house was held on resulting trust for them in equal shares, and an order for sale.

The majority of the House of Lords (Lords Browne-Wilkinson, Jauncey, and Lowry, Lords Goff and Keith dissenting) held that the plaintiff did not need to rely upon her illegal

---

[24] *Cf.* E Lim and F Urbina, 'Understanding Proportionality in the Illegality Defence' (2020) 136 LQR 575.
[25] *Patel v Mirza* [2016] UKSC 42, [2017] AC 467, [113] *per* Lord Toulson.
[26] *Simpson v Bloss* (1816) 7 Taunt 246, 129 ER 99; *Fivaz v Nicholls* (1846) 2 CB 501, 512, 135 ER 1042, 1046 *per* Tindal CJ; *Taylor v Chester* (1869) LR 4 QB 309, 314 *per* Mellor J; *Taylor v Bowers* (1876) 1 QBD 291, 198 *per* James LJ; *Farmers' Mart Ltd v Milne* 1913 SC (HL) 84, 87, (1914) 2 SLT 153, 154 *per* Lord Dunedin. But see *Pearce v Brooks* (1866) LR 1 Ex 213; *Scott v Brown* [1892] 2 QB 724 where the underlying purpose of an otherwise lawful contract was held sufficient to engage the rule.
[27] [1937] 2 KB 158.
[28] ibid, 163 *per* Lord Wright MR.
[29] [1994] 1 AC 340.

conduct in order to establish a resulting trust. All she needed to assert was 'the common intention that the property should belong to both of them and that she contributed to the purchase price'.[30] If however the parties had been in a relationship that would have given rise to the 'presumption of advancement', such as transfer of the title to a house by a father to his son, the result would have been that the illegality would have had to be relied upon to rebut the presumption, and so the result changed.[31]

The specific offence that the plaintiff was charged and convicted of was not discussed by the House of Lords or the Court of Appeal. Today it would probably be dealt with as making a false representation in order to obtain a benefit under the Social Security Administration Act 1992.[32] However the conduct was dishonest, and would also have been obtaining property by false pretences, a longstanding offence that was also created by legislation.[33]

The primary criticism of the reliance rule is that it is arbitrary.[34] It is clearly true that it is usually irrelevant to the justice between the parties on which side of the reliance line the claimant falls. However, as justice as between them is not the purpose of the rule this criticism fails to land. Fundamentally, the perceived arbitrariness is a feature of line drawing. When candidates for a degree are classified, the rubric for placing them into one class or another necessarily involves some fine distinctions. When we compare those who are just on one side with those just on the other there will be almost nothing to choose between them. Their different classification is not however arbitrary or unfair, but a feature of the use of rules for determining issues.

A secondary criticism is that the rule is uncertain, and there can obviously be debate at the margin as to whether a party is having to rely upon the commission of an illegal act or not. Fortunately, the courts had spent 250 years resolving this matter in disputed cases, exemplified by *Tinsley v Milligan*, thereby mitigating the problem.

E. Statutory Illegality

In the modern era, most litigated cases concern regulatory illegality sourced in legislation. In the criminal law we find the same pattern as we have already observed in private law. The common law initially recognised wrongs that are mala in se (eg murder, theft, bribery) whilst the legislature subsequently created offences that are *mala prohibita* for regulatory reasons (eg duties not to load ships so as to submerge the load line,[35] duties not to borrow foreign currency,[36] or the duty of landlords to provide tenants with a rent book[37]).

---

[30] ibid, 370–371 per Lord Browne-Wilkinson.
[31] *Chettiar v Chettiar* [1962] AC 294 (PC); *Collier v Collier* [2002] EWCA Civ 1095, [2002] BPIR 1057. In *Patel v Mirza* [2016] UKSC 42, [2017] AC 467, [238] Lord Sumption denied that in such cases it was necessary to rely upon the illegal scheme in order to rebut the presumption.
[32] Social Security Administration Act 1992, s 111A.
[33] Once the Larceny Act 1861, then the deception offences under the Theft Acts 1968 and 1978, today covered by the Fraud Act 2006.
[34] *Tribe v Tribe* [1996] Ch 107 (CA), 134 per Millett LJ; Law Commission, *The Illegality Defence* (Law Com 320), [2.13].
[35] Merchant Shipping (Safety and Load Line Conventions) Act 1932, s 44 considered in *St John Shipping Corp v Joseph Rank Ltd* [1957] 1 QB 267 (Devlin J).
[36] Defence (Finance) Regulations 1939, reg 2 considered in *Boissevain v Weil* [1950] AC 327 (HL).
[37] Landlord and Tenant Act 1962, s 4 considered in *Shaw v Groom* [1970] 2 QB 504 (CA).

Of course, today, many common law offences have been codified in legislation.[38] Some offences that are *mala in se*, such as the offence of dishonesty in *Berg v Sadler and Moore* and *Tinsley v Milligan*, have also always been found in legislation. However, the distinction between offences that are *mala prohibita* and *mala in se* is important and roughly tracks that between those created by legislation and those recognised by the judges at common law.

In his original formulation, in *Holman v Johnson*, Lord Mansfield stated that 'no court will lend its aid to a man who founds his cause of action upon an *immoral* or *illegal* act'.[39] In 1775 the distinction between the two would have been perceived as less significant than it is today, with the growth of the modern regulatory state.[40] However, where an action is not *malum* in se but *malum prohibitum* through legislation, the effect of that legislation on the enforceability of private rights is, irreducibly, a matter of statutory construction. The effect of such a statutory wrong should be determined by that statute.

Where a statute makes certain conduct illegal it may expressly stipulate that obligations concerning that conduct are void, unenforceable, or remain valid. Where legislation stipulates some private law effects of any breach, as increasingly modern statutes do, the court should be reluctant to add further consequences. Where a statute fails to deal with the private law consequences of a violation of a duty it creates, it is a mistake to think that the statute then falls away, and the common law 'takes over'.[41] Giving a statute further effects than, on its proper construction, it has, on the basis of 'common law illegality' was first suggested by Professor Burrows (as he then was)[42] and unfortunately this now has judicial endorsement in England.[43]

The effect of a statute must be determined by looking to its underlying purpose.[44] Would the validity or enforceability of the legal rights stultify the purpose of the law?[45] Whether the integrity or coherence of the legal system requires that private rights are nullified, unenforceable, or remain valid, can only sensibly be answered by reference to the statute and its purposes.[46] The process of construction is not therefore simply a matter of looking at the wording used. It is difficult to understand how *any* approach, other than the ordinary one of construing a statute's legal effects, may be sensibly or legitimately adopted by a court in cases of regulatory illegality created by legislation.[47]

---

[38] Eg Theft Act 1968.
[39] *Holman v Johnson* (1775) 1 Cowp 341, 343, 98 ER 1120, 1121 *per* Lord Mansfield (emphasis added).
[40] *Cf. Les Laboratoires Servier v Apotex Inc* [2014] UKSC 55, [2015] AC 430, [25] *per* Lord Sumption.
[41] A Burrows, 'A New Dawn for the Law of Illegality' in S Green and A Bogg (eds), *Illegality after Patel v Mirza* (2018) 23, 25.
[42] A Burrows, 'Illegality as a Defence in Contract' in S Degeling, J Edelman, and J Godkamp (eds), *Contract in Commercial Law* (2016) 435, 439.
[43] *Henderson v Dorset Healthcare University* [2020] UKSC 43, [74]; *Okedina v Chikale* [2019] EWCA Civ 1393, [2019] ICR 1635, [12] *per* Underhill LJ drawing on A Burrows, *A Restatement of the English Law of Contract* (2016), section 44; *Energizer Supermarket Ltd v Holiday Snacks Ltd* [2022] UKPC 16, [32] *per* Lord Burrows. *Cf. SR Projects Ltd v Ramperad* [2022] UKPC 24, [53] *per* Lord Leggatt.
[44] See eg *Cope v Rowland* (1836) 2 M&W 149, 150 ER 707.
[45] *Cf.* E Weinrib, 'Illegality as a Tort Defence' (1976) 26 U of TLJ 28.
[46] *Miller v Miller* [2011] HCA 9, (2011) CLR 1, [15]. In the contractual context this purposive approach was adopted in *Vita Food Products Inc v Unus Shipping Co Ltd* (1939) AC 277; *St John Shipping Corp v Joseph Rank Ltd* [1957] 1 QB 267 (Devlin J); *Archbolds (Freightage) Ltd v S Spanglett Ltd* [1961] QB 374 (CA); *Shaw v Groom* [1970] 2 QB 504 (CA); *Marles v Philip Trant* [1954] 1 QB 29 (CA); *Hughes v Asset Managers plc* [1995] 3 All ER 669 (CA). See also the statutory construction approach adopted in relation to an easement created by criminal action in *Bakewell Management Ltd v Brandwood* [2004] UKHL 14, [2004] 2 AC 519, *cf. R (Best) v Chief of Land Register* [2015] EWCA Civ 17, [2016] QB 23.
[47] *Gnych v Polish Club Ltd* [2015] HCA 23, (2015) 255 CLR 414, [36] *per* French CJ, Crennan, Kiefel, and Bell JJ.

An early example, pre-dating *Holman v Johnson*, is *Smith v Bromley*.[48] The plaintiff's brother was unable to pay his debts, and committed an act of bankruptcy. The defendant, his main creditor, took out a commission against him (ie put him into a bankruptcy procedure) but upon discovering that he was unlikely to receive any dividend, refused to sign the certificate that would discharge the bankruptcy. He then offered to give the certificate, but only if the bankrupt or somebody for him paid £40 and gave a note for £20 more. The plaintiff paid on behalf of her brother, and then sued the defendant for its recovery after the giving of the certificate.

Under the bankruptcy laws, the defendant should have signed the certificate of discharge only if the bankrupt had done all that was required of him. If instead he gave a discharge because of a payment by the bankrupt or a third party this would be a fraud on the other creditors. It was also an offence under the Bankruptcy Act 1731[49] for the plaintiff to have paid to obtain the certificate.

To have allowed the defendant to have kept the payment, which he had extracted through the plaintiff's affection for her brother, would have been flatly contrary to the purpose of the statute, which was to deter the granting of bankruptcy certificates other than when the bankrupt had done all that was required of him. Here, not only was the plaintiff's commission of an offence not a bar to her action, the illegal behaviour of the defendant was, as Lord Mansfield stated,[50] the foundation of her claim[51] as the purpose of the legislation was best fulfilled by awarding restitution.[52]

The 'coherence' or 'integrity' the illegality rule appeals to is therefore better understood as the coherence of the reasons underlying the various rules, rather than simply the formal coherence of whether a party is relying upon an action that constitutes a wrong. It may be speculated that if the criminal law were to be abolished, it would still be appropriate to withhold the state's powers of enforcement of private right to acts of murder, theft, bribery, and fraud.

On the other side of the line was *Boissevain v Weil*.[53] In Monaco in 1944 the defendant had borrowed 320,000 francs from the plaintiff in order to attempt to buy her Jewish son an exemption from being deported to Germany. She agreed to repay the plaintiff in sterling after the war. The loan agreement was contrary to the Defence (Finance) Regulations 1939 which stated that 'no person … shall buy or borrow … or lend or sell any foreign currency'.

Here it was the defendant, as a British subject, but probably not the plaintiff, a Dutchman, who had broken the regulation, but its purpose rendered both the agreement and the claim for restitution unenforceable. Lord Radcliffe stated:[54]

---

[48] (1760) 2 Doug 696n, 99 ER 441 decided in 1760 but not reported until 1781. In *Holman v Johnson* itself the contract for the sale of tea did not offend the purpose of the relevant revenue statute. *Cf. Atkinson v Denby* (1862) 7 H&N 934, 158 ER 749.

[49] 5 Geo 2, c 30.

[50] (1781) 2 Doug 696, 697 99 ER 44.

[51] C Mitchell, P Mitchell, and S Watterson (eds), *Goff & Jones: The Law of Unjust Enrichment* (9th edn, 2016), [25-207].

[52] See also marriage brokerage contracts where the policy behind their invalidation supports a claim for restitution of fees paid: *Hermann v Charlesworth* [1905] 2 QB 123.

[53] [1950] AC 327 (HL). See also *Kasumu v Baba-Egbe* [1956] AC 539 (PC). Compare *Shelley v Paddock* [1980] QB 348 (CA) where a *payment* made in breach of exchange controls was recoverable and *Bigos v Bousted* [1951] 1 All ER 92 (Pritchard J) which goes further.

[54] [1950] AC 327 (HL), 341.

[If] this claim based on unjust enrichment were a valid one, the court would be enforcing on the [defendant] just the exchange and just the liability, without her promise, which the Defence Regulation has said that she is not to undertake by her promise. A court that extended a remedy in such circumstances would merit rather to be blamed for stultifying the law than to be applauded for extending it.

The repayment in sterling, which the plaintiff sought, was the very thing the statute required not to be done. No court should compel to be done what it is illegal for the defendant to do. This refusal to enforce conduct by the defendant that would constitute a crime, even where the plaintiff has committed no wrong, is more common in the contractual context.

As elsewhere, this process of statutory construction is not reducible to any simple set of maxims (eg were the parties *in pari delicto potio est conditio defendentis*[55]). Although these maxims may provide a rough and ready guide as to the relevant considerations, they cannot substitute for the inevitably sometimes difficult task of construing the purpose of the legislation and its effects. A blunt application of the *in pari delicto* maxim would, for example, give the opposite result in *Boissevain v Weil* as it was the defendant, not the plaintiff, who was in breach of the Regulations.[56] Those who would reject a rule-based approach to illegality are right, to this extent, that the possible number of relevant considerations to take into account in construing any particular piece of legislation are potentially large, context dependent, and will vary.

Although often used, speaking of 'illegal contracts' is misleading. The law makes the conduct of persons illegal, and that conduct may include either the entering into of certain kinds of agreement, or the actions which constitute the performance of that agreement. It may also be possible to 'sever' obligations that are illegal to perform from others that are not. Contractual obligations may, as a result, be valid, void, voidable, or unenforceable. Contracts therefore are not themselves 'illegal'. It may be that both parties have committed an offence in entering into, or performing, a contract, only one of them as in *Boissevain v Weil*, or neither as in *Oom v Bruce*.[57]

A prohibition on entering into an agreement will, ordinarily, mean that a party so prohibited should also be unable to bring a claim for a *quantum meruit* based upon the failure of the agreed counter-performance. In *Awwad v Geraghty & Co*[58] the claimant, a solicitor, entered into a conditional fee agreement. Entering into such agreements was at that time a violation by the solicitor of the Solicitors' Practice Rules made pursuant to section 31 of the Solicitors Act 1974. Not only was the agreement thereby made unenforceable by the solicitor, the claim for a *quantum meruit* for the work done was also ruled out. In making out a claim for restitution the claimant would have to rely upon the failed agreed condition, that he had not been paid his conditional fee: the very agreement that he had been prohibited from entering.

---

[55] 'Where both parties are equally in the wrong, the position of the defendant is the stronger.'
[56] Similarly, the defendant in *Parkinson v College of Ambulance* [1925] 2 KB 1 was probably more morally blameworthy than the plaintiff.
[57] (1810) 12 East 225, 104 ER 87. Cf. *Eric Bieber & Co Ltd v Rio Tinto Co Ltd* [1918] AC 260 (HL).
[58] [2001] QB 570 (CA). Cf. *Tri Level Claims Consultant Ltd v Koliniotis* (2005) 257 DLR (4th) 291, 201 OAC 282 (Ont CA).

Similar is *Shaw v Shaw*.[59] The plaintiff paid the defendant £4,000 for a flat in Majorca. Restitution was then sought on the basis that it was a condition of the agreement that the consent of the Treasury for the payment was granted under section 7 of the Exchange Control Act 1947, and this had not been forthcoming. The Court of Appeal refused the claim. The plaintiff had not asserted any independently valid reason for restitution (eg they had not had title to the flat conveyed). The only basis of the plaintiff's claim was that they had behaved unlawfully in paying contrary to exchange control regulations. This result may be queried. Would the purpose of the legislation (preventing the payment of sterling out of the jurisdiction) have been better served with an order for restitution?

Usefully contrasted is *Mohamed v Alaga*.[60] Rule 3 of the Solicitors Practice Rules prohibited a solicitor from paying for introductions and rule 7 also prohibited a solicitor from sharing or agreeing to share his fees. The claimant, in ignorance of these rules, entered into an agreement to introduce Somali refugees to the defendant solicitors and to assist in the presentation of their asylum claims. Although it was only the defendant solicitors who had violated the law in entering into the contract, it was held unenforceable. A *quantum meruit* for the introductions was ruled out because, as in *Boissevain v Weil*, this would be requiring the solicitor to do what he was expressly prohibited from doing: pay for introductions.[61] But this did not prevent the claimant, who had broken no law at all, from bringing a claim for a reasonable sum for the translation services he had provided. The claimant was seeking to recover the value of work done under an (unenforceable) agreement where the condition of its provision had failed. He relied upon no illegal conduct in bringing that action.[62]

This is not to say that every decision was or is reconcilable or defensible. In relation to contracts of life insurance that are taken out where the insured did not have an insurable interest, the rule was that a client could recover his premiums where he had been induced to pay by fraudulent misrepresentation[63] but not where the misrepresentation was innocent.[64] Looking at relative fault seems inappropriate here. Allowing the claim for restitution, rather than denying it, is more likely to promote the reason for the invalidity of the contract, and thereby fulfil the statutory purpose.

The approach of the High Court of Australia has consistently been to adopt this suggested statutory construction approach, remorselessly focusing upon the purpose of the statutory prohibition concerned.[65] This process is not, of course, always straightforward. In *Equuscorp Pty Ltd v Haxton*,[66] the defendants had been made loans, the benefit of

---

[59] [1965] 1 WLR 537 (CA).
[60] [2001] 1 WLR 1815 (CA) cited with approval by Lord Toulson in *Patel v Mirza* [2016] UKSC 42, [2017] AC 467, [119].
[61] *Cf. Cotronic (UK) Ltd v Dezonie (t/a Wendaland Builders Ltd)* [1991] BCLC 721 (CA) where the payment for the work done was not prohibited.
[62] *Cf. Taylor v Bhail* [1996] CLC 377 where the claimant was seeking to rely upon a fraudulent conspiracy to which he was a party.
[63] *Hughes v Liverpool Victoria friendly Society* [1916] 2 KB 482 (CA).
[64] *Harse v Pearl Life Assurance Co* [1904] 1 KB 558 (CA).
[65] There is now a long line of cases: *Yango Pastoral Co Pty Ltd v First Chicago Australia Ltd* [1978] HCA 42, (1978) 139 CLR 410 (Banking Act 1959 Cth); *Nelson v Nelson* [1995] HCA 25, (1995) 184 CLR 538 (Defence Service Homes Act 1918 Cth); *Fitzgerald v FJ Leonhardt Pty Ltd* [1997] HCA 17, (1997) 189 CLR 215 (Water Act 1992 NT); *Master Education Services Pty Ltd v Ketchell* [2008] HCA 38, (2008) 236 CLR 101 (Trade Practices Act 1974 Cth); *Miller v Miller* [2011] HCA 9, (2011) CLR 1 (Criminal Code WA); *Equuscorp Pty Ltd v Haxton* [2012] HCA 7, (2012) 246 CLR 498 (Companies Code); *Gnych v Polish Club Ltd* [2015] HCA 42, (2015) 255 CLR 414 (Liquor Act 2007 NSW). See W Gummow, 'Whither Now Illegality and Statute: An Australian Perspective' in S Green and A Bogg (eds), *Illegality after Patel v Mirza* (2018), 293.
[66] [2012] HCA 7, (2012) 246 CLR 498.

which had been assigned to the plaintiff. The loans had been made with the sole purpose of facilitating the defendants entering into investment schemes with the lender. Contrary to the provisions of the Companies Code, no valid prospectus had been registered when the investments were offered. As a result, the loan agreements were, by clear implication,[67] unenforceable. Did the purpose of the law rendering the agreements unenforceable also rule out any claim for restitution? The majority held that it did. The protective purpose of the legislation ruled out the restitutionary claim against the party it was intended to benefit, just as much as the contractual action.[68] The dissent[69] argued that as the legislation specified criminal sanctions and contractual unenforceability, the court should go no further. The approach of the majority accords with House of Lords authorities holding that the protective purpose of consumer credit legislation that rendered certain agreements unenforceable (but with no illegality involved) also ruled out any claim for restitution against the party intended to be protected.[70]

F. *Patel v Mirza*

1. The Statute

Patel v Mirza[71] should have been a relatively straightforward case concerned with the correct construction of section 63(2) of the Criminal Justice Act 1993.[72] Unfortunately, it was seen by a majority of the UK Supreme Court as the occasion to re-write the entire area of illegality in private law by legislative action. In earlier decisions of that Court,[73] different judges had adopted different approaches to the operation of the illegality rule, and a nine-member court was convened to settle the matter.

Patel paid Mirza £620,000. He did so under an agreement that Mirza would use the funds for the purpose of share trading in breach of the insider dealing provisions of the 1993 Act. Their agreement was never carried out however as Patel's source of insider information, one Georgiou, ceased to provide it. Patel sought restitution of his payment. The trial judge denied the action, but this was overturned by the Court of Appeal and the Supreme Court upheld their decision.

How should the decision have been reached? The crime that Patel and Mirza were both committing by entering into the agreement was conspiracy[74] to commit insider trading. The first question that should have been asked was the effect the illegality had upon the contract.[75] Did it render it void, voidable, unenforceable, or have no impact? The majority

---

[67] The liability of the lender was expressly preserved by the legislation, implying that the liability of the borrower was not.
[68] French CJ, Crennan, Kiefel, Gummow, and Bell JJ.
[69] Heydon J.
[70] *Orakpo v Manson Investments Ltd* [1978] AC 95 (HL); *Dimond v Lovell* [2002] 1 AC 384 (HL); *Wilson v First County Trust Ltd* [2003] UKHL 40, [2003] 1 AC 81.
[71] [2016] UKSC 42, [2017] AC 467.
[72] But see *Henderson v Dorset Healthcare University* [2020] UKSC 43, [2020] WLR (D) 592, [74].
[73] *Hounga v Allen* [2014] UKSC 47, [2014] 1 WLR 2889; *Les Laboratoires Servier v Apotex Inc* [2014] UKSC 55, [2015] AC 430; *Bilta (UK) Ltd v Nazir (No 2)* [2015] UKSC 23, [2016] AC 1.
[74] Criminal Justice Act 1977, s 1.
[75] *Contra* Burrows, 'A New Dawn for the Law of Illegality' (n 41), 23, 25. See also *Patel v Mirza* [2016] UKSC 42, [2017] AC 467, [109] *per* Lord Toulson.

of the Supreme Court seem to have assumed that it rendered it invalid in some sense but unfortunately did not examine in which. As we have seen, in the law of restitution this should be the starting question, a performance rendered under an unenforceable agreement being irrecoverable unless the agreed condition of that performance has failed.[76] Lord Sumption (in the minority in the Supreme Court) and Gloster LJ (in the minority in the Court of Appeal) were the only members of either appellate court to focus on the effect of the statute upon the contract.

Insider dealing is (subject to exceptions) rendered illegal by section 52 of the Criminal Justice Act 1993. Section 63(2) of that Act states: 'No contract shall be void or unenforceable by reason of section 52'. Lord Sumption read that provision as only applying to contracts dealing in securities. The agreement between Patel and Mirza was a financing agreement preliminary to such a securities contract with someone else. He therefore read the provision narrowly as not protecting this anterior agreement.

This is, however, a difficult construction to accept. The contracts given protection by section 63(2) are not qualified. The better view was that of Gloster LJ in the Court of Appeal that 'in circumstance where the actual securities contract entered into on the basis of illegal insider information is not void or unenforceable (even, presumably, on the basis of the current wording of section 63(2), if the contract still remains executory), it is hard to see on what possible basis the public policy behind the rule against insider trading requires the anterior contract or arrangement for deposit of Mr Patel's funds with Mr Mirza, as Mr Patel's agent to be struck down as unenforceable.'[77]

Given that the contract between them was valid, what effect does this have upon the claim for restitution? Patel could not argue that Mirza had not been initially entitled to the payment: he was, that was what was due under the contract. However, the payment had been conditional upon the securities transaction taking place, which it never had. Should Patel have been barred from relying upon this condition in the agreement with Mirza, on the basis of the criminal conspiracy? The availability of this claim for restitution should have been determined by the validity of their agreement. There could be no objection to Patel relying upon the agreed condition because the legislation had, on its correct construction, stated that its validity was unaffected by the underlying illegality. Restitution was therefore correctly awarded. Gloster LJ's approach of determining the result through the careful construction of the statutory framework and its effect on the contract was the correct one. This accords with the result reached by the Supreme Court. However, no member of the Supreme Court (at least expressly) reasoned in this way.

2. The Minority

Lord Sumption (with whom Lord Clarke agreed) and Lord Mance, whilst generally adopting the view that the correct (indeed only) question was whether the claimant was seeking to rely upon his own illegal action, thought that an exception should be made in claims for restitution. Lord Sumption thought that restitution under an 'illegal contract' should always follow as the 'effect is to put the parties in the position in which they would have been if they

---

[76] But see [2016] UKSC 42, [2017] AC 467, [247]–[248] *per* Lord Sumption.
[77] [2016] UKSC 42, [2017] AC 467, [69].

had never entered into the illegal transaction, which in the eyes of the law is the position which they should always have been in'.[78] Lord Mance similarly stated that the 'logic of the principle is that the illegal transaction should be disregarded, and the parties restored to the position in which they would have been, had they never entered into it'.[79]

Such an approach would go much too far. First, it would treat all 'illegal contracts' in the same way, even where they had been fully executed, and regardless of the purpose of the illegality. This would be to treat them as uniformly void, when on the correct construction of the legislation they may be merely unenforceable or even valid. Second, and more startlingly, it would mean not only assisting in the recovery of unsuccessful bribes, as in *Parkinson v College Ambulance*, but requiring the law to assist even more egregious criminals, such as someone who pays for a murder, which the hitman incompetently fails to carry out. Lord Sumption did not balk at this conclusion.[80]

3. The Majority

More difficult to interpret is the decision of the majority given by Lord Toulson (with whom Lady Hale, Lord Kerr, Lord Wilson, and Lord Hodge agreed, and generally endorsed by Lord Neuberger).

Negatively, first they reject the 'reliance' approach to determine whether the offence was sufficiently connected to the dispute that had been used over many decades, exemplified by *Tinsley v Milligan*. Second, the effect of regulatory illegality contained in legislation was not perceived as solely a matter of statutory construction.

Positively, Lord Toulson commenced by endorsing Lord Mansfield's classic statement in *Holman v Johnson*[81] that a court will not assist a cause of action arising *ex turpi causa* or in transgression of the positive law, but then adopts an approach that does not follow this proposition. He also engaged, albeit in a 'somewhat cursory'[82] way, with the authorities from other common law jurisdictions, but adopts a view quite different from that of any other.[83]

Further, Lord Toulson, although not expressly endorsing the Law Commission's list of six policy concerns, did cite them with apparent approval.[84] He then confined himself to generally endorsing just two: 'One is that a person should not be allowed to profit from his own wrongdoing. The other, linked, consideration is that the law should be coherent and not self-defeating, condoning illegality by giving with the left hand what it takes with the right hand.'[85] Again, although less problematic than the longer list, these two policies may pull in different directions, as in the case of the hitman who misses his agreed target.

---

[78] ibid, [250].
[79] ibid, [197].
[80] ibid, [254]. See also Lord Neuberger [176].
[81] (1775) 1 Cowp 341, 343, 98 ER 1120, 1121.
[82] Gummow, 'Whither Now Illegality and Statute: An Australian Perspective' (n 65), 293, 294.
[83] The important Supreme Court of Canada decision of *Hall v Hebert* [1993] 2 SCR 159 was cited, but its approach not followed.
[84] [2016] UKSC 42, [2017] AC 467, [22].
[85] ibid, [99].

However, he then went on to endorse a list of eight factors, proposed by Professor Burrows,[86] that included a number of other goals as 'helpful':[87] '(a) how seriously illegal or contrary to public policy the conduct was; (b) whether the party seeking enforcement knew of, or intended, the conduct; (c) how central to the contract or its performance the conduct was; (d) how serious a sanction the denial of enforcement is for the party seeking enforcement; (e) whether denying enforcement will further the purpose of the rule which the conduct has infringed; (f) whether denying enforcement will act as a deterrent to conduct that is illegal or contrary to public policy; (g) whether denying enforcement will ensure that the party seeking enforcement does not profit from the conduct; (h) whether denying enforcement will avoid inconsistency in the law thereby maintaining the integrity of the legal system.' Lord Toulson also stated that he did not intend this list to be exhaustive.[88]

In concluding, Lord Toulson adopted what is presumably his definitive schedule of three factors, although the second could contain many others.

> The essential rationale of the illegality doctrine is that it would be contrary to the public interest to enforce a claim if to do so would be harmful to the integrity of the legal system ... In assessing whether the public interest would be harmed in that way, it is necessary a) to consider the underlying purpose of the prohibition which has been transgressed and whether that purpose will be enhanced by denial of the claim, b) to consider any other relevant public policy on which the denial of the claim may have an impact and c) to consider whether denial of the claim would be a proportionate response to the illegality, bearing in mind that punishment is a matter for the criminal courts.[89]

4. The *Ratio*

The primary difficulty with the leading speech is that it does not discuss how the proposed approach should be employed to dispose of the case before the court.[90] Would the presumed purpose of the offence of deterring insider trading be facilitated by denying the claim for restitution? What other relevant public policies were engaged? Would the proportionality of the response be impacted by the size of the claim?[91] Does 'integrity' have priority over the other considerations, or are they aspects of it?

However, and importantly, what was said was that in determining the case in issue the majority 'endorse the approach and conclusion of Gloster LJ'.[92] The *ratio* of the decision, or how the case before the court was actually decided, was therefore correct. The reason the court does not consider any possible countervailing policies or the 'proportionality' of holding the claim unenforceable was that it was unnecessary for it to do so. The dizzying array of incommensurable potential factors is *obiter dicta*.[93]

---

[86] A Burrows, *Restatement of the English Law of Contract* (2016), 229–230
[87] [2016] UKSC 42, [2017] AC 467, [107].
[88] ibid.
[89] ibid, [120], see also [101].
[90] Burrows, 'A New Dawn for the Law of Illegality' (n 21), 23, 28.
[91] *Cf. ParkingEye Ltd v Somerfield Stores Ltd* [2012] EWCA Civ 1338, [2013] QB 840, [39] *per* Sir Robin Jacob.
[92] [2016] UKSC 42, [2017] AC 467,[115].
[93] See Gummow, 'Whither Now Illegality and Statute: An Australian Perspective' (n 65), 293, 305, 'an unsuitable vehicle' for resolving the conflicting prior decisions on illegality.

5. The Future

The decision in *Patel v Mirza* raises two issues that are fundamental to the judicial method.

First, is it appropriate for a court, even an ultimate appellate court, 'to abandon basic principles going back nearly 250 years'?[94] *Patel v Mirza* is in tension with Lord Reed's warning that 'the wisdom of our predecessors is a valuable resource' and that 'the courts should not be reinventing the wheel'.[95] Should a court engage in an attempt to re-write an entire area of law, or should it more modestly attempt to resolve the case before it, whilst giving appropriate guidance as to how future cases should be decided? The court is not a legislature. It lacks both the technical competence to take into account issues that are not raised by the case before it, and the political legitimacy to reformulate rules for cases it has not heard. Although in *Patel v Mirza* the court did have the benefit of a number of Law Commission consultation papers and reports, the outcome of that process had been an inconclusive one. Initially the Commission had proposed legislative intervention to create a judicial 'structured discretion'.[96] However, this proposal was eventually dropped, partly because of the lack of any consensus agreeing with it[97] (and, no doubt, also because of a change in the Law Commissioner responsible).[98] The Commission had, in conclusion, left the law to judicial development whilst recommending that the reliance-based approach in *Tinsley v Milligan* no longer be adopted.

Second, and relatedly, the judicial power to make law is limited. Not everything that a judge, even an ultimate appellate court judge, says in a judgment is binding as law. If it were, a judge could, in deciding a case concerning the construction of a tax statute, read into the record binding statements on fundamental human rights. Such statements are *obiter dicta*. Even a set-piece nine-member panel Supreme Court, as in *Patel v Mirza*, does not have the power to determine in a claim for restitution how claims for damages in the law of torts should be determined, still less to overturn longstanding decisions of earlier ultimate appellate courts on that issue. Such statements do give an indication of how the presently constituted panel would decide such future cases, but that is all. If the Supreme Court wishes to overturn earlier ultimate appellate court decisions it should do so expressly by invoking the Practice Statement,[99] not by implication.

The *ratio decidendi* of *Patel v Mirza* is to be found in the construction of the statute that the case concerned, in the decision of Gloster LJ that is endorsed by the majority. The rest does not constitute the positive law.

For the law of illegality itself, the majority come close to endorsing the view of the minority that restitution should ordinarily always be awarded in cases of 'illegal contracts', Lord Toulson stating that:

---

[94] [2016] UKSC 42, [2017] AC 467, [187] *per* Lord Mance.
[95] *Investment Trust Companies (in liquidation) v Revenue and Customs Commissioners* [2017] UKSC 29, [2018] AC 275, [40].
[96] Law Commission, *Illegal Transactions* (LCCP 154, 1999), [7.43]. The Law Commissioner responsible at the time was Lord Burrows.
[97] See eg Law Commission Consultation Paper 189, 50 fn 145, 'Professor Andrew Tettenborn and Sir Guenter Treitel wrote very persuasive responses against the CP proposals'.
[98] Law Commission, *The Illegality Defence* (Law Com 320).
[99] Practice Statement [1966] 3 All ER 77.

A claimant, such as Mr Patel, who satisfies the ordinary requirements of a claim for unjust enrichment, should not be debarred from enforcing his claim by reason only of the fact that the money which he seeks to recover was paid for an unlawful purpose.[100]

On this approach, unlike that of the minority, if the contract is fully executed restitution should not follow, there being no failure of the condition under which each side has performed the agreement. However, the majority's formulation, ignoring the purpose of the statutory prohibition, does not fit comfortably with earlier decisions of the House of Lords that the protective purpose of agreements rendered unenforceable (but not unlawful) under consumer credit legislation, also ruled out claims for restitution.[101]

What if, in cases of statutory illegality, the agreement is executory and an action for the agreed sum is brought by a party meeting all of the ordinary requirements for such a claim? Presumably the converse to the restitutionary position is thought to apply so that any claim would always fail as this would entail performing the illegal contract? The illegality rule has not therefore been abolished. The better approach, by contrast, is to ascertain whether, on its true construction, the statute renders the contract, or specific obligations created by it, void, or unenforceable by one or both parties, or not. The availability of restitution should similarly be determined by the construction of the relevant legislation, rather than by a one-size fits all approach to 'illegal contracts'.

On the approach of the minority, the result of *Parkinson v College of Ambulance* would be reversed, and Lord Neuberger also expressly states that it should be.[102] *Parkinson* did not however involve a regulatory statute, the effect of which should turn upon its construction. Rather it involved what was then the common law offence of bribery, a serious crime of dishonesty.[103] There was no equivalent of section 63(2) of the Criminal Justice Act 1993 such as to make the contract between the parties valid. The majority judgment of Lord Toulson left the matter of Parkinson's correctness open, as was right in the light of how *Patel* itself was actually resolved.[104]

A legal system that gets itself into the position that bribes that do not succeed in their purpose are recoverable in court actions, or (even more extraordinarily) the recovery of payments for unsuccessful hit jobs actionable, is one that has confused itself.

Although the hope of the majority might have been that *Patel v Mirza* would settle the illegality issue, at least at appellate level, it has twice had to go back to the Supreme Court. In both cases the result was the same as that which would have been applied under the earlier approach (as indeed was true in *Patel v Mirza* itself). Neither concerned claims for restitution. In the first, *Stoffel v Grondona*,[105] Lord Lloyd-Jones for the court stated that it 'would not normally be appropriate for a court to admit or to address evidence on matters such as the effectiveness of the criminal law in particular situations or the likely social consequences of permitting a claim in specified circumstances'.[106] The question of what 'policy' required was to be determined by the ordinary process of construing the law, and not by

---

[100] [2016] UKSC 42, [2017] AC 467, [121]. See also [154] *per* Lord Neuberger.
[101] *Orakpo v Manson Investments Ltd* [1978] AC 95 (HL); *Dimond v Lovell* [2002] 1 AC 384 (HL); *Wilson v First County Trust Ltd* [2003] UKHL 40, [2003] 1 AC 81.
[102] [2016] UKSC 42, [2017] AC 467, [150].
[103] This crime is now on a statutory footing, but this should make no difference to the analysis.
[104] [2016] UKSC 42, [2017] AC 467, [118].
[105] [2020] UKSC 42, [2020] 3 WLR 1156.
[106] *ibid*, [26].

the judge's own assessment of where the policy balance lay.[107] The court stressed the lexical priority in the inquiry of the law's integrity as a formal matter, although unfortunately leaving in place the unanswerable question of whether the application of the illegality rule should be disapplied because 'disproportionate' in any given case. The four factors relevant at that second stage were said to be '(i) the seriousness of the conduct; (ii) the centrality of the conduct to the transaction; (iii) whether the conduct was intentional; and (iv) whether there was a marked disparity in the parties' respective wrongdoing'.[108] It is now clear that the court's role is not, as was arguable after *Patel v Mirza*,[109] simply to 'weigh' the full range of multiple possible factors counting for and against the application of the rule.[110] Where the illegality is found in a statute, the approach following *Stoffel* is close to the suggested one of determining the issue through the ordinary process of statutory construction.

Further, in *Ecila Henderson v Dorset Healthcare University NHS Foundation Trust*[111] (where the Supreme Court followed the earlier decision of *Gray v Thames Trains Ltd*[112] in refusing damages for loss caused by manslaughter committed by a claimant where this had been caused by injury to his mental state caused by the defendant's negligence), the Supreme Court denied that '*Patel* represent "year zero" and that in all future illegality cases it is *Patel* only that is to be considered',[113] as this would ignore and undermine the value of precedent. Previous decisions 'remain of precedential value unless it can be shown that they are not compatible with the approach set out in *Patel* in the sense that they cannot stand with the reasoning in *Patel* or were wrongly decided in the light of that reasoning'.[114] Given the extremely open-textured nature of the *Patel v Mirza* approach, the result is that almost all previous decisions remain binding. Indeed if, as is argued, the effect of statutory illegality is always and only a matter of the effect of the statute as properly construed, whether a decision of the Supreme Court could in principle require other courts to give effect to something other than the correct construction of legislation is a difficult question. Today, the best available reading of *Patel v Mirza* is that the court was seeking to identify factors that may, in an appropriate case, be relevant to the court's inescapable task of statutory construction.

Where earlier decisions on illegality are found in ultimate appellate court authority (as in *Boissevain v Weil*), the court in *Henderson* also stated that, even were they to be expressly challenged, it would be 'very circumspect' before overruling them.[115] At least at a formal level, therefore, even *Tinsley v Milligan*,[116] the result of which was irrelevant to the decision in *Patel*, remains the law until overturned, although in cases of first impression the reliance approach it adopted is no longer to be followed.

There is, therefore, at least the hope that *Parkinson v College of Ambulance* will continue to be followed. If it is not, a difficult problem of priority of claims then arises. An example:

---

[107] *ibid*, [26].
[108] *ibid*, [138].
[109] Burrows, 'A New Dawn for the Law of Illegality' (n 21), 23, 35.
[110] But see *Energizer Supermarket Ltd v Holiday Snacks Ltd* [2022] UKPC 16, [43] *per* Lord Burrows.
[111] [2020] UKSC 43, [2020] WLR (D) 592.
[112] [2009] UKHL 33, [2009] AC 1339.
[113] [2020] UKSC 43, [2020] WLR (D) 592, [77]. *Cf.* Burrows, 'A New Dawn for the Law of Illegality' (n 21), 23, 24, 'wipes the slate clean'.
[114] [2020] UKSC 43, [2020] WLR (D) 592, [77].
[115] [2020] UKSC 42, [2020] 3 WLR 1156, [87].
[116] [1994] 1 AC 340 (HL).

D acts as the purchasing agent for P1, a retailer. P2 pays D a £100,000 bribe to purchase goods from him.

As we have seen, D is obliged to account to P1 for the bribe he has received. Indeed, if traceable, the bribe or its proceeds are to be held on trust.[117] If P2 also has a claim for restitution of what he has paid, which has priority, or must D pay both?

The uncertainty created by *Patel v Mirza* is obvious.

G. Summary

The correct position may be summarised as follows.

(a) Where a party to litigation seeks to rely upon their commission of an offence that is *malum in se* (murder, theft, bribery, etc) the court should refuse to lend them its assistance. Claims for restitution should not differ in this regard from any other.
(b) Courts should not order to be done that which the law prohibits. This includes the making of restitution.
(c) The effect of statutory regulation is, all the way down, a matter of the correct construction of the effect of the relevant legislation by the court. There is no sensible point at which the effect of 'statutory illegality' ends and a different set of rules governed by 'common law illegality' begins. The purpose of making the entering into or performance of a contract illegal will often point in favour of the reversal of any performance rendered. The most common case where it will not do so is where the illegality rule exists in order to protect the defendant.

It is unclear to what extent the decision of *Patel v Mirza* will ever require any result to be reached that is inconsistent with these suggested principles. On the positive side, the decision does afford the opportunity for the courts to review those cases, such as those concerned with the refusal of recovery of premiums paid under contracts of insurance invalid because of the lack of any insurable interest, which are doubtful.

H. Illegality as a Ground of Claim

1. Restitution Founded upon the Statute

As we saw, in *Smith v Bromley*, the purpose of statutory illegality may not only mean that a party guilty of an offence is not disbarred from asserting a right to restitution, but also that the breach of statute may operate as a reason for restitution. Again, this is a matter of statutory construction. In England, the early statutes of bankruptcy, although providing for pro rata distribution of assets to creditors, were silent as to the consequences of preferences: a bankrupt choosing to pay one debtor rather than another before the onset of the

---

[117] *FHR European Ventures Ltd v Cedar Capital Partners LLC* [2014] UKSC 45, [2015] AC 250.

bankruptcy procedure. As the purpose of the legislation was to ensure fair distribution, the debtor was not permitted to decide that one creditor should be paid before another, and so preferential payments were recoverable as defeating the purpose of the legislation.[118]

The classic situation where restitution is appropriate is where the duty the defendant has breached was created for the protection of a class of people, of which the plaintiff is a member. It seems unlikely that the plaintiff needs to show that the defendant's duty was owed to him (ie that the statute created not just a public duty but a private right vested in him) such that he would also have a claim for damages for breach of statutory duty. The decision of the Privy Council in *Kiriri Cotton Ltd v Dewani*[119] is the usual illustration. The plaintiff paid the defendant 10,000 shillings as 'key money' in order to be able to rent a flat in Kampala. The Ugandan Rent Restriction Ordinance 1949 made it an offence for a landlord to ask for or receive any payment other than rent, but created no offence for the tenant who so paid it. Neither party realised that the demand was illegal. The tenant was entitled to recover the payment, despite the legislation not providing expressly for any such right to return. The purpose of the legislation, protection of the plaintiff, was best served through restitution.

2. Withdrawal

On the approach of the minority, in *Patel v Mirza* the illegality of a contract always provides a reason for its reversal, even where it is fully executed. On the approach of the majority, this is not so, indeed applying the actual *ratio* of the decision, all should turn in future similar cases upon the correct construction of the underlying statute under which the entering into or performance of the contract is illegal.

Prior to *Patel v Mirza*, there was some authority for allowing recovery where one party withdrew from the illegal transaction before it was performed, reflected in the Latin tag of *locus poenitentiae*, or a space for repentance.

The basis of such a rule is not repentance in the moral sense, of regretting wrongdoing.[120] Rather it would be the policy of encouraging parties to illegal transactions to withdraw from them so that they are not carried out. For example:

> P, an antique dealer, has a buyer prepared to pay a premium for an eighteenth-century jade carving. P knows that X has such a piece, and pays a cat-burglar, D £100,000 to acquire it by theft. The buyer then declares that he is no longer interested in jade. P informs D that the deal is off before the break-in happens.

It can be argued that the law ought to require D to make restitution to P. Although P may be thoroughly unrepentant of his behaviour, the policy of encouraging withdrawal, and thereby discouraging the performance of the illegal objective, may be thought to justify restitution. This would be an example of restitution justified by 'policy', unrelated to the justice as between P and D.

---

[118] *Alderson v Temple* (1768) 4 Burr 2235, 96 ER 55 (Lord Mansfield CJ).
[119] [1960] 2 WLR 127 (PC). *Cf. Green v Portsmouth Stadium Ltd* [1953] 2 QB 190 (CA).
[120] But see *Parkinson v College of Ambulance* [1924] 2 KB 1, 16 *per* Lush J.

Although there are many judicial statements invoking the *locus poenitentiae* idea,[121] the authority for its recognition is fragile.[122] In the leading decision of *Taylor v Bowers*,[123] the plaintiff was in financial difficulties, and attempted to defraud his creditors by transferring the possession of a steam-engine and some other machinery to his nephew. This was dressed up as a sale, with fictitious bills of sale drawn up. The nephew then double-crossed him, and executed a bill of sale of the goods in favour of the defendant, who was one of the creditors who knew of the arrangement. The plaintiff successfully brought an action in the tort of detinue for the recovery of the goods. If, however, we remove the illegality from the story, the result ought to be the same. The plaintiff had not parted with title to the goods and so could assert that title against the defendant.[124] Further the policy of the bankruptcy law that the plaintiff had been trying to evade favoured recovery: not doing so would potentially compound the fraud on the other creditors. In *Kearley v Thomson*,[125] where its application would have led to a different result, the Court of Appeal refused to give effect to the withdrawal principle where part, if not all, of the illegal purpose had been carried out.

The most important decision today is probably that of the Court of Appeal in *Tribe v Tribe*.[126] A father transferred shares into the name of his son, for a consideration that was never intended to be paid. He did this to safeguard his assets from his creditors; he was under notice as a tenant of an obligation to carry out costly repairs of premises. As things turned out, the clouds of bankruptcy passed, no repairs were ever carried out, and the father asked for the return of the shares. The son refused.

Although the shares had been gratuitously transferred to the defendant, the presumption of advancement that operates between father and son required evidence to be led as to the lack of donative intent. It was held that, despite relying upon his unlawful behaviour, the father could do so. He was withdrawing before any part of the transaction had been carried out, and so was not barred from proving his true intentions, as no creditors had been defrauded.

This is however a doubtful application of the withdrawal principle. It was no part of the illegal purpose that the father went into bankruptcy, indeed he had hoped that he would not. He transferred the shares into his son's name to put them out of reach of his creditors *in case* he went into bankruptcy. The illegal purpose had been completed, not withdrawn from.

A better justification for the result is that the purposes of bankruptcy laws do not prohibit the recovery of assets that have been transferred away with the intention of being unavailable for distribution to creditors. Quite the opposite, as restitution means that the asset is again available to creditors. If the father had gone into an insolvency proceeding, then the transfer of shares, as at an undervalue, would have been recoverable independently of any other ground for restitution. It should not matter if anyone is deceived.

---

[121] 'If money is paid, or goods delivered, for an illegal purpose, the person who has so paid the money or delivered the goods may recover them back before the illegal purpose is caried out': *Taylor v Bowers* (1876) 1 QBD 291, 300 *per* Mellish LJ.
[122] See W Swadling, 'The Role of Illegality in the English Law of Unjust Enrichment' in D Johnston and R Zimmermann (eds), *Unjustified Enrichment: Key Issues in Comparative Perspective* (2002), 283.
[123] (1876) 1 QBD 291.
[124] (1876) 1 QBD 291, 298–299.
[125] (1890) 24 QBD 742.
[126] [1996] Ch 107. *Cf. Collier v Collier* [2002] EWCA Civ 1095, [2002] BPIR 1057. See also *Symes v Hughes* (1869–1870) LR 9 Eq 465 (Ct of Ch).

The majority[127] of the Court of Appeal in *Patel v Mirza* followed *Tribe v Tribe* in holding that where an 'illegal contract' could no longer be performed (here because the source of information with which to commit insider dealing had run dry), the payor could withdraw from his transaction and reclaim his payment. Here, however, no policy of encouraging withdrawal could justify the result: the illegal purpose had independently become impossible to perform. The analysis of Gloster LJ in the minority, adopted (albeit in passing) by the majority of the Supreme Court, is to be preferred.

If the 'withdrawal' policy were truly accepted, it would indicate that anyone at all should have the ability to sue the payee for an order to repay back to the payor. The more the merrier, if our only goal is to deter the fulfilment of the illegal purpose. It is, again, a reason of the wrong form, and should be rejected as an explanation of recovery.

---

[127] Vos and Rimer LJJ.

PART VIII
APOLOGIA

20
Conclusion

A. Comparisons

The history of the German law of 'unjustified enrichment' is being repeated in the common law (and, in an even more direct way in Scotland[1]). A general 'unjust enrichment' doctrine is being divided.[2]

Much, but not all, of this work maps on to a fourfold classificatory scheme that should be recognisable by those familiar with the modern German law of 'unjustified enrichment'.

1) Claims to reverse a performance rendered without legal ground (*Leistungskondiktion*);[3]
2) Claims based upon the performance of another's obligation (*Rückgriffskondiktion*);[4]
3) Claims based upon the interference with another's right (*Einsgriffskondiktion*);[5]
4) Claims by a bona fide possessor who has made unauthorised improvements of another's property (*Verwendungskondiktion*).[6]

This division, the Wilburg/von Caemmerer typology, was originally proposed in 1934 as a way of dividing up the general enrichment provision in section 812 of the *Bürgerliches Gesetzbuch*.[7] It does not exhaust all of the material covered by works on the subject in the common law, including this one, which is much larger. Civil lawyers would not classify the *actio negotiorum gestio contraria* as within the subject of 'unjustified enrichment',[8] claims to vindicate rights to things are also outside,[9] and much of the law concerning claims to recover a performance rendered under an agreement is often treated as within contract law.[10] What is, in England, the duty of a fiduciary to account is dealt with as part of mandate or agency law.[11] The material covered under Equity and trusts has no direct analogue.[12] The German typology should not be confused with the laws of civilian jurisdictions generally,

---

[1] Modern Scottish works adopt the German typology: R Evans-Jones, *Unjustified Enrichment vol 1: Enrichment by Deliberate Conferral, Condictio* (2003) and *vol 2: Enrichment Acquired in Any Other Matter* (2013); N Whitty, 'Unjustified Enrichment Reissue' in *Laws of Scotland, Stair Memorial Encyclopaedia* (2022).
[2] *Cf.* A Burrows, '"At the Expense of the Claimant": A Fresh Look' (2018) 28 RLR 167.
[3] Chapters 3–6.
[4] Chapter 9.
[5] Chapters 15–17.
[6] Chapter 14.
[7] W Wilburg, *Die Lehre von der ungerechtferiften Bereicherung nach österreichischem und deutschem recht* (1934), 5, E von Caemmerrer, 'Bereicherung und unerlaubte Handlung', in *Festschrift für Ernst Rabel*, vol 1 (1954), 333.
[8] Chapter 10.
[9] Chapter 11.
[10] Chapters 7 and 8.
[11] BGB § 667.
[12] Chapters 12 and 13.

which are, if anything, more diverse and different than the various common law systems with which they are often compared, but it is at least generally also accepted as correct in Austria and Switzerland.[13]

However, this work differs from the orthodox account of the law in those civilian jurisdictions in two ways.

First, it is maintained that there is no unity of reason applicable to these different kinds of claim that binds them together. They are as different from each other as each is different from a claim that a contractual promise is enforced. As a result, it is impermissible to analogise across from one category to another, and to assume that the rules applicable in one area apply to another. We find these different kinds of claim not because of the history of one system or another, but because of the different reasons that exist for interpersonal obligations.

The Wilburg/von Caemmerer typology is not a clarification of the general 'unjust enrichment' provision found in section 812 of the *Bürgerliches Gesetzbuch*. It is a refutation of it.

Second, the subject matter of any claim in each of these categories is different, and is very rarely best understood in terms of 'enrichment'. It is not that 'unjust enrichment' should be restricted as an idea to the supposedly central 'transfer' or 'performance' cases. Rather, there is no useful category best understood in terms of enrichment at all.

In the performance cases, what is (in England) and ought to be (everywhere) reversed is the performance rendered (the payment, the service). The law should not be, and in England is not, concerned with the consequence of the payment or service. The payment or service need not have been enriching in any way.

Similarly, where an obligation has been discharged that ought to have been borne by another, we are not (unlike in the reversal of a performance) seeking to return to the world as it once was, but to go forward to the position that the correct obligor had borne the cost of the obligation. Again, enrichment is not our concern.

Where rights are interfered with, the usual quantum of any claim will be determined by the value of those rights. The interference may have left the defendant worse, not better, off but that is irrelevant.

Finally, the law of improvements by bona fide possessors is in England in something of a mess, at least in relation to land, But it can be said with confidence that the enrichment of one party by another is not its central concern.

That does not entail that these different species of claim are necessarily better re-allocated to other areas of law (eg claims dependent upon agreement into contract law, the improvement of things into an expanded property law, and so on). No clarification would necessarily be achieved by thinking of the right to contribution between joint tortfeasors as part of the law of torts for example. Still less should such claims be abolished as unjustified. Rather, we need to disaggregate the several different reasons in play, and this enterprise is not the same as that of constructing academic courses on contract, torts, equity, and property.

B. 'Unjust Factors' or 'Absence of Basis'?

Twenty years ago, the academic debate in England was dominated by the question of whether the English 'unjust factors' or the civilian 'absence of basis' approach to the law of restitution was superior. Unfortunately, as framed, this question is misconceived.

---

[13] N Jansen, 'Farewell to Unjustified Enrichment?' (2016) 20 Ed LR 123.

There are many reasons why restitution ought to be awarded in all legal systems, never just one. Even if we confined our topic to the reversal of performance cases, the ground for recovery in cases of illegality for the protection of a class, and that for payments made conditionally under agreements, are different from one another and cannot be satisfactorily explained in terms of 'absence of basis'.

However, it is also the case that where there is no objectively good legal justification for a performance rendered by the plaintiff to the defendant, exemplified by mistaken payments, it ought to be reversed. Payments of sums of money that are not due ought to be recoverable in all legal systems, subject to any countervailing reason why not. Here, there are not many reasons in play, but one. Outside of such 'performance' cases, the presence or absence of a legal basis is irrelevant.

It is not however the case that the various ways of nullifying contracts, gifts, and other justifying legal grounds (misrepresentation, duress, undue influence, and so on) are of no concern to the law of restitution. Rather, their relevance is not that they show that the plaintiff's consent to the defendant's enrichment was 'vitiated' in some way. Similarly, that there was a mistake as to whether there was an obligation to pay is frequently the best way of proving that there was no entitlement to a payment, but this does not reveal, as has been claimed, a fundamentally different conception to restitution being adopted by the two different legal traditions.[14] In fact, when properly analysed, it shows the opposite. What needs to be abandoned is not the legal significance of mistake, duress, undue influence, and so on, but rather the idea that (part of) the ground for imposing an obligation upon the defendant is found in the state of mind of the plaintiff.

The result is that there is truth in both views. The reason the Wilburg/von Caemmerer scheme of division of the subject appears so attractive is that it reflects the different reasons for recovery that there are in *all* legal systems. It is not an historically contingent or accidental division. What it simultaneously reveals, however, is the multiplicity of reasons for recovery: a number of 'unjust factors'.

In law, there is no scope for being a hedgehog concerned with one big idea, or a fox with many. We all of us must be both splitters and lumpers. Each reason must occupy the space it rightly has, neither more nor less.

C. Like Contract, Torts, or Neither?

A popular line of defence of the subject of 'unjust enrichment' is then to maintain that it is more like torts than contract.[15] Just as, so it is said, the law of torts is not reducible to any single kind of reason unified by a concept such as wrongdoing or the infringement of rights, so the law of unjust enrichment, unlike the law of contract, encompasses a diverse range of reasons.

If this is true, however, it necessarily requires the abandonment of the 'four-stage' structure of the subject employed by textbooks and now with judicial support, that was introduced by Peter Birks. We cannot safely reason by analogy from one group of cases to

---

[14] Eg T Krebs, *Restitution at the Crossroads: A Comparative Study* (2001), 1.
[15] C Mitchell, P Mitchell, and S Watterson (eds), *Goff & Jones: The Law of Unjust Enrichment* (9th edn, 2016), [1-108]. *Cf.* S Smith, 'Unjust Enrichment: Nearer to Tort than Contract' in R Chambers, C Mitchell, and J Penner (eds), *Philosophical Foundation of the Law of Unjust Enrichment* (2009), 18.

another if the reasons justifying the different claims are not the same.[16] We cannot assume that the meaning of 'enrichment' or 'at the expense of' or 'unjust' have any commonality at all. We must not start from the position that (subject to exceptions) the same defences apply to all of them.

In his last work, Peter Birks sought to identify single generic meanings for each of the three elements of the cause of action, and a set of defences that uniformly applied to them all.[17] Other commentators, by giving these labels separate and diverse meanings that have no genus in common, are *sub silentio* abandoning the idea that there is any unity at all. If restitution is, in fact, more like 'torts' than contract, then the reasoning by analogy between the different categories is misleading us. Importantly, civilian jurisdictions do not adopt this 'four-stage' approach, revealing a lack of unity to the subject as it is perceived. It is a mistake to try to mix and match these two approaches.[18]

Further, if it were true that the law of torts or the law of restitution are just a rag-bag of different things, it is unclear why it would ever be thought useful to write books or run courses concerning them. Such books or courses would be of much less utility than those on the law of the horse, which at least have the benefit of assisting those who wish to advise people specifically dealing only with one species of equine animal.

Although incapable of being defended at length here, the law of torts does have a unity of form (it is the law of wrongs that are constituted by the violation of a right of another) and reason (the obligation to pay damages is the 'next best' now achievable after the wrong has occurred) that justifies its treatment as a single subject.[19] The diverse topics covered by 'restitution' or 'unjust enrichment' have neither of these features. One indication of this is that no two books on the subject cover the same material, with some books varying in coverage from one edition to the next. The comparison of the two misleads more than it enlightens.

D. The Future

For the many books and articles written in the Anglo-common law world, based upon a model of the law that this book rejects, and now the cases decided that employ it, what is the implication if the central claims of this book are true? Does it mean for others, as Peter Birks wrote in the copy of the first edition of his book *Unjust Enrichment* that he gave to me, 'a life's work up in flames'?

The answer is clearly no. Most of these works discuss and analyse the law at a level of specificity that means 'unjust enrichment' theory could readily be dispensed with. Many discuss in detail issues this book has not covered, such as when a contract or gift can be set aside for duress or undue influence, that are left untouched by the criticisms of this work.

Further, the account given in this book could instead have been presented as a continuation of, rather than a break with, the history of the subject over the last 50 years. Since Robert Goff and Gareth Jones produced the first edition of their book in 1966, various

---

[16] But see P Birks, *An Introduction to the Law of Restitution* (rev edn, 1989), 20–21.
[17] P Birks, *Unjust Enrichment* (2nd edn, 2005).
[18] As modern Scottish authors do, eg Evans-Jones, *Unjustified Enrichment vol 1: Enrichment by Deliberate Conferral, Condictio* and *vol 2: Enrichment Acquired in Any Other Matter* (n 1); Whitty, 'Unjustified Enrichment Reissue' (n 1). The four-stage unjust enrichment scheme actually does little substantive work in these texts.
[19] R Stevens, *Torts and Rights* (2007).

authors have sought to separate out parts of what they originally discussed as distinct. Most obviously, claims based upon wrongdoing and claims for recompense by necessitous interveners, but also many others (eg attornment and, unfortunately, proprietary estoppel) that do not feature in more recent texts. This book could be seen as an attempt to take that process further.

A more cautious author might have confined himself to maintaining that 'enrichment' had a variety of technical meanings that differed in different contexts, and that it was important not to give the term the meaning that it has in everyday speech. Other authors have made similar claims along these lines.[20]

Peter Birks himself would not have been satisfied with such half-truths. If there is no single reason of justice or even some formal commonality such as enrichment as an element of each of the claims, 'unjust enrichment' as an organising idea is, at best, otiose, and, at worst, confusing.

For purposes of pedagogy and exposition, this book then poses a challenge. The great attraction of 'unjust enrichment' as an organising idea was that it proffered a way of making the law simpler and more readily accessible. It suggested that we can divide the law of obligations into three large categories (contract, torts, unjust enrichment). The third could then be presented in books and courses as a unified whole, with an easily accessible four-stage structure. In an era when the studying and teaching of private law is under pressure, shrinking to make room for more 'modern' courses, 'unjust enrichment' provided a way of keeping the barbarians at bay. As a result, it proved dangerously attractive to academics and practitioners.

In this respect I can offer no easy remedy or comfort. The law itself does not divide neatly into topics that can be taught in eight- or twelve-week courses. Private lawyers will always need more than three books on their shelves.

For courts and judges, what are the lessons? Two inconsistent forms of criticism of works of this kind are usually made.

First, it could be said that the thesis makes no difference in practice and that the law has been muddling along fine. If, however, this work is correct, we are in the midst of a longstanding and large systemic error. This book has been sternly critical of many decisions, arguing that several ultimate appellate court cases are either wrongly reasoned,[21] or, more seriously, wrongly decided.[22] Entire areas of English law have been condemned as being in a bad state.

Second, more plausibly, it might be said that the gap between this work and the law as it is is too great. Not only have common law cases of the highest authority been condemned, statutes have been criticised as misconceived.[23] English law is in a better condition than it

---

[20] Eg R Chambers, 'Two Kinds of Enrichment' in R Chambers, C Mitchell, and J Penner (eds), *Philosophical Foundations of the Law of Unjust Enrichment* (2009).

[21] *Lipkin Gorman v Karpnale Ltd* [1991] 2 AC 548 (HL); *Attorney General v Blake* [2001] 1 AC 268 (HL); *Menelaou v Bank of Cyprus* [2015] UKSC 66; [2016] AC 176; *Australian Financial Services & Leasing Pty Ltd v Hill Industries Ltd* [2014] HCA 14, (2014) 243 CLR 560; *International Energy Group Ltd v Zurich Insurance plc* [2015] UKSC 33; [2016] AC 509; *Patel v Mirza* [2016] UKSC 42, [2017] AC 467; *Moore v Sweet* (2018) SCC 52.

[22] *Baltic Shipping v Dillon* (1993) 176 CLR 3 (HCA); *Banque Financière de la Cité v Parc (Battersea) Ltd* [1999] 1 AC 221 (HL); *Dextra Bank v Bank of Jamaica* [2002] 1 All ER (Comm) 193 (PC); *Deutsche Morgan Grenfell v Inland Revenue Commissioners* [2007] UKHL 34; [2008] AC 561; *Samsoondar v Capital Insurance Co Ltd* [2020] UKPC 33, [2021] 2 All ER 1105.

[23] Law Reform (Frustrated Contracts) Act 1943.

was a decade ago,[24] but there is still much progress that needs to be made. Whether the criticisms made here are justifiable or not must be left for you to judge.

It cannot be expected that all others will swallow down these bitter pills and simply change their views. However, it is hoped that commentators and courts will cease to use the 'four-stage test' for liability in 'unjust enrichment' as anything more than 'broad headings for ease of exposition',[25] rather than as a way of disposing of actual litigated cases. The willingness to analogise across from one category of claim to another, in order to argue for changes to the law as it is, needs to be stopped.

Finally, this work should not be seen as an attack upon its subject matter. Rather it has sought to establish that it is richer, and more diverse, than any single idea.

---

[24] *Investment Trust Companies v HMRC* [2017] UKSC 29, [2018] AC 275; *Morris-Garner v One Step Support Ltd* [2018] UKSC 20, [2019] AC 549; *Prudential Assurance Co Ltd v HMRC* [2018] UKSC 39, [2019] AC 929.

[25] *Investment Trust Companies v HMRC* [2017] UKSC 29, [2018] AC 275, [41] *per* Lord Reed.

Index

For the benefit of digital users, indexed terms that span two pages (e.g., 52-53) may, on occasion, appear on only one of those pages.

absence of basis
   authority for 71–72
   bases defined 78–79
   comparative approaches 103
   corporate mistakes 96
   correct approach 416–17
   invention of "unjust factors" 100–1
   obligations performed 84–89
   positive thesis 7–8
   relation to "unjust factors" 72–76, 83–103
   theory of 79–80
   '*Woolwich* principle' 98–100
acceptance by defendant
   'enrichment' insufficient and unnecessary 48–49
   general principle 37–38, 46–48
accession
   identification of things 201–3
   improvements to goods 266–67
account of profits
   see also **profit-stripping awards**
   availability 344
   claims to gains through wrongdoing 295, 303
   date for attribution of profits 364
   positive thesis 14
actio negotiorum gestio contraria 415–16
actio perssonalis 104, 177, 178, 181–82, 187–88, 330, 370
administration of estates
   administrator's personal patrimony 220
   equitable property rights 218–19
   limitation of claims 331
   maladministered estates 39–41
   obligations to transfer rights 227
   rectification of gifts 53
   trustee's freedom to trade 223
   vesting on death or bankruptcy 226–27
advancement *see* **presumption of advancement**
agents
   acceptance by defendant 50
   ministerial receipt
      defence or denial 385–87
      overview 385
      scope of application 387–90
   necessity 180
   no right to transfer 33
   rental payments to agents 51–52
   requirements for performance
      acting through the agency of third party 42–46

      payments by agents 41–42
   reversal of payments made 60–62
agency of necessity 179
agreements
   delivery 197–98
   difference from contracts 111–15
   gifts 89–91
at the expense of the claimant
   core element of unjust enrichment 6
   correlative loss unnecessary 30–31
   failure of attempt to maintain the unity of 'unjust enrichment' 55–56
   performance as a necessary condition 29–55
attornment 53, 418–19
automatic discharge rule 160–61

bailments
   duty of care 285
   passing of title 197
   reciprocal duties 178–80
   tortious liability 330
   trusts distinguished 216
benefit *see* **enrichment**
bona fide **payees** 376–78
bona fide **purchases**
   general principles 376–78
   positive thesis 15
   recovery of things 209–10, 212–13
   restitutionary obligations which create trusts 241–43
breach of contract
   damages
      contractual right to performance 333–37
      leading example 332–33
      'negotiating' damages 338–44
   duty to account for profits
      general principle 320–23
      leading case – *Blake* 323–26
   failure of consideration
      relation to 117
   relevance of termination
      discharge of future obligations 127
      insufficient condition of recovery 125–26
      terminology 124
      unnecessary condition of recovery 126–27
   restitution claims
      payments against party in breach 130–32
      payments by party in breach 136–37

422 INDEX

breach of contract (*cont.*)
    services against party in breach 132–35
    services by party in breach 128–29
    reversal of performance rendered 57
    waiver
        conditions and breach 121
        estoppel 272
breach of statutory duty 326
bribes
    constructive trust 227
    counter-restitution 382
    duty to account 316–17
    illegality rule 22, 393–95
    title to bribes 227

categories *see* **legal categories**
causation
    account of profits 308, 317–18
    damages 296
    overpaid taxes 59–60
    rescission and money not due 102–3
    tracing 246–48
change of position
    defence rather than a denial 354–57
    genuine defence 59
    recovery of things 211–12
    relationship with estoppel 367–69
    scope of application
        conditional performance 359–60
        discharge of another's obligation 360–61
        general defence applicable to all claims 364
        property and trusts 363
        restitution of the value of rights to
            things 361–63
        unjustified performance 356–59
        wrongdoing 363–64
    which changes count 364–67
comparative approaches
    recovery of things 213
    unjust factors 103–4
    unjustified enrichment 415–16
    unjustified performance 103–4
    vitiation of consent 104
    wrongdoing 302–3
compulsion 7, 163–64, 169–70, 176
    policy 7
conditional obligations 159–60
conditional performance
    change of position 359–60
    conditions
        condition is to be found in agreement between
            the parties 110–11
        'fiction of fulfillment' doctrine 122–23
        general principles 109–10
        non-contractual agreements 111–15
        right or its performance 123–24
        'total failure of consideration' 115–16
        use in different senses 115–16
        waiver 120–21

interaction between contracts and restitution
    breach of contract 128–37
    frustration 137–46
    money, services and penalties 147–49
    overview 128
ministerial receipt 387–88
positive thesis
    condition found in agreement 10
    reversal of performance rendered 10
    rights to restitution 10
    'total failure of consideration' 10
termination for breach
    discharge of future obligations 127
    insufficient condition of recovery 125–26
    terminology 124
    unnecessary condition of recovery 126–27
confidential information
    damages for breach of confidencet 338
    duty to account for profits
        general principles 309–11
        scope of private information 311–13
    no right to information exigible against all
        others 260
consent *see* **vitiation of consent**
constructive trusts
    bribes 227
    duty to account for profits 318
    equitable property rights 217
    improvements to land 276–79, 280–82, 283
    justification for 262
    minimum conditions necessary to satisfy
        trust 222–23
    restitutionary obligations which create trusts 232,
        233, 236, 237–38, 241, 242
    trusts arising from contractual and other
        obligations 224–28
contracts
see also **breach of contract; services rendered**
    conditions
        condition is to be found in agreement between
            the parties 110–11
        'fictional fulfillment' doctrine 122–23
        general principles 109–10
        right or its performance 123–24
        use of condition in different senses 116–20
        waiver 120–21
    as defence for unjust enrichment 417–18
    frustration
        meaning of condition 119
        money obligations 137–42
        non-money obligations 142–46
        other jurisdictions 146
    interaction with restitution
        breach of contract 128–37
        frustration 137–46
        money, services and penalties 147–49
        overview 128
    quasi-contract
        French robationtion 24

label for rag-bag group of obligations 24–25
parallels with the modern category of 'unjust enrichment' 24
relationship with contract 24
rescission 36–37, 38
transfers of things 192–97
contribution
automatic discharge 160
discharge of another's obligation 155–56
establishment of loss 168
necessity
general average contribution 181–83
other examples 181–84
no defence of 'change of position' 167
rule against accumulation 170
convention
estoppel 288
no good reason for performance 79
conversion 179, 182–83, 191–92, 193–94, 199–200, 201–2, 203, 204, 216, 236, 345–46, 361
corporate mistakes 96
corrective justice
concept applicable only to wrongdoing 20
form of a rule 19
rights and the language of 'correction' 20–21
unjust enrichment 19
counter-restitution
leading case – Schools Facility Management 383–85
particular problem 378
positive thesis 15
restitution of payments against party in breach 131–32
valid contracts 383
void bargains 378–81
voidable bargains 381–83
countervailing reasons see **defences**
court orders
damages 341, 342
equity 216, 227, 257, 342
reversal 100
penalties rule 148
crime 80

damages
breach of contract
contractual right to performance 333–37
leading case revisited 344
leading example 332–33
'negotiating' damages 338–44
claims to gains through wrongdoing
definitions and distinctions 295–97
obligation to pay damages 297–99
gain-based approach
breach of contract 343
overview 332
torts 348–49
general and special damage 295–97
improvements to goods 265–66

'negotiating' damages
in lieu of specific relief 340–43
making good counterfactual loss 338–39
rejection of gain-bases approach 343
uncertain future loss 339–40
torts
gain-based approach 348–49
general damages 344–46
user damages 346–48
deceit
damages 296
rescission 381
account of profits 326–27
defamation 294, 312, 353
defences see also **illegality rule**
bona fide payees 385
bona fide purchases 376–78
change of position
denial rather than a defence 354–57
genuine defence 59
relationship with estoppel 367–69
scope of application 357–64
which changes count 364–67
claim specific and claim general distinguished 354
counter-restitution
leading case – Schools Facility Management 383–85
particular problem 378
valid contracts 383
void bargains 378–81
voidable bargains 381–83
criminal law approach 354
defined 353
ei incumbit probatio qui dicit 353
excuses or immunities 354
foundational arguments
illegality 22
labelling 22
lack of capacity 21
limitation statutes 21–22
limitation of actions 371–74
ministerial receipt
defence or denial 385–87
payments to agents 385
scope of application 387–90
multiplicity of justifications 348–49
passing on 374–76
positive thesis
countervailing reasons 15
illegality 15
recovery of things 211–13
rescission of a wholly executory contract 354
vitiation of consent 369–71
discharge of another's obligation
automatic discharge 160–61
bona fide payees 385
change of position 360–61
conditional obligations 159–60
contribution 155–56
joint and several obligations 158

discharge of another's obligation (*cont.*)
   methods of discharge 157–58
   necessity 178
   positive thesis
      claim for expense 10
      justification for claim 10
      no requirement for legal obligation 11
      ways of discharging obligation 10–11
   recoupment 154–55
   significance 153–54
disgorgement
   claims to gains through wrongdoing
      deterrence 300–1
      fructus rule 302
      institutional protection 301–2
      'no man shall profit from his own wrong' 299–300
      proxy for loss 300
      underlying problem 299
   profits 306
dishonest assistance
   duty to account for profits 318–19
   restitutionary obligations which create trusts 238

ei incumbit probatio qui dicit 353
enrichment of the defendant *see also* unjust enrichment
   baseline against which the improvement is measured 57
   core element of unjust enrichment 5
   defined 57
   reversal of performance rendered *see* reversal of performance rendered
   unjustified performance
      acceptance by all parties 48–49
      positive thesis 9
equitable estoppel
   conflicts with common law 216
   improvements to land 270–76
equitable relief against forfeiture 149, 216
equitable rules
   see also property and trusts
   central argument 214–15
   'equitable property rights'
      minimum conditions necessary to satisfy trust 222–23
      rights to rights 216–19
      significance 220–22
      two commonly held misconceptions 219–20
   nature of Equity 215–16
   positive thesis 13
   trusts arising from contractual and other obligations 224–28
estoppel
   claims under guarantee 112
   equitable estoppel
      conflicts with common law 216
      improvements to land 270–76
   improvements to land
      equitable estoppel 270–76

   evidential estoppel 269–70
   future re-configuration of 'estoppel' 287–88
   proprietary estoppel 276–85
   widening of estoppel by Australian court 285–87
proprietary estoppel
   claims under informal agreements 113
   improvements to land 276–85
   unaccepted improvements 14
   relationship with change of position 367–69
   reversal of performance rendered 69–70
'euro-torts' 87–88
evidential estoppel 269–70
expense *see* at the expense of the claimant

Failure of consideration *see also* conditional performance, 115–16
'fiction of fulfillment' doctrine 122–23
fiduciaries
   confidential information 309, 310
   duty to account for profits
      justification for duty to account 313–17
      quantification of claim 317–18
   relationship with wrongdoing 14
   restitutionary obligations which create trusts 231, 237–39, 244–45, 260
   reversal of performance rendered 64
foundational arguments
   corrective justice
      concept applicable only to wrongdoing 20
      form of a rule 19
      rights and the language of 'correction' 20–21
      unjust enrichment 19
   defences
      illegality 22
      labelling 22
      lack of capacity 21
      limitation statutes 21–22
   law and justice
      fact collation 17
      positive law as a social fact 16–17
      theoretical approaches 16
      what justice requires 17–19
   legal categories
      categories united by their legal form 22
      contextual categories 22
      those united by the reason why duties arise 23
   quasi-contract
      French ctionizingn 24
      label for rag-bag group of obligations 24–25
      parallels with the modern category of 'unjust enrichment' 24
      relationship with contract 24
free acceptance *see* acceptance by the defendant
French law 24, 43
fructus rule
   claims to gains through wrongdoing 302
   recovery of things 205
frustration
   justification 137

meaning of condition 119
money obligations
  common law approach 137–40
  legislative provisions 140–42
non-money obligations
  common law approach 142–43
  legislative provisions 143–46
other jurisdictions 146

gains *see* **profit-stripping awards;** *under* **wrongdoing;**
  unjust enrichment
general average contribution 181–83
German law 36–37, 105, 202–3, 296–97, 302, 378–79, 415–16
Gifts
  corrective justice 19
  good reasons for performance 78–79
  rectification of gifts 53
  vitiation of consent 89–92
  why claims fail 32
good faith purchases for value see *bona fide*
  purchases
goods *see* **things**

history 4–5
human rights
  judicial power to make law 405
  private and family life 312

identification
  mistaken payments 80–81
  things
    accession 201–3
    fructus rule 205
    mixtures 198–201
    overview 198
    specification rule 203–5
ignorance 100, 211
illegality rule
  bribes 392–95
  coherence of the legal system 196
  fundamental issues for future judgments 405–8
  illegality as a ground of claim
    restitution founded on statute 408–9
    withdrawal from transaction 409–11
  justification 22, 391–92
  leading case – *Patel v Mirza*
    construction of s 63(2) Criminal Justice Act 1993 401–2
    majority judgment 403–4
    minority judgment 402–3
    ratio of decision 404
  nature and effects 392–93
  passing of title 196
  positive thesis 15
  presumption of resulting trust 235
  reliance 395–96
  statutory illegality 396–401
  summary of correct position 408

improvements
  goods
    conditions attaching to specific delivery 266
    key example 264
    qualification to accession rule 266–67
    quality to priority of title 267–68
    quantification of damages 265–66
    tracing 267
    unjust enrichment analysis 264–65
  land
    equitable estoppel 270–76
    evidential estoppel 269–70
    future re-configuration of 'estoppel' 287–88
    overview 269
    proprietary estoppel 276–85
    widening of estoppel by Australian court 285–87
  positive thesis 13–14
  three key considerations 264
incapacity
  causation 103
  change of position 358
  counter-restitution 379, 384
  effect on contract 21, 235, 354
  necessaries 187
  passing of title 196–97
  trusts 235–36
incidental benefits
  claims by those who pay the debts of others 161
  why claims fail 34–35
increases in value
  mistaken payments 62–65
  services rendered 66–67
intellectual property rights
  claims to gains through wrongdoing 300, 302
  duty to account for profits
    fault requirements 306–7
    nature and purpose of rights 304–6
    overview 14
    quantification of claim 307–8
  equitable rights 218
  moveable and immoveable property distinguished 192
  restitutionary obligations which create trusts 240–41
  transfer of rights 193
'interceptive subtraction' principle
  attornment 53
  rectification of gifts 53
  rental payments to agents 51–52
  underlying problem 51
  usurpation of public office 52
interest 62–65
intervention in another's affairs
  discharge of obligations
    automatic discharge 160–61
    conditional obligations 159–60
    contribution 155–56
    joint and several obligations 158
    methods of discharge 157–58

426 INDEX

intervention in another's affairs (cont.)
  recoupment 154–55
  significance 153–54
  necessity
    contribution between common interests 181–84
    danger of over- ctionizing different species of rights and obligation 187–88
    discharge of another's obligation 178
    'exceptions' to general rule 177
    maritime salvage 184–87
    necessaries to those unable to contract out 187
    quantification of claim 176–77
    reciprocal duties 178–81
    two fundamental questions 173–76
  positive thesis
    discharge of another's obligation 10–11
    two possible responses 11–12
  unjust enrichment
    enrichment insufficient 164–66
    enrichment unnecessary 167–68
    establishment of loss 168
    unjust factor 169–72
  volunteers 161–64

joint and several obligations 158
judicial method 405
juristic reasons see absence of basis
justice
  corrective justice
    concept applicable only to wrongdoing 20
    form of a rule 19
    rights and the language of 'correction' 20–21
    unjust enrichment 19
  law and justice
    fact collation 17
    positive law as a social fact 16–17
    theoretical approaches 16
    what justice requires 17–19
  unjust enrichment 23

knowing receipt of trust property 236–41, 242

laches 371
lack of entitlement
  difference in practice 83
  justification for award 71
  knowing receipt 239
  limitation of claims 373–74
  mispredictions 102
  role of mistake
    nullification of services rendered 73
    proof 72
  unjust factors 169
land
  see also property and trusts; things, trespass to land
  claims to gains through wrongdoing 291–92
  conditional obligations 159
  corrective justice 19
  equitable rules 13

formality requirements 111, 112, 193
improvements
  equitable estoppel 270–76
  evidential estoppel 269–70
  future re-configuration of 'estoppel' 287–88
  overview 269
  proprietary estoppel 276–85
  widening of estoppel by Australian court 285–87
mistaken possession 133
rescuers 186–87
restitution for wrongs 8–9
services rendered 113
law and justice
  fact collation 17
  justification for private law duties 174–75
  positive law as a social fact 16–17
  theoretical approaches 16
  what justice requires 17–19
legal categories
  categories united by their legal form 22
  contextual categories 22
  those united by the reason why duties arise 23
legal compulsion 7, 163–64, 169–70
'liability mistakes' 73–74, 75, 88
limitation of actions
  administration of estates 331
  foundational arguments 21–22
  general principles 371–74
losses
  claims to gains through wrongdoing
    consequential loss 292–94
    justification for disgorgement 300
  contribution 168
  core element of unjust enrichment 6
  corrective justice 6, 7
  correlative loss unnecessary in performance cases 30–31
  correlative loss necessary for recoupment 168
  intervention in another's affairs 168
  legal categories 22, 23
  'negotiating' damages
    making good counterfactual loss 338–39
    uncertain future loss 339–40
  neither sufficient nor necessary for a claim to succeed 30–31
  reversal of services rendered 67–70
  why claims fail
    services rendered 30, 31
    unjustified performance 30–31

maritime salvage 177, 184–88
medical care
  necessity 181
ministerial receipt
  defence or denial 385–87
  payments to agents 385
  scope of application
    conditional performance 387–88
    unjustified performance 388–90

mispredictions 101–2, 110, 366
mistaken payments
  acceptance by defendant
    'enrichment' insufficient and unnecessary 48–49
    general principle 46–48
    payment of money without acceptance 49–50
  conditional performance *see* **conditional performance**
  corporate mistakes 96
  corrective justice 19, 20
  leading case – *Kelly v Solari* 71–72
  mispredictions 101–2
  mistakes as to recoverability 84
  mistakes of law 92–96
  positive thesis 9
    conditional performance 10
    four-stage test 5
    improvements 14
    unjust 7
    unjustified performance 9
  problem of labelling 25
  quasi-contract 24
  requirement for action
    acting through the agency of third party 42–46
    complex payments 39
    general principle 38–39
    maladministered estates 39–41
    payments by agents 41–42
  reversal of performance rendered
    counterfactuals 59–60
    increases in value and interest 62–65
    timing 58–59
    trustees and agents 60–62
  'spent' mistakes 96–98
  theoretical perspectives
    distinct roles of plaintiff's mistake 72–73
    identification of legal event and juridical act 80–81
    lack of entitlement as justification for award 71–72
    'liability mistakes' 73–74
    removal of juridical act 82
  vitiation of consent
    mistakes as to recoverability 84
    obligations performed 84–89
  why claims fail
    no right to transfer 32–34
    no 'unjust factor' 31–32
    overview 29
mistakes
  absence of good reason for restitution
    corporate mistakes 96
    mistakes as to recoverability 84
    'spent mistakes' 96–98
  difference in practice 83
  distinct roles of plaintiff's mistake 72–73
  gifts, wills and trusts 89–92
  'liability mistakes' 73–74
  misidentification by Birk 104–5

  mispredictions distinguished 101–2
  nullification of services rendered 74–76
  voluntary performance 76–78
mixtures
  recovery of things 198–201
  tracing 248–50
moral compulsion 7, 164, 176

necessity
  contribution between common interests
    general average contribution 181–83
    other examples 181–84
  danger of over-ctionizing different species of rights and obligation 187–88
  'exceptions' to general rule
    contribution between common interests 181–84
    discharge of another's obligation 178
    duty to provide medical care 181
    maritime salvage 184–87
    necessaries supplied to those unable to contract out 184–87
    overview 177
    reciprocal duties 178–81
  positive thesis
    actions on uninvited intervention 11
    general rule 11
    two possible responses 11–12
  quantification of claim 176–77
  reciprocal duties
    bailees 178–80
    duty to provide medical care 181
  two fundamental questions 173–76
'negotiating' damages
  in lieu of specific relief 340–43
  making good counterfactual loss 338–39
  rejection of gain-bases approach 343
  uncertain future loss 339–40
negotiorum gestio contraria see **actio negotiorum gestio contraria**
nuisance 159, 328

obligations
  see also **discharge of another's obligation**
  conditional obligations 159–60
  joint and several obligations 158

passing on
  general principles 374–76
  positive thesis 15
payments *see* **mistaken payments**
penal deposits 147–49
penalties doctrine 148–49
performance
  see also **conditional performance; unjustified performance**
  acceptance by defendant
    'enrichment' insufficient and unnecessary 48–49
    general principle 46–48
    payment of money without acceptance 49–50

performance (*cont.*)
  cases that do not require performance
    erroneous decisions 53–55
    'interceptive subtraction' principle 51–53
    overview 50–51
  discharge of another's obligation 157–58
  general damages for breach of contract 333–37
  recovery of things 191
  requirement for action
    acting through the agency of third party 42–46
    complex payments 39
    general principle 38–39
    maladministered estates 39–41
    payments by agents 41–42
  third parties 42–45
  three constituent elements 36–38
policy
  bankruptcy statutes 195
  breach of contract 129
  compulsion 7
  constructive trusts 280
  defences
    change of position 358, 359, 368
    limitation of actions 371
    ministerial receipt 386
    passing on 376
    vitiation of consent 370
  discharge of another's obligation 172
  excuses or immunities 354
  at the expense of the claimant 6
  flawed arguments 21
  'half-secret' trusts 222
  illegality rule 391–92, 394, 402, 403–4, 406–7, 409–11
  intervention in another's affairs 11–12
  necessity 11, 194
    blood donations 176
    necessaries to those unable to contract out 187
    rescuers 177
    salvage operations 186
  restitutionary obligations which create trusts 256–59
  rule against accumulation 170–71
  unjust factors 100
positive thesis summary
  conditional performance
    condition found in agreement 10
    reversal of performance rendered 10
    rights to restitution 10
    'total failure of consideration' 10
  countervailing reasons
    defences 15
    illegality 15
  discharge of another's obligation
    claim for expense 10
    justification for claim 10
    no requirement for legal obligation 11
    ways of discharging obligation 10–11
  intervention in another's affairs
    discharge of another's obligation 10–11
    necessity 11–12
  necessity
    actions on uninvited intervention 11
    general rule 11
    two possible responses 11–12
  performance
    conditional performance 10
    unjustified performance 9
  property and trusts
    equitable rules 13
    improvements 13–14
    things 12
  unjustified performance
    enrichment of the defendant 9
    largest category of case 9
  wrongdoing 14
presumption of advancement
  illegality 395–96
  lack of donative intent 410
  resulting trusts 235–36
procuring breach of contract 322–23, 329–30
privacy 311–13
profit-stripping awards
  breach of contract
    general principle 320–23
    leading case – *Blake* 323–26
  confidential information
    general principles 309–11
    scope of private information 311–13
  constructive trusts 318
  dishonest assistance 318–19
  fiduciaries
    justification for duty to account 313–17
    quantification of claim 317–18
  intellectual property rights
    fault requirements 306–7
    nature and purpose of rights 304–6
    quantification of claim 307–8
  overview 304
  torts 326–28
property and trusts
  see also **fiduciaries**
  administration of estates
    administrator's personal patrimony 220
    equitable property rights 218–19
    limitation of claims 331
    maladministered estates 39–41
    obligations to transfer rights 227
    rectification of gifts 53
    trustee's freedom to trade 223
    vesting on death or bankruptcy 226–27
  change of position 363
  constructive trusts
    duty to account for profits 318
    equitable property rights 217
    improvements to land 276–79, 280–82, 283
    minimum conditions necessary to satisfy trust 222–23
    restitutionary obligations which create trusts 232, 233, 236, 237–38, 241, 242

INDEX 429

trusts arising from contractual and other obligations 224–28
equitable rules
  central argument 214–15
  'equitable property rights' 216–23
  nature of Equity 215–16
  positive thesis 13
  trusts arising from contractual and other obligations 224–28
knowing receipt of trust property 236–41, 242
minimum conditions necessary to satisfy trust 222–23
policy 256–59
presumption of advancement 235–36
positive thesis
  equitable rules 13
  improvements 13–14
  recovery of things 12
recovery of things
  comparative accounts 213
  defences 211–13
  good faith purchases for value 209–10
  identification 198–205
  nature of rights 191–92
  substituted things 205–9
  transfers of title 192–98
restitutionary obligations which create trusts
  knowing receipt of trust property 236–41
  policy 256–59
  presumptions of advancement 235–36
  purchase without notice 241–43
  subrogation 252–56
  tracing 243–51
  transfer of rights without justification 229–35
  unjust enrichment 259–62
  unjustifiability of most trusts 262–63
resulting trusts
  illegality rule 395–96
  improvements to land 273
  unjust enrichment 259
reversal of payments made 60–62
reversal of payments made by trustee 60–62
'spent mistakes' 96–98
vitiation of consent 89–92
why claims fail
  no right to transfer 32–34
proprietary estoppel
  claims under informal agreements 113
  improvements to land 276–85
  unaccepted improvements 14
proprietary rights
  core element of unjust enrichment 8
  equitable property 216–20
  fructus rule 302
  improvements to land 283–84, 288
  intellectual property 304
  mistaken payments 63
  performance 40
  possession of things 192
  restitutionary obligations which create trusts 233–34, 245, 258

substituted things 207

Quantum meruit 67–68, 113–14
Quistclose trusts 225–26
quasi-contract
  French pecification 24
  label for rag-bag group of obligations 24–25
  parallels with the modern category of 'unjust enrichment' 24
  relationship with contract 24

reasons why a claim should fail *see* defences
rectification
  gifts 53
  title register 230
recoupment
  automatic discharge 160
  discharge of another's obligation 154–55
  establishment of loss 168
  no defence of 'change of position' 167
  rule against accumulation 170–71
  secondary liability 172
  subrogation distinguished 253
recovery of things
  bona fide purchases 209–10
  comparative approaches 213
  good faith purchases for value 209–10
  identification
    accession 201–3
    fructus rule 205
    mixtures 198–201
    overview 198
    specification rule 203–5
  nature of rights 191–92
  substituted things 205–9
  transfers of title
    contracts and conveyances 192–97
    delivery and conveyance 197–98
  unjust enrichment
    defences 211–13
    'ignorance' 211
    relevance 210
rescission
  constructive trust 229–30, 231, 233
  contracts 36–37
  counter-restitution 381–83
  executory contracts 38
  failure of an agreed condition 69–70
  gifts 92
  misrepresentation 65
  revesting of title to goods 193–95
  termination distinguished 124
  vitiation of consent 83–84
resulting trusts
  constructive trusts distinguished 229–30
  illegality rule 395–96
  improvements to land 273
  Quistclose trusts 225–26
  unjust enrichment 259
retrospective law 60, 92–96, 105, 373–74

430 INDEX

reversal of performance rendered
  defined 57
  illegality as a ground of claim 409–11
  meaning of words 70
  mistaken payments
    counterfactuals 59–60
    increases in value and interest 62–65
    timing 58–59
    trustees and agents 60–62
  positive thesis 10
  services rendered
    enrichment higher than market value of service 66–67
    enrichment lower than market value of service 67–70
    service and its consequences 65–66
    termination unnecessary condition of recovery 126–27
Roman Law *see also actio negotiorum gestio contraria*
  commixtio and *confusion* 199
  condictiones 36–37
  criminal law 300
  fructus 205
  discharge of another's obligation 160
  specificatio 203

sale of goods
  breach of contract 320
  frustration 141
  general damages 333, 336–37
  insufficiently completed agreements 113–14
  rejection of non-conforming goods 180
  restitution against party in breach 139
  specific goods 321
  transfer of title 193–94, 210
  waiver of condition 120
salvage *see* maritime salvage
services rendered
  see also contracts
  conditional performance *see* conditional performance
  enrichment 5
  positive thesis
    conditional performance 10
    unjustified performance 9
  quasi-contract 24
  reversal of performance rendered
    enrichment higher than market value of service 66–67
    enrichment lower than market value of service 67–70
    service and its consequences 65–66
  theoretical perspectives
    identification of legal event and juridical act 81–82
    nullification on the basis of mistake 74–76
    voluntary performance 76–78

why claims fail
  grudging gifts 32
  no loss 30, 31
  overview 29
specific delivery
  improvements to goods 266
  requirement for payment for work done 14
specification rule 203–5
'spent mistakes' 96–98
statutory illegality 396–401, 406, 407
subrogation
  contractual right to reimbursement 157
  ground of recovery 162–63
  guarantors 163
  inconsistency of the law 261
  recoupment distinguished 155
  revival of lien 54–55
  tracing 252–56
substitution
  recovery of things 205–9
  tracing 243–48

theoretical perspectives
  good reasons for performance
    customary convention 79
    gifts 78–79
    legal obligations 78
    natural or moral obligations 78–79
    rescuers 79
  mistaken payments
    distinct roles of plaintiff's mistake 72–73
    identification of legal event and juridical act 80–81
    lack of entitlement as justification for award 71–72
    'liability mistakes' 73–74
    removal of juridical act 82
  operative facts approach to unjust enrichment 79–80
  services rendered
    identification of legal event and juridical act 81–82
    nullification on the basis of mistake 74–76
    voluntary performance 76–78
things
  see also land
  improvements to goods
    conditions attaching to specific delivery 266
    key example 264
    qualification to accession rule 266–67
    quality to priority of title 267–68
    quantification of damages 265–66
    tracing 267
    unjust enrichment analysis 264–65
  mistaken possession 133
  recovery of things
    accession 201–3, 266–67
    bona fide purchases 209–10

comparative approaches 213
fruits 205
good faith purchases for value 209–10
identification 198–205
mixtures 198–201
nature of rights 191–92
positive thesis 12
specification 203–5
substituted things 205–9
transfers of title 192–98
unjust enrichment 210–13
scope of application 361–63
torts 170, 323–26
see also **wrongdoing**
apportionment defence 156
claims to gains through wrongdoing
definitions and distinctions 292
general and special damages 296–97
leading case – *Edwards v Lee's Administrator* 291
comparison with 417–18
corrective justice 20–33
damages
gain-based approach 348–49
general damages 344–46
user damages 346–48
duty to account for profits
general principle 326–28
waiver of tort 328–31
'euro-torts' 87–88
improvements to goods 265–66
improvements to land 286
joint and several obligations 158
legal category 23
popular line of defence for unjust enrichment 417–18
positive thesis 9
reversal of performance rendered 57, 58, 62
rule against accumulation 170
unaccepted improvements to property 14
volenti non fit iniuria 76, 164
waiver 24, 25
'**total failure of consideration**' 115–16
Tracing
Clayton's Case 249–50
improvements to goods 267
lowest intermediate balance rule 249
mixtures 248–50
pari passu approach 250
proportionate share rule 249
"rolling charge" approach 249
subrogation 252–56
substitution 243–48
wrongdoing 250–51
transfers of value
enrichment lower than market value 68
law of subrogation 261
principle of 'interceptive subtraction' 51
why claims fail 35–36

trespass to land
account of profits 291–92, 327–28
damages 266
waiver 271–72
trusts *see* **property and trusts**
trustees
claims against 60–62
condition of trusteeship 232
strict liability 237

user damages 332
unjust enrichment *see also* **enrichment of the defendant**
central dilemma 9
comparative accounts of unjust factors 104
core claims for recognition
central negative thesis of this work 9
enrichment of the defendant 5
at the expense of the claimant 6
four-stage test 5
generation of proprietary rights 8
restitution for wrongs 8–9
unjust 6–8
corrective justice 19
defences 15
different kinds of private law claim 3
implication if central claims of book are true 418–20
improvements to goods 264–65
intervention in another's affairs
enrichment insufficient 164–66
enrichment unnecessary 167–68
establishment of loss 168
unjust factor 169–72
misidentification of mistake and unjust factors by Birk 104–5
modern history of the subject
Anglo-Commonwealth approach 4–5
Scott and Seavey's American Restatement 1937 4
US approach 4
operative facts approach 79–80
parallels with quasi-contract' 24
popular line of defence 417–18
positive thesis *see* **positive thesis**
recovery of things
defences 211–13
'ignorance' 211
relevance 210
restitutionary obligations which create trusts 259–62
reversal of performance rendered *see* **reversal of performance rendered**
unified reason of justice why legal duties arise 23
unjust factors
central case in unjust enrichment theory 7
comparative approaches 103–4
correct approach 416–17
intervention in another's affairs
legal compulsion 169–70

unjust factors (*cont.*)
    policy 172
    rule against accumulation 170–71
    secondary liability 171–72
    invention of specific grounds for recovery
        'ignorance' and 'powerlessness' 100
        payments made under court orders 100
        'want of authority' 100–1
        '*Woolwich* principle' 100
    recovery of things 211
    role of mistake
        'liability mistakes' 73–74
        nullification of services
            rendered 74–76
        voluntary performance 76–78
    why claims fail 31–32
unjustified enrichment
    comparative approaches 415–16
    no loss 30
unjustified performance
    absence of good reasons for
        restitution
        corporate mistakes 96
        different causal rules 102–3
        gifts, wills and trusts 89–92
        invention of 'unjust factors' 100–1
        mispredictions 101–2
        mistakes as to recoverability 84
        obligations performed 84–89
        rescission 83–84
        retrospective law 92–96
        'spent mistakes' 96–98
        '*Woolwich* principle' 98–100
    cases that do not require performance
        'interceptive subtraction' principle 51–53
        overview 50–51
    change of position 356–59
    comparative approaches 103–4
    failure of attempt to maintain the unity of 'unjust
        enrichment' 55–56
    ministerial receipt 388–90
    mistaken payment *see* **mistaken payment**
    performance defined
        acceptance by all parties 46–53
        requirement for action 38–42
        three constituent elements 36–38
    positive thesis
        enrichment of the defendant 9
        largest category of case 9
    reversal of performance rendered *see* **reversal of
        performance rendered**
    services rendered *see* **services rendered**
    theoretical perspectives *see* **theoretical
        perspectives**
    vitiation of consent
        gifts 89–92
        mistakes as to recoverability 84
        obligations performed 84–89

    rescission 83–84
    why claims fail
        exclusion of incidental benefits 34–35
        grudging gifts 32
        no loss 30–31
        no right to transfer 32–34
        no 'transfers of value' 35–36
        no 'unjust factor' 31–32
        overview 29
usurpation of public office 52

vitiation of consent
    comparative accounts of unjust factors 104
    general principles 369–71
    gifts 89–92
    mispredictions 101–2
    mistakes as to recoverability 84
    obligations performed 84–89
    positive thesis 15
    rescission 83–84
    role of mistake and other "unjust factors"
        reply to a defence 76–78
        nullification of services rendered 75
        overview 72
    why claims fail 31–32
volenti non fit iniuria 76, 164
volunteers
    creation of trusts 227–28
    equitable easement 277
    intervention in another's affairs
        general principles 161–64, 370
        secondary liability 171–72
        'unjust factor' 169
    voluntary performance 76–78

waiver
    conditional contracts 120–21
    consent 387
    contractual variations distinguished 121
    equitable estoppel 270–72
    multiple different concepts 115
    quasi-contract 24
    torts 25, 304, 328–31
waiver of tort 328–31
'*Woolwich* principle' 98–100, 358–59, 370, 376
wrongdoing
    change of position 363–64
    claims to gains
        definitions and distinctions 292–97
        leading case of *Edwards* 291–92
        overview 291
    comparative approaches 302–3
    corrective justice 19–20
    definitions and distinctions
        consequential gains 294–95
        consequential loss 292–94
        general and special damages 295–97
        justifications 297–302

    wrongdoing 292
justifications
    disgorgement of gains 299–302
    obligation to pay damages 297–99
legal categories 23

negative thesis 4
positive thesis
    gain-based responses 14
    restitution for wrongs 8–9
tracing 250–51